The Allure of Battle

THE
ALLURE
OF BATTLE

*A History of How Wars Have Been
Won and Lost*

CATHAL J. NOLAN

OXFORD
UNIVERSITY PRESS

OXFORD

UNIVERSITY PRESS

Oxford University Press is a department of the University of Oxford. It furthers
the University's objective of excellence in research, scholarship, and education
by publishing worldwide. Oxford is a registered trade mark of Oxford University
Press in the UK and certain other countries.

Published in the United States of America by Oxford University Press
198 Madison Avenue, New York, NY 10016, United States of America.

Library of Congress Cataloging-in-Publication Data
Names: Nolan, Cathal J., author.
Title: The allure of battle : a history of how wars have been won and lost / Cathal J. Nolan.
Description: New York : Oxford University Press, [2016] |
Includes bibliographical references and index.
Identifiers: LCCN 2016016391 (print) | LCCN 2016017567 (ebook) |
ISBN 9780195383782 (hardcover : alk. paper) | ISBN 9780199874651 (Updf) |
ISBN 9780199910991 (Epub)
Subjects: LCSH: Battles. | Military history.
Classification: LCC D25 .N65 2016 (print) | LCC D25 (ebook) | DDC 355.409—dc23
LC record available at https://lccn.loc.gov/2016016391

3 5 7 9 8 6 4 2

Printed by Sheridan Books, Inc., United States of America

"Battles decide everything."

CARL VON CLAUSEWITZ, *1812*

"Instead of a war fought on to the bitter end in a series of decisive battles . . . everybody will be entrenched in the next war. . . . The spade will be as indispensable to the soldier as his rifle. . . . It is very doubtful whether any decisive victory can be gained."

JEAN DE BLOCH, *1899*

"Modern war is a war of motors. The war will be won by whichever side produces the most motors."

JOSEPH STALIN, *1941*

Contents

Acknowledgments

I AM GRATEFUL to the production staff at Oxford University Press for their careful attention to detail and patient editorial assistance in helping prepare the manuscript of this book for publication, along with its accompanying maps and illustrations. I am especially grateful to Executive Editor Timothy Bent for his strong guidance and support from first proposal through editing of the text to completion of the book. I thank him for his patience and sound advice throughout an always complicated processes of the proposal, external review, and editing and revising. I am deeply grateful to two anonymous reviewers for Oxford University Press whose insights and criticisms caused me to clarify and, I hope, argue with more nuance and accuracy a number of key points made in the book. I also wish to thank for their comments on selected portions of the book, while in proposal or manuscript form, Professor of Classical Studies at Boston University Loren J. Samons II; Professor Michael Kort of Boston University; Professor Carl Hodge of the University of British Columbia; Professor Danny Orbach of the Hebrew University of Jerusalem and Professor Alex Roland of Duke University. I am of course forever grateful, and profoundly indebted, to my wife, Valerie, for all that she does by way of support and encouragement, and for so much else.

Cathal J. Nolan
Natick, Massachusetts
June 12, 2016

List of Maps

List of Illustrations

The Allure of Battle

Introduction

MILITARY HISTORY IS hard history perhaps precisely because it seems so easy. At first glance war appears full of obvious turning points that center on decisive battles. These concentrated events draw the mind as well as the eye, to facilitate the conclusion that the dramatic events of an hour or a day determined the course of whole centuries and civilizations.[1] This idea of world historical battles has retained a hold on the public imagination from the works of the first historians and propagandists of the ancient world. More recently there has been a strong, and mostly justified, reaction against writing even military history as a sequence of major battles. The preference is to explain virtually all major change as arising from *longue durée* social, economic, cultural, intellectual, technological or other causes. There is much to be said for taking a longer view of causation and change, as well as for studying the social impact and experience of armies in addition to top-down planning and execution of wartime operations. Yet recent academic hostility to traditional military history has gone too far, as has a related professional drift away from major wars as an explanation of wider changes.

Many modern historians are indifferent to military history. Some are openly hostile. Or they redefine the history of war as a branch of social history that looks at its effects on the armies and societies that wage it, rather than looking at war itself. Many are strongly opposed to any claim that decisive wars have been main agents of lasting change. The trend in the profession to dismiss the big claims of older military histories is reinforced by a more general turn away from the idea of large narratives of decision, toward social and cultural histories of smaller folk, littler things, and everyday circumstances, materials and experience. Yet war remains hugely important in explaining much history and wider human affairs. Indeed, it may be the most important thing.

Armed conflict is too important to be reduced to bromides that "war doesn't solve anything." War in history has in fact *decided* many truly important things. Major wars have altered the deep course of world history, not least at critical modern junctures: the turns of the 18th and 19th centuries and first half of the 20th. Such war-filled times showed yet again, if more evidence was ever necessary, that war remains the most expensive, complex, physically, emotionally and morally demanding enterprise that humans collectively undertake. No great art or music, no cathedral or temple or mosque, no intercontinental transport net or particle collider or space program, no research for a cure for a mass killing disease receives even a fraction of the resources and effort humanity devotes to making war. Or to recovery from war, and to preparations for future wars that are invested over years and even decades of always tentative peace. That is a very different point from arguing, as this book does, that battles did not usually decide the major wars of the modern era that decided most everything else.

War's fundamental importance in world history means that non-military historians will surely return to consider it more closely one day. Meanwhile, military historians have already shifted their focus from battles to the study of permanent armed establishments; systems of finance and logistics as the sinews of war; the roles of industry, bureaucracy and mobilization; and how war is recalled or, at least as often, misremembered and obscured to serve other public purposes. Others study modes of combat and detailed operations—the intermediate level of warfare between small unit tactics and war-winning (or losing) strategies—that remain near the center of all military history, only now informed by fresh insights from other branches of history and from other disciplines.[2] In the end, we are all looking to explain the dynamics of immense wars that acted as accelerants and shapers of profound change. How did Europe get to the Thirty Years' War? What really underlay the explosion of nationalism and mass violence of the French Revolutionary and Napoleonic Wars? What exactly were the cataclysms of the two World Wars? Why did ordinary people agree to fight them, and extraordinary people frame plans that led not just into world wars but to deliberate mass exterminations, to destruction of social orders and all the old empires? These are questions that really matter, to both historians and the wider public.

We seek clarity in war. Yet that is something it does not always deliver. We speak of "victory" and "defeat," but these are emotive terms, subject to passions that distort memory and understanding. They mean less to policymakers than to a public with a binary view of conflict. More often, war results in something clouded, neither triumph nor defeat. It is an arena of grey outcomes, partial and ambiguous resolution of disputes and causes that led to the choice of force as an instrument of policy in the first place. This lack of clear resolution means war is likely to happen all over again as irresolution encourages war, and war begets more war. We fight to force some great decision on an enemy but fall short, pause to recover and rearm, then fight all over again. Exhaustion of morale and matériel rather than finality through battles marks the endgame of many wars. Even of most wars. Almost always of wars among the major powers in any era. This was especially true for the largest states struggling for military and political primacy in the modern era, for the Great Powers that seemed best able to sustain the enormous effort and cost of the biggest wars but fought to exhaustion all the same.

"Decision" is a more morally and politically neutral term than victory or defeat, and more useful in describing a war's outcome. A war is usually deemed to have been decisive when some important strategic and political goal was achieved in arms, gaining a lasting advantage that secured one side's key values and hard interests. Historians traditionally looked for the key moments that turned wars toward finality, pointing especially to lopsided and grand-scale battles as the key mechanism of decision by force. Yet, is a "decisive battle" the true metric of victory? Does the usual claim hold even about the most famous instances, bearing names so familiar they are fixed in our minds as having achieved a great victory under a heroic or at least a memorable leader: Marathon, Cannae, Leuthen, Trafalgar, Waterloo, Gettysburg, Midway, Stalingrad? How do we know that a victory in battle was "decisive," in the larger sense of fixing the outcome of a war? The term "decisive battle" is also too often used simply to indicate that one side suffered more dead and wounded than the other. Is such a raw accounting of casualties a true measure of decision? Even less helpful is using "decisive victory" loosely to mean a merely technical or tactical outcome, such as holding the field at the end of the day's fighting upon forcing the enemy army or fleet to withdraw, or retaining maneuver initiative in a longer campaign after a single battle is done.

That may be a reasonable way to record who has won or lost a given battle, but it does not make victory or defeat in war certain. Many who won hugely lopsided battles went on to lose the wars of which they were a part: Hannibal won at Cannae; Napoleon at Ulm; Hitler's panzer armies took 650,000 prisoners outside Kiev in 1941, yet all three went on to defeat. In each case, strategic losses came after protracted attritional wars against enemies who refused to accept those earlier tactical outcomes as decisive in the greater conflict. Many grand-scale battles thus lacked the long-term strategic impact their authors and later historians suggested. They might be better seen as accelerants of attrition, which really decided victory and defeat in long and larger wars. If the term "decisive battle" is to illuminate rather than obscure military history, it must be used more narrowly, to mean singular victories or defeats that created lasting strategic change, leading directly or ultimately to the decision in the war that framed them. Truly decisive battles translate into a lasting political outcome in the war of which they are a part, and that is actually quite rare.

In protracted wars, some of which lasted decades, most single battles accomplished little more than to accelerate underlying rates of human and material attrition, which this book will show are far more important in determining outcome. Winning the day of battle is not enough. You have to win the campaign, then the year, then the decade. Victory must usher in political permanence. If it does not, after a pause to recover and rearm the war will continue. Or later, a new fight will probably start over the same old causes in a chain of linked wars lasting decades, such as the Hundred Years' War, the wars of Louis XIV and Louis XV, the long wars started in haste by Frederick II, the wars of the French Revolution and Napoleon, and the modern thirty years' war more often discretely recorded as World War I and World War II. In such immense and protracted wars, single battle defeats and victories ultimately faded in importance as attrition became the overwhelming strategic reality. Remarkably, this was not always understood even by some of the very greatest battle generals, or by the governments of modern war states such as Napoleonic France, Imperial Germany and Imperial Japan. Generals and governments instead succumbed to the allure of battle, seeking swift tactical victories in lieu of harder strategic effort.

Although grand-scale battles are far less decisive in history than is commonly believed, the idea of them fascinates. We are drawn to celebrate battles because they seem to deliver a *decision*. We are also pulled toward the theater of battle by the allure of the senses, because of how they open: with a blast from a war horn signaling the advance of legionaries, armor glinting and weapons ready; or with a king's wave, releasing a colorful pageantry of mounted knights formed for a heavy cavalry charge; or with a curving line of galloping ponies in a Mongol horde. Grand battles are open theater with a cast of many tens of thousands: brightly colored condottieri and Renaissance militia, or samurai under signal kites, or Manchu and Chinese elite infantry organized into primary color and bordered banners. There are mahouts mounted on elephants, or a Zulu impi rushing barefoot atop lush grasses toward a redcoat firing line; or Aztec jaguar and eagle knights in gaudy feathered headdresses raising obsidian blades to contest against muskets and Toledo steel swords and breastplates. Battles open with battalions dressed in bold red, blue or white, flags fluttering, fife and drums beating the advance; or with billowing canvas down a line of fighting sail, white pufferies of cotton balls erupting red in broadside volleys; or in a file of jagged panzers hard-charging across a torn Russian steppe; and with helicopters whirring low, Wagner and rail guns blasting. What comes next is far harder to watch, let alone to comprehend.

We may teach sadder sorts of poetry in college courses on war in literature, and stand solemn and silent in cold rain at a cenotaph for a few minutes once a year. Yet after every war we also write more heroic poetry and books preaching "the old lie."[3] We bury the dead while neglecting survivors. We mourn awhile, perhaps for a generation but often much less than that, then write more war songs and speak of "pouring out the sweet red wine of youth" to another generation of boys breathlessly eager for war.[4] We bury more dead, erect more granite statues, and write lists of soon-forgotten foreign place-names scored with acid in brass on stone. We admire oiled images of oafish, mounted generals in silk and lace who led armies to slaughter in endless wars over where to mark off a king's stone borders. Perhaps most of all, we watch films with reassuring characters and outcomes which glorify war even while supposedly denouncing it.

This tendency is especially pronounced when it comes to World War II, despite its being the most horrifically destructive of all wars. Complex social and political issues seem beside the point, as an uncritical hero literature results: greatest-generation tales of Allied soldiers in a long morality play of good and evil, with perhaps just a garnish of moral ambiguity.[5] The "good war" has become callow entertainment. Too often it reduces to mere cartoon in slick films, in new media blogs and video games. Worse is explicit indifference to moral issues or basic causes of the immense and necessary multination fight against Nazism. Documentary films retrieve something of the sights and sounds of war, but even they detach us from hard realities with black-and-white and too distant images, and dull professorial narrations. Combat memoirs may quell our naïve desire to view modern war in heroic terms, but popular histories are written even now in a drums and trumpets style, with vivid depictions of battle divorced from hard logistics, daily suffering, and a critical look at the societies and cultures that produced mass armies and sent them off to fight in faraway fields for causes about which the average soldier knew nothing.

All these media play on what we want to see: displays of raw courage on red days, the thrill and spectacle of combat removed from the full context of modern warfare; enticement by explosive and the allure of battle. For war naturally evokes our fascination with spectacle, and there is no greater stage or more dramatic players than on a battlefield. Sir Michael Howard aptly refers to an abundance of combat literature that fails to speak to larger issues of armed conflict as "a kind of historical pornography."[6] On the other hand, Victor Davis Hanson decries the resort to "euphemism in battle narrative or the omission of graphic killing altogether." He adds: "War is ultimately killing. Its story becomes absurd when the wages of death are ignored."[7] Both are surely right, but where does the historian and reader draw the line between a mere voyeurism of slaughter and due respect for hard and brutal facts?

Despite battle's abiding allure, we must study war and not just battle.[8] Yet the shift from viewing combat to the context of larger and more complex conflict is hard to make. We want, and perhaps we need, to believe that the suffering that took place in some great battle decided issues of real moral salience and lasting importance. We seem to insist that battles are preferable to attrition, and think they must be more decisive. We say they had to be more than a mere sum of spectacular destruction of machines and dismemberment of men over an hour or a day that still left the issues at stake unanswered. How else but by a spectacular battle could we have won? Fearing to find tragedy without uplift or redemptive meaning in raw attrition, we give in to a powerful emotional need to believe that battles were more important, more heroic and decisive.

This is more than a *post facto* problem. The allure of battle has repeatedly enticed to war planners in aggressive but weaker states who could not otherwise conceive how to defeat or defy larger military powers or coalitions arrayed against them. From this a pattern of stumbling into wars of attrition emerged. A lesser power sought a decisive result right at the outset, through a singular annihilation of the opposing army in a sharp and quick victory. The vision was victory via the decisive battle, waged and won before enemy superiorities in troops and matériel could be brought to bear. The gambit seemed to offer a shortcut to decision and let the weaker power succeed at aggression, while avoiding a harder and longer war. In most cases, this was to chase an illusion. Dominant powers suffered from a similar misreading, especially after the Napoleonic Wars. Miscalculation sometimes led them, too, into unintended long wars of moral and material exhaustion. By 1914 the short-war illusion, the allure of quick victory by decisive battle, was universal.

Yet it was attrition rather than battles that decided most modern Great Power wars, though seldom by choice at the onset. More often, strategic attrition followed an opening flurry of indecisive fights, to take form as ruthless and relentless determination to endure until final victory, until the other side collapsed from casualties and exhaustion first. This book will not assess ongoing theoretical arguments over which is the preferable strategy in war: annihilation or exhaustion, seeking to win by an overwhelming blow against the enemy's main force at the outset or wearing down his will and capacity to continue fighting by raising his costs through attrition over time.[9] The argument here is that whatever the initial choice, few battles in the wars among Great Powers since the 17th century have proved to be more than locally or tactically decisive. In the largest wars fought among the biggest powers, a shared feature emerged instead: protracted stalemate born from a rough strategic balance, broken only after attritional wearing turned wars into contests of endurance. Exceptions were rare, such as the Austro-Prussian War and Franco-Prussian War, rapid victories by Prussia that only increased the allure of battle for Germans, contributing much to the miscalculations they made leading into the two world wars of the 20th century.

Arguing that battles were usually indecisive during the so-called "Age of Battle," and after, is not the same as saying that war was not worth waging. It is not true, as one historian of battle contends, that war long ago lost the virtue of decision.[10] Whether or not wars represent the best or only means of resolution of disputes, they have decided a great many things. We should not confuse the indecisiveness of grand-scale battles with the ultimate decisiveness of the biggest wars, whatever their short-run course and outcomes. Wars among the major powers have in fact rearranged history. While we are perhaps more uncomfortable with such thoughts than were our predecessors, what we share with them still is a longing to believe that battles decide wars, because wars really matter. Why else have we fought so many? Attrition seems to drain combat of its higher meaning and urgency, of a sense of moral purpose. Battles appear to better justify war by containing it to a limited theater and time, with a clear beginning, middle and end. The temptation to view battles that way reveals a persistent hope that they offer a place for something greater than we find in our own lives and daily affairs: heroism and genius.

Since 1815 the allure of battle has been manifest in war-planning and strategies pursued by key political leaders and military professionals and in the dominant theoretical literature. It was increasingly accompanied following the Napoleonic Wars by belief in an elusive military genius, that rare general who sees through to the essence of war and leads armies to decisive victory. The idea has intoxicated generations of generals and military theorists since Frederick and Napoleon. The ideal of leadership by the "great captains" of war reflects a core belief in battle as the canvas for genius in warcraft, or the so-called art of war. As such, it informed leading theories in the 19th century that became dominant in operational and strategic thinking, especially in Prussia and then Germany, into the middle of the 20th century.

Commanders said to have won modern history's greatest battles were singled out for a supposed innate genius with which only they saw through the thick fog of war, to its essence and to victory. Historians thus pronounced the Duke of Marlborough as unmatched in pluck, drive and skill. Frederick II's innovative "oblique order" was said to reveal a unique brilliance. Napoleon was the embodiment of genius, even when he failed to show it at Borodino or again at Waterloo (blame his subordinates or illness, or the weather and terrible mud). Lesser generals and subordinate decisions sometimes robbed a genius of his proper glory. Marshal Ney should never have advanced with cavalry alone at Waterloo. Why didn't he wait for infantry support? Robert E. Lee should not have sent Pickett's division to ruination at the center of the thick blue line on the third day at Gettysburg. According to his generals, Hitler should not have turned the panzers south toward Kiev, though by doing so he won the greatest encirclement victory and prisoner haul achieved to that point in the history of war. On small decisions turn battles, on singular battles turn the fortunes of war, and on the outcomes of war turns the history of the world.[11]

> For want of a nail the shoe was lost.
> For want of a shoe the horse was lost.
> For want of a horse the rider was lost.
> For want of a rider the message was lost.
> For want of a message the battle was lost.
> For want of a battle the kingdom was lost.
> All for want of a nail.[12]

In the major wars of the last three centuries, it was rarely the case that a single action would have led to a different outcome in a decisive battle, which then would have shifted the outcome of the war. The search for hinge moments that say otherwise seems almost desperate in its urgency to rescue the idea of heroic genius and decisive battle. Yet the idea of genius in war and in modern generalship persists, not least in order to affirm our connection to classical greats and ancient glory. Too many historians have overly celebrated Gustavus, Marlborough, Frederick II and yes, even Napoleon, at the cost of sweeping aside understanding of the greater role played by attrition in modern wars. Court historians conspired with poets and propagandists to obscure the harder realities of long wars at least until the 20th century, when total war obliterated individual genius and all short-war illusions alike, along with entire cities and tens of millions of lives.[13]

Even in wars fought with total means to the goal of total destruction, the allure of battle has endured. We look at great and long wars of attrition and see them not as heroic and meaningful but as tragic and wasteful. Tales of anonymous trenches in Crimea or in front of Mukden, or on the Isonzo and Western Fronts of World War I, or along the dreaded *Ostfront* in Russia in World War II, are generally told as morality plays of soldierly courage sacrificed to command stupidity; futile attacks by dull-witted generals or dictators; tragedies of wasted youth and lost generations.[14] Since Verdun and the Somme and Ypres, and many more mass bloodlettings, the dominant image of attrition warfare is that it proved utterly useless. Worse, it was immoral. The result was to call for a return to wars of movement, to restoring genius and mobility and quicker decision; to demand that war be fought in the old ways to bright new ends. Yet the trenches saved lives and reduced casualties relative to losses suffered in such maneuver battles as those fought in autumn 1914, and again in the German and Allied spring and summer offensives on the Western Front in 1918. Soldiers and armies dug trenches during the Great War and other wars because they provided protection from arcing shells and machine guns and bad plans. Defense also wins wars, even if with lesser allure.

Much in this book will be familiar to readers of military history, but I believe it is freshly presented with a perspective emphasizing a sense of how short-war thinking and battle-seeking by aggressor states in particular has evolved over time. Aside from the closing chapters—which concern Japanese planning and strategy from the first Sino-Japanese War in 1894 to the last dramatic days of World War II—the focus will be on the interplay between battle-seeking and abiding defensive realities as revealed over several centuries of Western warfare. It focuses on the biggest wars among the major powers because Europe's empires and wars drew in peoples and resources from around the globe until European domination ended in total war, and because of war, in 1945. Among the Great Powers during the period of European imperial ascendancy the allure of battle tempted most greatly. It was there that the appeal of short war was strongest and most enduring, dominating nearly all military thinking with ever more disastrous consequences to culminate in two protracted world wars decided by attrition in the first half of the 20th century.

The book does not argue that battle-seeking was always the wrong strategy throughout the period covered, or that all the wars considered were decided solely by attrition. However, it argues that, with few exceptions, the major power wars of the past several centuries were in the end decided by grinding exhaustion more than by the operational art of even the greatest of the modern great captains. Military history has too often ignored studying defense due to a distorting fascination with generalship in offense, as successive generations strove to overcome both deep natural and new technological advantages accruing to positional war and defensive postures. Traditional military history focused too much on Gustavus Adolphus' articulated lines, Frederick II's angled movements, Napoleon's "art of war" entire, Helmuth von Moltke's rapid movements to battle and overthrow strategy. Much is written still about efforts to restore mobility to wars that continually bogged down into position and attrition. Yet defense was also integral to major wars among the Great Powers, which very often reduced to victory by grinding rather than genius.

I believe it is important not to present cherry-picked examples to fit the argument. That is one reason I have included chapters on the success of Moltke's strategy in the Austro-Prussian War and his lasting influence over strategists everywhere even after his less convincing success in the Franco-Prussian War. Yet even these exceptions go some distance to establish the book's wider observation: Prussian twin triumphs with the "battle of annihilation" in the mid-19th century encouraged German operational hubris in the face of insurmountable odds and logistics issues in the first half of the 20th, when radical battle-seeking led to defeat in two long wars of attrition. Operational arrogance plunged Germans into wars that proved to be, and maybe always were, unwinnable struggles of matériel, additionally marked by the "peoples' war" Moltke and his followers so feared and sought desperately to avoid. German planners knew they could not win attrition wars against the hostile coalitions that their own aggressive policies and operations would create. The idea of a huge decisive battle at the very outset was their one way out of the strategic cul-de-sac, an operational solution to a political and strategic problem. It failed and brought the world to total war instead. The same allure beguiled Imperial Japan into starting what it thought would be "sharp decisive wars" that also ended in appalling attrition and defeat.

Although the lion's share of this book deals with modern European military history, it does not enter directly into debate over the so-called "Western way of war" thesis, the notion that modern war as waged by Western powers is uniquely rooted in classical traditions of legal and civic militarism and that it emphasizes battle-seeking and carnage as the essence of military culture.[15] Suffice to say that the practice and history of war in the West, or anywhere else, does not reduce to some Rosetta Stone of a single cultural model, or of claimed universally valid tactics or civic-military pattern or principles of war. No one fighting doctrine or stratagem is applicable in all places and times.

There was no single approach to combat in the jagged history of the West, let alone in the wider world. War is not reducible to one thing, be it a presumed tradition or fighting style or even the idea of decisive battle. Enemies adjust. War evolves. The real military history of the modern period was therefore far more muddled than any one theory encompasses. It was filled with tactical stumbling and unintended mayhem more than a singular culture, all well beyond mastery by any uniquely skilled general with a supposed genius for war.

This book highlights the clash between idealized generalship and iconic views of battle on one hand, and the powerful reality of moral and material attrition as the main determinants of outcome in wars among the Great Powers on the other. It does not suggest that ultimate decision by attrition is the inevitable outcome of all wars, or even of all Great Power wars. There was room in the past, as there appears to be in the present and likely will be in the future, for quick and complete victory if circumstances and events work out just right. That is why the allure of battle was so enticing, and so dangerous. When some Great Power faced an isolated small power in war, the outcome was usually as expected—though not always, for chance and war are linked because war takes place always inside a miasma of contingency. It was different when the Great Powers clashed directly, where misjudgments as to the real balance of power and military strength were more common; where chance or hubris or incompetence played an unexpected hand. It therefore took the wars themselves, not sudden but drawn out and exhausting the last resources of kings and states and then empires, to clarify or overthrow the old balance. Europe's wars increasingly became not king-to-king or state-to-state affairs but long contests among Great Power coalitions. Once that happened the opportunity to strike hard and fast, to march an army over a shared border and dictate terms before the summer was out, ended with the first snows. The chance to change the old order by resort to quick war was gone, though not the temptation to try. Time and again, challengers moving in a prewar fog thought they saw an opening and struck. Each time, they provoked into war a grand coalition dedicated to stop them. The culmination was the calamity of the two 20th century world wars. That is a central tale of this book.

The book starts with a short chapter reviewing the image of battle that preceded dramatic late medieval and early modern expansion of infantry armies. Next are discussed dramatic changes in gunpowder weapons and fortification, as well as the expansion of infantry under rising fiscal war-states. The "artillery fortress" retarded battle even as there was a revival of interest in classical military history by Renaissance thinkers, then again in the Enlightenment. A search got underway for better technologies to break through stone defenses, but also for new kinds of battlefield leaders who more closely embodied classical virtues and who would make war seemingly as of old, with clever maneuvers leading to a definitive clash of field armies. Yet, fixed stone defenses remained dominant even as early modern guns and infantry pointed the way to evolution of "new model armies" that emerged in the 17th century, to culminate in a different kind of tactical stalemate in linear warfare in the 18th century. Even so, Enlightenment writers pronounced that modern great captains had at last arrived on the battlefield, where they achieved a perfected understanding and practice of battle through applied reason. They were wrong: stone remained dominant. Battle-seeking only slowly came to the fore over the course of the late 18th century, ushering in a ferocious moment of revived movement to battle in the early 19th.

The Napoleonic Wars reflected a profound historical shift in command thinking, from battle-avoidance to what may only be described as veneration of battle. Napoleon's early and remarkable success at the tactical and operational levels of war obscured his ultimate defeat, as the Allies turned to attrition in Spain and Russia. After pulling his armies out of both those losing theaters, Napoleon's last campaigns in Germany and France exposed the fact that he lacked any strategic goal or plan beyond the next battle or campaign. Waterloo was not the moment of his decisive defeat, which really came a year earlier. It was his anticlimax. Even so, the Napoleonic style of battle-seeking aggression was elevated to the ideal, even perfect, form of war in the rigidly rationalist theories of Antoine-Henri Jomini and others. These highly influential early 19th century theorists distilled from Napoleon's maxims and practices, from his warcraft, a set of supposed universal principles they said reduced the eternal gamble that is all war to fixed rules about how to win or avoid defeat in all circumstances, times and places. Less influential at first but rising to dominate military theory and thinking later were differently admiring, yet similarly awestruck, views of Napoleon upheld in Carl von Clausewitz's deep Romantic idealism. For Napoleon's worshippers and Clausewitz's acolytes, the Philosopher's Stone became the military genius who transmutes maneuver into decisive annihilation in a climactic battle or campaign. It was an unstable chemistry that ultimately led to disaster.

For a great paradox arose in which battle-seeking became battle-worship, not just in the face of deeper attritional realities but *because* of them. The allure of battle, or put another way, the short-war illusion, came to dominate theory, tactics and operations into the first half of the 20th century. It did so in no small measure because the most effective strategies and key factors in victory and defeat in major-power wars nearly always proved in the end to be attritional.[16] Nobody wanted to accept that at the outset of the next war, since that made war as policy less attractive. Furthermore, attrition was viewed as a defensive and therefore long-war strategy that suggested stalemate, whereas genius always went on offense in search of quick and decisive victory. Battle innovation was thus the preferred solution for weaker aggressive powers facing high-cost and longer wars they knew they otherwise could not win. The idea had huge appeal for German and Japanese war-planners in the 20th century, weaker but highly aggressive powers that felt themselves ringed or hemmed in by opposition to their geopolitical ambitions. War came to be seen as at base a problem of command, which was malleable, not a struggle of matériel, in which they were overmatched from the start. It thereby retained utility as an option in national policy to further international ambition and aggression.

Morevoer, it was an article of faith in decisive battle theory that only genius could overcome the problems of stalemate, of fixed fortifications and long-war attrition. It was by sheer will and brilliance, by genius applied to military art, that great and natural generals could overcome long odds of strategic obstacles or inferiority. Had not Frederick II and Napoleon cut through Gordian knots of stalemate with their sharp Alexandrian swords? Did they not show that battle again could be decisive, if only one's commander was a genius? Yet the problem remained: how did one produce a genius, a great captain like Alexander or Napoleon, to triumph over the long odds against fast aggressive war in a world of balancing forces and Great Power coalitions? In an age increasingly devoted to science understood as discovery of a set of fixed rules in Nature, and dedicated to idealized rationality in all things, genius could be mapped. The instinctive insight into universal principles of war made by the natural genius, and its example, could be captured in prose and studied. Learn the campaigns of the great captains, remember their witty maxims and maneuvers, emulate their eternal principles of battle and war.

If genius revealed itself only once a campaign was actually engaged, at least it might be approximated by newly professional study. Prussians thus tried to institutionalize genius in their Great General Staff. It was a step back to Frederick and Napoleon, part of a "German way of war" that looked to *kurtz und vives* ("short and lively") wars of total and swift victory that could obviate deeper disadvantages of the Iron Kingdom's exposed central position and weak material basis for war.[17] It seemed to work. In 1866 Chief of Staff Helmuth von Moltke moved armies quickly along purpose-built railways to crush Habsburg Austria in six weeks, winning primacy in Germany. In 1870 he and Prussian Chancellor Otto von Bismarck isolated and defeated France in six months, winning hegemony in Europe. It seemed that Moltke's genius had broken the stalemate, leading to decisive political and strategic gains for Prussia. His name rose up the list of those to be studied and emulated.

Yet, well before Moltke's successes seduced Europe, two widely separated mid-19th century conflicts confirmed the continuing salience of attrition in modern warfare: the Crimean War and the American Civil War. Yet few right conclusions about attrition were drawn by planners of the next war in Europe from the appearance of trenches, long sieges, and mass casualties in the Crimea in the mid-1850s. Even less attention was paid to the trenches and high casualties that curled around Richmond in 1864–1865. The American Civil War was better known then (and arguably since) for its grand-scale but mostly indecisive Eastern battles than for its more decisive Western campaigns that savaged the overextended logistics and outer states of the Confederacy; or for its slower drama of fixed trench warfare in the last year in the East, the strangling Union naval blockade, and hard war by Union armies riding iron horses to tear apart the economy and destroy the will to continue fighting all across the deep South.

Europeans instead looked to the speedy Wars of German Unification, thence backward to Napoleon and Frederick II. Prussia's victories were indeed remarkably achieved, though not without major stumbles and scares. Carefully planned and prepared diplomatic circumstances by Bismarck, and then the astonishing shortness of the fighting season as conducted by Moltke, insulated the rest of Europe from these aggressive wars so that the German wars did not descend into general conflagrations, as well they might have. France was distracted by unrest at home and an imperial misadventure in Mexico, letting the Prussians destroy the Habsburg armies and win Germany. Four years later, Russia and Britain were distracted by conflicts within their respective empires while Prussian artillery encircled Paris. And so the King of Prussia was raised up to become Kaiser of a newly unified Germany, as Bismarck declared the creation of a Second Reich from inside the halls of Versailles itself. The shining allure of Prussia's decisive victory at Königgrätz in 1866 and brilliant glare from another triumph at Sedan in 1870 dazzled imaginations over the next several generations. The exemplar of the quick German Wars of Unification drove all thinking about mass armies and fast mobilization, and about how to fight and win the next war. Everyone said it must be done quickly, via even larger, faster, more ambitious campaigns and total victories, all planned and intended as war-winning knockout blows.

This was the fateful delusion with which all the major military powers planned for war long before it approached in midsummer 1914.

Moltke's field victories seemed to confirm that it was possible to break from the modern tendency to attrition, to escape the wearing high-casualty consequences of the mid-19th century "rifle revolution" and new rapid-fire artillery. A hugely damaging lesson was drawn from the wrong midcentury wars. Attrition fights, what Germans called *Materialschlacht* ("struggle of matériel"), could be avoided even when fighting another Great Power. You had to plan and conduct a lightning-fast campaign that replicated the winning maneuver tactics of Königgrätz or Sedan or Ulm, modern Cannaes all. It was still possible to send corps and armies flying across the countryside in search of the enemy and decisive battlefields, just as Frederick and Napoleon did, just as Scipio and Hannibal did. One might still find, fix and envelop whole enemy armies and wring political and strategic finality out of tactical and operational brilliance. Firepower advances that reinforced defense, basic matériel and manpower disadvantages, were not everything after all. There was room for genius still. There was a place for an iron national will to roll Bismarck's iron dice. War thus remained available as an instrument of policy, a continuation of diplomacy by other means, a cost-effective solution to geopolitical problems.

Less appreciated in 19th century Prussian military theory and 20th century German war-planning was the portentous people's war that in fact marked the end of the Franco-Prussian War. For fighting in France continued for months after Sedan, as the French populace was mobilized, new armies were raised and armed from abroad and national will to resist the Prussian invaders grew well after the French Army lost the opening battles. This resistance placed huge strains on the Prussian occupation, sustaining long-war fighting for which the Prussian Army was not prepared. Yet the opening successes fatally entrenched the allure of the battle of annihilation for Germans. For everyone else, it increased fear of losing that initial battle and thereby the next war. Decisive battle-seeking, with all its gambler's potential for strategic miscalculation and lack of logistical readiness to wage a more likely long war of attrition, was elevated as the new military standard for all the major powers. It became sheer dogma among German officers before 1914 and again before 1939, contributing to reckless prewar plans and then high-risk decision-making throughout both world wars.

In retrospect, it is clear that midcentury Prussian success was the exception to a larger pattern of rough strategic balance and long-war attrition as determinants in modern Great Power conflicts. Moltke himself warned that his day of cabinet wars was over and that only people's wars among aroused nations-in-arms lay ahead. He backed away from the idea that a Great Power could again be isolated and defeated as he and Bismarck isolated and broke Austria and then France. He warned against emulating his strategy, predicting that only long and wearing wars of attrition lay down that path. His own successors did not listen. Just as they remained indifferent to lessons of the trenches and killing fields of Crimea and Virginia, limited attention was paid to the battlefield lessons of the Russo-Japanese War of 1904–1905. There, high casualties were taken by both sides when facing machine guns, rapid-fire rifles and supporting artillery in fixed defenses.

The world's major militaries confidently said that in the next war *they* would avoid such problems via battles of maneuver, that *they* would overcome defensive firepower with some version of what the French called *élan vital*. A cult of the offensive and belief in the moral factor in war held sway everywhere.[18] All expected the next war to be one of rapid mobilization to the frontiers followed by short, sharp campaigns leading to decisive battles that would shape the outcome. They also feared the same thing coming at them from the other side, for it was another accepted lesson of Moltke's swift war example that speed to the opening battle somewhere along the frontiers was everything. So get there first, with every man you could muster, even if you had to shut down most of the economy to do it. If the enemy mobilized first, he might win the short war that everyone planned for and expected, and so the race to mobilize immense armies and move them at speed to the frontiers became all. This military concern added to the crisis atmosphere that led to profound feelings of vulnerability in July 1914, then to the speed at which the nations shifted from peace to war in the first days of August.

As future war planners worked for decades before 1914 from fear and fast-war assumptions, the Great Powers were all expanding their armies, and more, a capacity for social-material mobilization of millions of men and the supporting resources of entire nations. The stage was thus dressed for catastrophe in the two 20th century world wars. This is illustrated in chapters on the three most spectacular examples of decisive battle-seeking arising from short-war illusions. First, desperate German planning before World War I and the long war that resulted. Next, an even more profoundly delusional belief in the fast "war of annihilation" by panzer armies, given a sinister extra meaning by the Nazis. Finally, Imperial Japanese dedication to the same core idea of an opening war-winning battle, this one fought at sea, traced from the First Sino-Japanese War and the Russo-Japanese War through to long-war stalemate by attrition in the China War and defeat of staggering Japanese delusion in the Pacific War from 1941 to 1945.

Military historians already know these things. They are not the intended audience of this book. Its goal is to help correct distorted public memory of battle's place in modern war, to start to replace popular images of the decisive battle with somber appreciation of larger material and national commitments in wars decided by prolonged fighting that killed many hundreds of thousands in the 18th century, millions in the 19th, and tens of millions in the 20th. In these modern wars, fought on ever more massive scales to increasingly total ends by whatever means industrial technology and science provided, attrition nearly always proved the path to victory and defeat. Yet the old ideal of generalship, of a heroic genius on horseback singularly able to cut the hard knots of war by willpower and clever maneuvers, still haunted military imaginations and the battlefields. The allure of battle, an almost quaint throwback in the face of modern industrial and mobilization realities, helped deliver long wars instead of promised short ones. It helped bring about wars in which mass death and destruction, on scales hardly foreseen at their outset, became the ultimate means of reaching a lasting decision in quarrels among nations and empires. In attenuated form, it is a problem that abides still.

I

Battle in History

A WIDESPREAD BELIEF persisted, not for centuries but for at least two millennia, that when world history turned it did so on a few days or hours of intense violence, in major battles waged and won by great captains of special courage and genius. The ascent or toppling of dynasties and empires could be explained by a singular clash of arms so complete that the winner dictated the political and cultural direction taken by the loser. War's quick release of pent-up tectonic force, rather than slower processes of social erosion or cultural deposit, reshaped history in a red moment. Inside decisive wars, decisive battles shifted, shook and split apart deeply layered cultural and political foundations of civilizations.[1] Causality of complex change was reduced to a day of blood-soaked drama that decided whether ancient empires and cultures prospered or failed and how past eras would be framed or forgotten. A calamitous fight would stretch over just a morning or afternoon of intense drama. A crucial campaign might last only a spring or summer. Yet decades or even centuries of built-up pressure for change were released in sudden shudders of history-making carnage. Great wars and the battles that decided them were deep faults violently slipping to open critical fissures, breaking the bedrock of an ancient order and resetting the borders of whole ages, shaking empires to ruins, ending one era and uplifting a new one. Morally grotesque as brute contests of blood and bone might be, these spectacular battlefield clashes of muscle and machine were touchstones of political and cultural extinction or survival. Battles and wars lost or won fixed the fate of kings, countries, peoples and cultures.[2] Battle *was* history. War was destiny. Defeat was forever.

This approach is less often encountered in modern military history, though it is still not entirely absent. It retains some hold on an influential corner of the field and dominates popular accounts written for general readers.[3] Yet to view field battles as the soul of war and war as the soul of culture was always a gross misrepresentation and oversimplification of military *and* cultural history alike.[4] For it is also true that strategic victory even in many ancient wars was not always decided by the intervention of great captains of special genius who won spectacular battlefield victories, even before the limiting modern era of major-power balance and long wars of physical and material erosion. Ancient warfare also gave rise to protracted campaigns of endurance and to extended sieges; to exhaustion of men and matériel supply; to brutal treks and weary campaigns across hard, sun-beaten geography; to wearing out armies from bad weather and worse water and food. Playing a supporting role to physical attrition was moral exhaustion, until a war paused in stalemate or a limited victory was reached where one side's will or ability to resist eroded and flagged.

The persistence of decisive-battle thinking is less surprising when it is recalled that the notion germinated along with what is often described as the first writing of history (*historië*), a rudimentary empirical inquiry into causes of major events that was invented in Greece in the 5th century B.C.E. by Herodotus. He made the first known, serious endeavor to compose a fact-based account of events, or at least supplemented with facts the usual repetition of cultural myths and attribution of causation to the gods.[5] Herodotus proposed that at Plataea in 479 B.C.E. an army of 100,000 ordinary men did an extraordinary thing: they saved Greece from conquest by the Persian Emperor Xerxes, preserving the uniquely dynamic culture of the Peloponnese by force of arms and their wondrous moral and physical courage. He praised as well the Greek victories in the Persian Wars at Marathon, Salamis and Mycale, the latter fought in Asia Minor on the same day as Plataea.[6] Thus was born along with writing history the idea of battle as the great hinge turning the story of much larger things, and endless argument over causation and contingency. Is some great personage worthy of our praise or to blame for losing a cause or a kingdom in an afternoon? Was defeat foreseeable to reason or the Fates before a battle was even fought? Did an empire fall not through any hubris or moral fault but instead, as the rhyming medieval proverb put it, for some small and chance contingency, for simple "want of a nail"?

Dispute was immediate, as other Greeks emphasized the fight at Marathon as the truly decisive day in the long Persian Wars. They even pointed to a precise moment, the climax of a desperate charge by a hoplite phalanx that stopped, then broke, the advancing Persian line. The long-disputed hoplite charge is probably true in fact, if not detail. Most scholars believe it began not, as once said, from eight stadia (9/10ths of a mile) but at about 200–300 yards, or once the Greeks came within bowshot of Persian archers. The view of Greek courage being decisive at Marathon is not controversial, but the view of Marathon as uniquely decisive in the long war with Persia is. The claim likely originated among city propagandists pushing Athenian leadership in the contemporary affairs of Greece. With the ascendance of Athens, this version of the Greek-Persian wars became *the* epic legend, more powerful than the facts of a much wider war with the Persian Empire, at least as Herodotus presented it.[7] Marathon is still regularly described as the watershed moment in the rise of Athens, and so it was: had the Athenians failed on its field that day, their city-state must have succumbed to the Persian invaders, likely never would have built its famous and immense fleet, and might never have risen to become a first-tier power among the Greeks. Some battles in the Persian War were truly decisive. Marathon likely was one of several, as the defensive victory there proved key to the history of Athens in the larger Greek world after 490 B.C.E. It pushes things much too far to say, however, as some do, that on the fulcrum base of Marathon teetered all Western civilization over the next two millennia.[8]

The main point to be made here is that a powerful precedent of competing claims to decisive battle was set at the very beginning of *historiē*, of the art and practice of the historian. That led to disputes ever after about which battles were decisive and which were not, which era ended or began in some great war, and what civilization rose or fell on and because of a raw day of courage and gore. Sometimes the thesis is sustainable. Single battles did launch or end careers of city-states or imperial ambition and set the parameters of political competition and succession. This was almost certainly truer in early classical warfare than later in the period, notably in Greece before the 5th century B.C.E., when wars could be won or lost in a single battle. However, that changed with the Persian invasion and the rise of the Athenian empire, which led to larger and longer wars that had to be conceived and waged at a strategic scale of time, distance and multiple battles over long campaigns.[9] Witness the career of the greatest of the ancient captains, Alexander the Great. He won at Gaugamela in 331 B.C.E., but only as part and culmination of a much longer campaign of marches and city sieges across the Persian Empire. He later continued this protracted campaign strategy into India.[10]

Long strategic competition was as characteristic of Rome as of Greece. The First Punic War between Rome and Carthage lasted 23 years, ending in 241 B.C.E. in a narrow Roman victory on land and at sea, and then only after both sides faced internal rebellions and third-party tribal or mercenary threats to their respective frontiers. After a brief interval of peace, at the start of the Second Punic War came a spectacular but also highly risky invasion of Italy in 218 B.C.E. It was carried out by the supremely able Carthaginian general Hannibal Barca, another of the universally acknowledged great captains of antiquity. The campaign started after he crossed the Alps with Numidian cavalry and thousands of Gauls in close alliance. He won two sharp and bloody victories over Roman legions and their allies at the Trebia and Lake Trasimene that gave him control of northern Italy. Hannibal then effected total destruction of an entire Roman army at Cannae in 216 B.C.E. His crack Numidian cavalry pinned down the Roman left wing, buying the time needed for Hannibal to curl his heavy horse around the Roman right wing to suggest an envelopment. He was in the center while the bloody work on the wings continued, holding to prevent a Roman breakthrough in what remained most essentially an infantry battle. His cavalry took the Roman cavalry out of the decisive equation, and then the battle was finished by Hannibal's infantry turning inward on the advancing Roman infantry at the vital center. That enabled him to carry out his plan to annihilate, rather than simply defeat, a larger Roman force.[11] He inflicted the deaths of tens of thousands of legionaries and Roman allies (perhaps as many as 70,000), at a price of about 5,000 dead on his own side, mainly expendable men collected in Gaul. Survivors of the broken legions were thereafter exiled by Rome, sent off in disgrace. So devastating was the defeat that frightened Romans carried out human sacrifices, including of children, to appease their gods.[12]

Yet not even that single greatest battle and worst defeat of any army to that date in Rome's history sufficed to win the long struggle for Carthage. Rather than face and fight Hannibal in more costly field battles, fresh legions led by Quintus Fabius Maximus resumed a strategy of maneuver, deflection and harassment first employed after he was appointed dictator upon the defeat at Trasimene. It was readopted after the catastrophe at Cannae proved that facing Hannibal in direct combat would be unwise. The Romans also relied on their fortified towns and cities to stymie the Carthaginians. Refusing to fight Hannibal's army in the field except when absolutely necessary proved so effective it has entered the lexicon of strategic language as "Fabian strategy," or one relying on exhausting the enemy by battle-avoidance, to instead attack his supply and morale. Hannibal was unable to overcome this Roman refusal to meet him in open battle, where he expected his superior tactical skill would prove fatal to Rome. It has been called by some a huge miscalculation, even the most important error of the entire Second Punic War.[13] That may be unfair, considering he could not foresee such a novel approach to war. He still managed to tie down Roman legions and keep his army intact and in Italy for more than 15 years. It was a huge achievement, even if not a war-winning one.

Another claimed unforced error by Hannibal was to accept the defection from Rome by Capua, the second-largest city in Italy, but then not force its men into his army. Five years later, in 211 B.C.E., the Romans took Capua back after a long siege. It was an augury of Roman recovery to come. Mistake or not, this outcome was less a core weakness of Hannibal's strategy than a testament to Roman strengths that even his great skills could not overcome. He still won tactical moments that no Roman general could match, and few dared to come out to try against so feared and skilled an opponent. When challenged directly to do battle, he always won. Thus, he exceeded his earlier kill count at Lake Trasimene by eliminating another 16,000 Romans at Herdonea in 212 B.C.E. when the local governor foolishly came outside the walls to challenge him in battle. However, that was one of his last victories. After that, his position was worn down over time.

Hannibal's brilliant tactical feat at Cannae was the exemplar of the classical world's battle of annihilation of whole enemy armies, even the exemplar for all time.[14] Yet he gained no sustainable result. He was instead forced by his enemy's residual strength and Fabian strategy to conduct strategically indecisive annual campaigns up and down Italy's peninsula. His 15-year effort to undercut local Latin and Italian alliances on which Rome's power relied enjoyed some success, but ultimately proved vain. Carthage offered him less than full support by deciding to reinforce its armies defending Iberia in preference to aiding Hannibal's stalled offensive in Italy. In the strategic contest that ensued, stretching over years and from Spain to Italy to Africa, it was deeper Roman reserves, Hannibal's inability to force a second and then a third Cannae, and his failure to break down Roman city walls to win by sieges that told the strategic tale. His strength waned as Roman capabilities recovered, then waxed. Rome utilized its navy to prevent reinforcement of Hannibal's army in Italy as three Scipios in succession crossed over to Spain at the head of fresh Roman armies. They undertook a brutal and successful assault on the bases of Carthaginian finance in Iberia, and thus its long-term capacity to wage war against Rome. By way of first invading Sicily, with the moment prepared, Scipio Africanus invaded Africa in 204 B.C.E. and proceeded to devastate the Carthaginian homeland.

With realigned Numidian allies alongside, who posed an additional threat to Carthage, Scipio's foray into Sicily and Africa forced Hannibal's recall from Italy. The great Carthaginian general led a last army out to meet Scipio, himself a sometime imitator of Hannibal's innovative battle tactics. Hannibal suffered a crushing defeat, his first, at Zama in 202 B.C.E.[15] These are well-known facts of his career, yet one still encounters the argument, wrapped in an assumption that all wars are won by tactical genius acting through decisive battles, that the most important truth of the Second Punic

War was not Hannibal's ultimate defeat but his situational success, his surely brilliant tactical innovations rather than his and Cathage's strategic stumbles. On the other side is presented the comparable brilliance of Scipio Africanus, said to be another of the ancient great captains. Which to choose? One historian writes: "All things being equal, it is probable that Hannibal would have been the victor at Zama because he was the greater of the two generals."[16] That misses the whole point of Roman strength and strategy, which was to ensure that things were *not* equal. They almost never are in war. It was not Hannibal's losing one battle that lost the war. It was strategic erosion in protracted fighting in Iberia and on the water that reduced Carthage from a rival for Mediterranean hegemony to a future vassal of Rome.[17] It turns out that in the Second Punic War running a deliberate strategic and military marathon to its conclusion, not seeking to always fight Marathons, was what really mattered. Only then could the coup de grâce to end the war be delivered at Zama.

There is no doubting the human drama of the earlier fighting in Italy and the spectacular carnage brought about by Hannibal's tactical brilliance at Cannae. Yet the crucial truth about his generalship and battlefield victories was that tactical success in the most vaunted battle with Rome did not transmute into winning political or strategic results for Carthage. It seems an obvious point. Yet in the centuries and millennia that followed, Carthaginian defeat in the Punic Wars did not stop modern planners and generals from elevating Hannibal's tactic of envelopment at Cannae to an ideal war-winning strategy. Over 2,000 years later, in planning German operations before World War I, Cannae was invoked by Chief of the Imperial Great General Staff Alfred von Schlieffen as the model for a German war-winning campaign in Europe.[18] The abiding call of Cannae as the model of the battle of annihilation again exercised an inordinate influence on German thinking before and during World War II. It is not entirely coincidental that, just as Carthage was worn down in a long war and Hannibal ultimately endured crushing defeat on the field at Zama, his latter-day German admirers suffered catastrophic reverses that twice forced them into long wars they could not win, leading to ever more desperate throws of the iron dice as attrition brought complete defeat in 1918 and absolute defeat in 1945.

Not even Julius Caesar triumphed quickly or easily in the war that made his career, the conquest of Gaul. He needed eight years and extensive fortified defensive lines and works to vanquish the Celts and occupy Gaul.[19] Farther frontiers in Germany, the Balkans and the eastern Mediterranean saw chronic border wars marked by long Roman and enemy campaigns of cruel and vengeful slow war, rather than rapid conquest via great battles. Germania never succumbed to Rome. Instead, punitive raids and frontier campaigns, mixed with local truces and compromises, stretched over decades and even centuries. Despite these long campaigns, later commentators often attributed the Roman failure to conquer Germania to a single battle, pointing to three autumn days in 9 C.E. when wilder tribes ambushed and obliterated three legions, along with all their families, led into disaster in the forest by Publius Quinctilius Varus.[20] The defeat encouraged Augustus and most of his successors to be more conservative in their grand strategy approach to setting outer limits to imperial expansion. Yet the supposed world-historical import of the fight in the Teutoburger Wald was trumpeted too loudly by 19th-century German nationalists. Poets and historians alike exaggerated those three days of slaughter and their architect, Arminius, to a determinative role in all European history that followed. Similarly, a notable Victorian chronicler of world battles, Edward Creasy, oddly ascribed Britain's independence in the mid-19th century to a single leafy victory by German tribes "to which we owe our freedom." German nationalist insistence that Teutoburger Wald was the "sister of Cannae" probably spoke more unintended truth about the underlying attritional nature of the long fight with Rome than was realized by romanticizing poets and chauvinist historians centuries afterward.[21]

The Roman Army fought many battles and lost quite a large number of them, along with possibly hundreds of thousands of dead legionaries and auxiliary troops along the way.[22] The real question is what made it dominant for centuries nonetheless, despite an initial paucity of natural resources in the Italian homeland and early vulnerability to powerful rivals? If singular battles decide wars, how did Rome recover and thrive after its thrashing at Cannae? The answer lay, as it usually does in drawn-out war, not in brilliant tactics or operations or superior generals but in superior social organization and a deep capacity for logistics. In the case of Rome, it lay also in the war ethos of the ruling oligarchy; in ruthless civic discipline that translated into tough army discipline and long-war prowess; expectations of sacrifice by a long-service conscript army that was constantly at war, and thus always well trained and usually experienced; underlying economic and demographic strengths of an immense empire; lack of a serious challenger to political or military primacy after its defeat of Carthage; and carefully constructed alliances that supplemented Roman martial endurance over multiple campaigns during protracted wars that ultimately took down serial enemies.[23] Virtually every class of Roman benefited from imperial military policy. The ruling class gained political power and career advancement, while the lesser classes gained conquered lands to exploit and some political recognition. That is why so many Romans were willing to fight and to die in the effort to gain and keep these advantages. Destroy one legion and another marched out to fight, in an extraordinary display of unmatched strategic depth and strength.

It was not a record of winning field battles per se that made Rome the dominant military power of its time, though its best generals won more than their share of open fights against less well-organized, trained or supplied enemies. What mattered more was the Roman state's ability to replace its losses from a vast military establishment (standing army) and thus to continue fighting; to come back at its enemies in wave after demoralizing wave of fresh legions and auxiliaries, and with highly capable engineers and supply units moving armies over excellent roads or by galley atop closed Roman seas. This strategic capacity to absorb a defeat, even a catastrophic defeat, was rooted in economic, social, and cultural reserves and enforced martial and civic unity, more than in superior tactics or generalship. It was vital, for example, that the ruling class was willing to expand the civic franchise, in contrast to Athens, which restricted citizenship to those born to two Athenian parents. Rome had a strategic capacity for war that compensated for occasional tactical inadequacy by poorer generals and less capable legions. This reservoir was unmatched by any enemy, at least until the Empire fractured and the end arrived. Even then, the last act played out very slowly, as many "barbarians" served in the Roman Army while others fought against it in centuries-long armed conflicts that were always wearing and hardly ever spectacular.

Rome's final defeat had more to do with cultural decline than battlefield losses; with governing elite and army corruption, military mutinies, protracted civil wars, and too many emperors' reigns lived in fear and cut short by an assassin's dagger. Defeat at Adrianople in 378 C.E. was perhaps the closest thing to a decisive battle in this period, since it resulted in the Goths permanently taking up residence in the Empire.[24] Otherwise, it is hard to find determining defeats of Rome in its protracted frontier wars, against invading armies that are often better understood as the leading edge of slow migrations of well-armed peoples. From the 3rd through the 5th centuries C.E., alien military cultures and powers encroached on Rome's frontiers until they also exerted influence over the core areas of the empire, so that power flowed out from the center to the provinces. Tyrants and generals came and went in Rome, while the imperial frontiers were assailed and overrun. Edward Gibbon, magisterial 18th-century chronicler of the so-called "Fall of Rome," thought this was a long and decadent decline marked by a procession of ineffective general-emperors from "the barracks, to the throne, to the grave." However, modern scholars have demonstrated that it was less a sequence of lost wars than a slow and complex interaction of barbarian cultures with late-day Roman efforts to adjust to and control the migrations, while also including drawn-out fighting with military enemies far more sophisticated than once thought.[25]

***

WHAT OF THE long interregnum of medieval warfare, between the slow passing away of the last uniformed legionaries in the Western Empire and the rise of early modern states in Western Europe by the 15th century? It used to be said that a collapse into darkness came with the "Fall of Rome." In the early medieval period, populations were forced to huddle near private forts that hardly resembled vanished legion garrisons. Religious authorities proclaimed moral law in lieu of state law that was mostly unenforceable, as baronies and rudimentary kingdoms laid conflicting claims to political loyalty and secular jurisprudence. Roads and river routes fell into disuse while personal security and commerce waned. With no central military authority to enforce edicts and laws, taxes went uncollected or unpaid and justice along with order devolved into private hands. Cities declined, production and population declined, and in the minds of too many later commentators something essential in the quality of war also declined.

This older view of the period held that it was difficult or impossible to impose political will by force of arms over a large area, or to raise revenue from the great rural magnates who employed armed war bands to defy the writ of kings, and themselves dominated nearby towns and the countryside. Fighting was characterized by raiding along unmarked marches (disputed frontiers) and violent contests in the country as minor nobles heading private retinues clashed over local issues and squabbles.[26] Unprotected populations were said to have shriveled until large swaths of fertile land were allowed to overgrow or reverted to marsh. As supplies of coin and trade fell, wage-based armies dwindled, too. Most fighting involved magnate suppression of minor local revolts or opposition to weak kings by powerful provincial warlords. Given reduced populations and lesser social capacity to field or sustain large armies, grand-scale battles were said to be rare.

Modern scholars dispute much of this outdated view of medieval warfare, seeing even the early medieval period as exhibiting far more military sophistication than previously believed.[27] However, it remains a dominant popular image in which fragmented peoples of the Latin West suffered long defensive wars against external raiders and invaders, cleaving to whatever motte-and-bailey or other castellan security they could. Terrifying barbarian raids were followed by migration-invasions by aggressive peoples decanting swiftly over open frontiers on land and by sea: Eurasian nomads like the Magyars rode out of the east; Vikings descended in fast longships from the north, scouring coasts and following rivers as far inland as Paris and Kiev; Muslim invaders swelled out of the Middle East and across North Africa, thence into Sicily, reaching southern Italy and Iberia, penetrating briefly into the south of France.[28] Much of the older tale of a cacophony of endless small raids and woe has been replaced by understanding that Vikings and other raiders had only limited effects. Besides, the Western Roman Empire, too, had been beset at the end by protracted frontier fighting and internal military and political divisions. It, too, faced powerful invaders, including Huns and Goths. It also lost territory and traditional civic liberties as the standing army merged slowly with the new arrivals over its last centuries. Comparable conditions thus marked the late Roman period and the early medieval world. The vaunted descent and break from Rome once said to be fundamental and deleterious in all things military and cultural was actually less sharp or complete than once thought and taught.[29]

Writing in the Renaissance glow of admiration for all things ancient and rediscovered, and parallel contempt for most things medieval, early modern thinkers like Niccolò Machiavelli disdained what they saw as a muddled mayhem of medieval warfare in a lesser age following the classical and preceding their own.[30] It was asserted and regretted that successor states to the Western Empire had no standing armies, no far-flung garrisons of uniformed troops to project power and guard their frontiers. Armies and set-piece battles alike were said to have lost utility for impoverished and inferior post-Romans. Kings were monarchs mainly in title, their petty states fragmented provinces of a sunset imperial glory. Worse, with the decline of standing armies and fixed battle the successor kingdoms lost civic virtue along with martial skill. The old military and aristocratic classes drawn from Roman towns and cities were replaced by illiterate, grubby rural nobilities. Generals were boorish pretenders to the arts of war, while the helter-skelter armies they led were little more than armed rabble. A medieval warrior surely had skills, but he fought merely as an individual or with a few retainers, not as a soldier. This was the myth of the pinnacle knight, rather than the reality of medieval armies and *milites* as armed retinues drawn from a wide range of social backgrounds, who had varying and often considerable military skills.

It was a powerful, negative myth. Compared to Greece and Rome, what had medieval sieges, mad mêlées, seasonal soldiers and roving companies of mercenaries to offer the rising ambition of the city-states of the Italian

Renaissance? Unedifying, slow sieges marked indecisive wars. Where were the great battles to break the stalemate? After the passing of Charlemagne, no great captain rivaled in noble deeds a Hannibal or Scipio or Caesar, and even Charlemagne was suspect.[31] There was no medieval Marathon or Salamis. Where were the medieval Cannae or Actium or Adrianople, fulcrum moments of spectacular violence to balance the scales of civilization and move glory and history forward?[32] Surely a battle was better than a siege? What use were frustrating summer campaigns aimed at vulgar collective theft, or even grand *chevauchées*, the great and terrible "ridings" of cavalry and dragoons that burned out huge swaths of France during the Hundred Years' War?[33] What had medieval experience to teach early moderns, compared to the eternal and more heroic lessons of the Peloponnesian War or the Punic Wars or the Roman conquests of Gaul and Britain? Medieval warfare lacked all that was best and admirable about war in antiquity: discipline, civic militarism, large armies and major engagements, and most of all, the inspired genius of the great captains. Wars were also said to have been fought for the wrong reasons: in the name of God and to the purposes of the Church, not as they should be, for the interests of the rising secular states of the Italian Renaissance and at the behest of their princes and the sovereigns of Europe.

This hypercritical, dismissive view took hold during the Renaissance and held on for centuries. As late as 1885, an influential medievalist, Charles Oman, still described medieval warfare in hoary terms born of Renaissance and Enlightenment critiques, reinforced by the 19th century's seduction by Napoleonic battle.[34] Oman dismissed all medieval warriors as tactical amateurs, their armies as primitive and uncaring about operations (then called "campaign tactics"), their leaders as ignorant of what is now called grand strategy. In the wake of the 18th- and early 19th-century revival of field battle outside the window of his study, in the aftermath of Frederick and Napoleon and Moltke, Oman thought he saw that the proper path to victory in war only and *always* came from decisive battle, and he just could not find any in the medieval record.[35] Medieval armies, it was said by later critics, waged a false form of warfare. Chronic fighting was not true war, as Greece and Rome practiced the high military arts of generalship and strategy. Not the kind of virtuous civic wars to which Machiavelli aspired or the beautiful linear fights envisioned by the Enlightenment, filled with rippling arpeggios of musketry and crescendos of cannon guided in tight orchestral splendor by a marshal's baton. Not the kind of war 19th-century writers identified with revived battle-seeking under the guiding genius of modern great captains. Oman's work still exerted influence into the middle of the 20th century. It was not just generals and kings who succumbed to the allure of battle. Scholars, too, were drawn to the siren's song.[36]

They also began a search for a medieval pedigree worthy of remembrance and glorification, for battles and heroes who might link early modern Europe to the classical world, erecting the first on the sturdy shoulders of the second.[37] A modern equivalent is the "Western way of war" thesis that asserts a tradition of lethal, linear war running from 20th- and 21st-century Western societies back to the citizen armies of Rome and Greece, oddly skipping almost entirely the nonlinear military history of the Middle Ages. Such searching through medieval military history for its missing heroes and epic fights sometimes led to invention almost from whole cloth. Edward Gibbon believed he found a key moment in a grubby skirmish at Tours-Poitiers in 732 (or 734) C.E.[38] There, in what by ancient standards was little more than a blocked cavalry raid, Charles Martel led a Frankish army against a scouting party of encamped Moorish horsemen. Gibbon proclaimed that the bold Franks stopped no less than an entire alternate history that autumnal day, blocking an unbroken march of Islamic conquest 1,000 miles in extent, poised to pour into Europe. Had Islamic horse soldiers won at Tours instead of the Franks, he famously opined, "the interpretation of the Koran would now be taught in the schools of Oxford, and her pulpits might demonstrate to a circumcised people the sanctity and truth of the revelation of Mahomet."[39]

The claim took hold in spite of a lack of evidence. Even the great empiricist 19th-century German historian, Leopold von Ranke, recorded Tours as a vital moment in protecting Western civilization from being overrun by invading Islam, while Edward Creasy numbered Tours among the fifteen most decisive battles in world history. Hans Delbrück affirmed not only that Charles Martel "saved the state from the Moslems" but indeed, there was "no more important battle in world history." Others argued that Tours-Poitiers was decisive in another way, linking the fight to a once dominant but since discarded military theory of feudalism. The threat from Muslim horsemen, it was written, compelled the Franks to turn to heavy cavalry. Within just 50 years, Carolingian armies adopted shock tactics of charging mounted knights, inaugurating centuries of profound social, political, military and cultural domination by the horse-borne warrior class. Frankish victory at Tours-Poitiers was also widely celebrated in poetry and painting.[40] Even Adolf Hitler, who knew little real history and understood less, was perversely impressed by what he thought Tours represented. He believed it led to the cultural disintegration of Europe, opining that it would have been preferable if Islam—which he saw as a triumphal warrior faith, as opposed to decadent and weak Christianity—had conquered instead. *Contra* Gibbon, Hitler held that if Europe had become Muslim in the 8th century Germans would have achieved far more in world history by his own day, smoothing Germany's path to world historical greatness.[41]

How decisive was Tours in reality? Today most historians see Tours-Poitiers as a minor engagement and point out that the rise to dominance of heavy cavalry shock tactics developed much later, over the 11th–12th centuries.[42] Two leading military historians *explicitly* excluded it from a study of important battles on the ground that it lacked either contemporary or any lasting significance. It did not even make their index.[43] Yet entrenched belief that decisive battles have changed world history, and hence the old view of the importance of Tours, dies hard, if at all.[44] That the fight at Tours was upheld in later centuries as a world historical moment central to survival and all later history of the West says more about the abiding temptation to overstate the importance of singular battles than it does about real history. Add Hastings and a few more bloody days, and it is still a hard case to make that the medieval period saw hinge moments akin to certain of the great fights of the classical world.[45] Worse, fixation on the search for decisive battles overlooks the fact that while centuries of medieval warfare were not for the most part battle-centric, the wars of the period were still vitally important to all those involved.

Modern scholarship has instead revealed that there was real sophistication in the strategy and mobilization capabilities of late medieval societies. The period's emperors, kings and generals probably had just as sophisticated (or just as weak or inept) an understanding of tactics, campaigns and higher strategy as anyone else, including their classical predecessors and early modern successors.[46] That is why they decided that battles most often were *not* preferable to sieges. It was still true, as Tacitus wrote, that *pecunia nervus belli* ("money is the sinew of war"). A siege was usually more profitable than a battle won and less risky than a battle tried. If a renowned fortress capitulated to besiegers, lesser forts often surrendered, too, swinging whole regions from one overlord to another. A successful siege gave the victor not just laurels but lands, portable booty and a ready fortress or two to defend his gains. Battlefield victories sometimes had a similar effect, giving the winner a reputation for invincibility that made conquest look inevitable and resistance seem dangerous and futile. However, field engagements were much riskier to fragile armies than a summer's siege that could be tried again next year if unsuccessful. Open fighting was usually avoided unless one side was forced to fight by the need to relieve an ongoing siege or interrupt a *chevauchée*. The latter tactic was hugely destructive and also more strategically efficacious than risky field battles: a hard riding to raze crops and rural infrastructure (mills, barns and granaries), scorch the enemy king's resources, perhaps provoke him into offering open combat while also threatening his legitimacy by exposing an inability to defend his subjects. It had a core logistical purpose, too. Riding out on *chevauchée* permitted a marauding army to live off the enemy's lands and hurt his war finance while paying one's own hired troops with plundered goods and prisoner ransoms rather than hard-to-come-by money wages. Many of these principles and practices were so useful they survived well past the end of the medieval period.[47]

A key difference from Rome was that medieval societies lacked the capacity to support large armies for very long, so that sharp limits of weak finance and logistics curtailed large-scale fighting.[48] This was not for lack of will or want of wit. Territorial conquest was also retarded by fortification of large towns and a remarkable motte-and-bailey, and later stone, encastellation of the countryside. Yes, that meant radical military decentralization compared to Rome. However, it was not decadence. It is better understood as adaptation to new social and military realities: political domination of the demesne and superiority of defensive technologies over offensive capabilities.[49] Why risk an enormously expensive army in a terrible mêlée? Why commit to battle and possibly lose in a day precious human and material resources husbanded for years and needed for defense and political suppression as well as conquest? Field combat was just too risky, because too bloody. From the 11th to the 15th centuries in Western Europe, a losing side in an average battle suffered between 20 to 50 percent of its men killed outright.[50] Risk-averse kings and generals would continue avoiding large-scale battles long after the end of the medieval period, well into the 18th century. Mostly, that was wisdom.

Weak royal finances and limited logistics, not proclaimed devotion to a liege lord or the raised cross, were the true medieval Gods of War. In addition, baronies, bishoprics and even large towns all asserted a range of military rights of attack and defense, leading to nearly interminable conflict. Fragmentation of the legal and moral claim to exercise the right to go to war (*jus ad bellum*) rested atop rudimentary recruitment systems, undercut by a lack of coin to pay hired troops. Adding in supply issues, a king's authority was difficult to enforce beyond a few days' or weeks' march. Once there, he quickly met sturdy resistance from magnates in control of private armies, forts and castles. Thus, the dukes of Normandy and not the kings of France ruled that rich province from a great stone castle in Falaise, as did other lords protected from kings or emperors in stone forts across Europe. Later, urban militias emerged that were jealous to defend from behind city walls old civic rights and medieval privileges against aggressive barons and monarchs alike. There was even micro-fortification *inside* the walls of the city-states of Italy.[51]

Overlapping loyalties and strategic impasse along ill-defined frontiers led to chronic if unspectacular fighting in which many conflicts lasted decades, while some lasted centuries.[52] The *Reconquista* by Iberian Christians waged on and off against Muslim al-Andalus from the 9th century did not end until the fall of Granada to a Christian siege in 1492. It was dominated by orders of ecclesiastical knights ("warrior monks") such as Calatrava, Santiago, and Alcántara, among others. These were warrior knights (*miles*) who adopted elements of monastic rule, but whose armies also included paid troops.[53] Another armed migration disguised and justified as high crusade saw forced conversion and castellan occupation of north Germany and the western Slav lands, as the Teutonic Knights brought the terror of the cross to the Baltic shore, Poland and Lithuania.[54] The more famous crusades to the holy lands of the Middle East by ecclesiastical knights engaged in military campaigns

Castelo de Feira.
Courtesy of Wikimedia Creative Commons.

driven by religion occupied almost 200 years of Norman and Latin Christian effort.[55]

The popes also preached a formal Albigensian Crusade in southern France. It was carried out over two generations by French knights against Cathars declared heretic, and to suppress Languedoc independence. It wreaked that province with *guerre mortelle*: a savage campaign of terror waged without pity or quarter. Over its dread course there were few set-piece battles. The Cathar Wars were instead a sequence of cruel sieges of hunkered-down defenders inside fortified homesteads (*castra*), and one or two great stone refuge castles like Carcassonne. There were brutal *chevauchées* and lesser cavalry raids to burn out villages and wreck the countryside; deliberate terror and indiscriminate slaughter of whole towns; atrocities on a wide scale, including mass ritual burnings.[56] Another drawn-out conflict of late medieval times, though with less deliberate terror and destruction, was the papal-imperial-baronial struggle known as the wars of the Guelphs and Ghibellines. It spanned parts of northern Italy, Austria and southern Germany for nearly two centuries and continued in attenuated form as factional division into the early Renaissance (and into Dante's *Inferno*).[57]

If there was no direct line in heroic military endeavor from Caesar to Tours to the Renaissance, or to the later armies of enlightened French or Prussian kings, a different approach was needed to link the classical to the early modern and modern. If the successor states to Rome were dismissed as squalid entities struggling through centuries of "Dark Ages," retaining only faded memories of lost martial vigor and the glory that was Rome, the task ceased to be finding missing heroism in the medieval mud but to ensure that the Renaissance and the Enlightenment left the Middle Ages behind entirely, returning directly to the ancients in war as in all other valued things. How to get there, when there was so little to build on in the post-Roman military history of the West? The answer many came to was to literally overlook the medieval in direct emulation of the ancient world, where the Italian Renaissance and French Enlightenment thought they saw ever-lasting verities and warfare glorious in battles conducted by armies led by the great captains of antiquity.

Partly, this conclusion grew in reaction to the frustrating fact that slow and indecisive siege warfare continued to dominate over field armies for centuries more, deep into the wars of the Renaissance and after, and into the Enlightenment era as well.[58] Defending or besieging walls remained the main form of engagement, steering armies around fortifications or forcing them to stop maneuvering and dig trenches at their base. A great irony of Machiavelli's time and reform ambition is that siegecraft and defense against besiegers, rather than field battles, were alike boosted by the new rationalism. Fresh advances were made in fortification by the Italian city-states that, when exported to the rest of Europe and beyond, came to be known as the *trace italienne*. This was a real and important achievement reinforcing the dominance of sieges (positional warfare), and thus far from the ideal of revived battle-seeking by republican and citizen militia armies upheld by admirers of classical warfare and by reformers such as Machiavelli.[59] The new geometrical warfare that began in Machiavelli's Italy culminated later in the perfect symmetry of rational fortresses, sieges and trench lines in Louis XIV's France.

***

A GENERAL SHIFT to infantry as the backbone of later medieval armies is known to period historians as the "infantry revolution" of the 14th century. Even before that, in certain locales a greater role for infantry was evident, such as in English armies as well as in urban militia in Flanders and Italy. Displacing service nobilities and lordship retinues as the iron in the soul of late medieval warfare, armies in Western Europe moved toward inclusion of lower-class and lower-skilled, and hence cheaper, infantry units. In contrast, armies in Eastern Europe and Russia remained centered on cavalry. That was not because they lagged in reform and modernization, but because there were fewer natural obstacles or fortifications in the east, and distances between towns were greater. Hence, foraging was harder in Poland, Ukraine and western Russia. The new troops in Western Europe were armed with bows, longbows, crossbows, axes and halberds, all protected from heavy cavalry assault by hedges of foot soldiers presenting iron-tipped spears—pikers, in one guise or another. Swiss *Haufen* ("heaps") or squares guarded halberdiers, axemen, crossbowmen and later also musketeers, showing hedgerow edgings of iron-tipped pikes to charging horsemen. Scottish schiltrons were circular pike hedges. Flemings fought in ranks with short pikes (*goedendags* or "hello" spears). In sum, pike-and-bow (and later, pike-and-musket) infantry formations and tactics developed that challenged the dominance of heavy cavalry and their supporting men-at-arms. The changeover took time, but was marked.[60]

Change and adaptation were in part a function of population recovery, and partly due to wealthier economies and monarchs reshaping armies to new centralizing purposes. Foot soldiers, often mercenaries, bulwarked weak kings against truculent nobles. Old-style mounted, armored warriors were vastly pricier than the new-style cloth-and-crossbow or axe soldiers. The old warrior classes were, moreover, too often less than obedient to royal authority. Also pushing the hereditary warrior classes from their old central place on the battlefield was technology. Velocity and accuracy-at-distance improvements came to all projectile weapons, with infantry rearmed over time with greater killing-power-at-distance as short or long muscle-drawn bows gave way to mechanically cranked, then to all-steel crossbows. Primitive long guns known then as hand cannon (or "handgonnes") pointed the way to later arquebuses, and eventually to fully developed matchlock muskets. Weapons thus became available that were increasingly capable of piercing the heaviest body armor.

Reloading steel crossbows required both hands (and often also a foot) to draw or crank and fit the quarrel. Matchlocks gripping smoldering fuse (a length of match rope) on arquebuses were extinguished in a breeze, and pan powder flew into the air at a canter or gallop. Since these weapons could not be used easily or even at all from horseback, they were put in the hands of new and far more cheaply trained and armed infantry. Even so, transition to the new infantry dominance in battle still took many decades. Heavy muskets at first had to be held and fired by two men, or from a tripod rest, or mounted on wagons (*arquebus à croc*), or hooked over a castle or town wall. Later and much lighter matchlock muskets still had the problems of matches that were too easily extinguished and powder that became too damp in rain or mist or humid weather, while even later fusils (flintlocks) still retained the pan and wind problem. Nevertheless, progressively over time, the return of soldier's wages, the interest of centralizing kings in monopolizing military force, and new weapons technologies conspired to raise the role of infantry and lessen that of hereditary heavy cavalry, a change with enormous social implications as well. With ever larger field armies as the overall trend, the late medieval shift included an inching back to battles as a deliberate choice by some commanders. Slow war of stone and siege remained overwhelmingly dominant, but the incidence of field engagements increased as roving armies encountered each other more often and in greater numbers.[61]

The critical change was in the way the new weapons were used and what this meant for those who used them. To be truly effective against more traditional horse armies and similarly armed infantry armies, projectile and puncturing weapons that took two hands to load and fire absolutely necessitated fighting in unison, with some foot soldiers armed with pikes or halberds protecting the missile troops. This was seen in many different forms, though none so intimidating or successful as in the advanced tactics of an attacking Swiss square, or two or three moving in echelon with a small "forlorn hope" of skirmishers thrown out ahead to distract and confuse the waiting enemy.

The need to fight in close unison, as soldiers, meant a limited revival of drill to learn marching and fighting moves on which the life of each man in the pike unit depended. Drill and fighting together in turn raised levels of esprit de corps among lower classes entering upon the battlefield in large numbers. Class animosity came with them, as when Welsh and English archers slaughtered noble French prisoners at Agincourt, where French knights also rode with lethal contempt right though hired Genoese crossbowmen on their own side.[62] No one gave much quarter in victory or received any in defeat, particularly as proliferating foot soldiers from self-governing Flanders towns or kingless Swiss valleys and cantons fought the old martial aristocracies of France and Austria, with extremely violent results. Heavy cavalry could and did still win against the new infantry-heavy armies, but over time new-style and lower-class infantry unhorsed the mounted aristocrats at least from their military primacy.[63] It took centuries longer, but lowly infantry with better muskets, later self-protected from cavalry by bayonets, would in time unseat aristocracies from privileged positions in social and political arenas as well.

The first real surprise for the old order came outside the walls of Courtrai in Flanders on July 11, 1302, where urban militia with eight-foot *goedendags* and long-handled axes trapped, hooked, dehorsed and slaughtered over 1,000 fathers and sons of the French nobility. Pulled off their mounts with hooked pikes and halberds, or dismounted by horses gashed and screaming and bucking beneath them, knights turtled in constricting armor on the ground and were dirked or spiked where their armor lapsed: under the arm, into the groin or through a visor. Or they were hacked apart with two-handed axes. This axe slaughter of knights and their expensive trained warhorses (destriers) is known to history by the gentle, romantic name "Battle of the Golden Spurs," after the dead horsemen's accouterments that Flemings rinsed off and hung in their town church. That clinking boast inspired the French nobility to come back decades later to claim their grandfathers' spurs in an orgy of blood and class revenge.[64] Nevertheless, the damage to the reputation of heavy cavalry was permanent and severe. At Bannockburn, across the Narrow Sea, in 1314 Scots on foot faced and defeated English knights from inside packed schiltrons, a kind of piker hedgehog. Over time in the English-Scottish wars, knights were forced to dismount and fight on foot, too, supported by men-at-arms and longbowmen covering each flank. Once the English beat the Scots back north, Edward III took these innovative tactics to France and won at Crécy (1346). His son, the Black Prince, combined the old ways with the new when he finished a grand *chevauchée* with a second triumph of his father's tactics on the field at Poitiers (1356), as the first phase of the Hundred Years' War was won by English armies over the French nobility.[65] Change descended also from the Alps, out of the Swiss cantons and valleys. In 1315, an odd lot of Swiss infantry launched into military history at Morgarten, shocking all of Europe's mounted and privileged aristocracy by slaughtering an army of Austrian (Habsburg) knights and men-at-arms in a mountain pass, which they blocked at both ends with rolled logs. In time the Swiss came down to the plains and won there, too, fighting from pike-and-crossbow squares. Then they hired out to kings and popes, dominating the mercenary market because they did not lose once for the next 200 years. *Pas d'argent, pas de suisse* ("no money, no Swiss") became a proverb, and for two centuries having no Swiss on one's side usually meant defeat—always if the enemy did. They had no kings or nobles. They fought instead under elected officers, with deadly accurate crossbows and long axes wielded from behind protective pikes. They ran faster than some cavalry armies chose to move, adding surprise and battlefield flexibility by fighting in multiple squares. They were a justly feared and fearsome infantry, much admired by Machiavelli and hated by their enemies and imitators, the German *Landsknechte*. Finally they did lose, as nearly all players in the long game of war eventually do. In 1515, partway into the Italian Wars (1494–1559), they were bloodied by the French at Marignano, located 20 miles (32 km) from Milan. There, after 200 years of battlefield dominance, they were finally overmatched by too many cannon, muskets and pistols firing into underarmed and too densely packed squares.

Great change was afoot, for the infantry revolution that began in the 14th century did not end there. New infantry-heavy armies reinforced a key shift in the social bases of European warfare, beginning a trend toward expansion and professionalization that marked off late medieval armies from their forebears.[66] As shown below, these changes continued through the chronic wars of the Italian Renaissance and into the later Italian Wars, then again in religious contests across Europe in the 16th and 17th centuries, when Europe's wars first carried its armies and influence overseas as well. More inflation of infantry and the scale of fighting came with decades-long wars during the 18th-century Enlightenment. The French Revolution then vastly expanded the role of infantry in modern warfare and of social mobilization for war leading into the early 19th century. This long-term pattern of growth in the size and importance of infantry armies further accelerated in the second half of the 19th century, culminating in armies comprising millions of men, then tens of millions, in the first half of the 20th century.

2

Battle Retarded

THE HUNDRED YEARS' War (1337–1453), sometimes called the "Great War of the Middle Ages," was a time and a theater of fundamental change in military history. It waxed and waned for generations, saw bold aggression meet stone defense and creative military experimentation clash with crusty conservatism. It saw new dash and some battle-seeking and innovative tactics, as well as the same slow destruction and devastation by the old ways: siege and fire and *chevauchées* that tore asunder and ruined as much as a quarter of France. It ushered in the infantry revolution of the 14th century, spearheaded by raiding English armies that spawned later French imitation and, more important to the outcome, a late-war reform of the French state and army and adoption of gunpowder field cannon. France suffered and lost for nearly a century, then it changed the way it waged war and the armies it fought with, forged gunpowder weapons and related new tactics and reforged a social compact between the monarchy and nobility that enabled it to win the war.[1] In contrast, England's fortunes declined from lopsided early victories won by innovative early tactics developed against the Scots to technological and military conservatism, domestic and fiscal crisis, and final battlefield defeat and expulsion of its armies and influence from France and the continent.

As in most wars of vast complexity and duration, for both sides the idea of victory by decisive battle proved a chimera. This was additionally inescapable given the strong superiority of fortified defenses, at least until about 1435, when the advent of more powerful field and siege guns tipped the balance in favor of a reforming French state and modernizing army. France eventually won, partly by use of improved cannon in the war's final phase, but more by uniting its ruling elites and reforming its finances to wage more effective war. However, that was accomplished only after several spectacular defeats and far more costly deep cavalry raids and occupations by both English armies and free-ranging mixed companies of mercenaries. Inability to expel the invader and suppress smaller regional foes in Burgundy and Gascony over many decades finally forced the ruling classes to start thinking in more "national" terms after 1422. Only then could Charles VII, soon restored to the throne with the help of Jeanne d'Arc, the "Maid of Orléans," overcome the alienation of the noble classes and tap into religious and almost protonationalist feeling to win the war. In the last two decades of fighting the French pursued an ever more unifying and effective anti-English strategy, enabling them to conduct a closing series of war-winning campaigns from Normandy to Gascony.[2] In sharp contrast, the English clung to their old ways too long, and thereby lost all that they had gained over a century of armed conflict and lucrative occupation.

The Hundred Years' War arose from deeply complex and overlapping dynastic claims of law, vassalage and sovereign right. It was urged and sustained as well by the usual lusts for land, loot, honor and prestige. Battles took place down the decades, but they remained rare relative to other forms of armed conflict and extortion, not least because they were such high-risk affairs. Over its multigenerational course, highly aggressive English warlord-kings, starting with Edward III from the 1330s to 1370s, continuing with some interruptions through the reign of Henry V after the turn of the 15th century, won several spectacular fights. However, even in the glory days of marauding and battle-winning English armies, the core strategy always was to bring economic and moral pressure to bear on the Valois monarchy by a war of exactions and destruction, a war against the land more than against the French king's army, waged summer after summer, campaign after campaign, year upon year over decades. This approach allowed England to wage a long fight it otherwise could not afford, to make a war in France that paid for itself (*bellum se ipse alet*) by feeding and rewarding English armies from plunder and ransom.[3] The preferred methods were summertime raids and sieges once pastures turned green, ransoms of noble captives and other hostages, confiscations of property at sword-point and armed extortion of towns, monasteries and other places of portable wealth with threats of destruction by fire and murder by sword. There was wholesale wastage and plundering during great *chevauchées* that lasted months and tore asunder the countryside. These deep cavalry and dragoon raids and burnings were so devastating that at times they forced the French to come out in battle array and fight in the field in spite of clear and proven English tactical advantages, most notably in longbow archery.[4] There was also fighting at sea, less well-known today but very important, for control of the rich coastal trades.

Several celebrated field engagements were won by English armies at the start, notably bloody routs at Crécy (1346) and Poitiers (1356), where open-field battle lopsidedly favored innovative English tactics of dismounted knights fighting as heavy infantry, with archers (longbowmen) slightly forward on either flank.[5] Yet sieges were more frequent and characteristic events than battles, along with *chevauchées* grand and small, and more local destruction by fire and terror by armed foragers reaching each side of the havoc radius along the English line of march. France was also ruined by independent roving bands, by *routiers* and marauding Free Companies. These were often mixed gangs of English, Flemings and French who carried out private extortion and plunder under names such as Smashing Bars and Arm of Iron, the White Company and the Great Company. The latter had as many as 10,000 men. They served the English when the wider war made silver flow, and served themselves when it did not. During intermittent truces between the kings and royal armies the free bands committed terror and murder to extort *appatis* (ransom) from towns and villages, local noble estates and rich monasteries. They were a scourge, spreading chaos and rapine through much of France; for example, between 1356 and 1364, more than 450 locales were held to ransom by bands of *routiers* or Free Companies. Occupation could last a considerable time—15 years in the case of the Abbey of Louroux.[6]

The nadir of French fortunes came when King Jean II was captured at Poitiers in 1356 and held for a literal king's ransom. He was also compelled to sign a draconian peace. There followed a decade of *routiers* both taking English silver and forcing local *appatis*. They operated from rural strongpoints, continuing economic war against the French crown and thereby undermining its claims to legitimacy by demonstrating its inability to secure the countryside. In some ways, this second phase proved as brutal and wearing as the *chevauchées* of 1339–1356. However, by 1369 Charles V partly reconstructed the monarchy and rebuilt the royal army, so that by the mid-1370s the French won back much that was lost at Poitiers and in the ransom of Jean II and the forced peace. It did so not by winning field battles against still dominant English armies, but by forcing enemy garrisons to capitulate in a series of small sieges.[7] This pattern would repeat: English field victories and conquests followed by slower French recovery, until a final surge of destruction of English garrisons and relief armies became the winning strategy leading to French victory at the very end of the Hundred Years' War.

However, that shift to offense and martial success by the French lay a long way ahead. For several more decades, English power was reasserted and France set back hard on its spurs, humiliated and demoralized. A new low in French fortunes came in the famously catastrophic defeat by a smaller, retreating and cut-off English army led by Henry V, in a battle that dehorsed and killed many French nobles at Agincourt (October 25, 1415). Less well known is that far deeper damage to France's strategic fortunes flowed from Henry's follow-on campaigns of sieges and extortions, with renewed threats of waging indiscriminate *guerre mortelle* ("war to the death") against whole towns that refused his terms.[8] Along with Agincourt, another important loss came at sea off Harfleur (August 15, 1416). Ravaged on land and beaten on the water, France temporarily accepted Henry's claims and occupation of great swaths of the countryside and many important towns.[9]

Yet there was still no lasting result for England, not least because France was heavily fortified and thus unconquerable in the end. It was vast and rich, with latent military potential England could never hope to match. Finally, following Henry V's death in 1422, it tapped that potential and altered the course of the war. After decades of raids, rapine, ransom and violent *jacqueries* (peasant rebellions), the French monarchy revived and reformed. French armies then employed a modified Fabian strategy, rooted in broad popular support for the war effort, to force the English to give up Guyenne. Next came Normandy, and finally Gascony. English field victories of prior decades were thereby revealed to have had only tactical significance in a long war France won because of its strategic capacity for endurance and which England lost due to its relative strategic weakness, specifically an inability to overcome long-term costs of military occupation.[10]

Neither the early clashes at Crécy and Poitiers, won by means of the aggressive tactical innovation of Edward III, nor the more famed victory at Agincourt by brash Henry V and his men-at-arms and longbowmen decided the greatest war of the age in England's lasting favor. Yet these remain the best-known events of the war for English-speaking audiences, made still more famous, long after the war was lost, in William Shakespeare's royalist propaganda and Winston Churchill's imperial histories.[11] Yet all proved indecisive, and certainly less so than late-war French victories over English armies at the battles of Formigny (1450) and Castillon (1453), sharp field fights that took place within a larger context of lengthy siege campaigns. The importance of these last battles lay not so much in reaching a final decision by French armies on the battlefield as in how they opened the way or responded to French sieges that reduced English and Gascon garrisons and resistance until both collapsed completely. The *Agincourt Carol* might proclaim that God was forever on King Harry's side, but the kings of France prevailed anyway by more secular means.[12] They won by reasserting royal authority over a truculent nobility and earning support even from the lower social orders to expel destructive invaders and occupiers. With those key changes came more money flowing to the king's coffers, used to wage extended war with more and better guns and troops.

It helped the French that England's royal warlords and armies in the latter stages rested cocksure on old battle laurels won by their fathers and grandfathers, failing to adapt longbow tactics or recruitment and finance to the increasingly black-powder face of late medieval and early modern war. It also helped that Henry V died at age 35 in 1422, the same year the Dauphin Charles began his rise to the throne, even if he did not mount it until 1429, with Jeanne d'Arc watching in a state of religious ecstasy in Reims Cathedral. Yet it was probably already too late to save the English cause by the time of the English king's death. Having used war to promote a sense in England of a union of crown and nation, Henry V and his generals failed to understand that invasion and occupation by marauding foreign armies would provoke much the same response within France. When it did, France harvested its once fallow military potential and the war turned permanently and decisively in its favor.

More important in England's defeat than the death of its storied warrior king and his succession by a one-year-old, Henry VI, was a form of victor's disease. The infant king's advisers and Parliament failed to adapt to what historians call the "fiscal-military state" model pioneered in Italy and now also taking shape in France. Aided by the advent of Jeanne d'Arc, newly crowned Charles VII (*le Victorieux*) was able to rally France around the revived monarchy to wage a new kind of war to expel the hated English and fashion a final victory, not merely tactical or lasting over a campaign or two but strategic and permanent in its outcome. He did so in good part by creating one of the first and most powerful fiscal-military states in Europe, thereby pointing to the future way to success in war as it would evolve there over the next two centuries. Fresh strength in arms came from activating latent national resources—moral, social and economic—to wage a long war that isolated and wore down dozens of English garrison towns over time. The last campaigns told the tale and delivered complete victory. Set-piece battles were also fought but had less to do with the final outcome, and in more than one case resulted most directly from English efforts to lift an ongoing siege.[13]

Two decades before the war's official end in 1453, it was clear that French armies were adapting, the monarchy reforming and the tide of war turning.[14] A modernizing royal French army took the field starting in the 1430s. New taxes bought more powerful siege cannon and more mobile field guns that proved indeed to be *ultima ratio* ("the last argument") of French kings. New guns were cast by talented *maîtres d'artillerie* ("master gunsmiths"), such as

France after Henry V (1422).

Courtesy of the Department of History, United States Military Academy at West Point. Redrawn by George Chakvetadze.

the Bureau brothers, Jean and Gaspard, who became exemplars of a new kind of military specialist and contract entrepreneur. The French army and kings still relied on the *gendarmerie* (noble heavy cavalry) and men-at-arms, but added paid infantry organized in pike-and-crossbow units, also employing a few early muskets. The new-style cast cannon and cloth infantry supported, even if for social reasons they did not yet supplant, the mounted and armored aristocrats and men-at-arms defeated at Crécy, Poitiers and Agincourt. Old arms and new thus mixed in the late-war armies fielded by the king of France, but new mattered more. As a result, Charles VII soon earned another appellation to go along with "The Victorious." He was also called *le Bien Servi* ("Well Served"), a comment more on key changes in France than on his person.

The shift entailed more than adopting new gunpowder technology, such as more powerful corned powder and better casting methods. It arose from more than adoption of new infantry weapons and fresh artillery tactics, though ranging cannon fire before the horsemen charged played a role. It came from nothing less than basic reform of the emerging French state, and with it the monarchy's relations with the nobility. It came also from reform of finances and tax collection as a compact between crown and the castellan classes was affirmed. From 1435, the new French armies smelled blood as they smashed apart more conservative and too-confident English and Gascon forces with loud reports of iron. Driven from the field, the English huddled inside old-style fortifications built before their great-grandfathers' time, fearful to come out and fight and terribly mistaken in the belief that the old walls would hold. That illusion was shattered by plunging iron balls and stone splinters. More English castles and towns surrendered without resistance when they saw the big siege guns arrive and hordes of military laborers dig them into place, under the guidance of Jean and Gaspard Bureau. The brothers made ready to make iron fly, to crash metal into stone walls and bring them down like so many Jerichos. If a more stubborn garrison refused to give up its gate keys and surrender arms, big siege guns fired accurately and often, hurtling solid iron balls to crack brick and stone. Then the siege train moved on to the next castle or town, and the next. That is how the French king's armies extended and consolidated royal control over the encastled countryside, in time breaking England's hold also on the ports and reclaiming the rich water-borne trades in wine and foods and cloth that traveled the coast.

Recognizing the altered balance of forces, Burgundy switched sides by signing the Treaty of Arras with France in 1435. It also restored Paris, which it had occupied for decades, to the ever more confident and successful Charles VII. More sieges and campaigns followed, until most of Gascony was recovered to the French by 1442. Rouen surrendered in October 1449. Harfleur fell to besiegers that December. Honfleur quit resistance in January 1450. Now it was the endgame.[15] That April, a small English army of 4,000 men, three-quarters still armed with longbows, was pursued until trapped and forced to battle at Formigny. The French dragged two culverins, long-barreled and long-range but lightly cast cannon on wheeled carriages, onto the battlefield. With these they enfiladed the English archers, firing down the enemy's line from the flanks. Out of range of return longbow fire, the culverins shot into the dense pack of still-forming longbowmen, sending solid iron shot tumbling through the archer ranks at a rapid rate, tearing apart limbs and lives. Desperate to strike back, the longbowmen gave up the principal advantage of their weapon when they charged the guns. They overran the smoke-belching culverins but the French quickly brought more guns to bear to pound the now-exposed English. A second French army arrived, 1,200 trotting horse trailed by 800 panting crossbowmen. The reinforcements pushed the English back into a defensive arc that became so densely packed many longbowmen inside the cramped formation could not shoot. The final assault came from two directions at once, until the defense collapsed under intense close-in crossbow and arquebus fire from the new French infantry. The whole English army was killed or captured or fled the field, running in dread and panic. The one-sided outcome left England without a relief force to support its last fixed holdings in Normandy. The garrisons at Falaise and Cherbourg quickly gave up the fight, and Normandy was French again.

England failed to reform and modernize its fiscal-military state until defeat in France was imminent, and still it could not do what was needed, for it was also overextended and distracted by war with Scotland and rushing pell-mell toward civil war between the flowered houses. Moreover, the day of the longbow as a battle-winning weapon was already long past, save for a last gasp in the civil Wars of the Roses, in which antiquarian weapons and tactics were employed on both sides.[16] English troops fled their last holdings in Normandy and Guyenne, often without firing a shot. Garrisons capitulated out of fear of French siege artillery and lack of any field army to relieve them.[17] After a brief revival and stand in Gascony, the coup de grâce was delivered on July 17, 1453, as a result of the siege of Castillon in southern France. There, in a battle provoked by the siege, cannon under personal direction of the Bureau brothers pounded the last English and Gascon resistance into permanent submission.

The last fight of the Hundred Years' War thus resulted from an English effort to raise a siege, when a last relief army rushed to relieve the Castillon

garrison but fell into a trap. It was met and stopped by field guns, then slaughtered by enfilading crossbowmen and arquebusiers. Guns inflicted devastating losses on the English and Gascons, with culverins again firing from well
beyond the range of the longbows. French knights wielding lances and swords
waited out of return-fire range until the cannon did their raw work, then
charged. Next came the new-style infantry, firing crossbows and arquebuses
into packed longbowmen at close range. The French deployed perhaps 300
guns of all types at Castillon, mostly *coulverins à main* ("hand cannon"), but
also bigger pieces. That was more than in any battle to that time in Europe.
Yet this was not merely a triumph of gunpowder weapons over longbows,
because French archers also took a heavy toll. Still, if revenge was wanted
by the French for the misery and humiliation of their fathers and grandfathers at Agincourt, it was taken in equal and full measure on the bloody field
of Castillon. The casualty count actually mirrored Shakespeare's Agincourt
numbers: about 100 French dead against 4,000 English and Gascons, or
nearly all who huffed to Castillon intending to attack the siege camp, enduring a 30-mile forced march. Sometimes, amid the killing in these final
fights, hot-blooded French attackers shouted out "Agincourt!" It had been a
long war in which the French waited on vengeance for decades, and so took
understandable pleasure in it. Other troops in other armies seeking payback
for some never-forgotten torment did the same in later fights. Thus, Irish
serving in French armies shouted "Remember Fontenoy!" as they attacked
redcoat lines; Union troops bellowed "Fredericksburg!" at men in grey and
butternut across a Pennsylvania or Virginia wheat field; and Russians yelled
"Stalingrad!" as they shot down Germans in the streets of Berlin in 1945.

With the submission of Bordeaux to the French crown, the Great War of
the Middle Ages finally ended. English troops sailed home from La Rochelle,
leaving only a small garrison at the Pale of Calais allowed by treaty. The halcyon days of invading English kings and armies, of plunder and *chevauchées*
and longbow dominance, were done.[18] The outcome of the Hundred Years'
War proved yet again that long wars are not so much won on the battlefield as they are in the treasury and by endurance, by tapping into deeper
social strength and political support and then outlasting the other side. In
the 1430s, France finally actualized its dormant military power and went on
offense, overmatching England with expensive new cannon that only kings
could afford to purchase in large numbers, and with paid new-style infantry supplementing its old-fashioned service nobility. Its gunpowder weapons
aided the triumph over staid and stale English tactics, which still deployed
longbows that grew ever more outdated in the final decades. Yet technological

inadequacy or lack of able generals was not England's true Achilles heel. That was continued reliance on a rudimentary system of state finance and recruitment in the old ad hoc style of fifty or a hundred years before, even while fighting a whole new war against a bigger and richer state with much deeper resources and a renewed will to resist and win.

The war transformed France from an old medieval military power into an emerging, early modern war-state: a gunpowder state with centralized finances, able to suppress regional unrest, enforce domestic loyalty and make more effective foreign war. Emerging at last from a jagged puzzle of private baronial armies and weak political allegiance, the French king's army was newly elevated above all internal rivals through a complex process of renegotiation that ended resistance by jealous provincial castellans. The crown asserted its legal and social primacy and legitimacy when it caged private war, including putting an end to ravages wreaked by *routiers* and Free Companies. As a result, some of those hired men were displaced over the Alps to instead torment Italy during the Renaissance.[19] The old nobility still played a major role in French armies, well into the next century. Yet, by centralizing authority over the financing and conduct of war, the French crown acquired the tax base needed to pay for new foundries and cannon, for siege trains and military laborers and for the new-style hired soldiers. This would be the way of all future war: contracted soldiers, whether national or mercenary, and rising professionalism and firepower.

***

HALF A CONTINENT away in that same summer of 1453, the newfound power and prominence of gunpowder artillery against old-style fortifications were again demonstrated spectacularly, and seemingly beyond question. With huge bombards (great stone-throwing cannon) and even more impressive logistics, an Ottoman army led by Sultan Muhammad (Mehmed) II finally broke the 1,000-year-old Byzantine fortifications ringing Constantinople.[20] The Ottoman Empire thereafter loomed as a threat to the Latin West, starting in the Balkans and later encroaching on core Habsburg lands. The fall of the Byzantine capital was long-expected, even overdue.[21] It did not clearly bookmark the end of the Middle Ages and start of the early modern period, as was once widely said and taught. Nevertheless, it sent shock waves into Renaissance Italy and across Europe and beyond, with implications for culture and politics as well as for the practice of war.[22] The Latin West henceforth claimed the role of guardian of classical antiquity; Muscovy claimed leadership of the Orthodox world and the dropped Byzantine ideological mantle, proclaiming that Moscow was the "Third Rome"; while the Ottoman sultans restored Constantinople to its venerable role as a major imperial capital, albeit of an empire of a wholly different sort than had ruled there for over a thousand years.

In the years and decades that followed the fall of Constantinople, Ottoman armies would advance deep into the Balkans and along the Mediterranean coast, pressing as far west as the Adriatic.[23] Yet, the military threat from the east was quite real even before 1453 and the end of Byzantium. Ottoman forces had already defeated a large Hungarian army and assorted volunteers at Varna in 1444. Then, over three extremely bloody days at Kosovo Polje (October 17–20, 1448), they beat another Hungarian-led army that had sought to smash and stop the Muslim invaders but was soundly defeated instead. These victories over the frontiers of Europe by the sultan's armies were just the start of a period of rapid and aggressive Ottoman westward expansion. Just four years after the slaughter at Kosovo Polje, lead engineer units of the sultan's unmatched war machine headed to Constantinople to make ready gun pits for what became the great siege of the age. It was an endeavor carried out by a more organized and greater military power by far than any in Europe at that time.[24] Hungary, Austria and the Balkans would all be hard pressed by Ottoman armies after extinction of the Byzantine rump and

Hoop-and-stave bombards (15th century).
Courtesy of Wikimedia Creative Commons.

barrier, even if the old Eastern Roman Empire was long past its former glory and military power before 1453.

The fall of the Byzantine capital to Islam was accepted as inevitable by most Latin contemporaries for many years before it happened. It was reports of the manner of the sultan's great military achievement that surprised and worried when the deed was actually done. Renaissance military and cultural thinkers were much impressed by what was believed to be the destruction of Constantinople's strong defenses by gunpowder cannon. The city boasted the greatest combination anywhere of ancient and medieval fortifications, 14 miles of multiple lines. In over 1,000 years, no one had broken them.[25] And yet the walls came tumbling down under pounding by stone-throwing iron bombards and shiny bronze cannon. Or so it was reported and widely believed, as the legend took hold that the famous walls of the ancient City of Constantine had fallen to Ottoman bombardment. That claim was not strictly true, as toward the end the Ottomans shifted from bombardment to far bloodier tactics of siege towers and direct assault. Nevertheless, the tale of defeat by cannon power was believed at the time and became one of the most influential claims in the annals of early modern war.[26]

In early April 1453, Muhammad's troops and siege train reached the banks of the Bosporus, while his navy curled around the shore to supply his huge army and to enforce a water blockade. After nearly a year of engineering preparation, Constantinople's defenses were to be bombarded by huge purpose-built guns ranging from iron and stone-throwing bronze culverins to mortars hurling smoking balls of fiery tar, and possibly also Greek Fire. Most impressive of all were great bombards that took sixty oxen, many carts, and several months to move into position. They hurled granite or marble balls cut on-site by skilled masons, weighing almost 700 pounds (300 kilograms) and flying a mile across the Bosporus. The greatest was cast by a Hungarian master smith in the employ of the sultan, but most other guns used in the siege were cast by skilled Ottoman smiths.[27] The fort built to house the wall-smashing monster was called *Boğazkesen* ("Cutter of the Throat").[28] Cannon were hauled into position there and at another fort 6 miles south of the city, a cracked veteran left over from a long-ago failed siege. Assault troops and lighter guns were ferried across the Sea of Marmara, taking landward positions to surround and attack the western walls. That isolated the city from hope of reinforcement by land, not that much help was on the way, despite repeated appeals to the largely indifferent West made by the Byzantine emperor and the Latin pope.

The sultan's navy blocked all relief by water as well; only a handful of galleys were able to dash into the Golden Horn during the siege, bringing in pitifully few reinforcements or supplies. The bombardment started on April 5. Iron and stone hail fell for two months, pounding the outer walls and also lobbed over them, to rain down on the city. Great booms and cracks of distant sound skipped over the Straits, and rising clouds of acrid black smoke sailed high above the banks of the Bosporus. Muhammad's highly skilled gunners found the range quickly and battered the outer defenses. Iron and stone smashed with enormous kinetic force into old-fashioned square brick towers and walls built centuries earlier to stand against lower-velocity torsion artillery, and made high and thin to fend off ladder and siege tower assaults. Other heavy shot arced into the city, smashing rooves and crushing civilians under falling rubble. Balls of smoke-trailing incendiaries came next, setting things ablaze. People huddled in their homes and in dozens of churches, including the famed Hagia Sophia cathedral dedicated by Emperor Justinian I in 537 C.E.

Holes and breaks made by the heavy shot in the outer walls were not so much repaired by undermanned defenders as filled in with barricades, stockades and trenches dug behind them.[29] As stone, iron and flaming oil-and-tar projectiles fell against the walls and on the city, Ottoman sappers and miners moled toward the long ring of outer walls, the first line of hardened defenses. Small breaches were made, and bloody attempts to storm were met and repulsed in savage hand-to-hand fighting. Janissaries and "berserkers," as some Greeks and Westerners called fanatic Ottoman troops paid extra to lead near-suicidal attacks, rushed the gaping holes.[30] Men killed and died fighting face to face: shot, stabbed, falling with a hacked-off limb or a spilling gut. Bodies filled up the holes, impeding the onrush of more attackers. At night, enemy wounded were dispatched and piles of dead removed from the ragged gaps in the city walls, which were repaired as best the few defenders could. Patchwork interior defenses were thrown up and preparations made to resume hand-fighting the next day. And so it went, on and on for 55 days in all. The old capital endured a deluge of iron and stone and incendiaries; more crazed assaults; more terrible, gashing wounds; more suffering and terrified civilians.

Muhammad ordered 30 galleys hauled overland to bypass the sea wall on the north shore of the Golden Horn. The ships were pulled along a road made by his superb combat engineers. They moved past a great chain boom blocking access into the inner harbor, deployed back into water and closed the last seaward access into the city. On May 6, an assault into a small breach was stopped only by a makeshift barrier erected during the night, then

held with pikes, swords, muskets and sheer courage. It was the kind of warfare familiar all over the Mediterranean world for many centuries: slow siege
approach, then assault, biting into a protracted defense, not armies looking
to some special general to decide the issue in a set-piece meadow fight over
a spring or summer's afternoon. Multiple saps snaked toward and under the
walls. More assault holes appeared. The pummeling of the bombards and
mortars was unabated over a grim three weeks. Mines met countermines,
leading to underground fights in pitch dark with knives and clubs. Still,
the saps crept closer. Large mortars were now brought into range, lobbing
huge ordnance and more tar-and-fire balls into the city's streets, smashing,
burning, demoralizing the dwindling defenders and survivors. Siege towers
reached and touched the walls, where they were burned and thrown down. At
last, on May 29, 1453, the end came. Muhammad's *Bashi-Bazouks*, tribal mercenaries in mufti or other irregular dress, joined janissaries and "berserkers"
to make an all-out assault.[31]

The city did not succumb in the manner Europeans later thought, from
cannon bombardment that knocked down its ancient walls, tumbling them
over to let a horde of Muslim troops rush a huge breach and gain the inner
city. In fact, only a few attackers got inside a small lower breach, then ran
along the boulevard inside the city walls to strike into the exposed flank of the
last cluster of defenders. Constantine XI Palaeologus, last of the Byzantine
emperors, died amidst his guards. Then came massacre in the streets. Homes
and churches, markets and public squares all saw scenes of slaughter as the
city was sacked and civilians were put to the sword or taken away to be sold
as slaves.[32] Later, Muhammad ordered blackened pools of blood washed from
the floor of Hagia Sophia. Triumphant, he proclaimed the city his imperial
capital. It rested strategically and symbolically at the center of a confident
and rising empire, linking his Asian holdings to the promise of an expanding
sphere of Islam in Europe. Later sultans added minarets around the dome
of the erstwhile cathedral, converted into one of the world's great mosques.
No one expected anything less.[33]

It was a remarkable and impressive achievement of Ottoman military
transport and engineering just to get the great guns to the Bosporus, along
with smaller cousins and a vast supporting cast of engineers and assault
troops.[34] Everyone in Europe knew that now that the sultans were across the
Straits to stay, more sieges of European towns and even capitals must surely
lie in the future. More worrisome, the coincidental fall of Byzantium and the
defeat of the English coastal forts in France that same summer rang a clarion
warning that extant medieval defenses could not survive against improved

gunpowder artillery. That fact was reinforced by endemic sieges and bombardments with new cannon already underway in Italy. It was not at all unreasonable to draw a central conclusion: if Constantinople's famous walls, the greatest fixed defenses of the time, could be felled by cannon, then no old-style fortresses were safe. A race was already on to redesign, refinance and rebuild outdated fortresses and city walls all across Italy. The events on either end of Europe in 1453 gave the competition new impetus and urgency.

Militarily, the events in the east in 1453 may have been misunderstood, but culturally that year did indeed mark a reformulation of thinking about the Ottoman threat to the Latin world in the 15th–16th centuries, helping to forge key ideas that shaped early modern and then modern European culture.[35] The end of Byzantium and its connection to the Hellenistic world reinforced a Renaissance self-image as the essential bridge to the wisdom and practices of antiquity. Many humanist thinkers, enamored of the ancient Mediterranean world, believed that its only recently rediscovered cultures were lost to, and debased by, the Muslim conquest. They also believed that much had changed militarily.[36] Widespread propaganda fears about Turks took hold, along with real fears of military vulnerability in the face of the huge and ominous Ottoman state that had demonstrated unmatched logistical and military capabilities. Yet this shift in perception of the East occurred just as European states were themselves centralizing and modernizing their armies and defenses and gaining secular confidence in the face of older claims to universal religious authority.[37] The beginning of the "Rise of the West" thus closely coincided with the ascent of an Islamic empire that in turn deeply influenced European military and political culture.[38] Recent scholarship thus reconfirms an older view of 1453 and the fall of the Byzantine capital as indeed a formative date in Renaissance and European history.[39]

The demonstrated supremacy of gunpowder cannon over stone walls at both ends of Europe, along with the threat to walled Italian city states posed by advances in black powder artillery, was confirmation of this change. The threat from cannon dramatically increased urban insecurities and demand for more modern defenses. The result was a combination of new fortification design and defensive gunpowder firepower that reshaped war for three centuries to come.[40] Military thinking underwent a profound change, launching a centuries-long effort to rebuild outdated fortifications and erect stronger ones that incorporated cannon in defense as well as in sieges and assault. The coming turn to artillery fortresses that became exquisitely geometrical in design then drove reform in the composition of armies as well. This would have meaning for wars far beyond Italy, where it began in the chronic warfare among the Renaissance city-states. Upon intervention in Italy in the 1590s by the Great Powers of the day, Spain and France, the new Italian military advisers and ideas and fortress designs would be exported across Europe and beyond. That meant vast new military expenses were needed just to stay in the same place defensively, and that sieges would remain the dominant mode of war in Western Europe for another 200 years. That was true even though battering infantry armies and gunpowder artillery continued to evolve outside the walls of cities and stone borders of emerging early modern states. Europe thus remained far from revival of battle-seeking armies, distant as ever from war conducted by great captains.

At the same time, increasingly secular imaginations recrafted the Ottoman image away from the medieval and crusader view of a rabid jihad or ghazi state into one of a princely state, a polity pursuing rational interests through diplomacy and war. The shift held even if some Renaissance humanists did not yet accept that the Ottoman state was fully legitimate, seeking to instead write its history as the rise of a barbarian culture that overran the higher Hellenistic culture of the East.[41] Calls by the pope for Latin Christians to sally east had been rebuffed, confirming the fracturing of even the ideal of the Latin West as forming a *res publica Christiana* ("Christian Commonwealth"). A weakened papacy was again proven unable to persuade any army from the West to travel east in what the popes said was a crucial Christian cause, although it could still stir handfuls of crusaders in Poland and other lands, because they were closer to the Ottoman threat. The old idea of a unified Christendom, of a single people under the Christian god, was always more aspirational than real; past calls to wage holy war in the East had also been ignored. Still, this was different. By the end of the 15th century, military power shifted wholesale to secular authorities, though at different speeds in different lands. Political power would still find it necessary to genuflect toward Rome from time to time, to wrap itself in a mantle of papal and Christian legitimacy, but unity was gone. It was not so much a decline in religious influence inside Latin societies, or over the armies which they produced and sustained, as it was a shift in the causes for which those forces might be used, to advance more local and princely interests. The long process began by which the West began to view the East, and politics more generally, in its own slowly emerging and increasingly secular image.[42]

As Ottoman military might impinged further on European territory and political concerns in the decades that followed, the Sublime Porte—as the Ottoman court was known—would come to be seen by other major powers in an emerging European state system as another Great Power player on the board.[43] Cultural reconception of the Ottomans as a secular rather than religious threat also signaled evolution in deeper theories about the nature and purposes of war within Europe itself, away from the divine toward the secular. Diplomatically, the turn toward secular realism that began in Renaissance Italy would not be confirmed until the 17th century, by Louis XIV during his War of the Reunions (1683–1684), when he secretly encouraged an Ottoman invasion of Habsburg Austria as a distraction from his own wars of expansion farther north. In between the insights of the Renaissance and the secular practices of the Age of Louis XIV lay Europe's own era of bloody and prolonged religious wars. Yet, beneath the surface of confessional argument and religious violence a more profound change was already taking shape. Machiavelli best caught and chronicled the new sensibility, while other humanists accelerated a basic redefinition of "the Turk" and his Islamic empire from religious enemy to secular strategic threat: to a power on the borders, not in the heavens. A power like all the others.

3

Battle Remembered

SO FEARSOME WAS the reputation of the new artillery of the middle to late 15th century that some towns and fortresses capitulated upon merely the threat of bombardment. This was unacceptable. Renaissance engineers countered with an innovative fortification design centered on an angled or arrow-shaped bastion: a shaped mound of earthen (later stone) wall forming two angles and two faces in relation to the longer curtain wall. It was built thick and low, reducing defense against scaling to instead support the weight of defensive guns. Its angled projection from the curtain wall thrust defenders forward, allowing them to shoot in enfilade (directly down the flanks) along connecting sections of curtain. A moat or dry ditch might further slow attackers and expose them to raking from the bastions. The key was to create overlapping fields of fire, so that defenders swept fire from the bastions on either flank of each section of curtain wall, leaving no place for attackers to hide. The development and spread of bastions kept the military advantage away from field armies, holding it to strongpoints such as fortified towns and new-style fortresses that bristled with defensive cannon emplaced to answer siege guns and smash assaulting infantry. The strength of a bastioned defense was remarkable. It was also handsomely mathematical, which appealed to the new Renaissance rational and empirical aesthetic. The logic of design when setting out mutually supporting fields of fire led by 1515 to architecturally beautiful polygons, geometrically regular artillery fortresses with all-round defenses and thus no flanks. As the bastion spread beyond Italy into Europe and the Middle East, it was called the *trace italienne*.[1] With expansion of European trading companies and overseas empires, it eventually reached the coasts of Asia and North America as well.[2]

Changing fortifications naturally forced changes in besieging armies, as even small cities added bastions and rulers built new-style fortresses to guard key road and river choke points. Bastioned forts were better protected against bombardment by their low earthen walls, which absorbed thudding iron hits

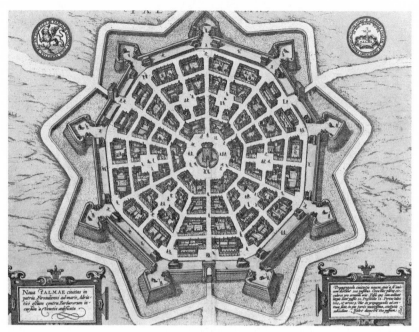

Trace italienne (bastioned town), 16th century.
Courtesy of Wikimedia Creative Commons.

better than the old, high and thin stone or brick. Fortresses and bastioned towns facing bombardment by siege guns could also effectively shoot back with counter-battery fire from low, sturdy, earth-protected gun mounts. Defenders fired out into the once-invulnerable siege camps of a surrounding (investing) army, driving attacking guns back or engaging and killing crews, military laborers and waiting assault troops. Moreover, attackers needed larger armies to defeat all-round defenses: a full polygon fortress had to be surrounded, demanding more saps (trenches) and troops, hence more time, money spent, and food for the men and horses.[3] Assault was made much harder even though the walls being assaulted were lower and more scalable. Attackers now were forced to approach through interlocking fields of fire by digging complex protective saps, as they worked inside the killing ranges of defensive cannons and gunmen while they sought to mine under the fortress walls. Shooting came from all sides of the mutually reinforcing, arrowhead-shaped bastions. Musketeers shot while standing behind solid walls or earthen ramparts, while attackers were cramped and cribbed by fighting from saps, or exposed in the open while making a direct assault. High casualties among investing and assaulting armies became more common. The ability to hold off besiegers until they quit or a relief army arrived was largely restored.

Siegecraft and fortification thus advanced in bloody point-counterpoint to arrive back at the beginning. Dominance of cannon over stone walls lasted only until military engineers reconfigured those walls, and in the process created kill zones between the bastions. Only the most callous or determined commander could sustain the high casualties that a hard siege now exacted. Fortunately for kings, there were lots of those, and lots of disposable common soldiers to hurl against the enemy's angled walls.

With hardened and angular fortifications so costly and difficult to break, even with ever more powerful siege guns in one's train, mobile field armies reemerged as a potential arbiter of war. Kings and generals faced a choice of a slow siege, which promised very high casualties to the attacker, or seeking to engage in open-field battle.[4] The costs of war were going up exponentially both on offense and defense, making the choice less clear than in the past. As the option of slow siege became less likely to hold down an attacker's costs and casualties relative to always-risky battle, the chances of more aggressive attackers choosing to fight it out in a field began to rise. However, such gamblers remained few for a very long time. The tendency of nearly all parties remained battle avoidance. Clever maneuvering to seize supplies by force and defensive siegecraft still offered higher odds. Let an aggressive enemy commander hurl the lives of troops and the contents of *his* city's or king's treasury against bastioned walls. Smart defenders refused invitations to fight in the open because battle still risked too much by way of resources and reputation. Besides, even if you won, your enemy could just retreat his remaining forces back into his bastioned forts and towns, and the war would go on.

Even so, rumblings began about returning to ancient practices, to fighting outside the walls by heroic captains leading larger field armies. No aggressor could win by staying in a fort or newly bastioned town. Armies must be raised, and wars must be fought outside the walls at times, by those who wanted to expand their power and territory rather than just defend it. Renaissance thinkers looking over the walls of their cities for inspiration found it in the rediscovered classical world. In war as in all else, they believed the ancients had a superior way to their own. In the military history of Greece and Rome, as reported by classical chroniclers and propagandists, humanists rediscovered an ancient view that battle was the soul of war. They thought that the great clashes of old expressed war's redemptive heroic sacrifice; that battles were supremely decisive; that victory was best achieved by articulated infantry whose recruitment, tactics, training and service cultivated worthy civic virtues; and not least, that battle allowed genius to strut upon the stage of history and achieve greatness—human greatness, not the medieval delusion that divine will was revealed by victory, while defeat was God's just punishment for wickedness.[5] There must be no more delusion that God takes sides in wars among princes. Renaissance delusions were more humanistic: belief in the virtue of war and war by a virtuous armed citizenry.[6]

It is therefore deeply ironic that, along with the great stories of ancient military history, the key classical source of military wisdom for Renaissance thinkers was *De Re Militari* of Publius Vegetius Renatus, a 5th-century Roman civilian administrator. This somewhat plodding compendium of the lessons learned and the practices of classical warfare (what some might call a late-Roman "principles of war" text) was written in either the late 4th or early 5th century C.E. It had become influential in medieval thinking as early as the Carolingian period, continuing through to the Late Middle Ages, but the Renaissance overlooked that fact, too, in asserting a unique claim to a restored link to the ancients.[7] As well as being read in Latin, it was translated by 1500 into six European languages. Indeed, until publication of Carl von Clausewitz's *On War* (*Vom Kriege*) in the 19th century, *De Re Militari* was the most widely read military treatise in Europe. The leading expert on the legacy of Vegetius, Christopher Allmand, notes that like the names Sun Tzu and Clausewitz today, for a thousand years after his death the name Vegetius was a synonym for war.[8]

De Re Militari focused on issues of administration such as recruitment and provisioning, with which Vegetius was likely directly familiar from his administrative work and which he seems to have regarded as the most pressing military problems facing the Roman Army of his day. He dispensed generic advice on leadership and the importance of morale, concentrating instead on the need to rally and recruit widely. He had much to say about infantry but almost nothing of import about cavalry or how to attack towns (Rome's enemies in his day rarely lived in towns, fortified or otherwise). Vegetius assumed that military-historical lessons from the period of Rome's rise and domination were still applicable during its period of decline. He thus offered a sum of systematized solutions to problems of war, based on reading earlier and more famous Roman military texts, most of which had been lost before the Renaissance and hence were available only secondhand in *De Re Militari*.[9]

With a mantle of authority conferred by its classical origins, *De Re Militari* spoke to Renaissance experience of at least some familiar issues, arising from the early modern shift to fiscal and military centralization. The text insisted, as did Machiavelli, that rulers ("princes," in the Florentine's language) must study and know war, and that their leadership was critical to success at it. Machiavelli took a particularly keen interest in developing civic militia in

Florence on a Roman model, to resolve the problem of moral and political duplicity of mercenaries he and others believed underlay chronic city-state wars in Italy and a dangerous military weakness relative to the Great Powers of Spain and France.[10] *De Re Militari* also appealed in its argument for a central army of well-trained, disciplined and virtuous soldiers. It even mapped out how to make one, with detailed drill and tactics that seemed superior to the chaotic medieval mêlée in both form and outcome, and to the parasitic mercenary companies that crossed over the Alps from France and Germany to plague Italy during the Renaissance.[11] As it was thought had been the case in the old Roman legions, drill and discipline were slated to become more important than courage or personal honor as defined by the Church and old medieval warrior classes. The shift was already happening outside Italy in growing infantry formations armed with pikes and arquebuses, weapons that required men to practice collective movements and to fight in cohesive units.

A further irony was that while Vegetius argued from and for "the authority of generals," his main operational advice to commanders in the last days of the Roman Empire was to avoid battle. He said generals ought not to seek destruction of the enemy army in open combat but should rely instead on clever ruses and stratagems, accepting a major clash of arms only when it could not be avoided. That advice actually fit the infamously cautious practices of condottieri, men hired under *condotte*, or military contracts negotiated by their captains. They were men whom Machiavelli deeply despised because large mercenary companies could and did easily switch allegiance according to who filled their purses last in the endless wars among rich Italian city-states. Initially, they were hired for a summer's campaigning and required to provide their own armor and weapons. Like the Free Companies in times of truce in France, to which some condottieri owed their origin, this left them unpaid and unemployed over the winter, with predictable results of marauding, rape and pillage. At their height, they held entire cities to ransom and stole vast amounts of wealth. Many were Germans, but Hungarians, English, French, Iberians and Italians also joined. One condottieri captain had a motto engraved on his breastplate that can stand for the cruelty of all the rest: "Enemy of God, Enemy of Piety, Enemy of Pity." After a condottieri army was devastated by the French at Fornovo (July 6, 1495), their way of war came to an end in Italy. Then the earlier pattern of military migration reversed, as condottieri fought for pay outside Italy, notably for Charles the Rash, last and ill-fated Duke of Burgundy.

Savage and thoroughly mercenary as they were, condottieri reflected rather than caused chronic Italian indecision in war and perpetual insecurity in Renaissance politics. The wars they fought were tame by comparison to what was coming in the wars of religion across Europe, and the even more violent wars of secular ideologies after that. Nevertheless, Machiavelli depicted them caustically. Their inconclusive ways of war did not suit the classically inspired and more aggressive thinking of that driven Florentine reformer.[12] His bias against them in favor of what today would be called citizen-soldiers, fighters with a personal stake in the state they defend, was repeated by others in later centuries.[13] So, too, was his view of battle as the highest mode of fighting, as supposedly proven in antiquity.[14] He wanted something more than administrative reform from the Renaissance rediscovery of ancient military art and the lessons of classical military history. He hoped to alter the basis of Florentine and even all Italian armies, reforming them away from untrustworthy foreign mercenaries toward a more reliable state militia of citizen-soldiers (or at least residents) organized in civic militia. In sum, he wanted to revive the legions as a means to inculcate civic virtue while promoting fundamental change in order to restore *decision* to the interminable warring among the city-states, and to ready Italy for greater wars to come. He also sought to re-establish battle in the central place he and others thought it had occupied in Greece and Rome. He wanted civic militia on the ramparts and before the gates of Florence, but he wanted more than a republican army. He wanted republican virtue to infuse that army and the inspired leadership of princes. And he wanted new great captains to lead the new armies of civic virtue, not mercenary contract captains. He wanted nothing less than a new Heroic Age of War.[15]

Machiavelli mined military insight from the entirety of the historical record in his desire to protect Florence and all Italy from external threats. Like other Renaissance theorists, he looked for the model for open and decisive battle less in basic military manuals like *De Re Militari* than in his reading of ancient military history. He believed that a secular prince's strength was best expressed in leading inspired civic militia in battle, not in relying on condottieri in slow war, or on ruses. His celebration of the secular heroic ideal of classical warfare was a fundamental rejection of the medieval style in war, due to its perceived inability to deliver real political and strategic decisions. At least part of this turn sprang from his and other humanists' keenness to create distance between their time and the preceding centuries, including in the way they thought battles *should* be fought and wars *should* be waged and won. Also, the expansion of infantry in the 14th century seemed to point to a future of war led by inspired generals in a new round of brilliant campaigns and decisive battles. Yet the actual and more complex reality of Renaissance warfare did not fit with this desire to return to the Classical Age in nearly all things military: civic virtue of republican militias vs. merely seasonal forces, or what were (wrongly) assumed to be always feckless mercenaries; centralized control of war finance, forges and fortresses, armories and foundries; erection of permanent military establishments (standing armies) in place of service nobility or vassalage and bought loyalty; civic motivation along with tactical rigor and drill discipline in locally raised militia, which would then fight for their city-state or country with a real stake in the outcome.

Machiavelli recognized that avoiding battle was less risky to an army and to a prince's cause than the uncertainty of field combat, yet he also railed against the waste and wantonness of sieges and the indecisive combat strategies of the condottieri. As an administrator, and only later as a writer of the treatise the *Art of War*, he looked above all to ancient history to model reform in his own time. He therefore became a lifelong champion of republican militia on the Greek and Roman models, looking to replace the condottieri, who he falsely said would never fight but only gestured at combat.[16] As a contemporary model, he pointed to the republican Swiss Confederation whose infantry squares or *Haufen* ("heaps") were undefeated for 200 years, from 1315 to 1515, from Morgarten to Marignano. He did not extend his general contempt for hired soldiers to the Swiss. Indeed, he saw in the *Haufen* a reinvention of classical infantry formations and flexibility, comparable to the tactics of the ancient phalanx in some ways. Moreover, he thought that even hired Swiss taking foreign gold fought from the right kind of civic base: solid, republican cantons. Swiss had no hereditary officer class or aristocracy, no king or warrior caste to rule over them. They elected their officers and served under cantonal banners, bearing not heraldic devices of some great baronial or royal house but commonplace images of a ring-nosed bull, an erect bear, even a lowly pig. He was so smitten by these armed commoners from the northern mountains that he referred to them as "the new Romans."[17]

The Italy in which Machiavelli matured was divided among a collage of weak city-states that were nearly constantly fighting.[18] The interminable condottieri wars before 1494 that he so despised arose mainly from a rough balance of power among the five largest city-states—Venice, Milan, Florence, Naples, and the Papal States—which progressively consumed smaller neighbors but could not overcome each other. Their balance was always unstable. Yet in time it produced a model for diplomacy that helped to reshape European interstate relations, and ultimately modern world politics, not least by speaking to how states must deal with issues of perpetual threat of war and instability in a system of multiple powers. Machiavelli also bequeathed

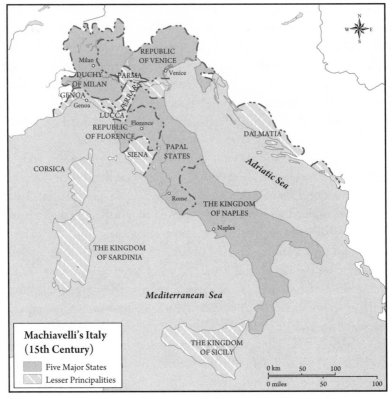

Machiavelli's Italy (15th Century).
Courtesy of the Department of History, United States Military Academy at West Point.
Redrawn by George Chakvetadze.

the world a new secular analysis of politics, expressed in a frank language of
power today called "political realism." He knew that only the ongoing distraction elsewhere of the Great Powers, of France and the Habsburgs of Spain
and Austria, preserved divided Italy from invasion and from falling under
foreign domination. The chronic cycle of small wars among the city-states of
the Renaissance culminated, as he feared it would, in a baleful swirl of conflict that brought in foreign armies to quell local quarrels in the name and
interest of outside powers. French armies arrived in the north in 1494; Spain
invaded Naples the next year. Habsburgs then straddled the French in Italy
from Austria and Spain, leading to a series of wars in and over Italy that lasted
until division of the immense Habsburg dynastic inheritance by Charles V in
1555 and 1556.[19]

Out of Renaissance Italy's political chaos and constant warfare in the 15th
century two key themes emerged. First, the city-states did not function in a

system ruled by law and moral constraints. They lived or went extinct in conditions of naked competition for power and in search of princely interests, restrained mainly but only minimally by a rough balance of power among the five largest. The system included the Papal States but rejected papal authority. Cynical warrior-popes might sputter about their claim to universal moral and religious primacy and lecture everyone that the laws of God were superior to the will of men, but the princes did what they chose. The days when princes bent the knee before the ideal of the Just War were done. Canon law bowed to the iron law of cannon. Henceforth, there would be just war, or as Machiavelli put it: "War is just when it is necessary."[20] Second, the early modern state was developing as a new kind of polity, in Italy and well beyond. Behind a veneer of principled law and respect for old religious authority, of poses of right and just government and legitimacy sanctioned by the divine, the rising states rested most fundamentally on their capacity to organize for war and to make war. They might still invoke God, as states and sovereigns would again during the coming era of wars of religion, and virtually every war since; but concealed behind princes' robes and ritual genuflections, as beneath the pope's purple soutane, was cynicism and venality. Politics was revealed in the Renaissance to be not the pretty lie of higher community the Church said it was and should be. Politics and war were together far more important than that. They were an ugly eternal truth: the calculus of power.

Machiavelli was the first to fully apprehend this, an achievement of the highest order for which much of the world has yet to forgive him. He is justly most famous, or infamous, for his clear and uncompromising depiction of the workings of interest and power and force in politics. He understood the new balance of power and the predatory nature of the wolf-like states of the Renaissance and the emerging European system. He saw that force was paramount in all politics, domestic and interstate, and that a primal lust for power curls beneath the covers and camouflage of even the most silken idealism. He was insightful, instructive and brilliant, if not always right. The Catholic Church banned his works, putting his books on its list of prohibited writings, the *Index Librorum Prohibitorum*. Still today, he is the only person whose name is used to describe attributes of Satan, called by some a "cunning Machiavellian."

Innovations in ballistics and fortification (the *trace italienne*), as well as ideas about the balance of power and other recognizably modern diplomatic notions and practices, migrated across the Alps during the Italian Wars to reshape much of European and then modern international politics.[21] Going

the other way, larger actors and armies poured into Italy, submitting it to
the whims and woes of Great Power wars as Valois France fought Habsburgs
from Austria and Spain in Italy.[22] These foreign armies and occupations initially aided Machiavelli's personal climb to office and power and allowed him
to experiment with militia reforms in republican Florence. However, restoration of the Medici in 1512 crushed his hope to lead a rich public life engaged
in military reform and political influence. Instead, the end of the Florentine
Republic led to his arrest, torture and banishment from office by the restored
Medici family. During his enforced retirement he wrote *The Prince* and his
major works on war. For all the political insight these works provided the
world, his military ideas about militia and classical stratagems were mostly ignored in Florence then submerged by larger events and control of the Italian
Wars by external military powers. Moreover, condottieri combat proved
tame compared to the mass atrocities that were coming to scour Germany,
France and the British Isles during the brutal religious and civil wars of the
16th and 17th centuries. And their excesses were as nothing next to the far
greater horrors that would be wrought by kings and secular ideologies after
that, in long wars scripted and waged by absolutist princes served by battle-
seeking generals leading mass armies of citizen-soldiers that ravaged dozens
of nations in the 18th, 19th and 20th centuries. In Italy not least of all.

***

INTO THE NORTH Italian mix also came the Swiss, but not as Machiavelli
wanted. They were at the height of their power and reputation for invincibility in battle at the turn of the 16th century. For 200 years their armies bested
all comers, from Habsburgs to Burgundians to French. They utterly destroyed Burgundy, which had boasted one of the most modern armies during
the latter 15th century, with many fine cannon in one of the largest artillery
trains. It was an oddly organized army, however, principally cavalry using a
unique four-horse formation called a "lance." The Swiss-Burgundian War
started when Duke Charles "the Rash" tried to connect his core holdings
in the north with rich Italian lands to the south by carving a corridor right
through the Swiss Confederation. The Swiss would not let him pass. The first
fight was at Héricourt (1474), where mature Swiss infantry tactics exhibiting
a barefoot and Zulu-like marching speed allowed separately maneuvering infantry squares to trap a Burgundian heavy column of armored cavalry. The
horse soldiers were slaughtered, with the usual Swiss disregard for quarter. At
Grandson (1476), the Swiss captured the Burgundian artillery train—over
400 of the best field guns in Europe, along with all ammunition and supply

wagons. The armies met again at Morat (1476), where 12,000 Burgundians and allied mercenaries in lances fell to unstoppable Swiss push of pike, and to the spears and pistols of cavalry from Lorraine who fought alongside the cantons (the Swiss had no cavalry of their own). They captured another 200 cannon at Morat. The final axe fell at Nancy (1477), where Charles lost everything: the battle, the independent future of Burgundy, and his life. His cavalry lances and tactics were overcome by disciplined Swiss foot, who attacked his horse soldiers with crossbows and halberds and pikes. Charles was hooked from his mount by a halberdier and hacked to death on the ground. A unique cavalry and cannon army built up by successive dukes across the course of a century was completely destroyed by commoners from the Alps.

Next it was the turn of the Swiss to fail to adapt to change, in yet another example of the working of victor's disease in military history. Their demise came at Marignano (September 13–14, 1515), outside Milan. The Swiss were occupying Milan in a rare act of hubris, having come down from their mountain valleys to take advantage of the chaos in northern Italy. A brash young French king, Francis I, wanted Milan for France. He brought 60 bronze cannon and an alliance with Venice to meet the Swiss, endeavoring to bribe them out but ready to fight if the Swiss would not negotiate a solution under the threat of his guns. Some indeed took his gold and left, but most stayed to fight. French cannon were of widely varying caliber. That was common in a time of nonstandardized casting, but it complicated dispositions and ammunition. Even so, the French guns greatly overmatched any firepower on the Swiss side. Francis had some 10,000 French infantry armed with arquebuses, halberds and pikes; ranks of steel crossbowmen; and mounted lancers and men-at-arms of the traditional *gendarmerie* (noble heavy cavalry). He also brought to the fight over 19,000 German *Landsknechte* ("country lads"), mercenaries from the Black Band. It was a famed company-for-hire that fought in infantry squares in imitation of the Swiss, while wearing bizarrely colored and deliberately puffed, torn and tattered clothing. It comprised 12,000 pikers, 2,000 two-hand swordsmen, 2,000 arquebusiers and 1,000 halberdiers. *Landsknechte* hated the Swiss *Haufen*, commercial and martial rivals they had never beaten. This would be a fight without mercy or quarter.

Francis divided his army into three parts. His van was closest to Marignano, where a line of arquebusiers guarded the artillery line, positioned behind a dug ditch and flanked by 10,000 French infantry and 10,000 *Landsknechte*. In a second camp he placed another mixed group, the bulk of the *gendarmerie* and 9,000 *Landsknechte*. About two miles away was the third grouping, in an all-cavalry camp.[23] The Swiss remained behind the city walls in

Milan as the opposing armies settled in for a lengthy negotiation, but a battle was provoked on September 13 when French scouts ran into a small party of Swiss and fighting broke out. At noon, church bells rang out across Milan, calling 20,000 Swiss infantry to make ready for combat. They marched out in silence, intent on surprising the French in their forward camp. They had just 200 cavalry in support, horsemen from the Papal States, and eight small guns in their artillery train. Most were shoeless and wore no armor, though some had mail or plate or greaves or helms taken off dead enemies in prior victories.

They reached the first French camp around 4 p.m. in three *Haufen* of 6,000–7,000 men each. The waiting French and Germans came alert, seeing rising dust approach above so many thousands of tramping feet even before they saw the *Haufen*. The Swiss moved into a hard trot, three ranks of pikers in front in each square, a moving grove of pikes held upright behind them, with missile troops and axemen protected in the middle and at the rear. Just before slamming into the arquebus and artillery line the square faltered with a stutter-step, slowing attack momentum. It was the ditch dug across the line of attack, in front of the camp, that did it. A caterpillar stagger-step slowed and stuttered the lead square, lessening its mass impact and shock effect as it slammed into the line of guns. The famous Swiss infantry-shock tactic had failed. The *Haufen* did not deliver a stunning, smashing blow directly and bluntly into the enemy line, with the full weight and force of a whole square. Shock had been key to Swiss tactical success for two centuries. Now it failed right at the start, and all that was left was push of pike. That came as the Swiss recovered, overran the line and pushed aside the French infantry, before smashing into 10,000 *Landsknechte* moving at a steady trot in a single massive square, behind a pike wall of their own. Two great blocks of infantry slammed into each other, and push of pike commenced.

The front ranks of the colliding masses were mutually impaled or crushed or suffocated from the weight of men pushing from behind. Corpses were held upright, wedged between locked squares by the pressure of thousands pushing hard on each side, hands on the shoulder or back of some stout fellow in front, knowing men were dying up there. Many in the front ranks could no longer use their weapons, their arms pinned and useless.[24] Some wriggled free to stab at an enemy, but for most death came from inside the squares, as guns and crossbow bolts were fired at point-blank ranges into men's faces and swinging halberds reached over to lop off heads and limbs. Dense packs of humanity pushed at each other like immense, demented sumo wrestlers, only at Marignano the penalty for losing one's footing was dismemberment and death. Men fell from exhaustion and exertion, or when stabbed or hacked, adding blood to a wide, slick pool spreading over the grass beneath the locked squares, causing yet more men and boys to be killed as they slipped and fell. Slowly the Germans were pushed backward, each yard of loss and gain measured in death and wounds.

Men died by the hundreds, then thousands: stabbed, clubbed, hacked with axes, impaled, or shot down with crossbow quarrels or musket balls. Dead or alive, those who fell were trampled under 20,000 boots and bare feet, churning and driving the push of pike, slipping on hundreds of gallons of blood greasing the autumn grass. Sometimes a line of sight opened in the smoke as the locked mass of bodies heaved by, and a big gun would fire at intimate range. Chunks of bone and flesh flew as iron balls tore gaping holes in the Swiss ranks and files, killing a dozen or more men with each blast, obscuring with billows of smoke the carnage that they made. The infantry kept pushing, holding each other in a death embrace. French cavalry rode hard to the sound of the guns, toward infantry shouts and popping arquebuses and muskets and clanging of metal axes on armor and bone. Dukes and princes and men-at-arms slammed into the sides of the Swiss pike square, in a stamping mêlée of bloodied men and horses, stabbing with lances and shooting weak pistols from just eight or ten feet away.

Younger men were held in place in the squares by greybeard veterans, sergeants who beat them and threatened death. For running by any caused panic, and panic meant death for everyone else. In an infantry square you fought and won together or you lost and died together. So densely packed was the main mass of contending squares that some French knights speared two men with one lance thrust. The Swiss stabbed and shot back at their tormentors. Crossbowmen hit horses and men with high accuracy at short range, piercing armor and flesh. Halberdiers hacked the legs off horses or gashed open their bellies to topple riders into killing reach. The carnage went on for hours, two masses of infantry locked in hand-to-hand, face-to-face combat, horsemen circling around the flanks and rear. Men and boys dropped from heat, thirst and exhaustion. Older men had heart attacks. Circled by French cavalry that rode past shooting pistols, Swiss stabbed out in the dusk with pikes and crossbow quarrels, to be met in turn by lances and more pistol shots in the dark. Neither side gave ground, neither side offered quarter as they fought close to midnight under an autumn moon. At last, the moon clouded over and darkness forced a pause in the killing. The armies pulled apart, in places no more than 25 feet on either side of the shallow artillery ditch.

Men huddled in darkness in clusters of thirst and wounds, as all around other men lay dead and dying, groaning or sobbing. Also all around was the screaming of wounded horses. Some men crawled a few feet to find aid or comradeship and had their throats cut as they discovered too late that they had moved the wrong way. About 4 a.m., the bloody masses rose with the new sun, as captains on both sides ordered survivors to form ranks so that the slaughter could begin anew. The French blew tinny trumpets and formed a new line of battle. The Swiss blew deep-sounding mountain war horns, called "Bull of Uri" and "Cow of Unterwalden," reformed three reduced and wounded *Haufen*, and attacked. After their assault was repelled on the right flank, each side shifted men to the left, where the last standing *Landsknechte* clashed with the largest remaining *Haufen*. Cannon and handguns tore raw holes in the Swiss files, and hand-to-hand fighting saw more stabbing and hacking and gore. What finally broke the Swiss on the rack of combat was a line of cannon and more handguns than they could match or cope with: they were raked, again and again. Around 8 a.m., a charge was made into their flank by late-arriving Venetian cavalry, shouting their city's battle cry "San Marco! San Marco!" It was enough. A grim and sacrificial rearguard of 400 men from Zurich let exhausted, wounded survivors of the three defeated *Haufen* pull back to Milan.

Gravediggers stopped counting when they reached 16,500 dead. Other men died later of horrific wounds or lived out their lives missing arms or legs. The Swiss gave up the city and signed the Perpetual Peace, a treaty with Francis I and with France. They did not fight the French again until Napoleon invaded their cantons in 1798.[25] So sharp a defeat of the Swiss, until then regarded as the most lethal and reliable infantry in Europe, stunned the military and political worlds. France's military reputation rose to unfamiliar heights while that of the cantons and their dense pike squares fell precipitously, never to recover. The admixture of old and new tactics and technologies and varied fighting styles, on the field all at once at Marignano, encapsulated basic changes underway since the infantry revolution began in the 14th century, now reaching into the 16th. Dominance of the battlefield by massed infantry in preference to cavalry was affirmed. The ascendance of guns over archers, though not yet indisputable, was clarified and the trend to infantry firearms accelerated. It was also clear that the day of pike-and-crossbow tactics and the infantry square was over. After Marignano, Spanish *tercios* ("thirds") displaced Swiss and German squares as the dominant infantry formation and fighting style in Western Europe, winning a convincing and even decisive victory over the French at Pavia in 1525, where Francis I was both humiliated and captured.

Change continued apace. Spanish infantry continued reforming, somewhat thinning and lengthening blockish *tercios* in order to avoid the rising power of field guns, and to bring additional arquebuses and heavy muskets to bear in longer firing lines in modestly rectangular formations. These were still very heavy formations, however. Most 16th century *tercios* had 3,000 men, but heavier *tercios* could field up to 6,000, in 50 to 60 ranks with 80 men to a file. They remained slow units, albeit of disciplined pikemen and arquebusiers, with some heavy musketeers and perhaps grenadiers on the corners. To contemporary observers they appeared as "iron cornfields." They won through shock and weight rather than any clever maneuver, of which they were not capable because they remained unarticulated and hence too inflexible. Others saw in them a "walking citadel" whose corner guards of clustered musketeers appeared like a mobile castle with four turrets moving on the battlefield. Even reformed, longer *tercios* later in the century presented 30 or more ranks of thickness, though over time pikers were further reduced and all archers replaced with musketeers or grenadiers. This represented a hesitant start toward an evolution into musket and fusil linear war. However, the shift took another century to complete.[26] *Tercios* thinned even more as decades passed, yet they remained clunky and rigid, vehicles of infantry combat weight over maneuver. Breakthrough reform leading to linear formations waited on late 16th century innovations introduced by the Dutch and then advanced in the early 17th century by the Swedes.

***

MEANWHILE, MORE AND bigger wars spilled across Europe. Along the northern rim of what was once Latin Christendom, the First Northern War (1558–1583) devolved into a protracted round of fighting that saw Poland-Lithuania, Muscovy (Russia), Sweden and Denmark fight one another in various and shifting combinations, mainly over spoils of conquest in Livonia and a long contest for dominance in the Baltic. That conflict ended indecisively, ensuring that fighting resumed to scourge and burn all the northern countries over the course of the 17th century, lasting into the first quarter of the 18th. The central issues in these extended wars were dynastic and territorial, with the principal powers of Denmark, Poland, Sweden and Russia facing off during decades of "Troubles" over competing aspirations to mount vacated thrones or lay claims to free cities and each others' rich provinces. Thus there came the Smolensk War (1632–1634), Torstensson's War (1643–1645), the Second Northern War (1655–1660), the Thirteen Years' War

(1654–1667), the Scanian War (1674–1679) and finally the Great Northern War (1700–1721).[27]

Politics and fighting were complicated by confessional hostility, born of the worsening clash of Protestant Reformation and Catholic Counter-Reformation as Christianity in Europe insisted on a last ritual slaughter, before giving way to the much greater slaughters by princes of the new realist politics waging wider secular wars from the 18th century onward. In the East and North, confessional disputation crept into state policy as Lutherans and Catholics added fierce conflict over doctrine to issues of dynasty and territory. Confessional allegiance was used to assert or undermine dynastic claims and legitimacy and enforced against once-free cities and principalities internally and across the Baltic region. The most important consequence was Sweden's emergence and then spectacular intervention in Germany under Gustavus Adolphus, starting in 1630, in support of the Protestant cause and Swedish interests in the Thirty Years' War (1618–1648).[28]

While wars of religion finally ended, for the most part, in central Europe with the Peace of Westphalia in 1648, regional wars over core issues of the secular sort remained unresolved.[29] The main motif in the North was Sweden's spectacular rise, then catastrophic defeat in the Great Northern War that ended its century of *Stormakstid* ("Great Power Period"). Karl XII invaded Russia in 1708, advancing to disaster as Peter I ("The Great") retreated into Ukraine, moving the local population back and scorching the crops and earth in front of the invaders, as his successors would do in 1812 and again in 1941. The Swedes endured a hard winter, losing over half their complement to starvation and bitter cold. An army of sick and weary survivors was then beaten at Poltava (July 8, 1709). An admixture of old religious cynicism and the new realism found expression in Peter's dispatch from the field: "God in his great mercy has granted us a matchless victory over the enemy. In short, their entire force has been defeated." With Sweden's field army broken or captured and Karl XII languishing in Ottoman exile, where he was forcibly kept for years, Peter battered now-exposed border fortresses with new-made artillery and knocked Sweden from the top tier of Great Powers in Europe, bringing Russia into the European state system in its place.[30]

In the West, protracted and pronounced wars of religion attended and then overtook the long argument among monks that finally broke into the open with Martin Luther's declaration of theses of dissent at Wittenberg in 1517. Theological disputes at first only lightly overlay the more usual fighting reasons of local quarrels, issues of succession, material interest and vain princely motives for war. As conflict dragged on for decades and depredations of war and religious cruelty hardened views, confessional impulses and justifications became violently corrosive of civil order inside countries and of the general peace between and among them. Thus, after the Habsburg-Valois wars over Italy ended, France collapsed into decades of regional and confessional civil war known as the Wars of Religion, or alternatively as the French Civil Wars. Characterized by unholy cruelty, fighting between French Catholics and French Calvinists (Huguenots) waxed and waned and waxed again from 1562 to 1629. The bitter conflict was marked by the usual cruelties of all war but also by ritual drownings (death by symbolic baptism) and burnings (death by purification by fire). Thousands of civilians were butchered in such ways by religious mobs, and many more in dozens of sieges and small battles fought by Huguenot and Catholic armies.[31]

At the same time, as much from piety as politics, Philip II launched Spain on a perpetual crusade to crush a Calvinist rebellion in Flanders, then reached over the water to threaten "heretic" England under the Protestant monarch Elizabeth I, who was aiding the rebels. His faith caused him to rely on hope in miracles and other divine assistance whenever he was told by his best advisers that his resources in ships and armies or taxes were insufficient to meet his military goals. This led to baffled interpretation of defeats that were best explained in secular terms as an expression of divine judgment on his statecraft. He once chided an official whose zealotry was less than his own: "You are engaged in God's service and in mine, which is the same thing." To pious ends, he encouraged the persecutions of the Spanish Inquisition, sent inquisitors north to scour Flanders, supported Jesuit missions across his overseas empire, and established courts of Inquisition in Lima and Mexico City by 1570. This devotion to the Counter-Reformation did not mean that Philip always got on well with popes. In 1557, Pope Paul IV excommunicated him and declared war on Spain, but the pontiff was tamed within a few months when Philip cut off Rome from its Sicilian grain supplies as a demonstration of whose sovereign writ really ran in Italy. Thenceforth, Philip was deeply involved in wider Church politics and in the affairs of the Papal States, intervening with money and threats and arms to prevent the election of any pope who might oppose his policies.

Philip called his plans his "grand design," in which he was further encouraged by a paralysis of French diplomacy and military resistance resulting from 40 years of confessional civil war between Huguenots and Catholics. That left him free to intervene even in France when he chose, rather than face stratagems of a powerful once and future foe of his ambitions. France's misfortune was Spain's opportunity, and Philip used it to prosecute a long war against the Dutch rebels in Flanders, on France's northern border, and to intervene repeatedly in the south. The Dutch crisis deepened into a war that would last eight decades in and around Flanders, to 1648. The Eighty Years' War (1568–1648) that Philip bequeathed to his successors also saw naval fighting against Dutch *Gueux* ("Beggars")[32] expand to all the world's oceans. Meanwhile, at home in Granada a rebellion by forcibly converted Muslims ("Moriscos") broke out, while in 1570 the Ottomans resumed a very old war for control of the eastern Mediterranean by attacking Cyprus. Philip failed to take full advantage of the religious wars underway in France to hamstring that enemy permanently. Instead, he was repeatedly drawn into conflict with the Ottoman Empire and the Barbary States, while also fighting religious rebels in Flanders. At Lepanto in 1571, his fleet won the last great galley battle, a bloody infantry engagement at sea with troops fighting from the decks of hundreds of ships grappled and lashed together. His galleys and allied Venetian galleasses destroyed the Ottoman fleet, killing 40,000 men. Yet this seemingly decisive naval battle actually settled little, for Philip failed to follow up victory on the water with occupation of the eastern islands that controlled the rich Mediterranean trades.[33] His attention instead lurched back to his other wars, most of all against the Dutch Calvinists and their Protestant ally, Elizabeth I of England. Philip appeared a colossus, but beneath the surface of his power serial bankruptcies driven by too many long wars all at once eroded the will and endurance of his country and empire. Miguel Cervantes, one of his soldiers, famously portrayed the overly devout king as a broken-down old crusader tilting at windmills of heresy.

Against all advice, Philip sent the "Invincible Armada" north in 1588, loaded with cannon and marines. His intention was for the Armada to escort his Army of Flanders, a powerful force fighting the Dutch rebels, over to English shores to reconvert Elizabeth I's Protestant kingdom to Catholicism. To that end, the fleet also carried inquisitors and hundreds of priests. Poorly sailed and worse conceived, the great Armada was attacked at night while at anchor off Calais, riven and scattered by explosive fireships modeled on Dutch "Hellburners." These were special fireships, not just hulks splashed with pitch over tinder, dry wood and canvas. Their holds and decks were filled with kegs of black powder, their cannon crammed with double-shot and chains, waiting to blow apart when iron turned red with the runaway flames. They were towed inward by skiffs before being left to drift crewless on a rising tide into the inner harbor. The Armada came asunder as galleon captains cut cables and fled, floundering out of the blazing port and into pell-mell battle with the English fleet waiting for the scattering ships to come out.

It was chased into the Channel, where it raggedly reformed, then was forced to run the long way on a "Protestant Wind," as English propagandists called it, all around Scotland and Ireland.

It was a bleak and hopeless voyage filled with thirst, disease and threats of mutiny. So lacking in potable water was the fleet that hundreds of horses were cast overboard into the North Sea. Shipwrecks were next, as poorly crewed vessels struggled off the Atlantic coast of Ireland in storm-churned waters unknown to and uncharted by Iberian pilots.[34] Philip only hardened more in defeat, puzzled by the fate of his fleet and cause, unable to comprehend that his god had forsaken him in his great hour of military need and personal and political devotion. Even after losing the Armada, in 1591 he still said: "The cause of religion must take precedence over everything." Spain thus continued the Eighty Years' War against Calvinist Dutch in Flanders and at sea, while also fighting the Muslim Barbary States and the Ottomans in the Mediterranean. Was Philip or Spain making a bid for mastery in the latter decades of the 16th century, the first in a line of would-be hegemons who drove the Great Powers of Europe, and thereby also their overseas empires, into war after war from the 16th through the 20th centuries? Historians still argue the point, a dispute foretelling another ongoing scholarly argument over Louis XIV's declared policy of *la défense aggressive* ("defensive aggression") in the second half of the 17th century.[35]

Drive for hegemony by Imperial Spain or not, for eighty years Dutch rebels and Spanish armies of occupation and Inquisition spilled treasure and blood for competing Christs, over the rights of kings, and over who would control the rich seaborne trades. Fighting occurred across the high seas and along the coasts of far-off islands, colonies and continents, as well as in the heavily populated and often water-logged fields and byways of Flanders. An advanced economy with major banks and a rising stock market enabled Dutch leaders to pay troops on time and in full, and sometimes extra. This gave the Beggar cause a huge advantage over the Spanish, whose troops were usually owed many months' (sometimes several years') back pay. As a result, they fought with less enthusiasm and mutinied dozens of times during eight decades of war. The worst incident, remembered still as the "Spanish Fury," caused lasting damage to the Spanish cause in Flanders when mutiny over lack of rations and missing pay led to the ravaging of the countryside, then a two-day sack of Antwerp (November 4–5, 1576). More than 1,000 buildings were razed, thousands of people were raped or robbed, and hundreds were murdered. Dutch propagandists claimed 18,000 dead, almost certainly a wild exaggeration, contributing to Spain's "Black Legend" of cruelty and

Inquisition.[36] The long war ended in Dutch independence in 1648, but not before it merged with the greatest of all wars of religion: the Thirty Years' War (1618–1648), centered on Germany but drawing in all the major powers of Europe before it was done.

The Thirty Years' War was the climactic confessional conflict. Originating in Bohemia and from Imperial politics and Habsburg ambitions, it spread across the Holy Roman Empire and beyond. It ushered in decades of wastage, pillage, massacres, atrocities, witch burning and bloody-minded fighting over emerging princely and secular issues. It was also waged, at least to start, to decide whether the "one true faith" on one side would triumph over the "one true faith" on the other. At its end, Germany's population was diminished by almost a quarter. Whole provinces were laid waste and cities sacked and put to the sword, most notoriously Magdeburg in 1631. This prolonged armed struggle at the center of Europe affected much more than narrow clerical arguments over transubstantiation or the predestination of souls, or other issues contested by theologians and religious authorities. It constituted a massive upheaval at all levels social and political, completing the final cultural transition from late medieval to early modern and from wars of religion to wars among states.[37] It was from the start a conflict caught up in, and defined by, this core change from wars fought in the name of God to wars waged openly by and for the interests of secular rulers. The greatest and fiercest of the religious wars brought God and princes onstage at the same time, mixing the fanatical fundamentalism of some key figures with the raw secular ambition of others. It crescendoed into the Great War of the 17th century (every century seemingly has its own Great War), pulling in most surrounding powers before petering into lasting confessional stalemate and compromise at Westphalia in 1648.[38] The great peace framed there confirmed and codified princely rights as supreme in politics, a secular balance of power, and a new diplomatic system modeled on Renaissance principles and sustained initially by revived French military strength.[39]

The person whose policies more than any other shaped the endgame of the Thirty Years' War and the lasting settlement of 1648 did not live to see the great peace. Cardinal Armand Richelieu, Louis XIII's first minister from 1624 until his death in 1642, was the most powerful statesman in Europe. Despite his church office, he was also heir to the spirit of Machiavelli's secular realism. He wore red robes and a red zucchetto, but placed his king and state (and, it must be said, also his purse, his family and himself) above his Catholic confession. He singularly framed the nature and course of French absolutism, preshaping the coming Age of Louis XIV in France. He made the balance of power and support for the perpetual division of France's enemies his foreign policy. A cardinal of the Catholic Church, in 1630 he intervened to support the Swedish king Gustavus Adolphus and the Protestant side in the Thirty Years' War against the Habsburgs. In doing so, he moved Catholic France from defense of the Faith to defense of itself, to what he called *raison d'état* ("reason of state"), or roughly what is today termed "the national interest." Paris rather than Rome hosted the cathedral and ultimate loyalty of the *éminence rouge* ("red eminence") of the Bourbons.[40]

The limiting principle of the Peace of Augsburg (1555), a failed effort to end the wars of religion before they grew worse, as they did during the Eighty Years' War and the Thirty Years' War, was *cuius regio eius religio* ("whosoever controls the territory decides the religion"). After decades of confessional war it was abandoned in the Peace of Westphalia in 1648, with minor exceptions.[41] Talks held at separate sites, one Catholic and the other Protestant, took four years to complete. As one Catholic delegate put it: "In winter we negotiate, in summer we fight." Still, ideas of security through balance and toleration, and hence the secular primacy of princes over the eternal claims of prelates, found resonance on either side of the exhausted confessional divide. The winning ideas were long on the roads north, traveling not from hardened theological homes in Rome or Wittenberg but from Florence and Venice. They came from the quill of Machiavelli and the ruthless examples of the doges and the Medici of the Renaissance, where even the Papal States had been ruled by warlord popes who behaved in war as did any other prince. They arrived over lands ravaged by burnings and battles in the name of God but waged more for the interest of burghers and to set borders agreed by secular rulers. At long journey's end, they delivered a profoundly secular understanding of war and power politics, moved to center stage in place of a fatally divided and clearly moribund *res publica Christiana*.

In clear new language stripped of reference to God, except for the usual banal and nonbinding pieties served up as cultural and political garnish, the princes of Europe in 1648 agreed to bar confessions and clerical concerns from the realm of high politics, elevating themselves and the ideal of secular sovereignty to exclusive roles.[42] The recognizably modern principle of princely or state sovereignty permeated the treaties and settlement, raising up a new norm of "nonintervention in internal affairs" (then meaning religious matters) that survives more generally in international law today. Secularism would henceforth inform the new order in international politics. The political pretensions of the popes were ignored, including by the gathered Catholic princes, who were just as jealous of sovereign prerogative as their Protestant counterparts. This pragmatism among the Catholic delegates meeting at Osnabrück caused Pope Innocent X to fulminate that all articles affirming confessional tolerance were "null and void, invalid, iniquitous, unjust, condemned, rejected, frivolous, without force or effect, and no one is to observe them, even when they be ratified by oath."[43] No one paid attention anymore.

Rail as the pontiff did, Reformation and Counter Reformation alike had failed to achieve confessional or doctrinal exclusivity. Not in the face of a balance of power among secular states. Not after more than a century of war. As one weary Catholic phrased the new reality, "It is lawful by urgent necessity to enter into perpetual peace with heretics." No more would rituals or the public oath of a cleric, a hard doctrine or church law, rude tracts published to provoke in Geneva or Paris or Rome, or religious pogroms in Bohemia or the Palatinate shake the high affairs of princes. Instead, the Peace of Westphalia proclaimed and codified the rules of an emergent secular political order, sanctioning in law and legitimizing in practice a rejection of any authority above sovereign princes. It was a change long in the making, this overthrow of the transcendent claims of popes and Holy Roman Emperors in favor of an ascendant secularism of kings and states.[44]

Monarchs still persecuted confessional minorities, but mainly to complete absolutist centralization of early modern states by enforcing conformity inside their realms. Thus Catholics were persecuted by English occupiers in Ireland, heretics were banished from Spain and Louis XIV hounded any of his subjects who were Huguenots, forcing them into conversion or exile. He ordered *dragonnades* that billeted dragoons in Protestant homes, enforced mass conversions, and issued the infamous Edict of Fontainebleau (1685) ending toleration. He banned Protestantism from public display, authorized burnings of Huguenot churches, ordered Catholic baptism of all newly born children, and forbade Protestant males from leaving France on pain of condemnation as galley slaves. Additional edicts forbade enlistment of Protestants in French regiments (foreign regiments in royal service were not affected) or on royal warships. Protestants who wished to remain in his service were given bounties for converting. Louis sent more dragoons to repress the Revolt of the Camisards (1702–1705) in the Cévennes. Yet all this had more to do with his political instinct for absolutism at home than any personal dedication to claims of a universal faith. These were policies of a prince, an ideologue of royal conformity and absolutism rather than of faith.

Behind the foreign policy that brought Louis XIV 29 years of war were a new language of politics drawn from Machiavelli, a secular diplomacy from the Renaissance as newly mediated by Richelieu and new-style artillery fortresses that permitted monarchs like the Sun King to mark and defend harder frontiers with stone and iron. If idealism remained in the face of such cynical realism it was to be found in something else that was new, what today we call "international law." This was defined and codified by the great diplomat and jurist Huig de Groot, or Grotius, in his principal works: *Mare Liberum* ("Freedom of the Seas"), first published in 1609, and *De jura belli et pacis* ("On the Law of War And Peace"), published in 1625. In the absence of any Church law to at least try to govern a community of polities fractured by war, principles of diplomacy laid out in his jurisprudence and agreed upon by treaty were vitally important.[45] Yet war and its politics remained dominant. And war, like Nature, remained "red in tooth and claw."

What really changed was the purpose for which future wars would be fought, as well as the expanding scale of the fighting to come. Faith would still be used to rally allies in a proclaimed religious cause, such as 18th-century calls for war against the Ottomans and Ottoman calls for jihad against their enemies, or Protestants against Louis XIV and Catholic France, or French support of Catholic rebels in Ireland and Scotland. However, no longer would sovereigns make war to impose one confession over another one in a different country. The Peace of Westphalia confirmed that a tectonic shift had taken place in the cultural order as well as in the military and political balance of power. The move was away from the churches to the states, from clerics and canons commanding in the wars of God to generals and cannons deciding the wars of princes. Popes and preachers henceforth were told to mind their pews, not to meddle in the affairs of monarchs and nations. The next wars would be bigger and just as protracted, but fought for other reasons. The wars of religion were over. The wars of kings and empires were about to begin.

4

Battle Reformed

RISING LOGISTICAL AND administrative demands on early modern states accompanied expanding armies, expensive cannon, and garrisoned artillery fortresses. In turn, armed force was increasingly monopolized by states as private interests could no longer compete with expanding and centralized tax bases, as they had in medieval times. It was a long-term pattern, evolutionary in pace but revolutionary in effect, as more powerful monarchs cut the legs out from under the horses of mounted aristocracies, and other entities such as free cities that had once enjoyed real local and military autonomy. War was getting more expensive, thereby limiting participation to fewer actors while concentrating armed power in royal hands, reinforcing the legal and social authority of monarchs even while expanding their means to wage protracted conflict against other kings. Players in the game got fewer but stronger, fighting more organized and lethal, with larger infantry armies and hardened borders guarded by fortifications of stone mounting gunpowder artillery.[1]

On the ground, a basic transformation in weapons, tactics, supply and practices of armies was underway.[2] Some historians identify these changes as a "Revolution in Military Affairs" (or RMA). The theory was first broached by the military historian Michael Roberts in the mid-1950s concerning the narrow period 1560–1660. He highlighted tactical reform, musket drill and other innovations in Flanders and Sweden. Another historian, Geoffrey Parker, deployed the term over a longer period, starting earlier and ending later, and asserting that the RMA advanced European power globally in the centuries that followed. The debate continues still, around a central thesis that a revolution occurred in which military technologies, war finance, infantry drill and gunpowder weapons drove immense changes in the face and conduct of war and in the societies hosting the new armies, first across Europe then far beyond, traveling along filaments of trade and imperial defense.[3]

The core idea involved changes to infantry due to gunpowder weapons, from arquebuses to muskets, and introduction of the first truly mobile or field artillery in Sweden by the 1620s. Also critically important in the theory are the *trace italienne* bastion, leading to full geometric artillery fortresses raised against more powerful siege guns which, as discussed above, helped drive the expansion of armies needed to besiege from all sides at once. One dynamic is said to have reinforced the other, in an expanding cycle of technology and social changes that brought new weapons wielded by new social classes onto the battlefield, expanding the scale of war and broadening the classes and elements of society that directly participated in it. Even after the early changes of the RMA were fully incorporated, a secular trend in military expansion is said to have continued that was centered on ever-larger infantry armies in wars of expanding participation and destruction. Thus, in 1567 the army that marched up the Spanish Road to repress the revolt against Philip II in the Netherlands numbered some 10,000 musketeers and pikers in three *tercios* of 3,000 each, with 1,000 cavalry in support. That was considered a large army at the time. Thirty years later, its successor as the Army of Flanders was swollen six times over, to 60,000 men, and it was but one of several theater armies maintained by Spain. Three decades after that, and armies of 100,000 or more marauded over Germany during the Thirty Years' War. And so on, despite brief periods of contraction, as armies expanded over time to eventually reach hundreds of thousands in the early 19th century and tens of millions of men under arms in the mid-20th century.

The other central tenet of the RMA is that gunpowder technology changed not just the face of battle but also host societies, through intense centralization of armed power and finance. The military revolution thereby created war states, elevating and sustaining more powerful monarchies whose legitimacy and efficacy relied above all on an ability to make war.[4] Bastioned artillery fortresses reached impressive new dimensions that imposed new costs, adding to the burden of sustaining expensive large armies and world-girdling navies. Some advocates argue that it was the RMA that subsequently elevated Europe to global dominance, as unique broadside artillery platforms arrived off foreign shores in the form of ships of "fighting sail," and bastioned fortresses were built to protect coastal enclaves before armies and political influence alike penetrated inland. Military domination is thus said to explain European political and trade domination, after the defeat of local galley or junk navies and more traditional armies even in territories that already had guns, such as India and China. In sum, the RMA is credited by some with having driven the whole trajectory of modern world history, starting with the ascendance of small fiscal-military states ruled by European kings in the 15th–16th centuries, spreading European military power and then cultural and political influence globally after that.

Other scholars dispute that a military revolution occurred at all, or note the theory's too-narrow focus on Western Europe. They point out that in Eastern Europe, Russia and nearby Ottoman lands, cavalry was dominant much longer, as infantry trying to traverse the wide plains and thinly populated steppes wore out legs and supplies. Cavalry moved farther and faster in the sprawling East, covering more ground in open space quite unlike the cramped and wet flats of Flanders, densely populated France and Germany, or urban and mountainous Italy. Geography made a difference. The need for slow foot soldiers was minimal in long-distance wars against fast horse armies of Cossacks and Tatars, who kept few if any garrison towns and none defended by bastioned walls needing reduction by long-haul siege guns and infantry armies. Eastern armies recognized that, other than dragoons and other mounted infantry, foot soldiers could not make up with musket firepower what they lacked in mobility in a theater where space and movement was more important. Cavalry remained the principal arm not because armies or polities in the East were militarily or technologically "backward," but because they understood the topography and supply issues of their theater.

Some military historians further set the RMA idea in a global context, viewing the thesis as incompatible with highly effective non-European militaries that enjoyed real success in regional wars.[5] Others charge the theory with being technologically deterministic, focusing too heavily on guns and gunpowder.[6] Where adherents argue that guns *drove* large social changes, others counter that the evolution of warfare was more a consequence than a cause of those changes. Did lower classes pour into and remake the face of war because of guns, or were guns manufactured to arm masses of men coincidentally, as they participated more broadly in war for other reasons? Did the "musket make the democrat," as some contend, or did firearms fortify states and kings and dictatorships against their peoples, as seems to have happened far more often? Finally, it may be doubted that any historical process taking several centuries to complete can be termed a "revolution." Moreover, military technologies always comprise a social dimension in addition to the technical.[7] How to resolve this debate when, even for fellow historians, it can reduce to an unprovable argument over which came first, gunpowder or the match? It probably makes most sense to see fundamental changes in war and society as symbiotic, with guns and social forces interacting at many points in different ways, producing an evolution of composite adaptation that had genuinely revolutionary effects over time.[8]

A good place to start is in the late 16th century, with the revival of drill for close-order musket work, including volley fire, first in the Netherlands and then more generally. Under the best conditions, an experienced and well-trained musketeer before 1600 could get off one round every two minutes or so. Muskets of the era were complex and hard to reload, a problem that could be fatal in combat. Two minutes was more than enough time for enemy infantry to close ground and return fire or resort to *armes blanches* (bladed weapons). It was an eternity when facing charging cavalry. Fire by volley was the only solution, but it was very hard to do. It called for better-trained troops who could stand ground as well as shuffle their ranks to fire and reload as the enemy advanced. If it could be achieved, it would significantly increase infantry rates of fire and hence both defense and offense. The solution was renewed emphasis on drill and other infantry innovations in a "new model army," the first of several to acquire the appellation, created in the 1590s in the Netherlands by military reformers strongly influenced by Machiavelli's views of Rome's civic and military discipline.[9]

In 1594, Willem Lodewijk introduced volley fire to the army of the United Provinces, then three decades into its Eighty Years' War with Spain. In his system, the front rank fired, then the second rank advanced through the front rank, followed by the next, and the one after that. There were in all ten ranks. Lodewijk's more famous cousin, Maurits of Nassau, added the countermarch, in which each rank fired in unison, then retired to the rear to reload, allowing the next rank to step forward to fire and retire. Reducing the depth of infantry stretched the firing line, adding flexibility in maneuver to superior rates of fire. Well-drilled Dutch regiments could now keep up a fairly steady fire by volley that devastated older, more stolid and less mobile formations such as the *tercios* of the Army of Flanders. Spaniards were additionally handicapped by deploying very heavy muskets firing a 3/4-ounce lead ball, universally called "Spanish muskets." They did so from thicker formations that presented far fewer muzzles along the firing line and thus achieved much lower rates of fire. The trend was set by the Dutch reforms. Within 25 years, the Swedish Army reduced ranks to six from ten and added the devastating "double volley," a drill wherein the first three ranks fired as one with front rank prone, second rank kneeling, third rank standing. Then they countermarched to permit the back three ranks to fire, and so forth.[10]

Others emulated the Dutch and Swedish reforms as faster rates of fire were produced by more reliable, more quickly reloadable and more accurate and lighter muskets. Everyone was forced to adopt the new systems of drill, though the Spanish resisted longest. Ranks dropped from ten to six, whereas infantry even in a reformed *tercio* might still form 16–20 ranks. Thinner and longer lines meant more muskets presented by each company or regiment or brigade, while volley fire by rank increased the weight of flying lead. Always, the trend was to more muzzles. This slow evolution toward what became "linear warfare" was spurred by the need to deploy guns and then more guns, and still more guns. Rear ranks became places to reload for the next volley, while also serving as a built-in reserve to step into the firing line as casualties fell. Grenadiers put down their hand bombs and took up muskets, though they retained the old name and unique tall and brimless hats. Pikers were progressively displaced, but still needed until the late-17th-century advent of the bayonet introduced in France.

It was once thought that fire by volley was unique to Europe, reinvented there in direct emulation of classical tactics such as javelin volleys. That is probably wrong on two scores: it was not a gunpowder version of the Roman javelin volley, and it was not uniquely European. It seems more likely that volley fire was a natural evolution from the nature of improved firearms. Volleys likely came from armies learning by trial and error, from experience in using muskets in real fights rather than imitation of Romans in rediscovered texts. Where the genuine cleverness of reformers contributed was in training Dutch and Swedish soldiers to do this faster and with more practiced skill than anyone else. Advances were also made through successful experiments in countermarching, enhancing the move to infantry firepower and away from shock. These were genuine innovations that bore emulation, and over time reshaped the face of battle.

In Europe, fire by volley was unknown beyond the Netherlands before the 1620s, but it is now known that both Japanese and Ottomans employed independent versions of volley fire much earlier than that. Musketeers under the Japanese shogun Oda Nobunaga used volley fire at the Battle of Nagashino in 1575, nearly twenty years before the first Dutch experiments. They had little or no knowledge of classical warfare, and did not learn the technique via diffusion from Europe.[11] Ottoman janissaries fired in volley in 1605, and possibly even earlier. They did this without known reference to Western classical models or any direct contact with Dutch troops. Janissary firearms drill also significantly predated musket drill in Europe. Ottomans in 1600 also had more advanced commissary and logistics systems and a sounder basis of war finance and supporting military bureaucracy. They fielded larger armies and siege trains and maintained a permanent establishment with advanced pay and pensions, and had far superior medical capability to anything then in Europe. Divergence in the quality of guns from those in Europe did not handicap the sultan's armies before the 1680s. Imported master gunners such as the Hungarian who cast the great bombard used at Constantinople in 1453 joined local masters to cast cannon and manufacture muskets broadly comparable to anything used in the West, at least into the late 17th century. Only then did the Ottomans fall behind in the arms race with Europe.[12]

***

IN 16TH-CENTURY EUROPE, field battles represented a small fraction of military effort and expense. Very few were fought between 1495 and 1600, and many of those originated in siege relief or from pressing issues of army resupply (including once, a shortage of beer). Problems of logistics and movement were so grave that even the most eager commanders devoted to battle-seeking often ended making marches that missed the enemy entirely, due to lack of information or insufficient speed on the march. A general could hardly shift his cumbersome army from camp onto the roads, let alone achieve decisive tactical results by clever maneuvers with troops not trained to make them. Offensive campaigning meant activating a massive logistics support system, adding a heavy tail to each army. Even regular foraging, let alone a campaign strategy to "eat out" the enemy's lands, consumed huge effort.[13] An opposing general had only to outwait the more talented tactician, not outwit him—or just leave before his enemy arrived.

He was likely leaving anyway, since no army could rest in place long due to food and fodder needs. The rule became move and requisition, preferably by stealing supplies from the enemy's lands and towns, or starve and wilt. Campaigns became almost indistinguishable from this constant search for provisions, in which hungry armies missed each other in passing. This could consume months or even years without forcing tactical, let alone strategic, decision by battle.[14] Under such conditions, 16th- and 17th-century warfare is best viewed not as a clash of armies in sequential field fights but as an administrative and war-management contest, a grinding competition of endurance. For defenders, it made most sense not to field an army looking for battle but to sink down behind breastworks and into trenches. War did not reduce to sanguinary clashes of armies to decide everything, nor even to a siege or a string of sieges to at least decide some things. Wars were driven and largely determined by finance and administrative capacity, or lack thereof, to sustain military infrastructure and pay the infantry. That is more often what decided victory or defeat. For when gold or coin to pay soldiers and for supplies ran

out, hired men left, or they mutinied and destroyed and plundered instead
of defending. Or worse, they surrendered the fortress or the city they were
supposed to guard to the richer paymaster on the other side.[15]

That is why logistics became everything. The search for supplies provoked
devastating campaigns by opposing armies, especially by mercenary contract
generals whose main loyalty was as paymaster to their troops rather than to
the monarch who hired them. Supply most often came down to seizure of
money and requisition of goods along the line of march, or all around an
encamped army during a siege. Military entrepreneurs took big armies on
campaigns of slow maneuver, seldom meeting the enemy in battle, though
sometimes brushing up against each other while in search of food and fodder.
Promissory notes on the royal treasury were often issued but less often actually paid. Over time, that wore down a sovereign's ability to make war as a reputation for nonpayment encouraged peasants and sutlers (large merchants) to
hide grain and fodder from a passing army. Food seizures eroded support for
any cause, as even friendly armies were compelled to eat out whole valleys
or scour fertile plains as they moved over allied lands. Richer cities paid off
extortionist commanders to go around their supporting territory, deflecting
them to pillage a neighboring town or valley instead. Yet a passing army also
could be good for business. Sutlers carted bulk goods out to the armies or
followed them with loaded wagons as part of the baggage train. Or they sold
from pole-driven barges as an army marched along a river route and camped
along the shore. Or they contracted to provision a garrison or siege camp.
Armies were, in a real sense, large mobile markets. Since they often traversed
the same invasion routes nearly every summer, sutler markets and stations
became more or less permanent over time. Mercenary captains and large sutlers were partners in the ongoing business of war.

States still lacked the bureaucratic capacity to push armies past where sutlers and gold ran out. The solution was to exact *Kontributionen* ("contributions") imposed by force on enemy lands. Contributions started as a form of
lawful military tax, but under the great pressures of the Thirty Years' War
they changed into an impost levied under threat of indiscriminate mass violence. Payment lists were issued as an army arrived. If the imposed tax was
not paid in full and on time, reprisal followed: whole villages were burned
down, and hostages from the list were executed. It was a ruthless but efficient
method of extortion at sword and pike point. Habsburg generals relied on
these forced cash levies paid into their *Kriegskasse* (war chest), a literal strong-
box of monies used to meet wages for the troops and to buy foodstuffs and
fodder. Contributions ensured that troops were paid regularly, relieving them

of the need to forage widely just to keep body and soul together, or in search of portable plunder in lieu of pay. Paying wages from a war chest damped down mutiny and made troops more acceptable to merchants, because contributions flowed back into the local economy from the army's camp. Eager sutlers thus brought food and goods to sell to armies and camp followers, mobile armed towns moving over the countryside (many armies were in fact more populous than all but the largest cities of the day). It was a supply system only just better than outright theft, but it worked, and was soon adopted by all sides.[16]

However, the solution came with a political price. Contributions kept armies in the field and denied men and resources to the enemy, but they also made military contractors virtually self-sufficient by attaching soldier loyalty to the general as paymaster. Ultimately, this posed such a threat to the Habsburgs in the case of their great mercenary general and entrepreneur, Albrecht von Wallenstein, that Emperor Ferdinand II secretly dismissed him in 1634, then sent assassins to kill his best general. From 1635, Imperial garrisons were no longer provisioned and paid solely from contributions. Taxes were voted instead by the Imperial Diet, which exacted a different kind of political price from the Habsburg emperors. After 1648, high taxes originating in the Thirty Years' War were kept in place by princes and monarchs across Europe to support new and enlarged peacetime or standing armies.

In the decades-long wars of the 17th century, fundamental problems of logistics discouraged rulers and generals alike from resort to high-risk battles to decide larger military outcomes. Tactical advantage shifted to defense, as offensive operations became more costly with bigger and expensively equipped armies that were hard to maneuver and even harder to supply. Meanwhile, as shown below, strategic and political indecision still characterized most of the battles that were fought. Always, even after a lopsided victory in the field, the bulk of enemy troops remained securely behind some hard-to-overcome fortifications someplace else. Sieges thus still dominated, while trending toward a scale greater in blood and spent treasure than before. Only the greatest late-medieval sieges exceeded in cost and casualties the *average* 17th-century siege, carried out by much larger forces and with more cannons firing from both sides of low stone walls.[17] These fundamental features of 17th-century warfare, along with underlying trends and reforms pointing to a new linear warfare to come, are best illustrated in the careers of two of the greatest reformers and innovators of the era and, some argue, also the first of the modern great captains of war: Maurits of Nassau, *Stadholder* of Holland and Zeeland, and Gustavus Adolphus, King of Sweden.

***

MAURITS WAS A close student of Machiavelli who similarly admired ancient Roman drills and civic discipline in war. He trained the Dutch new model army relentlessly in small unit maneuvers, coordinated musketry and volley fire, and the countermarch. The volley system the Dutch employed eventually ensured that firepower displaced manpower in waging and deciding battles, but in Maurits' time it was still more important for its encouragement of group cohesion, of infantry esprit de corps and group discipline. To accommodate volley fire, he and Willem Lodewijk standardized the bores and patterns of muskets. Maurits also standardized siege and field artillery, eliminating odd and excessively numerous bores at a time when irregular castings and calibers were common in all artillery parks and siege trains. He settled on just four calibers, each prematched to its own shot, significantly improving the reliability of ammunition supply and rates of fire for the guns. Next he limited design and types of carriages. His reform of infantry drill and experiments with volley fire dominated early RMA scholarly discussions, but some of his most notable reforms actually came in logistics: using barges to supply field armies and to move his largest siege guns. It was a skill in which he excelled beyond any other contemporary commander.[18]

Maurits moved massive artillery trains along the great interior routes carved out by the rivers Lek, Maas (Meuse), Rhine and Waal. This enabled him to bring big guns to a siege or battlefield unreachable by road, with speed that nearly always surprised the Spanish garrisons, who thought his train must be bogged down elsewhere. He also made contributions to siegecraft. He wisely gave preeminent roles to engineers and logistics officers, and made his troops dig in the guns and erect field works. He even issued entrenching spades as a regular part of his soldiers' kit. By providing extra pay for this labor, an indulgence permitted by the wealth of the Netherlands, he overcame the standard prejudice of that era against soldiers digging gun pits and doing other military labor, which was most often done by women camp followers or other non-soldier laborers.[19] That set a standard of behavior for professional troops that enabled Dutch armies to maximize effort and to throw up siege or field works in record time.

Maurits was also a new-style commander who at times actively sought battle, eager to deploy his proficient and tactically disciplined forces. However, that did not mean he actually fought many battles. Like most other generals, Spanish commanders in the long war with the Dutch tended to avoid battle even when Maurits sought it out, so that even for Maurits sieges remained the main and default strategy.

In 1590 he took Breda, today located in the southern Netherlands, in an assault whose speed stunned the Spanish garrison and contemporary military thinkers. The attack involved a mere 10,000 foot and 2,000 horse, but a large train of guns. The next year he captured Zutphen after just seven days, took Deventer in eleven, and received the surrender of Nijmegen in six. These were all very quick surrenders, induced by his powerful cannon along with offers of generous terms. In 1592–1593, he had more siege successes and took more cities from the Spanish, even as he ran into significant political restraints at home. He retook the town of Geertruidenberg, but only after a celebrated four-month siege in 1593. The next year, he cleared Groningen. In 1597, he took the garrison towns Oldenzaal, Enschede and Grol.[20] After a forced march of 20 miles in barely nine hours, a remarkable speed for the time, he stunned the Spanish by inflicting 3,000 casualties in an open battle at the Flemish town of Turnhout (1597), located in Antwerp province in modern Belgium. After years at war with his new model army, despite his eagerness he had fought just one battle.

His only other field battle came three years later outside the privateer port of Nieuwpoort in Flanders, from whose dunes he drove the Spanish away with heavy casualties. Then it was back to defense at Ostend, fending off a Spanish siege lasting three years (1601–1604). He kept the city supplied by sea but could not lift the long siege. In 1602, he took an army of 19,000 foot and 5,400 horse on a campaign planned as a sweeping strategic maneuver to liberate Brabant and Flanders, the heart of the Low Countries. He loaded 700 wagons with flour, and with millstones and ovens to bake bread en route. He arranged for more foodstuffs to follow by barge. His artillery train had 13 massive cannon, 17 half-cannon and 5 smaller field pieces, most of which he transported by canal or river barge. His advance, which was typical of the period, consisted of several periods of five or more days' march broken by three or four days spent in camp baking bread. He invited the Spanish to accept battle, but they refused. He then retreated to the Maas, having exhausted his food supply. This was 17th-century war, and his Dutch political masters grew tired of such pricey maneuvers with big armies that did not deliver cities and wealth in return. He had promised victory from this campaign with his new army, yet delivered little except bills for wages and supplies. So they forbade his too ambitious idea of invading Flanders next. He besieged the city of Grave instead, in north Brabant. He had trained a new model army for battle but was forced by the response of his enemy and by domestic constraints into waging an old-fashioned war of position.[21]

Maurits vehemently opposed the Twelve Years' Truce (1609–1621) with Spain, a mutually agreed interruption in the Eighty Years' War. The United Provinces neared civil war as he led opposition to extending the Truce, then launched a coup d'état in 1618.[22] Alone at the helm of state, he goaded young Friedrich V to claim the throne of Bohemia in 1618, sending him money and 5,000 Dutch troops and thus helping to provoke the outbreak of the Thirty Years' War which ravaged Germany and Europe.[23] Maurits then led the Dutch back to war with Spain and the Habsburgs in 1621. The truce ended as the renewed Eighty Years' War blended with the Thirty Years' War getting underway in Germany over who would control the Holy Roman Empire, the wider Protestant and Catholic military and confessional causes, and much else besides. He backed more Protestant princes with rich Dutch subsidies and Beggar troops, or hired German mercenaries, even as the Habsburgs accelerated efforts to crush what they still insisted was an illegitimate rebellion by their rightful Dutch subjects.[24] In the midst of all this, Maurits died from fever while trying to relieve a siege of Breda in 1625. So it was that the Dutch and Spanish resumed a fight already 50 years in the making, even as all the rest of Europe also tumbled into a huge war over the next three decades. More offensives and counteroffensives, more attrition during long sieges like the one at Maastricht from 1629 to 1632. After Maurits died both wars continued, widening and worsening for 23 more years, ultimately drawing in additional powers, including Sweden and France, in a general conflagration as destructive in its day as the world wars of the 20th century.

***

GUSTAVUS ADOLPHUS, THE other key reformer of the 17th century, was crowned king of Sweden at age 17. His country was poor and sparsely populated, but already the ambitious young "Lion of Midnight" (that is, of the North) intended to enrich it with new lands and looted wealth. The only way to do that was by war, so he set out to reform the army. He soon proved to be a superb reformer and administrator within Sweden, and later emerged as an even more able strategist and general in Germany. Over his first decade as king, he transformed the army into a national force and built up the navy to protect his supply route to Poland and Germany. As Gustavus modernized the weapons, drill and fighting techniques of the Swedish army, he also professionalized it, by shifting recruitment away from a traditional levy of ill-trained peasants raised locally to create a national army of well-trained regulars secured for long-term service by conscription. He took the best Dutch innovations out of the waterlogged, compact and canalized environment of the Netherlands to maximize their revolutionary potential on the broad battle plains of Poland and Germany, where a war of maneuver was more likely to lead to field battles and more able to achieve success. Like Maurits and other Dutch reformers, he newly emphasized drill and infantry discipline, centered on learning volley and double-volley fire. In disposition for battle he deployed by brigades, freeing his troops from the old infantry blocks, reorganizing into flexible and more linear formations. Thinning was achieved at some defensive cost, as lines exposed flanks when moving in ways that a pike square of 50 × 50 or so ranks and files did not.[25] The trade-off was worth it: all this cleared the way for Sweden's ascent into the ranks of the Great Powers, to intervention in the Thirty Years' War for Swedish gain and the Protestant cause.

Before he left for Germany, Gustavus also experimented with shortening and thinning the extremely heavy barrels of his cumbersome *Murbräcker* ("wall-breaker") large-caliber siege guns. *Murbräcker* barrels were often inscribed with boasts of their special prowess in knocking down fortifications, praise for their royal owners or religious pieties that dominated Swedish (and German) service. Gustavus was not impressed. He trimmed barrel length to reduce haul-weight, as well as the number of horses or oxen and wagons of fodder needed to move his siege guns. He also cast innovative small-caliber cannon called "leather guns." These were cast from iron, but lined with brass or copper and reinforced with alloy. Barrels were bound with wire and rope splints, then wrapped in canvas secured by wooden rings. Hard leather was nailed to the exterior. They weighed about 600 pounds, making them highly mobile as well as cheap. They became famous, but were not a true success. All-iron casting proved superior in the end, leading even Gustavus to prefer small *regementsstycke* ("regimental guns") that then became standard. By around 1640, leather guns were retired by Sweden in favor of all-iron cannon, and only used after that by mercenaries returning to fight in the Wars of the Three Kingdoms (or English Civil Wars) in Scotland and Ireland.[26] His less famous but more successful regimental guns were standardized one-and-a-half- and three-pounders. Although cast all in iron, they were light enough to be pulled by one or two horses, using a two-wheeled carriage that allowed off-road maneuvers before battle and repositioning of the artillery during battle, something no other army could then achieve. These excellent small cannon also had rates of fire exceeding the top rates of good musketeers. They gave Swedish armies more maneuverable firepower in battle than any other army of the time.[27]

Gustavus understood the role of shock in combat, of delivering a stunning, smashing attack directly and bluntly into an enemy with the weight and force of a whole military unit. He maximized it by double-volley fire by infantry, hard charges by cavalry, and a range of big guns as well as small leather guns and regimental pieces. His light guns were supported by less mobile heavies standardized at 6-, 12- and 24-pound calibers. He also standardized charges and shot for each caliber. Powder was bagged in measured sacks, improving reload times, rate of fire and repeat-fire accuracy. Cannon traveled with the siege train hauled by large teams of draught animals, or moved by barge, the army marching down a river's shore alongside the floating guns just as Maurits had moved his big guns in Flanders. Other generals left their largest guns to follow their armies in cumbersome land-bound siege trains, intending to use them to batter forts or city walls. Their oversized and immobile cannon could be positioned just once in a field fight, at the start of a battle. Most enemy cannon were too big to reposition as the Swedes shifted out of the line of fire, leaving the big enemy guns uselessly misplaced while repositioning their own lighter field pieces. Gustavus made sure his light guns moved with his infantry and cavalry, always ready for deployment. In battle, he positioned the small-caliber regimental guns ahead of the infantry, moving them as his foot soldiers moved, uniquely able to shift position to cover a suddenly exposed flank, or sometimes to spring a trap with a battery deliberately hidden by a cavalry or infantry screen.

Gustavus adopted wheel-lock muskets that were much smaller and lighter than the heavy-caliber Spanish musket, a matchlock that required two men or a forked rest to fire. He greatly increased the proportion of musketeers to pikers in the ranks, enhancing infantry punching power. He even shortened pikes to 11 feet from the more common 18 to 21 feet, making his last pikers as light and maneuverable as the musketeers they protected from enemy horse. Three or four brigades formed a flexible, articulated, extended battle line. Each brigade subdivided into three squadrons of about 500 each, providing even more flexibility and chance to maneuver. Whenever flanked, Swedish infantry quickly articulated to bring musket volleys to bear from a newly right-angled line, along with easily repositioned one-and-a-half- or three-pounder guns. Reducing firing ranks to six and using double-volleys meant that all interior and back ranks had clear fields of fire, while each brigade was confident that half its number always stood ready with muskets loaded. Putting the regimental guns forward added killing range and firepower in mobile attack *and* defense.

Gustavus modeled his cavalry on superb Polish horse units, characteristic of Eastern European warfare but largely unknown in Western Europe. He stripped armor from men and mounts alike, fielding lighter horses and hussar-like cavalrymen dressed in hard leather and simple cloth. He replaced with sabers and lances the wheel-lock pistols used to such little effect in the tactic called caracole. That was a wheel-lock pistol-and-cavalry tactic prevalent in Western Europe in the 16th century, especially among German cavalry (*Ritter*). It had some use against units of pikers alone, but almost none against musketeers protected by pikers. The caracole abandoned the physical and psychological shock effect of the horse charge with lance or saber in favor of riding in short columns at a trot, one by one or two by two, up to a pike-and-musket hedge, discharging pistols (each rider carried a brace), then whirling away to reload at a safe distance before returning to fire weapons a second or third time. Since pistols had a range barely past ten feet, if that, and the average pike was 18–24 feet before Gustavus' reforms, human nature encouraged shooting from outside effective range. The caracole thus presented great danger to attacking cavalry but offered little offensive punch against musket infantry.[28] Trouble mounted, or rather dismounted rather violently, when aggressive infantry with hooked pikes or halberds attacked, or a musket volley hurtled lead at too carefully approaching horsemen.[29]

Gustavus wanted shock restored, so horses in the Swedish cavalry were retrained to canter and gallop rather than caracole trot toward the enemy, while their riders were told to pull sabers and use lances, to reinstate the fearful cavalry charge of old. He thereby returned to the horse arm its ancient role in providing shock, but did it by favoring light cavalry speed over heavy cavalry mass. This reform took advantage of the widely noted Swedish martial ferocity and his cavalry's desire to pursue a defeated enemy. The advantage was immense as long as other cavalry still deployed in overly dainty and ineffectual long columns to perform the caracole, only to be easily dispersed. In battle, his horse always deployed on the wings, where its first obligation was to block enemy cavalry from taking offensive action. Only secondly was it to exploit gaps or exposed flanks and any opportunity to attack created by the superior firepower of his hard-punching infantry, firing double volleys, and his mobile artillery occupying the flexible center of his line of battle.

Gustavus stressed pre-battle preparation and deliberation, but also an eager offensive spirit that sought to carry war to the enemy. He was among the first to employ recognizably modern techniques of combined arms by coordinating attacks by mutually supporting infantry, artillery and cavalry units. Similarly, he pioneered fire-and-movement tactics, while reviving the

ancient principle of concentration of force at a chosen point of local superiority. The weight (and shock) of a Swedish attack came from the infantry and
field artillery. Batteries of little guns peppered an enemy square or line with
canister at intimate ranges, punching bloody gaps in opposing ranks. Then
infantry closed to maximize the effect of their double musket volleys. After
firing two or three salvoes at most, front ranks charged with short pikes level
and muskets reversed and used as clubs. Through all this, three back ranks
(countermarched into place) always stood ready to exploit a breakthrough or
pivot to defend their brigade's flanks, or to counterattack if arrayed for defense. Always the cavalry hovered, light and able and lethal. Skilled Swedish
armies could do terrible violence to more staid and conservative enemies. It
was awful and brilliant all at once.

When Gustavus was done remaking and reforming the Swedish army,
it was one of the finest and most deadly of the era: well-drilled and disciplined, infused with a conjoined spirit of martial patriotism and fervent
Protestantism, and uniquely able to shift from offense to defense with a battle
speed and efficiency unmatched by any other force in Europe. He tested
its mettle, and his generalship, in Poland. In 1627, he attacked Danzig. At
Dirschau (August 17–18), then in Pomerania but today called Tczew and in
Poland, he was seriously wounded in the neck and arm but won the field.
This was one of several times where the young king led from the front. He
was nearly killed, and was defeated as well, at Stuhm (Sztum) on June 27,
1629, in what is today northern Poland.[30] Gustavus withdrew to recover from
his wounds, prepare fixed defenses and reconsider the campaign. The wily
éminence rouge in Paris, Cardinal Richelieu, took advantage of the lull to arrange the Truce of Altmark with Poland's Sigismund III, who agreed to re-
nounce his claim to the Swedish throne. It was 1630, and Gustavus was at last
ready to enter the war in Germany, which was going badly for the Protestant
princes. His alliance with France gave him yet more incentive: a subsidy of
400,000 thalers annually and a powerful ally on the other side of the Holy
Roman Empire.[31] Protestants across Germany and Europe begged him to be
their champion. As did Cardinal Richelieu, although he was pursuing secular and monarchical *raison d'état* for France in open opposition to Catholic
Habsburg power in Vienna and Madrid.

Gustavus appeared to be a sincere Lutheran, leading troops in singing
hymns as they marched into battle and ordering prayers said twice daily by
the whole army under the supervision of pastors he assigned to each brigade.
Accepting Richelieu's mediation of his old dispute with Poland so that he
could move into Germany instead, Gustavus took his Swedish version of a

17th-century new model army into the Thirty Years' War, singing Lutheran hymns along the way. His Nordic blend of piety, drill and black-powder aggression would give his armies unusual discipline and cohesion in combat. Napoleon later compared him to Alexander the Great, naming Gustavus as one of the first of the modern great captains. The comparison seems exaggerated, even if, like Alexander, he would be cut off in the flower of his military prowess, killed leading a wild battle charge in Germany in 1632.[32]

He landed at Peenemünde in July 1630, with just 14,000 men. He had 80 field guns to go along with larger siege cannon. The ratio of nearly 10 artillery pieces per 1,000 men in his army compared to just one cannon per 1,000 men for the Imperials. Despite his reforms, he could only rely on about 10,000 fresh Swedish recruits each year, so around the hard national army core of well-trained Swedes he wrapped mercenaries as he proceeded into Germany. With a smaller war chest than his Imperial foes, he needed even more to make war pay for itself by battening and billeting his army on other people's estates and cities. He moved deliberately, gathering intelligence, conserving combat power, growing his forces, knowing he did not have strength enough to force the issue all at once. All the same, as the inherently weaker side, Gustavus kept the option of an aggressive battle in his pocket, ready to take it out if opportunity presented.[33]

So began the Swedish intervention in the Thirty Years' War that was to change its course, turning it away from the Catholic-Habsburg victory that loomed in 1630 toward the confessional stalemate and negotiated secular peace of 1648. Gustavus' spectacular success in the two years that followed, lasting until his death at Lützen in 1632, arose less from any battlefield tactical genius than from intense advance preparation of the army and from his acute sense of weaknesses in the enemy's psychology and politics. He exploited flaws he saw in his enemies positions, but not always or even mainly by hard action driven by a *coup d'oeil*, that quality some great generals have of seeing immediately to the essence of a how a fight will develop, based perhaps on an innate ability to read terrain and position and the balance of available forces. He had that natural commander's gift, but he waged campaigns more by way of threat and daring maneuvers and long marches. He repeatedly got his army behind the main enemy force, causing Habsburg generals to rush back to defend some important holding or damp down the emperor's fright in Vienna. It was a variation of old-style war by maneuver by the mercenaries, but always with a sting of battle at the ready should the enemy flag or challenge. Like all superior generals he was flexible in tactics and operations rather than committed to a system, with an eye always on the strategic goal.

He would fight battles if needed, but preferred to achieve gains by marching against the enemy's supplies whenever possible. He used armies to threaten Habsburg political and prestige interests as much as he threatened their hired soldiers and stiff artillery fortresses. He saw battle and maneuver as closely related, not as opposing strategic choices, all one or all the other.

In search of food and fodder Gustavus moved beyond Pomerania, which was already eaten out. He followed the rivers of northern Germany, subjugating and garrisoning towns, securing rearward lines of supply and contributions and putting a territorial buffer between Sweden and its enemies. Then he settled in for the winter, recruiting and training tens of thousands of German (and Scots and Irish and other) mercenaries in his reformed—rather than Reformation—way of war. Winter increased his strength but exacerbated logistics, forcing him onto the road with the spring thaw of 1631.[34] He marched into Brandenburg to feed his army and force its elector to join the war. He ambled south, taking the fortress of Cüstrin (Kostrzyn nad Odrą), then westward to Berlin to reduce the fortress at Spandau. That secured the confluences of the major navigable rivers of north Germany, which he needed in order to shift guns and supplies by barge toward the southern Habsburg heartlands. On April 13, he stormed Frankfurt an der Oder, smashing eight Imperial regiments and slaughtering a third of its 6,400-man garrison in reprisal for earlier Catholic atrocities. With his army shrunken by wounds and illness and the needs of spread-out occupation and resupply, he could not reach or relieve Magdeburg, a major Protestant center under siege by a large Catholic-Habsburg army. Without Gustavus to protect it, Magdeburg's walls were breached and its population put to the sword, starting on May 20, 1631. Some 20,000 died in a *guerre mortelle* revenge for resistance, killed by Imperial troops and the allied Army of the Catholic League, led by General Johann Tserclaes, Count von Tilly.[35]

Magdeburg was the worst atrocity of the Thirty Years' War and became the benchmark for all later 17th-century atrocities, echoing across Europe for decades; the city remained largely a ruin until 1720. At the time, the sack of Magdeburg strengthened Gustavus by raising levels of fear and resolve among Protestants everywhere: pamphleteers kept printing presses rolling with lurid tales and fine etchings of horror. Meanwhile, Gustavus cleared Pomerania of Imperial armies and garrisons, then marched into Saxony, forcing it into the war. Now he was ready to meet Tilly and the Army of the Catholic League in battle. Between July 22 and 28, 1631, he waited for the Catholic League army, blocking the road north at Werben with 16,000 entrenched Swedes. Tilly blundered into the position and attacked with his heavy *tercios*, twice in six days. Repulsed by firepower from double volleys and regimental guns,

Tilly left over 6,000 dead in front of the fieldworks at Werben. He withdrew into Saxony on the twin mission of eating out Gustavus' new but always reluctant ally and to bind his own army's wounds while feeding his men with Protestant grain, sheep and wine.

There was time for one more battle before winter, and Gustavus was looking for a fight. He needed to shore up shaky German alliances by proving to cautious Protestant princes that his new model army could indeed hold its own in battle against the immense Imperial resources of the Habsburgs of Austria and Spain and their allies in Catholic League states across southern Germany. He got his wish on the plain at Breitenfeld, northwest of Leipzig, on September 17, 1631. He had 24,000 Swedes and mercenaries retrained in the Swedish way of war, as well as 18,000 Saxons and others from a small-state Protestant alliance, the *Leipziger Bund*. These shakier troops took positions on his left flank. Facing him were 35,000 Spanish veterans in big *tercios*, on loan to Holy Roman Emperor Ferdinand II. Tilly's veterans were supported by a few thousand Bavarians, some Croats, and others from the allied Catholic League. The armies stood facing each other, pawing and praying, cursing and cajoling, each man and unit readying to play a part in what would be the biggest battle of the Thirty Years' War.[36]

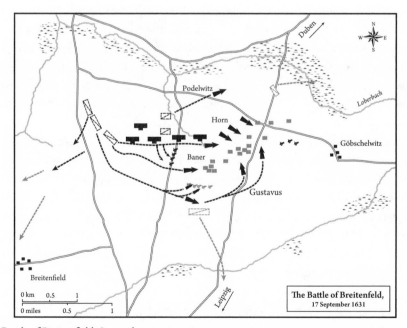

Battle of Breitenfeld, September 17, 1631.
Courtesy of the Department of History, United States Military Academy at West Point. Redrawn by George Chakvetadze.

Provoked by a peppering from regimental guns, Imperial cuirassiers on the right charged, and were cut down by Swedish musket volleys. There ensued a cavalry mêlée on the flank lasting two hours. Gustavus' lighter and more nimble horse finally drove the enemy cavalry away. More Imperials attacked on the left, where well-dressed but poorly motivated Saxons quickly wavered, then ran, leaving all their artillery behind. However, the suddenly exposed Swedes held the line, articulating as they had been trained to meet an onrush of Imperial horse. With regimental guns and double-volleys of musketry they shattered the surprised cavalrymen, who expected to roll up an exposed infantry flank. More musket volleys and canister from small cannon ripped into the Imperials, big men on heavy horses. The Swedes then rushed en masse to recover the abandoned Saxon cannon, which fleeing gunners had failed to spike. Gustavus again articulated his line, moving his units with a speed that the clumsy *tercios* simply could not match. He quickly enfiladed the opposing infantry, now exposed by disorderly withdrawal of the Imperial cavalry, pouring musketry into heavy ranks and files from both front and side. He ordered his heavy cannon brought up as well, dragged forward with great effort into killing range of the men packed in the dense *tercios*.

His quick cavalry moved around and to the rear of the stolid Spaniards, who held their ground, slashing into their back ranks with sabers and charging to stab with lances while light and heavy cannon and musket volleys committed carnage at the front and flank. The fighting lasted hours. Gustavus personally led a Finnish reserve of 1,000 horse in a fierce charge into an enemy who had been bled all day by superior firepower and left exposed by the flight of its own cavalry. Tilly was also in the middle of the combat. He was wounded thrice and finally had to be carried by his bodyguards from the field. Many men were crushed or trampled in the panic that ensued as the fight at Breitenfeld was lost by the Imperial army, and became a rout. Casualties were 6:1 in Swedish favor, not counting prisoners: 12,000 Imperial and Catholic League troops dead or dying, against 2,000 under Gustavus. Also lost were all the Catholic artillery and 120 regimental or company standards, seized from an army hitherto undefeated over 12 years of war. The majority of the 6,000 prisoners taken, most of them mercenaries in any case, volunteered or were impressed into the "Swedish" army. Gustavus won a smashing victory, despite being abandoned by his Saxon ally at the outset. The wounded were tended to and food and fodder gathered along with forced contributions, then both armies headed for winter quarters. Along the way, the triumphant Protestants invested several fortress towns. At Würzburg, defenders begged for mercy but met only cries of "Magdeburg quarter!" and died on the points of Protestant principles and swords.[37]

Europe wondered: with the Habsburg field army destroyed, would Gustavus move next to unite and convert all Germany under an ascendant Swedish and Protestant empire, a triumph over the Habsburgs' imperial claims and for his confession?[38] Catholic opinion panicked, leading Emperor Ferdinand to recall to high command a general he had earlier dismissed and would later assassinate, Albrecht von Wallenstein. The agnostic mercenary took command of all Imperial forces and began to repair the Habsburg army. In the meantime, in the spring of 1632, Tilly sallied out with a new Catholic League army. He wanted to avoid another loss like Breitenfeld, but Gustavus marched to intercept him. The clash came at Rain (April 25, 1632), also called the Battle of Lech. The Swedes daringly forced the River Lech under fire, covered by an artillery smokescreen. Tilly suffered a mortal wound when his leg was smashed by a cannonball; he died five days later, the last of the great *tercio* generals. That old formation could no longer stand against more flexible, articulated Swedish line tactics. Rain proved that once and for all. This second defeat left Catholic and Imperial opposition to Gustavus weak and scattered, but resolved a tricky leadership issue: with Tilly dead, Wallenstein was named *Capo*, commander-in chief of all "Catholic" forces. The wily Bohemian rallied mercenaries from all over Europe. They came to rejoin their old general for prospects of a share in plunder and pay from contributions, rallying to his name and reputation for success in war—not to fight for the Catholic canon or for the Habsburg dynasty and emperor. As the make-up of the field armies on both sides changed, so too did the war on the ground.

With Wallenstein still gathering forces and no Catholic League army of note left to interfere with his movements, Gustavus was free to eat out a Habsburg ally in Bavaria or move directly against Vienna. He paid his men and filled his supply wagons from forced contributions from the cities of Nuremberg and Augsburg. Nevertheless, he was impelled by the always thin logistics that hampered armies of that day to keep moving into fresh Catholic country. This was critical, as he had already consumed supply from his northern base in Pomerania and Brandenburg, and further demands up north might bring unwelcome political consequences in his strategic rear. So his army foraged and fed through enemy countryside instead, moving and eating its way along the course of the Danube. He occupied Augsburg and took Munich, chewing Bavaria while readying to either feint or drive to Vienna, hoping by that threat to lure Wallenstein out and beat him in another Breitenfeld. His army still had a core of disciplined Swedish countrymen, but the rest were mercenaries from all over Europe. At the peak of his power and ambition, Gustavus commanded coalition armies in excess of 100,000 men, including 10,000 Scots, supported by river barge supply from half Germany. He planned to raise 200,000 men and invade the Habsburg heartland from multiple directions at once, with five armies, in something of a precursor of Napoleonic movement by separate corps or even Ulysses Grant's grand strategy to invade the Confederacy with five armies in 1864. Such long-distance coordination and strategic ambition was probably beyond the capacities of his day. In any case, Gustavus would not live to try it.

Wallenstein was impressed by Swedish artillery prowess and linear flexibility, and by Gustavus as a general. He chose to avoid battle. Instead, he moved north in a set of brilliant maneuvers designed to draw Gustavus away from Austria. He resisted calls to turn east and relieve the beleaguered Elector of Bavaria, Maximilian I, ally of the Habsburg emperor, who was frantic over a Protestant horde eating out his country. Instead, Wallenstein moved into Bohemia where he attacked and defeated a weak Saxon army which was only reluctantly allied to Gustavus. He next curled around Gustavus into Saxony itself, taking Leipzig and wasting the land, trying to pull the Swedish army away from Vienna. He thereby cut Gustavus' lines of supply and blocked the Swedes from their base area of recruitment in north Germany. Gustavus prudently withdrew his threat to Vienna and marched north to Nuremberg. When the armies finally closed Wallenstein again declined to attack a force he knew to be superior in training and firepower, though inferior in numbers to his own. Instead he dug in, as did the Swedes in response. Wallenstein chose to dig in first and so took the best defensible ground. The two armies hunkered down into a series of wary, parallel fortified trenches where they remained for the next several weeks.

Quickly, the logistical limitations of 17th century warfare began to tell against this strategy as each side grew weaker from disease and hunger and desertions. The supply problem only worsened as both entrenched armies were constantly reinforced. Immobile armies could not forage or eat, lacked the supply capacity for sustained trench warfare, and therefore could not remain for long where they were. Wallenstein used his light horse to harass Swedish foraging parties while the Swedes probed the Imperial lines looking for a breachable weakness, but only provoked several minor skirmishes. Moved by the hunger of his men and his desire to engage in a decisive battle, and provoked by Wallenstein's hussar raids, Gustavus cracked first. He attacked Wallenstein's earthworks at Fürth and an old fort called Alte Feste (August 24, 1632). He was rebuffed with a loss of 2,000 men. While the action was not militarily significant in itself, this first check to the great Swedish general's campaign in Germany scarred his reputation for invincibility.

The effect reverberated through the strategic calculations of Europe. Because this made the Swedish position less secure politically, and therefore ultimately also militarily, Gustavus felt compelled to draw Wallenstein out of his trenches and defeat him in an open battle between the main armies. He thought he could entice Wallenstein from his fortified earthworks by moving south into Bavaria to once more ravage territory allied to the Habsburgs and threaten a dash toward Vienna. To draw Wallenstein out of his fixed position, but also desperate to feed his own army, Gustavus pulled out of the trenches and marched off to threaten Vienna again. The Imperials were now free to come out to forage, too. This was the moment when Wallenstein showed a superior strategic ability. He declined the bait and invitation to battle dangled by Gustavus in the south and instead struck out northward. Rather than follow the Swedish king, Wallenstein marched back into Saxony to again threaten Swedish lines of supply and eat out a southern Protestant state and Swedish ally. The main armies thus separated, hungry herds of armed men marching off in mutual feints and to gnaw at the other's allies.[39] Gustavus was again halted by a brilliant strategy of maneuver that avoided battle yet twice pulled the Protestant army back north by threatening its strategic rear. The two greatest generals of the Thirty Years' War were proving their worth as commanders not in battle but in the main warcraft of their era: in campaigns of strategic movement, maneuver and supply.

Wallenstein had partly adopted Swedish tactics when he reformed the Imperial Army after its defeat at Breitenfeld, marginally increasing the flexibility of the *tercios* and significantly increasing their firepower by multiplying the number of musketeers they presented. Moreover, while the Swedes retained a clear qualitative edge, they were a reduced force in numbers and quality from the crisp professional army that crossed the Baltic two years before. Two years of marching and fighting, of disease and desertion, and Sweden's limited manpower reserves and small population, meant that its army in Germany by 1632 was actually close to 80% foreign mercenary. However, it was still commanded by Swedish generals and was organized and trained to make war in the Swedish style. Also, its critical field artillery was still predominantly Swedish. It was also the turn of the "Lion of the North" to display his own advanced command skills. Making use of the markedly superior training and maneuverability of his Swedish regiments, joined now by thousands of mercenaries and allies he had trained to make war in the Swedish way, Gustavus took the great mercenary general's bait and marched

north to find him, determined to win a great battle and end the threat from
Wallenstein, and perhaps thereby win and end the war.[40] He moved north
with far greater speed than any contemporary army could achieve or commander imagine, so that the two armies met at last and joined in battle at
Lützen on November 6, 1632.

The morning broke with the armies nearly wholly concealed from one
another by a thick and persistent fog. That reduced the ability of Gustavus
to take full advantage of his army's greater maneuverability and increased
the comparative fighting value of fixed Imperial heavy infantry. Wallenstein
chose the ground, placing his 35,000 troops in a broken line protected by a
natural double ditch which he had his men deepen into fighting trenches,
lined with ranks of musketeers. He thought this obstacle would blunt the enemy's expected cavalry assaults and obviate the superior training and mobility
of the infantry on the other side, while maximizing the defensive firepower
of his *tercios*. Gustavus was also confident. He breakfasted, led his troops in
singing a Lutheran hymn, then sent a small cavalry force to open the battle
with an attack on Wallenstein's right, which was anchored on the small village of Lützen. Meanwhile, he personally led the bulk of Swedish cavalry in a
long ride right around the Imperial extreme left, to cut off Wallenstein's immediate lines of resupply and retreat. The main body of Swedish infantry was
positioned at the center, deployed in their usual six ranks per line, two lines
deep. As usual, mobile field artillery moved along with a mass of infantry at
the solid center of the Swedish battle line. As cavalry attacked each Imperial
flank, Gustavus' infantry moved toward the tight ranks of Imperial musketeers awaiting them in a line of double ditches. The heavy fog concealed all
movement, so that only the tramping of thousands of boots from somewhere
inside the morning mist was heard by waiting Imperials. Then the Swedish
infantry broke out of the mist and came into view of the Imperial musketeers,
already at close quarters. Both sides opened fire at close-range. Then they slid
into a heavy, prolonged small arms fight at the center of the battle.

Swedish regimental field guns were quickly maneuvered into an enfilade
position to support the capture of immobile Imperial guns by swift moving
cavalry on the flank. Under threat of capture, many big guns were spiked
before their crews ran for cover with the Imperial infantry. With the guns
overrun, large blocks of Imperial pikemen standing in rigid *tercio* formation
were exposed to the Swedish cavalry, but with little of their usual firearms
support because so many musketeers were already felled by mobile artillery fire or tied down by the fight at the center over control of the line of
double ditches. In the face of deadly fire and cavalry assault the overmatched

pikemen retreated, pressed by ferocious charges by Swedish and Finnish cavalry on either flank of the Imperial line. At the center, the slaughter continued. Swedish rates of musket and cannon fire were likely three times that of the Imperial side, as volley after volley tore into men penned in static *tercios*. On the right, Gustavus again led from the front, recklessly crashing into and through Croat light horse at the head of a Swedish cavalry charge that cut and slashed with *armes blanches*. The momentum of the attack brought him barging into more able Austrian cuirassiers, with whom a close fight ensued. Gustavus was struck by three musket balls. The fatal third opened his skull, spilling his brains. One of the new great captains was gone from war, his talent and career foreshortened at age 38. He fell even as the wider battle dissolved into a desperate struggle among clusters of men oblivious to all else but the enemy in front of them, gusting in-and-out of view through billowing clouds of fog and smoke. Swedish regiments continued fighting, most troops unaware until the day was over that their king and general was dead.[41]

Wallenstein counterattacked with his surviving *tercios*, rolling up the Swedish left where there was fewer cavalry and retaking part of the ditch line that was lost in the initial infantry attack. Meanwhile, 8,000 Imperial horse successfully counterattacked the mass of Swedish cavalry on the right, which was strung out and entangled with the Imperial baggage train. Unprepared to receive this counterattack, the Swedish horse took heavy casualties. It was the rapid-firing Swedish artillery that saved the day, cutting down Imperial troopers and horses with blasts of shot and canister, turning survivors away in disorderly retreat. The reserve line of Swedish infantry now showed its mettle. It swept forward, retook the part of the ditch line Wallenstein had briefly recovered, fired double musket volleys and fought furiously hand-to-hand with comparably brave and desperate Imperials. Wallenstein's last *tercios* wobbled and broke under this assault, then turned and fled as Swedish infantry smashed through the last Imperial line with a fierce charge that carried right over the ditches and captured the whole artillery train. Triumphant shouts quickly caught in Protestant throats, however, as word went out that Gustavus had been carried bloody and dead from the field. More mourning followed the body count: at least one-third of the Protestant army, about 10,000 men, were dead or wounded, lying intermingled with 12,000–15,000 Imperial dead and many more thousands wounded.

Lützen was a sharp defeat for the Catholic and Imperial cause. It shattered the Habsburg military system rebuilt by Wallenstein and ensured that the war would go on, and thereby the survival of the major Protestant states of Germany. It was in that sense a genuinely decisive battle, certainly the most decisive of the Thirty Years' War. Yet even Lützen was determinative only in the immediate sense, for it did not directly shape the final settlement at Westphalia in 1648. The death of the Swedish warlord did not force Sweden out of the war, but it robbed the Protestant cause of its most dynamic champion and greatest general. Never again would a Protestant prince alone decide the strategy of the anti-Habsburg coalition. After Lützen, Sweden remained in the German war but it was Cardinal Richelieu of France who took the lead in setting alliance policy, controlled the larger course of the war, and principally shaped its outcome as a secular agreement among princes rather than a confessional peace. The victory for Swedish arms at Lützen therefore was most important for making it more probable that a military stalemate would be the final result in the long contest between Catholic and Protestant in Germany and Europe more generally, even if many more years of bloody murder and mayhem was needed to drive the point home to all sides.

Wallenstein did not have long to live, either. He rebuilt the Imperial army after Lützen, adopting as many of the Swedish reforms as his differently trained and motivated troops and officers could absorb. Most notably, he returned to a shock role for cavalry, thinned infantry ranks and replaced more pikers with musketeers in the *tercios* and added lighter and more mobile field artillery. While Wallenstein skirmished and maneuvered with the very able commanders Gustavus left behind, he also intrigued in secret with Catholic and Protestant powers alike, seeking bids for what was really his army more than the emperor's. His plot-too-far was proposing to forge an alliance to force Ferdinand to agree to a peace that took no cognizance of the emperor's Catholic crusade, his sense of religious mission. Admirers say Wallenstein was trying to end the war by creating a unified and tolerant Germany. Others believe he sought all the titles and trappings to go along with the substance of Imperial power, that he may have been planning a coup. In either case, spies told Ferdinand about his general's secret talks, and he determined to finish Wallenstein for good. Reinforcing the decision was the fact Spain was preparing to formally enter the war in Germany but would not accept Wallenstein's demand that he alone have supreme command over all Catholic troops. Ferdinand secretly stripped Wallenstein of all his offices, declared him outlaw and traitor, condemned his hiring of Protestant officers and ordered his arrest pending a judicial murder. Wallenstein learned of the secret orders and fled toward the Protestant lines, sending word ahead asking for sanctuary. He was refused. Escorted by a troop of Irish dragoons whose commander was in secret contact with agents from Ferdinand's court, Wallenstein reached the fortress of Eger. There, two Scottish officers who had served him for years and a French mercenary captain agreed to join the Irish in assassinating him. After dining with their victims, they slew all Wallenstein's companions, entered his bedchamber and hacked him to death with their swords and a halberd. [42]

In 1632 the Protestants lost the best strategist and most able general in the whole war. Not long thereafter, the Imperials lost their best general, most able quartermaster and mercenary recruiter. It was a recipe rich in ingredients for strategic stalemate. All that remained was more dying. For the Swedish intervention did not win the Thirty Years' War for Protestantism, or the building coalition of Protestant and Catholic powers opposed to Habsburg hegemony. However, Gustavus did ensure that the war would not be lost by the Protestants, and that was the next best outcome. And so the armies found new generals, new battlefields, even new causes, and the Thirty Years' War dragged on for another sixteen years. Armies and towns across Germany and adjacent countries shrank as the land groaned under locust swarms of brutal and ruthless men who ate out city hinterlands and abandoned farming vales for a third or fifth or seventh time. Hyperinflation hit Germany hard. All trade declined as urban and rural economies shrank. Disease and famine spread. Livestock vanished. Fertile fields overgrew with scrub, left unfurrowed and unplanted by absent and incapable dead. Some 15 to 25 percent of the civilian population of Germany perished before it ended, making the Thirty Years' War the most deadly war in European history, its mortality rate exceeding by three or four times each of the world wars of the 20th century.[43]

Some scholars argue that varying skill and personalities of generals rather than opposing military systems explain the course and outcome of the latter half of the Thirty Years' War, attributing the final military and political stalemate to a deficit of generalship on the Habsburg side in particular.[44] That surely understates the determinative role in the last years played by moral, physical, military and fiscal exhaustion. It was not so much lesser generals that led back into stalemate as the fact that Gustavus' tactical and weapons innovations were emulated on all sides, countering the initial Swedish advantage and once more limiting the role of generalship in battle and of battle in war. Twenty years after Gustavus and Wallenstein departed, key differences between the ways the armies armed and fought was far less than when Gustavus met the *tercios* at Breitenfeld and exploited their heavy slowness of foot and far lower rate of fire with his well-drilled volleys and his light field guns and cavalry. The enemy had by then adapted, as is usually the case in war, even as the always too small Swedish army grew more tired and ragged.

The war ended not with any confession's triumph but in stalemated, and therefore also negotiated, tolerance at Westphalia in 1648. Its last period saw Cardinal Richelieu intervene not as a fierce Catholic champion but as a preeminent statesman, pursuing *raison d'état*. Catholic marched against Catholic and Protestant fought Protestant, in sure revelation that the greatest and transformative of all the wars of religion also ended them. It was always a struggle for power and prestige, taxes and territory, as well as partisan faith. Now the pretensions of prelates ended in a peace decided by princes: secularism stood over the corpse of medievalism. Habsburgs had learned the lesson of the emergent balance of power among secular states when a triumphal religious hubris in the Edict of Restitution of 1629 was blunted the very next year by a Lutheran king intervening with secret support from a Catholic cardinal of the Church. Next, it would be the turn of Louis XIV to challenge the balance of power, and of France to pay the price of a king's pride.

***

MAURITS AND OTHER Dutch reformers had pointed the way to enhanced infantry firepower. Gustavus Adolphus then showed the tactical possibilities of flexible lines, speed and mobility. Quicker musketry, lighter artillery, swifter cavalry allowed a good general to launch a combined arms attack mixing shock and firepower, to defeat thicker and more cumbersome formations. But as almost always in war, success breeds imitation, imitation restores balance and balance leads back to stalemate. Generals everywhere imitated the Dutch-Swedish way of war, insisting soldiers drill while thinning lines to deploy more muskets. New model armies took the field elsewhere over the rest of the 17th century, as Europe translated Dutch drill manuals and copied Swedish models of guns and triple infantry lines. They volleyed and double-volleyed and made the countermarch. Foundries everywhere cast lighter, more mobile cannon and carriages were built to haul them to the battlefield. Most cavalry gave up caracoles to wield sabers or lances and charge for shock effect in the Swedish style.[45]

Next came a shift from the old matchlock to the more powerful and reliable flintlock musket (fusil), implemented everywhere. After 1690, the ring or socket bayonet also quickly replaced the inefficient plug bayonet atop the fusil. The new-style bayonet fitted over the end of a musket rather than on a wooden plug jammed into the barrel. It let lines of musketeers fire and reload, yet fend off cavalry on their own by presenting a hedge of blades. That quickly eliminated all pikers in favor of yet more fusiliers in even longer, thinner lines. The French army did it first, as the French of that era did so many things first and best in war. Only if not enough fusils were available did pikers sometimes still appear in early 18th-century battles. The English resisted longest: British infantry used pikes on the continent as late as 1704. Such military conservatism and penury was another old tale, but one that was about to change dramatically.[46] Standardized weapons and the new, more flexible formations looked to some generals to promise a fundamental offensive breakthrough, toward maneuver to and in battle, and to battle as decider of wars. Yet they also enhanced defensive firepower and the long-term trend to reliance on infantry, and they reduced command opportunity for innovation once all units looked and fought about the same.

Musket infantry henceforth enjoyed a tremendous firepower advantage that most often trumped the superior mobility of cavalry armed with lances and sabers, unless cavalry caught an infantry battalion in march column and cut it apart. By 1700, the basic linear formations and standardized weapons of drums-and-fusil warfare were more or less set for the next hundred years.[47] Was it an advance? Linear battle did not always lead to easy maneuvering that granted decisive tactical advantage to the better mind and general. In fact, it conduced more to bloodier battles by volley, in which casualty rates of 30 to 50 percent were common and the winner could expect as many dead and wounded as the loser without a technical victory necessarily deciding any vital question. This did not change before the mid-18th century tactical innovations by Frederick II. Even then, as we shall see, the advantage he gained was brief, and there were in any case few tactical options beyond the obvious: an attempt to march around or break or turn a flank by an assault on the wings. Mostly, what changed were rates of fire and rates of death and maimings, as linear battles deteriorated into infantry brawls testing not line flexibility or maneuver or command genius, but which rows of ordinary men would break and disengage first, throw down fusils and run from a king's fight that was never their own.

Once 18th century armies were set in echeloned battle lines by the new ways of war learned and tested in the 17th century, banging by volley and cannon and dying and howling ensued, as each side shredded the other's infantry with mass casualties from fusil fire and hammering artillery. Generals watched through veils of smoke and uncertainty for gaps to appear in an opposing line caused by leaded hail or, more often, by confused movement in all the smoke and fear that forced separation between battalions. If a battalion in an approaching battle line lost contact with its fellows on either side, it presented a local flank. Then alert generals tried to drive home to victory through the gap with *arme blanche,* either sending in a shock attack by bayonet if they were French or, more usually, charging cavalry held in reserve to scatter the orphaned battalion and make the gap a gaping hole, with more flank attacks to break morale and make the enemy run. There was always more commoner or impressed infantry to replace the dead in one's own ranks, although skill declined sharply after a battle or two and green recruits stood trembling in the firing lines instead.

The door to winning command was left ajar by Gustavus, but not so wide that *any* general might squeeze through. Warfare was still the domain of stone and logistics, making for slow seasonal campaigns and long and mostly indecisive conflicts. Leaving aside the Swedish warlord's success in a few battles, what impresses more is his strategic sense, his ability to campaign against his enemy's supplies, recruiting base and politics and morale. His well-crafted operations rained heavy blows upon Habsburg prestige and undercut Habsburg alliances; his long marches across the Holy Roman Empire's political stage stand out as much as battlefield success. Gustavus understood that campaigning was a form of warfare, as well as constituting politics and exhaustion and defeat of the enemy by other means. Wallenstein had an eye for it, too, and did it so well that his emperor killed him for fear of his talent and popularity among his hired troops.

Still missing was reliable competence in handling the new armies in battle, which under mediocre and even quite good generals could reduce to trading murderous volleys between roughly equally weighted units, ordering hard cavalry charges into withering defensive fire, or standing in formation under the usual artillery pounding until one side broke before the other. Generals of talent and tactical imagination were wanted. Many applied, but few succeeded. Could the 18th century produce great captains such as Gustavus and Wallenstein, equal to the task of commanding new armies reshaped and thinned out and made more lethal by the lessons of older ones? As in all things, the Enlightenment was confident that it could make war better, and make better war.

5

Battle with Reason

NEW MODEL ARMIES paid for by monarchs wore the king's colors—white, blue, red—and the many vivid hues of hussars. Except for the colors, they started to look the same, drill the same and fight the same, absorbing universalization of fighting doctrine and style. They shared a culture of discipline and the tactical value and moral virtue of forbearance under fire. They moved toward partial professionalization of officer corps with systems of royal commissions, and relied on limited but increasingly meritocratic recruitment of officers. They had standardized unit sizes and fighting formations to match standardized tactics and weapons.[1] Many soldiers were now paid professionals, though no longer mercenaries: they were on the whole volunteers who took military wages. This wasn't exclusively the case, of course. Some states more than others used armies and navies as repositories for social undesirables, for their criminals sentenced to military service, the indigent, the unskilled, and unlucky foreigners seized by the press gangs.[2]

Behind each army stood a more modern and maturing state: secular, bureaucratic, collecting centralized taxes to pay for a full-time military. State capacity made year-round or standing armies possible, and then necessary (everyone else was getting them, too). These were not yet national armies, however. They were still the king's army, and officers especially formed an almost international class. The officer corps remained noble for the most part, especially in the always more conservative cavalry. Yet there were more openings for middle- and lower-class men of proven talent, notably with the artillery and engineering corps, where merit mattered more than pedigree, knowledge more than ancestry. Ever more men from the bourgeois classes took the "king's commission." The rank and file were not as yet citizen-soldiers; that radical change awaited the French Revolution. However, unlike the old mercenaries, they were uniformed in the king's cloth, fed and barracked year round, armed and trained by the state and paid state wages. They drilled and dug gun pits and erected field works, as well as marching and countermarching and serving at times in stone garrisons. In return, they could be harshly disciplined for even minor infractions, made to drag cannonball and chain or run the gauntlet or pilloried or hung. So in all armies they drank heavily and deserted in large numbers.[3] Yet there were always plenty more disposable men to take the place of those who were killed in battle, or ran away or were hanged for desertion, or died of "camp disease" (usually, typhus). As these armies increasingly deployed the same weapons and trained to fight in the same ways, it seemed clear to those who wanted more that only superior generalship could make them different in war. Was now come the time of generals, perhaps even of modern great captains who could deliver decision by battle?

Not yet. As wars got bigger and costlier, generals and their reputations seemed to grow smaller. Nothing secured finality, not money or lives spent. John Lynn, the leading historian of the greatest army of the age, the French army of Louis XIV, dryly recounts: "The ancien régime provides few examples of battles that ended major wars . . . Conflicts tended to drag on until exhaustion settled the matter."[4] Each aggressive move by Louis XIV, or later by Frederick II, brought coalitions into existence and opposition. Beneath the political and diplomatic balance resided a rougher military balance, arising from a lack of capability by any one power to change the overall political equation by force. So wars deepened, widened, lengthened, over seemingly trivial causes such as family inheritance or a king's vanity. Four of the 18th century's larger wars in Europe were triggered by disputes over dynastic claims to one succession or another (Spanish, Polish, Austrian, Bavarian). Kings quarreled, and the peoples fought. The armies marched out to stone borders, invested a fortress or city and marched home again. Then they did it again next summer, and the next, and the one after that. War in the 18th century was fought on a larger scale at greater expense, but it was nearly as chronic and indecisive as it had ever been in the much-criticized Middle Ages.

Position dominated war. Fortresses large and small dotted the landscape like stone mushrooms, hundreds of them in compact territories. Much of a general's and an army's effort was spent marching among and attacking or defending fortresses.[5] Even more of the king's funds were spent to build (or at least update with bastions) fortified sites and prepare field works to protect the frontiers and block the passage of armies. They formed interconnected defenses known as Lines that crossed sections of countryside connecting fortresses and towns, bridges and river crossings and key crossroads, all stoned and guarded to stymie armies. Lines so choked off movement that a "passage of Lines," moving an army through a fortified frontier, was rare enough to be viewed as a pinnacle act of war, a measure of highest generalship, whatever the result on the other side. Like entrenchments during World War I, 18th-century Lines comprised communications and support trenches as well as fighting trenches, redoubts, blockhouses, gun pits and strongpoints. They differed from 20th-century versions in two main ways: smaller armies guarding them could not cover their whole length, and they were not built to protect soldiers who occupied them from incoming fire but rather to block the enemy from ravaging rich hinterlands behind. Lines represented a posture of strategic defense, one seeking permanence of a border in stone. Yet they had two offensive functions critical to the disposition of armies and the economy of war: sheltering food and supply magazines serving armies about to jump off into invasion, and providing a fixed base from which small garrisons could raid and forage and pay for their own upkeep, or just ravage enemy territory.[6]

Rulers continued to abhor battle, as it invoked too much the role of chance. They sought to minimize risk to expensive forces by avoiding field battles, looking to limit not casualties but cost. They feared being fiscally ruined by a misfortune of war, by one of the fateful accidents and unexpected outcomes that always mark war's course. Standard practice was for armies to fight in short hops from fortification to fortification, dense in number and each positioned to guard the next turnpike or canal or river passage or taxable town. Garrisons were most often content to stay inside, or were kept inside by "armies of observation." Win a battle or take down a fortress somewhere in the Lines and more fortresses awaited, defended and intact. It was against this style of limited and territorial war that Clausewitz later railed, calling for unbridled battle violence aiming instead and always at physical destruction of the enemy's main force, and an endgame of dictated not negotiated terms.[7] His was a later century's philosophy of admired offense and aggression, looking to Frederick and Napoleon as exemplars. Yet for defensive-minded powers 18th-century Lines worked quite well, raising costs to aggressors and keeping foreign armies beyond the frontiers.

Still, lack of sufficient troops to defend all the masonry might allow a clever enemy to breach the Lines by means of surprise maneuvers, such as a rapid concentration after several marches that suggested a farther destination. The other army marched in parallel to the protected frontier while keeping spies and scouts in close observation, so it was hard to slip away ("steal a march"). Attackers also needed sound intelligence about where the enemy's forces really were. That was hard to come by in any era, continuing into the 18th century, when horse or boat courier were still the fastest forms of military communications.[8] Besides, the main point of maneuvering was not to seek out the enemy army to do battle but to evade it so as to capture the enemy's depots, drain his food supplies, and rob his taxes and morale—to exhaust him into quitting. If your aim was defensive war, this tactic combined with well-sited Lines or smaller choke-point fortifications worked. And so the wars dragged on, and on and on. Lines were dug, artillery fortresses erected, towns were besieged, armies marched.

One set of Lines crossed the United Provinces for 100 miles from the Maas to the Atlantic, connecting canals, rivers, natural rises and ridges; deepening ditches and adding trenches, high watchtowers, and earthworks lined with infantry-firing steps and premounted cannon. The Dutch incorporated canals and dikes and floodable polders into extensive water defenses in their "Holland Water Line." Sébastien de Vauban built new Lines for Louis XIV in the Spanish Netherlands as his armies advanced, in imitation of the grand Norman strategy of the conquest of southern England by motte-and-bailey forts, but on a scale to fit the rising Sun King. The twin "Lines of Brabant" were modeled on the disposition of fusiliers in battle. They passed in front of Antwerp to travel 130 miles to the Meuse, below Namur and the junction with the Sambre.[9] Unlike his king, Vauban was principally defensive-minded. Louis was slowly forced to become more so with each fresh defeat in his later wars. As the *Grand Monarque* aged and moved from territorial aggression to just trying to hold what he had already taken by force in his youth, he asked Vauban to hermetically seal off France from raids and invasions.[10] The great military architect of the age, even of all time, conceived and built for Louis a new set of Lines, a *pré carré* ("dueling field"), a stone and cannon position to defend France's expanded but by then overextended borders.[11]

Vauban built more and more Lines once Louis went over to defense, including the "Lines of Lauterbourg" along the Rhine frontier near Strasbourg. The Dutch erected opposing Lines of fortresses in Flanders and along the Rhine. They built the short (10 miles) "Lines of Stollhofen" in Germany in 1703, demonstrating with a serious financial commitment their preference for a positional strategy over the battle-seeking of arriving English commanders. Louis ordered the "Lines of the Var" built in Provence from 1708, in anticipation of an invasion of southern France. Three years later, he undertook a formidable set of inner Lines, the *Ne Plus Ultra* ("No Further" or literally, "go no more beyond"), which was about 200 miles long. Marshal Villars started construction after the Allies broke through Vauban's older connected forts in the *pré carré*. The *Ne Plus Ultra* ran from the coast past battlegrounds old and to come at Arras and Cambrai, on to the Sambre and thence to Namur, incorporating parts of the by then partly broken Lines of Brabant.

Stalemate was the order of the day, reflecting the stopping power of stone but also the roughly matched strength of the states at war in the era of the Sun King. Military power was too balanced for fighting to do more than force marginal changes to borders or swaps of overseas colonies, to be traded back or away after the next war. The Great Powers therefore waged decades-long wars filled with weeks-long sieges, whole summers of marching or investment of Lines, years of blockades and *guerre de course* (commerce raiding) at sea. French privateers like John Bart along with royal-built and commissioned cruisers preyed on Dutch and English merchant shipping, while the Dutch and English navies scourged French shipping on all the seven seas, exporting Europe's wars to far-off shores in contests mixing overseas investment and military enterprise. There were land and sea battles and lots of hard endurance as moral and material attrition set in at the strategic level, until political fatigue and national bankruptcy forced a pause. An armed truce then ensued, rather than a peace. Until it started all over again.

Lines and forts were a serious barrier to decisiveness, not something to be overcome by sheer will to battle by some great general.[12] As a contemporary observer wrote in 1677: "Field battles are in comparison scarcely a topic of conversation. Indeed, at the present time the whole art of war comes down to shrewd attacks and artful fortifications."[13] Similarly, an English officer lamented, in a manner that revealed his class origin: "We make war more like foxes than hounds; and you have twenty sieges for one battle."[14] Unforgiving stone underlay the power of defense, a fundamental resistance to deciding the struggle for dominance with inadequate offensive means. Each wearying war reached stalemate, then another coalition was provoked to stop whoever upset the balance next, first Louis XIV, then Frederick II of Prussia. Both human resources and matériel were committed and consumed in serial rounds of limited or "cabinet wars," discretely named conflicts perhaps better understood as campaigns in far longer and more fundamental struggles such as that between France and the Netherlands and its allies, and that between France and Britain. These wearing fights spanned much of the globe and most of the 18th century, before France finally descended into revolution in the 1790s and much of Europe therefore descended into yet another full generation of all-out war.

What of the armies? Inside one's own territory, soldiers were paid wages from a central state treasury, but the towns and wealth of foreign lands were still seen as fair play for rape, plunder and punitive destruction in wartime. Logistics remained a basic problem. Despite innovations such as magazine systems in which supplies were prepositioned along the line of march of

Marlborough's 10 Campaigns (1701–1711).

Courtesy of the Department of History, United States Military Academy at West Point. Redrawn by George Chakvetadze.

ZUIDER
SEA

MARLBOROUGH'S GAINS
IN TEN CAMPAIGNS

The War of Spanish Succession

0   25   50
SCALE OF MILES

C   D

Utrecht

Arnhem

Coesfeld   Munster *Ems* *River*

Nemegen

Grave   Gennep   Wesel   Dorsten   Hamm
                          Wesel *River*

Eindhoven   Rheinberg   Essen Bochum   Dortmund
             Geldern   *Ruhr River*
Venlo   Duisburg

Lille St. Hubert   Dusseldorf

Peero   Roermond
Helchteren   1702

Asch   Slevensweert   Bedburg   Siegen
        Demer R.   Marburg
18 July 1705   Julich   Cologne
        Maastricht   Alsdort   Duren   Sieburg   *Lahn* *River*
                          Aachen   Bonn

Liege   1703   WESTERWALD   Wetzlar
Limburg
Huy   *Ahr R.*   Coblenz   Limburg Friedberg

Cincy   *Ourthe River*   Mayen   Frankfurt
Marche   Boppard   *Main River*
La Roche   EFFREL   *Nahe* *River*   Mainz
ARDENNES   Bastogne   Bitburg   Trarback   Darmstadt
                          Vianden   Kreuznach   Oppenheim
ibramont   Worms
                          Trier   HUNSRUCK   1704   *Glan River*
Arlon   Ludwigshafen   Mannheim
Luxembourg   Kaiserlautern   Ladenburg
Virton   Blenheim
                                                              13 Aug. 1704
Meuse River   Thionville   SAAR   Homburg   Philippsburg
                          Saarlouis   Schellemberg
Etain   2 July 1704
GONNE   Verdun   Metz

LORRAINE

BLACK FOREST

NOTE: Phase lines are very general, showing the situation
at the end of each year. Both sides held fortified places in
"enemy" territory throughout. Furthermore, either side
could maneuver almost anywhere except through entrenched
Lines. Nonetheless, the general trend of Allied advance and
French withdrawal is clear.

Stollhofen

C   D

traditional invasion routes, armies still marauded and foraged widely past
their supply depots. Once they moved onto enemy land they often acted like
locust swarms, consuming everything, just as their 17th century predecessors had. Slow wars were marked by indecisive campaigns and seasonal sieges,
often of the same fortresses, and making war pay for itself by marching and
camping and living off enemy territory.[15] It was not always about self-supply.
Sometimes this style of war-making was about denying supplies to the other
side, about making economic war and political coercion by extortion and even
terror. Civilian dead mounted along with solidifying national hatreds born
of a new practice of "devastations," in which whole provinces were torched
to coerce a local prince or deny the land and resources to the enemy's army.
The turn toward generalized ferocity was signaled when Vicomte Henri de
Turenne's army ravaged the Palatinate in Louis XIV's name in 1674. Armies
had marauded before, of course, while foraging or when in mutiny against
a commander or for pay or against internal discipline. But this was the first
time one undertook systematic destruction of a whole territory as an instrument of state policy.[16] It was a portent.

Worse was to come, as in a second and more complete "Devastation of
the Palatinate" in 1688–1689 by a fast cavalry army acting under Louis XIV's
infamous destruction order to *faire bien ruiner* ("ruin it all"). The destruction was planned on a map by François Le Tellier (Marquis de Louvois),
right down to specific châteaux marked for burning: maps have been a tool
of atrocity ever since they became accurate. Beyond the châteaux of local
nobles who opposed the king of France, even laborers were forced to burn
down their small homes, farmers to burn fields and orchards. Louvois then
gutted and dismantled, stone by stone, large parts of the cities of Mannheim,
Heidelberg, Oppenheim, Worms, Speyer and Bingen. Twenty large German
towns and hundreds of villages were completely destroyed. In damage to his
reputation and inspiration to his enemies, along with the revocation of the
Edict of Nantes which had granted toleration to Huguenots, the ruination
of the Palatinate came to be seen as one of the major errors of Louis XIV's
reign.[17]

Field marches were made in battalion formation, frontage varying from
8 to 20 files of soldiers according to road width or if going cross-country, reforming into line and reserves whenever battle loomed. Once engaged, battle
tactics were constrained by short-range and largely inaccurate weapons. Fusils
were incapable of reliable hits beyond a few hundred feet. Such short range required multiple lines of men to march within shouting distance before opening fire—if they even chose to fire first, for it was not uncommon to instead

receive a first volley, or more, without firing back. One side took fire on a long dead man's walk, marching closer while the opposing line fired and then hurriedly reloaded. You took casualties, but you ensured through tactical and moral forbearance that your first volley did maximum damage at point-blank range. Some fights ended in a bayonet charge, but not many. Usually, infantry stood in bright-colored coats (necessary to avoid friendly fire through all the smoke) banging away at each other's lines until one side had enough and withdrew.[18] Even rankers came to appreciate the value of such battle patience, of holding fire while closing on enemy infantry or a gun battery. The courage and discipline shown by ordinary men finally convinced more officers to see them as something more than armed sheep, to be herded into combat by sergeants barking like border terriers at the corners of lines and squares. French officers would get there first, even before the French Revolution. As discussed below, the shift in perception would then lend strength to massive conscript armies after 1792 as *esprit* merged with the *levée en masse,* as mass conscription was called in France.

Meanwhile, adjustments were made to battle tactics by fresh innovators over the course of the 18th century, including attacking directly out of march column, increasing numbers of skirmishers, dragging more cannon to the battlefield, and reorganizing troops into battalions and brigades and divisions, units that could both march and fight.[19] Yet heading out to seek battle in the first place remained constrained by rulers and budgets, all the stone and defensive artillery obstacles to decision, and by political intolerance for mass casualties in battles that seemed to have little other effect. All armies arise from and reflect the societies that raise and support them. Therefore, in the mid-18th century the armies of Europe were not yet capable of recovering from the kind of destruction later wrought by Napoleon's wars, and after. It took the French Revolution and *levée en masse* to change that, too, by assuring generals that even should they gamble and lose an army in an afternoon of combat, the fully mobilized resources of a whole nation would supply them with another. In 1700, that societal ability to absorb mass casualties lay far in the future. Even so, battle-seeking by military pioneers was coming sooner— high-risk and bloody, but coming all the same. Some generals insisted on it.

A few 17th-century battles had indeed reached a decision, if the term is defined tactically. Some ended a campaign or stopped a summer's or a year's fighting, but none ended the long wars that hosted them. No battle may be fairly said to have determined the outcome of a major war, though Breitenfeld and Lützen perhaps came closest in changing a major war's main course. Not so the fights at Nieuwpoort or Rocroi, battles numbered among the more

famous European engagements of the 17th century. Those fights had some
political effects, but mostly raised material and human costs in a bigger, wearing conflict or achieved no lasting purpose at all. Moreover, and far too often
for the comfort of the kings and parliaments who paid for the armies, ambitious generals might win some field of glory that added to their personal reputation but at a huge cost in casualties and crippling expense for their sponsors.
Victory in almost every grand battle of the era was so bloody and costly it was
hardly distinguishable from defeat.

Late-century states were stronger, with better finances and bureaucra-
cies and fewer or no domestic challengers. With the long 17th-century civil
wars finally over in England, France and Germany, armies were not needed
as much for domestic repression and became available to fight more abroad.
Troops were more skilled and better armed, as armies began growing again
after shrinking briefly during the latter Thirty Years' War. At the Battle
of Rocroi (May 19, 1643), just 23,000 French faced 20,000 Spanish. In the
1660s, the French army of young Louis XIV still numbered only 50,000–
60,000, but by 1678 it fielded 279,000. That was more than any army in
Europe since the fall of Rome. It climbed to 340,000 in 1688, to reach a
peak wartime strength of about 400,000 during the 1690s. However, these
numbers can be deceptive, since most troops served in garrisons and Lines
rather than in mobile field armies out roving and looking for a fight. That
was actually the key to overall army growth. It was spurred not by a military culture changing to battle-seeking but by the need to garrison mush-
rooming fortresses and besiege, or at least to threaten, those of the other
side.[20]

Victory and defeat thus remained cocooned in wars where the dominant
mode of fighting remained slow siege on land, blockade and *guerre de course*
at sea. Year after year, Austrian, English, Dutch, French, Italian and German
armies undertook annual campaigns of maneuver, conducted sieges of fortresses and Lines, or carried out savage devastations. War fleets met and sailed
past each other in parallel lines of battle, firing mostly harmlessly beyond inflicting damage to individual ships and lives. Privateers and commerce raiders
did more extensive and lasting harm to enemies than such indecisive naval
battles. A province might change hands or a local border move ahead or back
when each *danse macabre* ended, as exhausted states and societies paused to
recover, regroup and refinance. British redcoats and Dutch in blue fought
French in Bourbon white and blue, summer into winter into spring, year after
year. They marched, suffered, killed, and died of wound sepsis or camp disease in summers, then paused to wait out the winter snow. They might serve

the king and colors for 20 years or more, then sons took their places. Still the wars ground on, without lasting decision.

After advancing to take a fortress town or key fort holding a river-crossing, armies rebuilt the forts they had just burned or knocked down in order to hold the position gained. In almost every case, in wars among major powers it proved impossible to win quickly. Victories left the losing side too much time and too many resources to recover and resume fighting. Even aggressive governments and marching armies thus returned to older tactics that departed from a battle-seeking strategy, relying on investing strongpoints, hunkering behind field works, eating out the enemy's lands, intercepting taxes and draining a foe's treasury with devastations and economic warfare. Ultimately, the arc back to attrition forced aggressive generals or their political overlords to accept negotiated settlements. The pattern continued campaign after campaign, war into war, decade upon decade. Yet not everyone was prepared to submit to indecision. Some generals longed for glory or looked to escape from long wars of maneuver and sieges of fortified towns or Lines with a return to battles. They wanted to force political settlement or reduce the cost of protracted war on their treasuries, or to relieve strain in a difficult alliance by winning fast, or just to locate personal fame by claiming a blooded meadow at the end of a day of combat. With more and better guns and more professional troops available, the old vision of battle was back, at least for some: the thought that brilliance of special generals might end wars quickly in sudden and decisive violence. More generals began to seek, fight and occasionally win battles. Yet still only a few, and only now and then.

***

MOST OF THE European wars spanning the turn from the 17th to the 18th century centered on Louis XIV, *le Roi Soleil* who sat on the throne of France for 72 years, ruling for over half a century. One cannot understand them without pausing to review his policy, for his serial aggressions ensured France would hardly see one year of peace in every two during the 54 years of his rule. Louis did many memorable things as the great monarch of an era to which he lent his name. But because he embraced war all his long life, he must be judged above all else by war's results. In the "Age of Louis XIV," war was the *métier du roi*, the measure and business of kings. In that arena he wrought mostly misery, destruction, futility and failure. From 1661 to 1715, Louis spent 32 years at war as he sought territory for France, absolute security along its claimed "natural frontiers," and above all *la gloire* for his own person and dynasty. He was no unrestrained conqueror, not a would-be Alexander or Napoleon. More of a vainglorious fumbler beyond his borders, he cursed his era with expanding war all the same. He sought for France an absolute security that must come at the cost of insecurity for everyone else, only to be shocked when accused of aggression. He fixated on winning petty gains by exploiting obscure legal claims, odd historical precedents, and never compromising the dynastic rights of the unforgetful and unforgiving Bourbon family he headed. His was a personal foreign policy, not a national one. He spoke for Louis, yet the French and much of Europe went to war. The human and material costs of his ever lengthening and ever more expansive wars plunged France into disaster as the brilliance of his long reign faded into a twilight of defeat and decline.[21]

The French army under Louis XIV was a marvel, thanks to unmatched funding and a succession of superbly capable military and civilian administrators.[22] They built a permanent, large and professional army that, before Louis launched into economically ruinous wars, rested on a sound fiscal base. Like the Roman Army, it was kept on a near-permanent war footing, guarding the borders or marching over crenellated and river-coursed terrain into neighboring countries. It bound the old nobility in a new form of royal service, as colonelcies of regiments became a key path to social success and to building client networks for leading noble families.[23] Bourgeois joined for other reasons. France was changing, and expenditure on the Sun King's wars was a cause of a new if limited social mobility and incentive to enlist. Peasants, on the other hand, were impressed into serving. Versailles glittered over all, boasting of the preeminent power of France and the leading person of the age. It would take a large coalition of many other powers to defeat this preeminent army and dominant state. That is precisely what Louis gave rise to with his aggressive military policies and unforced diplomatic errors.

Young Louis gained Alsace and parts of the Rhineland with some diplomatic finesse, but his march into the Spanish Netherlands in 1667 started the two-year War of Devolution that scared the Dutch into permanent hostility to his ambition. Territorial demands were characteristically mixed with insistence on absolute security for France at the expense of all others, and so Sweden and England joined the United Provinces in fighting Louis, closing out the long Anglo-Dutch maritime wars to do so.[24] Louis backed down in the face of this opposition, only to smolder with resentment and return to invade the confederation of the United Provinces itself in 1672. He thought he would win easily in a single campaign, but triggered six years of the Dutch War (1672–1678) instead.[25] A pattern was set in which Louis repeatedly failed to predict the depth of opposition his actions must provoke or the size and length of the conflicts that he started. None of his wars except the War of Devolution were as short or straightforward as he expected.[26]

After 1674, Louis never faced small, isolated countries again. He fought instead against widening coalitions he provoked into existence. No one opponent matched the reserves of his treasury or the size and power of the French army, drawn from 20 million subjects. However, the combined strength of the coalitions did. All around his frontiers from 1675 were enemies with growing military assets increasingly organized into an insistent balance of power aimed at blocking French dominance. Nevertheless, Louis insistently pursued minor but provocative legal claims which he and his minister, without any irony, spoke of as *le défense aggressive*. Later, he moved back to direct military aggression. This was classic Louis XIV, even classic hegemony thinking. Philip II of Spain said more or less the same of his distant campaigns and wars, that he was acting in defense, not committing aggression. Austrian Habsburgs made the same claim at the start of the Thirty Years' War, and into Louis XIII's time, until Gustavus and Richelieu stopped them with built-up coalitions. The pattern would repeat several times more after Louis XIV. French armies would strike across the national borders in 1794 and after to defend the Revolution by exporting it at point of bayonet. Many Germans thought the same about their aggressive 19th-century Wars of Unification in 1866 and 1870, and yet again about their hemmed position in 1914: we are encircled; we must attack, break the iron ring of enemies to gain security. In most cases, early success would lead to hubris and long-war catastrophe, as opposing coalitions formed in direct response to aggressive provocation. It is one of history's oldest tales, frequently forgotten and therefore too often relived in new storms of blood and steel.

Louis' policy of erecting iron and stone walls along all France's frontiers, as unilaterally defined by him to include much surrounding and disputed territory, frightened all the neighbors. No one saw anything defensive about his huge standing army. Not when he lost patience with legal processes while trying to secure small "reunions" (border annexations), including the city of Strasbourg, or in his overt seizure of the fortress city in 1681, which sparked the War of the Reunions (1683–1684). Seizures of other Imperial free cities, and denial of their traditional liberties and new treaty rights as framed in the Peace of Westphalia, permanently frightened the German states, which had seen enough of war and an Imperial drive for hegemony from the Habsburgs. Louis also annexed the Principality of Orange, on the Rhône, from a hated but exceptionally talented opponent, William of Orange. That made the *Stadholder* of the Netherlands a permanent enemy. The full effect of this error came much later, when William mounted the English throne following the Glorious Revolution of 1688. Thereafter, he would bring the rising world power of Britain into a Dutch alliance in the French wars. England's military thereby also became more professional, with an infusion of Dutch expertise and direct hiring of exile officers (the Anglo-Dutch and Scots Brigades). The timing fortuitously matched Dutch martial skill and leadership to British financial power, state reorganization and rising national assertiveness in matters of trade and war and empire.[27] Louis thus paid a far higher price than he could ever have imagined, just to annex the tiny and non-threatening enclave of Orange.

Making more enemies, to divert the Habsburgs Louis secretly encouraged the Ottomans to invade Austria, leading to the great siege of Vienna in 1683 and another in a long series of Austro-Ottoman wars, this time lasting from 1683 to 1699. He was playing an arrogantly foolhardy game. By 1700, the Habsburgs opposed him in the south and faced him also with an Imperial army from across the German frontier to the east, the Dutch blocked him in the north, while the British opposed him at sea and were readying to do so on land. The *Grand Monarque* was directly responsible for the creation of the Grand Alliance that stopped him in his next war, called the Nine Years' War (1688–1697). He began by sending Louvois to devastate the Palatinate in 1688, once again falling into the delusion that he could freely ravage in Germany and then stop, with all goals achieved and opposition and the fighting ended whenever he chose. France fought instead for nine years against an ever more powerful coalition pressing on its stone borders.[28] Defeated, financially distressed, even chastened, Louis went over to strategic defense. It was too late. The longest, most destructive of his wars followed when he would not compromise on the issue of the Spanish succession, which he insisted go unadulterated to the House of Bourbon. In 1702, Britain, the Netherlands, the Habsburgs of Austria and the Holy Roman Empire all declared war on France, reforming the Grand Alliance that would encircle and nearly break France during the War of the Spanish Succession (1701–1713). In all, from 1688 to 1713, he forced another 22 years of war on France and Europe; years of blood and taxes, battles and sieges and strategic futility.[29]

Louis XIV's lifelong habit was to meet foreign weakness with unalloyed aggression and to address his own weaknesses with even greater aggression, whether in diplomacy or war. After spending decades pursuing the chimera of aggressive war, from 1700 he was compelled to convert to reliance on defense, which actually proved the wiser and militarily and strategically more successful course for France. Even so, it took over a decade more of destruction and desolation of wide swaths of territory until his borders and the succession in Spain were alike decided, in a compromise that a less aggressive king probably could have reached through peaceful negotiations. For despite Louis XIV's desperation to end the Spanish war, as famine and costs came close to breaking France and he offered terms to the Allies in secret in 1709, peace could not be agreed until *both* France and the Grand Alliance reached military, political, moral and economic exhaustion. That state of affairs was codified in the Treaty of Utrecht in 1713, after years of talks in secret, then in the open. What does history remember of all that today, the sieges and garrisons and blockades on land and at sea, the famine in France and ruin of towns and national economies in a dozen states? Mostly we recall Louis and the glory of his high court at Versailles, along with a handful of battles made famous on the other side by court propagandists and nationalist historians.

***

THE LIMITS OF logistics, of the arms and armies of the day, meant that even highly energetic and battle-seeking generals still primarily fought the old, slower way. Most rulers, too, retained sober doubts and deep fear about the utility of battles at all. Generals were profoundly aware, or were made aware by their political masters, of a too often demonstrated failure in prior wars to leapfrog protracted conflict by risking their king's precious army on a roll of battle dice. Field combat remained a gambler's chance, not much more promising than a draw of numbered ivory beads in the popular parlor game of *cavagnole*. For the most part, they cleaved to conservative tactics, laid in sieges and marched their armies to avoid rather than meet the enemy in battle. Only a relatively few field battles therefore marked the extended wars of Louis XIV, and since those that were fought were astonishingly bloody and only rarely decisive, the deterrent point held.

Nevertheless, given the grating of slow war, the idea of faster resolution through battle called more loudly to some at the start of the 18th century, particularly as Louis XIV shifted to a strategy of positional defense of his earlier gains, such as they were. Most notable of the battle advocates on the other side, now moving to offense against France, was John Churchill, later 1st Duke of Marlborough and ancestor of an even more famous descendant and ardent admirer, Winston Churchill. John Churchill once fought *for* Louis, during the Dutch War. As a young officer under Marshal Turenne, he led an English regiment in battle against the Imperials at Entzheim (October 4, 1674). He would return to the continent 30 years later as a general leading armies of the anti-French coalition. In the interim, there had been a renewed

British dynastic struggle in which Churchill commanded the royal army for James II against the Duke of Monmouth's larger but far more ragtag force at Sedgemoor (July 15–16, 1685). That ended "Monmouth's Rebellion" while also securing for Churchill the special favor of that Catholic king. Churchill grew disillusioned along with the country, however, and broke with James when William of Orange landed with a Dutch and Protestant army at Torbay (November 15, 1688). In the moment of crisis that likely decided the Glorious Revolution, Churchill deserted his king. He brought the bulk of the royal army with him to bend the knee to William, a new sovereign (and patron). Along with considerable military talent, he also brought to William's court profound personal greed and high political ambition. Ever the schemer, for many years he stayed in secret correspondence with the exiled king and leading Jacobites. Even a highly favorably disposed biographer admits that he "lived on the margins of treason."[30] Or stepped right over them, eagerly and with both boots.

The new king, William III, never entirely trusted John Churchill, but needed him to plan the campaign in Ireland which led to royal and Protestant victory at the Battle of the Boyne (July 11, 1690). Dwelling in a shadow of royal suspicion after that, Churchill spent a decade out of favor, to 1701, before being reinstated to fight in William III's wars against another old patron in Louis XIV. In the interim, Britain had reformed its currency, land tax system and war finances, and was in a far better position than France at the start of the struggle over the Spanish succession.[31] For the next ten years, Churchill, now elevated as the Duke of Marlborough, commanded Allied armies of British and Dutch and various Germans. His political star rose higher upon William III's death because his wife, Sarah, was close to Queen Anne. That gave him a political base at the highest levels, over most at court and even above Parliament. It also made him enemies. He did not slip from favor until Sarah fell out with the Queen in 1710. By then, Britain was scandalized by Marlborough's personal corruption and tired of promises of victory but deliverance mainly of battlefield butchery. The party politics that once lifted his fortunes now doomed them, as the Tories displaced his Whig friends and undercut his support at court and in Parliament. He was recalled in January 1712, as the new government moved aside a corrupt and discredited old soldier who was trying to block its efforts to negotiate a peace treaty with France.

Marlborough had a lifelong habit of extreme self-promotion that helps explain his easy changes in political loyalty. He was always a secret plotter, in high finances and high politics, between dynasties and over alliances, and sometimes also across enemy lines. He padded his fortune and stoked his own reputation, while belittling contributions by the Dutch to the long war with France.[32] He resented the Dutch commissioners who paid for half his armies, or more, and who worried that he was reckless in command of their troops. He dismissed them as fussy, ineffective mediocrities who preferred sieges and timidity where he was a true visionary of decisive battle. It was not right that grubby Dutch paymasters demanded that he subsume offensive genius beneath their incompetence and conservatism, forcing the great man and great captain to bow before crass burghers and bankers who did not understand his new and special art of war.[33] It is a jaundiced portrait of Dutch allies that persists in nationalist histories that proclaim Marlborough to have been "Britain's greatest general."[34] All the while, Marlborough pocketed a fortune in finagled public and army money for a scandalously expensive palace he named for his greatest battle: Blenheim.[35]

Dutch effort in the French wars actually exceeded British on land in terms of men, funds and matériel. The small, confederal United Provinces bore the main burden of land warfare against neighboring France, with sea blockades and French privateers also raiding their key overseas and coastal trades. At sea, the Royal Navy outpaced the Netherlands, but naval warfare was not critical against France after fights off Barfleur and La Hogue in 1692 established Allied dominance. Besides, Britain after 1700 was already pursing a global naval strategy for its own reasons, only partly related to the French wars.[36] Marlborough could not reconcile himself to the fact of a decentralized and shared Allied command structure, though he better appreciated a key partnership with Imperial Field Marshal Prince Eugene of Savoy.[37] Marlborough also benefited from taking command of Allied armies at a point when French military fortunes were waning and England's were ascendant, not least due to the fact that the redcoat army had excellent staff and logistics officers, particularly Quartermaster-General William Cadogan. Marlborough's achievements were real but not his alone, despite what he and his acolytes in the English press and Parliament of the day, and later his most famous descendant, all proclaimed.[38]

Marlborough is remembered today for believing in battle, said to be the signature of his command style. It's why some consider him one of the great captains. He might even deserve the appellation if offense were all there was to war, and if day-of-battle tactics were all that was required for victory. However, at a more basic level his battle-seeking and poor alliance-management proved inadequate.[39] Marlborough believed he needed to win fast in order to please impatient political masters in London, and before funds and armies were cut back by his suspicious paymasters in Amsterdam. It is true that he fought against not just French armies but France's demographic and geographical advantages. Yet it is also true that he gained lasting advantage from Louis's dire and chronic fiscal problems after 1700, as well as from the advent of political and religious unrest in southern France just as he arrived on the scene. Several times he would benefit also from French errors in dispositions in battle or on the march, but such are the fortunes of war, and he made the most of them. The main reasons for his successes were Britain's rising military power, critical Dutch and English finance, very fine Dutch and British troops, many able subordinates, and an equally talented co-commander in Prince Eugene of Savoy.

Marlborough mounted the stage of Louis XIV's wars in July 1701, promising to break the stalemate with a strategy of relentless offense. He was an exceptional practitioner of the so-called art of war, within the limits imposed by the technology of his era.[40] Yet like Maurits a century earlier, Marlborough was forced by logistics and enemy fortresses into waging more sieges than battles, and into wastage campaigns that did not result in ultimate decision over Louis XIV or France. Moreover, his claims to battle-seeking and battle-winning results were ambiguous at best. He fought just four grand battles, despite seeking many more: Blenheim (1704), Ramillies (1706), Oudenarde (1708) and Malplaquet (1709). His admirers proclaim that he won all four, and that all four were decisive, yet it is possible to maintain that claim only by the convention that victory attends to which general holds the bloody field when fighting stops. As we shall see, his troops held the ground after Malplaquet, but he left far more of his own men dead and dying there than Frenchmen, while his enemies rightly believed that they, not he, had won.

Marlborough invited Louis's generals to fight numerous times, but the Sun King ordered them to avoid risky engagements. French strategy from 1701 was to husband troops and supplies in strong positional defense of heavy stone, to hold along the Lines, with occasional sallies to recover a lost fortress or on limited offensives into Flanders.[41] His Dutch allies were similarly unwilling to risk their armies in battle, declining to do so at the end of the 1701 campaign while Marlborough champed at the bit, even though the fighting season was over. Frequently, with both allies and enemies declining open battle, he was forced to march and besiege just like all the other generals. He marched better than others, but that does not mark him as a genius. Several times he used clever ruses, forced marches and quick concentrations (and information from his net of spies) to steal a march or breach a set of Lines. So did other generals. He failed, however, to persuade his political masters of the benefits of battle, or of his proposed and self-named "Grand Design" to break past the Lines of Brabant in 1703 with a large amphibious landing to flank and circumvent all three sets of France's northern defenses. The plan was vetoed by the Dutch, and Marlborough settled for a siege of Huy instead.[42]

Dutch leaders simply did not trust the most secretive and duplicitous man in the Alliance, perhaps in all of Europe, a man who could be accused of changing loyalty as another man might change his coat. They knew him as a schemer with private networks of spies and agents on *both* sides of the war. Even had his Grand Design gone forward and succeeded, they knew better than he did that the Allies did not have the armies or resources or domestic support to exploit such a breach, let alone invade France. Generals must understand the wider politics of the war they are fighting. Marlborough did not, and never succeeded in persuading the politicians who mattered of the military need for his grandest proposals, merely theoretical campaigns he never carried out yet later claimed would have won the war. After fighting Louis for just two years, he failed to appreciate that the Dutch already had been fighting for a quarter century. It is telling that the Dutch struck a commemorative medal for their limited military successes in the positional war against masonry of the 1703 campaign, which stayed battle-free as they wanted and he did not. It read: *Victory Without Slaughter.*[43] Marlborough could hardly conceive of such a thing.

On the other hand, there was Blenheim. In 1704, Marlborough made a virtuoso's bid to have his name added to the list of great captains of maneuver and battle. He began by shifting a smallish British-Allied army to the Danube, where no one expected it or him. He picked up reinforcements along the way, then forced the enemy to fight and lose a genuinely decisive battle. His move south and success at Blenheim gained more strategically than any of his other campaigns, by keeping Austria in the anti-French coalition while shutting off south Germany permanently to Louis XIV. Blenheim did not win the war, but it inflicted serious and lasting strategic hurt to France. It was Marlborough's masterpiece, and also that of Cadogan and the Allied armies.

Marlborough deftly deceived his watching opponents about his destination, starting with a diversionary pontoon-raft bridging of the Rhine in a place that implied he intended to move into France. That fixed on the other side French armies sent to observe and block him, which might better have pursued and harried when he left. He kept them standing in the wrong places with more clever feints and ruses. Then he turned outside Cologne on May 19 with 20,000 troops in pay. He was soon joined by battalions of Hanoverians and Prussians. It was not clearly the greatest and unequaled march of all time, as often said in British histories. It was at least matched if not exceeded by John Sobieski 20 years earlier; that Polish general had moved an army 400 miles in six weeks in relief of the Ottoman siege of Vienna in 1683, once marching 220 miles in just 15 days.[44] Marlborough's march was impressive nonetheless. Over five weeks he marched the Allied army 350 miles without exhausting men or mounts or eroding combat fitness.

Marlborough and his redcoats and Germans were able to do it because Cadogan expertly managed a remarkable ad hoc supply system after Allied magazines were left far behind at the Rhine. He arranged for supplies to be positioned ahead of the moving army, with towns encouraged to store food and fodder at preset rest stations or depots (*étapes*) for purchase by arriving troops.[45] Cadogan oversaw all supply wagons and dealt with the local sutlers, reloading 2,500 carts at the prearranged depots. The army camped every four or five days to resupply and to bake bread in portable ovens. The Allied force divided into parallel columns of horse and foot moving on separate roads in order to ease strain on the depots. Known widely in English histories as the "scarlet caterpillar," the march actually made two redcoat caterpillars (striped with Dutch and German black). It was a triumph of logistics more than speed, but a real triumph it was. While Marlborough shares credit with Cadogan and an excellent quartermaster corps, he deserves his own for securing vital intelligence from his agents along the way and for providing personal command drive and choosing the right march captains. He also mapped the route.[46]

More Germans arrived in the camps or joined the columns as they moved, swelling the number of battalions and straining even Cadogan's supply system. To move faster, Marlborough left behind all heavy siege guns and avoided assaulting fortresses he could better bypass. However, stone blocked his way at Donauwörth on the Danube. Without siege guns in his artillery train, he had to force an enemy camp protected by the imposing Schellenberg fortress. He pushed past this smaller Franco-Bavarian force not with any tactical cleverness but with blunt-force trauma: a direct storm by 18,000 men, front ranks with fusils shouldered while carrying brush and cordwood fascines for protection against long-range fire. It ended in savage hand-to-hand fighting: fusils empty, men dropped weapons and tore and gouged each other with bare hands. One assault was not enough to take the camp, so Marlborough sent in dismounted dragoons to finish the job. When it was done, Cadogan was wounded and one-third of the 18,000 men Marlborough sent to attack the Schellenberg were dead. A recent biographer calls this assault "a masterpiece."[47] It was not. Nor was it genius. It was tactical success by bloody and bloody-minded force majeure.

Having captured Donauwörth as a forward base, Marlborough was finally past the stones and free to devastate Bavaria. To make the enemy fight, he let the army pillage and burn, writing humbug laments to Sarah that this was all the fault of the enemy; he would desist if only a Bavarian army offered to meet him in battle.[48] He linked up with Prince Eugene's fast Imperial cavalry and dragoons on August 11. The big fight came two days later at Blenheim. The location was decided when the Allied cavalry screen blundered into the French encampment. Marlborough and Eugene personally scouted ahead, climbing a church tower to observe the camp some 5 miles from their own. They saw its cooking fires smoking, tents laid out in rows behind a marsh and a stream with a high bank. They also saw that one flank rested dangerously on the Danube while the other was anchored in wooded hills. Seeing their best chance in an immediate and surprise attack, they hurried back to break up the Allied camp just after midnight, then night-marched to do battle with 52,000 men. They reached the French picket line at first light and deployed off the march, moving efficiently from column into line.

Marlborough and Eugene shared command and fought that day with coalition forces acting as one army; the enemy generals did not, fighting as separate armies on the same field. The British and Imperials and Dutch faced 60,000 French and Bavarians, many of whom were hungry, having been on short rations for days. Many French cavalry mounts additionally suffered from an outbreak of glanders, an infectious disease of the lung. Some men were half-asleep, others breakfasting; foragers were still out when the shooting started. British, Dutch, Imperials, Danes, Hessians, Prussians and Hanoverians advanced in a proper three-rank line, but Marshal Camille Tallard's men were slow to respond to first contact with skirmishers to their front. Also evident from the start were superior Allied rates of fire and better discipline, especially by tough redcoats in an army just then coming into its own as a skilled professional force. The Allies advanced "locked up" tight, meaning rank against rank, closing fast against a scrambling enemy packed too closely in hasty deployments to properly form an opposing line. Perhaps the main French mistake, in a day of smoke-obscured confusion, was to leave cavalry unsupported by enough infantry at the center. Marlborough saw his chance there and initiated what became his trademark tactic: attacking the enemy's flanks to draw troops away from and weaken the center, where he then landed the killing blow.

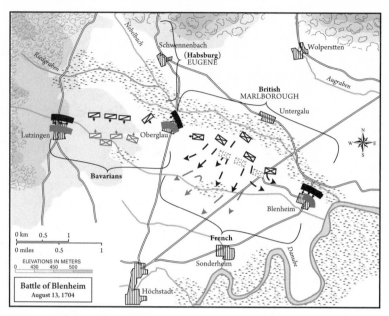

Battle of Blenheim (August 13, 1704).

Courtesy of the Department of History, United States Military Academy at West Point. Redrawn by George Chakvetadze.

The raggedy French line was five ranks deep and anchored on two small villages, Blenheim and Oberglau. The Allies attacked these at noon to draw off troops from the center. It worked, though only after a sequence of hard-pressed fights in and around the villages. A feint toward Oberglau was repulsed by a counterattack of Irish in service to Louis XIV in the *Brigade irlandaise*, fighting for a French king as their Catholic fathers and grand-fathers had served French kings before them in various regiments of *Géanna Fiáine* ("Wild Geese"). Marlborough reinforced while Eugene's cavalry rushed to plug holes. Tallard fed thousands more into the fight for the two villages, men in white coats stained with powder and soot. After two hours the *maréchal* committed his main reserve, although his troops were so crammed many could not bring weapons to bear on enemies they could not see through choking black-powder smoke and swirling ash from the burning buildings. Men felt the arriving shot and musket balls, however.[49] Marlborough had massed his reserve at the center, behind a grand battery of 40 guns. His first cavalry attack was repulsed, despite his taking away ammunition in order to encourage horse shock *à l'arme blanche*, just as Gustavus had taken away his cavalry's pistols and made them charge with sabers and lances instead. Frederick II would later do the same.[50]

Next came a full, combined arms attack. Infantry advanced behind the horse soldiers while solid shot thudded and ricocheted along the hard turf. Iron balls ripped right through men, some sending hurtling body parts as human shrapnel to kill and maim more. The French cannons also found killing range, one ball just missing Marlborough's hard-stamping charger. He ordered reserve infantry to lie down, a tactic imitated later by the Duke of Wellington in Portugal and on the ridge line at Waterloo in 1815. The French fought desperately and bravely under heavy bombardment, taking infantry volleys, receiving repeated cavalry saber and lance assaults.[51] Tallard committed his last reserve. The final combat was a cavalry-on-cavalry mêlée, artillery and infantry pouring in fire wherever horsemen appeared somewhere inside the smoke. The French line broke at 5:30 p.m. with the cracking and folding of a thinned-out center. Each village was still filled with French troops fighting hand-to-hand and house-to-house, but isolated from the main affair. The French in Blenheim village refused to quit until blasted into surrender by Allied cannon. When Marlborough refused requested terms, Tallard surrendered the rest of the army to spare lives from further slaughter.

In easily the most decisive battle of the War of the Spanish Succession, about 20,000 French and Bavarians were killed or wounded, including 3,000 cavalry who drowned trying to cross the Danube, horses and men sent spinning downstream to lodge and rot some other place, some other day. Another 14,000 French were taken prisoner.[52] The Allies lost 14,000 killed and wounded, 9,000 from Marlborough's wing alone. Out of 102,000 men who fought, 34,000 were either dead or wounded. The amputations began immediately. No one knows or ever counted how many of the wounded died later of mortal hurt or sepsis, as they always did. Thousands of horses were seriously wounded, too, but you could shoot a wounded horse. Dutch fatalities were about the same as the British, at 2,200 killed in each contingent. All of that made Blenheim one of the hardest days in European history in several centuries. Allied casualties suggest that it even could have gone the other way, for want of a nail or a missed order or dead courier or wafting smokescreen concealing a charge into a gun battery or exposed battalion flank at a critical moment. Battles remained extremely high-risk and even victories carried enormous costs.

Ignoring all Allied contributions, Marlborough wrote to Sarah: "Give my duty to the Queen and let her know her army has had a glorious victory."[53] It was not only Louis XIV who made war for reputation, too easily spending other men's lives for *la gloire*. Still, it was a clear victory for Marlborough and Prince Eugene. They won because of French mistakes and their own superior firepower and better firing lines and troops, and because of generalship. They scouted and understood the lay of the battlefield, pinned down the majority of enemy troops in heavy defensive fighting, managed reserves so well that they created local superiority at the point of their choosing at the center, then ordered the main attack at the critical moment against a French line badly weakened by bleeding off men to defend the flanks. It was the first time in the living experience of any but the very oldest soldiers that a French army had been so badly defeated. The campaign and battle framed a major *defensive* victory that may have rescued Vienna from French capture. It kept Austria in the war, also helping indirectly to weaken a major Hungarian rebellion (led by Ferenc Rákóczi). After Blenheim, Louis XIV lost the means to interfere in south German or Austrian affairs. The victory thus preserved the Grand Alliance and emboldened its shift to strategic offense, with France confirmed on defense for the rest of the war and duration of Louis' reign. Blenheim therefore was a genuinely decisive battle, with a lasting political outcome. It didn't win the war, but it altered its strategic direction and put permanent limits on what Louis and France could achieve by force of arms. Offense would be harder.

From 1705 Marlborough fought again in soggy Flanders, where Cadogan's Horse, led by the general quartermaster himself, forced the Lines of Brabant, an ambitious project Marlborough first proposed in 1703. It was a highly touted achievement, but not much more than a tactical one. Louis refused battle, while the Dutch hesitated to risk their troops in another bloody affair like Blenheim. However, in the next year's fighting season Marshal François de Villeroi came out from behind the lines, on his king's changed mind and unwise order. He had 62,000 men in two thick columns to try to seal the prior year's breach of the Lines. Marlborough gathered 60,000 Allied troops and met him at Ramillies on May 23, 1706.[54] Villeroi established a battle line along a slight rise, overextending his army across 3 miles, at two regiments deep. His center anchored on Ramillies, partly protected by marshy ground. The flanks were slightly forward, curving the battle line at either end. Villeroi locked his position on several small villages he thought would strengthen his defense, but they would in fact prove too far apart to serve as bastions that could lend each other mutual support. Bavarian exiles were in the fight, too, on the left of Villeroi's line just in front of the Petite Gheete River. A scattering of Spanish troops was there as well.

Marlborough formed a shorter convex line with his mostly Dutch and British troops, giving him a real advantage of interior reinforcement of either flank. Then he set 120 field guns to pound the overmatched French. The

Battle of Ramillies (1706).
Courtesy of Wikimedia Creative Commons.

bombardment began at 1 p.m. Again, he caught a French commander seeking to defend a broad plain while overly concentrating his infantry in flanking villages, thus exposing a correspondingly weak center. During several hours of heavy fighting, Dutch troops took two small villages on the French right. This was actually a feint, but Villeroi misread the maneuver and counterattacked with both infantry and dragoons. These unfortunate troops were run down in the open field by Allied cavalry. Redcoats assaulted the other flank for over three hours, but failed to break through. This also was a feint, in force. Villeroi did not fully take the bait. He reinforced the flanks, but only lightly. Each side committed cavalry at the center. Nearly 25,000 crashed into each other in a great mêlée, one of the largest cavalry fights of the century. Obscured by terrain and smoke, Marlborough's strong reinforcement went unobserved by Villeroi, until measured in killed and wounded.

Marlborough also made mistakes. Almost 20 years older than Gustavus when the Swede was killed at Lützen, he led a cavalry attack from the front and was nearly killed when his horse was shot from under him. By 4 p.m., both French flanks were under heavy fire and one was isolated from further reinforcement. The fight was still in doubt at 6 p.m. when the French right

wing suddenly gave way. Marlborough seized the moment he had been waiting for. He moved more infantry to the center, weakening his right. A simple
ruse of leaving battle flags in place while his troops moved under concealment
worked. Fully a third of the French army stayed in place facing flag poles and
small color parties, unaware of the true weakness opposite or that the hinges
of battle were turning out of their sight and about to slam an iron door on
the day.

A heavy combined arms assault at the center shattered the French line.
French, Bavarian and Spanish units broke and ran, abandoning guns and
casting aside fusils and packs as Villeroi lost all control of his side of the
battle. Allied troops pursued and mercilessly cut down the fleeing enemy.
When it was over, the toll was 1,066 Allied dead and 2,560 wounded, the
majority from Dutch battalions. French losses exceeded 13,000. Afterward,
Marlborough and his lieutenants rolled up sections of Lines abandoned by
fleeing garrisons, exploiting a rare battlefield victory to take down the real
enemy: stone and bastions. Even he later admitted that despite all exertions
and destruction of the French army at Ramillies, and rolling up of parts of
the Lines, he was still and always "surrounded by garrisons and enemy strong
places." Stone and iron still ruled. So the campaign staggered on for months,
while the war lasted seven more years.[55]

Two more years of hard positional warfare followed Ramillies, maneuvers and marching and battle-seeking on one side but battle-avoidance on the
other. Then Marlborough and Prince Eugene met Marshal Louis Vendôme
at Oudenarde on July 11, 1708, where they commanded 80,000 Allied troops
against 85,000 French. These massive armies did not intend to fight when
and where they did, but stumbled into each other while on the march, initiating a battle of encounter. Oudenarde began when Cadogan's Horse, leading a cavalry screen ahead of the Allied advance guard, brushed into cavalry
of the French rearguard. A bloody mêlée ensued, attracting more and more
units to the fight, both on horseback and afoot. The main infantry were still
strung out in thick traffic jams along the roads, with cannon even farther
back. Regiments of quick-marching foot arrived along with more cantering
or galloping squadrons of horse, all helter-skelter. Each unit engaged piecemeal while slower regiments hurried cross-country, rushing out of column
into opposing battle lines. All were drawn to the cricket chatter of constant
musketry and the first thumping cannon reports. Reinforcement went on all
day, but so strung out were the march columns that probably no more than
60,000 on either side made it into the fight before it ended.[56]

Caught by surprise by a chance encounter while crossing the Allied army over the Scheldt, Marlborough and Eugene reinforced the hurriedly forming battle line. So did Vendôme, but since the French had to turn around to reform, the Allies got there first. Again, quickness and luck mixed with skill told the tale. With most artillery on each side too far away to engage, with heavy cannon and caissons stuck in long columns, the battle turned into an infantry and cavalry fury of fusils, sabers and lances. By evening, the French were forced back at the center (as always, Marlborough's favorite point of main attack) and nearing defeat on either flank. Eugene and Marlborough cross-marched to try to envelop the entire enemy line and cut off all retreat. Now fortune favored the other side: nightfall allowed a mass escape by survivors of Vendôme's beaten army. Casualty estimates vary widely from 8,000 to 15,000 for the French and their Spanish allies, with a more reliable figure of 3,000 killed and wounded on the Allied side. It was another sharp victory for Marlborough and Eugene, permitting them to spend the summer rolling up towns and a few isolated fortresses, including some of Vauban's finest masonry near Ypres. Louis was also compelled to abandon his small recent reconquests in Flanders.[57]

More sieges and maneuvers, more fortress reduction campaigns followed, until the last and bloodiest of Marlborough's battles by far: Malplaquet, on September 11, 1709. Marshal Claude Louis Villars lobbied Louis to let him come out from behind Lines to fight, confidant he could match Marlborough by luring him into attacking a prepared defensive position. After Ramillies, Louis was hesitant to chance another battle, but Villars won him over. His army numbered 75,000, including some Bavarians, Irish and Swiss.[58] Many were not line troops. They had been recently pulled from garrisons or were raw recruits. However, Villars' shrewd tactics absorbed this fact. He knew he did not need first-rate men drilled in deft maneuvers just to stand in hard positions and shoot at oncoming Allied infantry and horse. But he also had with him ancient and veteran regiments and brigades from Louis' household guard, the *Maison du Roi*, as well as the elite *Gardes Françaises* and *Brigade irlandaise.* This was a French general who knew how to fight with the army he had and against the enemy he faced. He would stand and hold ground, and let the enemy's overconfidence break on his strong redoubts. Indeed, Marlborough was too confident, bringing 110,000 men to his last battle, a hodgepodge of Danes, Dutch, English, Irish, Hanoverians, Hessians, Prussians, Saxons, Scots and Swiss, along with 100 cannon. He, too, was looking for a fight.

To reach Malplaquet the armies moved through places that lent their names to awful battles past and to come: Courtrai, Tournai, Ypres, Mons, the Somme, as well as earthworks and trenches old, present, and to come as well. Heavily outnumbered and outgunned, Villars chose wooded ground, dug in his infantry and cannon behind field works, and waited for a day. He knew the Englishman would be driven to seek him out and then attack, and he was right. The assault began right after breakfast, with Austrian and Prussian infantry advancing against the French left. Ancient regiments from Picardy and the Champagne region stopped them. On the right, Dutch Blue Guards and the Scots Brigade of the Allied army were repulsed with very heavy losses, sustained while assaulting well-prepared defenses and thick lines of fusiliers. At 10 a.m., Marlborough reinforced each attack. He was up to his old game of trying to weaken the French center by drawing off troops to the flanks before making his main thrust. Villars had studied his tactics, which were therefore stale and defensible. He stood fast, holding back his reserve.

As they had before and would again in Europe's wars, Irish troops fought on both sides of other nation's battles. The *Brigade irlandaise* in blue counterattacked on the Allied right with the usual ferocity of the famed "Wild Geese." They were repulsed by Royal Irish in red coats, fighting for pay and for Queen Anne. Marlborough countered and the French line sagged, then gave way on the left. At noon Villars issued a movement order he was most loath to give, knowing what his enemy wanted. He committed to reinforce the sagging flanks from his central reserve, with troops he hoped would meet Marlborough's expected and signature killing blow when it came. Then he was severely wounded and carried from the field. Marlborough thrust his sword, sending 30,000 horse at the infantry-poor and weakened redoubts in the French center. They were met by a countercharge of French horse. A cavalry mêlée ensued as Allied infantry assaults continued all along the line and the cannons boomed overhead from both sides. Slowly, weight of numbers and superior guns on the Allied side began to tell.

In the absence of Villars the French made an orderly retreat, skillfully organized by Marshal Louis François de Boufflers. He first led a counterattack with the horse of the *Maison du Roi*, then disengaged the entire army in disciplined good order around 3 p.m. The field was left to the Allies, men in blue and red and black. Retiring Bourbon regiments in white and blue left 11,000 casualties behind. Yet an astonishing 24,000 Allied killed and wounded lay upon the field, including Prince Eugene. That amounted to nearly a quarter of the Allied armies. It was the bloodiest battle of Marlborough's and Eugene's careers. It also had far more strategic impact on the Grand Alliance than on Louis XIV and France, for whom Malplaquet was a well-fought defensive victory against a far superior force.[59] Marlborough nonetheless depicted it as *his* great victory, as did his admirers at the time and still today. He intended it as a culminating blow to win the war by forcing Louis to accept terms, and later claimed that it had. In fact, he had gambled and lost, but politics in London and Amsterdam forbade him to say so. His choice was to assert that he had won the battle, because the French left him in possession of the field, or accept political defeat and a reduced command. It did not really matter who held the field when evening covered so many dead men in quilts of night and widow's grief. The lie therefore gained him only a little time, until appalled governments in London and Amsterdam saw what the real cost was of offense in a single battle, let alone what might result from his proposals to invade France. Never again did they let Marlborough take their armies into open battle. The Dutch especially never recovered, or trusted him again.

Malplaquet *was* a decisive battle that pointed to the eventual peace, but for the French rather than the Allies. French generals had underestimated Marlborough before losing for the first time in 50 years at Blenheim, which they saw afterward as their bad fortune rather than a case of being outfought. They reconsidered his talent after Ramillies and Oudenarde, but never doubted that the fight at Malplaquet was their own clear-cut victory.[60] So it was: a thorough defeat for Marlborough, for the Dutch and British armies, and most of all for Allied political will to continue fighting for little more than marginally better terms. It was an impressive defensive stand by Villars that showed continued French resilience, even if France itself was wounded by too many years of Louis XIV's wars. The butcher's bill delivered in London and Amsterdam shocked Allied political elites far more than that given to Louis in Versailles. Moreover, Marlborough had sought and fought his bloodiest battle while Louis was facing famine at home and already secretly pushing to make peace in talks with Dutch envoys, and near to acceptance of the harsh terms the Dutch offered. Instead of driving home hard Allied terms, the outcome of Malplaquet somewhat revived the Sun King's fortunes and depressed the Dutch, just enough that the war continued with a greater sense of grim French resolution and Allied worry.[61] Louis understood this and celebrated a rare victory of his later years, issuing rewards to all French commanders. Villars got it exactly right when he told his king in response to Marlborough's claims of Allied victory: "If God gives us the grace to lose another similar battle, your Majesty can count on his enemies being destroyed."[62] Villars then recovered from his wounds and led French armies to fresh victories and small gains from 1710, mainly on the German frontier. By then Marlborough's star had fallen.

The Dutch would not lend the English captain their armies to be so blooded again, recalling also that he had lied to them in 1708, saying he would not seek battle with their troops and then doing exactly that.[63] British politicians were also tiring of his great promises and ever bigger butcher's bills. The essayist Jonathan Swift used his formidable quill to savage Marlborough, and his ink was worth a battalion of Brobdingnagians.[64] Marlborough had taken an army massively superior in numbers and guns into battle and lost 24,000 men. His own government thereafter limited his freedom of command, joining the Dutch in doubting and suspecting him. Parliament focused on his politics, past betrayals and ongoing scandals, ignoring his claim to have just won a decisive victory. In 1711, the Duke achieved his last military success, breaching the incomplete Lines of the *Ne Plus Ultra*. He did it by bluffing Villars out of Arleux by telling Cadogan to dissemble in defense of the causeway there, before doubling back. Marlborough used this diversion to cross between Arras and Vimy Ridge, locales made infamous in yet another Great War in the 20th century. He passed the *Ne Plus Ultra* without meeting resistance or casualties in September. He might have marched to threaten Paris, but was called home in January 1712, as peace talks commenced in the open at Utrecht. Later, he was censured by Parliament for corruption and went into comfortable exile.

Marlborough has a reputation for revolutionizing warfare by single-handedly reviving a preference for battle over positional fighting. It is said that while his peers were rigidly fixated on mere maneuvers and sieges, he saw through to the decisive battle. If his battles did not result in victory in the war as a whole, this was because of lesser military minds blocking the great English military genius from carrying out his best plans.[65] It is more accurate to say that he was thwarted by water and stone defenses, long Lines of fortresses and real limits to mobility, combined with a shrewd policy of strategic defense by France after 1700, and in the end by a French general who met and matched him in the field. In ten campaigns from 1701, he fought just four grand-scale battles and two small ones, but conducted 30 sieges and fortress assaults and three passages of Lines. When the French remained on strategic defense, it was their positional warfare that controlled the course of the war, not Marlborough's persistent battle-seeking.[66]

Marlborough's claims to genius, frustrated by feckless allies who would not fight to win, were circulated by a wide circle of clients.[67] They were repeated by nationalist historians and one exceptionally famous descendant. Yet, despite what Winston Churchill and other nationalists protest, Marlborough was not even Louis XIV's main foe. The Sun King's true bête noire over decades of high politics and war was William of Orange, later William III of England. Marlborough took the field on the continent in the last phase of fighting, with France already pushed over to strategic defense by William's successful policy of coalition containment of Louis' ambition. Military historians who later ranked Marlborough among the modern great captains were too enamored of tactical offense in war, without taking sufficient account of the limited strategic results he achieved. Perhaps also military historians have been overly impressed by innovators, generals who restored movement to war, in one century or another, where the common practice was siege or war of position. That might be because modern historians look back from more terrible wars of exhaustion of their own day and tend to exaggerate offense as an ideal type, against the persisting superiority in defensive firepower in fact.[68] Yet tactical offense is not inherently or strategically or morally superior, even if more daring. It is also more subject to blundering into carnage, as at Malplaquet. Nor is defensive war less noble or brilliant. Victory can be won on defense, too. The Dutch held off Louis XIV for a quarter century with positional defense, only to balk at the cost of Marlborough's minimal gains for maximum cost on offense. Villars won with defense, too, at Malplaquet.

Marlborough also benefited from commanding an unusually fine army over his 10 campaigns. The Dutch lent him solid battalions, though their army was entering a long decline as the United Provinces more generally were eclipsed by larger and rising powers. The British Army was just coming into its own as an instrument of national power, as the Royal Navy already had. It finally absorbed professionalization and tactical lessons of war from militaries on the Continent, especially from the Dutch via William but also from returning Scots. It especially benefited from excellent logistics officers in service to a rising commercial-military state with a developed global strategy. Redcoated troops and senior officers were of a high comparative quality. They made generalship if not easy, then at least more able to take advantage of presented opportunity.[69] Marlborough had the wit to seize such opportunities for battle and in battle, even if he lacked the wisdom not to grasp at every chance.

It is fair to say that Marlborough was a more daring general than most of his allies, except Prince Eugene, and all of his enemies, except Villars. However, his dash came at a high cost in dead and, perhaps more importantly, in wasted strategic gains and opportunity after 1709. Villars, who is less well known to English-speaking audiences, was Marlborough's opponent from 1705 and just as skilled at war.[70] A great French commander, he nearly matched Marlborough as a master of march and maneuver and clearly bested him at Malplaquet, during which he was badly wounded by a musket ball that smashed his knee. As or more importantly, he kept the ear and trust of his king and thus more nearly linked his fighting strategy to France's waning means and late-reign defensive strategic goals. He had courage and forbearance, riding with his wounded leg tied to his saddle during the 1710 campaign. In the Rhineland, he won a small but strategically important battle at Denain (July 24, 1712). Thereafter he rolled up Allied garrisons, taking 10,000 prisoners. That last success cleared the way to diplomatic agreement on terms of the treaty being negotiated at Utrecht, formally ending the war in 1713.[71] Arguably, given these political accomplishments, Villars was the greater and more decisive general.

War is too important to reduce to a parlor game of ranking generals. Marlborough was clearly a very good general for and in his time, even if his reputation was swollen in his day for political reasons and exaggerated ever since for nationalist ones. It was more important that he stood on the cusp of a wider change in battle culture. Someone had to be first to try to break stone with bullets, to get around the long stalemate of fortifications with tactical movement. It happened to be Marlborough. His failure was a measure of how little had changed in his time in the deeper tensions that always exist between offense and defense as approaches guiding tactics and operations; his successes were a measure of what might yet change before the 18th century was done.

***

ONE DID NOT need to fight wasting battles to wage wasteful wars. Time and again over the course of the 18th century, evenly matched powers or opposing coalitions of powers would fight drawn-out wars that decided little. These were protracted contests of roughly matched foes that resulted in grinding casualties and other steeply rising costs, leading to exhaustion. They were marked less by an "Age of Battles" than by land or sea blockades, more sieges and investments of Lines, more devastations and wastage campaigns, and near-permanent commerce raiding on all the high seas. Wars lasted years, overlapped each other across decades, consumed whole reigns and generations of taxes and effort and poor, expendable men. Then they petered into overseas swaps or minor border adjustments but left basic strategic indecision, resulting in pauses that no one really wanted but everyone was forced to accept.[72] Jeremy Black is surely right to say, contrary to the commonly held view dating from Clausewitz and after, that the era of cabinet wars was "neither limited nor static."[73] This was widely forgotten after Louis XIV died, full of regrets, in 1715. For a generation, an unusual quiet settled over Europe. It grew so quiet for so long that the silence of the thousands of waiting cannon was mistaken by early thinkers of the Enlightenment for the beginning of perpetual peace.

The French Enlightenment's most famous intellectuals, the so-called *philosophes*, saw war as they saw everything else, as a problem that could be understood and resolved by the application of Reason. With the exception of Voltaire, who mostly endorsed Louis XV's and Frederick II's midcentury wars, mainly to curry royal favor, many proclaimed principled if naïve antimilitarism, while a few proposed fairly wild-eyed schemes to bring about universal peace.[74] Jean-Jacques Rousseau, Claude Helvétius, Paul-Henri Holbach, Étienne de Condillac, Guillaume Raynal, Montesquieu and others thought and wrote very little about war. When they did, they usually expressed a set of fairly shallow views that boiled down to the notion it was an unnatural thing, a disharmonious and wasteful invention, or a criminal pursuit to be scorned by refined minds.[75] Diderot wrote only vaguely about war, along the lines of Immanuel Kant's late-century distaste for all standing armies and objection to inhumane treatment of soldiers under harsh military laws and punishments. He never systematically considered war the way he did most other social issues, or even seemed to be fully aware of the import of the wars raging all around him at midcentury.[76] Most *philosophes* saw war as just another resolvable social problem, but one removed from their more pressing concern for progress through science, education and reform, a matter to be studied and resolved in some distant future.[77]

As with Diderot, their most urgent social concern focused on the problem of honor and the behavior toward the lower ranks of gentlemen officers (reflecting class bias, they did not expect any honor in the ranks). Their main political distrust was of the influence of standing armies as a threat to prospects for *liberté,* and they were concerned on humane grounds about state abuse of common soldiers. *Philosophes* as a whole conceived of *fraternité* as a natural bond of peace, the direction in which the harmony of society was already moving, away from its violent and barbaric past toward a future of perpetual peace bound by law and comity among nations. This view did not make them all pacifists, however, although that was the distinct conclusion of some, like the Abbé de St. Pierre.[78] The common thread was belief that war, too, was mappable by science; that it, too, could be restrained and governed by Reason, reshaped to science-ruled modes of regrettable but natural organized violence. Already, war was becoming more humane in a blessed century freed from superstition and religious motivations that underlay the long wars of religion of the 16th and 17th centuries. The assumption was that secularism could never descend to the same dark places as religious hate; that the pride of princes and nations would not lead to the same pits of cruelty and torment in war as pride led Lucifer or the gods of antiquity.[79] As it turned out, the *philosophes* underestimated the allure of hard and cruel war for "enlightened despots" like Frederick II, and wholly failed to anticipate the secular rage of the French Revolution and its discontents.

Lesser and less well-known thinkers of the so-called *militärische Aufklärung* (Military Enlightenment) in Germany took a different tack. Broad thinkers like Johann Zedler, who wrote a *Universal Dictionary* at mid-century, along with the fervent war and battle poet Johann Gleim, who celebrated military brotherhood and the wars of Frederick II, framed a wider, self-conscious effort to rework and refine the theory and practice of war. Reformers in France wanted to rework military theory and law to accord with broader Enlightenment cultural and intellectual ideals of empirical investigation and reform.[80] In Germany, too, they looked to make war more humane, but also to make it more effective, moving past rigid discipline to release deep psychological forces that might better motivate troops than merely naked fear of savage punishments. They wanted more free will in the ranks, as everywhere else in society; more self-aware motivation among soldiers for why they fought, so that they would fight better. In return, they asked that soldiers be treated decently. They thought they found a great champion of these reform ideas in Frederick II. In 1735, he wrote a wholly cynical *Catechism for War* in the style of a basic Lutheran instruction to children, an odd and probably mocking choice for a ruler who despised established religion. It was issued as training advice for Prussian soldiers after he succeeded to the throne in Berlin.[81] Yet they were deceived. Frederick would treat his soldiers in war and peace as utterly disposable, more harshly than any other ruler in Europe mistreated his or her soldiers. Except for the tsars.

Everywhere, by midcentury Reason was being newly applied to the art and science of war. Theorists drew mathematical applications of Strategy and Tactics and Maneuver and Battle and Siege. They refocused attention and theory on battles as the sharp point of war, concealing with cold intellectualism and salon tastefulness war's real-world sharp points. Purely theoretical work was crafted outlining parallel applications of mathematics to ballistics, to congruent fields of fire in fortification design, to countervailing siegecraft. The effort reached perfect elegance under the draft pens of Vicomte de

Turenne, in artful schematics as applied to battle, and Sébastien Le Prestre de Vauban, in scientific principles applied in fortification and siegecraft. Art and science merged in linear war, especially battle. Combat was orchestrated, and crescendo violence returned to its rightful place in the Temple of Mars, where war was the amphitheater of genius as heroic exertion. The best minds laid out in mathematical regularity how to slaughter perfect lines of soldiers in a field, or all around a polygon fortress, altars of secular sacrifice to the Ascent of Man. Even bewigged salon guests and silk-and-lace courtiers played the game of comparing military geometry and linear tactics. It was a favored pastime at court in every major capital.[82] Everyone agreed that the perfect linear dispositions were exquisite, that the clash of arms and empires was as arousing as the highest art.

Architects, gardeners, urban planners, kings and generals were in love with imposing straight lines on stones, on nature, on people. High culture delighted in perfect straightness in everything from hedges to grand boulevards to buildings, in sieges and battles as well. One thing was missing, however. Entwining the rational and beautiful geometric, a supreme military intellect was required to gild battlefields in a union of beauty and brutality. War needed and called upon genius to complete it. Versailles and the French army both reflected this aesthetic sensibility, a newly refined taste for linearity. Reason produced fine, predictable parabolas and perfect trajectories of cannonballs; bounced clever ricochet fire inside fortress walls; made more mathematical precision and eye-pleasing artillery fortresses with interlocking fields of fire; it showed how to rationally dig approach saps and blow mines; it led to geometrical battle plans drawn on linen paper with a ruler and protractor.[83] Not a twig or trooper can be out of place; trim the hedges in Louis XV's gardens; make the bastion angles in his fortresses perfect and beautiful; straighten and refill the ranks in his *Gardes Françaises* as men fall down with a lead ball inside. The king would even ride out to watch.

Linearity was fine in positional defense and before a battle started. Fortifications were solid and fixed, and troops must deploy from column into line. Iron flew as iron flew, but battle moved. It was fluid and intensely human. This required genius, the one thing not subject to final dissection by Diderot and others who tried.[84] The idea was reduced to little more than a catch-all term for the human element in command that could not be so easily systematized as bastioned walls and linear dispositions; the quality of a great commander even beyond a *coup d'oeil* that sees to the essence of battle and war and strikes in just the right way to achieve victory. Genius for the Enlightenment stood atop an architectural foundation of scientific understanding that uncovered universal truths. These must include observed or deduced principles of war that would be good for all times and places, climaxing in supreme artfulness what had begun in ascendant science based in Reason. It was, in fact, a start down a path away from pure Reason back to the old heroic Romanticism, leading at century's end to veneration of Napoleon and the idea of military genius in the work of German military romantics, especially Carl von Clausewitz.[85]

In the interim, a treatise on war by Marshal Maurice de Saxe, the most famous and respected French general of the 18th century prior to Napoleon, remained among the era's most influential military works. He wrote *Mes rêveries* in 1732 but published it only in 1757, his narrow theoretical views unchanged by the years of real war and carnage in between. Instead, echoing Machiavelli and his later and lesser imitators, Saxe argued for reorganization of armies on the model of Rome's legions. Oddly but influentially, he also called for a return to hand-to-hand fighting with edged weapons. Avowing the superiority of maneuver warfare, he claimed he did not believe in field battles, saying: "I do not favor battles, particularly at the beginning of a war. I am sure a good general can make war all his life and not be compelled to fight one."[86] Yet he became famous for fighting several highly bloody ones. His singular triumph was a bloodbath at Fontenoy (Tournai) on May 11, 1745, during the War of the Austrian Succession (1740–1748).

Fontenoy was fought on a fine spring day with Louis XV himself in resplendent attire and attendance. Bourbon battalions in white waited with elite *Gardes Françaises* in dark blue and the similarly dressed Wild Geese of the *Brigade irlandaise*. The battalions were positioned by Saxe behind a sunken L-shaped road, atop a low ridge bordered by thick copses. Watching with him was the king and many curious nobles and courtiers, as two dense columns of disciplined infantry tramped upslope toward the waiting French. The British were under the command of the Duke of Cumberland, third son of George II and later infamously portrayed in Tory propaganda as the "Butcher of Culloden." Austrian and Dutch infantry allied to the British and wearing grey and black were already turned back on the left flank. The main attack into the strong center of Saxe's blue and white line wore red coats that day. Batteries on the right flank, dug into the woods, raked the columns with shot and canister as the battalions moved uphill as if on parade, 15,000 men in thick columns, fusils shouldered. Officers drew swords, sergeants barked orders, serried ranks stepped the march; flags fluttered, boys beat out time on drums, fifes and oboes played, bagpipes wailed. Close ranks of men in red marched upslope in lockstep, boots thumping the ground in unison.[87]

Saxe and Louis XV at Fontenoy (1745).
Courtesy of Wikimedia Creative Commons

It had started hours earlier, with the Allies forming for battle at 2:00 a.m. and coming under first cannon fire before dawn. Allied artillery replied ineffectively. Nevertheless, Dutch infantry had advanced, fighting through two small villages on the Allied left before being cut down by French sharpshooter and cannon crossfire from well-placed redoubts. Dutch cavalry broke in panic and the infantry withdrew, bleeding and torn. If Cumberland had studied Marlborough's tactics at Blenheim, there was little evidence of it in his dispositions and orders at Fontenoy. He did not weaken one or both enemy flanks before attacking the heavy center, where the bulk of Saxe's regiments waited for the red columns to come into range of their loaded fusils. He ordered British and Hanoverian infantry to advance straight upslope, against the strong advice of his senior commanders. They tramped upward at a steady pace, into a half-mile-wide gap between the town of Fontenoy and a thick wood, each flank full of waiting French cannon and sharpshooters. The narrowness of the redcoat approach forced by the terrain bent the lead ranks back at both ends, like a drawn and tautening bow.

As the ranks and files in red coats formed and advanced, Saxe said, in comparison to the blue-coated Dutch repelled earlier, "Now we come to the English and they shall be harder on the digestion."[88] Cumberland set the march cadence deliberately slow. Men moved up the hill past the mouths of big brass cannon firing from an undisturbed redoubt in the woods on the right, with more cannon and sharpshooter fire coming at them from the left. Under falling solid shot, then ripping canister, the steadily tramping men did not fire until they reached 30 paces from the sunken road, to crest the ridge and face the massed French infantry line. Then they stopped and loosed mass volleys at the French, receiving leaden hail in return.

It was magnificent, celebrated in verse and art and memory for decades afterward as one of the great infantry advances of the century, not least in a quick history by Voltaire.[89] This was war as the *philosophes* thought it should be, as the best minds conceived it, painted it, wrote of it in poetry, as troubadours recalled it to ardent youth. In fact, Saxe sent his cavalry to assault the British line and all dissolved into a mêlée of red and white and muddy brown; of shattering by musket balls; of saber cuts and bayonets and riderless horses. When it was over, after mutual volleys at point-blank range and hand-to-hand fighting with spent fusils used as clubs, after the British formed a compact square and withdrew in good order downslope, 6,000 French lay dead or dying among twice as many redcoats.[90] Saxe was pronounced the glorious victor because when the carnage ended he held most of the field and had half as many dead. Louis XV showered him with royal favors, including a victory château. He wrote in reverie, though lacking reverence, about generalship over men such as fought for him at Tournai (and before, when he served as a young officer in the bloodbath at Malplaquet): "Courage of the troops is so variable ... the true skill of a general consists in knowing how to guarantee it by his dispositions, his positions and those traits of genius that characterize great captains."[91] For the Enlightenment, combat such as blooded the slopes and L-shaped road at Fontenoy was coolly rational.[92] War was beautiful. Genius in war was sublime.

Genius would win battles and wars, as it would settle all great issues of the Age. The question was, where to find it? It might be assumed in persons of highest quality, in enlightened despots like Louis XIV and Frederick II, and in one or two of their generals. As for run-of-the-mill matters, such as actually moving and fighting real armies, the mere conduct and application of dull mathematical tactics, why, anyone of education and sensibility could master *that*. Conduct of sieges and moving armies in the field, and supply and combat, all subsumed under the term "tactics" in the 18th century—that was no more than a child's lesson or two in spatial geometry, and rote recital of universal principles of war revealed by Reason and recovered from history and written down as tactical manuals for officers. Strategy was the domain of genius, the reserve of rare high intellect. It belonged, said Paul de Maizeroy, one of the most prominent of the period's military reformers, "to the most sublime faculty of mind, to reason." Writing in 1777 after nearly three decades of draining worldwide wars by land and at sea, he still believed the rigid wisdom of a wigged and saloned century that called itself enlightened: "Tactics is easily reduced to firm rules because it is entirely geometrical, like fortifications."[93]

Because the Enlightenment's high aesthetic of war was as a clash of forces decipherable by mathematical principles and the rightful stage for discovery and expression of humanistic genius, it eschewed any serious understanding of what combat truly was. It denied the hate or fear and passion needed to stick a bayonet into another man's gut, to fire again and again into a huddled mass of infantry across a sweetgrass meadow, or blast grapeshot to mangle and mix horse and human flesh, or slash a saber down from horseback to carve open a boy's cheek, or cheer a callous call to "Take no prisoners!" Court historians instead wrote paeans to kings and generals in baroque language, of war as a concerto of force and resistance, of battle as full of crescendos of cannon and rippling arpeggios of musketry and sighing string sections of leveled bayonets; and overhead, bare-breasted Nature in resplendent flowing silk gazing down in awe at the heroic works of Man. They wrote as if a clash of armies was no more than a risqué but courtly dance between Louis XV and Madame de Pompadour. Enlightenment war was battle as theater, exquisite in human geometry arrayed with elegant wit, a playground of genius and the sport of kings, a grand spectacle to be watched from a hillside while sipping brandy. Not the bloody business of butchering it was in fact.[94]

Pieter Bruegel had broken from the older, heroic vision of war in the 16th century to paint it as social criticism, evoking horror and the suffering of ordinary people in *The Blind Leading the Blind* and *Massacre of the Innocents*. In the 1630s, Jacques Callot etched *Miseries of War* with graphic images that still shock, or should. Although court painter to Spain's Philip IV, Diego Velázquez subtly portrayed moral doubt in *The Surrender of Breda* and *Mars*, and Peter Paul Rubens made unequivocal condemnations in such works as *Peace and War* and *The Horrors of War*.[95] Too many Enlightenment artists depicted war on canvas solely as a clash of geometry, marveled only at the symmetry of a battle line, drew the high nobility and genius of kings and generals. The dead and dying were nowhere to be found in paint; no real men, taking and losing real lives, dying real deaths. All we see in châteaux then and on gallery walls now is frozen regularity, a collage of lines and squares. We see ardor only for regular form and officer heroics, the falsehood of a beau geste in place of red and wounded humanity in Louis van Blarenberghe's *Siège de Tournai par Louis XV*. We meet rational sensibility again in *Bataille de Fontenoy* by Edouard Detaille. No blood stains mortally wounded General Wolfe's cuffed white shirt as he implores heaven with dying eyes in Benjamin West's *Death of General Wolfe*. Instead, America is personified on the Plains of Abraham outside Québec as an Iroquois brave looking on in wonder at such gloried nobility come from Europe to teach the New World good form and highest manners even in death. Coming full circle as the *Siècle des Lumières* ended, the old heroic themes in military art would return as full-throated propaganda in the Napoleons of Jacques-Louis David.[96]

Outside the best Paris and Berlin salons, beyond the gilded windows of Versailles and Sanssouci Palace in Potsdam, real war was never Euclidian or Newtonian or Enlightened. Battle on the blood-greased German plain, on sloped Austrian mountainsides, or in sodden Flanders was not some baroque concerto to delight the senses and thrill the intellect. It was a slaughter in which the killed and wounded often reached 35 percent or more on the *winning* side. Its carnage added to even more copious death in sieges fought as engineered and slow-motion battles. Add that to uncounted dead civilians in ravaged provinces as armies passed, to starvation as crops were torched, to shrunken commerce from blockades on land and sea. Add it to dynastic wars of vain kings lasting decades, to the Anglo-French wars that lasted over 100 years. Wars were not mere disruptions of unreason on the surer path to enlightened and perpetual peace, bookending the Age of Reason with irrational passions of religion on one end and unleashed nationalism on the other. It was the Age of Reason and Enlightenment that was the unnatural interregnum in Europe's wars.

6

Battle Restored

AFTER THE SUCCESS of Marlborough at Blenheim and Ramillies and that of Villars at Malplaquet and Denain, at least the idea of the decisive battle was back in play. It was not yet conceived as a war-winning or war-opening knockout blow. "Decisive" was still a modest concept, culturally limited. Battle was merely added to other stratagems that could be employed by generals to gain the things most valued by their kings: rolling up Lines, capture of border cities, annexing a small hereditary holding or province. Limited war still required inflicting insupportable costs until the enemy tired and quit the fight. However, terms demanded were never close to "regime change" or social transformation, as would be the case in the 19th and 20th centuries. Fight awhile in orderly geometric formations or spoked saps all around a polygon fortress, then diplomats would make a settlement to appeal to reason and moderation. This was an enlightened interregnum between the wars of religion and the wars of ideology. Or so the Age of Reason might have said and believed about itself if it could have foreseen the bookend calamity coming at end of century.

Lying in his deathbed, Louis XIV warned his five-year-old grandson, the soon-to-be Louis XV: "Try to remain at peace. I have loved war too much."[1] So had much of Europe. The Great Northern War, fought between failing Sweden forced out of the Great Power club and Russia rising to replace it under Peter the Great, lasted to 1721. Otherwise, with minor regional exceptions, Europe's thirst for war was slaked for 25 years after the *Grande Monarque* died in 1715. Major powers took that long to repair finances and rebuild sentiment, to restore will and the ability to fight. Conventions of geometry and conceits of social class thus dominated 18th-century thinking about warfare for decades more. Old-school officers like Marshal Saxe spent the last years of peace studying military geometry and mathematically deduced principles of war and writing his reveries. When war returned in the 1740s, they were unprepared for its new ferocity, and so sent commoners to fight and die in the same old lines and same old ways. Uncommon generals like Frederick II stumbled in their first battles as well, before refining the mature conduct of war with horse-and-musket armies.

Others spent the last years of peace celebrating retired generals, reading Marlborough's or Villars' memoirs and letters or assessing the glories of warrior kings. Those more commonly literate read penny-packet histories of wars long since cooled, of the "I was there" kind that appear like grass shoots in springtime after every war and wherever veterans grey. For people who were not there, the horrors of Blenheim and Malplaquet and a hundred sieges faded in memory, displaced by manufactured memories of kingly and national vanity by other means. Some thought about how to win future battles, but peace had broken out and there was no way to test their ideas as Europe slumped into weary indifference to old and new arts of war. In its own green fields, at least. Overseas was another matter. Empires of fighting sail clashed over spice and slaves, fish and fur and mast-tall virgin timber. There was room enough in the Canadas or on the Malabar coast of India for eager young men to fight. There was profit in it, too. One day, colonies in such far-off places might even be worth a war in Europe.

Kingdoms and empires growing richer in peace and using weapons that produced huge amounts of obscuring smoke now dressed their troops in full uniforms after a millennium mostly without. Exceptions had been rare: Welsh longbowmen in forest green; Italian and Flemish militia in shared, simple town cloth; proudly baggy janissaries in white *börk* hats; *maison du roi* in France and other royal household troops, like Peter I's praetorians in the Preobrazhensky and Semenovsky Guards. One of the persistent cultural memories of the period is the rich look of its armies: their vivid colors, bicorn and tricorn hats, gaiter buttons, white trousers, broad leather straps. We see them in portraits of the famous and in grand murals of battles, in children's toy soldiers and elaborate museum or tourist dioramas, and especially in films. Cavalry became more uniform in appearance, too, but dressed more gaudily, as horse soldiers clung longer to older traditions, such as bits of polished armor like the cuirass (breastplate) still worn by French cavalry in the opening battles of World War I in 1914. Saxe commanded that they use bladed weapons (*arme blanche*), as would Frederick II and most cavalry generals of the period. The horsemen also adopted flamboyant hussar colors and braids, and took to wearing big fur hats or stiff plumed shakos (*csákó*) imported from Poland, Hungary or places farther east or south.

Armies still employed nonregulars, such as Habsburg *Grenzer*[2] from the Balkans who wore local clothing instead of standard uniforms, as well as border and mountain *partisans*[3] and part-time militia. Otherwise, armies were attired in standardized uniforms that were ever more national, although they had started out as royal and dynastic and wore coats of many colors. It began in the late 17th century, evolving into distinctive national colors by the 18th. As in most things fashionable as well as militarily useful, the French army led the way. Captains received clothing allowances or deducted pay to purchase cloth to make a regiment's uniforms. Intendants or other local agents inspected these purchases to reduce theft of funds or buying shoddy goods by officers, who would then pocket the price difference. Uniforms made desertion harder, since it was difficult to get away when the color and cut of your only clothes declared you were the king's man; they also raised morale by elevating unit identity, along with regimental names, facings, patches and standards carried by proud flag-bearers. Coats were long-tailed and made from coarse wool (broadcloth), worn over a white or buff waistcoat. Late in the 18th century, a shift began to shorter-tailed coatees.

The 18th-century British soldier was entitled to a full set of uniform clothes annually, or a comparable cut of cloth. The cost was deducted from enlistment bounties and as part of standard deductions called "off-reckonings," amounting (for all items) to up to a quarter of daily pay. Royal regiments initially wore blue breeches, while regular regiments wore red cloth—not bright scarlet, but a ruddy, darker, beet-like shade.[4] Belts were worn over a fastened coat into the 1740s, with hanger and bayonet hitched on. Grenadiers were known for tall hats, originally made brimless so as not to impede overhand motion when throwing grenades. When fusils with enhanced ranges made grenadiers less effective, they evolved into units of elite fusiliers themselves. Still called grenadiers, they wore special tall shakos denoting their origin and elite status. Some sported a white pom-pon that recalled puffs of grenade smoke from battles past. Room was usually made for regional variation in national uniforms, such as Highland dress regiments in the British Army, Balkan accouterments in Habsburg battalions, and more exotic hussar and Cossack looks that migrated from Ukraine and Poland to nearly everywhere else in Europe.

The main purpose of standardizing vivid royal and later national colors was to make more visible friendly troops in smoke-filled combat and thereby avoid casualties by "friendly fire." But specific colors were chosen more often for frugality than for fashion. British coats turned red over time because red dyes were among the cheapest available. Danes also wore red. Blue was more expensive, and in any case was reserved to royal guards and other favored regiments in most armies. In the *Königlich Preussische Armee* (Royal Prussian

Army), the *Königs Leibgarde* (King's Guard) wore bright yellow jackets. A few armies dressed all rankers in blue despite the cost. Swedish troops wore blue, while Prussians wore a dark blue-black. Bavaria had pretensions to greater power and status than it ever enjoyed, and perhaps partly for this reason dressed its infantry in sky-blue. Russians in Peter I's reformed army mostly wore green. In France royal blue was for elite units like the *Gardes Françaises, Brigade irlandaise,* and so on. French regulars wore simple undyed cloth, a "Bourbon white" just as visible as cheaply dyed red coats but even cheaper because they took no dye at all. Austrian, Dutch and Spanish infantry wore dull whites or light or darker greys for the same reason.[5]

Everywhere that new model armies appeared standardized colored uniforms arrived soon after, as in Britain by parliamentary order in 1645 (though not required across all regiments until 1707).[6] British infantry officers were initially identified by gilt-handled swords, epaulets and crimson sashes tied over hips. When they finally put on full red coats, made of finer-spun broadcloth than the rough wool given to rankers, they kept the epaulets, but sashes shrank over time into trimmings. Officer uniforms in France tended to be more gilded, though many officers in all armies dressed in peacock fashion if they could. The exception was Prussia, where even officer uniforms were fairly plain, reflecting the prudent frugality and penury of that state's kings, except when it came to the gaudy canaries of the *Königs Leibgarde.* Italian and Austrian officers came from warmer or more cosmopolitan cultures, and so indulged elaborate trim and tall plumage. Officers who later served in Italy from more distant armies often adopted a more braid-and-feathers look, especially French generals. Some of Napoleon's marshals who served or lived in Italy, notably Joachim Murat, even in battle appeared to be draped in pounds of gold and silver braid with medals prominent on chest. Not quite the look of an Aztec eagle or jaguar knight in peaked hat and high plumage, but close.[7]

In whatever finery they wore, class distinctions dictated position at least at the start of a battle. Many junior officers took too many chances because they were young and aristocratic or just impetuous, choosing to be in the middle of the carnage, for their honor. Quite often, even senior officers were directly exposed to the enemy by the pell-mell sweep of combat. Generals in 18th-century armies were usually positioned in the rear of a firing line or behind the guns to start, but often they were swept into the middle of a fight whether they chose to be or not, subject to the winds of war and flying musket balls and shrapnel. Tallard was taken prisoner at Blenheim; Cumberland might have been killed leading the bloody up-slope march at Fontenoy; Marlborough and Frederick II also led from the front at times, and each had horses shot out from under them. Villars and Cadogan (not for the first time) were wounded at Malplaquet. Other generals *were* killed. Many regimental and divisional commanders did not survive a battle. Generals may not have stood anymore like the Black Prince or Henry V right in the front rank, sword or mace in hand, but they were in real physical danger in most battles, since they still commanded literally on the field, not from some rear HQ.

Most 18th-century European armies were polyglot, not national, especially in their officer corps. Coalition armies usually had several sets of Germans or Italians, men from regions that were still geographical and cultural concepts rather than countries. Irish and Scots and Balkan mercenaries served in many armies, sometimes in long-established regiments and brigades. Even within individual regiments, there was ethnic and other diversity and usually at least some Germans: the "German soldier trade" was considered by monarchs across Europe to be a highly convenient and efficient means of filling their ranks. Nor did press gangs discriminate by origin when filling a hard quota in order to get their own pay.[8] Frederick II's father, Frederick William, sent press gangs far and wide to lure or kidnap men of all nationalities into the Prussian Army. He especially wanted tall soldiers for his regiment of "Potsdam Giants," big grenadiers dressed in bright red and dark blue. Such internationalism continued into the early 19th century. Napoleon's *Garde Impériale* (Imperial Guard) was another international force, numbering over 100,000 in 1812. That same year, young Carl von Clausewitz, a Prussian officer then in his 20s, served in the Imperial Russian Army. There was a rough fraternity of men at arms across armies, too, forged from habits of march, military law and the common experience of fighting. Furthermore, there was an egalitarian ethic in the ranks, more so as the 18th century lengthened.[9] However, this shared culture of martial and professional respect did not extend to irregular fighters, or even to the Continental Army in the American War of Independence. British and other professionals from Europe (French and Germans) saw American soldiers as little more than jumped-up militia, no matter how blue their coats.[10] Actual colonial militia were viewed with deep contempt, as being closer to lawless *Grenzer* than to real soldiers.

In an 18th-century army, a regimental officer's duty in battle was motivation, direction, and keeping the ranks in order and fighting.[11] He might physically punish men who broke ranks, beating them with the flat of his sword or a baton or, more rarely, even shooting them *pour encourager les autres,* as Voltaire put it dryly in *Candide* in reference to the Royal Navy execution of Admiral John Byng (March 14, 1757), for failing "to do his utmost."[12] The threat to kill men who broke ranks was always present. Usually the threat alone sufficed, but not always. That's when pistols were drawn and sometimes even used. Only actual combat experience taught regiments and armies how to fight, by fighting. It enhanced the skill of surviving officers and men and made veteran units significantly more effective in follow-on battles than companies of green recruits. However, given the scale of casualties inflicted even on the winning side in most battles, there were always green and scared youngsters standing in the ranks and firing lines on both sides in the next one.

Facing other European armies, officers expected they would not be specially targeted by marksmen in the opposing battle line. Of course, they told their own men to return the courtesy due to class status and rank. Not so when fighting irregulars like *Grenzer* or American rebels. In North America, European officers removed signs of rank and status such as unusual headdress or gold braid, since Native American marksmen and Ranger sharpshooters armed with rifles did not defer in choosing targets. Nor did *Grenzer* back in Europe, which made them despised and earned them little quarter if captured. Disappearance into the ranks by removing outward signs of one's commission would occur again in the Boer War and in the trenches in World War I, where snipers ruled no man's land, and officer insignia—or just being saluted—was enough to get you killed. However, in 18th-century Europe, regimental officers were expected to show fortitude under fire, the same quality of forbearance demanded from rankers but to a higher and more publicly obvious level. They had to show personal courage while leading from the front in an attack or defense, which got a great many junior officers killed or grievously wounded in the first volley or two. Even if seriously wounded, a culture of displayed officer courage sometimes manifested as refusal to leave the field.[13]

At midcentury, more powerful but lighter field artillery started to change battle tactics and raise casualties. However, not all powers gained equally from the new guns. The French Army had achieved supremacy in artillery at the end of the 17th century but went into a steep decline during the 18th. At the start of the Seven Years' War in 1756, it easily had the poorest artillery arm of any major power. Scholars show that this resulted from heavy spending before 1713 on larger guns used in siege warfare and to arm fortresses and Lines, as Louis XIV left deep deficits behind that permanently weakened military spending under his successors. Bad decisions on procurements and poor gun design also played a role. As armies took more cannon into battle in infantry-support roles, debate ensued among master gunners and tacticians over reducing weight to increase mobility. Austria and Prussia reduced their biggest field guns somewhat, but the French Army reduced to much smaller calibers, leaving its batteries outclassed in field battles during the midcentury wars. The royal military establishment was humiliated and set in motion reforms and recasting of new model guns that laid a basis for the huge success of Revolutionary and Napoleonic artillery in and after the 1790s.[14]

During the Seven Years' War, the bayoneted fusil remained the main infantry weapon of linear battle. Its effective range was about 300 paces, but it was seldom fired before 200. Volley fire took time to learn, so there was strong emphasis on drill while in barracks or field camps. Cross-country marches taught units how to shift from column into line and back; how to advance at a steady pace, reload and volley fire; and how to retire in "good order," meaning still capable of fighting in self-defense and with no panic. Failure to deploy quickly or properly always led to higher casualties and sometimes to outright defeat, as Allied troops beating the French into battle lines at Oudenarde showed and Prussians would later demonstrate more conclusively at Rossbach. Usually, two main battle lines positioned on opposing sides of an open field, each making two parallel lines in echelon (*Treffen* in German armies), with each echelon three ranks deep. Some armies retained four or five ranks in each parallel well into the 18th century, but the trend was to reduce still more over time. The front echelon was the firing line; back ranks were a close reserve. They might stay 200 or more paces back, according to terrain.[15] Cavalry were deployed on the wings to flank guard the main infantry (a practice dating to Gustavus), with other squadrons at the center held back for shock attack at the crisis moment of the battle (following Marlborough), or to make smaller gap attacks (standard practice by everyone) should a space open between battalions standing or moving across the field.

Light artillery supported infantry on either flank of each battalion, usually at a ratio of two or three guns to a battalion. A concentrated or "grand" battery might be positioned at either flank or the center, according to a general's attack or defense plan or terrain advantages or defects.[16] Guns were deployed forward to pound the enemy line and ready to move in support of an advance. Cannon and howitzers fired solid shot (12-pound iron cannonballs) that smashed men, horses, caissons and guns at ranges up to a mile or more. Iron balls arced up in clearly visible parabolas. Once the range was found, whole batteries commenced fire that ripped apart densely-packed formations and field works. There was no way for infantry to retaliate. Only counter-battery fire could do that. If the ground was dry, solid shot ricocheted among the ranks, wreaking true havoc, physical and psychological, on formations standing still while awaiting orders to move or engage. Long-range fire did the same to men in the second echelon, usually standing with fusils shouldered. If the ground was wet, the *thud!* of solid shot embedding into turf gave some relief. Otherwise, morale plunged along with the incoming shot. Nevertheless, in most battles in the 18th century most units in most armies stood and took it. Individual courage and unit discipline was astonishing. Closer in, light mobile field batteries of three- and six-pounders interspersed with the infantry did more harm. Solid shot at level angles whipped though standing files killing and grievously maiming two or three or a half dozen or more at once. Worse, the forward guns fired case shot (canister or grape) in shotgun blasts at intimate range, shredding men and horses and wreaking companies.[17]

With lines still too far apart for infantry-on-infantry fire, a more aggressive general advanced in an approach march (*Anmarsch*) to close the distance. A linear advance was made most often by battalions in line or echelon, with each unit endeavoring to maintain contact and act as part of the whole advancing army. There was considerable incentive to keep in contact with the battalions on one's flanks, for if contact was broken or the line gapped or bulged as units advanced or retreated on different axes and at different speeds, a battalion might be cut off and attacked on its flanks by predatory cavalry waiting for just that opportunity. Or worse, the whole echelon might break if the gap between center and wings, or just between two battalions somewhere in the line, grew wide enough for enemy cavalry to rush in. Cavalry squadrons were kept behind the infantry for exactly this purpose: to attack enemy gaps during an advance or hurriedly plug them as they appeared in one's own line. Companies within each battalion similarly strove to stay in sight and physical contact while on the move, emulating miniatures of battalion tactical principles. Exceptions existed for light companies and lines of skirmishers, especially in French armies later in the century. It all worked on an HQ map or salon intellectual's etching, but in almost every battle bad dispositions by commanders or bad terrain, or simply advancing though billows of smoke or a morning mist, orphaned whole units and exposed them to enfilade and slaughter. Meanwhile, cavalry vs. cavalry mêlées on the wide wings of the battle lines were almost standard, as opposing generals adopted similar dispositions that used cavalry as flank guards.

Once the infantry lines were close enough one side fired first, according to which line of frightened and excited men could forbear receiving the first volley and which could not tolerate or endure the wait. Then both engaged with volley after volley of massed fusil fire. Firing was by platoon and company at first. To maximize morale and the shock effect of mass volley-fire, shooting might be done in volley by battalion. Usually, each battalion was arrayed in three lines and eight firing units. That was later reduced in British (and also Prussian) infantry to two lines, as unlike the French Army the British Army stressed infantry firepower from the start of the 18th century right to its finish. Each battalion would fire by platoon starting from the center out or the wings in, then repeat, so that fire was constant as men reloaded. The whole battle line kept up constant fire once it began, though with reduced discipline and effect as fear, smoke and rising casualties reduced the rate of fire of units bleeding and psychologically raw from taking as well as giving volleys.[18] The problem was that such tactics could hardly lead to a bankable victory in a field engagement; they most often led instead to a mutual, brutal and indecisive mauling.[19]

There was a direct parallel to this result in 18th-century "line of battle" naval warfare. Fleet-to-fleet fights could be sanguinary for crews but were hardly ever decisive, not even leading to heavy ship losses that would threaten a whole fleet or to turn the fortunes of war at sea. Most 18th-century sea fights ended inconclusively as one battle line broke away under cover of smoke and with the "weather gage," the advantage of assuming the windward position in relation to another fleet or ship. Running on a following wind was critical in fighting among ships of sail, as it permitted the attacker to bear down at speed on the enemy, fire broadside guns, then turn away to reload while firing rear-facing chase guns. As a result, hours or even days might be spent before a fleet action in seeking to gain the weather gage, and thereafter to keeping it or disputing it. If the fight went badly, if one side took a much harder close-in pounding than the other, the admiral with the weather gage could turn away most easily, obscured by smoke and with a modest speed advantage that was most often insurmountable by his opponent. At least, that was the way things went until Royal Navy captains disobeyed their "Fighting Instructions" from the Admiralty and broke from their own line of battle in order to "cross the T" and break the enemy's line. Admiral George Rodney probably did this unintentionally at The Saints in 1782. Horatio Nelson did it by design at Trafalgar in 1805.[20]

Back on dry land, if the first volleys from a firing line had the intended effect of ragging or dispersing the enemy's line, or if a significant gap between enemy battalions appeared for any reason, supporting or reserve cavalry went in at a gallop. Charges by infantry with naked bayonets also occurred. The decision to use bayonets was governed in part by national styles of fighting. French armies followed Saxe in emphasizing psychological shock, to be achieved by sword or lance or bayonets after a few "softening-up" volleys, or none at all. His idea of attacking with *arme blanche* was not so much to stab at as to frighten off the enemy, to break his will to stand and resist. Seldom did a fight with bayonets on both sides occur, as infantry mêlées were rare.[21] Fixed bayonets interfered with firing accuracy as they weighed the end of the barrel, pulling it down and causing the shooter to fire low or into the ground. Armies that preferred shock therefore ordered infantry to advance to bayonet range without firing, while being hit with volleys themselves. Prussian troops were not allowed to consider bayonets until they reached 30 paces from the enemy. Only then could they charge. Advancing to close distance required enormous discipline and courage and casualties, but it maximized the psychological impact of massed fusil fire by holding the first volley until absolutely lethal and accurate close range. The tactic also spoke to aristocratic officer doubts that letting ordinary men pause the advance to fire and reload would make it much harder to get them moving forward again. So sergeants barked at the corners and lines kept moving as men fell dead or wounded in the ranks.

***

MOST OF THE fighting that resumed in Europe in the 1740s was marked yet again by chronic combat without real clarity, by exhausted pauses in desultory warfare on land and at sea. Wars of imperial conflict and European affliction had already dragged on for decades, expanding around the globe as Europe's endless search for military finality pulled in faraway places and peoples of whom the fighting states knew little and cared less. More battles were lost and won, new place names etched in stony honors in ever-lengthening lists on a chapel wall or tall cenotaph in a small town's central square. Then they were forgotten. Portraits of the upper class in uniform hung in mansions, and great public murals recalled commissioned and mounted aristocrats in lace and silk. Hero tales were told to encourage daydreaming apprentice boys and farmer's sons to follow the "drum's discordant sound," to put on a king's colors and go off to foreign wars. The darker sensibility of John Scot's 1782 *The Drum* was rare:

> I hate that drum's discordant sound,
> parading round, and round, and round.
> To thoughtless youth it pleasure yields,
> and lures from cities and from fields,
> to sell their liberty for charms
> of tawdry lace, and glittering arms.
> And when Ambition's voice commands,
> to march, and fight, and fall, in foreign lands.[22]

There would be more battles to fight, more sieges to levy or lift, more gloriously odd names of unheard-of foreign places to etch in books and cold church stone with intonations of each nation's virtue and pride. More men and boys dimly recalled by those hurrying on with life. More graves to kneel on wearing widow's black, to weep over in grey hairs. Whole generations spent at war.

Yet out of this ruin and rubble of the second half of the 18th century one reputation for decision by battle emerged and held, despite the grimmer facts of his career. Frederick II (1712–1786), King of Prussia, would be called *der Grosse*: great intellect, great reformer, great captain of war, great illuminator of Reason in vital action, greatest of all Germans.[23] Whatever he did was deemed to have greatness in it. He was idealized by Prussian and German historians and by the great English historian Thomas Carlyle, who spent 12 years writing a biography of this admired foreign king.[24] Frederick was acclaimed as the sculptor of modern German history and listed by some with the most important figures in modern world history. He was praised or condemned in his day and since as an amoral champion of *Staatsräson*, the pursuit of "reason of state" above any other consideration, and for defining the interest of the state more harshly than in Richelieu's *raison d'état*. He was admired as a brilliantly innovative tactician and said to be a strategist who won even from weak positions. He was denounced as the inventor of the first and model predatory state, who supposedly sent Germany hurtling down a so-called *Sonderweg* ("special path") into shame and disaster in the 20th century, a thesis and concept rejected by historians today.[25] Or he was blessed by nationalists, called the savior of Prussia and even Germany from other predatory states that unfairly hemmed it all around. Voltaire fawned, and was not alone. Maria Theresa of Austria did not. She famously called Frederick a "godless, lawless" monarch.

In military history he is acclaimed as a genius of offensive tactics, of daring flank attacks leading to overwhelming victories. He is heir to Gustavus and precursor to Napoleon, a modern great captain and warlord worthy to stand with Alexander, Hannibal and Scipio. In an age that believed itself enlightened, that wanted its heroes to walk in the sandaled footsteps of Greece and Rome, his exploits evoked the classical battle of annihilation, clashes of glory and *fortuna* like Marathon, Gaugamela, Cannae and Zama. An irony of this reputation is that in his own military writings, kept hidden as secret papers of state during his lifetime, he emphasized military education and theory closer to standard Enlightenment rather than classical approaches. He did not admire antique battle uncritically, or much at all. He thought modern generals like himself had nothing to learn from Caesar or Scipio. He believed all useful insight into command and war in his time began with the gunpowder battle experience of Maurits and Gustavus.[26] He learned to excel within the constraints of his time because he knew he would have to fight its battles, either forced upon him or by choice. However, he was never an annihilationist or an ideologue like so many Germans who followed him. Rather than always driving his army toward decision via a clash of main forces, he understood that battles were one arrow in a general's quiver. There were others.

Another irony of his reputation for battle-seeking is that Frederick feared the inevitable carnage of 18th-century battles. This was not from care or concern for his men, for he despised his rank and file, viewing ordinary men and soldiers as fodder to his ambition for Prussia. He was not alone in that. Wellington infamously said of British troops in 1813 that they were "the scum of the earth, the mere scum of the earth. It is only wonderful that we should be able to make so much out of them." One French minister of war similarly described troops raised among his own countrymen as the "slime of the nation, and all that is useless to society."[27] For Frederick, fighting a battle was less often a direct strategy and more often an act of desperation, the last resort when his less costly political or military options failed or evaporated as he provoked conflict with more powerful or more numerous foes. Although sometimes a battle presented itself as a chance to be seized, should an opposing general make a fatal error on the march or in camp or in his dispositions. If that happened, Frederick more than most was able to take advantage of the opportunity. A third irony is that Frederick had battles thrust upon him by his foes for the same reason he is said to have sought them out. Other generals leading richer and larger armies thought they could break the under resourced Prussian Army and spank its upstart king in battle, achieving decision in the wider war with a singular blow.

As we shall see, in his first battle the Austrians humiliated him personally and nearly did break his army and ambition right at the outset. In time, however, Frederick proved that he had genuine tactical gifts. He learned how to conduct battles and campaign operations not just in theory but in fact. The gravest charge to lay against him is that, much like Louis XIV, he failed as a long-term strategist—the cardinal virtue demanded of the king of any state, but especially one determined to make and lead a war state. As we shall also see, his invasion of Silesia in 1740 was planned as a *kurtz und vives* ("short and lively") fight to quickly gain the population and revenues Prussia needed to become a Great Power. Instead, he set off wars among the European states that were unresolved for a generation, and which nearly broke him and Prussia before they ended. His gambler's thinking in 1740, and his greater gamble in 1756 that began the Seven Years' War, pulled Prussia and all the powers of Europe and their world-girdling overseas empires into long conflicts that forced Frederick into desperate defense against much bigger treasuries and armies that his small kingdom could not defeat alone.[28]

Frederick was raised in cruel austerity and trained in stern barracks virtues by his father, Frederick William II. The apparent contrast between their sensibilities could not have been greater: the father brutal in habits, narrow and mean in mind, vulgar in action, Spartan in tastes and outlook; the son scholarly, apparently gentle and refined, Athenian in sense and sensibilities. At 18, Frederick tried to run away from his oppressive father, to England. He was seized and returned to Berlin, where Frederick William threatened his heir with execution for desertion, then forced the young man to watch the beheading of his companion and possible lover, Lieutenant Hermann von Katte.[29] Well before Frederick succeeded to the throne at age 28 in 1740 and tumbled all Europe back into war, he was damaged and embittered, a prematurely cynical and complex misanthrope. He concealed this cynicism, but also revealed it, by writing *Anti-Machiavel*, a high-minded critique of the Florentine realist.[30] Voltaire edited and endorsed it, adding only a garnish of his own scorn for religion to Frederick's. *Anti-Machiavel* enshrined the young Prussian prince as the paragon of a new type of enlightened despot the Age of Reason celebrated and thought it had now produced. As king, he ruled in fact as Machiavelli would have admired, as a calculating sovereign who paid most attention to his army as the instrument of *Staatsräson*. He was a prodigy in many things: a composer of real talent, a writer of learned treatises on government and philosophy, an administrative reformer and state-builder of restless drive and perseverance. Yet there were limits to his vision. He did almost nothing to alter the hard Prussian social contract between state and Junker landowning class; he was a patron of fine arts and letters and founder of public libraries who sometimes burned books and had conventionally anti-Semitic and strongly misogynist personal views.[31] He corresponded with the literati of the age and was adored by them, holding conversations over 42 years with Voltaire. He also dressed mostly in blue velvet that in later life was always stained with dribbled Spanish snuff.

Prussia in 1740 was still small and scattered (noncontiguous), with few resources and a low population. To gain a seat in the councils of the Great Powers, Frederick needed both more subjects and tax revenue to build up his army. War was the only way, though it was an abrupt departure from the cautious and slow accumulation of hereditary claims over decades by his predecessors. He could not hope to win at slow war against the revenues and resources of Great Powers such as France or Russia or Britain, or even Austria. If war was to be this minor statesman's choice to cut geopolitical knots tying down the Gulliver of his ambition, it had best be a sharp war, starting and ending in a decisive blow to produce a fait accompli. Not a decisive battle, however. Battles were still too risky even for this hasty Prussian. He intended to force the issue at what is today called the "operational level" of war, or the conduct and movement of armies above small-unit tactics but less than the level of war-winning (or losing) strategies, such as joining a coalition or settling on defense in preference to seeking out the enemy to destroy his main forces. In his day, that came down to the command and movement of armies over the course of a summer or at most a year's campaign, with some looking ahead to setting the stage for the next year's fighting. If tactics were how he won battles, skill at movement to the right targets was how he would win campaigns. Strategy he thought less about, if at all.[32] He launched lightning campaigns to seize what he needed while avoiding battles if at all possible, then let diplomats fuss over compensation and violated promises and broken treaties. While they talked, he would build more regiments and cast more guns. He always looked for high-risk, high-payoff results from his throw of the Bismarckian iron dice, to gain in a campaign the resources and power for Prussia he wanted. He cared more for that than any salon reputation endorsed by Voltaire or praise from all the glittering and chattering classes.

Within months of ascending to the throne in May 1740, Frederick moved to steal the province of Silesia from Austria's Habsburgs in a localized and lightning-fast war. His sudden strike instead started a new round of much wider Great Power wars, beginning but not ending with the War of the Austrian Succession (1740–1748), which took its name from a crisis touched off by the death of Austrian and Holy Roman Emperor Charles VI in October 1740. Rival claimants to the throne challenged the Habsburgs because the Imperial succession in Germany was barred to women, and upon the old emperor's death most interested powers repudiated the "Pragmatic Sanction" he had negotiated to permit his daughter to succeed him. His long effort, begun upon Maria Theresa's birth in 1717, had cost diplomatic and territorial concessions that conveyed the impression that Austria was fatally weakening.[33] Thus, as Maria Theresa came into her Austrian inheritance in Vienna, she was challenged by claimants to her other inheritance in the Holy

Roman Empire (Germany). With conventional prejudice toward her gender and a nod toward her youth, it was widely assumed that she was unfit to rule. She quickly proved capable and high-spirited, marshaling for war and refusing to accept the loss of Silesia to Frederick's invading army.[34]

Contrary to contemporary views of Habsburg decline, before 1740 Austria built a standing army and reformed its scattershot political institutions to allow it to compete with the other Great Powers. Behind the comedy of diplomatic errors that comprised the Pragmatic Sanction, the mid-18th century was actually a period of strengthening of the Habsburg Empire and Austria. Major reforms militarized the state, enabling it to compete with Prussia in Germany and Russia in Poland. Like those rivals, Austria had lingering medieval privileges still in place and kept old regional structures and allegiances that hampered the concentration and exercise of central political authority on the French or British models. Still, it faced rebellion in Hungary and won. It faced war on several frontiers and held its own. It pushed back the Ottoman threat to Vienna and across the Balkans in a series of wars in the first half of the 18th century, and nearly defeated Prussia during the second half.[35] It succumbed only temporarily to invading armies led by Napoleon in the early 19th century, to reemerge as a leading Great Power and member of the winning coalition that defeated France and drove Napoleon into permanent exile.[36] It came through the 19th century while surviving revolution and partial partition, and defeat by Prussia in 1866. It reached the 20th century in a state of perpetual internal crisis, to expire along with several other empires at the end of, and because of, World War I. Austria's reputation and many misfortunes before that endgame spoke to core internal weaknesses, but its survival for over two centuries after 1700 also showed that empires can successfully decline for a very long time.

Even so, it was the perception of Maria Theresa's and Austria's weakness in 1740 that tempted other powers to defy Habsburg claims in Germany and Frederick to seize the rich province of Silesia. She then proved to be his greatest enemy for 40 years, until her death in 1780. She called Frederick "that wicked man," but to counter him she mimicked his practices, including his habits of war and annexations (hers came from Poland). "Old Fritz," as Frederick was nearly universally known in his old age, said of Maria Theresa: "She is always weeping and always annexing." Another time he said of her, in comparison to himself and Catherine the Great of Russia as well-known predators: "Catherine and I are simply brigands; but I wonder how the Queen-Empress manages to square with her confessor."[37] Her ambivalence about war as policy and about double-dealing as a necessary instrument of *Staatsräson* was hard for him to understand. He broke treaties and made war without regret or tears.

Within a year France joined Prussia in the so-called First Silesian War. Britain, Hanover, Saxony and smaller German states of the Holy Roman Empire were provoked or coerced to back Austria. Maria Theresa ceded Silesia for just half a summer in 1742, but then Prussia and Austria immediately fought the Second Silesian War of 1742–1744. On the larger European stage, Frederick's aggression reopened festering disputes everywhere as other conflicts merged into the issue of the Austrian succession. Soon, Austria and Britain were allied with the Netherlands and the smaller German states to fight France, Prussia, Bavaria and Spain.[38] Sweden fought Russia in the Baltic from 1741 to 1743, with every other state watching the Pomeranian front and noting the rising reach and military power of the tsars.[39] France and Britain reengaged their dormant world conflict, sending convoyed merchants and fleets to carry armies and war to North America, the West Indies, the Mediterranean and contested enclaves in India.

Voltaire sneered in *Candide* that the powers "are fighting over a few acres of snow on the borders of Canada."[40] Maybe, but also for fish, furs and timber, straight tall trees that could no longer be found in the exhausted forests of Europe, to make composite masts for the big First-rates, the largest class of men-of-war battleships. And more masts and timbers to build more big ships of fighting sail, the Second- and Third- and Fourth-rates; and lots of Fifths and Sixths to fill out the battle lines; and swarms of frigates to scout and escort them, and to make fast commerce raids against distant ports and trade routes. They fought in the snow also for the prestige of kings and the vanities of emergent nations. As Voltaire knew well, just a little south they fought also for richer lands and river navigation into the interior of a brave new continent, a new found land, and broad trades in molasses, rum, sugar and slaves. There was a second continent below that one, and they fought there, too. As a chained and twice amputated slave in Suriname said to Candide: "It is the custom here . . . and it is at this expense that you eat sugar in Europe."[41]

Was blood splashed onto snow any different from that greasing the green grass at Fontenoy in 1745, a battle Voltaire fawned over to please his king and win a place at court? Saxe and Louis XV came out from their siege of Tournai to meet the Duke of Cumberland and left 21,000 geometric dead in neat rows where they fell, face down in the vainglory of kings. Also in 1745, Bonnie Prince Charlie landed in Scotland and a panicky Parliament recalled its armies from Flanders. The Jacobite Rebellion scoured the north, until a highland charge broke against lines of redcoat fusils at Culloden Moor

(April 16, 1746), where Cumberland allowed a sheering and slaughter of wounded and prisoner Scots, and hard repression of suspected Jacobites after that. The dead at Culloden included men of the *Royal Écossais*, a regiment come from France where it served Voltaire's king in nearby wars and battles the *philosophe* better approved. Yet blood scattered over a few acres of heather hardly seems different from English, French, Irish and Scottish blood spilled on Canadian snow.

Fighting in renewed rounds of war in Europe paused with the Peace of Aix-la Chapelle in 1748, an armed truce masked as peace. Other than Prussia, which kept Silesia, no major power was satisfied with the settlement. They only apprehended war, pausing to reassess and to refill drained treasuries. Fighting did not stop even then between the French and British in India or along the wild frontiers of America, just because far-off kings finally settled the Austrian succession, which went to Maria Theresa after all. Frederick consolidated Silesia into his war-state, but he knew the fight was not over. Austria and Spain nursed deep grudges, as did most other powers, all left wounded or unrequited in some way by the peace. They all desired and planned for more war, pausing only to reassess and to refill drained treasuries, raise new battalions and squadrons, cast hundreds more cannons and lay down keels of mighty warships. Fighting thus resumed on a greater scale in the Seven Years' War, a more far-flung and destructive round of conflict that broke out in 1756 and was not resolved until 1763.

The new war also arose from Frederick's original 1740 aggression, because Maria Theresa refused to accept the loss of Silesia and instead changed centuries of Habsburg policy to try to get it back. In 1756 she secretly allied with Russia and France, Austria's new enemy in the east and old enemy in the west. Her initiation of what is sometimes called the "diplomatic revolution" of 1756 advanced a central war aim to crush "that wicked man" and dismember Prussia itself. Frederick turned in desperation to Britain, now bereft of its old Austrian flanking ally against France but a rising global power with unmatched wealth and reach. This realignment of all the old alliances lasted throughout the Seven Years' War, and beyond.[42] Frederick had smashed apart a hornet's nest with his aggressive ambition and grab for Silesia. Europe was never the same.

Prussia was a poor state, but Frederick had still led the fourth largest army in Europe (83,000 troops) into the maelstrom of war in 1740. The men of the Prussian Army were schooled in "Frederickian drill," built atop the tough style, regulations and severe punishments of his father and grandfather. It was imitated in other lands, though it was always less draconian outside Prussia.

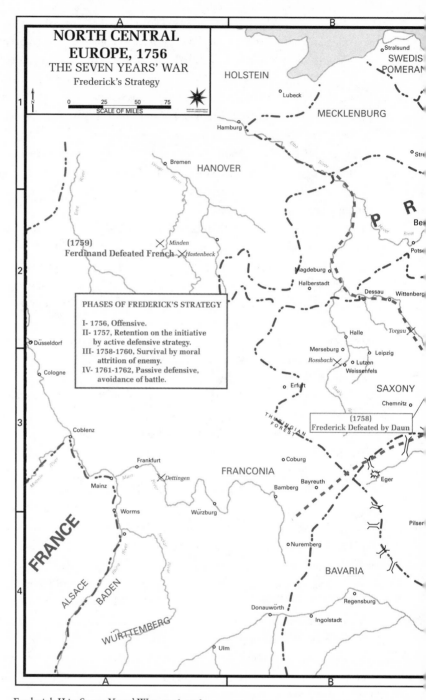

Frederick II in Seven Years' War, 1756–1763.

Courtesy of the Department of History, United States Military Academy at West Point.

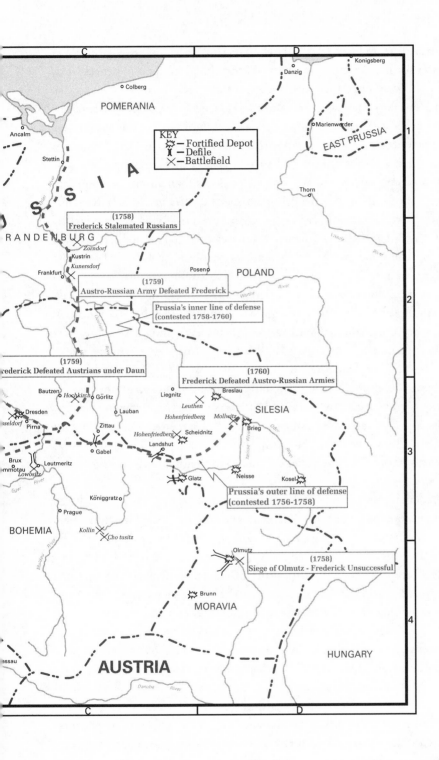

Frederick further maximized infantry firepower by compressing his lines of fusiliers so that Prussian lines were shorter than any opposing enemy. His army had been superbly trained and supremely disciplined in 1740, more so than a few years later, when casualties and green replacements were felt as he grew weaker and his enemies stronger with each campaign. His troops were more practiced on the firing range than any others except British redcoats. They loaded and shot fusils in volleys four to five times per minute, firing by platoon or company. Prussians were also quicker than anyone moving from column into line in their initial deployment on the battlefield. They maneuvered precisely, uniquely practicing and executing Frederick's famously daring "oblique orders," the maneuver most closely attached to his reputation for a superior warcraft.[43] This trademark tactic refused (held back) from close engagement a weakened wing of the battle line, using detached troops from its second echelon to conduct a wheeling march around the far enemy flank. The movement worked often enough to be notable, and to become the signature of his reputation for subtle tactical genius, then and afterward. Robert Citino, preeminent scholar of a "German way of war" of movement that is often traced from Frederick down through World War II, argues that his approach to fighting was actually more basic and brutal than finesse: "He usually saw one path to victory, and that was fixing the enemy in place ... to give himself a favorable position for the attack, and then smashing it with an overwhelming blow from an unexpected direction."[44] What mattered was not elegance or brilliance. What mattered was that it worked, until it didn't anymore.

Frederick was a great general in his era, probably the greatest. As with Gustavus, however, much of his later success in battle rested not on tactical genius but on prewar preparation. His and his predecessors' devotion to the Prussian Army gave it advanced skills that translated into real advantages in battle—except for the Prussian cavalry, which he badly neglected until the war started, costing him an early defeat. The armies facing each other from 1740 deployed nearly the same weapons systems and had similar fighting habits and doctrine (with the key variation of whether to emphasize infantry shock or firepower in attack). Skills learned prewar and in later training, the mental and moral discipline of the troops, and command and control (generalship) could make a critical difference at the margins in battle. The question remained whether Prussia's early advantage would be enough to overcome the dominance of defensive firepower and the greater resources of its enemies.

Frederick's tactics indeed surprised opponents and gained him successes. As time wore on, however, and the Prussian Army's early advantages wore out, he would be forced to reduce his preference for infantry shock in the French manner. High casualties ultimately forced him to adopt more defensive, artillery-reliant formations and tactics. That slowed his armies down while on campaign and between battles by adding many more caissons and ammunition wagons to an already heavy artillery train, reducing his command flexibility and making Prussian armies march and fight more like all the others. By then, his enemies had far more men and guns and money, and at least some opposing generals had learned from their experience of defeat by Frederick and his novel tactics. His enemies learned to anticipate and counter his oblique movements until fresh victories became elusive, then rare, then desperate and distant. That put his fate and Prussia's in hands other than his own. As we shall see, a similar pattern attended Napoleon's career, as French armies declined in skill and other superiorities after 1809 and opposing armies ascended in professional and combat ability and looked and fought more like the French, then outfought and defeated France. Frederick barely escaped the same fate, and far more by diplomatic luck than his vaunted warcraft and reputed military genius.

Frederick broke the long peace in Europe in order to gain Silesia, and thereby force elevation of Prussia from the second to the first rank of powers in Europe. Yet he could never hope to win unaided the bigger wars he started, which meant he must push all Europe into war, then seek to maneuver through the wreckage.[45] It was the short-war illusion as well as arrogance that told him his special talents and unique Prussian Army could shorten such long odds, and win quickly any war he began. This delusion would lead Frederick, as it led Louis XIV before him and others to follow in his wake, into long wars and near-calamitous defeat. For a rough strategic and military balance among the rotating Great Powers still governed, and dictated that a planned short and limited war for limited aims would go long and general instead. Superior tactics and operations were never enough, given the strategic imbalance and military odds against Prussia. That it and Frederick survived and even expanded by the end of his reign therefore impressed observers then and afterward as a mark of his genius for war and statecraft. In fact, even Frederick knew better. Famously agnostic, he would nevertheless call an unexpected political salvation from Moscow, that collapsed the anti-Prussian coalition on the brink of his contemplated suicide and occupation and dismemberment of Prussia by his enemies, the "Miracle of the House of Brandenburg."

***

WITH NO FORMAL declaration of war issued to undercut tactical surprise, the Prussian Army crossed the snowy border into Silesia on December 16, 1740. Austrian defenders fell back as the Prussians advanced to take possession of towns and countryside and lay siege to fortresses at Glogau, Brieg and Neisse. Frederick had acquired his new province seemingly at little cost, but the Austrians spent the rest of the winter reorganizing their armies for a spring offensive to take Silesia back. Before the spring of 1741 fully thawed the ground, 19,000 Habsburg troops came out to fight, led by Field Marshal Wilhelm Neipperg. He marched well, cutting off Frederick's lines of retreat and supply and forcing him to fight. Frederick's first test came at Mollwitz on April 10, not because he chose to fight but because the enemy compelled him to accept combat. Frederick wrote: "Battles decide the fate of a nation."[46] Yet real war was different from the Berlin parade ground or annual field practicing he was used to overseeing. For the first time, he led troops into an actual fight against a skilled enemy commander. Although on the morning he achieved march surprise and arrived undetected at the Austrian camp, he squandered that advantage by tardy and inept initial dispositions of his army. He thus failed in his first command before any fusil shots or slashing saber cuts were ever made.

As the Austrians recovered from surprise at his sudden appearance outside their camp, Frederick too slowly set his cavalry in traditional style as flank guards on either wing. The rest of his deployment was also badly made. He left nine regiments orphaned from the main battle line and failed to anchor his right flank against defensible abutting terrain, leaving it "in the air," or open on one flank, and hence subject to cavalry attack and turning off the line. That is exactly what Neipperg tried in the opening move of the battle. Frederick's 21,600 men were hit on the hanging right by an aggressive Habsburg cavalry assault. The Prussian horse was outnumbered 8,000 to 4,000 on the field as a whole, and comparably on the assaulted flank. Weaker in numbers, poorly trained and much neglected by Frederick before the war, the Prussian cavalry broke in the face of attack by 4,500 Habsburg riders and fled en masse toward Hermsdorf. In the first minutes of his first battle, it looked like Frederick had lost the fight and might soon lose the rest of the army.[47]

Worse, he ran away, galloping off while his thin blue lines of infantry stood in the field where he left them. He did not run from cowardice. His courage cannot be doubted since at Mollwitz, and in several later fights, he overly exposed himself to musket or cannon fire and several times was nearly killed. He fled instead to escape capture by fast-closing Austrian hussars, an outcome which would have cost him everything before his career as king had really begun. He would have been delivered to Vienna and perhaps held there, just as Charles XII was held for five years in Constantinople after losing to Peter the Great at Poltava. After his invasion of Silesia, would anyone blame Maria Theresa for that? Instead, the superb Prussian infantry rallied without their king to watch them. Double lines advanced with exceptional discipline, turned right and fired into the now exposed flank of the Austrian cavalry. The rapid fusil fire made slaughter of Austrians still milling around dead and dying Prussian horsemen. The volleys continued until the Prussians started to run out of powder and shot, forcing them to scavenge from nearby wounded and dead. A second Austrian charge on the left flank failed after an initial breakthrough, when it met more hailing fusil fire. Infantry met infantry at the center, pushing the Austrians off the field and into retreat to the fortress of Neisse. Frederick lost nearly a quarter of his field army at Mollwitz (4,659 to 4,551 Austrians), but he learned two big things: he needed to improve his own command skills and he needed to reform his cavalry. He was also reinforced in his belief that he must win fast campaigns or lose at war.

He reorganized his cavalry, trying to raise it to the standard of the now proven infantry. He added more light cavalry hussars, to gain mobility. He needed his cavalry to do its main and traditional job of protecting his line infantry's flanks in battle, but he was also thinking about making true and innovative combined arms attacks with infantry and cavalry supported by light artillery. More importantly, he gained an immensely powerful ally that summer in Louis XV, who decided to support Prussia against France's old enemy the Habsburgs. A diplomatic upheaval to be initiated by Maria Theresa in 1756 to help her win back Silesia and destroy Prussia with French and Russian military aid still lay years in the future. However, already Prussia was noticed and Frederick put on notice: he was playing now in the great game of power politics. It meant his war with Austria would grow larger and longer, and more demanding of his skills and wearing of Prussia's scant economic and manpower resources.

After Mollwitz, Frederick was forced to spend troops on defense of his supplies, as Austria resorted to what was then called *petite guerre* ("little war") by the French and *kleine Krieg* by Germans. *Petite guerre* distinguished small-scale harassment and attacks by irregulars from grand-scale sieges and battles, or *grande guerre*. In little war, attacks were made on Prussian supply columns, on farms and foragers and couriers, by irregular Habsburg troops usually outfitted as light mounted infantry. They were either local partisans in mufti recruited from Silesia and in Germany or costumed *Grenzer* brought up from the Balkans. They carried out a wearing campaign of ambush and hit-and-run assaults that harried and eroded the occupiers all that winter.[48] This was a style of irregular warfare long practiced by Habsburg armies in the *Militärgrenze* ("military frontier"), a long and violent, semi-fortified mountain border zone with the Ottoman Empire.[49] Partisan warfare of this kind was actually fairly common across Europe. Kingdoms from Hungary to France kept several hundred to a few thousand partisans in border garrisons or armed villages, paying them a percentage of what they looted. They scouted and foraged, attacked the other side's foragers, and killed or ransomed stragglers. They collected forced contributions in money and supplies, took hostages and killed any not ransomed as demanded, made fast raids ("courses") into enemy rear areas, burned crops and villages, harassed garrisons, carried out mountain pass ambushes, and dispensed to local civilians brutal punishments and reprisals for any losses. Soldiers of *petite guerre* were especially skilled at stealth and deception. They were highly mobile, almost always riding to battle as dragoons, but sometimes double-riding with light cavalry hussars. Croat partisans and *Grenzer* thus did real harm to Frederick's troops and supply system, until his near-starving army was forced to retreat without forcing the decision by battle that he both wanted and needed.[50]

When spring came his retrained cavalry helped him win the war's second set-piece battle, at Chotusitz (Czaslau) on May 17, 1742. The situation was fluid as terms were agreed at Breslau on June 11, ending the First Silesian War with a temporary cession of that province to Prussia. The treaty was merely a truce. Neither Vienna nor Berlin thought the fight was over. Frederick's win-fast gambit therefore failed. This highly aggressive field commander had still not shown either any tactical or operational skill that exceeded that of his own generals, let alone any that might frighten a more numerous and well-led enemy. To his credit, he agreed that his performance was a major problem. So he undertook to relearn his craft and remake the Prussian Army to suit his personal command style, to make it the most aggressive in Europe. He spent weeks working on battle tactics, experimenting with light field artillery in combined arms attacks along with cavalry and infantry. The main trick he came up with would become famous as his oblique order: marching the second echelon of infantry from behind one flank, usually screened by terrain, leaving it undermanned and vulnerable but timing the move to achieve an overweighted and therefore overwhelming attack on the other side. Flanking was always his goal, by marching or in battle. This was opposite to every Marlborough battle plan that looked to attack the wings as a means of preparing the enemy center to receive the killing blow. Frederick instead overweighted infantry on one flank to march to the enemy's opposite flank, moving (in neat theory and on maps, at least) at an inclined angle across the battlefield and in echelon. Sometimes he moved infantry behind a screen of cavalry or, even better, blocked from view by high ground. Once or twice he did it in full view of the enemy.

Now Frederick did something else typical of his war-making. With ink hardly dry on the Peace of Breslau, he broke the truce by invading Bohemia in August, starting the Second Silesian War. Widely separated by entire provinces, he marched three columns over the border before reconcentrating outside Prague in early September. (Napoleon admired, copied and ultimately perfected this method of rapid movement by his corps before concentrating for battle. Helmut von Moltke tried it, too, only moving with separate armies rather than corps in invasions of Bohemia in 1866 and France in 1870.) When the French failed to draw off sufficient Austrian troops in the west as Frederick hoped, a large Habsburg force moved against the Prussians in Bohemia. He gave up Prague and retreated into Silesia, having gained nothing even as Saxony changed sides, taking 17,000 troops out of his order of battle and adding them to the list of his enemies. Only 40,000 Prussians made it back out of 66,000 who invaded. Half the survivors died over the following winter.[51] Exposed by this poorly managed campaign, and repeatedly outmaneuvered, Frederick worked all winter to learn from his having fought badly how to fight better. In the spring, he was finally ready to offer battle, to try to achieve in a day what he failed to gain in summers of maneuvering and winters of occupation. He wanted to win, and win decisively.

He sent his agents to the Austrians to spread disinformation that his army's morale was failing, hoping to entice them to move out of their garrisons and fortresses to meet him in the field. It worked: they and the Saxons came out looking for him, seeking to do battle. Frederick marched to engage them with a springtime army of 59,000. The Allies were confident, too, for they also had 59,000 men, coming down through the mountain passes to beat the supposedly demoralized Prussians. Frederick broke camp at night to force march to the foot of one pass, hoping to flank the arriving Austrians. He missed their arrival, so the armies met and fought instead at Hohenfriedeberg on June 4, 1745, barely a month after destruction of the redcoat columns and other Allied troops by Marshal Saxe at Fontenoy. Frederick attacked with his much-improved cavalry, which defeated an Austrian cavalry attack one-third again as large. He advanced his always excellent infantry next, with light artillery in forward support. Fighting swirled around three small towns. Casualties mounted.

Marlborough always attempted the death blow into a weakened center, after feints in force on the flanks to thin the fatal attack point by drawing wide the enemy's reserves. Frederick instead always tried to get around his enemy's flank. While it worked at other times, it did not work so well this day. Gaps opened as the angled move was made, and a still inexperienced commander in Frederick and unpracticed Prussian Army failed to complete the special maneuver. However, Prussian soldiers made up in discipline what their general still lacked in command skill and the army as a whole lacked in battle experience. The infantry on both sides stood and matched the other's terrible volleys, tearing front ranks apart. Prussian dragoons and light cavalry, mainly hussars, smashed one Austrian wing with a massed charge. Twenty infantry battalions were broken and scattered and 2,500 Habsburg prisoners taken, for Prussian losses of 96 men.[52] One more fight came at Soor (September 30, 1745), but after that everyone felt the fiscal burden of keeping large armies in the field so long. On Christmas Day, 1745, the Peace of Dresden was signed by exhausted belligerents, ending the first Austro-Prussian war. It left most of Silesia still in Frederick's hands. Maria Theresa signed the treaty but smoldered with thoughts of vengeance against the wicked man in Berlin who stole her rich province. Prussia was out of the war for now, though Austro-French and Anglo-French fighting in the much bigger war Frederick had started lasted to 1748.

Continued fighting elsewhere in Europe and overseas was a sign that Frederick had stirred things among the Great Powers far beyond his control, and possibly past Prussia's ability to survive.[53] Yet he had won his fame and general's reputation. He was seen as the paragon of the well-ordered Enlightenment general, his Prussian Army as nearing perfection in the practice of horse-and-musket war. His generalship was admired and his central role in Prussia's success acknowledged, but it was the Prussian Army's training and professionalism that had gained victory. Its use of compressed fusilier lines, drill and more rapid volley-fire, and above all its discipline won through. The bad news was that all those things were replicable, learnable skills and not talents.[54] And that meant something of the successful Prussian system was soon adopted by rivals, insofar as they could fit it inside their own military cultures. Other powers had more resources, too, bigger revenue streams and larger populations from which to draw replacements and recruits. Frederick turned to foreigners to fill out his regiments and squadrons as he ran out of eligible Prussians, but he needed money for that, too. Silesia was not enough. Clearly, if Prussia was going to take the next step up the Great Power ladder he was going to have to start another war one day. He must try to steal another province. The Electorate of Saxony, richest land in Central Europe and just below his borders, would do nicely. From 1756, his foragers and armies would move in and bleed Saxony white.

Arguably, the interregnum between the War of the Austrian Succession and the Seven Years' War, which Frederick also started, was his time of real glory, the time of *der Grosse* in other things than war. For the moment, war had more than paid for itself. It gave him personal prestige for the ages, and it secured Silesia. Yet all through the years of peace he knew he was not done with defending his recent conquest, and longed to try to seize more territory and power to elevate his state into the first rank. He wondered whether he could use decisive battle to make up for Prussia's vulnerabilities in army size and strategic shallowness, which his aggression had exposed for all to see. He spent the next years practicing his oblique-order tactic, perfecting it for battles yet to fight. However, he was not yet fixated on seeking battles as his first choice. He was preparing for whatever shape campaigns might take, including culmination in field battle. He expected to join a battle at some point, by his own choice or his enemy's, but he was not yet wedded as one day he would be to the idea of obliteration of his enemies in a single fight. His greatness at war, such as it was, never lay in the oblique order or battle-seeking per se. It lay in his willingness to take advantage of whatever circumstance war at the operational level, over the course of a campaign, offered: battle if useful, maneuver and exhaustion of enemies whenever possible, defensive or offensive attrition if unavoidable.

Attrition, always Frederick's least favored option and weaker Prussia's worst chance, was indeed going to be unavoidable. Frederick knew that his enemies were legion, but was as yet unaware that he had set in motion decades of war by attacking Austria in 1740. Prosperity and contented peace were to be overthrown for a generation in favor of sieges, marches, countermarches, burnings, invasions and mutual blockades. Before it was over, he would nearly lose everything: his power and his kingdom, as his decisions led to fiscal, military and moral exhaustion of Prussia and most of Europe. He had started it all, willfully. Louis XIV had not known he was embarking on 29 years of war either, when he first pushed his armies to reach the "natural frontiers" of France, and in so doing violated the actual frontiers of his neighbors. In each case, short-war delusion was profoundly costly for the aggressor monarch and nation and tragic for millions more.

***

PRUSSIA BEFORE THE start of the Seven Years' War was a power with an army grown too big to be ignored by the other Great Powers, but was still far too weak to stand on its own. Frederick succeeded in elevating it to the vulnerable cusp of greatness, to attention as a known threat and a target for Habsburg vengeance and Great Power intervention. Austria refused to stop trying to retrieve Silesia, even when it signed the province over to Prussia a second time. Soon it would send more and larger armies against Frederick and into Prussia itself. Peacetime meant only that Maria Theresa and the Habsburg allies were training fresh armies. He knew that, and so spent those years retraining his own. What he did not know was that she planned a stunning surprise to shake all Europe, precipitating a diplomatic revolution in 1756. She would make an alliance of Austria with its old enemy France and with rising Russia. She would ring isolated Prussia with other strong monarch's armies in addition to her own before she struck. She was a worthy enemy.

Frederick was surrounded by enemies. Some arose from Prussia's geographical position, others in direct reaction to his policies since 1740 and the threat he posed to do more. Others partook of brilliantly revanchist diplomacy by Vienna, Maria Theresa's coming diplomatic revolution rooted in revenge and desire for return of her stolen province. As always, in peacetime Frederick readied for war, the main driver of his domestic administrative reforms as well as his foreign policy. If war came one border at a time, he might survive. If it came all at once, Prussia was too weak to stand alone. Each season, the problem of Prussia occupying the central position in the midst of enemies would keep him marching back and forth to block new threats almost constantly. Therein lay a part of Frederick's military greatness, for during the Seven Years' War he would use Prussia's shorter interior lines of movement and supply to fight off widely spaced enemies one by one. It was a skilled operational adaptation, but to a political and strategic problem he caused in the first place with a diplomacy of repeated deceit and annexations. Militarily, it was inspired. Yet in the end it was diminishing, arguably not worth the bones of one grenadier let alone hundreds of thousands of wasted Prussian lives.[55]

After another naked aggression to gain in Saxony the resources and people he wanted to stay at the Great Power table, and needed to hold on through a much greater war, Frederick would go over to strategic defense. Like the Sun King after 1700, Old Fritz would seek in his later years only to keep what he took by force in his youth, after beginning what would amount to the first worldwide war of the modern era. He started it coldly and deliberately, for

Staatsräson. Characteristically, he struck first and without warning, invading Saxony to secure that territory to his treasury, gain a near monopoly control of commerce on the Elbe and make one less border to defend. Later, he sought to transfer all blame for starting the Seven Years' War onto his enemies, pleading that his own motives were solely defensive, pointing cynically to other powers fighting over that million acres of snow in North America as the true trigger and the place the war had started, in a skirmish around Lake Erie. It was a calculated lie, technically correct and wholly misleading.[56] He readied the Prussian Army for years, planned the subterfuge, and started the war in Europe when he saw the moment ripe with other conflicts that might mask his latest aggression. He did so knowing that his second unprovoked aggression must take place inside a much larger conflict, the worldwide struggle between France and Britain. Just for the aggrandizement of another stolen province to Prussia, he set the powers at each other's throats and deliberately wrecked the general peace.

The Lisbon earthquake killed anywhere from 60,000 to 100,000 innocents in 1755. It thus badly shook Enlightenment confidence and assumptions that Nature was orderly and benign. The Seven Years' War that broke out the next year would shake the *philosophes* and emergent nations of Europe even more. For it was a ferocious worldwide conflict with a global maritime dimension not seen hitherto except as precursor. Fighting was dispersed from the Baltic to Spain, from West Africa to the West Indies, from Guyana to North America, from the Philippines to the South Seas, from the Carnatic to Bengal. Logistics and finance played critical roles in deciding the outcome, perhaps even the decisive roles. Much of the key history of the war simply did not take place on its battlefields or in naval fights on the high seas, but inside the counting rooms of great trading houses, in secret intrigues of political salons and on the pages of the political press, in parliaments and in the council chambers and bedchambers of prime ministers and monarchs.[57] Domestic politics in the belligerent nations decided its outcome as much as key battles. Regular armies fought each other but also irregular partisans. Investments in both senses, physical and financial, were again paramount in its outcome as cities and whole provinces and countries came under siege of one form or another.

Before it ended, Frederick's gambit cost Prussia alone nearly 400,000 of its 4 million subjects and saw the devastation of its lands and wealth. Habsburg lands similarly suffered, as Bohemia and Moravia were invaded by Prussia. Together, the armies lost 500,000 killed in combat and at least as many again wounded.[58] Civilian losses were high but less well counted, and so they remain largely unknown. This was no *Kabinettskriege* (cabinet war) waged among royal courts and cabinet governments, employing minimal means to secure limited objectives. All countries around Prussia were tempted in, or pulled in. Even Sweden, which was unable for decades to sustain the military spending necessary to play at high stakes in the European system, jumped into the war. Its leaders, too, thought they could win swiftly and change the power calculus of decline in a short, sharp fight. Instead, Sweden would be gravely burdened as fighting in the Baltic turned into grinding low-intensity combat in Pomerania, which spilled over into Central Europe and Germany.[59]

Frederick struck first, of course. He sent armies snaking into Saxony and Bohemia but barely defeated an Austrian army in a bloody fight at Lobositz (October 1, 1756), where he personally mistook the enemy main body for the rearguard and blundered into battle. Austria had prepared for war, too, reforming its army and recruitment system to make long-war fighting possible. It was a state much less centralized than others but was readier to fight than Frederick realized.[60] After months back in winter quarters, in the spring of 1757 he sent 115,000 men into Bohemia from bases in Saxony and Silesia. As was now his established operational practice, four corps marched in widely separated columns over 200 miles to fight outside Prague (May 6). Then he marched 35,000 troops away from the city to fight an Austrian relief army of 50,000 at Kolin (June 18). He was badly beaten, leaving thousands of dead behind as he retreated out of Bohemia. It was a major defeat and a huge blow to an until then unblemished reputation for invincibility he should not have had, given what happened at Mollwitz and Lobositz. Already, the enemy was adjusting to his battle tactics. At Prague, his effort at an angled flank march met Austrian redeployments and was blunted. He did it again at Kolin, where the Prussian oblique movement broke down, facing greater numbers of enemy infantry and guns.[61] Given years of rearmament and preparation, the scale of casualties already dwarfed those in the first Austrian war: 24,000 Habsburg troops and 18,000 Prussians at Prague alone. More death was on the way.

As the Prussian Army recovered slowly from two maulings, two more Allied armies marched east together to fight Frederick. The larger one was French. The smaller contingent was the *Reichsarmee* or "Imperial Army of Execution," a collage of over 200 separate, and also small and unruly, contingents from the Holy Roman Empire. Many of its men were about to be lost at Rossbach (November 5, 1757), largely through the fault of quarrelsome and incompetent generals on their own side as well as Frederick's skill in seizing advantage from luck. Together, the Allied armies initially numbered 60,000. The *Reichsarmee* was polyglot, but so were most armies, especially coalition armies and even national ones like the French and Prussian. Diverse ethnicity was not the problem with the Allied armies. The problem was that, like the Franco-Bavarian armies at Blenheim, the combined force was a two-headed creature of joint but uncooperative command. Its generals could not even agree whether to contend with the Prussians by maneuver or seek out battle. Frederick had just 25,000 men, but at least he was in charge.

As he readied to fight, a courier brought news that an Austrian cavalry raid-in-force had battered through the city gates into Berlin (October 16), departing with 200,000 silver thalers from his treasury. Frederick lurched toward his capital, but turned around to offer battle when the Allies made a mistake in maneuvering and split their force. Now he faced only 41,000 combined enemy with his 22,000 Prussians.[62] Like Marlborough and Prince Eugene at Blenheim, Frederick personally reconnoitered before Rossbach. He found the enemy camped with a flank badly exposed and decided to attack. He advanced on November 4, to find the exposed flank repaired with a solid set of field fortifications. It looked as if a classic set-piece battle would ensue the next day as the armies stood in echeloned battle lines 2.5 miles apart. Regimental flags fluttered, drums beat, horses stamped and whinnied, sergeants shouted and generals paced, and nothing happened.

The Allies instead decided to disengage in order to make a wheel flanking move around Frederick's known position. They started in late-morning and planned to march most of the day on November 5, to catch him in poor position when they completed the maneuver either late that day or in time to open the battle on the morning of November 6. It was a too-leisurely movement, incompetently executed. Frederick learned that the Allied armies were still marching in column and took advantage of this remarkable opportunity to strike a lethal blow. It was another example of his exceptional *coup d'oeil*, the natural ability of a great commander to see and read a battlefield's terrain and all its possibilities, where other men struggle to see more than hills and fields and woods and therefore plonk down units willy-nilly or unimaginatively. He was also audacious. Taking the moment by the muzzle, he sent his cavalry wheeling around the head of an unwary approaching column, his squadrons completely screened by two low hills. It was a rare chance to catch an enemy on the march and he made the most of it.[63]

This was not just another example of his repeated tactic of the oblique order. Seizing the moment with his cavalry and taking advantage of terrain were the two keys to the Battle of Rossbach. Not every general could have done this, or had the freedom of authority to risk it. The Prussian cavalry, led by youthful General Friedrich Wilhelm von Seydlitz, moved fast with

38 squadrons around the low hills. When the rest of the Prussian Army also passed out of sight, the watching Allied generals assumed it was retreating in face of their greater strength, and continued to march in column. Prussian cavalry completed the encirclement without being seen or molested. The cantering squadrons reached around both the hills and the Austrians and suddenly appeared. The opposing generals were stunned to see seven regiments of Prussian horse then break into a fierce charge in echelons of 15 squadrons, followed by 18 more. Their own cavalry was caught in march column, infantry strung out behind, the big guns even farther behind them.[64] On came the Prussian squadrons, thundering echelons at full gallop with lances down or sabers out. A crashing, slashing, steel-tipped mêlée ensued, with hand-to-hand fighting with sabers and pistols too. The whole Allied cavalry fled the front of the collapsing column and skedaddled off the roads. Squadrons fled right though the infantry, galloping helter-skelter cross-country away from the fight and pursuit.

Meanwhile, Prussian infantry crested the hills in battle echelon, 15,000 men appearing in front of bewildered Allied troops and their befuddled commanders. Three columns of French infantry approached, bravely closing to intimate range. Both sides held fire until the distance between them was just 20 paces. The Prussians were in perfect flanking position and already deployed in line. Drummers beat frantically trying to get the confused French into ordered lines, with shooting to commence when the drums stopped. The advancing French columns were still scrambling to mirror the Prussian firing line dispositions but too surprised and congested to do so in time to be able to match volley for volley. When the Prussian line opened fire it furrowed all three columns, slaughtering whole French battalions at the head of the Allied army. More French infantry bravely advanced into the fusil hail, but the Prussians extended their line to form a V-shaped firing wedge and poured in musket balls from two sides. Volley after volley shot and tore the French from either side, all along the V. Next came case shot from artillery on the hills, then a massed cavalry charge, and it was all over except the carnage.

The Allies lost 72 cannon, or nearly all their guns, as their broken infantry columns, long since abandoned by fleeing Allied cavalry, collapsed into a river of overflowing woe, tumbling backward and over the sides of a road damned by Prussian echelons pouring in volley fire, pounded also by merciless cannon on the heights. Battalion crashed into battalion as the rearward flight began, folding the whole army in segments like a caterpillar being slowly crushed from the head. The Allies lost over 5,000 killed and wounded and another 5,000 who threw down their weapons and surrendered. Days later, 10,000 discarded muskets were dredged from a nearby river. Prussian losses were 169 dead and 379 wounded. Robert Citino concludes: "It was unique, the easiest and most complete victory in Frederick's career. It had taken just ninety minutes."[65]

The easiest victory, but not his greatest. That description is usually reserved for Leuthen in Silesia, where the Austrians were making real gains in retaking the province from Frederick's garrisons, driving the Prussians he left there back across the Oder River. Frederick crossed the border on November 28 after a hard, early-winter march of 140 miles through mud and the first snows. At this point he faced a serious morale problem among retreating, defeated troops. So he shrewdly if cynically shed his normal royal aloofness and loathing of his own men and sat and talked with them in their camp, as if he was concerned for them and not just their fighting fit. Then, in a famous war council held on December 3, he told his top commanders and their staff officers that the coming battle must mean his victory or their deaths, and possibly also his own. When the cold raw day came on December 5, he and just 35,000 Prussians faced 65,000 entrenched Austrians and Imperials. The Prussians were also outgunned 235 to just 78 cannon. He attacked. It was that or lose Silesia, at least over the coming winter but perhaps for good.

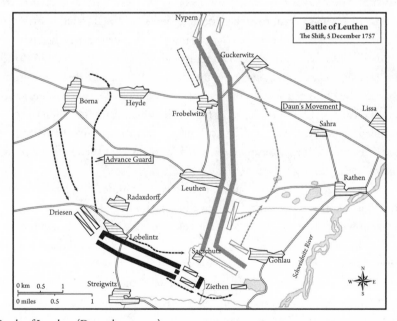

Battle of Leuthen (December 5, 1757).
Courtesy of the Department of History, United States Military Academy at West Point. Redrawn by George Chakvetadze.

Fortunately for Frederick, the Allies left their works and advanced on December 4. He knew the ground well and overnight devised a complex march plan. A huge wheel would be made by his infantry in columns, marching to the south flank of no-longer-entrenched Allies at a distance of 1.8 miles. As at Rossbach, the move was screened behind a line of low hills, barely more than mounds in fact. His key, novel idea was positioning cavalry as if readying to send in an attack on the other Austrian flank. This fixed the Habsburg infantry in place as his own infantry moved south to full flanking position, completely unobserved. Again his luck held, as an early morning mist hid the marching Prussians. A second wheel made left and eastward by the infantry put his redeployed battle line square up against the Austrian flank. The Prussians were already in echeloned lines, making a double top of a T formation relative to the enemy's now flanked battalions. It was a high-risk march that paid off, a three-stage commitment of all his strength to a right-flank movement in order to catch and roll up the enemy's open left.

It was brilliant but also more than a little lucky. All the marching by wings of his army, then by lines deploying into firing positions, was hidden by thick winter fog as well as the smudge of low hills. As the final Prussian advance and shooting started, the first companies at the end of the exposed Austrian-Imperial line of battle were simply shattered: they died en masse, and many survivors ran. Austrian commanders scrambled to redeploy, trying to wheel their whole line, then 1.8 miles long, to face Prussians who appeared suddenly out of the heavy fog. Too many battalions were crammed into too little space, creating a terrible jam up to 100 ranks deep. Lead units were cut apart as they fought back in desperation, ripped up by Prussian infantry volleys and cannon fire, both shooting from full flank advantage. Then the great jumbled mass of disordered Allied infantry met the oncoming Prussian lines and a horrible carnage commenced, swirling around Leuthen's village church and over and through its graveyard.

Volley after volley poured into the Austrians, pounded also by thundering booms as hundreds of iron balls plunged into a huddling mass from batteries firing down from the low hilltops. The center of the Allied line disintegrated and broke apart, men running in every direction except toward the Prussians. Only darkness prevented further carnage and complete destruction of the two Allied armies. Frederick's men suffered, too: 6,000 Prussians fell at Leuthen. But 23,190 Allied troops were casualties, including 13,343 missing or taken prisoner. Dead and wounded were found the next morning, each forming a little quiet mound under a crisp overnight snow. It was as pretty a battlefield as one could ever hope to see on the morning after. Similar scenes appeared along the Somme at Christmas 1914, at Verdun in 1916, on the Eastern Front after many a fight in World Wars I and II, and in the Ardennes in 1944: corpses appearing to be peacefully blanketed in a light snow. It was of course illusion atop horror, as every thaw revealed.

Leuthen was a decisive victory not solely due to the casualties inflicted on the Allied side, but more because in its aftermath Habsburg armies were cleared from Silesia as garrisons chose to surrender their fortresses: 40,000 Austrian troops quit the fight and their positions before the year was done.[66] That was a real strategic gain. Yet the war went on, for it was a war of coalitions now and Prussia could neither win nor get out on its own. Frederick faced 45,000 Russians next, presenting a new threat to Berlin. This time, he *was* determined that a grand-scale battle was the way to win, for the stunningly decisive successes at Rossbach and Leuthen impressed even him. So he hurried to make contact with the Russian army even after securing a good defensive position to protect Berlin that it would have been wiser to hold. He aimed to intercept right off the march, but he missed the target.[67] A younger Frederick might not have so eagerly pressed for battle yet again, fearing to lose more than he stood to win. But the mistress of battle had Frederick enraptured now. He was all in, filled with longing for another Rossbach or, best of all, another Leuthen, as he would be over the rest of his career as a general. As would so many who came after him in Germany, forgetting how this war ended for Prussia.

His dance of march and maneuver resumed until the Prussian and Russian armies met and fought at Zorndorf (August 25, 1758). Things did not go as they had at Rossbach and Leuthen, confirming that to win against the odds Frederick needed luck as well as his skill. His advance guard and left wing were destroyed, as was one Russian wing, when the battle dissolved into an hours-long cavalry and infantry mêlée in which orders and movements by commanders on either side were superfluous to what the ranks and artillery did to each other. Contrary to the clean portraits of linear war that hung in the salons and galleries, then and later, Zorndorf was another slaughter with axes more than a quick cutting with dueling rapiers or even officer sabers. The Russians lost nearly half their men, some 22,000. Frederick lost a third of his, at 13,000.[68] He bemoaned his own tactical failure to "Leuthen" the Russians as he had intended. He later said, ignoring all the dead and dying in Prussian uniforms, "for the first time, my troops let me down."[69]

He had reason to worry. There were not so many Prussians left in the north, given the rate at which he was losing men in battle and to *Grenzer* campaigns run out of Vienna against his occupations in the south. Worse, there were a lot more Russians than he had killed at Zorndorf moving against him in other armies, and more behind them arriving from the vast recruitment catchment of the tsars. Russian armies and interests and interference were coming to Europe to stay after Zorndorf, as Russia committed to intervening in the wars and politics of the European state system as it never had before. Prussia and Europe in 1758 had Frederick to thank for that, too. So the war went on, with most of it yet to be decided well after Rossbach and Leuthen, and Frederick's fate, too, in theaters far beyond his influence let alone control. He spent more years on campaign. He fought and won or lost more battles that moved diplomacy and the war a touch this way or that, but he could not settle the truly vital issues because the Seven Years' War moved on from still-little Prussia to competition among the British, French, Austrian and Russian empires. That was not a game Prussians could play for another century.

More often now, Frederick did not win decisive victories. He fought only bloody battles that he lost or that settled little. He lost at Hochkirch (October 14, 1758) when he camped too close to the enemy despite a warning from one of his field marshals that he had put the army in danger. He dismissed the caution with characteristic arrogance, a vice that grew ever more pronounced as he aged into irascible Old Fritz. The Austrians duly attacked before dawn, smashing his regiments. He lost 20,000 more men and most of his artillery at Kunersdorf (August 12, 1759), where Austrians and Russians joined to crush his army and whittle down his reputation. He lost despite introducing his latest field innovation, squadrons of horse artillery towing guns cast as mobile firepower that could keep up with cavalry.[70] He tried to replicate Zorndorf by moving around the flank of an entrenched opponent, but this time the maneuver failed. During the fight, Frederick's coat was holed by musket balls and two horses were shot dead underneath him. He wrote that night: "It is my misfortune to be still alive ... Everybody is in flight and I can exercise no influence over my men. At Berlin you ought to be thinking of your safety. I shall not survive this cruel turn of fortune." The Allies lost 5,000 killed, 15,000 in all from a starting force of 65,000. With killed and wounded, adding panicky desertion by 25,000 green and undisciplined Prussians, barely 3,000 men remained intact out of Frederick's army of 51,000. Again, he blamed the catastrophe he made on chance and the wavering of "my wretched infantry."[71]

Blaming others for bitter misfortunes he fathered, by clinging to his aggressive tactics with a lesser army than he had in the first and second Austrian wars, was by now an almost daily habit. Catastrophe followed catastrophe.

Frederick barely escaped from Liegnitz (August 15, 1760), against heavy odds and with more casualties that he could ill afford. In the first week of October, a large-scale cavalry raid by 18,000 Russians reached and briefly occupied Berlin. The blue velvet king decided to dislodge an Austrian force from a strong ridge position at Torgau (November 3, 1760), northeast of Leipzig. Yet again he attempted his trademark long and wide flanking maneuver, too long and wide as matters turned out. Torgau was a best a narrowly technical but strategically Pyrrhic victory. He held the field at day's end, but on it lay at least 16,700 Prussian casualties and possibly as many as 24,700, traded for 11,700 Austrians. Those dead secured him a winter of peace to recover, but no more. Financial costs were growing heavy, too, for everyone. To pay its insupportable war debts, Russia resorted to issuing paper instead of coin, simply declaring receipts valid as payment for supplies by tsarist *ukase*. Mere proclamations thereby replaced hard silver coin, ruining merchants and weakening both Russian resupply and Allied trust in Moscow's ability to stay in the coalition fight. At least the war was not being fought on Russian territory, wreaking havoc on towns and crops and killing up to 10 percent of the population, as was the case in Prussia.

At Vellinghausen (July 15, 1761), the main belligerents gathered 157,000 men and made more bloody murder that settled nothing. The war had moved past individual battles, no matter how much bigger the armies grew or how long the casualty lists. Now it was a world war of empires trying to grind each other down across the seas and several continents. France had lost badly to the British overseas in 1759, Prime Minister William Pitt's and Britain's *annus mirabilis* ("year of miracles"). It continued the naval war but reconcentrated its armies and main effort in Germany, to win different chips to play at the peace talks table. With the British secure in India and North America after 1759, redcoat regiments poured back into Europe. Austria was as fiercely opposed to Frederick in Germany as ever, where Prussia's elevated grandeur and power or abasement and destruction were the only options considered by Vienna before 1762.[72] Prussia remained a modest power that looked mostly just to survive the maelstrom Frederick had stirred. In an often overlooked irony of his reliance on stone over his reputation for battle, had the great Prussian fortress at Magdeburg not held fast at the Elbe over the length and depth of his deepening misfortunes, he might not have survived the war.[73]

Fortunately for him, before 1762 the Russians accomplished little in the east beyond minor fortress-taking and frontier adjustments in Poland, while the French achieved even less in Germany and pulled back. Even so, he fell into despair as he contemplated another looming year of war and invasions

of Prussia, a mood made worse by age and chronic illnesses. He spoke of suicide and told his ambassadors to make ready to seek surrender on terms that
might leave a rump of the Iron Kingdom intact for his heirs.[74] Another irony
of his wars launched to make Prussia rich is that it survived invasion in good
part because it was so poor. Allied armies had trouble living off its infamously
infertile and hardscrabble land, made even less productive by wartime depopulation. So they marched and fought elsewhere, to resupply. Frederick's foes
were thus deflected by bad farms and poor roads as much or as more than
by his military exploits and brilliant use of interior lines. Facing calamity,
he clung to the fantastic hope of some miraculous event to save him from
what he had done, including fantasies of a devastating Ottoman invasion of
Austria. Yet he never imagined what finally enabled him to survive, for a quirk
of politics and personality in the Russian court saved him from the trap he
had made. The sudden death of Empress Elizabeth in January 1762, brought
Peter III to the throne, a position he occupied for just six months before the
far more formidable Catherine II led a conspiracy to depose him. The young
tsar was childishly enamored of Frederick. In the brief time left before his
own death he called back Russian armies advancing on Berlin then agreed to
a separate peace with Prussia. This "Miracle of the House of Brandenburg,"
as Frederick called his stroke of sheer dumb luck, collapsed the anti-Prussian
coalition.[75] That was fortunate for Fredrick's reputation in history as much as
for his survival in power.

The opposing coalition he had forced into existence in 1756 fell apart
as the military and diplomatic balances shifted with events in Russia, as
unpredictable fortunes of war and far more predictable patterns of deceit,
treachery and diplomatic betrayal took their usual course. Maria Theresa
despaired of the coalition's will and resources. She admitted secretly to her
ambassador in Paris that her hopes for invasion and reduction of Prussia to a
minor power, and recovery of Silesia, exceeded her means. It was, she wrote,
"a chimerical idea and impossible to achieve."[76] Frederick therefore held on
to modest territorial gains as an old man that he had made as a young one,
only after waging backbreaking defensive wars that Prussia could ill afford.
He survived more by dint of diplomatic fortune (his alliance with Britain)
and by accident (the shift in Russian court politics) than by earlier battlefield
successes. Frederick had started Europe on a path to decades of indecisive
war that Prussia barely survived. The fighting did not end until every major
power was bloodied, near bankruptcy and morally and politically spent,
Prussia most of all. He went to war in 1740 over an Austrian succession. He
was saved from war in 1762 by a Russian succession. Between the two chasms

of accidents of royal birth and death was a bridge of his great military talent, but also much sheer *fortuna*.

Frederick was aided by the repeated failure of clumsy coalitions to coordinate politics and military efforts, to bring to bear the greater weight of their material prowess on him and Prussia. He followed the same basic pattern traveled by Louis XIV: provoke enemies all around by aggression based in part in short-war illusions, then hunker down and fight protracted defensive wars that drag on for a generation. Frederick is admired for his virtuoso ability late in the Seven Years' War, his conversions of tactical turnings into battlefield success even in the face of superior numbers. In fact, he also lost often and badly, and at least once so calamitously that his army of 50,000 men simply dissolved by nightfall. He barely survived the wars he started. He kept Silesia in the end, in the process gaining a reputation for ruthless military brilliance that displaced his original reputation for enlightened despotism. However, his ranking among the modern great captains must be weighed in scales of judgment that place on the other side his succumbing to fantasies and his taking a middling power into an expansive set of Great Power wars that nearly destroyed his dynasty and kingdom. His lightning aggressions led not to short and lively wars but to geopolitical futility over two decades of wearying war and bleeding finances.

The price of Frederick's misjudgment of the utility of war was high. Again like Louis XIV, he spent much of his life in desperate wars and expended too many lives and too much treasure on fighting just to keep a stolen province, then another. Sustained fights with more powerful enemies threatened to knock his overmatched kingdom from even the lower tier of powers and overthrow him from his throne. His militarily strategic use of advantageous interior lines, marching armies back and forth to each of Prussia's borders to fend off serial threats, was close to brilliant at the operational level. That he needed to do it, however, arose from a more fundamental failure of strategy and his utter misreading of Austrian reaction to his Silesian aggression. His enemies adapted, as long-war opponents always do. They had bigger populations and deeper treasuries to make more big battalions on whose side, Voltaire once said, one always found God.[77] They studied Frederick's tactics and countered at Kolin and later battles. For military success and familiarity breeds not just respect but emulation and countervailing tactics. His were too invested and practiced by the Prussian Army to ever abandon, yet too well known to work forever. It is the way of all tactical innovation. Shifting to a late-war strategy of fortification and hunkering down behind stone was more realistic for Prussia, given the fraying of its Army and of the coalition formed against it. To his credit, he made the change away from aggressive campaigning and battle-seeking to more cautious war, and to a strictly utilitarian concern about taking casualties that he could no longer afford. Too late. His enemies still gathered to march on Berlin. Only luck intervened to save him.

In the aftermath, Frederick's Prussia was a weakened state in much need of time to recover and rebuild. He kept rich Silesia at the cost of a ravaged land and diminished population in Prussia itself, along with a drained treasury and permanent Habsburg enmity. War had also brought a powerful and predatory neighbor in Russia closer to his eastern borders and permanently and more directly looming over calculations of the Great Power game. The swelling of Prussian power and expansion of its territory that raised it to the first rank of Great Powers came later, in predatory diplomatic cooperation with Catherine of Russia at Poland's expense. It came also when he no longer wanted war, and by means (a three-way diplomatic partition of Poland) intended to *avoid* war with Austria. Moreover, the great innovator left behind at his death a reactionary Prussian Army inured to serious and much needed adaptation and reform, run by old generals who thought the highest "art of war" was merely to drill and arm and fight exactly as he had done a half century after he first did it. When they led this anachronism into battle against newly dynamic and reformed and much larger armies of revolution it would be shattered in a day, and Prussia occupied and reduced.

Yet Frederick retains in military history a prior reputation as a paragon of the battle-seeking general, a warlord who raised Prussia from among the minor powers not by diplomacy but by his brilliant wartime operations, through politics and diplomacy by other means. Indeed, he showed that tactical and operational mobility and decision on a given day was possible, and exhibited a genuine talent for command unequaled by any enemy he faced on the battlefield, even if he did not always win. His flanking tactics gave him focused superiority in battle, for a time, while his skill and maneuver from interior lines provided operational superiority as he moved from front to front. He succeeded, sometimes brilliantly, other times not, at tactics and operations. But he failed repeatedly before 1762 at the most important level of statecraft, that of strategy. His policies and naked aggressions forced into existence coalitions that threatened not just to roll back his gains but to destroy Prussia, a danger his excellence as a general never overcame.

Frederick's strictly military admirers too often elide his provocation of Europe into a generation of war, and fail to recall that before it ended he nearly lost Prussia to partition by a grand coalition that formed to have done with him.[78] They see the result of an enhanced Prussia when he died in 1786, and some wrongly proclaim that he got there by a straight road of battle-seeking. They acclaim him for surviving against stark odds and superior enemies by virtue of all his virtues, idealized as his supreme wit, shrewd daring and high military skill in pursuit of necessary territorial expansion.[79] Ignored too often by later German nationalists was the fact it was his strategic miscalculations and aggressive policies that caused the mortal threat to Prussia to begin with: the admired bold strike of 1740 and reckless second gamble in 1756.[80] For generations of Prussian and German war planners who followed over the next 200 years, and still in romantic military history more broadly, he became the all-in-one idealized statesman-general, the *König-Feldherr* or *roi-connétable*. The language matters less than the legend, far less than Clausewitz's idea that a brilliant mind in command was the counterpart to "friction." Tragically for later generations, German military thinkers and planners who followed in the 20th century would look backward to Frederick II as they, too, planned *kurtz und vives* wars to obviate disadvantages of the Reich's exposed central position and relative weakness. They, too, would seek quick victory via battle and campaign virtuosity, only to plunge Germany into vastly destructive and losing wars of attrition and ruin.

***

BY 1763, AFTER a generation spent mostly at war, only minor decisions were achieved in the affairs of the Great Powers. Alliances had formed and been dissolved or betrayed; capitals burned or fell to foreign raiders; provinces were overrun or retaken; impressed men wore the king's or queen's black or red or green or blue and fought each other in battle after battle. In the end, it led to small adjustments of continental borders and odd little swaps of nonvital overseas colonies. Then came a hiatus called "peace" in the great Anglo-French war of the 18th century and ancillary conflicts touched off by Frederick's aggressions that had rolled into a worldwide war. Even the loss of all New France to Britain in the settlement of 1763 did not end the long wars of indecision that marked the reigns of Louis XIV and Louis XV. That loss did not even settle the North American question as so often claimed, by Britain supposedly winning America on the fields of Germany. For France quickly returned to war against Britain, critically intervening in the American War of Independence and fighting as well in the Caribbean and in South America.[81]

Back in Europe, most 18th-century armies still could not win decisively enough in field battles to impose strategic decisions in war. It took the French Revolution and accompanying *levée en masse*, then the spread of the nation in arms and wars of aroused peoples far beyond France, to change that fact of 18th-century warfare. Enlisted nations would absorb extraordinary losses that royal armies of the 17th and 18th centuries simply could not. The odds against any one battle being decisive remained high, while the cost in casualties would only go up. What was about to change the face and ferocity of war was not some new military revolution in technology or tactics or command. It was much more fundamental. What would transform armies and war were deeper changes in the societies that raised the armies and sent them off to fight. The Enlightenment project to tame war with Reason was about to end in an outburst and indeed a celebration of mass social and political violence that would topple kings and pale their more limited wars and ambitions. Napoleon would then try for a Europe-wide empire built by decisive battle, by his will to war at the head of mass armies of an entire nation placed under arms, contesting against other nations aroused to arms. Cool and reasoned intellectualism about war as elegant and limited would collapse in a cacophony of secular rage to rival the old religious hates, and of revolutionary and counterrevolutionary war that would surpass the violence of the old religious wars. The peoples' wars that would close the Revolutionary and Napoleonic era in turn left deep legacies of elite fear and recurrent violence and atrocities over the next hundred years, or more. War was not tamed by the 18th century. It was unleashed.

7

Battle Decisive

RECOVERY FROM THE losses and debts of the wars Frederick started was slow, but arrived just in time for Europe to begin another generational round of war lasting to 1815. First, the century-long French and British war was triggered by the rebellion of the American colonies, drawing French troops back into North America and involving fleet actions and amphibious invasions in the West Indies. French intervention in Britain's war with its colonies was critical, contributing much to the final success of the American Revolution. Even then the great contest for global mastery between France and Britain was not over. After adjusting to the loss of New France by Paris in 1759 and that of New England (and much more) by London by 1783, the global contest ripened for a final harvest that reaped all the other powers as well. From 1792, for yet another full generation war was waged on the seven seas and around and over the borders of France as fighting moved inward, from the Atlantic to central Europe and on to Russia, until it stretched from Barcelona to Moscow and back to France again. A pause and false peace, and then the Hundred Days campaign, Napoleon's last, ending at Waterloo in June 1815. The conflagration changed military and world history, helping to shape all the major wars to come.

The strains of a half-century of taxes and war since 1740 frayed all political and social contracts across Europe. However, in France the cracks and debts went all the way back to Louis XIV. By 1789, they were insupportable. This is not the place to review the complex causes of the great Revolution in France, an earthquake so profound it is still conventional among historians to divide what came before as "not modern" and what came after as "modern." Yet a quick narrative is essential to set the context for the generation of war the rupture in France caused and spread, for the violence of the wars was also revolutionary as things fell apart, the ancien régime did not hold, and near anarchy was loosed into Europe and the world. The French Revolution brought radical upheaval with immediate and permanent military consequences, amounting to a second revolution in modes and scales of war. The idea shift at the center of change was a turning over in the concept of political and then social legitimacy, from the asserted absolute right of kings and traditional rights of nobles and the Church to the natural Rights of Man and Citizens and "popular sovereignty." In a tectonic break from the past, the relation of ordinary people to the state changed from *subject* to *citizen*, thence and inexorably from "king's men" in royal armies to "citizen-soldiers" of the nation-state. Revolution changed many things that needed changing. It also allowed, then forced, the states to mobilize whole nations for war.

Two truisms of military history are that armies reflect the societies that produce them and that success in war always prompts emulation. Hence, even as the French Revolution brought into existence anti-French and anti-Revolutionary coalitions, the profound changes in social and military organization that began inside France spilled over its frontiers to affect all the Great Powers, including conservative monarchies that hated all that the Revolution stood for as they braced against France in serial coalition wars from 1792 to 1815. Before it subsided, this radical upheaval set in motion change that ultimately delivered to all states an engorged capacity to mobilize their societies for war. The radicals quickly lost control, however, ceding mass armies and the nation's war aims to political reaction and then to the "Man on Horseback," the Romantic hero riding the wave of military change to become the greatest of the modern great captains. A young Corsican nobleman, dispossessed from his island inheritance by the low overthrowing the high, gifted with superior intellect and driven by unmatched will and ambition, trained from boyhood in artillery science and the "art of war," Napoleon Bonaparte coursed like the comet of 1812 over a generation, dominating his moment in history as few men ever have.[1]

The immediate trigger of the French Revolution was a deep fiscal crisis which arose from debts incurred by the monarchy in its century of war for dominion fought against Britain since the 1690s. Just before the Revolution, 75 percent of the state budget regularly went to debt service and the military. The monarchy was so burdened by war debts that it was compelled to assess egregious taxation, while exempting whole classes and social categories that would not yield their historic privileges. Taxes were mediated through a hated and corrupt legal system that favored nobles and holy orders, so that the heaviest burdens fell on the mercantile classes and on peasants. Beneath surface tension over high taxation was deeper class and social conflict: a crisis of rising expectation and frustration over a range of stymied social, economic and political reforms.[2] Fermenting longer were fruits of the French

Enlightenment, the trickle-down teachings of *philosophes* proclaiming the deep virtues of *liberté* and *fraternité*, the natural Rights of Man (*les droits de l'homme*) and public and participatory rights of citizens (*et du citoyen*). These views found a ready audience among a newly literate, self-conscious and socially ambitious bourgeoisie. Peasants also resented taxation by a distant king and serving by compulsion in his endless royal wars. Finally, nationalist resentment toward the king rose as France lost prestige in a series of diplomatic crises which desacralized the monarchy. Many believed that Louis XVI was too weak and indecisive to properly protect and project the interests of France. A modern nation was finally emerging beneath the old client networks, and outgrowing its kings.[3]

Revolution began politely, with consultation by the king of the *États-Généraux* (Estates-General) that met at Versailles from May 5, 1789, until late June. The three Estates representing the "order of the realm" (the clergy, the nobility, and the broad bourgeoisie) were convened by the king solely to levy more taxes, to pay for past wars and current upkeep beyond the *taille*, the direct tax that kings of France collected without consultation. This right of permanent and direct royal tax meant that French kings after c. 1500 and before 1789 normally did not consult the *États-Généraux*. Even through the wars of Louis XIII, Louis XIV and Louis XV, internal and class divisions of the Estates left the kings free to rule as they wished. However, decades of accumulated war debts were an extraordinary burden presenting an exceptional political opportunity. Demands were made for more consultation, quickly swelling into calls for conversion of France into a constitutional monarchy. Oaths were taken not to disband until Louis agreed to undertake reform, as a double echo of old British constitutionalism and new American Revolution sounded in Versailles, a shout akin to "no taxation without representation." Louis reluctantly conceded to convene a National Assembly, while also mobilizing troops around Paris. Before either side could act, revolution moved into the streets. On July 14, Parisians saw royalist troops surrounding their city and broke into the Bastille prison looking for guns. First blood was spilled by the mob, of guards and prisoners. And blood changes everything in revolutions. Not for the last time, a Paris mob reset the course toward more radical political demands and widening social violence. A set of "August decrees" remade the legal and social order, and a *Déclaration des droits de l'homme et du citoyen* was proclaimed against the absolutist claims of the monarchy. Henceforth, whatever the king, nobility, clergy and high bourgeoisie might negotiate or want, the threat of street theater and violence by the *sans-culottes*—the common people and working classes—of Paris was backdrop to all deliberation, and later to radicalization leading to mass public executions before cheering crowds.

Radicalization picked up from July 1790. Rising demands for a republic gripped the Revolutionary Convention (the renamed National Assembly). The movement fed off the king's obvious desire to return to his old, absolutist ways. Then Louis decided to flee with his aloof Austrian wife, Marie Antoinette, to return with a Habsburg army to crush his subjects. He was discovered in disguise, by a postman who recognized his face from the coins. He returned to Paris, a well-treated prisoner in the Tuileries Palace, not yet put in a common cell. Nonetheless, this royal betrayal of the nation, the king's plotting with a foreign sovereign to invade France to prop up a Habsburg daughter and Bourbon son-in-law, cinched the fate of the monarchy. It was only a matter of time.[4] The promise and potential that France might export its chaotic and violent change to Europe, and the French Revolution's fundamental challenge to the international principle of the sovereign legitimacy of monarchs, prompted formation of an anti-French First Coalition. Prussia allied with its old enemy Austria in a portent of anti-Revolution and anti-French coalitions to come, one after another and ever larger over the next 23 years of war.[5]

War was declared by the Revolutionary Convention on Austria on April 20, 1792. By midyear the Revolution was also at war with Britain, Naples, the Netherlands, Prussia, Piedmont and Spain. War changed the course of the Revolution, hastening the overthrow of the monarchy and permitting Jacobin emergency powers and repression. A theory of revolution also informed the war: France declared war on foreign tyrants, not peoples. The age of the ideologies arrived, wholly secular in their policies of overthrow but in their passionate intolerance fundamentally similar to the old wars of religion. On August 9, a Jacobin insurrection set up a fiercely radical Commune in Paris. Henceforth it was a race to the left, to Terror and the guillotines. External danger sped everything up. Verdun fell to the Prussians in late August. Urged by fear of invasion and by Jean-Paul Marat[6] and radical Jacobins, once again Paris mobs drove policy by taking lives. In a half-week of semi-spontaneous murders from September 2 to 7, priests and royalist prisoners were massacred in the street or inside their cells in the Bastille and other prisons. Over a thousand died. The royal family was jailed and the monarchy abolished. France was declared a republic on September 21, 1792, following the "September Massacres" and a small battle against the Prussians at Valmy (September 20).[7] Just as Charles I had been tried for treason by Cromwell and Parliament, citizen Louis Capet was now tried and convicted of treason against the French nation. He surrendered his head to the people's basket on January 21, 1793. The queen's head followed on October 16. Their son did not live to become Louis XVII. He died of scrofula at age ten, after two years in a dank republican dungeon. Rumors of his murder were widely believed by émigrés.

Revolution progressed to Terror.[8] State ties to the Catholic Church were already cut. Now, accelerating formal secularization—some of a quite comical kind under the clerically stiff and humorless Robespierre—spurred a revolt by peasants in the Vendée region of western France. They demanded a double restoration, *pour Dieu et le roi*, that Paris restore God and the king to their rightful place at the center of national life. The revolt was treated as a *jacquerie* against the châteaux would have been under the ancien régime, with ruthless violence from the center, this time republican rather than royalist but to the same bloody outcome for the Vendée peasants. Revolutionary zeal produced terrible savagery and wanton killing of Vendéens by the people's government and army, which marched in "infernal columns" to massacre and burn out whole villages and hunt down resisters.[9] The Vendée descended into a cruel and chronic war of small ambushes, scorched earth, mass drownings, executions and killing without quarter asked or given during or after battles and raids. Already the Revolution was encouraging extremes of social violence, for and against.

Following the deposed king's execution, a sense of siege gripped an actually encircled capital and France. The country faced a threat of multiple invasions while the Revolution faced revolt in the west and accused traitors (officers and aristocrats and other supporters of the ancien régime) at the highest levels of the republican state and army. Vast treasonous plots were rumored in this phase, which is reached by all major revolutions sooner or later. Nevertheless, not even paranoid Girondists and Jacobins were always wrong, for real plots existed. Beyond the king's proven treason, many ancien régime officers and nobles were determined to reverse the Revolution by force. Could the generals be trusted? What about other noble officers in the Army of the Republic? In April, a coup threat by a former defense minister was thwarted, after which he went into a conspirator's exile in Vienna. An already radical Committee for Public Safety (*Comité de salut public*) moved left even faster, led by Georges Danton and Maximilien Robespierre, in further straining the quality of Revolutionary justice.[10] Several noble generals were arrested and executed in the purges that ensued. Fear that the Revolution would be crushed by enemies both internal and foreign sent thousands of condemned to the guillotines. Robespierre's personal and cruel jealousies sent more.

What came next was truly astonishing and more important even than the
Terror: the *levée en masse*.

***

WARS OF THE 17th and 18th centuries are not usually regarded by historians
as useful in explaining the character of modern warfare (although the Seven
Years' War is being reassessed). War as practiced by French Revolutionary
armies, especially as led by Napoleon, is more often said to mark the start of
modern war. Still others would point instead to the "rifle revolution" of the
mid-19th century as the demarcation line. In fact, technology was not the main
driver of the dramatic change that came out of the French Revolution. There
was actually little difference in weapons technology from the time of Marshal
Saxe and Frederick II to that of Napoleon and Blücher or Wellington. With
small exceptions, in 1800 soldiers fought with comparable weapons to those
used 50 years earlier—in the case of the Prussian Army until 1806, exactly the
same: 1754 model fusils. Rifled muskets and some rifled cannon were used,
but sparingly. Rifles were generally issued to skirmishers and snipers but not
to the mass of regular infantry. Every army clung to smooth-bore muzzle-
loading infantry weapons, with 6- and 12-pounder smoothbore cannon the
basic guns, dating back to Frederick. The notable exception were French
12-pounder "Gribeauval guns," cast lighter by one-third.[11] Cavalry stayed
devoted to combat with saber and lance, attack by shock of the charge, although
light cavalry proved more adaptive.[12] Where some do see a "military revolution" was in command.

War in the 18th century was stupidly slow and indecisive, everyone
agreed. A stale "art of war" had been overly idealized and locked in by geometric masonry that only allowed for fortress-bound positional war on defense. Frederick's career suggested that something else might be possible,
and Napoleon's confirmed it. At least that is what contemporaries said, as
well as all 19th- and many 20th-century theorists. They proclaimed that
Napoleon reconceived war itself, returned to its essence of decisive battle by
sheer strength of will and force of intellect. Everything that came before was
precursor to his genius, said his admirers then and an older military history
long afterward. The battlefield reforms of Maurits and battle-centric tactics
of Gustavus, battle-seeking by Marlborough and Frederick, all culminated in
Napoleon. Even if the Prussian king did not always seek battle, he pounced
on opportunities whenever his opponent made an error. He would release
the wolf straight for his enemy's throat, with an aggressiveness few generals
possessed and fewer still had the tactical and operational skill to make work.

Ferocity was a cardinal virtue of generalship, and Frederick had that quality. Even so, the real master of war wore French blue, not Prussian black.

Napoleon was the Wolf of Battle incarnate. Everything changed when *he* made war. Genius at last arrived on the battlefield, indisputable and glorious.[13] He was mind on horseback, imbued with a ruthless will that looked direct to the essence of war, to total annihilation of the enemy in battle. He said once of his method: "I see only one thing, namely the enemy's main body. I try to crush it, confident that secondary matters will then settle themselves."[14] He surpassed all contemporary generals in skill and reputation by 1800, then became a *roi-connétable,* a statesman-warlord seemingly without peer, once crowned emperor in 1804. He promised to cut ancient Gordian knots of choking politics with his sword, then benignly bring Europe universal law under his personal empire. Clausewitz, who fought against him in the Prussian and Russian armies, called him the "God of War." He actually had no system of war, only supreme talent and self-confidence. It was others, then and still today, who sought to impose a rigorous and systematic frame around his every thought and act.[15]

What really changed is that the armies doing battle after 1793 were different from any seen before. Already during the Seven Years' War, a trend toward militia armies had begun, as wars starting as arguments among kings took on something of the early character of national wars. By the end of that war, in some countries an emergent public opinion far beyond the salons celebrated their men in arms and thrilled to reported victories or swooned with news of defeats, once deemed the affairs of monarchs alone.[16] Starting in France in 1793, war shifted definitively and spectacularly into this new era. Propelling change was the modern state's ability to mobilize vast human and material resources, to field and support multiple large armies capable of waging long campaigns and sustaining longer wars of endurance. It happened first in France because the urgent military need to fend off invasion married Revolutionary ardor to an emergency national army of surprising new size and power. Amassed around an extant professional core were initially ill-trained *soldats-citoyens*. Few expert military men at the time thought such an ad hoc army of common volunteers and conscripts could defend the frontiers, let alone the Revolution, even with a forest of fusils and bayonets.[17] They were proven wrong.

Thus, a profound cultural and military shock was felt in every capital and HQ, and also in working quarters and villages across France, when tens of thousands marched off to battle and once there unhorsed and unhinged armies of foreign professionals. Their motives varied widely and changed over time with new conscript classes and varying experiences under the Republic and Empire.[18] But overall, success by French conscript armies made it inevitable that copycat forces would spread to belligerents as varied as Prussia and Russia, as for regime and political survival all the powers marched some distance toward putting their own nation-in-arms. By 1812, mass conscription forced by military necessity transformed the armies of even the most reactionary monarchies, as scions of old wealth and power grudgingly agreed they would rather enlist and arm their own workers and peasants than be beaten by someone else's.

Military stalemate against so small a power as Prussia in the Seven Years' War, despite so much expended blood and treasure and effort, was deemed by professionals both a disaster and unworthy of France. Army reform therefore began well before the Revolution, focused above all on assumed moral causes of indecision such as "soldierly lassitude."[19] That problem at least seemed solved by the new republican politics even before conscription. Starting with the volunteer class of 1792, French soldiers were no longer impressed subjects of the king, indifferently or sullenly waging a king's wars. They were *soldats-citoyens* of the nation and Republic, many truly ideologically committed devotees of the nation-in-arms. The change was twofold and fundamental, causing war to change in scale and intensity. The first nation-in-arms was a republic, its armies expressing republican idealism and also emergent national sentiments and loyalties. The *levée en masse* proclaimed the next year was the first universal male conscription, ensuring mass participation in soldiering. That dramatically escalated the scale of war across Europe, starting in French armies and then everywhere in necessary emulation. The high ideological motivation of new citizen-soldiers and their engagement of real national feeling in country after country also increased the intensity of warfare.

In February 1793, the Convention declared a conscription levy of 300,000 men. It was resisted by peasants in the west and south, where objections were met with ferocious force and state terror from a regime already deathly afraid of the gathering armies outside its borders. Despite the inflow of recruits, the war news grew ever worse. Austrian and Prussian armies descended from the northeast; Spanish armies came up from the south; ports, coastlines and overseas trade were blockaded by the British. Key fortresses fell as France's armies retreated on every front from spring deep into summer. Panic took hold of Paris. On August 23, the Committee issued a second *levée*. Article I read: "From this moment, until that time when the enemies shall have been expelled from the territory of the Republic, all the French are in permanent requisition for the service of the armies."[20] Hundreds of thousands were conscripted and started basic military training before being rushed to defend the frontiers. Buying substitutes was not allowed; evasion was severely punished. Men called up by the open-ended draft of 1793 would in fact serve six years, until the Directory set up an annual conscription law in 1799 for all males aged 20–24.

Other articles requisitioned military animals, saddle horses as cavalry mounts, draught horses to pull supply wagons and the field artillery. All military-grade weapons in private hands were to be turned over to the Army of the Republic or carried to the war by the new soldiers. "Regulation caliber arms are reserved exclusively for [soldiers of the frontier armies]. Interior defense forces shall use hunting pieces and side arms only." The decree created a state arms industry, located in Paris, to supply the demi-brigades. All materials and skilled workers needed for this new industry and the wider war effort were requisitioned. "National buildings shall be converted into barracks, public places into workshops for arms." Siting war industries in Paris was not just to defend the capital against outside forces. Commune leaders also needed jobs for restless urban workers; violently unpredictable *sans-culottes* scared even them some days. The consequence was rapid national mobilization of men, industry and finance. Next came the public order to gather human waste. "Cellar soil will be washed in order to extract saltpeter."[21] Women joined in gathering saltpeter (potassium nitrate) from night-soil pots and the cellars and stables of Paris, separating it from human and animal waste for use in gunpowder manufacture. This was critical war work as a saltpeter crisis resulted from the British blockade. Paris was soon producing 5,000 pounds of the white compound per day.[22]

It did not matter that rougher-looking recruits from across France marching to save Paris in the Army of the Republic did not look as pretty or march as smartly as more professional armies. Not yet, anyway. It was enough that they had special *élan*, skilled officers and very good Gribeauval cannon.[23] They threw back from the frontiers all France's enemies, winning at Hondschoote on September 6 and at Wattignies on October 15 and 16, and more fights in 1794. Then they crossed over the borders, making aggressive war and eating out foreign lands. Initially, some *levée* units were poorly trained, to the point that they were not trusted to carry out more than basic maneuvers under fire. One unit was so imbued with radical egalitarianism it refused to obey a sergeant teaching basic drill in camp, denounced him as a tyrant and tried to hang him. He survived to later serve as one of Napoleon's generals.[24]

It was once argued that the new French armies won with ferocious patriotism and mass, from *élan* and sheer numbers, that simply overwhelmed smaller professional forces as battles culminated in frantic amateur bayonet assaults.[25] The Revolution caused such military chaos, many historians said, that only Napoleon was able to restore order along with traditional military values and a system of honors and rewards to replace those abolished by the Jacobins. He made the Directory army work, it was argued, and the army of The Consulate from 1799-1804. Then he turned his imperial army into the supreme instrument of his personal will, renaming it the *Grande Armée* in 1805. In fact, later research showed that *levée* troops in the Army of the Republic ("Army of Virtue") performed much better in battle than those crediting French success solely to Napoleon's subsequent leadership conceded.[26] Moreover, there were many continuities of reform that he built on or benefited from, dating even to the ancien régime but especially following an overt return to military professionalism with the overthrow of Robespierre.[27]

Revolutionary armies were *not* inchoate peasant masses, the countryside in arms. Nor were they just a step up from an armed but illiterate rabble, a French version of berserkers. They were politically educated and often highly motivated to defend the Republic, because many soldiers believed they had a personal stake in the state for the first time in their lives.[28] This republican spirit had real military effects. Not reckless and crude bayonet charges for want of combat skill, but in motivated learning of drill and tactics. The initial weaknesses of raw recruits in matters of drill were quickly made up by highly motivated soldiers eager to learn the craft of war and go defend the Republic. Their high morale was also reflected in historically low desertion rates compared to the Bourbon army of the ancien régime.[29] The 1793 *levée* came at the height of revolutionary fervor and fear, generally agreed as lasting from 1792 to 1794. It was seen by enemies of the Jacobins, their political foes at the time and anti-Revolutionary historians later, as a vast school of radicalism rather than a direct response to dire military need. In fact, the *levée* uniformed a mixed if also roughly radicalized intake of recruits, reflecting that there was also widespread and even violent refusal to serve, notably in the south and west.[30] The key point is that the *levée* raised huge armies to defend France and that these armies did so very well, giving green troops experience and martial confidence to replace fading republican idealism as they became veterans. Success also made them more aggressive, lending to French armies a fighting spirit no one else could match at first. This was not esprit de corps, however. The political masters of the Revolution's armies feared that natural military phenomenon in ways conservative powers did not, because they thought it might separate the army's identity from the people, or rather from the people's regime. That was precisely what conservative monarchs wanted, but in

France specific unit loyalty common in all armies was initially discouraged in favor of higher devotion to the ideal of the Republic.[31]

The *levée en masse* was intended by the Jacobins as a literal mass rising, a voluntary and idealistic defense of the nation by the nation. When that failed to raise enough troops, it turned into the first mass conscription, ballooning the Army of the Republic to 750,000 during 1793–1794 (one million, in paper strength).[32] That was 500 percent larger than the Bourbon army before 1789, which topped at about 200,000, which still made it a giant among all 18th-century armies. French numbers subsided under the Directory to an average of 380,000 from 1795 until 1804, or the same as maintained by Louis XIV at the peak of his wars. They swelled again for Napoleon, who recruited two million into the *Grande Armée* by 1814.[33] He also had access to tribute troops on loan from allies or temporarily conquered foes. From 1805 to 1812, he always had more troops than his enemies, a fact Owen Connelly persuasively argues "enabled him to commit greater tactical and strategic sins and survive with greater ease."[34] His enemies could not do the same until they, too, adopted mass conscription and mass armies to achieve military and strategic depth equal to or surpassing his. His losses in Russia and Spain, and Allied conscription, tipped the balance of forces against France after 1812.

Change was not just about size. Ambitious minor nobles like Napoleon committed to a military career with the Republic, as did talented bourgeois who rose to command on merit. With discipline and a uniquely flexible unit organization, and under the right officers, French armies gained professionalism in addition to advantages in numbers and aggressiveness and soon proved superior to their enemies—not always, but surprisingly often and quite early. They showed they could maneuver as well as all-professional armies to gain tactical advantage on the way to battle, and of course fought with more *élan* when they got there.[35] The importance of numbers was superiority over time, over a long series of battles during protracted campaigns and wars that went on year after year. The effects were Roman—newfound depth of reserves that could lose battles and yet send more armies out to fight again and again. It wore out France's enemies by cumulative casualties and the psychological threat of more battles to come. France had unmatched recuperative powers due to state requisition, conscription, and bureaucratic management of its wars. It could mobilize matériel and recruits to replenish battle losses or attritional losses by disease and desertion at rates that conservative and hence more conventional enemies could not match. Lessened fear of losing came from expendable conscripts and matériel, giving confidence that lost battles and even lost armies could be recovered. Win and we take Milan or Brussels. Lose and France will live to fight again.

French armies after 1792 also had an advanced administrative structure that their enemies lacked. Increased numbers were handled by a flexible system of much larger units than the old battalions, brigades and regiments, a reform underway before the Revolution but hastened in a greatly expanded national force. All-arms divisions (combining elements of infantry, cavalry and artillery) became standard in Revolutionary armies, later grouped into multidivision corps (*corps d'armée*) in the *Grande Armée* under Napoleon. A corps was about the size of a mid-18th century army at 20,000–25,000 men, though real numbers varied greatly by country and circumstances. Corps were meant to march more quickly because independently, while staying within a single day's reach of each other. They were to recombine only for battle at a prearranged junction or by "marching to the sound of the guns" when one of their fellow corps met the enemy and engaged. Ideally, this allowed concentration against an enemy who did not expect such rapid movement and would not be ready to fight. In short, the reorganization looked to maximize speed of movement and operational surprise. When it worked, it could also deliver local numerical superiority. By moving on separate axes, larger armies broken into discrete corps could also forage more widely and effectively than if a single mass followed one line of march.

All that also meant the enemy did not know the real object of the march until the army reconcentrated just before offering battle. Marching by corps risked each one being defeated separately by a superior—because still concentrated—enemy force, leading the whole army into a "defeat-in-detail," as this is known. In theory, however, a single corps with its own strong infantry, cavalry screen and supporting artillery was a miniature army that could stand at least for a one-day fight against a larger enemy army. It would hold its ground or wage a fighting retreat, while awaiting reinforcement by its sister corps marching nearby and with standing orders to move to the sound of the guns when any corps made contact with the enemy. The advantages were greater speed for the whole army, wider foraging and confusion of enemy scouts and commanders as to one's intended destination. Traffic snarls were also better avoided, with each corps assigned its own roads and line of march. Napoleon told his corps commanders where to go and when, then left it to them and staff officers to work out how and over what roads. Prussians used the same technique at the level of whole armies to outmarch the Austrians in 1866 and get around the French in 1870. They learned it from Napoleon, who took it from the smaller-scale practices of Frederick's invasion of Bohemia.

An unintended benefit of royalist officer purges by the Jacobins, and self-exile of still more aristocratic officers from service in the Army of the Republic, was to encourage professionalization of new officers from lower classes in *levée* armies.[36] Excesses of Jacobinism also swept away those officers who might have been loyal to the Republic but who opposed military changes, while the Revolution as a whole provided lower-born men of talent with real opportunity for military advancement. Something similar happened in the Red Army on a much greater scale as a result of Josef Stalin's bloody *Yezhovshchina* purge of 1937. In addition to purging far too many capable and innocent officers for alleged political unreliability or simply to fill quotas, the great purge of the Red Army also unintentionally cleared out a generation of Russian Civil War and Old Bolshevik incompetents concentrated at the top leadership level. That *felix culpa* opened paths to wartime generalship by younger officers, including Georgi Zhukov, who provided vitally dynamic leadership in the war against Nazi Germany.[37]

As the fever flush of the *levée* subsided by 1795, French armies became increasingly professional. They were led and trained under an experienced and highly skilled officer corps that worked inside a relative meritocracy, supported by a dedicated bureaucracy. Napoleon built on that foundation, but it was already there before the Empire and his reshaping of what became the *Grande Armée* from 1805. This was a substantial advantage over all other armies, where too many aristocrats still assumed command merely because high birth or blood relation to the monarch raised them above talent and knowledge. As for enlisted men, under Napoleon peasants were told they could become officers, an echo of the revolutionary promise he captured in his famous remark that each soldier might carry a marshal's baton inside his knapsack. It was not strictly true, of course, but it nevertheless caught a spirit of merit lingering from the days of republican war.[38] Anyway, it was truer for the French than others: in the Army of the Republic and later in the *Grande Armée* soldiers *could* rise above their original social stations. Yet one should not exaggerate the shift toward egalitarianism or underestimate the role the older nobility continued to play in French military affairs. After 1804 the officer corps of the newly declared Empire was still 60 percent old nobles, including four out of eight new-made *maréchals*.[39] Other nobles ran the Empire for Napoleon from thrones and other seats of privilege across occupied and allied Europe. It was a blend of ability and nobility personified by the minor Corsican aristocrat who rose by his talent to become Emperor of the French.

Selflessness seldom survives in life and never does in war, where sacrifice causes the least selfish to die and the rest to reconsider. Thus, not even the

Army of the Republic could rely solely on moral virtue or revolutionary *élan* for long, as pure ideological commitment to the Revolution faded with fighting and casualties. It proved difficult to maintain even after a year of victories in 1794, although it lasted longer in attenuated forms. In addition, the Committee on Public Safety professionalized Revolutionary armies from the start, recognizing that even through Terror compulsory public virtue could be fostered only to a point. Efforts to enforce it in the barracks and on the battlefield failed in an ambience of permanent crisis and war. Something else was needed, a realistic combat motivation to supplement and then replace fading republican spirit. Puritanical republicanism was already evolving into a more sustainable ideology of honor and national service under the Directory in 1795, which disdained radical secular idealism and overthrew and executed Robespierre.[40] By then, the *levée* troops of 1793 were veterans, grown more professional with time in service, alienated from the state and especially the Directory, most attached to their units and generals. Napoleon completed the inexorable and even natural shift, providing a new focus for soldier loyalty in restored martial honor and shared glory (and plunder). Of course, Revolutionary armies *and* their opponents in battle already had martial honor, and won battlefield honors. This was different. He restored celebration of honor as the centerpiece of military culture.

Napoleon brought back unit insignia, unique battalion flags, and later gave out the famous imperial eagles. He supplied battalion flags to the army

Napoleon distributes Imperial Eagles (December 5, 1804).
Courtesy of Wikimedia Creative Commons.

in Italy from 1797, and to the whole imperial army in a grand ceremony held on December 5, 1804. It is recalled in Jacques-Louis David's 1810 neo-classical mural *Distribution of the Eagle Standards* (*Serment de l'armée fait à l'Empereur après la distribution des aigles*), depicting Napoleon as Caesar before the legions. In more desperate circumstances, Stalin similarly discarded troop motivation by political religion and sacramental whippings of troops by Soviet political officers (*politruks*) and restored traditional insignia, unit and personal honors in the Red Army during World War II. In both cases, soldierly motivation thereafter tapped into values of denounced ancien régime aristocratic codes by successfully universalizing them to all classes. Napoleon also paid attention to (or took care to appear to) and rewarded courage and unit leadership, no matter what the rank. He took time to issue public awards, praise and promotions and to meet and play humble with men who showed the combat behavior and loyalty he needed, including from junior officers and plain soldiers. If Frederick similarly stooped to conquer troop loyalties by walking their campfires while concealing his contempt the night before the fight at Leuthen, Napoleon did it on a grand scale, like everything else he attempted.

He also played to notions of the divine, in a much different sense than the young and adoring Clausewitz meant when he called the Emperor of the French the "God of War." To many soldiers he *was* a god of war, almost a literal god, transcendent over their lives and the life of the *Grande Armée* despite its inherited anti-clerical and skeptical heritage. They saw their warrior-emperor as a near-divine, just as Catholic and Bourbon armies once saw the kings of France as semi-divine. It is not inconsiderable that, as the scholar Jean Morvan put it, during the Napoleonic Wars French troops "had with them a living god, a tangible providence, a being thanks to whom, amidst all the blinding action of war, they marched and fought with assurance [*à coup sûr*]: Napoleon." John Lynn adds to this thought: "This god of war was not a god of Virtue, but a god of Honor."[41]

Esprit de corps was encouraged again, in place of Jacobin fear that it might encourage an identity in the Army of the Republic separate from the people and the state. Napoleon set up a *Légion d'Honneur* as a nearly exclusive military reward: of 48,000 Crosses given out by his Legion of Honor, only 1,200 or so went to civilians. Rather than the national honor system it later became, it was a means of bonding soldiers to his person through a powerful sense of personal honor and connection. When he was done, the *Grande Armée* was transformed from Robespierre's utopian "Army of Virtue" to a more traditional and sustainable "Army of Honor."[42] His battles were fought by armies imbued with intense pride in their *roi-connétable*, and in their unit and personal honor. These were much different emotions than in *levée* armies a decade earlier, combining the traditional military with something new. With eagle banners held high over the columns and the Legion of Honor and his grace open to all, Napoleon led a *Grande Armée* that marched with sustainable combat motivations of unit identity and personal loyalty and a high conceit of imperial honor and its own glory, not with unsustainable ideals of public sacrifice and ultimate sacrifice. Not less important but less often said, he also paid his troops from tribute looted from foreign lands, as conquerors and their armies always do.

***

AS A BATTLEFIELD commander Napoleon could afford to experiment with more aggressive operations and tactics, a view also encouraged by revolutionary disrespect for all old, tired things of the ancien régime. French generals and their political masters in Paris were more willing after 1792 to accept the bloody wages of battle than were conservative monarchs whose professional soldiers were expensive to recruit and retain and much harder to replace. It was a decisive advantage. Yet one could not say out loud to civilians waiting on war news back home that heavy casualties among *soldats-citoyens* could be more easily absorbed than by armies in the wars of dead Bourbons, not without couching it in the romance of national sacrifice. So that became a feature of wartime propaganda everywhere in a new era of the nations-in-arms.[43] It was true nonetheless, and French governments and generals understood it was true. Knowing that they could endure higher losses in battle and even the losses of battles, and yet still win wars by eroding smaller enemy armies in battle after battle after battle, made them less averse to combat risk and to mass casualties. Huge armies on the move were more likely to find bits of each other and fight battles of encounter anyway. The casualties would have to be borne.

Points of contact and conflict multiplied in part because armies were too big to feed from domestic magazines, so they moved over the borders to forage outside national territory. Napoleon's vaunted practice of cutting loose from magazines to move faster by living off the land was also and even largely a response to logistical demands imposed by massive conscript armies which could not be supplied from the traditional magazine system. Better to keep moving like Gustavus and Wallenstein, to eat foreign sheep and grain, drain someone else's treasury and wreck the enemy's lands with swarming troops. Not much really new in that. Early reliance on private contractors was also replaced by a more centralized Jacobin administration as the whole French state bureaucratized. Napoleon inherited this more sophisticated supply system. Still, logistics added an incentive to deploy conscripts aggressively across the frontiers as field armies, rather than sit them in large garrisons. It was a small step from there to armies living off the lands they marched through. At the height of the Empire, tribute payments made to Napoleon in specie (as well as in foreign divisions barracked outside France's borders) further reduced the burden on the nation of supporting his vanity and the *Grande Armée.*

Napoleon understood the advantages in mobility and striking power conferred by the aggressive character of armies comprised of *soldats-citoyens.* He maximized advantage with shock tactics suited to this character, tactics already being worked out within the Army of the Republic by its professional officer corps before he took full command. Operationally, he liked to fight out of a central position from which he could split enemies and beat each part of their army or each coalition army separately; that is, in detail. Tactically, a key change came from experiments dating to before the Revolution: the use of heavy columns to break the mauling stalemate of linear battles by smashing though the enemy line, creating and attacking flanks. Well before Napoleon, the French officer corps settled on a new combat doctrine that favored columns in rapid approach marches and for closing the distance between opposing lines in battle.[44] The old parallel echelons were disdained for their exchanges of deadly volleys until one side broke, but the other one was usually left too shattered to exploit the gap. Attack by column was better, using weight and thickness and moral momentum to bash like a ram right through the thinner enemy line standing, in the case of British armies, just two ranks deep. It was an old argument, dating at least to Saxe. Attack with shock and *arme blanche* or stand and rely on firepower? The new French armies actually did both, and very well.

Other basic tactics preexisted the Revolution and Napoleon, such as sometimes shifting into lines to maximize infantry firepower (*ordre mince*); shock attack (*ordre profond*); sending *tirailleurs* or skirmishers ahead with rifled fusils to rag the enemy line; using heavy columns for assault, as just described. So, too, French use of all three formations (*ordre mixte*), which was actually the usual practice in most battles. Also, a French "column" was not really a column but more nearly a rectangular block at roughly 40 men wide and 12 or so ranks deep, on average; a sideways column, so to speak. A screen of skirmishes with rifles led the way, peppering the enemy line with aimed shots, softening it for the column armed with smoothbore muskets and mounted bayonets while preventing an enemy assault during the approach. The new citizen-soldiers of 1793 helped decide the issue because columnar attack better suited Revolutionary generals in charge of the first green troops of the *levée en masse,* who lacked experience or training to make the difficult transition from column into line while deploying for battle or inside a battle. Tactical innovations therefore included fighting from column rather than shifting into echeloned battle lines.[45] Even in the heavy column there was continuity from the ancien régime. French infantry at Rossbach fought in column, though to an unfortunate outcome. Pre-Revolution military reformers drilled columns well before 1789 or 1792, and tactical preference for attack with bayonets went back to Marshal Saxe in the 1730s and long before. However, the troops of 1793 did not stay green for long. Once they learned to fight, French armies became truly formidable as they applied line and column tactics old and new and mixed, as battle conditions and enemy dispositions warranted.

In a sense, French armies did on land what the Royal Navy discovered also worked against linear battle indecision in fleet actions at sea. Like Nelson at Trafalgar, they broke the stalemate of lines by conceding initial firepower advantage to the other side to instead batter through the enemy in columns, then rake the short flanks created by the ruptures. It worked, and Napoleon followed suit. When attacking an enemy line that insisted on fighting in the ancien régime style, standing thin to fire in volleys, his heavy infantry were trained to close rapidly and attack instead in columnar formations, to hit hard with momentum and shock, only shifting to firepower at very close ranges. His attacking columns took casualties at their heads from fusil fire coming from two sides, but as often as not they smashed through the thin enemy line, howling, brawling, stabbing and wrecking it where his artillery had earlier "softened up" the enemy's will and ranks. Infantry shot, bayoneted and even trampled enemy soldiers underfoot, opening gaping holes for cavalry to roll up battalion flanks, then pursue or kill fleeing enemy.[46]

Napoleon actively sought battle, which he saw as the climax of every campaign, the single greatest opportunity to break his opponent's will to resist by inflicting casualties and setbacks at critical psychological and political moments. He said: "It is upon the field of battle that the fate of fortresses and empires is decided."[47] There is no doubt he was a nearly singular military virtuoso with a both native *and* studied talent for war. A driving will to power and to battle, as well as speed in action and reaction on the battlefield, lifted him over all rivals and challengers. Not on every day, but on most. Yet the intersection of mass armies and horse-and-musket firepower never reached near-perfection at the tactical and operational levels under his *coup d'oeil* and quicksilver mind, despite what his least critical admirers aver. His combined arms tactics were instead the culmination of long-building trends in European warfare. He was far better at them than anyone else, but he was not the God of War or the perfection of war. He made mistakes, especially in operations leading up to battle. Severely so regarding movement and logistics once he left the familiar battlefields of Western Europe and fought instead in more open Poland and Russia in 1809 and 1812.

Napoleon made policy and war less like a great artist, who sees the whole landscape he will paint even on a white canvas, and more like a Corsican bandit—in fast, violent dashes. One of his severest critics, Owen Connelly, sees Napoleon as an opportunistic scrambler, if one better at using available tactics and weapons than any general of the time and less likely than most to make major mistakes.[48] It is perhaps enough to say that he was markedly superior at making war, though not at planning or winning wars. For his strategy was another matter entirely from his tactics and operations. Indeed it is not at all clear that he ever had one. Not having a realistic goal or sense of endgame beyond the opening or next round of campaigning and fighting, relying instead on the short-war delusion or assumption of one's own superior virtue or virtuosity to win through in the end, is a sure sign of failure to resist the allure of battle and usually a portent of disaster. Napoleon was not the first, and he would not be the last, to embark on a major war or series of wars without thinking through how to actually win, or ever thinking much at all about final goals and possible outer limits to his imperial drive.

As always, the system of war finance helped shape the nature of the wars being fought. In Napoleon's case, his highly aggressive warcraft was partly compelled by a need to supply the spoils of war to keep the domestic front calm and collaborating in his ever more ambitious imperial project. Literal spoils of conquest, then regular payment of tribute, must flow into his Empire from conquered provinces and countries all around, or his war-state would not be viable. He turned the old adage that war must pay for itself (*bellum se ipse alet*) into a grand system of collective theft and expropriation of wealth, up to small countries. Once his payment and honor systems displaced original republican idealism, the lasting impact of national conscription was to increase the *scale* of war rather than provide more or a different *ardor* for war. That is exactly why even anti-republican and reactionary monarchies were later able to raise and motivate mass conscript armies that in the end came out to match and beat Napoleon and the French.

In early 1796, Austria was the main threat to France, with the key theater of operations expected to be southern Germany. The Directory sent the
young Bonaparte to Italy to waste his time in the mountains and possibly
ruin his reputation, for already he was seen as a general with coup d'état on
his mind. Instead, in a series of bold moves, he threatened Vienna and then
forced terms that he negotiated personally. He showed dash and initiative
in moving lightly and fast by foraging away from his magazines.[49] It seems
that he had an unmatched ability to visualize both battle and large-scale
movements of armies, a *coup d'oeil* extended out to the operational level as
he explored terrain or a map.[50] He also believed in the efficacy of moving
against the enemy's capital as a prime military-political target, as he did in
Vienna and would again toward Berlin in 1806 and Moscow in 1812. In so
doing, he differed from Gustavus and Frederick, neither of whom ever moved
on Vienna. His Italian campaign of 1796–1797 swelled his reputation via a
sequence of smallish battles, none of them decisive except in the sense that
his reputation brought him closer to real political power in France. He spent
1798 in a spectacularly useless, failed and quixotic expedition to Egypt.[51]

In mid-August the next year, he abandoned his army in the Middle East
and returned to France, arriving in October to find a country unhappy with
the progress of its war against the Second Coalition and discontented with
the Directorate. He joined a conspiracy that carried out a successful coup
d'état on November 9, 1799. That made him "First Consul" and effective
dictator in a nominal triumvirate. The next year he invaded Italy, winning
at Marengo (June 14, 1800), his favorite battle in later memory. It was a
close-run affair, but translated into popularity and added political security
at home. In a rigged plebiscite in 1802, he was made First Consul for life,
firming up his dictatorship. After another rigged referendum, on December
2, 1804, in the great medieval cathedral of Notre Dame in Paris, he crowned
himself "Emperor of the French." Consciously aping Charlemagne, without
bending the knee as the Frankish king did, Napoleon took the crown from a
summoned pope's hands (Pius VII) and placed it on his own head. As he did
so he proclaimed himself the embodiment of the nation-in-arms, saying he
took the crown "in the name of the French people and the Army."[52] He then
crowned his indifferent wife Joséphine as empress.

Napoleon dazzled all who faced him, and particularly those who admired
him without question.[53] The cult of battle and Napoleon's imperial cult both
found political expression in propaganda and state-sponsored popular literature, and in a revival of heroic battle painting that marked his reign.[54] Deep
ambivalence can be found decades later in Leo Tolstoy's *War and Peace*,

less in the Napoleon caricature he presents than in the views of him held by all the others.[55] Napoleon's wit was cutting and legendary. His personality loomed over Europe from London to Moscow. Like Louis XIV, he burned his name onto an entire age, but in 20 years rather than 50. Like Machiavelli, his name entered language: grand things are called "Napoleonic." Like Frederick, he impressed everyone with promised law-giving and reform. Also like Frederick, who left Junker privileges over the serfs in place while proclaiming his enlightenment, Napoleon spoke of *liberté* and *fraternité* and left slavery untouched. Worse, he spent 20,000 men trying to force slavery back on Haiti, then tossed Toussaint L'Ouverture into a dank cell to die. He was capable of judicial murder as well, most infamously of an innocent man (the young duc d'Enghien).[56] He was the grandest patron of high society and the arts, and was framed himself in sycophancy in oils by Jacques-Louis David.[57] He funded architecture and libraries and made grand boulevards in reworked cities. And yet, also like Frederick, he is properly and primarily remembered for making war.

Discontented within just a few months of his coronation, he headed out to war. He was always restless for war, to test again his talent for conceiving a campaign as a strategic whole (though without ever conceiving of *war* at a strategic level, or as serving any purpose beyond *la gloire*). His policy was always and forever war, broken by temporary truces which he tore up whenever he chose or needed to, without regard for damage to his and France's ability to negotiate or achieve a lasting, stable peace. From 1801 to 1812, every power tried to make peace, to appease or submit or even ally with him.[58] Always, he bullied. Often, he invaded.

Italy was overrun and he was compared to Hannibal, a long-war fit more apt than the artist David realized.[59] He broke up harmless Switzerland and remade it into the "Helvetic Republic." The weak and archaic Holy Roman Empire was abolished so that only one emperor might rule in Germany. His marshals and his brothers were imposed on thrones ancient and newly made, stretching from Sweden and the Netherlands to Naples and Westphalia. Germany was occupied; Poland partitioned, again. Prussia was not allowed to sit out his wars, as its timid king desired; he broke the Prussians at Jena-Auerstedt and took Berlin in 1806. He invaded Portugal and Spain, where *guerrilla* war broke out against his occupying army. Austria was alternately bullied, beaten and bribed. He smashed the *Hauptarmee* at Wagram in 1809 and Vienna submitted to the upstart, giving him a Habsburg daughter as his wife in 1810 to displace Joséphine, be mother to his heir, and thereby secure both his legitimacy and his dynasty.[60] It did not suffice. He fought Austria again from 1813 to the very end. Tsar Alexander made a grand bargain with him at Tilsit in 1807. Napoleon seethed about Russia into 1811 and invaded in 1812, leaving Moscow a burned hulk and his own *Grande Armée* destroyed and abandoned during its fatal retreat. Britain sought to appease him repeatedly from 1801 (its self-congratulatory image of unrelenting and principled resistance to Napoleon must be set aside). It found him utterly unappeasable.

Napoleon was not in any sense a normal statesman or ruler. He was *roi-connétable*, yet far past the limited ambition of Louis XIV or the limited military power of Frederick II. Once Europe realized that he would never compromise but must dictate, the powers made a pact to dispense with him, to invade France from all sides and overthrow the disturber of their peace. They did it twice, the first time generously and the second with righteous anger. Without such a reckless warlord in charge of France after its Revolution, the balance of power must have been restored years before 1815, as almost any other French leader would have struck a deal—perhaps cynical but moderate Charles Maurice de Talleyrand, as he did in Vienna in 1815 after so much more blood and treasure lost to France and all its wounded enemies. Never Napoleon, who had a passion for war. As his wars and hubris expanded together, they became divorced from the ambitions of more and more French and the national interests of France. Making it all worse was that so much was lost to the pursuit of petty ends. The leading diplomatic historian of the era, Paul Schroeder, shrewdly concludes that Napoleon not only lacked a war-winning strategy, he did not even have a "final aim or coherent overarching scheme of empire behind his imperialism."[61] As with Louis XIV before him, it was all about vanity, a personal hubris and ambition to dominate, to push the hollow limits of *la gloire*.

Napoleon fought too many significant battles to even begin to review here.[62] Victories at Marengo (1800), Austerlitz (1805), Jena-Auerstedt (1806), and Wagram (1809) for a time left him master of Europe from the narrow sea of the Channel in the west to the Vistula in the east. The warlord sat uneasily in peace on a throne that ruled an empire the like of which had not been seen since Charlemagne, and would not be seen again until the even briefer military ascendancy of Adolf Hitler from 1940 to 1942. How and why he did has been the subject of two centuries of research, as has been the question of how he won so often in battle but lost the war. It seemed for a while as if he had found the Philosopher's Stone of decisive victory, yet he lost everything in the end. It is pointless and unpersuasive to assert that he won from genius when, with boastful humility, he said: "It is not genius which reveals to me suddenly and secretly what I should do in circumstances unexpected by others; it is thought and preparation."[63] It is less helpful to argue, as some seem to, that genius somehow deserted him at Borodino, came back for the 1814 campaigns, then abandoned him again at Waterloo. Less convincing still to blame subordinates like Marshals Emmanuel de Grouchy and Michel Ney for his defeats, talented generals in their own right who surely made mistakes yet served always at his direction. Or to blame the mud or cold or ill health or Fate. His final defeat went much deeper than that, to profound strategic realities he never mastered.

Napoleon headed back to battle in the summer of 1805 in defense of his proclaimed Empire and to reorder the oldest imperium in Europe. His coronation *à la* Charlemagne was a direct challenge to the status quo inside the Holy Roman Empire, to all Germany. He hoped to deter Prussia from joining his enemies by defeating Austria and Russia swiftly, before the full weight of another assembling coalition came to bear. Austria divided its armies, sending 90,000 to Italy in case he struck there. That left only 70,000 in Germany under General Karl von Mack, with 95,000 Russians under Field Marshal Mikhail Kutuzov marching to join with Mack but badly split into a van of 35,000 that was several days' march ahead of the main Russian body. Both were too late in any case. Napoleon crossed the Rhine with 200,000 men in seven separately marching corps, gaining weeks on his slower enemies. Mack invaded Napoleon's minor ally Bavaria, then moved to Ulm near Württemberg. It later appeared as if Napoleon had deliberately trapped him there. He did not. In fact, he nearly stumbled into a trap himself, but recovered in time to head to Ulm. Austrian confusion left just 27,000 to receive him after three corps fled from the French cavalry upon first contact days before. Having penned in the Austrians, he bombarded Ulm from October 16 to 20. Mack surrendered without a fight.[64]

Ulm was an operational more than a battlefield victory that, as we shall see, Austerlitz confirmed in short order, pushing Austria out of the Third Coalition. In the meantime, tens of thousands of Russians arrived. Some 38,000 led by General Kutuzov, one-eyed hero of the Ottoman wars. The Russian corps were spotted and pursued by Murat's cavalry, which cut up infantry stragglers each day until Kutuzov turned aside to wait to concentrate his armies. Murat and cavalry General Louis-Nicholas Davout could not resist taking their corps into the undefended Austrian capital, where they paraded giddily through its streets in plumed ranks on November 12. That allowed Kutuzov to join his two armies into one body of 71,000 at Olmütz, reinforced by 15,000 Austrians and Tsar Alexander himself. Napoleon had at that moment just 57,000 troops in his main body. Alexander unwisely took over command as Kutuzov cautioned against seeking battle, even with the advantage of numbers. However, the Russian emperor wanted to fight. Young and untested, he was eager to show that he was the match of his French counterpart.

Napoleon feigned further weakness as he moved north, in order to lure the Allies out. The armies collided on a frigid morning near the quiet village of Austerlitz, about 70 miles from the capital. It was December 2, 1805. Reinforcements brought Napoleon up to 73,000 with the hurried arrival from Vienna of Davout's corps. Against him were 86,000 Allied troops, a mix of Russian and Habsburg divisions and corps. Around 40,000 held the south flank, 16,000 were on the ambitiously named Pratzen Heights, and 14,000 were still in column coming up a main feeder road. The battlefield had a 7-mile frontage, ranging in topography from the low Pratzen to the Goldbach Brook, a slowly flowing creek that had more the look and character of a wide pond. Russian infantry tramped through snow-covered marshes, chilled and wet with cracking ice under their boots. Slowing but doggedly, they moved forward through the ice-marsh for their watching tsar, heading toward the French. The battle began on Napoleon's order, though Davout's corps was still only half arrived. It was a high-risk move that worked, yet might have gone another way. There was no subtlety at all in Russian tactics. The inexperienced and indeed militarily inept Tsar Alexander simply sent the infantry in thick waves across the breaking ice, straight into waiting French fusils and artillery. His right flank grew ever weaker as he fed more men into this slaughter, reinforcing futility.

With the main body of Russian infantry fixed against Davout's section, Napoleon sent Marshal of the Empire Jean-de-Dieu Soult to take the Pratzen. A counterattack by Russian Imperial Guards smashed a whole French division from under Soult, but Napoleon committed his own Imperial Guard cavalry in a heavy assault by his most reliable veterans. He reinforced Soult in place, with cavalry and infantry drawn from nearby corps, and concentrated artillery for a mass combined arms attack. He would commit his reserve at the critical moment. Napoleon's battle tactics at Austerlitz were a miniature version of his marching tactics on the way to the field. He presented what seemed a weak right flank to draw the Allies into an attack that must weaken their center, anchored on the Pratzen Heights. French discipline on the march meant that even as the Allied attack hit the flank, reinforcements were swinging into line behind Davout, so that his position held. Thousands of Russians floundered and died before Davout's fusil line and batteries firing canister and shot. Then Napoleon hit the Allied center with two full

divisions of his reserve, hitherto concealed by a thick morning fog rising over
the ice and marsh. Hours of bitter hand-to-hand fighting later, the Allies on
the Pratzen succumbed.

At 11:30 a.m., the French drove the Russians off the Pratzen down into
the frozen pools and marshes, already laden with dead and drowned men.[65]
Ninety minutes later, a follow-on attack into the huddling Russian mass
cracked the ice over deeper water, drowning hundreds more. As men scrambled to get out of the frigid water, Napoleon's guns mercilessly enfiladed and
pounded them. Water pooled as red as the salt tidal pools at Omaha Beach
140 years later. Still the armies fought, deep into a midwinter sunset that
came mercifully early amid a snowfall that started around 4 p.m. Darkness
gave relief to the unhurt, though a night lay ahead of solitary suffering for
thousands of wounded lying on or crawling down the Pratzen, or slowly
bleeding or freezing to death in the marshes and Goldbach Brook. What was
left of the Russian army slipped into chaotic retreat; corps, divisions, batteries, companies and individuals got out however they could. Full units and
smaller groups of stragglers moved in all directions that led away from the
French, who were confused by all the movement in the dark but too tired and
with too many wounded themselves to give much pursuit. Left behind in the
marshes and on the Pratzen were 10,000 Russian dead and 15,000 wounded.
French loses were 2,000 dead and 7,000 wounded.[66]

Austerlitz must rank among Napoleon's most decisive victories. In a
matter of weeks, the newly crowned Emperor of the French had smashed two
Allied armies and humiliated two fellow emperors from lines that towered
in history over his newly-minted and upstart dynasty, one a Habsburg, the
other a Romanov. In addition to inflicting over 25,000 Allied casualties in
a single day, the psychological nature of Napoleon's having snatched afternoon victory away from likely morning defeat at Austerlitz was so profound
it helped convince the Habsburgs to exit the war just days later. Defeat thus
sent the remnants of two Russian armies reeling back to the tsar's Polish
border, opening Germany and the Habsburg hereditary lands to a peace
dictated by Napoleon. Europe had not seen such deft battle tactics and lopsided decisiveness since Leuthen in 1757. Owen Connelly, an otherwise relentlessly critical analyst who believes Napoleon failed to properly manage
or concentrate his army prior to Austerlitz, leaving too many corps hanging
useless in other places, concludes: "Ulm was an improvised strategic victory;
Austerlitz an improvised tactical victory. They marked Napoleon as one of
the all-time masters of the art of military command."[67] There is no doubting
that. Technically and tactically, he was the master.

What Napoleon did politically and diplomatically with his victories was another matter. From Austria he took Venice, Istria, Tyrol and Dalmatia and handed them to client states. With these (temporary) rewards given to his minor allies, he inflicted a deep and lasting wound to the prestige and wealth of a Great Power enemy. He gained a free hand in Germany, too, and so proceeded to abolish the Holy Roman Empire and redraw ancient borders, cutting up with the tip of his sword claims and maps that stood for decades or centuries. He pushed Russia back to Poland, away from the frontiers of his own expanding empire, denying Alexander any part in settlement of "the German Question" lying between them. Only *he* would dictate terms. Not bad for an afternoon of other people's blood and lost sons. Yet his arrogant refusal to consult or compromise did not secure decisive military victories with lasting peace terms. It bought only enmity.

His demands and diktat cost him dearly, losing any chance of permanent peace with Austria, which he so vengefully stripped of territory the House of Habsburg held since the 14th century. The move guaranteed that a conservative but diplomatically moderate power henceforth became revisionist toward his Empire and his now revealed intention to unilaterally govern Germany and perhaps all Europe. He forewent any chance of permanent peace with Russia, too. It had lost two armies and much prestige. However, like France, Russia was Roman in its strategic military reserves, even without the *levée en masse*. The land of the tsars was wounded, not beaten. Britain watched and waited, and offered secret subsidies and encouragement to any European capital that would join in a future coalition to stop Napoleon. Gone soon enough was his chance for peace with Prussia, which he provoked against all the peaceful wishes of its timid king, who was no Frederick the Great. Prussia would now come out to fight, to try to stop him remaking Germany to fit only the interests of the French Empire, which was him.

That was a great deal to lose out of disregard of the need to have and follow a long-term strategy. Failure to convert military victory into lasting political victory lost him everything in time, from the high hubris of the battle victory moment to high-handedness toward every other empire's lasting interests. Napoleon was unmatched on the battlefield, yet he had not the slightest idea how to move from battle on the field to victory in the conference hall. Other French knew what to do. He never listened. After his stunning victory in 1805, hubris swelled until he barely heard advice at all.[68] It is a wonder that the mature Clausewitz so greatly admired such a *König-Feldherr*, who treated policy as continuation of triumphal war by the same means, ensuring that others must move to a policy of coalition war that finally overmatched and overthrew him.

Early the next year, Napoleon sent one of his *maréchals* and an army to conquer small, harmless Bourbon Naples. Just because he could. French troops did not cross over to Sicily, however, because the Royal Navy was all around that island. He put Murat on a fabricated Italian throne, set his brother Jérôme to rule an invented kingdom in Westphalia, and brother Louis on the throne of an unwanted kingdom forced upon the Netherlands. It didn't matter that the Dutch were loyal allies of France dating back to 1796. He formally ended the Holy Roman Empire (August 6, 1806), knowing Prussia must object. Technically, Prussia started the war that followed, but Napoleon caused it. It was short and sharp, for once. Prussia and Saxony moved too far ahead of the allied Russians, allowing Napoleon to move into Germany with 180,000 French, then gather 100,000 Germans from minor allies and Bavaria. This powerful army maneuvered to Jena-Auerstedt, southwest of Leipzig, to meet a force little changed from Frederick's day.

In discrete battles fought at Jena (the smaller one) and Auerstedt (more important and bloody) on October 14th, Napoleon and his marshals destroyed the reputation and ranks of the Prussian Army made famous by Frederick. It did not fight at Jena-Auerstedt like its predecessor. Or rather, it did, and that is why it lost. Fighting in three-rank echeloned lines by regiment (the Prussian Army had not yet adopted larger division and corps formations), the line at Jena readied to make the obligatory Frederickian angled attack. However, still deploying Prussians were shredded by French skirmishers firing rifled fusils, covering fast-moving heavy columns. The Prussians were then smashed in their compact regiments by much larger French divisions. Marshal Davout's single corps did better still at Auerstedt, where 27,000 French destroyed an ill-formed and poorly led Prussian army of 60,000. Masses of infantry surrendered as Murat pursued and cut off the Prussian retreat, which was chaotic and panicked in any case. Whole regiments and then strings of fortress garrisons surrendered without further fighting, as the French fanned over Prussia. Jena-Auerstedt was another great victory, driving Prussia from the war. Berlin was occupied by a detached French corps and Napoleon soon arrived to dictate terms in person, which were abject as usual. The king abdicated in shame, leading the caustic Napoleon to jibe about the queen: "She is the only man in Prussia."[69] In fact, there were Prussian men still in the field willing to fight, a single corps of 15,000 at Thorn, who would yet cause trouble for Napoleon. Others, like young Clausewitz, left to join the tsar's army, still contesting with Napoleon after Prussia succumbed and submitted.

Napoleon moved into Poland next, to finish the Russians. Saxony switched sides to join his winning cause and share the spoils, and other minor German states and rulers did so too. Poles grew excited as he arrived, thinking he came to save them from Prussians and Russians. They were wrong. Napoleon always posed as flag-bearer of the ideals of the Revolution and liberator of captive nations from other people's empires, but he harbored no such sentiments or intentions in fact. By late 1806, Tsar Alexander decided on confrontation in Poland, partly to save the Prussian monarchy and hence the wider European balance of power from complete destruction. He also wanted to maximize military surprise with a rare winter campaign. Alexander hoped that months of structural and other reform had already produced a more modern Russian Army overall. It was in fact still too dependent on illiterate serf soldiers and had too many aristocrats and foreign officers of dubious quality in command positions. However, like most Russian armies, the one he had in Poland had the virtue of size, which has a quality all its own. On the other hand, all commanders of enlarged forces were discovering command and control issues as early 19th-century technology proved inadequate to the growth of the era's armies. Two such engorged forces were about to slam into each other.

Napoleon chased down the Russians and the armies fought at Eylau (February 7–8, 1807) in four feet of snow and atop small frozen lakes. It was a bloody affair, including a rare overnight opening battle of the Russian rearguard and French advance guard grown to corps size. It raged into dark, illuminated by a burning and ruined town in a howling winter night of blowing snow and crackling wood and exploding shells. The next day, the full armies fought a winter battle on ice and crusty snow. Much went wrong for the French, as the Russians refused to sit still and be enveloped. In fact, Napoleon nearly lost his army and his own liberty as Russian infantry overran his HQ (conveniently located in a cemetery). He used his reserve early, the famed Imperial Guard. He had to, as in the afternoon 7,000 manly enough Prussians struggled through the snow and a howling gale from Thorn to reinforce the Russian left, which was weakening. General Gerhard von Scharnhorst was there to guide them in. A single French corps attack next went in against Russian guns hidden by smoke and ice fog. The Russians fired canister from 300 feet (100 meters) while French batteries also poured shot into the advancing columns, having mistaken them for the enemy. When the day was done and it was all over, bar later dying from sepsis and neglect, each army was mauled and bloody. It did not matter that the truth was hidden in Napoleon's falsified casualty lists and Antoine-Jean Gros's painted lies on canvas.[70] Because Napoleon held the field, he was called the victor. If so, his victory was nearer to Marlborough's claim for Malplaquet than his own clear-cut wins at Marengo or Austerlitz, for he lost 25,000 killed and wounded at Eylau to the Russian and Prussian 15,000. That was one-third of the *Grande Armée.* It was so battered it failed to pursue, as was its famous way and the means to turn slaughter into decisive victory. Ney let go an outburst: "What a massacre! And with no result."[71]

Both armies bound and healed their wounded and regrouped over four months before doing battle again, when Russia's last army in Poland was pushed across the border just 15 miles west of Eylau, at Friedland (June 14, 1807). Even Napoleon's most chauvinist admirers cannot claim he showed subtlety of tactics or any genius that day. Because he had the advantage of raw numbers he decided, as he would again at Borodino, to win at Friedland by sheer blunt force. He would concentrate and simply batter through and over the Russians with mass (*masse de décision*) and firepower. For the first time, he used his artillery in a new way, concentrated in what became known as the tactic and technique of the "grand battery."[72] It was a sign that even France and Napoleon were beginning to feel the loss of veteran soldiers, forcing a turn to firepower over direct infantry assault. It worked at Friedland because the Russian army there was poorly disposed, backed against the River Alle, with no place to go but into the river or onto the guns. In a long summer's day of concentrated killing, Russians were shot down or trapped in the town as it burned down with them inside, under bombardment from guns on the nearby heights. Or they were pushed by fire and fear into the Alle to drown. Packed and frightened infantry, Cossacks and horses, all crashed together in muddy water as a pathetic jumbled stoppage of burned and floating flesh, slowly breaking up later like a loosened logjam in a forest fire to drift downstream as single bits of char. In all, 30,000 casualties, including 15,000 killed, were traded for 1,400 French dead lying on dry earth, and another 8,500 wounded.

Russian commanders were as shocked by the day's losses as British officers were on July 1, 1916, when casualties in khaki numbered 19,240 killed and nearly 37,646 wounded on just the first day at the Somme. Mass death brought little to the war in 1916 but an answering round of more death, and more determination to succeed the next time, or the one after that. However, relatively comparable carnage was just enough in 1807 to encourage a pause in fighting, as stunned Alexander asked to parley. He met Napoleon on a covered barge on the Niemen at Tilsit on June 25. The two emperors appeared to like each other. They paraded and inspected each other's armies, walking past ranks of weary and wary veterans from recent battles, who must have marveled at how these demigods made talk and peace over their heads while they limped and marched hundreds of miles to bleed and die in ice and fire. A treaty was agreed between the bookend empires that settled the affairs of all the small states of central and eastern Europe lying between St. Petersburg and Paris, including a chastened, occupied and much-reduced Prussia.[73] All those years of war in the last century, and Frederick's gains from the partitions of Poland were gone in a few months in the new one.

Like Tsar Peter III, who was so enamored of Frederick he called back the Russian armies heading for Berlin to finish him off, Alexander was enthralled and charmed by Napoleon and left him all of Europe west of the Vistula. They pondered a joint campaign to conquer and dismember the Ottoman Empire, but nothing came of the idea. Some 45 years later, French and Russians killed each other alongside Turks and British in Crimea over the "Eastern Question." Alexander's brother Nicholas would be tsar then, a different Napoleon the Emperor of France, as the game of thrones and empires went on. For now, the French and Russian emperors straddling the Niemen partitioned Poland and Prussia and agreed to exclude British trade and influence from the continent. Britain was isolated. Austria was broken. Prussia was smashed. Russia withdrew east under cover of a forced agreement. Tilsit left Britain alone at war with France, and that fight was waged mostly at sea and by economic blockades. Napoleon was master of Europe from the Vistula to the Channel, the Baltic to Italy. He should have been content to rule in peace. He never was.

8

Battle Defeated

DECISIVE BATTLE MADE Napoleon Emperor of the French and de facto emperor of Europe. Attrition, on the other hand, would whittle him down to Emperor of Elba. It had started already. Napoleon typically took 100,000 men into battle, marching them in discrete corps. Then the 1807 campaign revealed serious flaws in his preparation for war and in operations far from France, in unfamiliar country with few and poor roads and too much space. It was what would bring him to defeat and disaster in 1812–1814. Fresh from destruction of Habsburg, Prussian and Russian armies, he did not appreciate that his successes must be a stimulus to military reform by his enemies, even as he reached the outer limits of French military power and his own ability to reshape events and whole countries by force of will expressed in arms. The signs were there to be read from late 1806. Although badly led, Russians fought well against two French corps in small battles that took place on the same day (December 26, 1806) at Pultusk and Golymin. At Eylau just weeks later, a Russian army beat Napoleon in person and knocked back the *Grande Armée.* He still had enough green recruits pouring out of France to fill out gaps in the ranks made by musket balls or cannon, but already the quality of troops and their morale was wearing out from too many casualties in too many battles.[1] One problem was that *les grognards* (literally, the "grumblers") were aging, or being killed off, including the old bearskin veterans who gave Napoleon victories in the first half of the decade.[2]

French artillery changed after 1807 for the same reason, yet Napoleon was compelled to turn to the hitting power of big guns to make up for what infantry increasingly lacked in skilled veterans. And still to come was a disaster in Russia in 1812 that would kill so many fine mounts he would need artillery to support a gravely weakened cavalry also, in defensive campaigns across Germany thence back into France in 1813–1814. In Napoleon's last three years at war, 1812–1815, he would resort more often to concentrated grand batteries to break enemy lines before sending in the infantry, usually also just crashing the center because he no longer trusted his armies to make more refined bat-tlefield maneuvers. He would try to punch a big hole in the enemy battle line with massed guns before sending infantry columns to hit with shock, then send cavalry in support of the infantry to attack into any flank gaps and make pursuit. It was brute and elemental. Even the head of his corps of engineers later remarked that he was too crude by the end, also accusing him of reckless-ness with the lives of his men.[3] He did it because he was losing the advantages of numbers and of veterans' skill, permanently. Where once the trademark of his tactics was to concentrate off separate march columns to achieve local numerical superiority and surprise, after 1812 he would more often face larger armies concentrating in superiority against *him*, forcing *him* to fight from the great disadvantage of inferior numbers. After the destruction of the *Grande Armée* on the retreat from Moscow he never had enough troops, or enough good ones, to go one-against-one, except when he had no choice. Even when he had the numbers, he lost more often than before.[4]

The decline began with the campaign of 1807, which consumed too many greybeards of the *Grande Armée*. After Friedland and because of it, Napoleon never again commanded mass armies confidently wrapped around a core cadre of the veterans who won so many battles for him in the past. He also mismanaged at the most basic level of command, supply of his field army. He seems to have misapprehended logistics in the more open East, which were different than in Western Europe. In the East, marching corps could not live off the land as easily as they were forced onto a few poor roads traversing much longer distances though much poorer farmland. Experience also showed that whenever the *Grande Armée* was short of food, trouble was not long in showing up in the form of increased desertions or whole units wandering off to forage, as well as general indiscipline. Nor could French corps maneuver as fast and unpredictably on fewer roads as they did on the dense road nets of Western Europe. That made it harder to surprise or flank or encircle enemies with the superior pre-battle speed to which French mar-shals were accustomed. Napoleon never learned this central lesson, as demon-strated when he repeated all the errors of the Eylau campaign five years later in Russia. Arrogant and deeply corrupted by amour propre, and by fawning sycophancy on all sides, he grew corpulent and quickly irritated. As a proven master of march and battle tactics, he became overconfident that his ad hoc tactical solutions and scrambling abilities would bring swift and final victory through battle, anywhere he chose. So he badly neglected the more basic lo-gistical and morale realities of long campaigns and longer wars, far distant from bases of supply and reinforcement.

From 1804, the *Grande Armée* expanded to an average of over 500,000 men, surging higher in major campaign years. Other states were forced to follow this lead of expansion via conscription. With national variations according to local social conditions, all major belligerents save Britain slowly approached universal conscription as the *levée en masse* was exported from France.[5] Deeply conservative monarchies in Austria and Prussia had avoided raising mass armies throughout the Revolutionary Wars, yet they were compelled to do so during the Napoleonic Wars. Defeat of the Prussian Army at Jena-Auerstedt forced major reforms on Berlin, while French monopolization of the "German soldier trade" eliminated a major source of hired men that had been dipped into by all monarchs for centuries. Outside Prussia and Austria, Germans increasingly fought for France in the armies of small allies like Bavaria, Saxony and Württemberg, or were recruited directly to French service as tribute units or as soldiers for hire.[6] As all armies expanded again after 1809 in order to match the French, so did the size of battles and attendant casualties. Wagram, Borodino, Lützen and Bautzen were all fought by armies totaling 250,000 men or more. At Leipzig in 1813, over 600,000 fought for four days. The time of French numerical superiority based on a unique *levée en masse* was over.

Kings and emperors worried at seeing so many bourgeois and commoners in arms, yet they did what was necessary to stop Napoleon. Still, the lesson took years and many defeats to learn, so great was the fear of monarchs of arming their own subjects while the smoke of the French Revolution still hung in the air. If the elites outside France were unhappy, conscription was far less popular among those forced to serve. In all armies the last years of war saw chronic high levels of desertion. Draft avoidance was also extensive, quite often by resort to self-mutilation. Knocking out one's own teeth made it impossible to load a fusil, because paper cartridges had to be torn open by mouth; a more radical cutting off of one's thumbs made it impossible to hold or fire a musket.[7] Death by disease in dreary camps did the rest, ensuring constant demand for replacements; hence new and more draconian drafts, leading to intakes of lesser quality men and yet more indiscipline and desertions.

Moreover, not all things French and militarily useful were importable. While conscription was necessary, it was always deeply threatening to the internal order of conservative monarchies. Armies then as now to a high degree reflected the societies that hosted them, bringing social and cultural characteristics into camps and barracks and even onto the battlefield. Other powers after 1800 could not just copy French systems of recruitment, citizen-soldier combat motivation, and a far more meritocratic officer corps that melded aristocratic military privilege with lower-class natural talent. They had to adapt within peculiar constraints and noble and other class resistance in each of their own societies. By the end, however, the exigencies of war meant that every major power except Britain mimicked core elements of the French model as best they could, and even Britain raised one million soldiers and sailors over the course of the wars.[8] Austria and Prussia both bit the conscription bullet, but only after defeat forced them to choose the lesser evil of putting their own people under arms. Prussia went furthest after 1806, having lost most badly, yet it moved to full conscription only in 1814. By then, even the staid, reluctant Habsburgs agreed to a conscript reserve. Russia already relied on a long-service system set up by Peter I starting in 1700, and so rooted in its peculiar autocracy and serfdom that no other power considered or copied it.[9] Britain resisted conscription, too, except for its militia and impressment for the Royal Navy. Each year from 1807 to 1812 it lost 15,000–25,000 military dead, mostly from disease. Another 5,000 were discharged as unfit for active duty, while up to 7,000 per year deserted.[10] Yet domestic distrust of large and standing armies, combined with subsidies to Allied governments, meant that only limited conscription was wanted, needed or introduced. British casualties were kept low overall by fighting Napoleon with other people's subsidized armies.

Except for Prussia, by the end of the Napoleonic Wars major French practices such as the shift into all-arms divisions and corps were widely adopted to manage the enlarged armies. Despite resisting that particular reform, the greatest military change came in Prussia, where an unprepared army and a war were lost in an afternoon at Jena-Auerstedt. The defeat of 1806 was a total and systemic military collapse, and everyone in Berlin knew it. The reasons were many, though all pointed to retention of Frederick II's model army past its due date. The Prussian Army in 1806 was still a professional force that included many hired foreigners, so it was far too small for the new era. It also still fought in echelon in three-rank firing lines, using a 1754 model fusil, and it was organized in regiments rather than the new divisions and corps used by the French. It lacked staff officers and relied on aged generals from Frederick's wars, even at Jena. Only three men stood out, and all three played a huge role in reform: General August von Gneisenau, General Gebhard Blücher, and Scharnhorst, who positioned the arriving half-corps from the fortress of Thorn that saved the Russian left at Eylau.[11] It was a moment of pride that reformers built on in 1813 and German officers still recalled as late as World War II. However, defeat was more important. In a "revolution from above," serfs and Jews were emancipated in law, bureaucracy was modernized, towns held the first local elections, Prussian patriotism was stoked and the Prussian Army was reshaped accordingly, to embrace a growing national and not just dynastic loyalty.[12]

The officer corps was opened to merit and in a limited way to all classes, though in practice the Junkers still dominated commissions and commands. A new Ministry of War was established in 1809, short-service enlistees were allowed in place of long-term professionals, and a *Landwehr* reserve decreed (March 17, 1813), slated for home defense separate from the main army.[13] In 1812, a new tactical manual introduced skirmishers and combined arms attacks on the French model, and brigades replaced regiments. Not yet divisions and corps, but at least moving in that reform direction. At command level, a General Staff was established along with the famous War College where Clausewitz would later teach.[14] From its graduates came staff officers to ensure that doctrine was understood by generals and line officers. In the liberation campaign of 1813, the changes proved their worth as the new Prussian Army harried Napoleon out of north Germany.[15] With large complements of Russian troops (up to two-thirds of the whole) under the command of three Prussian generals, it fought well at Lützen and at Bautzen. It fought superbly at Leipzig, then marched into France in 1814, fighting numerous corps-sized battles with Napoleon's scratch armies. It defeated Napoleon's last army at Waterloo in 1815. France still had deeper strategic reserves over the last two years, despite its resources diminishing with each new and younger draft class and long war and casualties. By then Prussia had allies who could play Rome as well as France, lending whole corps and armies to Berlin, while it fought instead like Sparta.

Habsburg troops in 1800 were still halfway between an instrument of the dynasty and a national army, a distance they could never close because Habsburg holdings were not a nation even in potential but a polyglot family and hereditary network. The empire was assembled over centuries, made and ruled by marriage as much or more than by war. The *Hauptarmee* already had 300,000 men in 1792, but it was an international force and in many ways backward. For instance, it still required formal knight service by Magyar nobles sitting on large landed estates. Militia were resisted in favor of long-service (up to 14 years) professionals. It was the disaster of 1805 at Ulm and Austerlitz that forced a minimum of reforms from 1806 to 1809. Generals were fired, logistics professionalized, and artillery was concentrated in a new division and corps system modeled on the French, but also reflecting a conscious shift to reliance on firepower over the old style of shock attack. However, the infantry retained line tactics and 18th-century drill. Not even defeat at Austerlitz in

1805 and again at Wagram in 1809 persuaded the Habsburgs to arm their divers and restless peoples. It was not until resumption of active war in 1813–1814 that more change came, when attack in columns led by skirmishers was introduced along with the principle of marching to concentrate for local superiority. Still no move was made to solve the bigger problem, to create a true national army. It just was not possible in a multinational empire tied together not by shared language or ethnicity, or even by common laws and customs, but by Habsburg hereditary claims and historic titles.[16]

In addition to a partial decentralization of command via the adopted corps system, in the last phase of the Napoleonic Wars there was an accompanying shift from line to French-style columnar tactics in most armies. By 1815, only disciplined British infantry still held the line in the old way when fighting against a French enemy lined up in heavy infantry column. Yet even Arthur Wellesley (elevated to a peerage in 1809 and created Duke of Wellington after Napoleon's defeat in 1814) did that in Spain, and again at Waterloo, only with cautious incorporation of high ground into defensive positions. In particular, he used reverse-slope deployment of infantry to protect from pounding French batteries, which by that point in Napoleon's tactical evolution were nearly always massed together. Other than in British armies, preference for infantry frontal attack over firepower dominated the last years of war. More than that, shock attacks remained the major tactical idea in European infantry warfare in most armies past the mid-19th century, including in Austria and France. Change did not come until Prussian infantry advanced in line shooting rapid firing rifles, Johann von Dreyse's famed *Zündnadelgewehr* ("needle gun") that shredded whole Habsburg corps in campaign preliminaries in 1866, then helped destroy Vienna's main army at Königgrätz.

Historians still wage war over column vs. line tactics of the Napoleonic era, often along national lines. British histories tend to "count muskets" and proclaim that the infantry fighting system that brought the most muzzles to bear from the line was necessarily superior. Of course, that means steady redcoat wait-to-fire tactics over French columns. British victories in the Peninsular War, as the war against Napoleon's forces in Spain from 1808 to 1813 is often called, are cited as proof. Waterloo is always the literal closing argument.[17] In balanced contrast, Paddy Griffith, a leading expert on Napoleonic-era tactics, notes that "musketry was more lethal than bayonets; but this is not to say it was more decisive. The most damaging form of musketry, after all, was aimed skirmish fire . . . specifically designed for attrition and not for reaching a decision."[18] British firepower smugness dates back to Wellington, who said in 1811 in Iberia, "Really these attacks in column against our lines are very contemptible."[19] There is a much deeper and more general reason for French defeats in Spain and elsewhere than supposedly foolhardy and rigid adherence to faulty columnar tactics in the face of superior British cleverness and firepower: the lessened quality of late-war French soldiers. Jean Morvan is harsh about the decline in the quality of French military education, poor discipline, and lack of campaign enthusiasm in the last years, attributing it to decay in the moral commitment of French soldiers.[20] One might put that another way: the nation was tired of endless war, and running out of veterans and quality recruits. Defeat and defeatism had more to do with 20 years of hard combat and rising casualties than any one or three or five tactical errors by Napoleon at Borodino, or by Ney in the heat at Waterloo. France lost in the end because long war wore it out. The signs were everywhere that French soldiers marched.

Recruits arrived in Spain in 1808 with low skill and little military training of any kind, some without having ever fired a fusil. They had low morale from the start, and their usefulness was minimal. French occupation forces then suffered a steady stream of morale-reducing casualties inflicted by guerrillas. These irregulars did great damage to garrisons and supply columns, turning the countryside into such hostile territory that French patrols and road convoys dreaded to venture out.[21] Yet the role of guerrillas should not be romanticized any more than the supposed decisive contribution of redcoat courage and musketry, in battles that were not actually decisive to the final outcome. Beyond the images of tragic heroes in Francisco Goya's painted memories, Spanish guerrillas could be little more than brutal bandits or gangs of criminals and deserters, as much parasites as liberators in the peoples' war.[22] Still, when garrisons went out to resupply, a lot of young French died. During 1810–1811, green recruits ("war levies") replaced 100,000 French casualties in Iberia. Those men were lost to chronic attrition while Napoleon was at peace everywhere else in Europe, though already preparing for war with Russia. In five years of the Peninsular War, the French Army lost a staggering 300,000 men. The vast majority never faced a British musket. Column vs. line was the least of French problems in Spain and the least of Allied advantages, if it was one at all.

It was defeat by disease, desertion and demoralization that decided the issue in Spain, and all of that worsened for the French from 1811 as Napoleon pulled out the best troops to invade Russia in 1812, then more for his fighting retreat through Germany in 1813. Lack of experienced officers left behind in Spain forced into command positions a number of mutilated veterans, a premonition of the toll of war to come inside France in the scrambling defense of 1814.[23] Wellington clearly commanded well in Portugal and Spain, but he never acknowledged fully the very real contribution of the Spanish nation-in-arms to Allied (not just British) victory in the Peninsular War. French defeat also resulted from critical logistical help from Portugal, and from its regular army: 20,000 Portuguese fought under Wellington at the Battle of Salamanca.

Historians point out the role played in Wellington's winning general-ship by sound logistics, his generally cautious strategy, and innovative "fast and light" tactics learned as a "Sepoy general" in India, as well as his keen sense of the connections among war, politics and strategy. It is not necessary to occlude such genuine insights into his talent with chauvinist language, comparative general-ranking or assertions of "genius" to explain success.[24] Wellington contributed solid leadership and real management skill over the largest British army fielded to that point in the wars against France, com-manding also Portuguese and some Spanish troops. He waged a traditional positional war in Iberia, using Lines and fortresses to wear out the always aggressive enemy before moving over to offense himself. The French inva-sion of Portugal in late 1810 began just as he started construction of the three parallel Lines of Torres Vedras, which he believed were impenetrable by less than 100,000 men. Facing just 67,000, he scorched earth as he pulled back, fought a delaying action, then reached and manned the Lines on October 14. That winter, the French lost 20,000 men to a mix of combat, disease and starvation.

Wounded by long years of small war, the French retreated back to Spain in March 1811, where that year's campaign was stalemated with the Anglo-Portuguese failure to take two fortresses guarding traditional invasion cor-ridors into northern Spain, Ciudad Rodrigo and Badajoz. There were two bloody battles in May at Fuentes d'Onoro (May 3–5) and Albuera (May 16), but already by the end of 1811 too many French troops had been pulled out to make ready to march to Russia to allow French defenses to hold in Iberia. Wellington took Ciudad Rodrigo (January 19, 1812) after a 13-day siege. He took Badajoz (April 6, 1812) after a siege of three weeks. Enraged at heavy casualties while storming the fortress, British troops ran amok and massacred many civilians. Only after that did Wellington face in a large set-piece battle a French field army at Salamanca (July 22).[25] Madrid fell on August 12, but Wellington's invasion sputtered out in a failed siege of the fortress of Burgos that September and October. He retreated to Ciudad Rodrigo, in bad weather and with more indiscipline evident in British ranks. Reports Napoleon re-ceived in Moscow that Wellington might invade southern France in 1812 were therefore fanciful. With the French in Spain fatally weakened by more troop withdrawals for Napoleon's 1813 defensive campaign in central Europe, following the disastrous losing campaign in Russia, Wellington again invaded with an Allied army in 1813. He drove the last ragged French army northeast and defeated it at Vitoria (June 21), where the Allies outnumbered the French by 75,000 to 60,000. Rearguard actions through the Pyrenees slowed the British pursuit, so that Wellington pushed over the border into the south of France only in the late summer of 1813.[26] Meanwhile, Napoleon was waging an increasingly desperate and much larger campaign in Germany.

Other factors contributing to French defeat in the Peninsular War—giving indications that the end was coming overall for Napoleon and France—included overly centralized military control exercised from Paris and jealous and quarrelsome senior officers in place in Spain. Too often, veteran officers and troops rotated out of the theater too quickly, taking with them vital field and anti-insurgency experience. The guerrillas thus got more experienced and better at mayhem as the French grew weaker, eroded by a wearing campaign of ambushes against their patrols, garrisons, supply lines and depots. Sometimes, French garrisons were forced to come out to fight before they ran out of food, too weak to maneuver effectively in hostile country and in any case blocked from foraging by local guerrilla bands.[27] Wellington's army struggled with desperate logistics as well. Spain was a dry, harsh and hostile place for armies trying to live off the land.[28]

Underlying this mess was strategic neglect of the war in Spain by Napoleon, who saw only *petite guerre* there and despised it. The French Army of that time actually had a tradition of what is today called "low-intensity combat," going back even before the Vendée revolt to the anti-Huguenot campaigns under Louis XIV and Louis XV. Closer in time, it had faced irregulars in Tyrol and Bavaria, fought *Grenzer* in the Balkans, and put down rebellions in Haiti and in South America.[29] However, only *grande guerre* interested the Wolf of Battle. Napoleon was made for battle, and in Spain there was only squalor and atrocity and flies. Its "little war," its *guerrilla*, was too small to fill up his sense of greatness. Where was *la gloire* in protecting supply wagon trains? Too much fighting there was too old-fashioned, over fortresses and the Lines of Torres Vedras. He thought he had time to spare. He would deal with Spain later, and easily, once it warranted his proper attention. He did not understand its place in the larger war, how it was bleeding his armies of men and skill, corroding morale and corrupting officers, just for a secondary front in the much greater contest of empires with Britain and Russia, and their allies in Prussia and Austria. He never understood the war in Spain until too late, when he was in exile and spoke bitterly of "the Spanish ulcer that killed me." Even that was a typically self-pitying, blame-deflecting exaggeration of the role of the Peninsular War in his downfall, which he could accuse because he never really fought there. The decisive theater of the war was far from the Atlantic, distant from Spain and even the Channel, moved years earlier to the fulcrum theater of central and eastern Europe where the land empires touched. Yet his lament held a large grain of truth about strategic attrition all the same.[30]

Napoleon let Spain bleed his resources as he marched off to beat the Austrians in 1809 at Wagram, where another telling sign flashed. Of the 200,000 men he took on that campaign, only half had ever been in battle before.[31] Overall, the definitive Wagram campaign history shows that the war in the central theater was changing at a strategic level, shifting advantage away from the *Grande Armée* as other powers reformed and refitted their militaries, fought better and recovered more quickly from defeats.[32] A portent of declining military superiority was in the air, and with it a renewed political and strategic balance among the Great Powers. That meant two things. First, Napoleon would be beaten more often by armies that knew his methods, adopted some of them, and blunted the rest. Second, the long war would be decided, as so often before and after, by exhaustion. It was no longer about "genius" in the saddle and command, if it ever was. It was about national endurance, and about strategic depth and vision. That is where Britain's major contribution to the defeat of Napoleon comes in. It did not arise from linear firepower tactics by redcoat armies or even the dragged-out war in Spain. Not from battlefield victories and sieges in Iberia from 1812 or the last campaign in Flanders in June 1815, when the contest was essentially all over save the final killing at Waterloo. That fight did not in any sense win the Napoleonic Wars. It merely ended them in more dramatic fashion than the real defeat of France, which actually occurred in 1814.

Britain's critical contribution to final victory came from its national endurance of war over 23 years, with only the brief interruption of the Peace of Amiens in 1802.[33] Essential to the final victory of the Grand Alliance and defeat of Napoleon were British loans and direct subsidies to Allies straining to keep large armies in the field with less modern economies, along with London's guidance of the economic diplomacy behind each rolling coalition. It came with sustaining a fleet of over 500 warships and feeding, servicing and supplying in excess of a quarter million Royal Navy and overseas British Army personnel.[34] Britain's naval contribution involved far more than decisive sea fights at the Nile, Copenhagen and Trafalgar. It involved harder years of close blockade of French-occupied shores, and marshaling a partnership of the state and private contractors into a coherent national supply system capable of nurturing men and sustaining ships around the world. It all rested on an extraordinary contribution of complex naval finance stretching back decades into the 18th century, that permitted 60 years of Royal Navy expansion into a truly global force while nearly always at war.[35]

More contributions to victory came from mobilization of British industry for war, amphibious transportation of armies and supplies, and strength of diplomacy. All of that took exceptional bureaucratic and administrative skills. British governments managed several severe financial crises and wartime inflation. Along the way, the political and social ruling classes also suppressed labor and rural dissent in favor of pursuing the war effort. This all culminated in a national effort to "organize for victory" from 1802 to 1815, with the critical period 1807–1812, when Napoleon straddled Europe as victor and tyrant from the Channel to the River Niemen.[36] British armies and will kept pressure on France in Iberia, then provided the Allies massive subsidies for the final campaign years, as well as smaller field armies. Without this fundamental structural support of the Grand Alliance it surely would have taken much longer to defeat Napoleon. There is no need to seek national gratification in exaggerations of the importance of redcoat fire tactics or enlarged claims of decisiveness of the brave but almost postscript battle at Waterloo.

***

UNAPPRECIATIVE OF ONGOING change in the fundamental structure of the war, Napoleon spent 1811 planning not how to defend the immense empire he already had but readying for an fresh invasion, of Russia. The tsar had dared to resume trade with Britain against Napoleon's wishes and their agreement at Tilsit, against his counterblockade of Britain, his grandly titled but actually quite porous Continental System.[37] Britain's blockade bit hard into his empire, as each Great Power pursued victory at the expense of all the other states of Europe, and far beyond, out to the edges of their world empires and also along American ports and shores. The Royal Navy was the bane of his every move at sea and London the financier of every coalition that formed against him. However, after he lost his escort warfleet at Trafalgar in 1805 he could not cross an army over the Channel, so narrow, yet too full of Royal Navy wood.[38] His own counterblockade failed to tighten the economic noose due to demand for British goods all over Europe. So he decided to break Britain's will by eliminating its last potential ally, in Russia. He would crush ever defiant London by taking newly defiant Moscow.[39]

Napoleon was warned by key advisers not to do it. He was a student of military history and knew that Charles XII had lost an army in the snow and vastness of Ukraine, lost his empire and Great Power status for Sweden. All lost to Peter the Great after dissolution of the Swedish army following defeat, too far from home and secure supplies, at Poltava (July 8, 1709).[40] In 1812, Napoleon was too corrupt from too much power held too long. He was irascible, contemptuous of all disagreement. He would find a way where lesser men said victory was impossible. He was also feeling his age. He had epileptic seizures, bad hemorrhoids that made riding a horse painful, and a gastric ulcer, and he was losing his hair. Like most middle-aged men, he had grown overconfident as well as overweight. For those reasons, for his vanity and for *la gloire*, once more he called the sons of France to war. A quarter million answered *Hurrah!* A few still meant it.

He demanded that his allies and tributaries commit their armies, too. All of Europe would invade Russia, not just France. As for his own army, he recalled the best divisions from Spain and took the Imperial Guard with him. Wrapped around greybeard veterans were the called-up classes of 1810 and 1811—green boys, still in their last teen summers. He left Paris in May, in a grand parade of hundreds of gilded carriages. Everything he did was *grande*. Across Europe the tribute armies stirred, making to join him in Poland to concentrate for the great push into Russia. The *Grande Armée* assembled slowly, its huge van camped along the Niemen, its main body and rearguard still assembling much farther back, stretched over Poland and Germany. Napoleon personally scouted the crossing and directed engineers building pontoon bridges during the night. He then led the advance guard across. It was June 24, 1812. There was no going back. Napoleon crossed the Niemen, but also his Rubicon. For the next three years it was a fight to the death. Not a war of kings or even emperors, but among nations and peoples. Europe would finally have done with this reckless adventurer, this man who must impose his will on everyone, who left no space for other nations' interests or pride or history, who was petty and vindictive in victory, melancholic and unaccountable in defeat, who would be bitter and deflect all blame in later exile. There could be no compromise. Napoleon must win in Russia or he and France would lose everything.

He took 640,000 men and a half a million horses into Russia in midsummer, 1812. One-third were French; 160,000 were Germans. There were Poles and Balts and Dutch, Italians and Austrians, conscripts from sullenly occupied lands, and tribute corps of minimal loyalty or none. He had over 500,000 infantry, 110,000 cavalry, 25,000 civilians, 130 siege guns and 1,200 field cannon, mainly 6- and 12-pounders (the latter still called "Napoleons"). Over 6,000 wagons carried provisions, while 2,000 more hauled powder and shot. Hundreds were filled with useless officer's baggage. Thousands of heavy army wagons moved, as well as simple requisitioned farm carts taken from across Germany and Poland; 150,000 local farm horses pulled them, most never before having been beyond their village market. These poor creatures were harnessed to the big guns and their caissons, and to ammo and fodder and supply carts. The *Grande Armée* was pulled by 340,000 draft animals. Another 100,000 cavalry mounts walked east as well. Almost none of these animals survived the invasion and subsequent retreat. The vast land armada moved along narrow dirt roads, making no more than 15 miles on a good day. Each division of 10,000 men and support wagons was strung out over three to four miles. It was the largest army in Europe in 1,500 years, and on Russia's poor, narrow dirt roads it soon made the greatest traffic jam in history. Carts, men, horses and guns were backed up over 200 miles.[41]

The *Grande Armée* advanced in three parts. The main body of 250,000 marched with Napoleon, who rode out of the beating sun inside a carriage, to spare jarring his painful hemorrhoids. Two smaller armies of 75,000 each marched on either flank. Behind came 165,000 replacements. It looked unstoppable. Yet from the moment it crossed the Niemen, things went badly wrong. Conscripts, especially foreigners, deserted in droves, melting away while on foraging expeditions or hiding out in the countryside or in a passed and abandoned village before turning to walk back home. Even Napoleon's brother Jérôme deserted his army and went home to sulk on his throne in Westphalia. Logistics failed right away. Supplies, bad roads, and requisitioned farm carts all proved inadequate. This under a warlord who famously proclaimed: "An army marches on its stomach." His warcraft had been refined in more crimped countries; it did not work so well in vast spaces. Nor was anything learned in Poland in 1807. Napoleon made the same mistakes in Russia in 1812.

The Russians withdrew before the advancing horde, declining battle but stretching Napoleon's supply lines; ever east, ever deeper, away from German and Polish depots. They poisoned wells and burned everything in front of the French, villages and crops and granaries as well as hay and grass for the horses. Just as Peter had burned everything in front of invading Swedes in 1708, forcing them to suffer a hard winter before defeat in 1709 at Poltava. Just as the Red Army would later wreck and scorch western Russia and Ukraine as the Germans advanced in panzers and strung-out leg infantry columns far behind the tanks in the summer of 1941. Russians also moved peasants and all stored food supplies in front of Napoleon, burning whatever they could not carry, as they would again in front of advancing Germans. As the French foraged ever more widely out of the burned zones, they found the broad flanks blocked by superb and harassing light cavalry.

Tsar Alexander and his generals had 410,000 troops, including a sprinkling of émigré officers who opposed Napoleon, the Revolution, or both. Too many thousands were tied down in garrisons or still assembling, but the Russians were of course better than the invading French at logistics in their own lands. It was more than just local familiarity at work. Minister of War Mikhail Barclay de Tolly had long planned a defensive war, to last two years or more. He knew from spies and observation of past practices that Napoleon wanted a quick decisive victory. He knew what defensive war was doing to the French in Spain and explicitly chose to imitate a strategy of attrition in defense of Russia. His generals dipped into six months' prestored food supply for their armies as they fell back and let the French advance. Food and potable water were denied to Napoleon's huge and already ragging formations, yet available to keep Russian corps supplied as they fell back on purpose and in good order, observing the *Grande Armée*.

Barclay de Tolly better understood Cossacks and peasants, too. Where Napoleon naively hoped both would revolt against the tsar, they rallied instead. Where he sought battle, Barclay de Tolly looked to draw him in and wear him out. The tsar's army had the same allies in 1812 that it had in 1709 and the Red Army would have again in 1941: time and space. It was not winter or battle that beat the French. Russians had to deal with the weather, too. It was awful logistics by a battle-seeking commander who didn't know what to do when his enemy refused to fight, choosing to meet him in a different way. It was an officer corps that left French and allied troops without tents or food or proper clothing or enough animal muscle to pull all the guns and wagons, as the horses started to die. Above all, it was the astonishing hubris of Napoleon, who invaded an immense and hostile empire without a viable plan about what to do once the *Grande Armée* got to Moscow, or any plan on how to win the war. He was looking to win battles. The rest would take care of itself.[42] Napoleon concentrated his corps, hoping to catch and beat inferior forces. It was always his way. Russians refused battle and withdrew into the vast open space, burning anything of use to their enemy. It was always their way.

Led by Murat's cavalry, the *Grande Armée* was marched too fast, wearing out draft animals and men in the intense summer heat. Ten thousand horses died within days, literally in harness. The first to go were the Polish and German farm nags, weak or older beasts hundreds of miles beyond familiar pastures. They died from too heavy loads and too many angry lashings by frustrated drovers, collapsing from heart attacks while pulling overloaded ammunition carts and multiple-ton guns. They succumbed to heat, as did men. It was unusually hot and dry. Thousands more horses died from colic from eating green or moldy fodder. With no dry hay (all burned), horses were fed damp thatch from rooves of abandoned village huts and swamp grasses from the Pripet Marshes. Bellies bloated with gas then burst open. Horses screamed in primal agony, demoralizing men nearby as cries of wounded and dying horses always seem to do. Ten thousand stinking carcasses soon lined the roads, adding disease and the stench of rotting flesh to the ordeal of troops strung out in long march columns. It was worst of all for the reserve.

Lack of potable water caused dehydration and more death. Unburied horses joined with defecation along the roadsides by hundreds of thousands of tramping men, and atop the roads by almost as many panting horses. That forced a march every hour and day through dangerous filth and an overpowering stench. Dysentery and more dehydration, and typhus spread by lice inside filthy uniforms, were heaped onto the weight of all the "things they carried" into Russia. Compounding the misery was dust, great clouds kicked up by 600,000 shuffling men and nearly half a million horses. It darkened the sky overhead, in black curtains that hung above the roads like a shroud. Then it rained, every day. It was the autumn *rasputitsa*, the season of rain and mud and dissolution of unpaved roads. The swamps of the Pripet Marshes swelled high and to the season's greatest girth, and dirt roads dissolved under foot, hoof and wheel. When the rains stopped, the mud dried into ruts as hard as concrete and so deep they ruined the roads entirely. The columns slowed to a crawl as axles broke, more horses died, and soldiers were ordered to turn laborers to manhandle guns and wagons with ropes and tackle.

The infantry slogged on this way, hot then wet, hungry and exhausted, for hundreds of miles. Men at extreme limits of physical endurance started to throw away the heaviest items in their packs: sacks of flour, powder pouches, lead balls. Still they drooped under empty field packs that somehow felt always heavier. Each step took them deeper into Russia: 300, 500, then 1,000 miles from homes in Saxony, Westphalia, Naples, Normandy or Provence. Those who could slip away, deserted. Those who could not, suffered and soldiered on. Desertion rates reached 20 percent. By September, 100,000 men had been lost to desertion, sickness or exhaustion. Whole battalions broke away to forage, killing and raping peasants, burning villages, many men never coming back as freedom from military discipline beckoned or Cossacks shot or slashed them down. Morale drooped in a land of endless sky and fields stretching always onward, empty and never-ending. Psychologically, it was profoundly oppressive. It would be again to churning panzers and leg infantry in summer *feldgrau,* victoried to death by Soviet distances and ferocious resistance in 1941.

Napoleon traveled in a commander's coach, hardly noticing the ruin along the way. He paused for two weeks to organize a useless occupation of Vitebsk. He insisted on reviewing his Imperial Guard in full dress uniforms each day. He was 300 miles inside Russia, had yet to fight a battle, and already he was missing one-third of the *Grande Armée,* lost to disease, desertion and assignment as guard units on his ever-lengthening flanks and lines of supply and communication.[43] This was deliberate Russian strategy, agreed to by Tsar Alexander and Barclay de Tolly well before the war. On August 11, Barclay wrote to the commander of the Army of the Danube marching in observation at Napoleon's rear: "The enemy's desire is to finish this war by decisive battles and we on the contrary have to try to avoid such battles . . . Our main goal must be to gain as much time as possible [to allow reserves to form in the interior]."[44] Napoleon was marching half a million men into a set trap. It remained only for the Russians to slam the door.

A small engagement was fought at Krasnyi on August 14, against just 7,000 Russians. The first big fight came outside Smolensk (August 16–18). Napoleon's attack again revealed deep problems in the *Grande Armée,* as it made a brute frontal assault on a fortified defense, repulsed with heavy casualties. After a second day of fighting, Barclay ordered a retreat, over the objections of generals who wanted to fight. Napoleon faced a choice, too. Should he stop in Smolensk and absorb the western Russian provinces, or continue in pursuit of a retreating Russian army? He pursued, through a forest zone. It was the wrong choice, giving the Russians more time and pulling him farther from his already inadequate supply lines. He threw away limits. He was pulled east, seduced by the idea of forcing a great battle, and by his need for one barring any other plan to win. He wanted to win everything in a single campaign, not winter in Smolensk and fight again in 1813. In a land as immense as Russia, he expected to win in a few months, as if campaigning there was the same as in the Rhineland.

As the *Grande Armée* marched deeper into Russia its flanks came under threat, as corps spread out over spaces so wide Napoleon's marshals were bewildered. They peeled off to deal with threats from roving Russian corps or to reduce garrisons the French feared to leave in their rear. They found that Russia was almost as wide as it was deep. Take out one garrison or arrive to find it was already gone, and there was always another and another, some-where wider on the flanks, beyond reach or blocked off by Cossacks or hus-sars. On August 29, the Russians got a new commander-in-chief in Mikhail Kutuzov, and morale soared. French morale sank with every befouled step taken farther from home. It was all predictable, and predicted.

As the invading *Grande Armée* drew to within 100 miles of Moscow, Napoleon was down to just 130,000 men in fighting fit. His supply line trailed 650 miles back to the Niemen and beyond. Just guarding the wagons stripped off tens of thousands from the main army. Nevertheless, Napoleon felt a surge of joy. Scouts said he faced a Russian army positioning to stand and fight him in front of Moscow. He was going to get his great battle after all. Kutuzov chose the killing ground, near the village of Borodino, 78 miles west of Moscow. He put his best batteries in strong redoubts (most famously, the Raevsky Redoubt) along a line of small hills at the center of a westward-facing line. His left flank was nearly open. It had no natural terrain advan-tages. There, he was forced to rely on three arrow-shaped earthwork flèches, each forming a salient angle in front with an open back. He had 24,000 Cossack cavalry but only 90,000 infantry, many ill-trained and readying to fight their first battle. The guns must hold.

The first French arrived on September 5, when a sharp little fight cost each side 5,000 men. The next day the main army arrived. French marshals saw the Russian line shaped as a salient and deployed to face it. When dawn broke over fields and woods still undisturbed by war on September 7, keen for the coming battle, Napoleon said to his nodding marshals: "Behold, the sun of Austerlitz."[45] Most of the Russians were packed into a salient along a narrow frontage. Kutuzov intended this position to force bloodletting on the French, at the price of suffering his own high casualties from artillery that was massed and at times in enfilade position. Kutuzov and other Russian generals weren't particularly callous. This was just the new way one made war, the way everyone had to from now on, with whole nations standing behind the armies and not just kings. Simply put, they knew they could replace their casualties but Napoleon could not replace his, not this far from France and not in time. Still, it was a brutal decision, intended to force Napoleon off his usual game of clever maneuver into a slugging match with cannon and mus-kets and other men's lives. Two Russian corps were poorly deployed, however, anticipating a French attack where none would come. They would not join the fight until much later. Their absence forced Kutuzov to deploy his reserve in the salient from the start, increasing target density for the French guns. Before the shooting started the Russians proudly paraded a famed icon taken

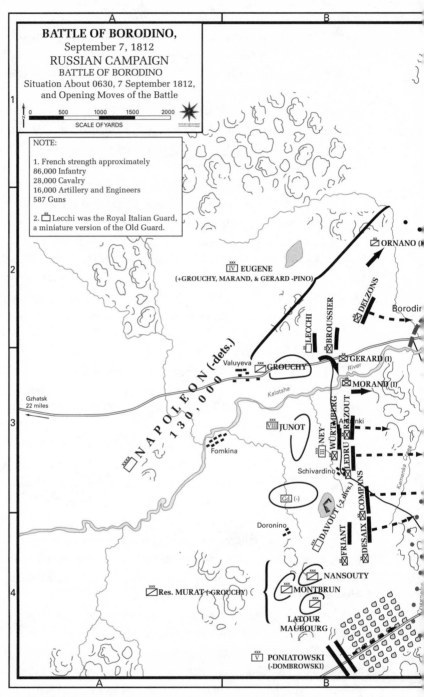

BATTLE OF BORODINO,
September 7, 1812
RUSSIAN CAMPAIGN
BATTLE OF BORODINO
Situation About 0630, 7 September 1812,
and Opening Moves of the Battle

0   500   1000   1500   2000
SCALE OF YARDS

NOTE:

1. French strength approximately
86,000 Infantry
28,000 Cavalry
16,000 Artillery and Engineers
587 Guns

2. ☐ Lecchi was the Royal Italian Guard,
a miniature version of the Old Guard.

ORNANO

IV EUGENE
(+GROUCHY, MARAND, & GERARD -PINO)

DELZONS

Borodir

LECCHI

BROUSSIER

GERARD (I)

Valuyeva   GROUCHY

River

MORAND (I)

Kalatsha

Gzhatsk
22 miles

NAPOLEON (-dets.)
130,000

VIII JUNOT

NEY   WÜRTTBERG   RAZOUT   Alekinki

Fomkina

LEDRU

Schivardino

COMPANS

Kamenka Creek

Gd (-)

DAVOUT (-2 divs.)

Doronino

FRIANT

DESAIX

NANSOUTY

Res. MURAT (-GROUCHY)   MONTBRUN

LATOUR
MAUBOURG

V PONIATOWSKI
(-DOMBROWSKI)

Battle of Borodino, September 7, 1812.

Courtesy of the Department of History, United States Military Academy at West Point. Redraw
by George Chakvetadze.

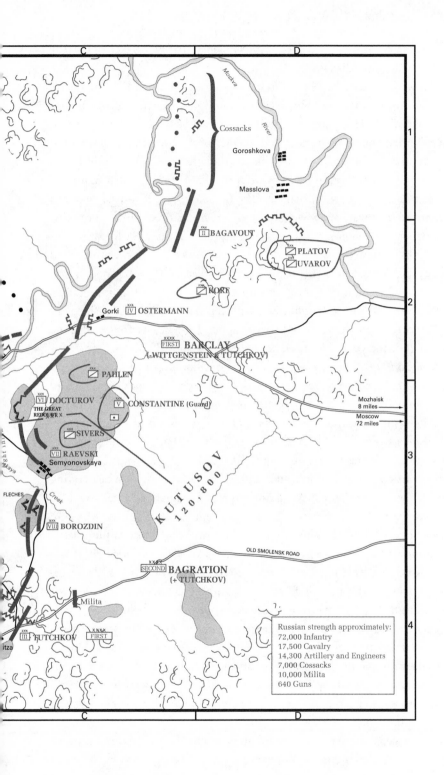

Cossacks

Goroshkova

Masslova

XXX
II BAGAVOUT

XXX
PLATOV

XXX
UVAROV

XXX
KORF

Gorki IV OSTERMANN

XXXX
FIRST BARCLAY
(-WITTGENSTEIN & TUTCHKOV)

XXX
PAHLEN

XXX
VI DOCTUROV

THE GREAT
REDOUBT X

XXX
V CONSTANTINE (Guard)

XXX
SIVERS

XXX
VII RAEVSKI

Semyonovskaya

FLECHES

Creek

XXX
VIII BOROZDIN

K U T U S O V
1 2 0 , 8 0 0

OLD SMOLENSK ROAD

Milita

XXX
III TUTCHKOV

XXXX
FIRST

XXXXX
SECOND BAGRATION
(+ TUTCHKOV)

Mozhaisk
8 miles ——→

Moscow
72 miles ——→

Russian strength approximately:
72,000 Infantry
17,500 Cavalry
14,300 Artillery and Engineers
7,000 Cossacks
10,000 Milita
640 Guns

with them when they pulled back from Smolensk. The French across the way watched with some disdain.[46]

Napoleon was advised by Davout to flank march around Kutuzov's redoubts with 40,000 men, but declined. He wanted battle right away, not more marching. He seemed to lack his old daring, disdaining all maneuver to instead order a massive attack into the center of the Russian line. He would do it again at Waterloo. It was not illness, though he was ill that day. It was not desertion in his hour of need by his tactical muse or supposed genius for war. It was his army, and his enemy. The *Grande Armée* had fewer veterans after 20 years of war; many were dead, others had retired. He did not trust green troops to maneuver, fight and win in the old ways, not like his thinning ranks of grey *grognards*. Nor did his enemy face him in the same failed old way. He was rooted to the terrain, fixed in place, unmoving and perhaps unmovable. His guns must blast or shift the Russians out of their redoubts, if mere boys in uniform could not. Napoleon had 587 cannon that day at Borodino, far more than he would have to pound at redcoats on the ridgeline at Waterloo; and yet it might not be enough.

At 6:00 a.m. on September 7, the French cannon opened fire on the redoubts. Some batteries were poorly placed and had to be repositioned under heavy counter-battery fire. It was not an auspicious start. Iron flew in both directions, smacking into earth, guns, men and horses. Cavalry and infantry skirmishers advanced. First contact came in the village of Borodino, which the French overran. Then came much heavier fighting around the flèches, whose earthen walls caved in under falling French solid shot and exploding shells. They changed hands several times as Ney, Davout and Murat attacked, trying to turn Marshal Pyotr Bagration's position and the flank. At 8:30 a.m. Napoleon was forced to commit a part of his reserve. Ninety minutes later, the strong attack on the Russian right was stopped by 300 cannon firing from inside Kutuzov's fixed redoubts. Raevsky Redoubt was overrun as French infantry advanced through thick smoke, assaulting cannon running low on ammunition. It was retaken by a Russian counterattack. The chief of the artillery was killed, as was Bagration. In 1944, the Red Army would name its greatest offensive of World War II after this tsarist general killed by an invading army, sending Soviet tanks and guns and troops to smash through fixed-in-place Army Group Center, breaking whole German corps. In a man's name, one war's violently heroic defense against invasion remembering and honoring another.

French generals were dying, too, at Borodino. Their infantry kept attacking in heavy columns, as it always did. Cavalry charged as well. Ney and

Murat attacked repeatedly, leading the cavalry personally. French and Polish and German courage was met by tens of thousands of Russian muskets and double lines of cannon firing canister to shred the advance. With guns, guts and cold bayonets the Russian line held. It bent backward, but it did not break. Napoleon was shaken. Cossacks attacked, riding from the north to threaten the French rear and sow panic on the left flank. At the other end of the battle to the south, on the Russian left, French cannon moved up to fire canister point-blank into infantry forced to stay in squares because of constant cavalry assaults; 1,600 fell. The squares retreated, leaving hundreds of shredded men behind, but did not break.

Napoleon refused to commit the Imperial Guard, as several marshals angrily demanded, saying the moment of crisis was here. Kutuzov used the time to dig his men in along a second defensive line. At noon, 400 guns positioned as a grand battery blasted apart the hard redoubts. Napoleon was in his tent, where he spent most of the day feeling ill, not even watching the battle he had marched so many so far to fight. At 2:00 p.m. French heavy cavalry attacked and overran the redoubts. It was an unusual tactic, sending horse alone against the guns. Nearly every Russian stayed with his gun. Everyone who did was killed or wounded by lance, sword or pistol in ferocious hand-to-hand fighting with the horsemen. Now 20,000 French infantry advanced to secure the redoubts. As they did, Russian cavalry counterattacked, leading to a ferocious mêlée. Napoleon again hesitated, again refused to commit his Old Guard, and lost his last chance at a smashing victory.

Few surrenders were accepted at Borodino. The war and the hatreds it produced had moved past noble gestures and personal honor, and perhaps also mercy. This was *guerre mortelle*, new-style. Kutuzov's line wobbled, bloody and torn. At 4:00 p.m. Napoleon came out to watch, mounting his charger with assistance and difficulty. His marshals criticized him to his face, yet he still would not commit the Imperial Guard. He feared what might happen if he lost his most dependable veterans 800 leagues from Paris. Turning his hopes once again to the big guns, he planned more artillery bombardment to win the battle on the following day. Kutuzov, too, wanted to fight again, but could not when he heard that the Imperial Guard remained uncommitted and that his own losses were stupendous. After 12 hours of close combat, the armies, if not their generals, had enough.[47] Whole divisions and corps were shattered, effectively destroyed. Kutuzov decided to pull out during the night, making a quiet and orderly retreat. He left his dead to camp dogs and carrion birds, his wounded to the mercy of the French. Amputations went on over four days and nights. Ten thousand wounded from many nationalities lay uncollected for days. Most bled out, untended and alone. One boy was found a week later, wrote the diplomat Armand de Caulaincourt in his campaign diary, "half his body buried in the belly of a dead horse, eating its raw flesh like a wild dog." His brother was a general of the cavalry, one of 16 French generals killed at Borodino.

Napoleon held the field and thus technically won the battle, at a cost he could ill afford. Against 45,000 Russian casualties, he lost 35,000 French (and Poles and Germans and others). His dead were harder to replace, his wounded more of a burden. Recovered from his illness, he walked the battlefield in deep and silent melancholy. For his lost men or his blunted ambition? Only he knew, but one may reasonably suspect the latter. The retreating Russian army had been mauled but not broken. As it passed though Moscow on September 14, the city's population was already streaming out. Reinforcements were moving the other way, toward Moscow from across the tsar's empire. Napoleon had none, except a few thousands still straggling up the Moscow road. The *Grande Armée* limped into a ghost city abandoned by its people on the order of its governor, Count Fyodor Rostopchin, who then set it on fire to deny billets to the French. Only the indigent, the insane, criminals and some foreigners were left behind, and a few hundred spies and saboteurs.

Napoleon rode into Moscow on September 15, brooding in his command carriage as it passed down silent streets lined with emptied mansions and onion-domed churches. He passed under the Kremlin gates at noon. The tsar's palace was empty, much as the British would find the White House a year later. He could not find his victory. He had misplaced his glory. He said to all who listened: "I have beaten them. I have beaten them. It means *nothing*?"[48] Despondent, he went to sleep in the tsar's bedchamber. At 8:00 p.m. the first fires broke out. By midnight the city was ablaze, burned by arsonists to deny shelter to the French. Scorched earth, scorched city. Awakened and shown the fires from a Kremlin window, Napoleon strained for breath in heavy smoke as he watched the center of Moscow glowing orange. He fled the fires and city that night, leaving an inferno burning all around his camped *Grande Armée* that consumed 75 percent of the buildings.[49] His army had few billets and little food. It was naked and exposed and wounded as a Russian winter approached. He had won only ashes in the mouth.

Napoleon had no plan, no strategy. Only hubris and hunger for battle which did not pay for itself any more. It fed on itself and him from the inside out, hollow and gnawing. Why was he even in Moscow? What was there he did not already have? Where was his victory and glory? He wrote to the tsar,

Napoleon in the Kremlin (1812).
Courtesy of Wikimedia Creative Commons.

deflecting all blame: "I have made war on your Majesty without animosity: a note from him before or after the last battle would have stopped my march."[50] He may even have believed it. Alexander refused to talk peace as long as French boots were on Russia's soil, but he also played Napoleon with hints and ruses. He wanted to hold the *Grande Armée* in Moscow as long as possible, while new Russian armies gathered alongside the road all the way back to Belorussia. Now came bad news from Paris, word of an attempted coup. It was quixotic and easily put down by Napoleon's loyalists, but perhaps a portent. Wellington had also won in Spain, he was told, at Salamanca in July. He might dare to invade France itself, absent its warlord emperor. Should he leave Moscow or stay? Winter was coming, soon. Napoleon had left behind several corps on the road to Moscow to protect communications and supply. These were now under constant harassing attack. If he stayed, the road might close behind him.

Hundreds were summarily shot by French firing squads—Russian saboteurs and accused arsonists, but also looters from disintegrating French units. Openly defying their officers, French soldiers stayed drunk for days. They made fires on abandoned tile floors of mansions and burned books and furniture to stay warm and to cook horseflesh. They looted everything, piled it around like conquistadores in the treasure rooms at Tenochtitlán, indulging a macabre gold lust among the ruins. Napoleon ordered more looters shot. It was too late. He had lost control. The *Grande Armée* was become a drunken, disorderly mob. Morale collapsed in a wooden city reduced to a burned-out tomb as four fresh Russian armies marched to cut off and encircle the hated invader. Napoleon had 102,000 men and 500 guns and 15,000 wounded from Borodino. There were not enough carts to carry the wounded and his supplies; not enough starving horses to harness over boney shanks. And yet he gave the fateful order. Anything was better than wintering in an alien and ember city made of ash pile and cinder buildings and burnt ambition. He left orders to blow up the Kremlin as he departed, as if the war was between him and the tsar and not between aroused nations-in-arms, full of hate. He understood less and less of what was happening around him, or in Europe.

On October 18, Russians ambushed Ney's corps in a forest at Tarutino, inflicting 3,000 casualties and capturing many guns and Imperial Eagles. The invaders were frightened. They were about to crawl from Moscow in disorder with several Russian armies positioning to cut off the retreat, to kill Napoleon's wounded ambition and the remnant of the *Grande Armée* before either reached the border. The westward dying of the *Grande Armée* began the next day, 35 days after entering Moscow. It had no fight left. Like armored Spanish thieves padding down the causeway, trying to sneak out of Tenochtitlán at night, the French were overladen with greed and loot: silver, furs, rugs, paintings, even marble statues and chandeliers ripped from the ceilings of great mansions. A lumbering column of carts slogged west over the same roads and past the same burned-out lands of the summer. On October 24, at the town of Maloyaroslavets, some 32,000 Russians fought 24,000

Italians to a bloody draw, inflicting 7,000 casualties on each side. The *Grande Armée* was nine days out from Moscow, had already eaten much of its food, and had hardly left the burned spires and onion domes of the city behind. Harassment of the ragged columns by Cossack light cavalry and hussars was constant and lethal.

There was food farther south, but the way was blocked by elements of 15,000 fresh Don Cossacks and another Russian army. A Council of War set the path back to Borodino, thence to Smolensk and on to the border. The column of woe already stretched 50 miles. Five days later, its lead elements passed the battlefield at Borodino, where there were still tens of thousands of unburied dead, some half eaten by scavenger birds and wolves. Severely wounded French soldiers left behind when the *Grande Armée* moved on to Moscow were still in unheated huts and a crowded monastery. Napoleon ordered them carried in his wagons, but the drovers later dumped them out. From there to the border, the retreat wound through burned lands and the broken detritus of war. Skeletal horses died daily from beatings and starvation or were shot and eaten, further slowing the jam. Stragglers and outriders were attacked nightly by Cossacks or partisans who murdered some and terrified the rest, once nearly capturing Napoleon, who actually drew a sword before being rescued by his Imperial Guards. Common soldiers who straggled or got lost in the night met peasants or partisans, who committed hundreds of private atrocities. They murdered and then mutilated, or mutilated and then murdered many lost boys, as their descendants would later do to fleeing German boys in late December 1941. Half the cavalry was already walking. It snowed heavily on November 6.

Now it all fell apart. Orders were ignored. Discipline was gone. Loot was dropped into snowbanks the same way the conquistadores had dropped their gold in the lake to run down the last yards of causeway. Cannons and caissons were abandoned. Horses were stolen by deserters, often by officers who rode off to save themselves. The wounded were dumped out of horseless carts by healthier men who stole all their clothes and left them to freeze or to be murdered by partisans. Temperatures plunged to −35°F. Men froze to death while sleeping, past care or caring. The dead were stripped of clothes and boots by the barely living. Some 200 were covered by blowing snow, forgotten under frozen earth until discovered in 2002, preserved huddled together in fetal positions just as they had died in 1812. Forensics showed their average age was 21. Thousands more were discovered in long rows laid down in a mass grave on the outskirts of modern Vilnius. Dutch and French and other corpses still in blue cloth, with flattened shakos and buttons of alloyed tin and copper with

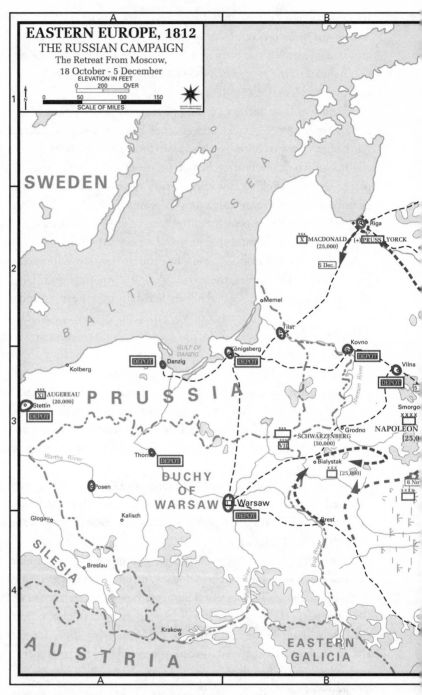

Retreat from Moscow, October 18–December 5, 1812.

Courtesy of the Department of History, United States Military Academy at West Point.

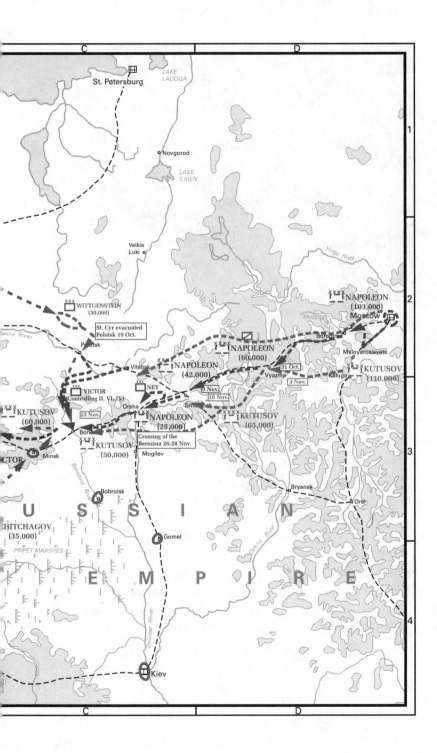

St. Petersburg

LAKE LADOGA

Novgorod

LAKE ILMEN

Velkie Luki

Volga River

XXX
WITTGENSTEIN
(30,000)

St. Cyr evacuated
Polotsk 19 Oct.

Polotsk

wina River

XXX NAPOLEON
(103,000)
(103,000)

Moscow

Moskva River

Borodino

XXX
NAPOLEON
(60,000)

Maloyaroslavets

Vitebsk   XXX NAPOLEON
(42,000)

XXX
VICTOR
(Controlling II, VI, IX)

XXX
NEY

31 Oct.

Vyazma

Kaluga   XXX KUTUSOV
(110,000)

3 Nov.

XXX
KUTUSOV
(60,000)

23 Nov.

Orsha

Smolensk

9 Nov.
16 Nov.

XXX
NAPOLEON
(25,000)

XXX KUTUSOV
(65,000)

Boris

XXX KUTUSOV
(50,000)

Crossing of the
Berezina 26-28 Nov.

Minsk

Mogilev

Bryansk

Berezina River

Bobruisk

Orel

R U S S I A N

TCHITCHAGOV
(35,000)

Gomel

Desna River

PRIPET MARSHES

E M P I R E

Dnieper River

Kiev

Night Bivouac, Retreat from Moscow (1812).
Courtesy of Wikimedia Creative Commons.

number stamps intact that showed they came from over 40 different regiments. One corpse still wore a cockaded tricolor helmet. Most had died of
starvation. They were reburied with full military honors, then further com-
memorated in a solemn international ceremony in 2011.[51] Not so the 30,000
other corpses carpeting the retreat within just two weeks of leaving Moscow.
Some were devoured by wolves, others by starving men. No cavalry worthy
of the name remained by the time survivors reached Smolensk. Russians had
severe winter supply problems, too, which helped save Napoleon from encirclement and possible capture by enveloping Russian armies. Many of his men
by then had enough. Whole divisions of starving infantry whose will ran out
with the last of the food, or whose officers ran away, surrendered to the pursuing Russians rather than go on. On November 9, elements of the Old Guard
refused orders for the first time. They ran amok, eating a week's supply of
food stored at Smolensk in just a day. When the rest of the army arrived the
city was a hollow ruin, a tomb full of murdered Russians.

Napoleon sent a courier to Paris, ordering a new levy of 300,000 men. He
meant to form a new army and fight in Germany. Wrapped in sheepskins,
he abandoned his no longer so *Grande Armée*. Slipping away by troika, he
crossed the frozen Niemen and raced for Paris. Of the 640,000 who crossed
that river with Napoleon in arrogance in June, fewer than 50,000 recrossed

it. Ney's corps of 15,000 fought as a rearguard all the way, and was reduced to 800 men by November 18. The remnants had to fight their way out under fire as they ran across the last pontoon bridge over the Berezina on November 26–29. At least 25,000 more were lost in fighting around that last bridge out, along with nearly all the baggage and guns.[52] Over the next three weeks, half those who got out died or were captured by more pursuit. When it was all over, the Russians had lost 48,000 men in the hot pursuit to the Berezina in exchange for about 100,000 broken French and allied troops taken prisoner. Yet the tsar and his generals were upset. They wanted to trap the whole French army and capture Napoleon, but he was gone ahead. The rest were simply gone, deserted or missing or dead. In the spring, the corpses of 400,000 men left behind by Napoleon were buried or burned by the Russians. A half million horses were also dead on the French side alone. Most importantly, 100,000 irreplaceable cavalry mounts that would be greatly missed in the last campaigns in 1813–1814.

Already, Napoleon blamed the Russian campaign on everyone but himself. His comment on the ruin of his plans typically focused on his reputation, not the half million French and allied dead he left behind. He told the Polish ambassador: "From the sublime to the ridiculous is but a step." Prussia allied with Russia on March 17, 1813. Britain granted subsidies to all who agreed to form another anti-French coalition. Some of Napoleon's marshals grew permanently disillusioned with his conduct of the war, and began to maneuver to save themselves should he lose it as they now suspected he might. Murat went back to Naples, still dressed in feathers and gold braid. Marshal Jean-Andoche Junot went mad. Jean-Baptiste Bernadotte, a former French marshal later crowned as Charles XIV of Sweden, brought his adopted country into the war against Napoleon as the Great Powers gathered their armies and declared war. Dresden in Saxony fell to a Russian army, and Bavaria asked out of its French alliance. Even Napoleon's father-in-law since 1810, Habsburg Emperor Francis I, joined this last and greatest of the anti-French coalitions. The powers agreed not to make any separate peace, to pursue Napoleon until he agreed to terms or was brought to defeat in Paris.[53]

By August 1813, Napoleon was at war with all Europe. Allied armies came at him from all directions, out of Russia, Prussia and Spain, from Austria and the Netherlands. France had made war for a generation and by 1813 was nearly bereft of fighting men, down to greybeards and kids and a few second-rate and third-rate garrisons in Germany. The combined losses from Spain and Russia were catastrophic, forcing Napoleon to call up ever-younger classes of inadequate recruits. Yet the bureaucracy gave him only 200,000 replacements for all the dead he left in the East and more across the Pyrenees. He salted the arrivals with survivors of the *Grande Armée* and added second-rate garrison troops and 50,000 Germans. But more of his tribute armies were vanishing or changing sides, or waiting to do so should he suffer further losses. From now on, he was always outnumbered two-to-one or worse in every fight he made outside France. His generals were disillusioned by his poor demeanor and worse generalship in Russia. His cavalry could hardly ride, lacking trained mounts. His infantry was mostly green. His batteries had fewer guns than before. So of course he hurried back to Germany to give battle against a vast coalition. He could not conceive how to stop.

As always after a defeat, all hope for Napoleon lay in the next battle. Even now he had the short-war delusion that the next victory would be decisive, redeem all his prior political mistakes, settle and fix everything he had ruined past repair. He met the Allies and won, though not easily, in a street brawl at Lützen (May 2). Then he fought a standing count prize fight at Bautzen (May 20–21), a mauling that brought both sides heavy losses. He wanted to go on offense, but the desertion rate skyrocketed. Troops did the usual sorts of things soldiers do when morale fails, but also self-mutilated in unusual numbers, cutting off trigger fingers, shooting themselves in the hand or foot or buttocks. Others faked wounds during combat in order to fall down and lie still under the enemy's musket balls when attacked, not firing back, and surrendering if possible. It was profound war weariness accompanied by a new popular realism in the face of overwhelming Allied superiority.[54] France knew defeat was coming. Napoleon did not share this growing view.

A truce was agreed on July 20, but not a peace. Each side regrouped and reinforced. When it ended, his father-in-law, grandfather to his son, brought 300,000 troops into the Grand Alliance against him. Russia sent more armies west. The Prussian Army was in the fight, too, and no longer the backward weakling he had beaten at Jena-Auerstedt. It was reformed and ready as it marched to war in Germany. His former marshal in Sweden brought 95,000 men with him, and beat Ney in a sharp fight. Murat secretly negotiated with the Allies, looking to survive by betraying Napoleon and adding Naples to his list of enemies. Wellington was emerging out of the Pyrenees with a veteran army fresh from victory in Spain. All told, 600,000 Allied troops were closing around Napoleon by the autumn of 1813. Generously, he was offered terms and peace. He refused. He thought the next battle, one more campaign, might change everything.

It did not. The Allies agreed to coordinate movement by three armies (called the "Trachenberg Plan"), to surround and trap him with overwhelming forces. They trusted nothing less, for he was still the Wolf of Battle and they feared his skill with reason. In deep mud at Dresden (August 26–27), he isolated one of the three circling armies and defeated it soundly, but he also lost 10,000 men. At last the Allies concentrated for superiority, driving him like hounds toward Leipzig, where they would kill this cleverest of foxes. For officers from the new Prussian war academy and General Staff, the fight at Leipzig would stand as a model for the wars they waged for the next 140 years, their first planned and successful *Kesselschlacht* ("cauldron battle"), a concentric mobile encirclement of an entire enemy army leading to its physical elimination.[55]

Over 600,000 men in all, an army from France facing armies from Russia, Prussia, Austria and Sweden, fought in the *Völkerschlacht* ("Battle of the Nations"), as Leipzig is also called. It lasted four days, from October 16 to 19, 1813. Napoleon still believed in the decisive battle, still thought that was how wars were won or lost in the new way of war. On its eve, he was heard to mutter "between a battle lost and a battle won the distance is immense, and there stand empires." He had 195,000 men and 700 cannon. His enemies had 410,000 men and 1,500 guns. Their numbers and skill forced him into a ring defense that was attacked from every side. There was no advantage of interior lines; there was only slaughter all around. Halfway through the fight and losing badly, he tried to negotiate. He was rebuffed. Blücher attacked at the head of the Prussian Army in the north. Other armies attacked the encircled French on different sides. As Napoleon pulled out of Leipzig the Allies raced in, smashing up his rearguard. Bridges were blown prematurely by someone in a panic, and four French corps were trapped. The Allies proceeded to do to the French trapped in Leipzig what Napoleon had done to Russians trapped with their backs against the water at Friedland. They drove them without mercy into the river, drowning thousands. Counting 30,000 who surrendered, Napoleon lost 68,000 against 54,000 on the other side.[56]

Napoleon retreated into France. He got over the Rhine with just 80,000 of the 200,000 fresh troops raised earlier. Again he was offered generous terms: stay inside France and rule it like an ordinary monarch and you may have peace; come out with an army again and you will be crushed and toppled, your dynasty overthrown. Again he refused to be cribbed or confined in his ambition. On December 1, the Allies pledged once again to make no separate peace and to jointly invade. Napoleon called on France to raise yet another army for him. It was as raw a force as could be, formed of even younger boys than before, hardly trained to march and badly underequipped. These youths became known as the "Marie Louises" because, in his absence,

Empress and Habsburg daughter Marie Louise signed their conscription notice. They joined with a hodgepodge of Young Guards, some bourgeois volunteers, and the desperation of a restored yet barely armed or competent militia, the *Garde nationale*. They were short of artillerists and ammunition, engineers, fusils and uniforms. Short of everything, especially veteran *grognards*. France was bled out. Not enough youths answered the call-up, or were allowed to leave home by desperate mothers, when Napoleon called out the classes of 1815–1820, ordering boys of 14 and 15 to take up arms.[57] Shame was a foreign country to Napoleon.

He was still a virtuoso, however. His last campaigns saw speedy movements and corps-sized battles, including several more small victories. The French Empire, like the Roman Empire, had built dense networks of roads to move its legions and war matériel. Napoleon knew these pathways well, and used them in a small-scale version of fighting from the central position to cut off and surprise several Allied corps, foolishly separate from each other when the Master was so near. Four times he beat a Prussian corps led by Blücher, in discrete fights in January 1814. He won two more frontier battles shortly after that. For a third time, the Allies offered him a reasoned peace. For a third time he refused. Having ignored Spain, he learned nothing from its style of fighting invaders, refusing to emulate its guerrilla war or what the partisans had done to his army in Russia. He eschewed advice to call a new *levée en masse*, in the original republican sense and spirit of a mass popular uprising to defend France from invasion. Only *he* could save France by seeking out and winning battles by superior will and talent. The war could not be won by some grubby *petite guerre*. He allowed a handful of partisan bands to form, but only on the condition that they must be led by trusted regular army officers.[58] Then he went back to battle-seeking.

He would win, he believed, if only his army did not melt from desertion along with the spring snow. Again he met Blücher's Prussians. This time he was beaten by them at Laon (March 9–10). He turned and beat off 20,000 Austrians at Arcis-sur-Aube (March 20), and looked to fight again. But the Allies were already done with him, debating who would replace him. They had five armies in northern France to his one and a few detached corps. He could not block them all. Two moved around his little force to march directly on Paris. He rode ahead with a half-dozen aides to within 10 miles of the capital, where he learned on March 31 that Paris had already surrendered. Paris was not France. He was France, he had once proclaimed to the Senate. He gathered 60,000 troops at Fontainebleau, saying he would march to retake his capital. Talleyrand had enough, and turned away. On April 4,

Napoleon was at last refused by Ney and the other *maréchals de France*. They said they would not march with or under him again. He was *not* France after all.[59] The Allies forced him to abdicate two days later then sent him into exile as "Emperor of Elba," a tiny island between his original home in Corsica and his adopted empire and ambition in France. Then they sat down in Vienna to make the peace they could never reach with him in the room, or on the continent.

He came back to trouble them one last time, in the most famous of his campaigns, though not his most important: the Hundred Days that led to his final defeat at Waterloo on June 18, 1815. All statesmen knew after Waterloo that peace required that Napoleon must be exiled not from France but from Europe. They sent him to live out his days on St. Helena in the windy south Atlantic. The British agreed to guard him until he died.[60] Napoleon's wars of Empire cost France 860,000 dead, and possibly closer to 920,000. Relative to population, that was roughly equivalent to France's losses in World War I, though stretched over a longer period. The numbers also represent a 38 percent mortality rate for males born between 1790 and 1795, the missing veterans in the armies that waged the last three years of war. Europe as a whole lost five million dead, again comparable to or worse than World War I.[61] Such mass casualties and the disruption of social, economic, political and cultural life that attended them are what ultimately decided Napoleon's wars, not the battles per se, which largely were accelerants of the more profound strategic attrition that decided the outcome. France finally quit fighting in 1814 because it was exhausted, worn out by war.

That was the year the war was decided, too, not the next year at Waterloo. Victor Hugo said Waterloo "wasn't a battle. It was a change of direction in the universe." It was not. It has been more aptly called a "glorious irrelevance."[62] Had Napoleon won at Waterloo it would have changed little except the length of casualty lists needed to beat him next time for good and all, and for the good of all. Wellington famously said of him that "his presence on the field made the difference of 40,000 men."[63] If true, it was still a downgrade from Louis XV, of whom Saxe said at Fontenoy "His presence is worth an additional 50,000 men to us." Whether true or not of Napoleon, it did not really matter. The Allies had far more men than that in 1815 and the will to use their huge armies to crush Napoleon whatever happened one day in Belgium, win or lose there. Already armies of the nations exceeding 500,000 men were nearing the borders of France, and there were more Allied armies behind them. Already the war was lost. Already morale was broken, willingness to surrender young men to Napoleon exceeded by French willingness to surrender them to the Allies and to peace. One or two or five more bloody and indecisive battles would not change that strategic calculus. It was not just the Old Guard who finally cried out when facing death and Blücher at Waterloo, *"Sauve qui peut!"* ("save yourselves, whoever can"). It was all of France.

***

NAPOLEON'S SPECTACULAR SUCCESS up to 1809 outshines in history his final failure and chronic lack of strategic planning. Yet he was as spectacular a grand failure at the strategic level of war as he was clearly and markedly superior at its tactical and operational levels. Believing in his own command skill above all else, his policy was always to make war, interrupted only by truces of convenience that he later broke without regard for severe damage to France's diplomatic reputation and the long-term need for a stable peace to secure dynastic and imperial gains. Napoleon thereby lost it all, gains from earlier battlefield victories like Ulm and Austerlitz and Jena-Auerstedt, his empire and his dynasty. While winning appears to make you a genius in military history, losing everything does not always strip the praise and title away, as it probably should. War is too important to be left to genius. It is also far too complex for anyone to actually control as Napoleon and his admirers thought he controlled it; too contingent for fortune, good or bad, not to play a large role alongside command skill and soldier courage in every battle's outcome and in the sound and fury of every war.

Through mists of memory, and the influence of Jomini and Clausewitz and a hundred admiring historians, Napoleon and the idea of the decisive battle dominated military thought for more than another century. Yet even in his time such victories were rare and anomalous. In an era supposedly marked off as an "Age of Battles," and over the career of the greatest battle general of all times, exhaustion by coalition in the end won the war for his enemies. His keen tactical exploitation of maneuver and encirclement no doubt expressed a uniquely skilled generalship, unmatched by any other commander. Yet his triumphs rested more basically on what proved merely temporary advantages afforded French armies by mass conscription, superior bureaucratic organization, inspired troop morale and military professionalism, all of which he inherited from Revolutionary armies and in part also from the evolving army of the late ancien régime that was so despised by admirers who claimed he changed everything.

Napoleon was the pinnacle and completion of 18th-century tactics and battle, of horse-and-musket war. He was not a major innovator per se. He was instead master and sometimes perfecter of changes and earlier innovations that showed how combined arms attack might succeed in circumstances of horse-and-musket battle. Even the crucial exception of his corps system that sped movement of armies, allowed wider foraging, and disguised direction of march so that he was often able to achieve surprise concentrations and local superiority just before a battle started had antecedents in the warcraft of Frederick II.[64] Nevertheless, Napoleon unquestionably had unique talents for foreseeing complex movements of armies and reading more staid enemy intentions, to get there first with more men and guns—at least until the enemy had so many more men and guns that getting there first no longer mattered. The moment passed, in his own lifetime. All he could do in his last major battles against superior numbers, in armies again coming to look and fight like each other, was to bash bluntly at enemies who now knew his tactics and so sat in defensive positions and took it, grinding his armies down with theirs.

Even the most reactionary regimes and armies caught up to his tactics, and beat him. So, too, the *levée en masse* and *petite guerre* engaged peoples other than the French, who then beat France. Within 50 years of Borodino and Leipzig, mobilizations produced armies so big that most of Napoleon's methods were defunct, even as the influence of his reputation continued. His fast movement and battle tactics fit armies of 100,000 or fewer, and no longer worked so well even in his last years and campaigns. The 1812 campaign showed that one could not march armies of a half million or more men and achieve real surprise or retain flexibility in movement, as he did only with much smaller forces. Nor could armies that big—and they were all going to get even bigger—rely on foraging, as his failure in Russia also proved. The 1813 campaign in Germany showed that when both sides had mass armies of hundreds of thousands of men the outcome of all the clever maneuvering was still to crash into each other and commence mauling by cannon and musket, a form of brute combat where the gods of war remained on the side of bigger battalions. Technology was changing, too. Napoleon was the greatest of the horsepower generals, but more importantly he was also the last. Iron horses were the future of war. Britain was already using steam engines to drive industry and move goods over a world empire. Within 50 years, major armies everywhere would ride railways into war and haul supplies after them on a scale of movement spanning countries and continents.

9

Battle Exalted

NAPOLEON'S BATTLEFIELD VICTORIES lingered in military imaginations. His words and career were studied in detail, shaping the thinking and writing of all his contemporaries, including Jomini and Clausewitz. As he dominated the wars of his own lifetime, so he dominated military thinking and theory into the 20th century. War was reducible to knowable principles, even if lesser talents than Napoleon must practice war as a shrouded art. So said a generation of theorists who saw the Master of Battle at work, then went to work to master battle. They watched him slip the restraints of magazines and fortresses to break into open country, moving along interior lines to seek local envelopment by maneuver to the enemy's rear (*le manoeuvre sur les derrières*). Theorists like Jomini in France, Clausewitz in Prussia, William Napier in Britain, and Denis Mahan and Henry Halleck at West Point thought the Master had made war in ways that forever changed it, leaving behind the stalemated past of stone and *Stellungskrieg*, of grinding positional warfare. He had moved deftly and with one purpose, to achieve the cardinal act of war, which was battle. They did not perceive that strategic exhaustion of a different sort, strung out year over year in battle after battle, accelerating costs and casualties among whole nations under arms, was more critical in the outcome of the Napoleonic Wars than a rare red day of decision at Ulm or Austerlitz. They believed that the culmination of war was revealed as battle, war's true Platonic form. They sought a Philosopher's Stone to transmute battle into lasting decision. They thought they found it in the idea of genius as the guiding hand of action, aiming always and with all possible force for an envelopment and *Vernichtungsschlacht,* a decisive "battle of annihilation" in the Napoleonic manner.[1]

The distillate of the past to guide future operations was concentric envelopment, not just turning a flank but engulfing a whole enemy army and then destroying it; preferably, his main force right at the outset of the next war. The goal would be utter destruction of the enemy's ability to continue military resistance, a military *Vernichtungsschlacht* leading into a political diktat.[2] Napoleon was the doctrine incarnate. His victories had been won by defying older wisdom, by dividing armies into flexible corps that moved swiftly and separately but with a paramount purpose: to approach the enemy from several directions at once, sever his rear communications and supply lines, and thereby force him to fight a great battle at fatal disadvantage. As his army did at Ulm and Austerlitz, your army should achieve surprise and local superiority by moving fast and then reconcentrating just before the climax of battle. Never mind the coming long war of matériel against a stronger enemy or a coalition, which your opening aggressive thrust will surely bring about. Win fast like he did and you win everything.

Most military thinkers at the close of the Enlightenment century still worked from the assumption that war was subject to perfect scientific rule-making. They looked to the deposed French emperor as the exemplar of what was possible, what was perfect and permanent and replicable in war. Initially, Jomini was the widest read of the new theorists. Over time, though not for decades, Clausewitz was acclaimed as the most original and important. He helped shape a different military theory that took root especially in Germany, a reaction against rigid military rationalism. Yet his theory of the art of war also worshiped Napoleon as a natural genius, as the "God of War," as he called him, whose penetration to war's essence let him act in accord with the highest rules reason revealed.[3] Clausewitz served as a young, impressionable officer with the Prussian Army and then with the Russian Army. In 1812, he observed the Moscow campaign from the opposite side to Napoleon. All around him was the scorched evidence of a strategy of attrition that denied Napoleon the all-decisive battles he wanted, then ruined the *Grande Armée*. Against his own experience and all the evidence, Clausewitz exclaimed in ink that year: "Battles decide everything."[4] He never quite got over this myopic admiration of Napoleon and decisive battle.

Enlightenment *philosophes* wrote that war was regrettable, though some embraced it even so if it was wielded in the duels of monarchs by the very best despots. They upheld a view of the "art of war" as coolly controlled and rational violence, of sieges and battles as high compositions using muskets and crescendos of cannon, concertos of action conducted by genius, brilliant concerts of combat to compare to the classical masterpieces of Alexander, Hannibal, Scipio and Caesar. Romantics reacted against the sterile and geo-metric formulae of perfect war, more impressed by the release of violent pas-sions in the French Revolution and the *levée en masse*. Romanticism about war aroused visions of change and domination made naked to force and the

will to triumph. One view exalted the secular genius of modern great captains; the other revered the released genies of peoples' war. Napoleon combined both indulgences, beguiling everyone with a dance of the furies. If
such a great captain's example and natural-born talent could be distilled and
taught, a science of generalship would be achieved. Clausewitz set aside the
pure rationalists' chimera of universal principles of war, reducible to precepts
and maxims. He also abjured the uncontrollable rage and violence of the war
of peoples he saw all around him. He wanted something both controlling of
decision in war and Romantic in unleashed power. The search for the distillate of genius was on.

Clausewitz believed that all warfare tended toward total destruction ("absolute war"), that the "battle of annihilation" located its true purpose. He
wrote glowingly of the importance of the "destructive principle" and "total
overthrow" of the enemy in war. He dismissed attrition with confident, even
sneering, certainty in decisive battle: "Gradually the units are burned out . . .
and others will take their place. So the battle smolders away, like damp gunpowder." Yet his own vaunted theory of war, like those of the 18th century
that he dismissed, was just as dogmatic.[5] Only late in life did Clausewitz correct that error, or rather stumble into a deep crisis of contradiction he left
unresolved at his death. For not all actual wars approached the absolute war
of his early theory. In fact, most wars in history did *not* reach for totality in
means or goals. War was *not* all about battles. To his credit, he admitted that
the abstract theory he had framed in his youth rested on grave empirical error,
as studying history showed that most wars did not become "untrammeled."
How could this be, when he had seen war reach toward the absolute in his
own lifetime? Because war was an instrument of policy, defined by social and
cultural and political interests that chose and mediated and limited military
means. In the real world, war-fighting was not some young theoretician's exercise in absolutist abstraction. Battles did *not* decide everything after all.[6]

Clausewitz never resolved his crisis of contradiction. His unfinished
masterpiece *On War* was published posthumously, crisis intact and in print.
People noted the difficulty or not, then everyone returned to talking about
tactics and battle-seeking campaigns. For a century, his first view of war as
tending toward absolute goals of total overthrow served by absolute means
took hold of military theory. Offense was everything. One aspired to make
war as Napoleon did, with climactic battle the purest and highest expression
of its true nature, or one did not really know how to make war. Movement to
seek the destruction of the enemy's armies was brilliance. Sitting in a strong
defense while the enemy wasted his army on your guns and redoubts was

contemptible. These ideas played some role in Prussian planning leading into the Wars of German Unification in the mid-19th century as Moltke won decisively at Königgrätz (1866) and Sedan (1870), seemingly affirming all that Clausewitz taught.[7] Germans planned an enormous *Kessel* (cauldron) campaign to win at the outset in 1914, but failed at First Marne and lost World War I by material and human exhaustion. They doubled down. Hitler's armies won huge envelopment battles in 1939–1941 on the way to losing an even more immense war of matériel. They all cited Clausewitz. Hitler even named a 1942 operation in southern Russia after the dead theorist whom he clearly had hardly read or absorbed. Clausewitz must not be blamed for what came after him, or in his name. His ideas did not lead the world to total war. Total war led the world back to him.

***

PRUSSIAN GENERALS HEADING into the Napoleonic wars looked to Frederick II as the model of a warlord king. They saw only his shrewd march and battle orders, not the bare-chance survival of his dynasty by aborted foreign invasion. Scientist formulae captured and illustrated perfectly geometric dissertations on his use of interior lines, singing praise hymns to a national genius. Then came the shocking defeat of their outdated professional model army by conscripts in 1806. Thinkers bathed in German Romanticism rejected Frederick's narrow military system and disdain for his own troops as no more than fodder for cannons. They looked to triumphant France instead, to somehow emulate or capture the benefits of its *levée en masse* and civic and more broad-based patriotism. They sought to institutionalize the genius Clausewitz identified as lordly in war, to lock it down inside their doctrine and their new Great General Staff. They stressed a raw side of war where there was room for, as historian of military thought Azar Gat puts it, "creative genius, moral forces, and the factors of uncertainty and chance."[8] Over the century that stretched from 1815 to 1914, from Waterloo to the outbreak of World War I, this idealized Frederickian and Napoleonic creative battle became *the* aim of General Staff officers in Berlin, transmuted into the well-planned, war-winning campaign.

Staff work and planning were at the core of a new Prussian "science" of operational planning and warfare, what some even called a German "genius for war."[9] The governing idea was a campaign leading to swift and total victory to be won right at the outset, thereby avoiding the longer *Materialschlacht* (battle of matériel) they knew they could not win. The models to be studied and emulated were Rossbach, Leuthen and Ulm (Schlieffen added Cannae to the staff curriculum in the 1890s).[10] The ideal war by swift movement to achieve a clear and crushing envelopment dominated officer training, budgeting, logistics, weapons and military-civil relations. It conduced to short-war thinking in which a superior army and doctrine triumphed, without contingency planning for the more likely longer wars among nations. The swiftly fought opening campaign promised the Alexandrian solution that Prussia, and later Germany, needed due to a profoundly vulnerable geopolitical position and pursuit of an aggressively expansionist policy. Conundrums of encircled geopolitics that had defied solution for decades could be resolved by triumphant short wars. Never again would Prussia suffer the bitter experience of defeat and occupation and lost territory, as it had in 1806. The Prussian Army would complete in the 19th century Frederick's unfinished 18th-century work. It would make Prussia dominant in Germany. Then it would make Germany dominant in Europe.

Over seven years, Prussia's political and military leaders would in fact conceive, prepare and execute three stunningly rapid war-winning operations. With Austrian help, they would assault Denmark in 1864. Then they would turn and crush the Habsburgs in the Austro-Prussian War of 1866. They would fight according to a bold plan worked out years in advance, via a rapid opening campaign leading to a lopsided victory which actually came at Königgrätz. Then they would move against France and do it again, trapping one French army at Metz and enveloping another at Sedan in 1870, taking Emperor Louis-Napoléon prisoner.[11] It would be a virtuoso performance. Moltke and Bismarck would blend war and diplomacy seemingly to perfection, to isolate and defeat Austria in seven weeks and France in seven months. A lightning-fast "war of annihilation" (*Vernichtungskrieg*) against each of two Great Powers in succession would thus appear to show that war remained available as an instrument of statecraft even when facing much stronger opponents. Their success would be a fateful example to Germans and others into the mid-20th century.

***

WITH PEACE RESTORED in 1815, no king or emperor, especially the tsar wished to retain a large body of armed men of suspect loyalty, pulled from the lower classes. Moltke later wrote: "Arms are quickly distributed but not so quickly taken back." Victorious reactionary regimes feared nationalism in almost any guise, but especially its military form in the *levée en masse*. Muzzling that potential uncontrollable force for revolutionary change meant repressing the nations-in-arms, at home and everywhere else. As Michael

Howard phrases it: "Whatever value Napoleonic warfare might have for a power trying to overthrow the states-system of Europe, it could have little for a statesman trying to preserve it."[12] The governing classes also wanted an end to disruptive peoples' wars. They knew conflicts must still arise in Europe, but looked to make more reasoned settlements decided by cool-headed governments. The nation-in-arms was a danger at home and a threat internationally. It had to be quashed.

Afraid of French-style *guerre à outrance*—all-out war by aroused nations, out of the control of their rulers—the elites wanted to return to *Kabinettskrieg* ("cabinet wars"), to smaller affairs of state fought by kings over the heads of nations left unaroused by war. Wars fought with smaller armies and for limited ends, not for revolution or overthrow of another state's government, let alone of its system of government. That meant an end to mass conscription and a return to long-service professional troops led mainly by aristocratic officers.[13] One exception was France, where the Revolution left too deep and permanent a social imprint to drive all non-aristocrats out of military service after 1815. In the French Army, a hemmed and confined corps of mixed nobles and lower-class careerists oversaw a long-service rank-and-file, recruited via seven-year conscription. Many men re-enlisted to take easy and steady peacetime pay, serving into their forties and even fifties. The other exception was Russia, which retained its peculiar system of peasant conscription for 25 years, dating back to Peter the Great. Until the mid-19th century, only hawkish Prussia retained short-term (three-year) conscription.

In all the other armies "social betters" once again tended to long-serving soldiers who lived in barracked units, physically separated from and hence uncontaminated by nationalist fervor. Armies were to be again beholden to monarchs rather than parliaments or demagogues. Such a near-return to pre-Revolution conditions necessarily incorporated some structural reforms based on lessons absorbed from the French wars. Yet, politically and socially, all armies of the post-1815 Concert system were devoted to maintaining a restored ancien régime at home and to fighting, if at all, only in limited wars for limited purposes. They were carefully and deliberately *not* "people's armies."[14] Fiscal and psychological exhaustion with excesses of violent revolution and climactic war encouraged a return to military conservatism. It and the peace lasted for a generation.

Generations die, new ones forget the last war, and technology keeps changing. By 1850 new communications, transportation and war-fighting technologies reshaped the playing table for leaders and citizens alike, who did not know or remember war and thought they might like to try it. The telegraph, railways, and new rapid-firing guns changed the roll of the dice. The telegraph in particular seemed to promise a command-and-control revolution, and it did permit communication among armies at vast distances. Electricity might allow fast communications that in turn would lead to rejuvenation of Napoleonic maneuver, so hard to do with larger midcentury armies. Fixed to poles and cables, the telegraph in fact proved more valuable in defensive war. Armies on the move across country could hardly benefit unless they were staying close to railways, as in American western campaigns of the early 1860s. As the Crimean War quickly brought home to Paris and London especially, together with newspapers and rising literacy the telegraph created a new political problem. It fed a rising demand for news from the front that helped shape the first mass public opinion about the politics and conduct of wars. Cabinet wars were going to be harder to keep limited with jingoistic publics clamoring for news of victories, with ordinary people thinking they somehow had a stake in distant outcomes.[15]

The military importance of railways first became evident when both revolutionary and counterrevolutionary armies mobilized and maneuvered by train across Germany in 1848. Not everyone drew the right lessons from the experience. Eleven years later, Austrians mobilized against Piedmont in the same way as their grandfathers, in a mishmash of divisions and corps struggling over narrow mountain roads into northern Italy. Railways revolutionized supply, however, allowing year-round fighting, since there was no need to stay in winter quarters when food and fodder caught up by rail, tapping into base areas hundreds of miles from forward military operations. Once again the technology was fixed, dropping off armies at known railhead positions. Since troops always arrived at predestined railheads, any opportunity for surprise was severely limited. It was limited also by the much greater size of the armies and the attending burden of logistics. Railways most directly affected faster mobilizations by shrinking geography, raising new vulnerabilities. Prussia's sense of insecurity increased in proportion to the French Army's ability to mobilize to the border by rail much faster than in the old days, moving on foot and by horse. The same thing was true in reverse. Once the armies left their domestic railheads behind, they resumed movement and logistics by horse and foot, with ill effects on execution of master marching plans that remained to be seen. Railways met additional degrees of cultural resistance and budget constraints, varying by country, such as a preference for building military march roads in addition to railways. Choices had to be made.[16]

Fighting was still too often reduced to lumbering masses of infantry scouting for each other with dispersed cavalry screens while maneuvering for suspected flanks, then finding each other and mauling in a set-piece affair that was hardly controllable by general officers. That meant the key technology was a new type of single-shot breech-loader that permitted much more rapid fire by infantry than older model muzzle-loaders. They were also rifled, and hence capable of aimed shooting over long distances. The new infantry weapons increased offensive firepower but far more dramatically enhanced firepower deployed in defense. It took many years to recognize the full import of this breech-loading and "rifle revolution." The British Army issued a few breech-loading smoothbores as early as 1776 and the East India Company used a breech rifle from the late 18th century. However, such early models used plug cartridges that were deemed not militarily efficient. Plug ammunition used a metal cup (*culot*) in the cavity that drove into the bullet on firing, increasing diameter and decreasing windage in the barrel, to engage its rifling. Later, this was achieved with a small wooden or clay plug. Then Monsieur Claude-Étienne Minié invented a conical, hollow-base bullet, or "Minié ball," that relied on expanding gasses alone to increase diameter and fill the hollow to grip the rifling. The British Army adopted the Enfield rifle as standard issue in 1853, just in time to fight the Crimean War with the new Minié ball ammunition.[17] It inflicted huge casualties on Russians armed with older model smoothbores.

By the 1840s many models of military-issue needle guns were coming to the arms market, including the Dreyse *Zündnadelgewehr* that would be made famous by the Prussians. All were breech-loaders using a needle-like pin to penetrate a paper cartridge, thence to strike a percussion cap that ignited the charge. Theoretically, they extended infantry ranges up to ten times that of Napoleonic-era fusils (to about 4,000 feet or 1,200 meters), and greatly raised rates-of-fire. Yet needle guns and other rapid-fire rifles met fierce resistance by some senior officers, despite the clear advantages. Because the old peace was long-lasting and the new guns and ammunition were expensive, there was insufficient incentive to change over before the midcentury Wars of German Unification demonstrated a clear superiority. Delay would prove fatal to the military fortunes of the penurious Habsburgs in 1866, after years of restricting shooting practice by infantry in order to conserve bullets. There was also wider resistance rooted in an older military culture. Rapid-firing rifles raised questions of resupply, but also whether troops could be trusted not to expend all carried ammunition in skirmishes or panicky firefights before the main clash began. Professionals at senior levels were uncertain. Their worry was that rapid rates of fire would exhaust ammunition, leaving effectively dis-armed troops subject to decisive direct assaults by the enemy, still the pre-ferred infantry tactic of the time. This actually happened in Prussian units several times during the 1866 war with Austria. Four years later, Bavarian units that ran out of ammunition early while fighting against the French simply walked off the field.

A shift from muzzle-loading smoothbores to breech-loaders was well in hand by the early 1850s, but adoption of the rapid-fire models was resisted into the mid-1860s. Absent real war demonstration of the effects of in-creased infantry firepower, the best conservative argument before 1866 said it was not yet clear that fundamental change was actually underway. Even in Prussia, the most militarily farsighted power of the time, there was op-position to needle-guns. Dating to 1836 and the first of its kind to be mass-produced, the Dreyse was adopted by the Prussian Army only in 1858, with design refinements after that. It was not until belief set in that Dreyse was decisive in the 1866 war with Austria that all major militaries, even severely cash-strapped Italians, rushed to adopt new-style rifles.[18] Rapid-fire rifles then forced basic changes in tactics to account for higher rates of fire by po-sitional defense. First, a breech-loading rifleman could reload while kneeling or prone, whereas muzzle-loading musketeers had to stand. New infantry rifles also meant that killing distances remembered from past wars or old military histories were out-of-date. The new distances had to be learned the hardest way there is, in combat. The main effect was to eliminate both old-style lines and columns, since it was impossible for erect infantry to advance across open space under long-range accurate fire, whether from rifles or rifled cannon. One solution was to increase skirmishers, with an overall effect of making infantry vs. infantry battles into firefights with each side in open-order formations.

Long-range rifles forced artillery back until the big guns were beyond the old tactic of reaching out to approaching enemy with canister. Now, when closing range in order to finally charge the guns, attacking infantry or cav-alry would brave fire from far-off batteries that dropped explosive shells onto them from much longer ranges and with more rapid and accurate rifled fire. All of that massively strengthened defense over offense, overall. Breech-load-ing, rapid-fire rifled artillery also had horizontal range that additionally widened the battlefield by making it harder to carry out tactical flankings of any position supported by artillery. Finally, the *mitrailleuse* introduced by the French Army was essentially an early machine gun capable of firing 75 shots per minute. Along with the new infantry rifles and rifled artillery, its introduction at midcentury suggested that in future wars the main tactical problem would be how to overcome walls of lead rather than of stone.

The long peace from 1815 was broken by the start of the Crimean War in 1853. Fought by Russians, French, British and Ottomans, it coursed along the Danube into the Caucasus, with minor clashes in the Baltic and White Seas. Its main battles were waged on the Black Sea and the Crimean peninsula, notably fierce fights at Alma, Balaclava and Inkerman in 1854. But battles mattered less to the outcome than wearing sieges. A siege of Sevastopol lasted for nearly a year, from October 1854 to September 1855. It is memorably recalled in a stark journey from naive nationalist enthusiasm to grim realism and growing pacifism in Leo Tolstoy's *Sevastopol Sketches*.[19] However, these odd and far-off events persuaded few in Europe's capitals that real change was coming. For one thing, the Western armies arrived by ship while Russian railways were appallingly bad, and so did not reveal the potential of that technology to move and supply large armies facing each other in static fronts. Professional study was neglected, deemed uninstructive by deeply conservative militaries and governments in the West that disdained and feared wars fought by masses of commoners in any case, and smugly assumed that little could be learned from catastrophic losses of illiterate peasant conscripts in the Russian Army.[20]

Antiquated weapons and stale tactics further obscured the firepower revolution underway in smithy shops and patent offices across the industrialized world. Most weapons used in Crimea were muzzle-loading, though British and French troops at least had newer rifled muskets. While the British issued muzzle-loader Enfield Pattern 1853 rifled muskets, the Russians used wholly outdated smoothbores and the tactics that went with them, such as columns for attack and other blunt-force assaults dating to before 1815. Nor was much learned by anyone from clumsy face-on assaults made by inept British commanders, some actual holdovers and others who were closer to spiritual throwbacks to their grandfathers' wars two generations old. Everyone had glory on their side, and favored gods and a sense of right. It was proudly said of British cannon by period nationalists, "everywhere, where right and glory leads."[21] Yet it was Russian guns that slaughtered a brigade of British light horse at Balaclava, compelling the poet Alfred Lord Tennyson to famously write in his 1854 *Charge of the Light Brigade*:

> Cannon to right of them,
> cannon to left of them,
> cannon in front of them

> volley'd and thunder'd.
> Storm'd at with shot and shell,
> Boldly they rode and well,
> Into the jaws of Death,
> Into the mouth of Hell
> Rode the six hundred.[22]

Everyone had guns. Everyone had pride in them. So the armies in Crimea clashed in the same old way, with sabers, lances, muskets and bayonets, shot and shell and shattered horses, but also in dreary trenches under a years-long fall of heavy rifled artillery.[23]

Something genuinely new was reporting by the first war correspondents, who sent dispatches over transoceanic telegraph cables to newspaper editors and the printing presses in far-off European capitals. Penny sheets gave voice to the fervent boasts of early jingoism, recalled in a beer hall song by a later generation also forgetful of their fathers' war and eager to try it themselves:

> We don't want to fight but by Jingo if we do,
> We've got the ships, we've got the men, we've got the money too.
> We've fought the Bear before, and while we're Britons true,
> the Russians shall not have Constantinople.[24]

For many in the West, however, even in belligerents such as Britain and France, the Crimea remained a faraway place of which they knew little and cared less. Especially as hints of future and less glorious wars were also seen in the sieges and trench fighting that followed early and wholly indecisive battles. There was more portent, of the increasing and more direct role of women in war, in field stations and hospitals where Florence Nightingale, the "Angel of Mercy" and leader of a growing contingent of volunteer female nurses, was at first rebuffed and unwanted by some in the British officer class but adored and welcomed by wounded men. Another warning came from the other side of the line, where most of the war's dead expired in far worse Russian hospitals or camps. Total war-related deaths were almost 750,000. The tsarist army lost 475,000 men, mostly conscript peasants felled by disease. Tens of thousands of civilians also died. Lessons were obscured by the fact that most of the Russians died from typhus, dysentery, cholera or other swamp or camp fevers that could be smugly blamed by Westerners on Russian backwardness. French losses were 95,000 dead, of whom 20,000 were killed in action or died later from wounds; the other 75,000 succumbed to various diseases. The British lost 22,000 dead, while the sultan's army, the forgotten ally, lost 45,000.[25]

The war could hardly have been less Clausewitzian, less decisive or marked by battles of focused climax. A war of sieges and entrenchments, folly and futility, it was stumbled into and stumbled through on all sides. An ignored tragedy. An overlooked forewarning. No general instruction was achieved about the changing nature of industrial warfare, of the greatly enhanced strength of defense. Smaller lessons were carried home from Black Sea ports, along with the wounded in body or mind. Each belligerent recoiled from the carnage in its own way, without a wider conclusion informing thinking about war. Ottoman sultans were saved in place for the moment, yet they remained existentially challenged by surging nationalism in the Balkans and eastern Mediterranean and by smoldering revanchism in Moscow. The Sublime Porte was finally and formally admitted to the European diplomatic system after the war, but that was more an indication of fading strength and new weakness and instability that might trouble the whole state system. To its last days the Ottoman Empire faced minorities' resentment and unrest, often supported by external powers. Austrian and Russian designs on Ottoman territory led to repeated Great Power diplomatic intervention, but nothing was resolved until Istanbul's foolhardy entry into the Great War of 1914–1918 struck the death blow to Ottoman rule and empire.

Russia was severely wounded, and so turned inward to reform decrepit social and economic structures. This was a reform turn taken principally in order to modernize the Russian Army for a long-term drive to restore sovereign rights in the Black Sea, limited by the 1856 Treaty of Paris at the close of the Crimean War. Tsar Alexander II abolished serfdom in good part to enable basic reform of the Army's utterly archaic conscription system. He also tried to reform the bureaucracy, justice system and education, all to modernize in ways that might attract foreign capital to exploit vast underdeveloped resources. The spur to build railways over the following years and decades arose in good measure from anger over slow military reinforcement and supply to the Crimean peninsula during the war, due to a lack of prewar lines. The main point of building heavy industries and other infrastructure was to sustain a modern army, to grow the economy to meet the demands of future industrial wars against other modernizing empires, and to support a continuing strategic ambition to remain in the front rank of the Great Powers.[26]

British nationalists were not happy with their tarnished victory in the Crimea. They were frustrated that the British Army had not fully "avenged" early defeats, and many accused the Royal Navy of improperly deploying a fleet of ironclad gunboats built to wrest control of the Black Sea from Russia. Political and military elites turned to mutual recrimination, and then the political class withdrew Britain from continental engagement that might lead to a future war over what seemed faraway places and other people's quarrels. The focus was on consolidation of overseas empire and the project of expanding and reforming British democracy at home. Britain would therefore sit idly by through all three Wars of German Unification during the critical decade to follow. And there was always the festering problem of Ireland. Fenians were active in the 1860s as the question of Home Rule roiled British politics and a lingering confessional quarrel across the Irish Sea threatened to lead one day to armed conflict that must draw in British troops. Trouble on that other island always loomed over Britain's politics and future.[27]

Despite formal neutrality, Austria was the great strategic loser of the Crimean War, as staying out won Vienna no friends. Instead, it was left profoundly isolated by a war it did not fight and a peace it did not negotiate or sign. It was already deeply antagonistic to Prussia over a decades-long and now intensifying struggle for influence in Germany. That polyglot territory was organized in a *Bund*, or German Confederation, of four free cities and 35 states. It was originally set up in 1815 to discourage Great Power quarrels over the affairs of Germany that might lead to renewed war, and to forestall German unification. By right of treaty, Austria was granted primacy in *Bund* affairs, but Prussia loomed in growing real-world influence.[28] Internally, the Austrian Empire faced a cracking constitutional structure and corrosive multi-ethnicity, made harder to manage by aborted and repressed revolutions in 1848. Austria's diplomatic isolation and political opposition to any form of nationalism as threatening its own multinational character led to an old-fashioned cabinet war with France and Italy in 1859, resulting in a quick and clumsy defeat. The Habsburgs were too prudent to pursue an aggressive diplomacy toward resurgent Italy after that, yet too weak not to respond forcefully to a core challenge to their status and role within greater Germany. That was precisely where the next threat arose.[29]

France looked like the major winner in 1856. Napoleon's less exalted nephew, Louis-Napoléon, seemed to sit atop a pinnacle of domestic support and international prestige in the Second Empire. In fact, his was a shaky perch on both counts. He thought he could discard the balance of power in Europe just as his famous uncle had, or at least that he could make Paris the hub of a dominant alliance within the wider system. He acted the provocateur rather than statesman, dangerously supporting minor nationalist movements and several small but open rebellions in southern and Eastern

Europe. He thereby alienated the conservative eastern powers, Austria and Russia. That policy also displeased more liberal Britain, which wanted no continental disturbances while it pursued reform projects at home and imperial adventure overseas. Next came direct French intervention in the Austro-Italian War of 1859. That venture was modestly successful militarily from the French point of view, but a strategically foolish gambit nonetheless. Defeat of Austria in support of Italy elevated a newly independent power on France's southern frontier without garnering the lasting gratitude of Italians that Louis-Napoléon needed and expected. Widely and properly regarded as a feckless incompetent, and already having isolated France within Europe, he sent French troops and fortunes on an imperial misadventure in Mexico that ended years later in humiliation and defeat.[30]

Louis-Napoléon's reputation for foolish behavior long preceded and underlay Bismarck's plans to trick him into war in 1870. Paris may have looked like the winner coming out of the Crimean War, but Berlin was the actual winner of a localized war over non-vital issues from which it had abstained. Bismarck knew that in international affairs, as at home, only the great questions counted in the affairs of states. And "the great questions of the time are not decided by speeches and majority decisions . . . but by iron and blood [*Eisen und Blut*]."[31] Now he intended that Berlin should gain from other peoples' broken iron and spilled blood, to emerge as the principal beneficiary of that foolhardy, distant war's destruction of the Concert of Europe, the system of Great Power cooperation set up in 1814–1815 following the defeat of Napoleon and France. His interest was unification of Germany under Prussian leadership, an ambition long opposed by several "flanking powers," as they were called in Berlin. Now, on the eve of the German wars, all were weakened and in retreat from wider engagements. Britain was sullen and ever more isolationist; Russia had withdrawn into efforts at modernizing internal reform; Austria was weakened by war, diplomatically uncertain and isolated as never before. France was ebullient but led by a reckless and overconfident fool who could be manipulated. No other statesman could match Bismarck's wit or guile.[32] Or the ruthless cunning of Moltke, who planned the serial military campaigns that would smash the old order and balance of power and unify Germany under Prussia.[33]

***

WHAT ABOUT LESSONS from across the Atlantic? Was more caution in order about the role of battle in deciding wars now dominated by defensive firepower, based on American experience? Few in Europe thought there was

much to learn from the American Civil War. Officers of the Prussian Great
General Staff did little to develop strategy in the sense of interrelated politi-
cal, economic and military goals. Before the war they studied battle histories
yet hardly paid attention to campaigns, let alone wars or war as a whole.[34]
Some Americans had foreseen a long war. Most had not. When it broke out,
General Winfield Scott famously predicted that the war must be long and
won in good part by blockade (the "Anaconda Plan") and exhaustion of the
South, rather than a few handsomely conducted and decisive battles. Colonel
Robert E. Lee similarly anticipated a long war. However, the temptation of
quick victory by heroic field battle swayed most politicians, and officers, to
think that the fighting would be decided by the opening battles. For the
North, General George McClellan devised an ill-conceived plan for a very
short conflict. In the South, General P. G. T. Beauregard brashly proposed
to march directly on Washington and end the war inside a month.[35] Naked
illusions about 90-day enlistments and winning the war in its opening campaigns to take Richmond, or to trash the Yankees and storm Washington,
were soon shattered in shockingly real and bloody battles that sobered military and civilians alike, starting at First Bull Run (Manassas) on July 21, 1861,
not far from the outskirts of Washington.

It was going to be a long, hard war after all. The Confederacy could not
afford to lose any territory or resources and hope to secure the international
recognition vital to its survival, and it needed to blunt Union belief in the
rapid certainty of Northern military victory. It also had expansionist ambitions. It set up a separate Arizona Territory and negotiated with tribes in the
Indian Territory, promising CSA statehood. Thus, it was mandated to undertake aggressive military operations that pushed the South into a generally
offensive strategy.[36] That ensured military provocation of the North not once
but several times, even into the last year of the war in Missouri and Kentucky.
Everyone shed short-war thinking as the battles multiplied, the armies and
enlistments grew and casualty lists lengthened. Each side, each people and
republic, committed to what became a long and draining war, slogged out
along railways and river routes that reached half a continent. The strategy of
attrition and economic and territorial reduction that the Union needed to
adopt to win, and did when President Abraham Lincoln finally found his
general in Ulysses S. Grant, was always difficult to carry out. The war presented huge logistical and territorial challenges on a continental scale, even
with the transition in logistics to railways and steamships from the horse and
carts of Napoleon's day. Armies on both sides moved great distances and supplied by rail, but still needed draft animals and had to forage upon departing

the railheads. The role of the telegraph in command and control of armies at distance also proved critical, in ways not yet available in Europe.[37]

Americans fought with some new-style breech-loading rifles, yet mostly with muzzle-loading rifled muskets, and of a dizzying variety of manufactures. The carnage was immense, about 640,000 dead out of a prewar population of 31 million—more than in *all* other American wars combined. Europe's armies had observers present on one or both sides at many battles and on long campaigns, but their analysis was ignored or dismissed afterward as reporting on a confused fight among amateurs, with few lessons to teach military professionals. The rapidly improvised armies of North and South were unlike any in Europe: a combination of militia, volunteers and short-service conscripts. It was not appreciated that a rifle revolution was on display at faraway places like Shiloh and Fredericksburg in 1862 or Gettysburg in 1863 or The Wilderness in 1864.[38] Even absent high rate of fire needle-guns, rifled muskets raised casualties. Infantry protected itself by digging in, fighting defensively from trenches or behind earthworks, resorting to skirmishing and sniping rather than assault. Cavalry and artillery were both pushed back and made less effective by longer-range infantry weapons. New technologies showed that they could prolong wars by strengthening the advantages of fortified defense, making battles less decisive than in Napoleonic warfare or contemporary German military theory. The gamblers in Berlin planning war were sure they knew better than bumbling amateurs, that they could achieve a war *kurtz und vives* where Americans had descended into siege trenches and slaughter. Yet war is always more unpredictable than knowable by military theory: full of confusion, effort, chance and hot wagers on iron dice and cold steel.

Berlin saw military blundering in Europe, too, but also a new potential threat in a war that is today nearly forgotten yet first tested all the new technologies of telegraph, rail and rifle: the Italian War of 1859. The French mobilized more efficiently and quickly by rail (and steamship) than the Austrians, achieving a sixfold improvement on the movement of Napoleon's speediest corps.[39] This confirmed to planners in Berlin that there was likely also a major French advantage in rapid mobilization by rail to the Rhine frontier. The efficiency of the French rail net in fact caused Prussian-German strategists real worry again and again—in 1866, 1870 and 1914. However, once across the Po River the French corps outran the rails to slog forward as a vast traffic jam of guns, carts, caissons, exhausted troopers and worn-out horses. Prussians learned far less from that fact than they might have, as their own troubles past the railheads would show persuasively beneath the surface of victories in 1866 and 1870, and disastrously in 1914. Moreover, despite rapid mobilization of the French Army to the Italian frontier the result was not a great battle of dash and decision. It was a series of smaller Austrian defeats at Montebello, Palestro and Magenta, followed by a high-casualty affair of 300,000 French, Austrians and Piedmontese who clashed at Solferino (June 24, 1859), a military muddle that leaned toward French victory. There followed desultory mountain fighting as the utterly disorganized and disunited Austrians, who also failed to take advantage of their superior rifles, withdrew to fixed defenses of the Quadrilateral. That was their fallback position, a system of four large and mutually supporting fortified towns at Mantua, Peschiera, Verona and Legnago, straddling a zone of Habsburg control between Lombardy and Venetia. Europe's diplomats awoke to the threat that the French might advance into Austria next, compelling Louis-Napoléon to back down in the face of threatened intervention. Emperor Franz Josef accepted the lethargic defeat with ancien régime equanimity: "I have lost a battle. I pay with a province."[40] He meant Lombardy, ceded by Austria to Piedmont in the peace settlement. The whole war was out-of-date and out of sync with the fast-changing military times.

Such a modest pose and restrained policy as Franz Josef displayed was only possible because all parties still fought within an agreed context of limited cabinet war. The emperor would not be so sanguine about the catastrophic outcome of his next war. Any loss to aggressive Prussia threatened to expel the Habsburgs from Germany while exposing them as permanently militarily deficient. In fact, Bismarck and Moltke intended nothing less than a total military victory so decisive it must remove Austria permanently as an obstacle to Berlin's domination of Germany. Bismarck would first isolate Vienna politically, allowing Moltke to exploit the backwardness of Habsburg weapons, training and tactics, an archaic and nepotistic command structure, and an inadequate rail and mobilization system. Seven years after Solferino, Vienna's barely reformed army faced attack by a modern Prussian Army, moving at speed by rail to the frontier thence marching with imagination and skill. More important, the point was not to capture a province but to clear the way to dominance of all Germany, not a *Kabinettskrieg* but a *Vernichtungskrieg*. It would be won with immediacy. It would break Austrian will to resist by removing its means to resist, through total destruction of its armed forces. Echoing Napoleon and Clausewitz, Moltke said that the Prussians could not win what they wanted in Germany "by any means other than . . . battle."[41]

Prussia had just half the population of the Austro-Hungarian Empire, while its territories were non-contiguous along its northwest frontier. On the other hand, where Austria staggered always near bankruptcy Prussia was enjoying a boom in the 1860s, one rooted in exploitation of coal and iron ore, economic advantages of a central geographical position, and trade with the *Bund*. However, Berlin saw mainly the disadvantages of its position, fearful of the reaction of flanking powers (France and Russia) that might crush Prussia should it challenge Austria inside Germany. Using a crude military metaphor like "flanking powers" in a broad diplomatic context reveals the pervasiveness with which military issues and solutions presented in Prussian thinking about geopolitical problems. Still, Bismarck was circumspect. His concern was that the Great Powers would unite against Prussia if it moved too aggressively to force by war the German state and nation he wanted gathered under Prussian dominion.[42] Urgent military reform was needed to refine war as a tool of Prussian statecraft. That responsibility was handed over to two other exceptional men, Moltke at the head of the Prussian Army and General Albrecht von Roon, Minister of War from 1859. Moltke reshaped the Great General Staff, which he headed from 1858 to 1888. Roon oversaw budgets and procurement and a critical reorganization of the *Landwehr* reserve. Together they upgraded and expanded the Prussian Army and more firmly rooted its support and position at the center of the state. They also gave it new infantry weapons and transport.[43]

Bismarck did not care for war. It was too politically messy and defaulted control from his own hands to the generals, whose foresight he discounted and whose ability he distrusted.[44] Still, he was willing to use war and the generals to advance national policy if the moment was ripe. Fear over a punishing reaction by other Great Powers governed Bismarck's caution during the Danish War or "War of 1864". The fight was lopsided and short, used by Austria and Prussia jointly to sunder the Elbe Duchies (Schleswig and Holstein) from Denmark.[45] The stakes in the north in 1864 were not high enough in Bismarck's view to engage a larger or more general war to advance an agenda of radical territorial change which would overthrow the balance of power inside Germany. That gamble must bring much higher returns than a strip of land taken from Denmark. The chance came two years later. Employing private manipulation of his own reluctant king (Wilhelm I) and a hardening postwar argument with Austria over disposition of the Elbe Duchies, he arranged to start the Austro-Prussian War of 1866 on favorable political terms.[46] This larger and more important war proved decisive for Bismarck's diplomacy and for Moltke's military strategy and reputation for masterful "operational art," although that term would have been foreign to him.[47] Together, they faced a woefully unready foe.

Austria's army was riven by ethnic divisions and deeply conservative in its approach to fighting, while its officer corps was simultaneously nepotistic, prone to paralyzing personal rivalries, and professionally incompetent at the highest levels. Under inept senior commanders, and in good measure because of them, it was defeated in the Italian War in 1859. It would be badly led again during its war with Prussia (and Italy) in 1866, though less so on the southern front than in the north against Moltke. It clung to the hoary tactics of the ancien régime for three reasons. First, Jomini's stilted and formalistic ideas dominated military thinking outside Prussia (where Clausewitz turned more heads, and Moltke and Roon turned to reforms). Second, the old ways well suited a long-serving army that was more royalist than popular and a regime that had distrusted conscription and the nation-in-arms even at the height of the Napoleonic Wars. Lastly, the old tactics were more defensive minded than what Moltke was contemplating, which better matched Vienna's status quo political goals and shaky finances by abjuring aggressive war.[48]

On the other hand, mass infantry attack rooted in columnar tactics dating to the Napoleonic Wars was fatally out of date given the new infantry rifles and rifled artillery. Nevertheless, Austrian tactics still relied on swarms of *Jäger* ("hunter") skirmishers preceding the main attack by columns of heavy infantry. A tragedy of 1866 was that inept generals cleaved to these tactics against Prussian firepower arriving from much greater ranges than those of 1815, ensuring severe casualties for any try at an old-style columnar attack. Moreover, Moltke incorporated into Prussian tactics radical advantages of rapid movement and decentralized command. Jomini's putatively eternal principles of war, as practiced by the Austrians, would face Clausewitzian all-out war as Moltke's innovations were backed by a cultivated fighting rage, by a *furia Teutonica* that aimed at nothing short of utter destruction of Austria's principal army.[49]

In 1855 the Habsburgs had issued upgraded, percussion-type muzzle load-ers, the "Lorenz rifle," to most (though not all) of their troops. However, Austria's high command and officer corps failed to adapt tactics to incor-porate rapid-firing infantry despite this weapon advantage in Italy in 1859, partly from reluctance to pay for all that ammunition in training exercises. During the 1860s cash-strapped Austria again refused to adopt newer and updated rifles, necessary given rapid technological change, because they had just spent large sums on replacing infantry weapons a few years before. It was too little reform too late from a penurious and staid regime that did not want war and could not afford to properly prepare for it should it come anyway. As a result, Habsburg troops armed with Lorenz rifled muskets headed into war in 1866 badly outclassed by Prussian infantry carrying Dreyse needle-guns. This failure occurred despite Austrian officers having closely observed Prussian field success with their rapid-firing breech-loaders during the Danish War. A main worry guiding rifle procurement by Vienna was, as elsewhere, that illiterate and poorly trained peasants would exhaust their ammunition before the critical moment in the battle arrived. Geoffrey Wawro points out that sticking with cruder shock tactics also "spared the emperor the considerable cost of rifle training and gave him the means to preempt language and morale problems by literally herding his ethnically mixed battalions together like cattle."[50] Astonishingly, the Austrian officer corps would essentially do this again in 1914, herding whole divisions forward into slaughter by even more advanced massed rifles, machine-guns and rapid-fire artillery.

Austrian mobilization capability was also decades behind the railway revolution going on all around. To move troops to preset defensive positions along the northern frontier to meet an expected advance by the Prussians, the Habsburgs built just one rail line, the *Nordbahn*. It was again too little too late. Strategy was just as outdated as tactics, relying essentially on networks of extremely expensive fixed fortifications built up over decades, all connected by static lines of communications. Too high a proportion of available forces was dispersed across these garrisons, which could be more easily isolated than before in a new kind of war where mass armies moved with speed by rail. The Quadrilateral system in northern Italy would again prove of worth in 1866, largely due to inept Italian generalship and planning. In the north, however, the great fortress of Königgrätz and its sister forts on which the Austrian forward-defense strategy relied would mainly serve to back-stop Moltke's grand envelopment of Austria's North Army.

In contrast, between 1862 and 1866 Moltke and Roon expanded and modernized the Prussian Army, moving it away from reliance on blunt shock tactics to making firepower assaults that made full use of Dreyse needle-guns. A partial exception was the artillery, whose smoothbore cannon lagged well behind more modern and mostly rifled Austrian guns, due to budget constraints in Berlin. The changes in tactics and operational and strategic thinking and planning were profound, as Moltke and Roon applied learned lessons of clumsy mobilization and operations in 1848 and 1864 to better utilize the new communications and transportation technologies of telegraph and rail in wars in 1866 and 1870.[51] Moltke began a study of the military potential of railways in the 1840s, well before any line was built in Germany. Funds thereafter were shifted from fortifications to installing a railway net. From 1861, Moltke and Roon pressed successfully for funds for accelerated railway-building, looking to move with French speed to the frontiers. They also forced enlargement of the Army through Prussia's legislature, swelling it beyond the needs of any cabinet war by tripling numbers to 300,000 in 1866.

At last, Moltke had the instrument to shift from tactical operations to planning wholesale envelopments that might decide a limited war at the very beginning. If Bismarck's diplomacy could first clear a way by isolating Austria for an attack that did not trigger a much wider and longer war of coalitions formed out of the balance of power. If his enemy did as he expected in the fields of maneuver to and in battle. If Clausewitz's "friction," the fog and breakdown of command intentions by unforeseen events and physical effort and enemy action, did not wear down his operations.[52] If his subordinates carried out his will and intentions, hastening to victory and thus shortening the chances that the war would spread to new fronts. If Prussia's opening gambit did not devolve into a grinding contest against much superior populations and resources in each of three larger neighbors, France, Austria and Russia. If his luck held and his plans worked. A lot of contingencies. A real gamble, whose success should not blind later observers to its high-risk nature. Most observers at the time, including Louis-Napoléon, thought that if war came Austria would handily defeat Prussia in what forcibly unified Germans later called their *Brüderkrieg* ("brother's war").[53]

The Prussian Great General Staff was indispensable in planning and executing these ambitious operations plans, deploying large armies more speedily over wider fronts than ever before. Yet there were other problems harder to plan for, starting with Prussia's own diplomatic isolation and scattered geography, both of which left it vulnerable to counter-invasion at many different points, even from all sides. Its historic eastern provinces of Brandenburg-Prussia were disconnected from its rich western territories of Westphalia and the Rhineland, with the intervening space filled by several independent German states including Baden, Hanover and Hesse. In 1866 there were 35 million French, the Habsburgs had 33 million ethnically diverse subjects, while the tsar presided over 76 million. The kings of Prussia had just 19 million subjects. That meant some 20 million Germans living in the scattered lands of the *Bund* were of potentially crucial importance to all four powers. Prussia had already attached that population to its dynamic and expanding economy via a customs union (*Zollverein*), but Berlin wanted much more, nothing less than political, and hence military, control of the *Bund* to double its recruiting base and vault into the front rank of Great Powers. The challenge was how to do so without provoking a general conflagration that pitted it against an unbeatable coalition. For all other Great Powers in the

European system the goal should have been to prevent Berlin from achieving its ambition to dominate in Germany, especially if the means was to be force of arms. However, in 1866 the powers were distracted or asleep.

Drawing directly from Clausewitz and thereafter cemented into the German military tradition, Moltke's solution to all these complex problems was to ensure that the Prussian Army was not just the best-trained in Europe but that it was designed to seek strategic victory via rapid mobilization and deployment leading to a war-winning campaign right from the outset. In short, it was trained to force upon the enemy and then win a new Rossbach, Leuthen or Ulm. Prussia's armies would rapidly mobilize and head to the frontier along a dense road system and a superior rail net, with multiple rail lines built in a well-conceived arc. Once reassembled, the whole Prussian Army must immediately attack, seeking a decisive confrontation. All movement was aimed at delivering armies swiftly to the frontiers, then conducting concentric enveloping marches to concentrate around the entire Austrian North Army.[54] As with Napoleon's corps, generals were told not to concentrate their separated armies until the moment of battle was reached. As in Frederick's thinking, even if a wider war erupted as a result of Prussia's strike, at least one enemy would be beaten before the others could mobilize and deploy. It was Frederick II's lightning campaign in aggressiveness and offensive spirit, utilizing Napoleon's practice of dispersed marches heading to last-minute concentration for battle in the initial deployment. Additional operations would evolve as improvised concentric encirclements.[55] The idea, as Robert Citino puts it, always was "pin the foe in the front with one army, then hit him simultaneously in the flank and rear with another."[56] If all went as planned at the beginning, the result would be a *Kesselschlacht*, a great cauldron encirclement in which the Austrians were to be trapped and cooked alive. If it did not, then the war would arc back toward attrition, as coalitions of Great Powers formed and fought to stop Prussia. It was the short-war, all-in gambler's pattern seen at the start of prior Prussian wars. It would be seen again in German wars to come.

Moltke's 1866 scheme replaced corps with armies as the keystone units of maneuver. This meant mobilizing, assembling and transporting several armies on dispersed march routes to enhance speed, so that the main enemy army was outmaneuvered and enveloped when the Prussians at last concentrated advantageously at the crucial moment. Confident that Prussia's multiple rail lines leading to the southern frontier gave him a critical time advantage in mobilization, Moltke proposed concentric operations along exterior lines. This would avoid congestion caused by too many troops on the move all at once, while enabling flanking and envelopment of North Army. It was also a clear violation of a widely accepted orthodoxy about the superiority of interior lines, said by Jomini to form the basis of Napoleon's success in battle and indeed of all success in war. Moltke intended to follow a different example. His dispersed campaign explicitly mimicked Napoleon's wide-march order prior to concentration and victory over Austria at Ulm in 1805.[57] The risk was that a dynamic and concentrated enemy might catch and defeat-in-detail each weaker Prussian army while it was still making its march. However, Moltke knew that was not the kind of enemy army, or commander, he faced. There was little initiative and no dynamism on the other side of the southern frontier.

Despite recognizing the grave dangers of breakdown and uncertain command, Moltke would send four armies (First, Second, Elbe, and West) on widely separated rail lines, with gaps between them as wide as 90 to 120 miles. Along the way, the Prussians must defeat the south German states whose contingents made up the *Bundesarmee* (Federal Army). Although it numbered 150,000 men, an impressive number on paper, these troops did not train or fight under a unified command.[58] After sweeping the Federals aside, all four Prussian armies would drive into Bohemia, concentrating a quarter million men to destroy North Army, expected to be tardy to the field in the usual Austrian way. Moltke's goal was not merely to re-create Ulm. This was no cabinet war, whatever he later said. It was to be a fundamental upheaval in the internal German and international order. He and Bismarck intended nothing less than to permanently eliminate Austria as a rival within Germany, smash the old *Bund*, and annex or newly intimidate the smaller German states in a new arrangement of hegemony by Prussia over all Germany. The plan called for a quick strike into southern Germany and Bohemia by dispersed but coordinated columns that would flank, then envelop and destroy, the *Bundesarmee* and North Army. Prussians would arrive at speed while their enemies were still deploying, then smash all opposing forces with superior firepower. This was the main idea of a so-called cauldron battle. Moltke conceived it as a war-winning operational maneuver to envelop the enemy's main force and devastate it as the culmination of a single campaign.[59] It was a high-risk gamble that brought together multiple strands of strategy and several historical examples. It was Clausewitzian in strategic conception and Napoleonic in operational audacity. It was all-in Prussian in its insistence that short-war success would overcome the chances of rolling iron dice into a wider and longer war that Prussia might not win.

In Vienna, the *Hofkriegsrat* (Court War Council) felt no similar pull toward climactic battle. That was an idea for aggressors, and Austria was a status quo power. Sticking to strategic defense, Habsburg generals would slowly advance North Army, numbering 245,000 men, to occupy a defensive position anchored on Olmütz in Moravia, there to await the arrival of the Prussians. The much smaller Iser Army (60,000 men and sundry garrisons) was dispersed widely across a line of older and outdated fortifications in Bohemia. Another 130,000 were tied down defending the southern frontier in Venetia against Italy, settled snugly into a holding position inside the Quadrilateral. In the event, even after inflicting a sharp and bloody defeat on poorly led Italians at Custoza (June 24), a cautious Habsburg general with South Army refused to venture out of the safety of the Quadrilateral to pursue a demoralized enemy. At least he did not lose *everything*, as the inept commander of North Army was about to do.[60]

The initial Austrian plan to sit in a defensive crouch at Olmütz was abandoned, but only after a fatal delay, as reports and rumors of Prussian movement reached Vienna. On June 16, the same day Prussian forces crossed into Saxony, the *Hofkriegsrat* ordered North Army to leave Olmütz and shift to the west, to block the Prussian invasion along a traditional defensive line anchored on large 18th-century fortresses at Josephstadt and Königgrätz. But Austrian officers had also studied Napoleon's dicta and campaigns, and thought they saw a chance to emulate the brilliance of the Master when facing a divided enemy with an already concentrated army. On June 17, General Ludwig von Benedek ordered nearly a quarter million men of his North Army to march for the Iser River. Where Moltke was looking to recreate Napoleon's success at Ulm, Benedek was inspired more by the Master's campaigns that met divided enemies and used numerical superiority to defeat each opponent separately. He thus hoped to catch and beat each of Prussia's smaller armies in turn, inflicting a defeat-in-detail on the invaders. Unfortunately, on the long flank march to the Iser neither Benedek nor his troops matched the old French march standard, let alone the new pace of war set by the remarkably speedy Prussians.

North Army set off for the Iser in three ponderous march columns, each stretching back dozens of miles. Agonizingly slow movement over the next ten days exhausted and demoralized many of the troops. Adding to their misery, alternating rain and heat beat down spirits while mud narrowed the choice of route. Logistics soon failed, so that men and horses were hungry as well as hot and tired and encaked. Like the *Grande Armée* tramping in the summer heat on the road to Moscow in 1812, weary soldiers discarded rucksacks, coats, even ammunition and rifles. Traffic jams of carts, caissons, wagons and guns staggered across Bohemia along muddy tracks.[61] This slow and bitter procession allowed Moltke's far quicker armies to move by rail into Hanover, Kassel and Saxony, thence to split and drive off elements of the cumbersome *Bundesarmee* away from a planned union with North Army. So far, all was proceeding to Moltke's plan.

The failure of Saxon engineers to destroy that country's railways allowed Elbe Army to race south and occupy Dresden inside two days. Scattered *Bundesarmee* units failed to mobilize fast enough, or maneuver well enough, to have an impact on the campaign. Most of its contingents were effectively shunted away from the main fight by the smallest of the four Prussian armies, West Army. That was so despite West Army's uncertain generalship, multiple avoidable delays, and several outright command blunders that drove Moltke to distraction. This so-called *Bundeskrieg* ("War of the Federals") culminated in a battle at Langensalza (June 27–28), in which Prussian *Landwehr* reserve units performed worryingly badly. Still, Hanover was knocked out of the war.[62]

With smaller Federal forces defeated or surrendered, or reeling in retreat, or refusing to come out from fortified positions to face West Army, three Prussian armies moved unimpeded across southern Germany. Moltke sped armies along march routes with the same facility that Napoleon once moved smaller French corps. He used Prussian railways and then the captured south German network to achieve the first part of his famous dictum, to "march separately, fight jointly." The question was whether he could now close the trap, catching Benedek with one of these dispersed thrusts, to use that initial contact to fix the Austrians against an anvil upon which his other two armies might concentrate and hammer. He needed to move fast, for Prussian divisions were already suffering serious logistical failures, including supply logjams after outrunning railheads. Prussian armies in Bohemia later would be forced to live off the land, stealing food and fodder in the same old way as armies in centuries past. Things grew much worse when physical exertion and poor nutrition and other privation contributed to an outbreak of cholera among Prussian troops in Austria. Fortunately for Moltke's plans, that did not happen until July.[63]

Beginning on June 23, the Prussians disgorged into Habsburg territory via three passes through the Karkonosze or Giant Mountains. The first fighting at the foot of the passes went badly for flank elements of North Army. Starting on June 26, in skirmishes and then larger clashes along the Iser, Prussians inflicted enormous casualties on Austrian infantry and cavalry flank guards (4:1 or 5:1 in every crossing battle). The latter fought bravely, even recklessly, but mostly uselessly. They charged repeatedly against Prussian rapid-firing needle-gun lines, bayonets mounted on Lorenz muzzle-loaders. Immediately revealed was the dangerous staleness of Austrian reliance on storm columns, in which troops were told to close to bayonet range without shooting.[64] Once-proud old companies and famed Habsburg regiments were devastated. The critical advantage given Prussians by their rapid-firing, breech-loading rifles and *Schnellfeuer* ("fast-fire") attack methods shredded all counterattacks, inflicting death and wounds at an appalling ratio of 1:5.

Troops in Prussian *dunkelblau* (blue-black) fired, reloaded at the breech and fired again. Over and over. Sometimes they shot from the hip as waves of rapid-fire mowed down stunned Magyar hussars, Slovakian *Jäger*, Polish cavalry and Romanian and German infantry in green or grey or yellow or black. Men lay in rows, mown down like summer grass. Even the best Habsburg units could take only so much of this new way of rifle war, these unbelievable rates of fire, before throwing down muzzle-loaders to raise up their arms in submission or just to turn and flee. In several close fights, thousands of Dreyse rifles clashed against Lorenz and bayonets while both artilleries engaged, ripping apart battalions clumped too closely together, cutting down cavalry charges. That is how the Prussians came down and out of the mountain passes, fighting into the flank guard of North Army and onto the plain below.

Thousands of men engaged in growing fights around the mouths of the passes at Podol and Vysokov, and twice at Trautenau. Meanwhile, the bulk of the cumbersome North Army was still struggling across the Bohemian flats, inching toward the fortress at Königgrätz and a hoped-for junction with 60,000 reinforcements from Iser Army, at last gathering out of its forts and on the move toward the crashing of the cannon. The union site was slated to be the town of Jičín. Along the way, multiple fights broke out between scouts and skirmishers from North Army and the lead units of three Prussian armies coming out of the mountains. These were followed by running fights at Münchengrätz, Burkersdorf (Soor), Rudersdorf and Skalice, over three days of bloody if intermittent contact (June 26–28).[65] Thousands more were lost to intense and bewildering rapid fire, fed into flank battles against disciplined Prussian firing lines in outdated columns better suited to Wagram or Waterloo, sent to attack by a confused and unready officer corps. Some broke and ran. Others surrendered to firepower for which their officers never prepared them and could produce no answer.

As Moltke's pincers blew past the flank guards and threatened to close around North Army, Benedek made the worst decision possible. Instead of trying to speed west to escape the trap of two enemy armies positioning to envelop, he turned to offer battle. He gave the order to stand along the Elbe, thinking that he must win because one of Jomini's major principles of war favored his "interior position." These rigid rules plucked from Napoleon's time and career were never rules even then, merely observed patterns of results. Yet Benedek clung to them in the face of changed technology and circumstances a half century later. He must win because his army had the crucial, decisive advantage of holding the critical interior. Military theory said so. History said so. Benedek told his staff he would turn his front northward to face and fight Second Army, defeat it quickly, then turn westward to defeat First Army as it strained impossibly over exterior lines to wrap around his flank and envelop his rear. An Austrian staff officer less enamored of Jomini's supposedly eternal insights recorded his appalled reaction: "What this *really* means is that *now* the Prussians can hit us from *three* directions. . . . What a stupid idea!"[66]

On the Prussian side, speed was causing real problems. Elbe Army and First Army were already out of food, having outrun rail supplies which were also badly jammed. Contrary to the image of Prussian troops as tightly disciplined, conscripts malingered or even deserted in rising numbers. The constant fighting was eroding Moltke's best planning. However, at Jičín on June 29, 40,000 Austrians and Saxons in Iser Army were introduced to rapid fire so intense that some Prussian infantry did not even form squares when facing Habsburg cavalry. They just stood in line firing and reloading, breaking every charge. Austrian infantry was also decimated by the force multiplier of needle-guns. The murderous rate of fire was exacerbated by outdated tactics and bewildered officers, as some units were repeatedly exposed to the massed rifles while others were left standing in place without orders as the Prussians advanced in erect lines, shooting and reloading as they came. Language differences between German officers and Polish, Czech or other troops complicated command and control, as they would again in bloodier catastrophes in Serbia and Galicia in 1914. Remnants of Iser Army staggered to the Elbe over the next two days. Benedek was close to despair about the campaign, but characteristically blamed his subordinates. He cabled the emperor: "Debacle of Iser Army *forces* me to retreat in the direction of Königgrätz."[67]

Speed was crucial to Moltke, who feared that without a rapid and decisive defeat of North Army the French might intervene militarily in the west to prevent Prussia from transmuting military success into strategic permanence.[68] The climactic battle took place on the left bank of the Elbe, in front of a 120-year old fortress at Königgrätz. The fight at Königgrätz, also known as Sadowa (Sadová), saw 450,000 men engage in a new style of war that also revealed a whole new scale of killing. It was the largest fight in Europe since the Battle of the Nations at Leipzig in 1813. So high were the battle's stakes, and so limited the command utility of the telegraph once armies left the roads and rails and entered enemy countryside, that Moltke came south to take direct line-of-sight control of the fighting. So great was the spectacle that Bismarck and the King of Prussia both came to watch. They would see tens of thousands of men killed and wounded in a single day.

Luck stood at Moltke's side along with brilliance, so that it is hard to say which counted more over the following days. First, Benedek remained on the wrong bank of the Elbe, cramming his entire army into a narrow camp that followed the line of the gentle Bystřice River, where it could be neither properly supplied nor fully deployed. There is lingering disagreement among historians of the war as to why Benedek did this. Gordon Craig argues that he stayed before the fortress complex in order to launch a counteroffensive that never materialized, while Geoffrey Wawro attributes Benedek's decision to depression and incompetence.[69] He made another major mistake by arraying his divisions in a crescent, projecting the center and refusing both wings. That effectively parted his stance into three discrete fronts, with the wings too separated from each other to provide mutual fire support or rapid reinforcement—hardly a classic of deploying to take advantage of the interior position. Moreover, he formed up too shallowly. Working from old fusil tactics and range tables 50 years out of date, he took no account of the extended range of the new Prussian infantry rifles and rifled artillery. That meant his reserve, standing or milling en masse, came under murderous fire almost from the outset and would be discombobulated and demoralized when he needed them. Finally, his HQ wasted much of the last day before the battle in arguments among the commanders, several of whom had premonitions of catastrophe and wrote preemptive and self-exculpating letters or backdated orders to put themselves in a better light when the great disaster was done.[70]

Moltke heard reports of the inexplicable Habsburg position and reacted quickly. He deployed Elbe and First Armies as an anvil to await the hammer of Second Army's 110,000 rifles, which he urged to force-march to the sound of the guns. It was already doing so. Benedek had more troops and cannon at his powerful center than Moltke anticipated, and he was not moving but waiting to repel the expected Prussian assault. Moltke attacked anyway, before Second Army arrived. He might better have waited, for he had only the 135,000 rifles of Elbe and First Armies available. Waiting was not his way or Prussia's way, however. Nor would it be the future German way in war.

All battles are high-risk, even when advantages of technology, field and foe are with you. Generals add more risk to the calculus of combat with decisions they make. Patience did not count among Moltke's virtues, so on July 3 he opened the fight at 8 a.m. with a barrage by 300 guns. Along with failure of several subordinate generals to understand or obey his orders during the fighting that ensued, this premature attack permitted three-quarters of North Army to escape the cauldron battle for which Moltke had so long prepared and dreamed of achieving.[71] Luckily for him, that made little difference, since Benedek truly was a rank incompetent who proceeded to lose the battle anyway. Still, Moltke's overly eager aggressiveness courted disaster before the Austrians at Königgrätz, so that the Prussians might well have lost their high-risk gamble.

Despite radically poor dispositions by Benedek, by noon strength of numbers and the tactical initiatives taken by several of his subordinates threatened to breach or flank the Prussians on the left. Meanwhile, superior Habsburg rifled artillery pounded and repelled an attack on the center by four Prussian divisions, pinning them to the ground. With no sign yet of Second Army, King Wilhelm wailed: "Moltke, Moltke, we are losing this battle!"[72] Moltke sternly rebuked: "Here there will be no *retreat*. Here we are fighting for the very *existence* of Prussia."[73] The iron dice were tumbling as he spoke, but yet to show final facing to decide the outcome of battle and the ruler of Germany. This was the climax moment, when it was still an open question which army might envelop the other as commanders on each side, excepting Benedek, sought to flank.

Worried staff officers around Moltke scanned the horizon for Second Army. It was coming, but slowed by rain-sodden roads, its march train strung out over 25 miles. Benedek's staff urged him to advance at the center against the stopped Prussian attackers, but he would not budge off his fixed position to counterattack or support the flanking effort by more assertive subordinates. Instead, he deferred all hope and outcome to the artillery. Hours filled with savage bombardment. Also thrusts, retreats, and local counterattacks. Just after 1:00 p.m. the first guns and charging Guard companies of Second Army finally arrived to join the fight, regimental bands playing. The sound of Prussia marching inspired beleaguered Elbe and First Armies but chilled and demoralized Habsburg troops who heard. Gaps opened in the Austrian lines as emboldened and reinforced Prussian infantry advanced, firing rapidly as they walked, reloading on the move in ways Habsburg infantry with muzzle-loaders could not. They swept away some Saxons, then destroyed an entire Austrian corps inside 30 minutes. Moltke verged on achievement of complete envelopment of North Army. Ecstatic, he poured in his last reserve troops and ordered up the last shells from reserve caissons. He was fully in the thrall of battle, urging commanders to press their divisions hard around the enemy flanks to force a "second Cannae."[74] He wanted more than victory. He wanted total annihilation.

Instead, the Austrian center-right around the key town and heights of Chlum dissolved, ceding over 8,000 distressed and bewildered prisoners to the advancing Prussians. Some units stood to fight brave rearguard actions and died in place. The most famous later was an eight-gun "Battery of the Dead." It briefly stopped a Prussian assault in Chlum but was devastated and overrun by rapid-fire from Prussian infantry.[75] Some battalions followed officers with raised swords in courageous yet futilely murderous counterattacks, but others fled. Survivors of the command breakdown at the center threw down haversacks and weapons and ran for the Elbe. Galloping cavalry passed right through the reserve corps, spreading panic. Just like the Allied cavalry at Rossbach, the terrified horsemen galloped though friendly infantry trapped in column. Others refused orders to plug yawning gaps in the infantry lines or try to staunch the headlong flight of the eroding center. Gun batteries hitched caissons and pulled out without orders, abandoning their assigned infantry to advancing Prussians. Frightened Austrians and Hungarians mistook retreating Federal troops for Prussians and fired into their panic. By 3:00 p.m. it was utter chaos. Benedek's whole army was collapsing. That's what saved it from total destruction.

From the center and both wings of the broken position came guns without caissons, mounted and riderless horses, tens of thousands of leaderless and panicked infantry from four corps. They poured as into a funnel, flowing through a 2.5 mile gap from Chlum to a single bridge leading to the fortress of Königgrätz on the far bank. They were desperate to make it across before plunging shells found the close-packed mass and Prussian flanking columns closed Moltke's trap. Two corps stood exposed by the mass flight away from the flanks and were defeated separately. Several futile, tactically perhaps even stupid, yet certainly courageous counterattacks were made out of old-fashioned columns. Prussian fire was so intense that Austrian fusiliers who tried to fight found they could not stand to reload in the gale of lead. One defile filled with so many dead and dying Austrians and Ukrainians it was later known as the "Way of the Dead." Habsburg VI Corps on its own lost 6,000 men inside an hour. An Austrian officer described the carnage: "Cavalry, infantry, artillery, trains, everything; we couldn't clear them out or restore any kind of order. Our columns were broken up. The enemy

directed his fire into this overfilled ravine and every ball hit home. We retreated, leaving thousands of dead."[76]

By mid-afternoon, North Army was defeated. By 5:00 p.m. it ceased to be
an army. This badly led force of 240,000 once arrayed in proud and ancient
regiments disassembled into a formless mass of wounded, of panic and fear,
of open disobedience and desertion. Survivors had one purpose, to escape
from under the hell of dropping Prussian shells and pursuing rapid-fire infantry by crossing the Elbe. Senior commanders abandoned them. Benedek
crossed the river downstream of the great jam of guns and divisions bulging
around the fortress of Königgrätz. He ordered four pontoon bridges taken
out of the river behind him, cutting off his own men but also any chance of
Prussian pursuit. Otherwise, he did little or nothing to aid the crossing of
the mass of his broken force. He chose instead to sit and compose an exculpa-
tory telegraph to his emperor, announcing the defeat and blaming it on that
morning's fog and on his subordinates. Meanwhile, the commandant of the
fortress of Königgrätz locked it tight against tens of thousands of armed men
pressing and hammering on the gates. Shots were fired in anger and confusion before part of the garrison sallied to force back the desperate, armed and
threatening mob of refugees and to guard the causeway. Hundreds drowned
trying to swim the Elbe and its fork, the Adler. Evening covered the battlefield with dark and mercy, subduing gunfire so that groans and cries for help
were more clearly heard all around. Austrian and Federal casualties were
24,000 killed and wounded and 20,000 prisoners. Moltke's losses were 9,000
killed, wounded or missing.[77]

The Prussians had won an immense battle after a short and lively campaign, although not at all as planned. There was no encirclement of the enemy
force, no cauldron battle lifted off the planning table and onto the field at
Königgrätz.[78] Success can be attributed to the superiority of Prussian weapons and prewar training, and far less to Moltke's purported genius on the day
than to mistakes by his counterpart. Moltke was greatly aided by Benedek's
faulty dispositions and refusal to adapt or take control. The plan to catch
North Army in a caldron worked after a fashion only because Benedek,
against all advice, turned to fight with his back against a river while in hopelessly spread out deployments that were also massed too close to the Prussian
guns. However, Moltke attacked too soon and impatiently with inferior
numbers and was quite fortunate that frozen Benedek refused to come out
from his stronger center position to follow up heavy Prussian losses to far
superior Austrian artillery.[79]

The pell-mell retreat of North Army to the Elbe bridge, combined with Moltke's decision to attack early that morning while Second Army was still strung out in march columns and hours from the field, conspired to deny the Prussians a full envelopment and complete devastation of North Army. Moltke's error was exacerbated by the poor performance of the Prussian cavalry, which had virtually no impact on the battle or the late-day pursuit. Instead of being destroyed, North Army slowly reconstituted 180,000 men on the far bank of the Elbe and crawled back to Olmütz, lethargically pursued by Second Army. It was another Benedek mistake, but the Prussians again failed to capitalize. The retreat to Olmütz opened the road to Vienna for First and Elbe Armies, but three hungry Prussian armies instead ate out the richest provinces of the Empire as they moved south. They were essentially unopposed, despite the fact that Austria was still in possession of a force of 200,000 men. Habsburg resistance had been smashed psychologically. On July 22, before Moltke could aggressively move on Vienna, a threat that might have brought other major powers into the war and thereby blunted Bismarck's plans in Germany, Vienna asked for terms.

The diplomatic settlement that secured this stunning military victory was all down to Bismarck. He blocked excessive demands by a usually cautious King Wilhelm I, who suddenly was avaricious for annexations. Bismarck insisted on no annexations of Austrian provinces, for that was too likely to provoke France and Russia. Instead, he moderated the armistice to dissuade other powers from propping up Austria or trying to reverse the meaning within Germany of the decision won at Königgrätz. Prussian armies withdrew from Lower Silesia and Bohemia as Berlin abjured annexations in the south. Austria and its *Bund* allies paid large indemnities (reparations) to Berlin but stayed intact apart from Venetia, which was ceded to Italy. The balance of power in Germany and in Europe was shattered, but Austria was so effectively isolated by Bismarck before the war, and so quickly defeated by Moltke during it, that the other Great Powers failed to react to this fundamental shift of wealth, resources and population in Prussia's favor.

Over the next two years, southern German states were bound to Prussia via defense treaties forced upon them. Vienna never again challenged Berlin within Germany. It turned inward, roiled by nationalism among non-German peoples, an acceleration of a long-standing internal crisis that would do much to bring about World War I in 1914 and the final dissolution of the Habsburg Empire in 1918. Reflecting internal division, the monarchy presided over linked but not unified German and Magyar holdings, and many smaller ones, and became known as the hyphenated Austro-Hungarian Empire in 1867. Each state maintained its own army. Each army had its own ethnic and budgetary base, recruitment areas and systems, separate command languages, and ethnically based units. The German-dominated and officered *Gemeinsame Armee* ("Common Army") was headquartered in Vienna, while a Magyar *Honvéd* ("home guard" or "fatherland defense" force) was jealously ruled from Budapest. An Imperial reserve, the *Landwehr*, made up the third part of a Habsburg army that was anything but unified and modern. However ancient, a house so divided could not stand. Discord over when to use the armies, and how or even whether to pay for overall Imperial defense, undermined the Empire from 1866 into World War I, ending with military and political extinction of the ancient Habsburg empire in 1918.[80]

In France after 1866, Prussia faced rising opposition to its ambitions for a takeover of all Germany, but benefited from Louis-Napoléon's feckless leadership and diplomacy, including fanciful Second Empire support for the "national principle" in Europe. Bismarck and Moltke had already secured far more from the other Great Powers than their king ever dreamed possible, including annexation of *all* the spoils of the Danish War; closing of all yawning territorial gaps in Prussia by annexing Frankfurt, Hanover, Hesse-Kassel and Nassau after beating Austria; and enlarging Prussia's wealth and population even as they sealed old vulnerabilities along the frontier with France. Other northern states and cities were left nominally independent, yet fell under Prussia's control via combination in a North German Confederation whose military and foreign policies were set in Berlin.[81] Moltke's high-speed military operations and Bismarck's *Schnellfeuer* diplomacy were so well planned before the war they were able to make on-the-run adjustments as military or political opportunity arose. Their flexibility ensured that Königgrätz proved a truly decisive battle in every sense of that term. It won and ended the war, permitting Berlin to impose a soft peace yet also an effective diktat on Austria. It elevated Prussia overnight to the main rank of the Great Powers. It led to physical connection of its eastern and western halves. It added millions of new subjects and thus delivered entire future corps and armies to Moltke and the General Staff.

In return for a moderate peace with Austria, Bismarck was freed to act more aggressively in the near future to secure the rest of Germany to Prussia by force. Austria was defeated. France was divided and ill-led. Russia and Britain were preoccupied with their own internal issues and what Russians called the *Turniry teney* ("Tournament of Shadows") in Central Asia, which the poet of imperialism and competitive empire, Rudyard Kipling, later made romantically famous among English speakers as the "Great Game."[82] Moltke and Bismarck thus readied to provoke another crushing war of hard and final decision, this time against France. Only defeating France would ensure Berlin's domination over all Germany, removing the last Great Power obstacle and objection to annexation of the south German states. That would add millions more subjects and 200,000 excellent troops then in *Bundesarmee* or state uniforms to the Prussian order of battle, vaulting Berlin to hitherto unknown levels of power and prestige. Bismarck and Moltke set out not just to defeat France but to humiliate it, raising Prussia-Germany *über alles*. Yet the coming war would hold surprises and reveal deep strategic facts about war that Moltke did not anticipate. His newly rapid way of operations and short war would be tested by protracted peoples' war, with results both predictable and worrisome.

Battle of Annihilation

IN THE DECADE before the Franco-Prussian War of 1870–1871, Emperor Napoléon III (Louis-Napoléon) had already stumbled into a useless war in Italy in 1859, then an imperial misadventure in Mexico. He even flirted with the idea of joint diplomatic and naval intervention with Britain in the American Civil War, to ensure survival of the Confederacy and the break-up of the United States. Most damaging, his impulsive support of minor nationalist movements in Eastern and Central Europe alienated France from the more conservative Great Power allies it needed if Prussia was to be stopped from forcing the creation of the most powerful state in Europe by unification of Germany under its domination. This vainglorious adventurer only awoke to the core threat from Berlin in late 1866, after Moltke's armies had already won at Königgrätz. His stirring came too late to stop Bismarck locking down the victory in crucial territorial gains in northern Germany, notably along the Franco-German frontier. Thereafter, it was a near certainty that tensions would rise and war would come between France and Prussia.[1]

Yet all wars are wars of choice, by at least one side and sometimes by both. The Franco-Prussian War of 1870–1871 was wanted and chosen by leaders on each side of the Rhine. The decision for war came amid great turmoil in the unsettled European balance, resulting from Prussia's stunning victory over Austria four years earlier and the subsequent reordering of internal German affairs. Prussia's raised power and status caused uncertainty about Berlin's next target and intentions, and made for general insecurity over shifting power relations.[2] As the powerful moved mountains, many smaller people listened to the thunder and thought they also wanted war. In the summer of 1870 the pride of nations and the vanity of rulers intersected, as they so often do, in the urge to fight. As would happen again in the summer of 1914, when war between Germany and France was declared in 1870 there was public rejoicing in the streets of Berlin and the boulevards and cafés of Paris.

Louis-Napoléon is something of an enigma even among period historians. Relentlessly ambitious, he was an erratic and insecure purveyor of grandiose political ideas, unrooted colonial visions and boyish military fantasies. Victor Hugo devastated his reputation with the dismissive appellation *Napoléon le petit*. Speeding France along the path to war was his need to distract from mounting opposition over his failing "Liberal Empire" at home and gross misadventures abroad. He wanted to close a yawning distance from the nation, where rising disdain for his person and policies threatened to bring him down. He grew desperate as national elections in 1869 renewed republican demands for an end to his dictatorship and the corrupt trappings of the Second Empire. His political insecurity and personal vainglory contributed importantly to the decision to make war.[3] Nevertheless, it is clear that Prussian policy was the primary cause.

Moltke and Bismarck coldly chose to complete by force the unification of all Germany under Prussia. Bismarck especially used cunning deceit and subterfuge at home and abroad to stoke public support for war, forcing an artificial crisis with publication of a carefully and cynically edited "Ems Dispatch" (*Dépêche d'Ems* or *Emser Depesche*) on July 13. The affair leading to a faked *casus belli* began when the French ambassador spoke directly with King Wilhelm at the spa at Bad Ems, communicating that Paris wanted Prussia to promise never to put a member of its Hohenzollern dynasty on the Spanish throne. Bismarck was sent a summary memorandum, edited it to make the French demands seemed more rude and more directly backed by threats of war, then released the doctored note to the national press and foreign diplomats. The furor over slighted national honor that followed in both countries produced the expected overreaction from Louis-Napoléon, giving Bismarck and Moltke what they wanted when the easily manipulated Emperor declared war on Prussia.[4] They planned and expected to win another short, sharp fight to complete their trifecta wager on three Wars of German Unification in 1864, 1866, and 1870.

When it came to decisions to make war, Bismarck nakedly summed up the problem this way: "A conquering army on the border will not be halted by the power of eloquence." He did not add that under his hand the conquering army was more often Prussian than not, the borders violated defended by someone else's troops. Moltke waxed more mystically about battle cutting through Prussia's problems to quickly advance its larger goals: "Eternal peace is a dream, and not even a pleasant one. War is a part of God's world order."[5] Bismarck joined King Wilhelm at a forward HQ with mobilization underway. He expected to be back in Berlin in a month, to dictate terms to

France after another *kurtz und vives* victory. In the event, he was not able to leave invaded France until March 6, 1871, after months of war. Not until after taking direct command to order prolonged artillery bombardment of Paris, restraining Moltke, who frothed at the bit to invade the rest of France to put down a peoples' war flaming all around.

As France and Prussia moved armies to the frontiers each expected a short and sharp fight, and to win easily and quickly. Like the Austrians in 1866, the French Army readied for battle in the old style, though with an important firepower modification. France would mass an orderly concentration of men and guns in a single body so big that, it was assumed by its *état-major* (General Staff), it must hold France's borders against any invasion and be irresistible once it chose to go over to offense. The French Army thought it would prevail over the Prussian Army by sheer weight, reinforced by advanced rifle fire-power it, too, had adopted a few years earlier. It was even more confident in its professional veterans. In fact, many veterans were unreliable and it was a badly outdated force overall. It had been reorganized in 1815 in the shadow of the Congress of Vienna, remade into a purely defensive force to serve a defeated, distrusted and bound-over nation. Minor reforms were assayed over the following decades, yet overall the French Army failed to keep up with the accelerating pace of military modernization from the 1830s to the 1850s. By the mid-1860s, after years of Second Empire distractions and corruption, most of its wartime experience was merely colonial, garnered in fights against ragged enemies in Algeria and Mexico that hardly tested its structures or fighting doctrine. It last fought a European power in 1859, but only against an even more blimpish Austrian force in a slogging campaign in north Italy. Since French mobilization, field maneuvers and fighting performance were easily the best of the three armies engaged in that war, there were few lessons learned and little done afterward to keep up with fast-modernizing Prussia.[6]

In 1870, the French Army's core was a professional long-service cadre kept in place by solid re-enlistment bonuses rather than merit. The system served to keep too many out-of-shape and older *grognards* in uniform far past their prime, some into their sixties. These veterans were profoundly unfit for war physically and psychologically. Too many officers were also poorly skilled. Some were illiterate. All partook of a retrograde culture that disdained hard technical education in favor of remembered (or imagined) *élan* over matériel, an attitude harkening to the glory of Napoleon I yet fatally out of touch with more open-order tactics against much greater defensive rifle and artillery fire-power. This was decidedly an army of the nephew's Second Empire, not his famous uncle's First Empire. It could not contend with the *furia Teutonica* about to hurtle to France's frontiers on hundreds of troop trains. Despite an excellent rail system, hastily assembled and poorly trained French divisions would be singularly unprepared for the speed of Prussian mobilization or the skill of many battle-tested German officers and units.[7] Worse, at the Army's head was Louis-Napoléon. In 1870, he was deteriorating badly, physically and intellectually as well as politically and diplomatically.[8]

The French had no reliable reserve, despite Louis-Napoléon's unkept promise to raise the *Garde nationale* to a million men to overmatch Prussia's *Landwehr* reserve. An 1868 reform extended service from seven years to nine, with four spent in a reserve dubbed the *Garde mobile*. After falling afoul of domestic opposition to the regime, on the eve of war this force had just 90,000 poorly trained men. When war came, it was mobilized late and badly. Many entrained without rifles or kit. A second, even less effective reserve was the *Garde nationale sédentaire*, which took men between 30 and 40 years old for garrison duty to free younger men to drill and fight. The French Army had barely 400,000 fighting men at the outset of war, with little prospect of reinforcement and only the shallowest of reserves. How could anyone contemplate fighting with this antiquated army against the battle-proven Prussians? Because of misplaced confidence in the fighting edge of the *grognards* and too much uninformed boasting in cafés and in the cabinet that France's older professionals would quickly and easily dispatch Prussia's hordes of green reservists and recent conscripts.[9]

As for the *état-major*, it was hardly worthy of designation as a General Staff. It was sharply inferior in organization and skill to its Prussian counterpart under the hard-driving Moltke.[10] It was severely handicapped by endemic corruption and gross misappropriation of Army funds, including by Louis-Napoléon. After making several abortive efforts a few years earlier, it had no operational plan to deal with the Prussian Army on the borders. The *état-major* lacked key administrative and logistical structures to mobilize or concentrate its troops even half as rapidly as the Prussians would reach the frontier, or to keep up with maneuvers by Moltke's corps and armies once they got there. It did not encourage initiative or instruct on how to execute a corps march lasting just a single day. It did not supply lower-level officers with proper maps, relying instead on centralized command, whereas all Prussian officers had excellent small-scale war maps (*Kriegskarten*). They were also rewarded for taking local initiative.[11] On the other side, staff failure to plan mobilization from peacetime footing to wartime on the accelerated railway schedule of the mid-19th century was about to cost the French Army and nation dearly.[12]

The Army of the Second Empire was not utterly hidebound. A few force-ful critiques made by officers and military writers before 1870 were accepted, taking into account also the firepower *surprise de Sadová,* as the French called the impact of the Prussian Army's needle-guns at Königgrätz. Republican critics wanted to return to the *levée en masse,* to universal short-service con-scription to raise a national army. The professional officer corps rejected the idea, but at least tried to keep up with modern equipment, weapons, commu-nication and transportation. An exception was the artillery corps. Cannon that proved good enough in Italy in 1859, or in Mexico, were deemed as still modern in 1870. In fact, these old brass guns were badly obsolete compared to powerful steel guns brought to battle by the Prussian Army, which finally upgraded its artillery after being outgunned by the Austrians in 1866. French artillery doctrine was similarly outdated, and too many shells would prove to be erratically and unreliably fused at point of manufacture.[13]

Prussian skirmishers at Königgrätz advanced in staggered, decentral-ized waves protected by rapid fire. Even low-level officers took initiative within the overall direction set by higher command. This became known as *Auftragstaktik* ("mission tactics"). It encouraged subordinates to aggressively pursue overarching goals and to move directly into attack in pursuit of a de-fined mission, rather than strictly follow a set of prescribed orders no matter what was happening nearby.[14] In contrast, in the French Army all firing was to be directed not by officers in local contact with the enemy but reserved to a central command. That built fatal delay into the system that reduced effective counterattacks and generally made French responses more sluggish.

At least the French high command recognized that the Prussian Army's upright firing lines were superior to the outdated tactics of the Austrian in-fantry, taught also to their own until 1866. No longer could one advance in shock columns and hope to win. The old way was therefore discarded in favor of rapid fire with chassepot rifles (discussed below) and a doctrine of advance by echeloned battalion. That still bunched infantry into dense masses, vul-nerable to Prussian rifles and long-range artillery. However, infantry were wisely told to dig in under Prussian hailing fire, to maximize defensive fire-power from their chassepots and *mitrailleuses.* As blue waves of Prussian in-fantry advanced, it was believed they would be cut down by French *feu de bataillon* ("fire by battalion"). Rate-of-fire advantage would be so great, it was thought, that it must prove decisive. With better rifles and unique *mi-trailleuses,* despite inadequate brass cannons at least a decade out of date, the French Army would defeat the Prussian Army at its own game of greater in-fantry firepower. Since this was deemed to be enough, other key reforms were shelved, including the thorny political issue of professionalism vs. expanded conscription.[15]

Where the *état-major* contemplated war, Moltke planned it. His preparations were more professional, precise and calculated, as he ruthlessly discarded ideas he believed outmoded, even his own. He diverted military spending to railways, specifically ordering more rolling stock and wider loading platforms and other facilities to move large numbers of men and horses west by rail. As he had in 1866, in 1870 he would again send out several smaller armies marching along discrete routes, to converge at the point of battle. He married rapid mobilization to his own direct command and control via the telegraph, all to try to replicate in France the victory over Austria, to bring about a singular envelopment and devastation of the enemy army in a cauldron fight. Like Clausewitz, Moltke believed military operations must aim to bring main forces into violent contact. Because of Prussia's vulnerable multisided strategic position, he went further, adding an urgent need not only to win the opening battle but to succeed so rapidly he must also win the war. This was his signature contribution to the German way of war that so absorbed the attention of the world from 1870 to 1945.[16]

Prussian short-service conscription drew on a much enlarged population from 1866, dramatically increasing troop numbers from 300,000 to 1.2 million in 1870. Conscripts served three years in the regular army from age 20, then four in the reserves. North German armies were fully incorporated by 1868, so that Berlin had a professional core of 300,000, plus 400,000 in the active reserve and 500,000 more in the *Landwehr*.[17] Prussian regulars were more literate than French counterparts and spent more time at target practice, in small unit training and maneuvers. That imparted a real advantage, even if so great an expansion in numbers between 1866 and 1870 meant that skill among the new troops and reservists was sacrificed to mass and speed as training lagged. One-third of the recruits who entrained for war in 1870 did not yet know how to use their needle-guns and had no training at all in basic tactics. This belied Moltke's own caution about the role of firepower: "In the next war our needlegun will not again be opposed by a far inferior rifle but . . . an entirely equal weapon. Superiority is no longer to be sought in the weapon, but in the hand that wields it."[18] It was another typical Prussian gamble. It was also a feature of short-war thinking coming to the fore in industrial-era warfare, as technology became ever more fast-changing and planning and military budgets could not keep up. When such hard material factors were unfavorable and the long war of attrition they suggested might result proved unattractive, appeal was increasingly made to moral qualities and the fighting superiority of one's troops that must surely bring swift victory.

Making matters worse, Moltke was actually wrong about the rifles. A French chassepot was not equal to a Dreyse needle-gun, it was markedly superior. The rifle invented by Antoine Chassepot and adopted by the French Army in 1868 easily outranged the Dreyse at 1,000 yards vs. 400 (realistic and accurate shooting range, not maximum), and it had a higher rate-of-fire, as high as 15-18 rpm compared to 4-5 rpm. Because a chassepot used a smaller-caliber and lighter (linen-wrapped) round, French infantry carried 105 rounds to a Prussian soldier's standard 70. Unintentionally, chassepot bullets had more stopping power because they tended to tumble, tearing jagged entry and exit wounds in men and horses.[19] Some Bavarian units marching alongside the Prussians carried a Werder rifle in 1870 that was roughly equal to the chassepot, but others were still armed with the badly outclassed 1858 Podewils that fared badly in combat. With the addition of the *mitrailleuse,* the French Army had a marked overall infantry firepower advantage, supported by lesser artillery.

Moltke allowed the Prussian rate-of-fire advantage to slip away after Königgrätz by upgrading artillery instead. He knew the old smoothbore cannon used in 1866 underperformed Austria's rifled guns, and was impressed that the majority of Prussian casualties were inflicted by artillery. So he poured funds into rapid-firing, breech-loading steel cannon made by the Krupp industrial firm. They gave the Prussians a decided advantage in artillery rate-of-fire, distance and accuracy, and fired much more destructive high explosive ordnance. There was a real trade-off, however. Spending on railways and cannon meant Moltke could not replace the infantry's rifles, even though just four years after winning at Königgrätz the Dreyse was already obsolete when facing chassepots. Forced to choose between cannon with high rates-of-fire or better rifles, and more impressed by the performance of Austrian guns at Königgrätz than by his own infantry fire-superiority, he opted for artillery.[20] He also counted on armies getting to the frontiers faster on improved railways, where they would envelop then overcome French infantry chassepots and *mitrailleuse* with high explosive storms erupting from "artillery masses" of steel cannon. The French Army went exactly the other way, ordering as many as three chassepots per soldier.[21]

Moltke did not accept the defensive implications of the ongoing revolutions in infantry and artillery firepower. He concentrated mainly on offensive potential of the new technologies, downplaying their impact on defensive strength and tactics. Moltke and the Prussian Army were all about offense. Defense was for status quo states, not revisionists setting out to reorder the power structures of Germany and Europe, goading decision from speed to battle. He denied that trench warfare or mass slaughter must result if other Great Powers also employed rapid-fire weapons. He simply was not as impressed by defensive firepower as were French generals, who were wrong on many other things but were not stupid when it came to firepower, which they maximized by having their troops dig in to receive attacks. Moltke could not accept that the new technologies and attendant tactics adopted by other nations might be defensive equalizers against temporary Prussian offensive advantages in General Staff planning and operational skill. If he did, Prussia could not make winning war. If he did, Bismarck could not justify using war as a continuation of Berlin's diplomacy by other means, by encirclement campaigns and decisive battles to break the iron ring of the "flanking powers" that hemmed in Prussian destiny. Denial of hard limits to military means was built in to overreaching political goals in Berlin. It was a basic problem and rigid habit of mind that only got worse before the world wars, each started under fast-war delusions, each leading to long war attrition and defeat by more powerful coalitions Berlin provoked into existence.

Moltke could not accept that the firepower advantage in modern combat went powerfully to defenders because it would mean he could not carry out the short and lively war against France deemed essential to complete the unification of Germany under his king. Insisting always that a mobile and skilled field army could inflict decisive defeat on the enemy, he modified tactical doctrine just enough. Where the French dug in to defend, his battalions would attack weakly into their central position, mainly to reduce the effects of concentrated defensive firepower. While a deliberately weak frontal assault fixed the enemy, the real attacks would curl around the flanks, seeking complete destruction. As always, even at the tactical level his goal was to move on the flanks toward a triumphal quick decision.[22] As a compromise between real-world obstacles and Prussian strategic ambitions, it was well conceived. However, getting corps and divisional commanders to obey his orders and follow his doctrine would prove another story.

Just as in 1866, in 1870 Moltke would divide his force in order to speed along several smaller armies (*getrennte Heeresteile*, literally "separated parts of the Army"). Each separated army would provision along its own route, and be just powerful enough to hold its own in any battle of encounter while all the other parts rushed to reinforce and then envelop. Alternatively, the main body of the enemy was to be located and then fixed by an army reconnoitering in force. Once in contact, its job was to act as Moltke's anvil, while the other armies marched with all speed to the sound of the guns and hammered the French flanks, attacking off the march. Moltke would only allow concentration once the main French strength was identified and fixed, moving to trap the whole French Army inside a vast *Kessel*, where he would then methodically eliminate it and win the war.

It was a design to wage and win an idealized Ulm or Cannae, achieving wholesale envelopment and overwhelming victory via more rapid maneuver, and thereby deciding the outcome of the war in its opening campaign. Moltke would alleviate the inherent problems of transporting and supplying a single massed army by instead sending three smaller armies on discrete march routes into France, as if they were Napoleonic corps. He already did this successfully in Bohemia in 1866 just as Frederick did when he invaded Bohemia in 1742, sending three columns over the border widely separated by entire provinces. This principle and practice of initial deployment in *getrennte Heeresteile* chanced defeat-in-detail of the separated parts. It was high-risk but also the only way to achieve speed in movement and thereby reach decisive victory in the short time available, before war against a Great Power devolved into a wearying fight by attrition, or other so-called flanking powers intervened to stop Berlin's offensive and political objectives.[23]

Moltke was confident that his technique of envelopment at the tactical and operational levels could provide strategic victory. However, he did not trust all officers to understand this method, so he issued regulations in 1869 that strictly forbade old-fashioned frontal attacks. He was right to do so. Many older officers were still drawn to the tactics of their grandfathers' day that had inflicted humiliation and defeat on Prussia when used by its most glamorous adversary, the *Grande Armée* of the First Empire. They still admired "moral shock" by attack column, although this invariably led to mass casualties against rapid and long-range fire by enemy infantry and artillery, as was proven at Königgrätz in their own experience. Moltke feared they would persist anyway, wasting divisions with blunt attacks into fixed positions that were well defended by cannon, *mitrailleuses* and chassepots.[24] Some Prussian generals would do exactly that when the moment came. On the other hand, Moltke's rapid-fire tactics against similarly or better-armed French would also lead to massive losses. Prussian armies would take 13 times as many casualties in 1870–1871 as they did in 1866, mostly from chassepots. Maybe offensive-minded Germans could have learned something from those amateur Americans after all, from so many repulsed Union attacks against Confederate rifles firing from behind field works around Richmond in 1864–1865? They no longer needed to look as far as that, having seen what their own rifles did to Austrians. They did not see, however, and would not for another half century, not until they stalled at First Marne.

***

WHEN FRANCE DECLARED war on Prussia on July 19, 1870, it had 492,585 men available for mobilization, including a small reserve. The *état-major* thought it could move its troops to the frontiers faster than the Prussians, along a solid and purpose-built rail net. However, the mobilization plan was inept, ending in a mad dash of units piecemeal as they became available in assembly areas. When fighting erupted two weeks later the French had only 304,000 ready at the frontiers, facing 426,000 Prussians (and other Germans). Moreover, French logistics were appallingly bad. Prussians at least began with adequate food, fodder and ordnance. The French Army was poorly supplied from the start. The calamity suffered over the next weeks and months was rooted in failure to raise or train enough men in advance, then inept movement and supply of the divisions it had. It did not get the *Armée du Rhin*, as its main force was called, to the borders in time to meet the Prussian concentration. Once it arrived and met mobile fury coming the other way, it fell back on inadequate fighting doctrine that it could not make up for a lack of officer training and a culture of discouragement of command initiative.[25]

France had four railway lines heading to the borders compared to Prussia's six, and they were not fully linked. Fewer miles were double-tracked, and a key fifth line (Verdun-Metz) was unfinished. Nor were there adequate plans to take advantage of a superior road system that might have eased the strain on the railways. Lack of planning led to muddled concentrations of French corps around Metz and Strasbourg, in great confusion after aggravated delays. No branch was fully mobilized. Infantry, cavalry and artillery were all delayed in jammed depots or departed them without assigned reservists. That left many units short of men and heavy weapons and dramatically short of horses, especially the artillery. Confused mobilization was confounded by inferior logistics. There was more than enough equipment, but the French supply service did not move troops and horses or guns and ammunition at the new speed of mid 19th-century railway war.[26]

French units making first contact with the enemy at the border were quickly outnumbered. Some commanders were hesitant or hampered by delays in reservists reporting for active duty or in reaching their muster points. Too many officers were woefully uninformed about the rail system that was so critical to mobilization *and* supply. A pronounced tendency to remain on the defensive as Prussians maneuvered for position arose in part from colonial warfare experience in North Africa and Mexico, where field reconnaissance was often so poor officers preferred to await the enemy attack in secured positions. Regardless of the mess at the frontiers, as Louis-Napoléon paraded out of Paris at the head of the *Armée du Rhin* he jauntily promised suddenly cheering, rather than jeering, crowds lining the boulevards that the army he headed would bring them a "second Jena."[27] Instead of his uncle's short and quick victory over Prussia in 1806, the nephew was about to lead the French into a catastrophe of Prussian fury and revenge.

The efficiency of Prussian mobilization has been exaggerated. Once beyond the railheads, Moltke's marching armies quickly ran short of supplies as a still experimental mobile staging system (*Ettapen*) failed to keep up with the combat divisions. One historian of the mobilizations of 1870 concludes that the Prussians won the battles of the frontiers "in spite of and not because of their supply organization."[28] Things would only get worse when the Prussians encamped outside Paris during months of siege later in the war. Something similar had happened when Prussians staggered toward Königgrätz woefully undersupplied, and after the victory had to forage widely in ways that large 19th-century armies could not sustain for long. Inadequate attention to logistics in favor of battle-seeking was a major flaw in the Prussian system that stemmed directly from the quick-victory delusion, which pushed resources and the best officers into the combat arm in preference to supply. It was a flaw that reappeared in German operations planning in France in 1914, and again in the invasion of the Soviet Union in 1941. Still, at least in getting to the railheads and frontiers in 1870 Prussian movement was an exemplar of the speed, reach and efficiency of railway war. Off-rail was another matter. That was still about horse carts and marching along dirt or mud roads in full kit under a summer sun.

Moltke moved his split forces over all six rail lines, with long double-tracked sections and specialized supply depots and wide loading bays specially built to support aggressive war, just as wide and straight autobahns would be built by the Nazis in the 1930s to speed armies into wars to come. His plan was to position in advance for later adjustment around the arriving enemy flanks, once the French dispositions and main march direction became clear. He had available 13 Prussian corps, supported by more south Germans. He divided these troops into three smaller, speedy armies. Second Army was the main strike force, moving at the center with 131,000 men. On the right he placed First Army, just 60,000 strong to start but reinforcing constantly. Third Army was the southernmost force, holding his left flank along the Palatinate border, yet ready to serve as an enveloping arm once French movement was fixed. Its 125,000 men were mostly south Germans.

Moltke's tripartite movement offered French generals a real chance to push flank attacks to defeat the Prussians severally and individually. That was always the gamble in any system of widely dispersed movement prior to concentration for battle. The key to success was speed rather than power, first in mobilization and then by rapid field marches once armies left the railheads. Moltke was fully confident he could get to the borders before the French finished mobilizing, just as French generals were confident of arriving first because of their denser rail net. Once there, he would disrupt the enemy and limit French options by attacking into one flank or the other of their main mass. No matter which way the French turned, if he got his armies there first they would be in a flanking position. Or he could fix the *Armée du Rhin* with First and Second Armies while sending Third wheeling around the south flank to cut off lines of supply, communication and withdrawal. In either case, envelopment would deliver victory and revenge. Jena and Auerstedt, the taking of Berlin in 1806 and the memory of humiliation ever since, all would be avenged with one swift triumph. And more important, all Germany would be won to Prussia.

Desperate to burnish his political fortunes with military success, Louis-Napoléon left just 15,000 men in Paris to meet anticipated popular dissent as he massed the *Armée du Rhin* under his personal command outside the fortress-city of Metz. In manner and vainglory he was much like his uncle. In political and martial ability he was by far the lesser man and leader, *Napoléon le petit*. Fearful of losing the limelight of war to rivals in the Army, and well acquainted in his own career with the power of coup d'état, he relegated his best generals to supporting roles as corps commanders or sent them on lesser missions far from the main theater to dim their chance for glory that might outshine his own. He rode from Paris in fuss and feathers, drawn to the frontier by the charms of battle yet inured to its peril. He would survive or fall with a roll of the iron dice.

Marshal Achille Bazaine, senior soldier of France, was denied overall command. Bazaine served initially only as a corps commander directly under Louis-Napoléon. A detached I Corps of 45,000 headed for Alsace, under Marshal Patrice de MacMahon. A bloated VI Corps assembled at Châlons, initially under Marshal François Canrobert. Needing to pose as offensive-minded, Louis-Napoléon sent an excursion to make an early military demonstration across the frontier, into the Saar. It was a mere gesture, a soufflé served to aroused national opinion and public pressure, topped with a sugar of forlorn hope to lure Austria, Denmark and Italy into the war. Otherwise, the Emperor sat with 22 massed divisions in the *Armée du Rhin*, holding in a purely defensive posture. Or rather, his subordinates fumbled through a still confused mobilization and early contact with the aggressively moving enemy armies, now away from their railheads and over the frontier into France. Louis-Napoléon in command of the *Armée du Rhin* had no real plan, and his men lacked a confident commander to tell them where to go or what to do next. The *état-major* before the war simply assumed that a massed and more professional French Army would somehow meet and block any Prussian invasion, only to find confusion and uncertainty and fear along the frontiers when war came. As for the emperor, Louis-Napoléon had no idea what he was doing or how to conduct field operations.[29]

Moltke was not impressed or deterred by French mass. He easily repulsed the small advance into the Saar, then ordered Third Army to move out of Alsace to search for the enemy's flank and rear.[30] So far, all to plan. Still, not everything went smoothly. Errors and indiscipline affected the occasion and flow of early fights as Moltke's order not to conduct frontal assaults was ignored by imprudent or insubordinate corps commanders. Flash fights disrupted his grand marching scheme with little battles he did not want. He was after massive strategic envelopment, not little puffs of glory. Yet this kind of command behavior was not uncommon. It spoke to the downside of following mission tactics, of standing encouragement of on-site officer initiative. It also encouraged vainglory. It would happen again at the level of whole German armies during the invasion of France in 1914, when generals in another Battle of the Frontiers attacked rather than falling back as ordered and helped set the stage for defeat at First Marne. It would happen yet again as panzer group commanders disobeyed direct orders, including from Hitler, after crossing the Meuse in May 1940, and fortunately for them (but not for Britain and France) raced ahead to reach the coast and split the Allies' armies in two. Yet again in 1941, Wehrmacht generals advancing into the Soviet Union were sometimes so eager for battle honors or to capture some onion-domed city they did not always stay with the march plan. Twice disobedient in senior command might be coincidence. Three and four times and more says it was a key feature of the Prussian-German way of war. Sometimes it worked, other times it traded solitary officer glory for greater disaster.

So it was in 1870 that division and corps-sized engagements developed as senior Prussian officers launched old-fashioned blunt infantry assaults against Moltke's orders, right into well-defended enemy positions. Sometimes the French dug in behind loopholed walls of stone forts centuries old, where archers once stood defending dead kings and old faiths. French snipers and skirmishers took cover in ditches, in low trenches as well as atop high ground. Prussians won all these small encounter battles, though at growing cost in lives and wounded men. French frontier defenders fought hard and well protecting national soil. Eager lads in dark Prussian *dunkelblau* and Bavarians in a lighter *hellblau*, as well as German conscripts in other shades of blueblack not quite as keen for war, were laid prone by crescendos of rippling fire from chassepots. Tumbling bullets left linen casings to come at them faster and at greater range than they could match with outclassed needle-guns. Or they heard the heavier *crack-crack-crack-crack* of a *mitrailleuse* as they fell, grievously wounded by that gun's larger rounds. Survivors dubbed the novel weapon *Höllenmaschine* ("Hell Machine"). Sheets of incoming fire at rates they could not understand made gaping holes in men and horses. It was an early example of the real genius of modern war, if such a thing exists at all: industrialization and science harnessed to purposeful destruction.

What saved the survivors was a standing practice of the Prussian Army to concentrate off the march at the point where any battle started. Nearby divisions and corps hastened to the sound of volleying gunfire. The dug-in French were thus outnumbered, and usually maneuvered out of their fixed positions by the end of each day's light. Senior officers in centralized corps HQs failed to reinforce defensive positions or countermaneuver around the attackers, even when they had advantage of numbers. Content to rely on superior firepower, they positioned infantry lines to maximize the dominance of chassepots but failed to widen them to protect exposed flanks as more Prussians arrived and curled around the ends of discontinuous lines. This was more like August 1914 than November 1914: flanks still existed and could be turned. French officers left whole divisions bunched in place, taking terrible punishment from fast-arriving steel guns firing high-explosive shells. The big Krupp guns were always vigorously pushed forward, traversing some rivers on rafts improvised by engineers. Outnumbered or outflanked at some point on each new day of combat, despite fighting hard and well, the French pulled back from the advancing artillery fury. German armies marched ever deeper into France, still seeking an envelopment.

The first big encounter battle took place at Wissembourg in Alsace on August 4. A detached division of Marshal MacMahon's I Corps was slammed into by forward elements of Third Army, readying to locate and attack into the flank of the *Armée du Rhin*. MacMahon's force was bruised and fell back. A larger, better-prepared defense took place at the nearby Froeschwiller Heights two days later, where 88,000 Germans faced 50,000 French. Third

Army's nominal commander, Crown Prince Friedrich Wilhelm, hoped this second match with MacMahon's floating I Corps might become a little cauldron fight he could claim as his own. Instead of fresh glory, one of his rambunctious corps commanders bludgeoned into French and Algerian troops well hidden and dug in on high ground, and was stopped with heavy casualties.

At the Froeschwiller Heights, also known as the Battle of Wörth, the defenders were in a half-moon of prepared trenches. With clear lines of sight for chassepots and *mitrailleuses*, they opened rapid fire at ranges that answering needle-guns could not match. Time and again, advancing Prussian infantry was scythed by rifle fire, helpless to reply in kind. In a straight infantry-on-infantry defensive battle the French would have prevailed, but they had officers who fell into a combat trance and ordered attacks instead. Like their Prussian counterparts ordering blunt assaults with visions of Frederickian annihilation in mind, too many French officers sought some misremembered Napoleonic glory in an infantry charge. The French also suffered from markedly inferior artillery. Eager to fight with old tactics for new glory, officers ordered well-protected troops out of trenches into needless open-field counterattacks. As the erect French at last came into needle-gun range, Prussian skirmishers and well-dispersed firing lines responded with a metal storm of their own.[31] Cavalry also attacked into the teeth of rapid fire. One charge surpassed in futility that of the British Light Brigade into Russian guns at Balaclava in Crimea, as needle-guns cut down over 800 French lancers out of the 1,200 who made the death ride. Not one reached the firing line. Cavalry played a subsidiary role in war well into World War II, but the day of charges across an open field against rapid-firing infantry was over.[32] The decision on the Froeschwiller Heights went to fast-arriving Prussian steel artillery, which blasted apart the heights and trenches and troopers. Of the 11,000 French killed or wounded, most were hit by shell fragments. Heavy ordnance in combination with superior numbers, not tactical brilliance or Prussian command genius, won the field.[33]

A third frontier fight broke out at Spicheren (Spichern) in Lorraine, also on August 6. Again, the battle was not of Moltke's design or choosing, as Clausewitz's inescapable friction abraded his grand plan. More friction at HQ approached *théâtre de l'absurde*, as a true farce was scripted and enacted by some of his most senior generals. The lead was played by 74-year-old Karl von Steinmetz, hero of the Austrian war now in command of First Army. Contemptuous of Moltke's maneuvering and envelopment plan, and expressing admiration instead for blunt old Marshal Blücher's hard charging at other

French divisions under the other Napoleon, he sought battle on his own. He disobeyed explicit march orders and took his eight divisions right across the path of Second Army, thereby blocking its advance and helping to ruin Moltke's plan for a cauldron battle in the Saar. It cannot be dismissed as just one old man's vanity at work. There were several similar episodes under other generals. This was the Prussian attack ethic and abuse of the idea of mission tactics all at once.[34]

Steinmetz attacked straight into a solid French position, through thick woods and then up the slope of a small mountain. Again, young men in *dunkelblau* were scythed down in bushels by rapid defensive fire from chassepots and *mitrailleuses*. Again, other corps marched to the banging guns to win the field for Moltke by day's end. Again, artillery masses finished the story, as heavy batteries of Krupp guns coordinated crossfire to obliterate French positions. Also helping were inept French generals, notably Bazaine. He stood by with four divisions yet did nothing to assist assaulted countrymen as the Prussians gathered around them. So the Prussians won at Spicheren. Nevertheless, from Moltke's point of view, a disobedient subordinate had caused unintended and fatal delay to his larger plan, which relied on speed and obedience, qualities now sorely lacking. He was not satisfied with trapping parts of the enemy army, he wanted it all. Now his plan to encircle the *Armée du Rhin* in front of Metz failed. Although the French Army was broken into two pieces and bleeding men and resolve, he must find his politically essential decisive battle someplace else.[35]

Atrocities in these frontier battles must not be passed over. Some Germans showed no quarter to surrendering *Schwarzen* ("blacks"), as they called Berber troops in French service. Bismarck later denounced those who did show mercy: "There should have been no question of making prisoners of those blacks. If I had my way, every soldier who made a black man prisoner would be placed under arrest. They are beasts of prey, and ought to be shot down."[36] Early days, yet a motif of annihilation in a different sense was already there in German military and political thought, taking on a sinister and murderous meaning beyond the Moltkean ideal of a crushing victory. When the peoples' war began later that year, it led to more atrocities against all colors. As Germans faced irregular resistance from real or imagined *francstireurs*, they reacted with collective reprisals and indiscriminate killings. Comparable and worse dark acts later stained German colonial operations against the Herero-Nama peoples, the opening battles on French soil in 1914, and yet again in 1940.[37] While all armies contain some men capable of such acts if unrestrained by conscience or their training and officers, there was more to this brutal pattern than the usual moral shrug of *à la guerre comme à la guerre* ("when at war, as at war"). There was also a building belief in the German *Machtstaat* ("power state"), at the cost of all else.

Despite unintended and outdated actions by Prussian commanders, Froeschwiller Heights and Spicheren nevertheless divided the *Armée du Rhin*, prised open the frontier and exposed France to deep invasion. Strategically, they cooled any possible ardor in foreign capitals for alliance with Paris. Not that there was much to start.[38] News of border defeats also spurred civilian dissent against Louis-Napoléon, against his imposition of martial law and call to the nation to rise up to support the Second Empire, so far from the misremembered glory of the First. The absence of any serious prewar or contingency planning by the *état-major* was fully exposed as the *Armée du Rhin*, now with a cumbersome and separated left wing, retreated in disorder toward the fortress city of Paris. Ill-health and strain finally caused Louis-Napoléon's full mental and physical collapse. He ordered the *Armée du Rhin* to turn aside from the Paris road and instead enter and hold Metz. Then he relinquished command to Bazaine. The French Army was split and lacking confidence and initiative after its battering along the frontier. The move into Metz threatened to trap its main force bodily inside a fortress complex. Yet the order was given to head to a defensive position there instead of more defensible Paris, where so large a force might have made the capital unwinnable by the Prussians. The reason was that Louis-Napoléon feared that a retreat to Paris might finish him, after parading out while promising the laurel of a "second Jena." Following the midsummer's nationalist excitement and expectations and promises of quick victory, retreat all the way back to Paris could provoke a revolution that would oust him at last. So the dictator chose Metz instead.

A sense of defeat, low morale and rising ill-discipline characterized the retreating *Armée du Rhin* as it entered Metz.[39] The situation was not helped by Louis-Napoléon's personal issuance of bad marching orders directly to the commanders of widely separated corps, or by overbearing interference in military matters by the distant empress and her supporters in Paris. Bazaine's oddly indifferent command once the army slogged into Metz only made things worse. On August 7, Moltke ordered all his forces to halt in order to separate First and Second Armies, whose march routes Steinmetz had hopelessly entangled. There was a three-day lull during which Bazaine might have counterattacked and done real damage to confused Prussian armies and plans, but he missed the moment. Dividing him further from other French generals was poor intelligence, strategic confusion, growing disobedience and jealous arguments over who had command authority. Already displaying defeatism, Bazaine openly sulked about interference by everyone and anyone, charging insubordination by his senior officers. He committed error upon error in conducting a lethargic retreat to Verdun, then in failing to concentrate 400,000 available troops in the face of three still separated German armies. The *Armée du Rhin* was not at all well served.

The Prussians were also in bad shape, tired from long marches, nursing wounded, short food and transport. Even so, most officers adjusted and tried to fix problems, keeping troops marching more or less in accord with Moltke's grand vision. The final reckoning for the *Armée du Rhin* was therefore merely postponed as Bazaine vacillated, dithered and sulked with 200,000 men at Metz even as a new but weaker French army gathered around MacMahon at Châlons.[40] On August 14, First Army clashed with the *Armée du Rhin* in a bloody little battle at Borny. The next day, Bazaine finally moved up the Verdun road toward Châlons, seeking concentration with MacMahon well after that had become impossible. Again, headstrong Prussian generals disobeyed Moltke to attack numerically superior French forces in a nasty encounter at Mars-la-Tour on August 16. The French inflicted 20,000 casualties before artillery masses of steel guns conspired with too-cautious French generals to win back the day and field. Bazaine gave up the Verdun road to pull back to Gravelotte that night. The *Armée du Rhin* sitting in Metz was cut off from Paris and isolated from the new army MacMahon was trying to form at Châlons.

In the other HQ, Moltke and Roon agreed it would be acceptable to take losses as high as 20,000 in another battle, seeing opportunity rather than carnage in their calculus. Moltke ordered four corps to stop advancing to the Meuse, to wheel around and seal the *Armée du Rhin* into Metz. The fortress could not house or feed its garrison, the civilian population, and a parked army of 200,000 that had lost or abandoned most of its supplies on the Verdun road or before. A decisive battle might yet be forced by Moltke not by envelopment off initial deployment—that plan had already failed—but if Bazaine could be enticed or somehow made to come out and fight. If not, then the old ways of investment and starvation should work, even for hasty Moltke.[41] Already gripped by foreboding, Bazaine ventured out to fight at Gravelotte–Saint Privat on August 18. This was the first set-piece fight where one army marched out to offer battle to another one waiting for it. All the others had been battles of encounter, where armies crashed into each other while on the march. It was also the war's grandest and deadliest fight, with over 360,000 men engaged. It was a uniquely horrific affair because it partly traversed ground littered with unburied corpses from fighting two days earlier at Mars-la-Tour.[42] A Prussian officer later recalled: "It was gruesome. We had to force our horses through rows of corpses . . . I'll never forget the sound of skulls cracking beneath our wheels and the dull thump of arms and legs caught in our spokes; all cohesion was lost as our horses frantically shied, trying to find a way around the dead." Similar scenes were witnessed by a distinguished visitor in the Prussian HQ, American Civil War General Philip Sheridan.[43]

At Gravelotte, Moltke hit the number he had discussed with Roon, as the French inflicted 20,000 Prussian casualties against 12,000 of their own. Prussian reliance on mission tactics was a real advantage overall, but sometimes the command initiative tended toward conservatism and outdated tactics or just got into wrong hands and thus threatened larger operations. So it was at Gravelotte. Prussian dead and wounded mounted as old-style generals once again committed whole corps to brutal direct assaults, having learned little from Moltke and nothing from Königgrätz or the frontier battles. Certain commanders simply bulled infantry into dug-in French positions and much higher rates of fire than their own troops could return. Moltke paced briskly with Sheridan, Bismarck and King Wilhelm, muting his rage over this futile waste of infantry. He accepted high casualties without demur over what it meant to the dying men, as he admitted to Roon, but only on the way to some higher operational goal. Other generals were not as calculatingly brutal in their necessary methods on the way to victory, they were just brutes.

Prussian infantry at Gravelotte (1870).
Courtesy of Wikimedia Creative Commons.

Wave upon wave of Prussians, Hanoverians and Hessians were shot down by the French, falling by thousands in a chassepot gap in which their needle-guns were out-ranged by all the tumbling bullets from the French firing lines, a gap they needed to advance across to close to firing range for their own rifles. Gravelotte was not Königgrätz. As Sheridan could attest, it looked more like the carnage inflicted on Union attackers by entrenched Confederates atop the heights at Fredericksburg. Defending from concealed, dug-in positions, chassepot riflemen on the ridge of Saint-Privat could not be dislodged by assaulting German infantry, so they were pounded to pieces by Moltke's artillery masses instead. A line of 270 steel guns threw 20,000 high explosive shells at the heights.[44] It was a hurricane of explosions and steel splinters in which men were blown apart by swirling winds of smoke and fire. Soldiers everywhere would learn to dig deep into clay and chalk to escape the terrible new artillery of the industrial age of war. Not yet, however. At Gravelotte, the French went into battle without entrenching tools and had no place to go except flat on the ground. Prone men were killed or wounded by showers of hot splinters from shells bursting overhead. Men in cloth hats or bareheaded had no protection and died in droves. The battered line was also stretched by aggressively maneuvering German infantry, until an undefended flank was found and turned, at great cost to both sides. The firepower revolution brought about by the new-style rifles and cannon was no mere theory. It was proven on the killing fields of Gravelotte.

Bazaine returned to Metz to nurse his wounded and his pride, to stew bitter resentment in the cauldron Moltke now kept him in, where he also willingly remained. He wallowed in moral and command lethargy, in a long-lasting and lethal ill mood so deep he never really attempted to break out of the trap. Just two desultory tries were made, on August 26 and 31. What was left of the *Armée du Rhin* then settled into despair and slow starvation. Bazaine even left crews of Prussian engineers unmolested as they tore down the last bridges and placed steel guns all around the city's perimeter.[45] Moltke was hugely helped by Bazaine's extraordinary passivity, which allowed him to leave just 120,000 investing Metz. He was so puzzled by Bazaine's paralysis that he concluded that the French commander must be playing a deeper political game. He would, but not until later, when Bazaine took part in two plots to overthrow a revolutionary republican government declared in Paris on September 4, three days after the defeat at Sedan and capture of Louis-Napoléon by the Prussians.[46] The timing of the plots does not explain Bazaine's inactivity in August or his indifferent behavior at Gravelotte, or the sulking disaster at Metz that led to surrender of the city and the rump of

the *Armée du Rhin* in October. It was all so odd and incompetent and humiliating that Bazaine was accused of treason and compelled to face a court of
inquiry after the war.[47]

With the broken *Armée du Rhin* and Bazaine locked into Metz, a new
Armée de Châlons formed under Marshal MacMahon, with a much subdued
Louis-Napoléon in tow. The question was whether this force of 104,000
should fall back to Paris to add its strength to the 150,000 garrison, a force
that had grown by the day from an original 15,000 and was still holding the
city. Empress Eugénie warned her husband, deep into a paralyzing psychological breakdown, that a retreat posed severe political risks. The *Armée de
Châlons* instead should move away from Paris to relieve the starving survivors
of the *Armée du Rhin* at Metz, to reconcentrate the whole French Army for
a deciding battle. It might even lure away the Germans besieging Metz, if
MacMahon could just outmarch his pursuers and get the new army there.
Then he could attack thick outward-facing Prussian siege "lines of circumvallation," while Bazaine sallied out of the bunkered city to attack the Prussian
inner-facing "lines of contravallation." In short, MacMahon should march as
a relief army to reach and raise the ongoing siege of Metz, coordinating with
Bazaine to make the attack.

Just before communication between the armies at Châlons and Metz was
severed a compromise was struck between the quarreling generals, in which
Bazaine committed the *Armée du Rhin* to break out and meet the *Armée de
Châlons* at a reconcentration point at Montmédy. In fact, neither army was
strong enough to complete its task, the *Armée du Rhin* to break out or the
Armée de Châlons to march to Montmédy to reconcentrate. Bazaine lacked
the command wit and the will to make the breakout work, while the ragtag
units gathered at Châlons were an army in name only, hardly capable of
maintaining cohesion, let alone a relief mission. They comprised elements of
MacMahon's twice bludgeoned I Corps and parts of VII Corps, the last of the
French reserve. Too many men were traumatized survivors from broken divisions that retreated to Châlons after Froeschwiller Heights or were worn out
in other overlong retreats. Others were combat virgins of the *Garde mobile*
who lacked basic equipment beyond rifles. A few scratch units (*régiments de
marche*) were pushed together out of stragglers, late-arriving reservists and
untrained conscripts. Some were picked up still waiting to deploy from when
the war began, stranded at muster points along the railways in the chaotic July
mobilization as hurried trains left them behind on suddenly quiet platforms.[48]

Reluctantly, MacMahon pushed unfed and ill-shod men past all physical limits, back out on the march with Prussians all around, but unseen and

unscouted. Where was Moltke going next? MacMahon was blind to the location of Prussian Third Army and unaware of a new enemy force Moltke had
formed, a 120,000 man Army of the Meuse made from two corps and some
loose divisions stripped from Second Army. It was still being reinforced by replacements and reservists pouring into France. By the end of August, Moltke
had 150,000 fresh troops in France to make up his losses, with 300,000 more
assembling in Germany. The *Armée de Châlons* in contrast had little supply
on hand and no open supply lines, no proper gun train, not enough horses
or wagons, not even complete personal kits for its soldiers. This saddest of
French armies lurched from one promised but already emptied supply depot
to another, harried and pursued by powerful enemy forces it could not outmarch or outfight. At last, it staggered into Sedan.

Moltke was also scrambling to recover, from the disobedience of his
generals, a fog of maneuver and missing information, several unexpected
and unwelcome frontier battles, and the breakdown of his original envelopment plan to a multitude of unforeseen contingencies and building
pressure of the intense physical and moral effort that is war. Failing to
force a decisive battle at the outset now meant stretching limited forces
to achieve three war-winning requirements: lock the *Armée du Rhin* into
Metz, destroy the *Armée de Châlons* and invest the fortress of Paris. To
accomplish all that he needed every available replacement, every last man
of the reserve still assembling or entraining in Germany.[49] As they arrived,
he sent 300,000 troops of the Army of the Meuse and Third Army to run
down and catch the stumbling, hungry, wretched souls marching through
a Slough of Despond who made up MacMahon's *Armée de Châlons*. They
were found crowding hopelessly into Sedan, now trapped as badly as the
Armée du Rhin at Metz.

The old fortress at Sedan was built to 18th-century standards and could
not hope to hold against the modern steel guns it now faced. MacMahon and
Louis-Napoléon also unintentionally collaborated in setting the fatal trap by
deploying on the wrong side of the Meuse. Moltke hurried his armies and
guns forward, seeing at last the chance for victory while also fearing that the
French would resort to a long defensive war if he could not land a knockout
blow.[50] In fact, he was about to get both results: destruction of the *Armée de
Châlons* at Sedan followed by months of small-war attrition across an aroused
France. His original plan for a decisive and annihilating single campaign was
already unraveling in ways that German nationalist histories and his successors on the Great General Staff later obscured, and popular memory and
much military history either forgave or forgot.

The Battle of Sedan began at 4 a.m. on September 1. Killing and dying lasted most of the day, but the outcome was actually decided well before the battle started. The *Armée de Châlons* was badly outnumbered, outgunned and outranged. It was so poorly positioned it could not maneuver. It had no line of retreat and little ability to hit the enemy with anything more than glancing blows. Its general was knocked out early when MacMahon was lacerated by shrapnel as big steel guns tossed 20,000 shells into Sedan from positions older French cannon could not reach or silence. Two sides of the triangular defense collapsed, leaving shaken *troupiers* to stagger back to the fortress. As happened at Königgrätz, a disorganized mass crowded the base of the fortifications while howling shells and waves of pursuing Germans chopped at their heels and killed them.

Many French units fought hard and well, in spite of all the fatal handicaps their position and commanders placed them in. Some went beyond doing their duty, to display foolhardy courage. In a repeat of the Prussian disaster at Froeschwiller Heights, a forlorn hope of ragged horse charged massed guns and German infantry, achieving only piles of mangled men and mounts and bits of useless slaughter smeared on medics' aprons. For those who sought cover or escape by flight, there was no relief from bombardment by a closing circle of 700 Prussian guns.[51] Stone splinters knocked out of the fortress walls by the cannonade added to metal shrapnel from the shells, and to fear, wounds and agony. So did heavy wood splinters from tree bursts, causing gaping tears in men's bodies akin to those afflicting Union and Confederate troops in the burning Wilderness forest south of Washington six years earlier. Seventy-five years after Sedan, German guns again firing high explosives into France would rip up young Americans with treebursts in the nearby Huertgen Forest and Ardennes. The same battlefields fought over and over again.

Louis-Napoléon declined to try to break out and race to Paris. In a final humiliation, he was berated for an hour during a meeting with Bismarck before agreeing to surrender the *Armée de Châlons* without conditions.[52] Where his uncle tumbled into glory and perhaps earned it, the nephew blundered into ignominy and certainly deserved it. French casualties at Sedan were 17,000 killed and wounded and 83,000 prisoners. The Germans lost 9,000 killed, wounded or missing. With Louis-Napoléon a gentle prisoner of King Wilhelm, the overthrow of his Second Empire and a radical government was declared in Paris. In six weeks, Moltke had split the *Armée du Rhin* and penned the greater part inside Metz, then crushed the *Armée de Châlons* at Sedan. It was not exactly according to his plan for a rapid envelopment and cauldron fight, but it seemed a decisive victory nonetheless. The surrender of Bazaine and the *Armée du Rhin* at Metz waited only on the ancient and certain work of starvation. The city saw mass desertion, a total breakdown of military and civilian discipline, and riots by trapped and starving French troops. The end came in a humiliating surrender on October 27.[53] It looked to all as though Prussia had handily won the war, and that it was over. Not so, for while the French Army was defeated at Metz and Sedan, the French nation did not accept the result.

Bismarck and Moltke had shattered not just the French Army but the French constitutional order. Both were deeply conservative men who supported everything about the established European order except Prussia's place in it. To change that, they violently smashed France and unintentionally let loose all its radical children, kept penned and hidden since 1815. Revolution broke out in France once again, along with calls for all-out resistance to Prussia made by a new *Gouvernement de la Défense nationale*. "Reds" in Paris wanted the war to continue by means of a radicalized reprise of the 1793 *levée en masse*. It was a call for peoples' war, even for a return of the Terror; for a full arousal of the nation-in-arms and executions of any and all declared traitors to the Republic and authors of the defeat. Some of this vengeance was carried out later under a radical Commune erected in Paris.[54] Political tumult raced like a prairie wildfire across France. Civil war loomed as well, as on the other end of the political argument bitter reactionaries held out for the Empire, muttering *mieux les Prussiens que la République*, "better the Prussians than the Republic." Their spiritual-political descendants in the run-up to World War II and under Vichy said "better Hitler than Blum," about Léon Blum, the prime minister they despised for being Jewish and for his moderate socialist politics.[55]

Paris was a large city that nonetheless ranked among the most heavily fortified places in the world. The first of 240,000 Prussian troops arrived outside on September 19. They quickly surrounded the fortress capital and settled down for a siege. They faced an immense task, digging trenches all around, hauling in food and fodder and ammunition, cutting all the roads to isolate the city, defending their own exposed camps and siege lines from harrying attacks. Their reliance on overlong supply lines, all the way back to Germany, meant that the besiegers suffered all the ancient and usual afflictions of idle and encamped armies: desertion and disease, despondent lethargy, decadence of pastime and passion, rumbling discontent, even talk of mutiny. Wide Prussian foraging along with a land blockade of the Paris food supply meant that a packed-in and swollen population suffered hunger leading toward starvation almost immediately. The city garrison stood ready to fight but was a huge burden on food supply at 400,000 strong, swollen by late call-ups who had mobilized while the eastern battles were underway. Communication between Paris and the rest of France was maintained by a postal balloon service that in turn led the Prussians to invent the first anti-aircraft gun. Messages still got out, calling for the nation to raise fresh armies and for intense irregular war, for *guerre à outrance* by all and any means available in every town and district across the country. Scorched earth and harassing attacks soon began, by small regular units and by *francs-tireurs* gathering in front, behind and all around the German invaders and occupiers.[56]

A *levée en masse* was called on November 2, consciously evoking the spirit of 1793 when relief armies marched to Paris, some singing *La Marseillaise*. Fresh if ill-trained regular divisions were formed by General Léon Gambetta around units pulled from small provincial garrisons or *Garde mobile* in the western and southern provinces. Weapons caches were secured. Imported Belgian arms were passed out to masses of recruits. French warships, an element of national power not understood in Berlin at the time, provided access to arms supplies from the Anglo-American powers. Before fighting ended in early 1871, France fielded nearly one million new troops. Ill-trained as many of these men and units were, swarms of *francs-tireurs* and other ragged outfits presented a real threat to the occupiers, provoking vicious collective reprisals by Germans against civilians and summary execution of any and all accused.[57] In short, the Germans behaved in France as they would again in 1914 and during World War II, but also as the French behaved toward Spanish guerillas and civilians 60 years earlier in the Peninsular War.

Moltke recognized the enormous economic, social and political strains that any protracted war placed on participants. As a conservative monarchist, he feared revolutionary social effects that must result with a shift from cabinet wars among kings to peoples' wars among nations. He now saw this fear realized by his own hand. The fighting in France was shifting in conduct and deeper nature from an extremely violent yet short war between armies to a potentially protracted and much worse peoples' war. There was no room for planning fresh Ulms or Cannaes against *francs-tireurs* who ambushed columns and harried patrols. Focused for over a decade on offense leading to climactic battle, Moltke and the Prussian Army were not prepared either for the trench warfare that developed around Paris or the brutally merciless *guerre à outrance* that set the countryside on fire. They had trained for set-piece fights, to mobilize with speed and concentration into grand battle masses, to envelop and contend with regular armies. Such skills did not matter against French guerrillas. Irregular *francs-tireurs* and quasi-uniformed guerrillas spread the

Germans out, exposing a grave weakness in their wholly inadequate supply system. The Prussian Army and its German allies were profoundly challenged by the irregulars, and they only occupied the north and east. Most of France had yet to see German uniforms or hear Prussian boots tramp into town.[58]

A grand destruction of enemy military resistance still eluded Moltke, despite victories at Sedan and Metz and the fact that his troops were all around Paris. Revolution had accompanied military collapse along the frontiers, but almost half a million men still defended from inside Paris and national defiance was hardening beyond the capital. He grew ever more agitated, then lurched toward a solution that was alien to the small cabinet war he planned but failed to complete in time. He issued orders to crush all resistance in a "war of extermination" against irregulars and any civilian supporters. His intent was total, to destroy all opposition in all of France, then impose a ruthless diktat.[59] He planned to invade the south to punish its raising fresh forces, and to extinguish all remaining national resistance to German will and control. If this change in approach failed, the Prussian Army would bog down in a long campaign akin to the French war in Spain half a century before. An invasion of the south was actually beyond the Prussian Army's means, far past its logistic or reserve capabilities. Most of all, an all-out conquest and occupation of a Great Power like France, no matter how wounded for the moment, must engage complex diplomatic problems Moltke could not solve with steel guns. Others knew it. Moltke was stopped from invasion of southern and western France by Bismarck and Roon. They worried about the reaction of other Great Powers and feared that invasion and occupation would only prolong fighting and enmesh the Prussian Army in a protracted war it was not designed to wage. What they wanted was a quick end to fighting to lock in German unification and geopolitical ascendancy.[60] That was the whole point of starting the war in the first place, a fact from which Moltke appeared distracted.

The result of this bitter dispute was that Bismarck took the military reins from Moltke, asserting a right to interfere directly with his use of 600,000 German troops inside France in order to serve *Staatsräison*. To more quickly end the war, he ordered Paris ringed with siege guns and bombarded with high explosives and incendiaries, to the express end of terror killing of civilians to compel France to surrender.[61] Moltke objected that shelling would only stiffen resistance, arguing for continuing the city blockade and for starvation instead. That was too slow for Bismarck, who won the argument. Paris was relentlessly shelled. When the French still did not surrender, it was Bismarck's turn to display calculated cruelty. He ordered villages burned and demanded reprisal hangings and shootings for the smallest act of resistance, such as boys throwing stones or spitting at German troops. His wife went further in private letters, writing that he should refuse to discriminate by age or gender. "Shoot and stab all the French," she advised her husband, "down to the little babies."[62]

Forgotten in this Prussian hatred of *francs-tireurs* were memories of righteous peoples' war waged with similar means and freshly raised armies by Prussians against Napoleon's men in 1813. It is noteworthy, too, that the same brutal responses occurred in 1914 when stories of *francs-tireurs* in the frontier battles contributed to comparable atrocities by Germans and to "hedge-fright," where fear of snipers supposedly lurking behind every country hedge led to collective punishment even in the absence of any crime.[63] Similar practices, and far worse, defined Wehrmacht and Waffen-SS behavior from the first day of war in Poland in 1939, quickly escalating from spontaneous atrocity to meticulously planned and morally demented behaviors. Along with *Auftragstaktik* and sweeping envelopments seeking *Kesselschlacht* and waging *Vernichtungskrieg*, and the rest of German operational art, language and theory bequeathed to military professionals, ruthless barbarities that swiftly elevated to military and state policy might also be considered an element of the German way of war. War makes no one tender. German theoretical and operational emphasis on the ideal of total annihilation made it worse, encouraging disproportionate numbers of Germans over several generations to behave as war criminals for reasons running deeper than can be explained by the usual heat of combat.

Three grand sorties were attempted by the Paris garrison, each more desperate than the last. The final one was made by 90,000 men on January 19, 1871. It was a gory failure that left 8,000 men killed, wounded or missing before ending in a pathetic search for potatoes by starving troops. By then, 4,000 Parisians were dying each week from starvation and epidemic diseases. Germans outside the city perimeter were better off, though still in rough shape. Moltke's plan for a swift war had descended into a wearing contest as the French adjusted to fit diminished central resources to a strategy of waiting and peoples' war. Some German battalions were attrited to company size by hunger, disease and fighting *francs-tireurs*; others faced several small French armies scattered and moving over the south and west. By the New Year, both sides neared break points. Winter hunger, more firefights lost to hard-hitting Germans in January, and Bismarck's ruthlessly constant shelling of Paris finally forced capitulation.[64]

***

A NEW GERMAN Empire (*Kaiserreich*) was formally proclaimed on January 18, 1871, in the sparkling Hall of Mirrors at Louis XIV's palace at Versailles, where the aging Prussian king was elevated to Kaiser Wilhelm I of Germany. An armistice took effect 10 days later, on January 28. Unlike his prudent generosity toward Austria in 1866, with Prussian hegemony and German unification assured Bismarck imposed harsh terms in the Treaty of Frankfurt forced on France on May 10. Alsace and most of Lorraine were directly annexed to Germany, and France was made to pay a war indemnity 60 times larger than Austria's five years before. It was a huge economic burden meant to cripple postwar military spending and politically undermine the Third Republic. To enforce these terms, 50,000 German troops squatted on French land until the indemnity was paid in full. Bismarck then capped the Wars of German Unification by coercing south German states into the new *Kaiserreich*. Old territorial buffers between Germany and France were gone, and a powerful military threat henceforth loomed along France's border. The old balance of power across Europe was gone, too, all pretense stripped away that there was anything left of the Concert system. Henceforth, while the forms and language of balance remained, Bismarck assured that Germany was *primus inter pares* in Europe.[65]

Like Frederick and Napoleon, Moltke was blessed in his enemies. Yet, he was only half-satisfied. His armies had utilized the telegraph, railways, and rapid-fire rifles and guns to smash poorly led forces from Denmark, Austria and France. His successes were celebrated then and since, sometimes called the work of "military genius." Yet he worried over the late-war transition by the French from conventional armies seeking battle at the frontiers to *guerre à outrance* across the whole country. The dirty war strained Prussian resources in unexpected ways, making it a real struggle to maintain a million men in the field for many months beyond the failed foresight of his original plan. As Moltke calmed and reflected once the fighting ended, he recognized a pronounced tendency of modern wars to shift from traditional contests among battle-seeking armies into peoples' wars, into protracted fights among angry nations-in-arms. He knew that such wars must in future strain the destructive capabilities of entire industrialized nations, girding them for attrition and victory or defeat by exhaustion. Force them into long wars without mercy or garlands or foreseeable ends. That portended dire things above all for Germany the next time the Great Powers fought.

Moltke and Bismarck showed just how obsolete "limited war" was during their invasion of France, ending in bombardment of the national capital and a punitive diktat. Gone was reasoned compromise around limited goals that respected the rights of other Great Powers. Compounding the lesson, they were forced into employing older long-war techniques, not decisive battle but blockade, starvation, bombardment, and urban and civilian terror. Younger officers admired and embraced the ideal of Moltke's tactical and operational ideas perhaps too well, enthused by national hubris and military victory. He worried that other powers would draw the deeper lesson of high casualties and late-war attrition in 1870. Germany might then lose the military advantage that initial speed into battle and superior movement gave its armies, returning future wars to the rule of the defensive firepower revolution he had worked to escape in the 1850s.[66] The question thus remained whether the Wars of German Unification were anomalous in their speedy conclusions, no more than an interlude between long attritional wars among aroused nations-in-arms. Even Moltke had doubts. The more he studied and thought in the calm of peace, the more his most basic doubts grew about the utility of war for Germany.

Moltke was right to worry. The French suffered a true *année terrible* in 1870. However, the new Third Republic recovered from the destruction of the Second Empire more quickly than anticipated. It introduced conscription in 1873, looking to make an army more culturally suited to its revived republican politics. Retiring its discredited *grognards,* the French Army looked to build on the late-war successes of Gambetta's hastily raised provincial legions. The hard indemnity was paid off more quickly than Bismarck expected, so that by 1873 the French Army was already recovered to the point that Moltke thought it was again capable of fighting Prussia's.[67] However, plunging birth rates were a grave problem if it hoped to match Germany division for division. It quickly became clear that France could not, that it faced permanent demographic and military inferiority when facing the swollen population base of a unified Germany.[68] Meanwhile, until the early 1890s Bismarck's deft diplomacy continued to deny France the ability to compensate for its shortfall of soldiers by forming strong military alliances with other opponents of Berlin.

France therefore adopted a defensive strategy by building a string of strong fortresses along its frontier, behind which it rearmed to await any return of German armies. Its reformed *état-major* was still not an independent war planning agency like its German counterpart. The French Army was also riven by the animosity of conservative officers toward the Third Republic, a profound division that emerged in the Dreyfus Affair of trumped-up charges of espionage against a Jewish officer in 1895. That drawn-out dispute poisoned civil-military relations and encouraged civilian interference even in fighting doctrine heading into World War I. Thus, in reforms enacted by the National

Assembly, *attaque à outrance* was reinstated out of a left-republican ambition to reduce conservative influence and democratize the French Army. It was a political impulse that would send massed infantry in close order straight into German artillery and machine guns in August 1914.[69] On the other hand, reform of transportation and mobilization protocols meant that the French Army matched the Germans in 1914 with the maneuver flexibility it had lacked in 1870, enabling it to achieve a vital victory at First Marne.

Importantly excepting Britain, other Great Power armies more or less followed suit, increasing short-service national conscription in place of the older, smaller armies of long-service professionals relied on before the Wars of German Unification. Issues of conscript service length, reserve strength, fortification and military infrastructure, and mobilization plans dominated national budgets and civil-military relations for decades. Fears of losing an opening and devastating campaign to a better prepared enemy in mass formations strained thinking about future conflicts, shaping recruitment and forcing civic militarization. Staff officers everywhere planned quick mobilizations and immediate mass offensive action at the start of the next war. Nearly all attention went to winning fast, like Moltke and the Prussians, on the assumption that future wars would look like 1866 and 1870 (but without the *francs-tireurs*), and would be decided just as fast. Almost no attention was paid to actually fighting long wars that might result despite the best laid plans of general staffs and budget offices.

The least change came in Germany, as often happens to the winning side in war. Although Moltke did not achieve full envelopment in either 1866 or 1870, his rapid deployments and pursuits set the mold for planning future wars that would start with well-planned, knockout opening campaigns. His operational theory upheld decision by battle in its most alluring and Clausewitzian form, while his practical example shaped a rising myth of quintessential campaigns of total overthrow. This trajectory in German military thinking triumphed across the political class and officer corps, despite rising expressions of doubt from Moltke himself that only deepened as he aged and witnessed changing geostrategic facts and threats. He eventually came to the conclusion that the time for decisive battles and short wars was past, that a war of nations was coming. In his last speech to the Reichstag on May 14, 1890, he warned: "The age of *Kabinettskriege* [cabinet wars] is behind us—all we have now is *Volkskrieg* [peoples' war].... No one can estimate its duration . . . It might be a seven or even a thirty years' war—but woe to him who sets Europe alight and first throws the match into the powder-barrel!"[70] The audience hardly heard him. His successors did not heed him.

German operational thinking split. Most planners and officers circled like moths around the flame of Moltke's proclaimed genius, celebrating its expression in victories at Königgrätz and Sedan. These were to be models for future German wars, added to Rossbach, Leuthen, Ulm and ancient Cannae.[71] The conceit of war as perfected in maneuvering around the enemy to make more modern Cannaes was thus elevated, becoming the ruling image in German operational art. Little thought was given to what came after years of wearing warfare that followed Cannae, when the Carthaginians lost a long war of attrition and any hope of competing against Rome; or despite the success of annihilation at Leuthen, when Frederick nearly lost Prussia in the end; or after Ulm and so many other victories, when Napoleon still in the end lost France. Planners instead designed sweeping opening campaigns that not even they believed in, then marched conscripts into the waiting guns of August 1914, and a long grinding and losing war after that.[72] Adding a more murderous and genocidal Nazi meaning to the ideal of annihilation, *Vernichtungskrieg* as operational doctrine was again the gambler soul of Wehrmacht practice from 1939 to 1941.[73]

There was a minority tradition inside German military thinking that looked instead to peoples' war in Prussia in 1813 and in France in 1870 as more likely models of future war. Moltke came to share this minority's doubt about the utility of any proposed *Vernichtungsschlacht* campaign fought singly, or several campaigns strung together to make *Vernichtungskrieg*. As we shall see, rather than impeding the short-war delusion, this different appreciation of modern war as attritional found an advocate in General Erich von Falkenhayn in 1916, who turned it into an effort at annihilation *by* attrition at Verdun.[74] Defensive firepower at Sebastopol, Fredericksburg, Froeschwiller Heights and Gravelotte, trenches and siege warfare around Paris, and swarms of *francs-tireurs*, had more to say about future war than Königgrätz or Sedan. In Berlin no one listened, not even to Moltke. The most recent example in military history is often the most powerful in shaping preparations for the next war, even if the lessons it suggests are wrong. His wartime efforts thus proved more powerful than his later conclusions and warnings.

Military and political fascination with reproducing a Leuthen or Ulm or Königgrätz or Sedan was not confined to Germans, for success in war always breeds imitation. The attraction of battle in quick-war scenarios received a critical boost in *all* military thinking from the success of Moltke's operational art, which appeared to confirm the best of Napoleon's and Frederick's. Other planners and generals in other countries listened to sirens singing of fast victory and low-cost diplomacy by war, of Königgrätz and Sedan fought anew in Africa or Asia; of sparing men and matériel and strain on long-war budgets by winning fast over the heads of quiet nations, before they were roused to long war anger with the first shots and dead sons. The song sounded sweetest to those in highly revisionist states, as it seemed to offer aggressors slicing military solutions to cut intractable strategic knots: Germany's geopolitical insecurity and weak resource base relative to larger empires that so worried Berlin before 1914; Italy's industrial backwardness and overpopulation problem, that twice helped entice Rome into colonial misadventure in Abyssinia; Japan's resource poverty and lack of access to closed markets in the 1930s that drew it into Manchuria and China.

Different lessons might have been drawn from the bloody yet indecisive battles, long sieges and trenches of the Crimean War and the American Civil War. That was not to be, given the huge distraction of Prussia's victories in Europe. Dazzled by Moltke's battlefield successes, and presuming a German or at least General Staff "genius for war," the militaries of Europe paid little attention to the bog of death in the Crimea. They paid no more to lessons of the American Civil War, whose wide vistas of bloody attrition and hard-spade fighting by armies of amateurs today seem far more pertinent in hindsight than Prussia's unusually swift defeats of Denmark, Austria and France. Total war was coming, already conceived and gestating as attrition and peoples' war behind the lines, though it was not yet released into the world. However, to borrow William Butler Yeats' famous words, soon the "blood-dimmed tide" would be loosed, for a "rough beast, its hour come round at last" slouched toward Flanders and Verdun to be born.[75]

Military history is not a tale of scientific laws or outcomes, only of recurring yet never quite identical patterns under circumstances of changing technologies and varying military cultures. So it must be said that even in an age when attrition was the dominant mode of Great Power war, some battles were indeed decisive, and Königgrätz was one. It framed the outcome of a war between two Great Powers and reshaped the history of both, and much else. Sedan was less clear. Not in the totality of French military defeat, but in its political decisiveness. It had more the character of a massive mopping-up operation than a battle of annihilation in the Moltkean sense. Astute observers, including Moltke, also perceived that a fundamental feature of modern warfare was revealed in the second half of the war in France that could become more important than the victories at Metz and Sedan. For even after losing their battle army, the French raised fresh corps and armies through a *levée en masse* that then scorched their own country with *guerre à outrance.*

Fighting after Sedan was devoid of grand-scale battles, yet it cost the Prussians dearly in men, matériel, and moral and political investment. Here was a different future for war, not decision by a decisive battle like Königgrätz but desolation. Moltke saw that beneath a surface of aristocratic and diplomatic restraint Europe's peoples would, *in extremis*, throw aside limits and cabinet wars and resort to all-out war by nations.[76] Therefore, Great Powers could not again be so quickly or easily defeated by a battle or single campaign strategy. Besides, winning changed everything, especially how other states saw the new and ascendant Germany. In the 1880s Moltke repeatedly warned politicians and fellow officers that future German armies would not face isolated and unprepared neighbors, as the Prussian Army had in 1866 and 1870. He warned against aggressive diplomacy that would surely lead to an unwinnable war on two fronts. He predicted that in the next war Germany would meet an alliance of two or three Great Powers coordinating military policies in order to prevent a repeat of his kind of war.[77] He was right about everything except the number.

Moltke's newfound caution and departing warnings were dismissed as an old man's feebleness. German officers preferred to back Alfred von Schlieffen, Moltke's key successor as chief of the General Staff. That mattered very much. The expanded Imperial German Army, the *Kaiserheer*, enjoyed a uniquely privileged place in politics and society, while the Great General Staff was virtually independent from civilian political control in setting military doctrine and planning.[78] Schlieffen ignored Moltke's later warnings and instead committed to his original idea of total overthrow of enemies, designing operations in accordance with *Niederwerfungsstrategie* ("overthrow strategy"). If anything, he elevated the doctrine to unchallenged supremacy by explicitly citing Cannae as a new exemplar within a hermetic military culture in which models of victory in 1866 and 1870 dominated operational planning. Opening "battles of annihilation" were seen as essential to winning any larger war. The idea of planning for them became an article of faith in a military theology of operational art as revealed by prior genius and transcribed as doctrine. Never mind that Moltke famously warned his officers that no battle plan "survives with certainty beyond the first encounter with the enemy's major forces." Planning was what General Staff officers did.

Armies everywhere studied German doctrine. Some as far away as Asia invited German instructors to train their divisions and adopted German-style uniforms to go with the drills. All major powers around Germany tried to emulate its efficient staff work, seeking as did Berlin to institutionalize a putative genius for war, to bottle the essence of Napoleonic and Moltkean success to be imbibed by following generations of officers. To some degree, all major armies succumbed to a related idea, the notion that if they inculcated an offensive spirit in officers and troops this higher moral quality would overcome recognized advantages of defensive fire. Scholars call this the "cult of the offensive," suggesting thereby a core irrationality in the face of technological realities that continued to evolve in the direction of shifting combat advantage to the defense: magazine-loaded repeating rifles; more destructive, nitrogen-based high explosives; smokeless powder; breech-loading, shielded, self-recoil artillery; heavy-caliber mortars; machine guns that realized in fact what the *mitrailleuse* only promised in 1870.[79] Behind this ideology of the offensive was a belief in the decisiveness of battle in modern warfare as had been practiced by Napoleon, idealized in theory by Clausewitz and embedded as governing doctrine by Moltke.

The idea that truly decisive battle was possible gripped the strategic imaginations of budget-aware politicians as much as it did professional soldiers, for short wars would also be cheaper wars. However, most governments outside Germany feared the new way of war rather than loved it, as the German officer corps did. They sought not to emulate the German way and example so much as to avoid the fatal errors made by Austria and France, and to defend against Germany and other revisionist states attempting to repeat Moltke's aggressive feats of arms. The limits to other Great Powers' embrace of short and destructive wars are more striking than similarities to the Imperial German way of war, for the same reason that after 1815 Napoleonic warfare fell by the wayside until Moltke revived and adapted it. A strategy of annihilation, of Clausewitzian absolute war, of *Niederwerfungsstrategie*, was not a style of fighting suited to defensive powers. It was the warfare of naked aggression. To adopt Moltkean operational art one first had to want to plan for offensive war. Most Great Powers did not. So they were content with smaller lessons incorporated into positional defenses or, at most, plans to rush into a forward defense with faster mobilization to the frontiers and more flexible field tactics and maneuvers, faster infantry rates of fire, and steel artillery massed for fire effect.

In his late career, Bismarck also showed more caution and restraint, but the damage was done. Lopsided victories in the Wars of German Unification embedded German belief in rapid campaigning. The victories of 1866 and 1871 would keep alive the ideal campaign in military thinking, even as those victories so changed the world around Germany that pursuit of a third rapid military overthrow of a rival Great Power must next time lead to vast killing fields. After 1890, after a generation of peace, Bismarck's and Moltke's more mature restraints were removed from diplomacy and military planning.[80] Coming into power was a younger and more ambitious generation of leaders who did not know war and decided to chance its horrors (bookish, to them). Imperial Germany's aggressive status-seeking from the 1890s, its pursuit of *Weltpolitik*, forced an anti-German alliance into existence to contain that ambition, starting with closer military relations between republican France and tsarist Russia. The honor of the nation and its sons therefore must be mobilized to break out of an iron ring of unjust Great Power containment. The rallying cry became *Weltmacht oder Niedergang* ("world power or ruin"). Facing an opposing grand coalition, Germans were aroused to issues of national prestige in crisis after crisis as war was openly contemplated—for some as a positive moral force, as social Darwinian ideas crept into political analysis.[81] Planners needed to find a way to avert a prolonged *Materialschlacht* they feared above all else, a slugging match of world industrial production of war matériel matched to population of whole empires to make total war. They knew that if the *Kaiserheer* did not win lightning wars of annihilation conceived as a sequence of battles of annihilation, Germany must fall into a protracted contest of endurance it could not win. And so the plans were drawn and redrawn in a fever of fear and ambition and delusion. And so catastrophe loomed.

Annihilation of Battle

LONG BEFORE THE last summer of peace arrived in 1914 there were bright assurances that the brave new 20th century would be one of ever greater progress. The peace movement was broad, from heads of state to religious groups to international lawyers. It offered treaties and conferences and draft constitutions of a proposed League of Nations. The tsar convened two peace and disarmament conferences at The Hague, in 1899 and 1907. Dozens of nations attended. They agreed on limits to arms races and affirmed the moral progress everyone expected, including banning aerial bombardment from balloons in any future war. Hundreds of arbitration treaties were signed, solemn promises to only seek peaceful resolution of conflicts among nations. Socialist leaders said that workers would never fight other workers in a future capitalist and imperialist war. Starting in 1901, the first Nobel peace prizes were awarded. They went to humanitarians who founded the Red Cross and Permanent Peace Bureaus, to esteemed international negotiators, disarmament proponents, pacifists and parliamentarians. It would have shocked everyone to know that no peace prize would be awarded in 1914, 1915, 1916, 1917 or 1918.

Serious people said that war could never happen again. Not that it should not happen, but that it *could* not happen. Panglossian economists and editorialists wrote that war's time was long past, that the world had entered a new era of integrated markets, historic material prosperity, remarkable scientific advances, social and even moral progress. In 1899 a Polish banker, Jean de Bloch, studied rapid-fire rifles, machine guns and the new artillery and published a widely read book subtitled *Is War Now Impossible?* He concluded that trench warfare must result from using these weapons, so that increased firepower could only produce paralysis on the battlefield as future war bogged down in one long siege of earthworks and mass casualties. Rather than a war "fought on to the bitter end in a series of decisive battles" in the old style, it would be "a great war of entrenchments . . . The spade will be as indispensable to the soldier as his rifle." Millions would fight, so many that it would be impossible for armies to maneuver. Logistics would fail, as would morale: "There will be increased slaughter on so terrible a scale as to render it impossible to get troops to push the battle to a decisive issue." A war of spades would make it impossible to feed armies *and* peoples. Under such conditions, the next war must lead to massive social unrest and revolution, repeating the Paris Commune of 1870 on a grand scale, perhaps continent-wide. War would be both unwinnable in vast trenches and too socially disruptive for elites to permit.[1]

Norman Angell's *The Great Illusion* was an international bestseller from 1910, widely deemed profound and prophetic. He wrote that the economies of all the major powers were so intertwined that war would no longer profit any country, as it must interrupt trade. Destruction wrought by fighting must always exceed gains, and rational interest would therefore preclude that choice.[2] Militarism and war were alike failures of moral evolution. They were extinct, and the long peace proved it. War was confined to barbarous cultures or a thing to be seen in history's museum, like dinosaur bones. Never again in advanced Europe. Jean de Bloch said war was unwinnable and far too socially disruptive to permit: the size of armies, sheer slaughter and fear of social convulsion would ensure peace. Angell said it was unreasonable and unprofitable, that sane people and rational and sensible governments would never turn to it. Peace was certain. H. G. Wells published a much darker vision with *The War in the Air* in 1908, foretelling countries overflown by fleets of strategic bombers during a future world war. No one took it seriously.

When the rush to war began in the last week of July 1914, Europe was stunned. How was it that a minor crisis in the Balkans, flowing from the assassination of a Habsburg heir unloved by his own people, had tumbled Europe and its world-spanning empires into crisis? Kaiser Wilhelm was on his yacht, and Paris was readying for its annual vacation rites. A peace delegation was on a slow boat to Russia, suggesting there was still time to avert the worst. Whitehall seemed detached and unworried. Only in Vienna and Belgrade were they preoccupied with diplomatic notes and military threats and what seemed squalid little quarrels to the rest of indifferent Europe. Then it all rushed together in just a week. Diplomacy collapsed, mobilization orders were sent out in country after country, a thousand trains began to raise steam. Millions of men reported to their muster points and fit awkwardly into uniforms of British khaki, French *bleu-rouge*, German *feldgrau* and Russian brown. They picked up rifles and shouldered kit, boarded huffing trains and headed off to the great adventure of their lives. They were cheered as the trains pulled away for the frontiers, though not everywhere or always.

It was one year shy of a century since the last general war in Europe; nearly 60 years since the bloodletting of over a half million dead in far-off Crimea; over 40 years since Prussians last marched into France and there were death lists in newspapers and low keening was heard while passing shuttered houses. A half century of aging into infirmity with only memories of a lost husband or child in an old photograph, weathered to faded grey on the mantle; since victory parades in Berlin but public inquiries in France into command incompetence and possible treason. All that time, there had been annual conscription intakes and constant preparations for the next fight among nations, but there was no war. The last war was so long ago, so removed from living memory that war again seemed a great adventure to many boarding the troop trains or waving from platforms. The trains pulled out one after another, all according to meticulous official timetables. Europe lurched from crisis to crisis in the decade before 1914. Why was this crisis different from the last one or the one before that? It was said all July that there was no need to worry, until the orders went out and the trains left nonetheless.[3] This time it *was* different.

Most people thought it would not last long. Weeks maybe, four or five months at the most. The poet Robert Graves claims he enlisted thinking war would not last beyond Christmas.[4] He was not alone. With some exceptions, newspapers and politicians in all the capitals boldly predicted swift victory for their side. In Germany, it was hard to get people to contribute to the Red Cross because most thought there would be little need for its services, certain that the *Kaiserheer* would win easily and quickly. Nearly everyone believed that their country's cause was both just and entirely defensive, a stand against foreign bullying or naked aggression.[5] Class conflict that had tensed politics for decades dissolved with worker embrace not of socialist idealism but defense of the homeland, in each homeland. Who started it? It was close to a playground moral sensibility, and the most commonly asked question at the time. It's the most common question asked of any war. International law asks it this way: "Who was the aggressor?" French and Russians thought it was Germans who started it. Germans and Austrians were sure it was the Serbs, French, British and Russians. *Their* government violated peace with too brazen demands, threatened our allies; *their* troops mobilized first, heading toward our borders. Our men will fight to defend the beloved *Heimat*, Mother Russia, *la patrie*, the Empire, the rights of small nations, law and civility, for civilization itself. Theirs fight for unholy causes. They are Huns, barbarians.

Enthusiasm for war was not universal. Although the excitement was real enough, if mixed in motive. As crowds gathered to hear the news there was excited talk of national honor. Also of personal adventure and escaping the dullness of daily life, though this was oddly more true in the cities than among the peasants who comprised the vast majority of conscripts. Most of those reporting under mobilization orders that went out everywhere were conscripts. Others volunteered, including 25-year-old Adolf Hitler in Munich, who a few months earlier was ruled unfit by an Austrian draft board. A more uplifting example is Stephan Kurt Westmann. Age 21, he left Freiburg University to enlist. He served in a combat unit in the kaiser's army until 1915, then transferred to lead an ambulance train until 1918. On the other side, Georges Blond remembers being an eight-year-old standing in a village wild with excitement and nationalist enthusiasm as a thousand French troops singing *La Marseillaise* rode past atop a train heading for the front.[6] Everyone knew history was being made and they were making it. Large numbers of women volunteered and were militarized from the start in national women's organizations formed to support the war effort. Fathers who never knew war themselves spoke proudly of soldier sons; mothers mostly worried, as mothers always do. There is little evidence parents felt anything like the English poet Rupert Brooke, who wrote: "These laid the world away; poured out the red sweet wine of youth; gave up the years to be . . . Their sons, they gave, their immortality."[7] Brooke died of an infection in 1915 aboard a French hospital ship bound for Gallipoli. One man lost inside a statistic: 10 million. Lost, too, in a romantic fog, his combat virginity intact. He never experienced a battlefield except in verse.

Had it just been poets and intellectuals who wrote paeans or ponderous editorials, or marked pins in newsprint maps in cafés and proclaimed where the armies should go even as they did not; had it only been the public that indulged the short-war illusion in nationalist outbursts, it would not be a great surprise. Or matter that much, except to cultural and social historians. What astonishes generations later is that all the governments believed in the quick-war scenario, too—in a hurried fight with massive armies that somehow was supposed to end in quick decision and not drag on, as it did in fact.[8] Some key decision-makers later lied that that they were surprised by the declarations of war, even when they had taken a hand at pushing their own nations into fighting. On the morning of August 1, 1914, German Chancellor Theobald von Bethmann Hollweg said, "If the iron dice must roll, may God help us." Yet he had a hand in the rolling. At 7:00 p.m. that same day, the first *Westheer* company forced the border into Luxembourg and captured a railway station at Ulflingen that was essential to the German mobilization plan. Over the next days, the storm clouds of July thundered into the guns of August all along the horizons of peace. Then they were into it. To those fighting the war, and those who also served who only stood and waited, it no longer mattered how it started. It only mattered that their own lives and everyone and everything they knew were somehow swept up in the war. Yet it did matter, and does, who started it all.

Was it nervous Habsburgs in Vienna who felt their long-declining empire under threat from component peoples pulled away from the center? Or the Romanov dynasts in St. Petersburg who feared modernization, yet needed it too? Or German elites, who feared being encircled or passed by other rising powers, especially Russia? Or republican France, insecure from yawning internal divisions over the shape and makeup of the French Army and because a falling birthrate meant conscript classes always fell short of Germany's? That was why Paris clung to its alliance with hugely populous Russia, a silent reserve of millions of troops. Did the balance of power cause the war, then? Was it because each antagonist made secret agreements with some of the others in anticipation that became self-fulfilling prophecy? Or was it because Britain defended its global interest and position too aloofly against all the rest, especially Germany's naval challenge to British supremacy outside Europe? Might London have been more engaged or accommodating of German interests? Was it the Anglo-German naval arms race that led to war? Did anyone know? Diplomatic historians have argued ever since about who started it in 1914. A greying and hung jury dressed in tweed.

Great wars seem to demand great explanations, but do they really have any that match what they became? It is hard to make persuasive, grand connections to any of the macro causes proclaimed at the time or proposed as primary since then: rigid and secret alliances, ferocious antagonistic nationalisms, imperial colonialism, competition for overseas markets, deep class conflict across Europe, rabid social Darwinism, frozen authoritarianism, archaic Junkerism, general militarism, naval and arms competition, reservoirs of revanchism from past wars, and unrequited hate. Later, to escape the argument down the decades, it became popular to say that no one wanted war or planned it.[9] World War I was all a tragic mistake, a kind of collective stumbling, as if governments and nations stampeded like buffalo pursued by Sioux, plunging over a precipice into a deep "blood kettle" below. But it was *not* all a grave misunderstanding. It was *not* a faultless mistake, a sleepwalker's stumble, or a mad stampede. World War I was, like all wars, the outcome of specific leaders making hard choices, of callous calculations of *Staatsräson* blending with blunders and miscalculations. Leaders of the five major powers in 1914 all made explicit decisions to save or enhance their state's interest, most often defined vaguely as honor or prestige. They knew that each move carried a high risk of war. They made that move anyway.[10]

The powers did not go blindly into war. Small cliques of decision-makers in the five Great Power governments either chose war or accepted war. Austria and Germany were the principal aggressors, agreeing secretly and jointly to initiate war during a partly fabricated crisis with Serbia. Weaker Vienna led the way for strong Berlin in plotting and planning to ensure that war broke out in the east, though they quickly got a different war than they hoped, spreading more widely than they intended. Austria wanted a war with Serbia that must also bring high risk of a second war with Russia. Germany either failed to restrain its vital ally or handed over a "blank check" of open-ended support that unleashed Vienna's intention to attack and punish Serbia. All of that provoked Russian mobilization in support of its small Serb ally.[11] There was contributing but not primary culpability from Serbs and Russians, as Moscow escalated a building crisis.[12]

There was no war lust in Paris in July, despite the cheering crowds that turned out in August. France was dragged into an unwanted defensive war, a fact obscured by its army fighting from the start with an engaged *élan* that tapped into the general cult of the offensive gripping all prewar militaries and doctrine. France was threatened. France engaged its defensive alliance with Russia. France would be attacked. It was not an aggressor. Similarly, Britain's leaders were passive. So passive that they probably bear responsibility for being too reactive too long, for slow and uncertain responses to key events and an unraveling diplomatic crisis in Vienna and Berlin, Paris and St. Petersburg. London worried about the Russian challenge in Asia as well as the threat of German hegemony and the sanctity of treaties, and doubted the wisdom of making a military commitment on the continent. Ultimately, Britain went to war for its empire and its preeminent position, dragging in its world-spanning overseas colonies, but also for honor and law.[13] Britain was also unique in expecting a long war. Secretary for War Lord Kitchener told the Cabinet on August 5 that the war would last three years and require raising armies of several millions. It was an underestimate better than most.

The war was started by small cliques of decision-makers in each of the major powers who did not always have general support for war even within the ruling elites. However, it would be sustained and eventually taken over by vast popular movements that lent their full consent to war, then demanded more war to advance the wider passions and purposes of whole peoples. The first key decision was made in Vienna on July 19, when an ultimatum was drafted purposefully designed to be rejected by Serbia so as to provide Austria with a *casus belli*. Some in Vienna wanted war to prop up a fast failing empire. Serbian terrorists gave them the opportunity, and they seized it. The ultimatum was duly rejected on July 25, though only in part, as Serbia tried at the last minute to damp down a conflict it had stirred for years. Mobilizations began immediately. Austria declared war on Serbia on July 28. Nothing happened, so Habsburg artillery was hauled to the border and symbolic shells fired across; then it was withdrawn.

Vienna thereby deliberately started what it expected would be a short and local war with Serbia, knowing it must also cause a much larger war with Russia. For that fight it expected German support. Leaders in Berlin had backed this policy in early July, giving Germany a vital role in the outbreak of war. Now the consequences of that blank check emerged. Vienna's ultimatum and calculated shots triggered swift responses in Berlin and Moscow that changed the dynamic from a Balkan quarrel to general panic and European mobilization, and then world war. This widening came from Berlin's operational war plan, which was dictated to some degree by Germany's central location. The *Kaiserheer* must choose one border to clear of enemy fast, then turn and face the other. General Staff planners chose to strike at France, then Russia, also violating Belgian neutrality in an act likely to draw in Britain and convert a European war into world war. Everywhere, fear of falling apart or falling behind was the most important motive behind the decision for war, with militarism and nationalism and other concerns lending secondary support, later rising to preeminence.

In Berlin, fear combined with an opportunity to preempt relative geopolitical decline by striking fast and hard to achieve dominance instead. Berlin's ruling elite saw the Reich as encircled, with Russia set to pass it on the road to world power. That they would not accept, even if the price to stop it was a general war in Europe. They chose war even though they knew it would spread far beyond the Balkans because of Russia's commitment to Serbia, and because their own war plan guaranteed war with France, and most likely with Britain as well. One reason Germany would strike at France through Belgium, though the probable price was war with the sprawling British Empire, was to avoid fortresses along the French frontier that pushed the *Kaiserheer* around their flank. This was the only way to win short and sharply, to not get hung up in a long war on the French frontiers while Russia mobilized in the east. In Germany, fast war was the only kind ever contemplated or planned.

Russia was wrenched by arrested revolution, social dissent, half-finished reforms; its elites felt aggrieved in their cultural uniqueness and deep historical humiliation, most recently by Japan in Manchuria in 1905. They would back client state Serbia come what may, ensuring that the war spread beyond the Balkans. France was deeply divided over army recruitment and officer issues dating to the Dreyfus Affair, and nursed dark and bitter memories of its defeat in 1870–1871. Those memories were faded, but would be easily revived to rouse popular support for a defensive war once France was attacked. Britain no longer felt splendid in isolation. It was stretched over a garrisoned Empire challenged in home waters by Germany and showing cracks from Afghanistan to Ireland. It would resist its main challenger and defend its informal but traditional obligations on the continent. There was no sleepwalking into war, no stumble in the dark. There was instead widespread fear, gamblers' calculations and deliberate choices made to fight.

In just days, Germany was at war with France, Russia and Britain. The latter's engagement meant that in World War I as in World War II, a regional war became global due to Britain's world reach, enabling it to draw upon imperial resources and peoples outside Europe to wage war in Europe. Also in both wars, but only after years passed in each case, core support for British resistance to Germany drew in the United States. The war was correctly seen at the time, in 1914 as in 1939, as a grand coalition fight against Germany's push for continental dominance. War breeds war, however. So over time other states entered to take territory out of the chaos (Japan, Italy, Romania); or more fundamentally and harder to control, to stave off impending imperial collapse (Ottoman Empire); or to serve world order security interests masked by grand moral principles (United States). New belligerents entered the war with similar short-war illusions to August 1914: Italians, Ottomans, Romanians, Bulgarians and Americans all thought they could win quickly where others had failed.[14] Human and material sacrifice deepened consent in all belligerent societies from the first contact of the armies, radicalizing aims and engaging popular support for the war, progressively deepening consent so that it quickly became a full peoples' war. Before it was over, all the world's empires, and all the distant lands and peoples attached to them by sentiment or by coercion, were committed to years of fighting the first true total war.

It began for the armies with lessons learned from prior wars, whether small and colonial or the more recent and larger-scale Boer War, Russo-Japanese

War, and Balkan Wars of 1912 and 1913.[15] From the start, Balkan states maneuvered for territorial gain in what they fought as another local war, with external support, to follow up their First and Second Balkan Wars.[16] The "Young Turk" reformers of the Ottoman Army had imbibed prewar doctrine from their German ally about striking hard and fast at the outset to secure quick victory in Cannae-like encirclements. They had tried it in the Balkans in 1912 but could not execute in practice what so compelled in theory. The Ottoman Army thus bogged down in a two-front long war in Thrace and Macedonia, and later a third front in Bulgaria and on a fourth front against Russia.[17] Only later did Ottoman leaders discover that their troops fought much better in defense than seeking chimerical decisive battles against technologically superior foes.[18] They learned and applied the lesson at Gallipoli in 1915, and across the Middle East and in the Balkans.[19] A supreme military effort proved insufficient to save the old Empire, but enough to prolong the fighting flaming all around its borders to 1918, and even after that. Nor did the Imperial German Army learn from the near-term experience of its Ottoman ally and the proxy defeat of its core doctrine in the Balkans in 1912–1913. That could be and was explained away as due to ineptitude by a lesser power and military, not a proven failure of the operational idea.

Instead, the Balkan Wars seemed to most European observers to reinforce the rightness of the cult of the offensive, as the successful choice was to attack and suffer extreme casualties but win, whereas conservative defenders preserved lives but lost.[20] German staff officers continued to map the older campaigns of Frederick or Napoleon to changes in firepower, though this task was complicated beyond the technical by domestic politics and national traditions. They still cited paragons of offensive destruction like Cannae and Leuthen, Austerlitz and Ulm and Königgrätz. Yet again they overlooked inconvenient bloodbaths like Malplaquet and Eylau, Inkerman and Gravelotte. They wholly ignored prior stalemates and long wars of the spade. Instead, they planned sweeping opening campaigns. And not just Germans looked to win fast. Most armies overestimated what they called the "moral factor," adding *élan* to calculations of offensive power but forgetting to add it to defense as well. They underestimated defensive ruggedness and the ever-rising logistical and movement constraints on million-man armies comprised mainly of reservists and poorly trained conscripts. They assumed flexibility on the move and overwhelming offensive abilities that the armies simply did not have. The Germans also failed to calculate the full effects of the balance of power in multiplying their enemies, an astonishing miscalculation for the land of Bismarck.

After decades of controversy, there is little doubt today that the gambling character of German diplomacy was a principal driver that turned the July crisis into the guns of August.[21] German support for Austrian recklessness was fatal. Nor was Austria just another clumsily contending power in the last summer of peace. It was not, as too often represented, a comfortably old-fashioned society, quaint and likeable, even if in thrall to a more belligerent Berlin.[22] In fact, Vienna was no less culpable as roller of the iron dice than its partner in fear and hubris. Most starkly put, the war began as a choice by Vienna and Berlin, out of Austria's efforts to arrest its own internal breakup on ethnic lines by smashing Serbia, which it thought posed an existential threat both as a nationalist magnet to its own Serbs and because of Belgrade's expansionist policies in the Balkans. Vienna knew that attacking Serbia meant war with Russia as well. It could only move, therefore, with full German support.

That is what made German policy key to the outbreak of the war. Berlin had long wanted to destroy the ring of enemies it believed encircled it, with a smashing victory over at least one so-called flanking power, France or Russia. As the Habsburgs secured German agreement to war against Serbia, both knew that also meant war with Russia. Breathtakingly reckless moves in Vienna and Berlin thus steered the eastern European herds over the cliff, with the rest of Europe about to follow into the blood kettle. As early as 1878, Bismarck had warned his fellow Germans: "Europe today is a powder keg and the leaders are like men smoking in an arsenal. A single spark will set off an explosion that will consume us all. I cannot tell you when that explosion will occur, but I can tell you where. Some damned foolish thing in the Balkans will set it off."[23] It was in fact set off by damn fools in Vienna and Berlin playing at iron dice *with* the Balkans, gambling with the peace of all Europe and much of the world. Austrian short-war triumphalism matched to military ineptitude positioned and shaped the southern and southeastern fronts of the long war to come, while German win-right-out-of-the-chute thinking and entirely predictable operational failures shaped the war's northeastern and western fronts. What remained was all the fighting.

***

HABSBURG EFFORTS TO reassert the Empire's core Germanness after 1900 had quickly backfired. Internal collapse accelerated as non-German minorities looked for more freedom from Imperial control, some also to Serbia or Italy for external succor and support. The Magyars already had autonomy in Hungary, including their own army in the *Honvéd*. By 1905 the minorities' problem was so profoundly divisive that the monarchy in Vienna secretly planned an invasion and occupation of its own territory in Hungary. The idea was to take back the Hungarian autonomy granted in the *Ausgleich* of 1867 that had produced the hyphenation of the Empire, the "Dual Monarchy" of Austria-Hungary. It was to be replaced with an utterly fanciful reassertion of German dominance. However, there were just not enough ethnic Germans inside the Empire to carry off the plan, while the dissolution of central power had already gone too far. Ethnic crisis followed upon crisis until the emperor was forced to use his most reliable troops, at that time Bosnian Muslims of the Imperial and Royal Army (*kaiserlich und königliche Armee*), to protect German towns from attacks by Slavs. Desperation over this internal weakness and Austria's regional decline was exacerbated by Serbian gains in the Balkan Wars of 1912 and 1913. When Serbian terrorists supplied the perfect pretext and outrage by assassinating the heir to the Habsburg throne, Vienna proposed to Berlin a short, sharp "punishment war" against Belgrade. What followed left a lasting memory of the Habsburg Empire as increasingly marked by the same decrepit and delusional character as its senescent and intermittently senile emperor.[24]

Archduke Franz Ferdinand, nephew to the Habsburg kaiser and successor to the throne, was a disliked, abrasive and unpleasant man, but he did not want war. On foreign policy, he was one of the more rational and moderate voices in immoderate Vienna, until silenced by Gavrilo Princip's assassin's bullet in Sarajevo on June 28, 1914. His death left unchallenged in power, at the court of an ever more feeble Emperor Franz Josef, the Chief of Staff of the Army, General Franz Conrad von Hötzendorf. Conrad proved to be a reckless diplomat and general who failed to grasp the limits of power or the demands of modern logistics of mass armies and the tactical lessons of rapid-fire rifles. His obsession with launching huge offensive operations beyond his army's ability would be pronounced all through the war. He would keep attacking on both the Italian and Russian fronts, with forces so inadequate he ultimately broke the Habsburg army into many pieces. It remains one of the true wonders of World War I that he survived in office to its very end, vacillating between grand personal fantasies and profound psychological despair.[25] He had premonitions before the war began of the course the final disaster would run by 1918. In January 1913, he wrote: "I believe more and more that our purpose will merely be to go under honorably, like a sinking ship."[26] His unfettered control of diplomatic and military policy goes far to explain the catastrophe suffered from the first shots fired in the war, by his artillery, and the mass casualties inflicted on disaffected and woefully commanded

Habsburg armies over the next four years. Berlin shared the blame, for not insisting that Conrad be dismissed when German troops were sent to save his armies, time and again.

Like his counterparts in Germany, in the summer of 1914 Conrad expected to fight lightning campaigns on two fronts, one after the other, aiming for a virtuoso double Cannae that was utterly beyond his or his army's capability. First he would invade and crush Serbia, then swing north to concentrate and beat in Galicia what was widely referred to as the "Russian steamroller." It was precisely the wrong plan carried out by exactly the wrong general, and conducted in the field more ineptly than anyone imagined possible. The leading historian of Austria's wars, Geoffrey Wawro, has written that this was fundamentally a "reckless gamble that the monarchy's internal problems could be fixed by war."[27] It all came down to war, even though for decades the southern kaiser's army was underfunded, undersupplied, underarmed and wholly unprepared for the aggressive two-front plan his ministers and generals proposed. The Magyars were divorced from imperial control by the *Ausgleich*. Magyar elites blocked central taxation and military preparedness, ensuring that Vienna's *Gemeinsame Armee* was ill-equipped and undersized as well as divided by language and loyalty. This was partly Bismarck's fault. For decades after the Prussian victories of 1866 and 1870, he supported the Magyars against Vienna to forestall an Austro-French alliance that might try to undo the Wars of German Unification. The result was that by 1914 Imperial Germany found itself tethered to a weak and even dying southern empire as its principal ally.

A mostly German-speaking Habsburg officer corps could not communicate well or at all with resentful, half-hearted troops organized in units based on a dozen ethnicities and languages. Appallingly bad march and battle performances in the first few weeks shocked German allies and Habsburg enemies alike. The Habsburgs had not even integrated small unit and firepower lessons from 1866, following a catastrophic defeat inflicted on them by infantry firepower half a century earlier. During the first fights in Serbia and against the Russians in Galicia in August–September 1914, Habsburg units massed densely just like their grandfathers at Königgrätz. When they made assaults in the same blockish style as their grandfathers, they were massacred by Serbian and Russian artillery and machine guns as a million Habsburg and Serb troops clashed along the Drina and more engaged advancing Russians farther north.[28] This military archaism arose partly for cultural reasons. Ethnically German generals did not think illiterate Slavic peasants could make complex maneuvers or fight independently outside the view of officers, so they massed the infantry instead of advancing in less vulnerable open order. Casualties were huge from the start, suppressing already low morale and fighting spirit and splitting German officers from sullen, beaten and badly supplied non-German field divisions.[29] Conscripts returned little loyalty to such officers or the Imperial cause, and surrendered in large numbers in 1914 and 1915. Later, some turned their coats and fought against the Habsburgs. Or it might be said that they asserted in arms the claims to independence of their own people. Treason depends on one's angle of vision.

We know that the Schlieffen concept in Germany initially planned to send 7/8ths of the *Kaiserheer* to invade France via a wide swing through Belgium, leaving the front in East Prussia barely defended. Conrad did not. He was never told that there would be so few Germans in the northeast, leaving the mass of the Russian Army free to march into Galicia and farther south. That is exactly what the *Stavka,* the Russian high command, planned to do in any case. On the other hand, Conrad never told the Germans that he had also changed the Austrian prewar plan, to shift weight against Serbia while weakening the critical Galician thrust. His counterpart, Chief of the Great General Staff Helmuth von Moltke, the elder Moltke's nephew, thought Habsburg troops would arrive in numbers sufficient to hold back and pin down the Russians in Galicia, allowing him to defend lightly in East Prussia while defeating France with the bulk of German forces. It was a first-order failure to communicate on both ends, leading Austria's armies into not one but two opening disasters on widely separated fronts.

Unforced errors proliferated from the first days, or even before. A most able Serbian general, Radomir Putnik, was arrested by Austrian officials at a train station in Budapest on July 25. He was returning from a spa to join the Serbian Army as its senior commander. Just three days before the start of a war engineered in Vienna and with the ultimatum clock clicking down, Habsburg officials released him, allowing Putnik to return to Serbia and assume command. By the end of 1914 he would blunt or break three Austrian invasions of Serbia, inflicting over 400,000 Habsburg casualties, then reverse the idea of punishment for the events in Sarajevo and aid to ethnic Serbs by counterinvading Habsburg lands. That was just the start. Austria's war was a nearly unmitigated series of calamities to the very end in 1918.

In the first two weeks of war Conrad sent Second Army south against Serbia rather than north to hold back the Russians, then panicked at Russian advances in Galicia and reversed the move before it was completed. Not only did this aggravate command confusion, he lost more time by disembarking Second Army from its troop trains 100 miles shy of the planned assembly area. Second Army marched to Serbia, returned to entrain for Galicia, then got out and marched a needless and exhausting distance. It was therefore in *neither* fighting theater to start the war, unused to any military purpose yet already worn out. It was one of the strangest, most wasteful operations of any army in the entire war, maybe in any war—a tragicomedy of errors of mobilization, deployment and command that ranks among the most incompetent in history. It was not the last time the main army command or HQ in Vienna, the AOK (*Armeeoberkommando*), would improperly deploy, grossly misdirect and fail its armies fighting desperate far-off battles. There was more bloody blundering in Galicia and Poland, where Conrad was so certain of quick victory that he appointed a military governor for Warsaw, then still held by the Russians. Everything went wrong: slow mobilization, failures of logistics, outdated battle tactics that lost half a million men, inept strategic direction by Conrad in the AOK. Out-of-date infantry tactics had been overmatched by firepower even back in 1866. Their retention and use in 1914 led to slaughter by more modern and much more destructive weapons. All Conrad's plans were ill-conceived as offensive, even after the defeat of the initial conceit of destroying Serbia in a swiping blow by armies on the way to the Russian front. Casualties were unsustainable. Nothing was accomplished. By the end of 1914, Austrian forces were expelled from Serbia for a third time. The armies in Galicia and Poland were devastated by the Russians, leaving 190,000 Habsburg dead on those fronts alone; a million casualties were suffered overall. Survivors were left freezing in defeat and misery and mountain snows on both fronts. There were far more Russians than feared, and fewer Germans than expected or would be needed to change things or even just to hold on in the east.[30]

Ahead lay a long war of attrition of men, morale and matériel, a war against Russian reserves so deep in all three factors Austria could never hope to match. It had already lost, and so completely that only German intervention saved Vienna's armies from total collapse. Things only got worse as in 1915 Austria became entangled in a third war with Italy, on top of the wars it started in Serbia and against Russia. Italy was bribed into the Entente, thinking it could defeat wounded Austria easily given Habsburg losses in Serbia and Galicia. The new front in the Alps stalemated quickly instead. Italy's army eventually broke at Caporetto in 1917, also called 12th Isonzo, a battle nomenclature that says everything about the utter futility of the Austro-Italian front.[31] Austrian troops fought in all the Isonzo battles, sustained on the high mountain front by the *Kaiserheer* as it was on other fronts. Already by 1915 Austria was a de facto vassal of Imperial Germany. Its armies were flailing and without basic military or food supplies. Already, no hope of victory was in sight and survival was in doubt. Far from the quick victory envisioned by Vienna during the forced crisis of July 1914, word went out to the officer corps that "we are in a new Thirty Years' War."[32] It would not take so long as that. Killing leading to collapse was compressed into four years, during which Conrad tried to win an unwinnable war of mass armies and matériel with new offensives that could not rescue his failed initial strategy. Death lists only lengthened as defeat and decline took their toll and catastrophe neared. History's dustbin for failed dynasties awaited the Habsburgs. Mass graves yawned under the peoples.

From 1915, Habsburg armies lost badly time and again, with a late-war exception on the Italian front at Caporetto (12th Isonzo), from October 24 to November 19, 1917. Morale was rock-bottom for most of the war, desertions sky-high. The main army divided into two parts, in addition to its already complex prewar structure. An "assault mass" was well fed and cared for by officers, but the reserve or "defense mass" was not. When the time came for the latter to fight as casualties mounted, whole divisions might melt away on first contact with the enemy. Overall, Habsburg troops on the Eastern Front suffered at Russian levels of undersupply, hunger and privation but from even worse command, especially at the highest level. The nadir came during the 1916 Brusilov Offensive, tsarist Russia's greatest of the war, which saw 350,000 Habsburg troops throw away their rifles and run toward Russian lines with hands held high, so eager were they to surrender.

Kaiser Karl I replaced his grand-uncle, Franz Josef, as emperor in November 1916, upon the old emperor's death. He wanted to talk peace and did so in secret, but was overruled by Conrad. In Germany, too, during 1916 tough-minded generals took control of the war away from the civilians and the other kaiser. Easy terms were offered to Vienna by the Allies in March 1917: restore Serbian and Bulgarian independence and forswear interference with Russian control of Constantinople, a lingering fantasy in Moscow dating to the fall of the Byzantine capital in 1453 that the Western Allies played to in secret treaties. A year later Karl's secret letters discussing his desire for peace were published in France, ultimately leading to astonishing subservience to Germany when he was given a tongue-lashing by General Erich von Ludendorff in May 1918. Austria was forced to commit to German offensive plans for 1918, resulting in total defeat six months later. Not allowed to get out of the war by its own generals or Germany's, Austria lost another 300,000 men at the Battle of the Piave (June 15–23, 1918). By the end it ceded to Berlin control of its railways, munitions factories and armies. At German behest, boys and pensioners were pushed into uniform over the last months of fighting and the army took the last skilled workers out of the factories to fill in hollowed out ranks of infantry. The war consumed the Habsburg state, and much more.[33] Austria never had a chance of winning. The great irony is that, had it won, victory would have meant annexing tens of millions more non-German subjects to aggravate its internal crisis. The war made no sense from start to finish. In the telling phrase of Geoffrey Wawro, Austria's war was all a "mad catastrophe."[34]

***

ON FEBRUARY 6, 1888, the Iron Chancellor made a bravado speech to the Reichstag. He told the gathered legislators: "We Germans fear God, but nothing else in the world." In fact, like most Germans of that day he also feared encirclement by hostile Great Powers. He spent decades successfully blocking France from alliance with Austria or Russia, but then he and Moltke retired. Theatrical pursuit of prestige that began in the 1890s spoke to Moltke's and Bismarck's departure from control of state policy, and to the erratic personality and ambition of the brash new kaiser, Wilhelm II. The nation, too, was restless, eager for Germany's rightful elevation in prestige and power to the first rank among nations, to *Weltmacht* ("world power") status. Under successive governments, German assertiveness shaded into needless aggressiveness in small crises that it usually made bigger, helping to cement the counterbalancing alliance of France and Russia on either flank that Bismarck had so carefully forestalled for so long. From 1904, France and Britain also drew closer in a series of informal agreements—the Entente Cordiale. British strength was lining up against Germany as well, in fact if not yet in a formal anti-German alliance.[35] Berlin thus felt encircled by a prewar grouping its own behavior largely forced into being, the Triple Entente of France and Russia and laggardly Britain.

Germany's recent ally Italy it did not trust. Its old enemy and new ally Austria it did not respect or believe could survive much longer, as its long-serving monarch aged and its minorities became more restless. Italy would in the event stay neutral when war came in 1914, then switch sides to the Allies in 1915. Germany's alliance with the Ottomans was promising, but the Sublime Porte was believed to be militarily weak. In any case, it could not protect the southern flank of Germany's central position as did Austria. German need for a strong Austria was so acute before the war that its diplomacy was too often reduced to supporting Vienna unconditionally, since its only other choice was to accept isolation and encirclement should the Habsburg state break apart. That is why, during the July crisis, Berlin agreed to Vienna's war against Serbia, to break that Balkan upstart on the wheel of war instead. Yes, an Austrian and thus a German war with Russia must surely follow, but the politicians and generals in Berlin were confident they could beat Russia. They had seen a woeful performance of the tsar's armies against Japan in 1905, then a fall into revolution and reaction at home. If they could isolate Russia as Bismarck had isolated Austria in 1866 and France in 1870, another short and lively Moltkean war should break the iron ring closing around Germany and its paltry allies.[36]

This was a major underestimation of the success of tsarist reforms over the nine years that followed war with Japan, and of latent Russian military strength. The Russian Army was modernizing fast, while railways and heavy industry were rapidly expanding.[37] Berlin also misjudged French determination not to be isolated again, and the fact that reform of military transportation and mobilization plans meant that the French Army matched Germany's in 1914 in the areas of mobility and flexibility it had so fatally lacked back in 1870.[38] German leaders also underestimated London's interest in sustaining the balance of power in Europe that so favored Britain globally, its commitment to uphold Treaty of London obligations to Belgium, and its strengthening if still informal military ties to France.[39] Navalist thinking played a role, too. Strategic "risk theory" promoted by Grand Admiral Alfred von Tirpitz built a *Kaiserliche Marine* (Imperial Navy) large enough to threaten the Royal Navy, though not to defeat it in a major sea battle.[40] Tirpitz deemed this "fleet in being," as the concept was known, as sufficient to deter British intervention in a continental war while the *Kaiserheer* quickly won the land battle.[41] A tiny British Army would not be a factor in that fight, added Schlieffen with real contempt. Moltke (the younger) disagreed. He thought that the war must be won before Britain mobilized its industrial economy and millions of troops for protracted land warfare, something it had never done before.[42]

Italy's *Regio Esercito* (Royal Army) had numbers but not combat power. It had no effective doctrine for winning in the mountains and not enough of the best weapons. It might not matter, therefore, on whose side Italy stood when it came to war. On the other hand, Moltke had secret intelligence on the appalling state of the Habsburg army, and knew it was inadequate to guard Germany's southern flank without help. Austria's army was a royal mess, but rather than deterring leaders in Berlin that fact pushed them faster to crisis and war. Things would only get worse if they waited, was the calculation.[43] In a swirl of gambler's risk-taking, Berlin committed to prop up

Austria-Hungary against Serbia come what may because Austria-Hungary was essential to its own security on the southern border. Its chosen method, planned and reworked for years by staff officers, was to wage a sweeping campaign to knock out France right at the start, then reconcentrate in the east for a somewhat longer but now winnable war against a fully mobilized and fearsome Russian steamroller. High risk all around, but the generals were certain they would score a victory over Russia, too. This most famous of all short-war delusions was a mixture of arrogance and panic, and all the more dangerous as a result. Belief that the *Kaiserheer* could fight discrete campaigns on widely separate fronts instead ensured a long and more general war in which Germany was forced to fight at disadvantage in the east and west at the same time, with more troops drawn south to prop up failing Habsburg Austria. It led to hitherto unimagined levels of death and destruction as a grand coalition of the nations rose into arms against Berlin's reckless gamble and ambition.

Alfred von Schlieffen was a less vital or original thinker than Helmuth von Moltke (the elder). Nevertheless, he was the fateful designer of the main operational concept worked out over six main drafts and multiple war games and staff rides up to 1906. It was implemented upon the outbreak of war in August 1914, with modifications by the younger Moltke. Schlieffen also left his mark on the German Army in the form of dozens of senior officers who remained fiercely loyal to his ideas long after the war. What was the essence of his scheme? At one level, to make war always on offense, seeking the great war-winning encirclement battle that would destroy the main enemy army and with it the enemy's will and ability to continue to resist. Call it by any heroic name one likes—Frederickian, Napoleonic, Clausewitzian, Moltkean—as long as all effort, all movement, all purpose, all will to war aims at *Vernichtungsschlacht*.[44] Schlieffen wanted a modern Cannae, winning via encirclement a total crushing victory that would defeat a Great Power in a single campaign. The *Kaiserheer* must go beyond what the Prussian Army accomplished at Königgrätz, about which he criticized the elder Moltke for not finishing the job of total destruction. He called his idea the *Schlacht ohne Morgen* ("battle with no tomorrow").[45] Normal victories would not serve. The enemy's armies rested atop reserves too vast to defeat with normal war. Germany needed Cannaes and Ulms. Anything less and it would lose. Defeat would be only a matter of time, as an opposing coalition gathered its strength and an iron grip closed. Knowing this as they did, more cautious leaders might have reconsidered the utility of war for Germany and adjusted its major geopolitical aims. In 1914 there was a shortfall of caution in Berlin.

It was Ulm that Schlieffen chose as his model for invading Belgium, linking that plan to Cannae as the model for defeating France. By 1905–1906 the core concept of annihilation was frozen hard as military dogma. Tinkering with the mechanism was allowed, and played out in several reviews by Moltke. Yet there was no challenge to the main ambition framed in a 1906 memorandum by Schlieffen entitled "War Against France," more often remembered as the heart of the "Schlieffen plan."[46] It was the central plank in a somewhat rickety scaffolding worked on since the 1890s, drafted and redrafted and tested in war games and staff rides, yet never quite completed to the satisfaction of its principal author. Moltke was deeply skeptical about the central concept before 1914, yet had no recourse but to implement it when war was chosen by civilian politicians during the crisis of midsummer. All railway and mobilization timetables were charted to its governing idea of crushing destruction of the whole French Army as the culmination of the opening campaign, to be followed by additional encirclement operations against the Russians. Moltke decided not to move through the Netherlands and shifted armies away from the right wing, but he could not discard Schlieffen's core assumption of a two-front, three-enemy war (France, Russia, Britain). There was only one way for Germany to fight such a powerful coalition: swift and absolute victory on one front before turning to the other. Either that or do not fight at all. Short-war dogma drove *Kaiserheer* deployments, which responded to harsh war aims, which guaranteed a long and general war.[47]

For years before 1914 civilian and military elites dreamed of a new Moltkean war to force an opening in the steel walls around Germany, despite warnings from no less than Moltke himself that this would not work. His immediate successor, General Alfred von Waldersee, confined operational planning to a one-front scenario, working out ways to destroy Russia in a great *Kessel* modeled on Königgrätz.[48] Moltke warned him in private that the time of such grand battles was over, that no Great Power could be isolated and defeated as he had done, that the time of short war was past. In that case, said the Schlieffen plan that superseded Waldersee's, we will just have to win on *two* fronts. First, catch all the French armies massing along the frontiers and scoop them up like "cats in a bag." The *Kaiserheer* would destroy the entire armed might of a Great Power in six weeks, then turn back to race across a continent to defeat an even mightier Great Power with far more strategic depth assembling armies in the east. It was breathless hubris.

While planning for future war before 1914, and given that Germany's position seemed to grow more cribbed and its rivals' chances better with every passing summer, the victories of 1866 and 1870 made it nearly impossible to

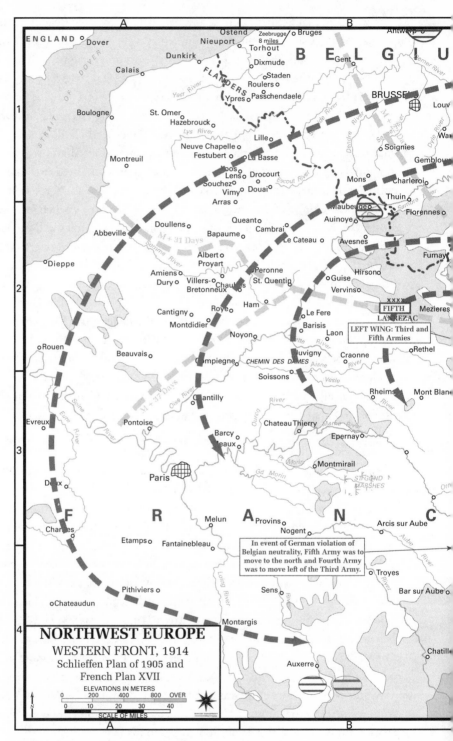

French and German War Plans, 1914.

Courtesy of the Department of History, United States Military Academy at West Point.

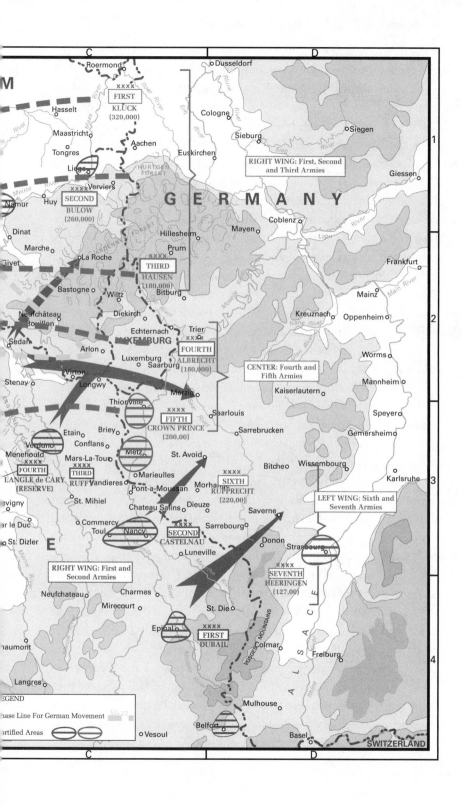

Roermond

Dusseldorf

C

D

XXXX
FIRST
KLÜCK
(320,000)

Hasselt

Cologne

Siegen

Maastricht

Aachen

Euskirchen

Sieburg

Giessen

Tongres

Liege

RIGHT WING: First, Second and Third Armies

HÜRTGEN FOREST

Verviers

G E R M A N Y

XXXX
SECOND
BULOW
(260,000)

Namur

Huy

Coblenz

Mayen

Dinat

Hillesheim

Marche

Prüm

Frankfurt

La Roche

Givet

XXXX
THIRD
HAUSEN
(180,000)

Bitburg

Mainz

Main River

Bastogne

Wiltz

Neufchâteau

Diekirch

Kreuznach

Oppenheim

Worms

Bouillon

LUXEMBURG

Echternach

Trier

XXXX

Sedan

Arlon

Luxemburg

FOURTH
ALBRECHT
(180,000)

Mannheim

Stenay

Virton

Saarburg

CENTER: Fourth and Fifth Armies

Longwy

Merzig

Speyer

Verdun

Thionville

Saarlouis

Gemersheim

Etain

Briey

XXXX
FIFTH
CROWN PRINCE
(200,00)

Sarrebrucken

Kaiserlautern

Conflans

St. Avoid

Bitche

Wissembourg

Menehould

Metz

Karlsruhe

XXXX
FOURTH
LANGLE de CARY
(RESERVE)

Mars-La-Tour

XXXX
THIRD
RUFF

Vandieres

Marieulles

Morhange

XXXX
SIXTH
RUPPRECHT
(220,00)

LEFT WING: Sixth and Seventh Armies

evigny

St. Mihiel

Pont-a-Moussan

Dieuze

Saverne

r le Duc

Chateau Salins

Donon

Strasbourg

St. Dizler

Commercy

Toul

Nancy

XXXX
SECOND
CASTELNAU

Sarrebourg

Luneville

RIGHT WING: First and Second Armies

Neufchateau

Charmes

St. Die

XXXX
SEVENTH
HEERINGEN
(127,00)

Freiburg

Mirecourt

Epinal

XXXX
FIRST
DUBAIL

Colmar

aumont

Langres

Mulhouse

EGEND

Belfort

Basel

SWITZERLAND

hase Line For German Movement

ortified Areas

Vesoul

C

D

resist the seductive pull of battles past. Never mind that Schlieffen's successor, the nephew Moltke, denied just as his uncle had that it all could be done again, let alone against two Great Powers at once (or three, if aloof Britain joined the fight, as the plan virtually guaranteed). It was against France that Schlieffen's blueprint proposed to hurl 7/8ths of the *Kaiserheer,* while holding with the last fraction against Russia's concentrated might in the east. Never mind that as chief of the Great General Staff following Schlieffen, Moltke feared Russia far more than defensive-minded France, whatever might happen in Alsace-Lorraine. Train schedules were set and locked. There would be mobilization according to the schedule, followed by a campaign by timetable aiming at a knockout blow against France. It was the legacy of 14 years of Schlieffen's planning and eight more of staff rides and war games and worried tinkering and adjustment at the margins by Moltke.

Even though the war plan was fundamentally flawed, maybe even fatally so, the civilians in Berlin still pursued foreign policies that pushed bordering Great Powers into a firming alliance against Germany. The generals made all operations plans separately from the politicians, strictly with military concerns in mind, guarding their war prerogative jealously. They drafted and designed and chose mobilization routes and set timetables, all in a military shop closed to politics and diplomacy, ignoring Clausewitz's warnings against such separation and their own ideal of a *König-Feldherr*, king and general all in one, just like Frederick or Napoleon. When the civilians forced a diplomatic crisis to war in July 1914, they forced the generals to implement the only plan they had, to take it out of storage, flawed as it was, recklessly inured to diplomacy as it was, blind as it was to the danger of arousing whole nations to peoples' war in the lands it proposed to transit or invade. Never mind that its narrow solution to a technical problem of fortification of the French border wrecked all its win-fast assumptions by violating Belgium, dragging Britain and its empire into the fight, ensuring that a European and world war would grow out of a Balkan quarrel not even Germany's own. The civilians' encircled worldview and policy was matched by doctrinal paralysis inside the Great General Staff. Thus the next war would begin with an over-thought operational schedule in service to goals that were always unachievable.

Overtly, everyone in Berlin on the eve of war spoke of the Frederickian and Moltkean past, so saturated was German political-military culture with those memories. Officers talked excitedly of another Rossbach or Leuthen, and of course Königgrätz and Sedan. Secretly, there were doubts. Among the civilians, too. That's why Bethmann Hollweg implored the divine as he walked away from the gaming table on August 1, the iron dice still warmly tumbling from his hands. The elder Moltke was not there to remind everyone that military operations must take account of strategic politics and that basic geopolitical conditions had changed for Germany.[49] Schlieffen was always cocooned from politics inside his staff and studies and the defiant principle of military primacy in all operations plans. His few expressed doubts were about whether there would be sufficient attack mass on the strong right wing he intended to sweep through Belgium into France, and lesser technical issues.[50] He never questioned strategic fundamentals.

The younger Moltke had command responsibility in 1914, but he was already frozen with fatalism. It was not possible to move millions of men and all their supplies and food and equipment, not with the speed and timing of the demanding ghost of Napoleon who lived inside Schlieffen's memos. He knew what was coming. In 1905 he wrote privately about his fears: "Future war will be a peoples' war, one which would not be concluded by a single decisive battle. [It will break down into] a long and protracted struggle." On the eve of war, he was wracked with doubt about facing all the enemy's men and spades and machines.[51] Critics were in a quandary, however, without a real alternative that left to Germany the option of war, thought necessary to its ambition to *Weltmacht*. If a future peoples' war might last years, then the best way to avoid such a calamity was to win fast, right at the start. Schlieffen at least proposed a possible way to do that. If the Great General Staff could not plan a successful short war because such wars were no longer viable, what use was war to Germany?[52] Germans were not pacifists. They would do what was necessary to win through to their national ambition. Moltke understood that there were only two choices facing him and Germany: roll the iron dice against long odds for a short war, or give up war entirely as an instrument of statecraft. No one in Berlin was ready for that; ready to be a quiet, ordinary power. Not when there remained a chance to win through war. He knew that Germany would fight, bad plan and all, high risk and all. Or it must sink down the ranks of Great Powers and never rise to become a *Weltmacht*.

Moltke could not simply tear up his predecessor's plan without a viable substitute, even if he did not believe it had much chance of succeeding. So he tinkered instead. Germany would not strike through the Netherlands, only Belgium, as it needed a Dutch "windpipe" for imports once war began. He put more men directly on the border to blunt an expected heavy French rush into Alsace-Lorraine that could threaten key industries in the Saar. He moved the needed corps from the right wing, for there were no others available. Still short of men, he added the *Landwehr* to provide mass to the initial attack, an all-in bet with the whole reserve on winning with concentrated local superiority. He would ask Conrad and the AOK to move troops to Galicia to tie down the Russians, even though he knew he should probably re-inforce in the east, because he received worrying intelligence reports that his ally's armies were too weak and fragile to stand. He might have to move more corps from the vital right wing, shift them all the way to East Prussia to hold there. All that, and he did not know what Conrad had decided not to tell him, that when war came Austria would reinforce into its invasion of Serbia, holding corps *out* of Galicia in the opening weeks of fighting against Russia.

Moltke was not a warmonger. Yet he pushed hard for war from 1911, even as his doubts deepened about a proposed two-front operation against three Great Power opponents. He had little hope that the two-front, two-war gamble would work. Even if it did, all that could be gained was a strategic delay, he thought, not the war-winning campaigns in east and west posited in Schlieffen's plan. In a few more years Russia would surpass Germany in several areas of industrial output, matching those gains and new railways to its already huge advantages in space and population. Falling behind Russia would close Germany's window of opportunity to become a world power. It was the fact of Germany's relative weakness that confirmed his sense of decline and increased the urgency of his advice to make war while some pos-sibility for limited success remained. Moltke was a military fatalist, seeing in his modifications of Schlieffen's plan at best a chance to buy time to strengthen the *Kaiserheer* for the much wider world war he believed was in-evitable.[53] On May 14, 1914, six weeks before the assassination of Archduke Ferdinand in Sarajevo began to unravel peace, Moltke confirmed his view that the Schlieffen concept would not work. At the same time, he affirmed that the *Kaiserheer* would implement it nevertheless. The blank check Berlin gave to Vienna that brought a general European war closer was sent in part at his urging. Over the days of crisis that followed, his pessimism was expressed as abject fatalism. On July 28, he wrote in secret to Chancellor Bethmann Hollweg that "a world war" was coming, once again confirming that the short-war concept built into the only available war plan was fatally flawed. Two days later, his Chief of Operations, General Gerhard Tappen, opened a steel safe inside the General Staff HQ and removed *Deployment Plan 1914/15*, the Schlieffen plan as revised by Moltke. Then the *Kaiserheer* took Frederick's and Napoleon's ghosts to war.[54]

Moltke's doubts raise the question of whether he and others in the clique of decision-makers in Berlin who chose war were delusional, or whether they knew Germany had little to no chance of winning a war that was almost cer-tain to go long and chose war anyway.[55] It seems that they did know. How else may one fathom General Erich von Falkenhayn—who later oversaw the worst bloodlettings at Verdun and the Somme—who on the first day of the war said, "Even if we go under as a result of this, it still was beautiful"?[56] Others had grave doubts. Logistics officers, for instance. All such objections were swept aside. Germany's leaders in 1914 needed to believe in a short war because they believed war was inevitable and the only road forward for their ambitions. Germany must win fast when war came or its whole geostrategic enterprise was untenable. The longer the strategic odds against winning a protracted contest with an immensely powerful anti-German coalition, the greater was the draw of battle to escape the political-military trap made by determined pursuit of *Weltpolitik*. Schlieffen planned an impossible, but short, two-front war because he thought Germany could not survive a long one. Moltke only hoped for a short war against France in 1914 because he believed a longer war against Russia, and others, was coming in any case.[57]

Either way, short-war thinking was built into the fiber of German military culture. So leaders and planners told themselves that Austria was strong enough after all, and that Russia was much weaker than it was in fact. They convinced themselves that Britain was indifferent to the balance within Europe, that attacking through Belgium would not trigger British intervention. They said London would not fight them as part of the anti-German coalition, and that its little army would be irrelevant even if it did, too small to make a difference in opening campaigns that would decide the war for Germany. The next war would be over so fast that London must then accept a fait accompli. Beneath all that surface, however, they knew the odds were long. Moltke teetered on the edge of a breakdown into despair on the very eve of war, so grave were his doubts. The main charge to bring against Germany's leaders in 1914 is not that they plunged Europe and hence much of the world into total war out of overconfidence and arrogance, but that they planned an aggressive war knowing it would probably lead them to stalemate or defeat.[58]

German leaders wanted to dictate timing, retain initiative, and strike with force before their geostrategic situation deteriorated further with advancing French reforms, Russian growth and Austrian weakness. They also lied, often and well. Bethmann Hollweg worried in private about bogging down in protracted war but said out loud that it would be a "brief storm." It was a storm of steel lasting four years instead.[59] Kaiser Wilhelm told troops departing for the front in the first days of August 1914, "You will be home before the leaves have fallen from the trees."[60] There was no fallback plan in the event it went terribly wrong, if fighting continued after the leaves had fallen. The political conceit of these and other leading civilians was a driving force behind Germany's urge to war. Operational conceit, belief in concentric encirclement, was dogma in a military faith accepted by virtually all German staff officers.[61] In addition, many German officers had conceit about their professional superiority over their enemies.[62] It was always rash hubris to think that Germans, because they were Germans, could overcome by sheer dexterity of command in the field the more basic wearing character of modern industrial war.[63] Disaster awaited, twice. For the same short-war illusion and delusion of superior military culture would inform the German officer corps leading into World War II.

***

THE ATTACK BY the *Kaiserheer* in the west initiated the largest fight by infantry armies in the history of war. Millions of men clashed as seven German armies collided with five (later six) French armies, the Belgian Army, and the small but highly skilled and fully professional British Expeditionary Force (BEF). The key to the opening moves was a thick system of French frontier fortresses built for the most part after the defeat of 1870. These forts pushed German armies around the end of the line onto an invasion route heading into northern France by a wide swing through Belgium.[64] Most German strength was loaded into this "strong right wing." Schlieffen said the right wing should be set at 7:1 to ensure it could overwhelm the French, but in 1909 Moltke reduced this ratio to 3:1 by deploying two armies to defend Alsace and Lorraine. He confirmed the change in 1913. After the war, officer acolytes and hagiographers of Schlieffen blamed this reduction for losing the critical fight at First Marne, a battle that set the stage for years of trench fighting to follow. This criticism was part of a general postwar denial of the real causes of defeat by 1918, which were not tactical or operational but basic and strategic.

Moltke sent five armies in a giant wheel marching around the nests of French frontier fortresses. The right wing ("the hammer") was to move fast while the left wing ("the anvil"), formed by two armies, waited on the French advancing east of Paris. The left wing was to fix the French Army for the arrival of the hammer, which would bring overwhelming force to bear and swift victory, releasing most of the *Kaiserheer* to move to Russia and do it again in a wider theater of war. The Belgians put up strong resistance, however, while the armies of the anvil did not wait on the French. Vain generals wanted their own little Cannaes and repeatedly disobeyed Moltke's orders. Instead of waiting for the French to advance, they attacked. Along with the inevitable confusion of large armies meeting in encounter fights, this led to serial Battles of the Frontiers that engaged a third of all forces during August

14–24, fighting from Alsace-Lorraine to the Argonne and Ardennes. These frontier battles were large, bloody fights leading to a staggering 520,000 total casualties. According to Schlieffen's redefinition, however, they were not even considered separate battles. They were merely tactical encounters subsumed in the larger grand battle that was the whole campaign.

However, most German army commanders could not think on that scale and were not ready to take Moltke's orders in any case. When they saw a French corps or army in front of them they tried to "Leuthen" it. As a result, from first contact along the frontiers German armies advanced rather than withdrew, as they were supposed to in the plan in order to pull the French with them deeper into a trap. Moltke's operational idea thus lost focus and concentration.[65] There were also problems with the immense hammer. Five armies advancing at best possible speed were trying to keep to a strict time-table: clear Belgium and reach the French frontier by the 22nd day; cross the Somme and Meuse by the 31st day; win the war in the west by trapping and obliterating the whole French Army by the 40th day, crushing it against the waiting anvil along the cramped frontier. All this to be accomplished by an unwieldy conscript army rife with organizational, logistical and command weaknesses.[66] Other armies in 1914 suffered from sharp structural problems. The point here is that they did not plan to win a two-front war on a tight timetable.

No one was sitting still in mid-August. All armies were on the move, millions of men all at once on four discrete fronts: Western, East Prussian, Galician and Serbian. Moreover, all armies began the war by attacking. The encounter battles that resulted were corps and army size, bloody and fluid on all the fronts, but with the decisive encounters in the west. There, huge masses of men in five French infantry armies and seven German armies sought each other out, with full old-style cavalry screens out front and entirely new and still unarmed aircraft scouting overhead.[67] Germans had farther to walk—across Belgium and northern France in full kit, in summer heat. Each German corps (four per army) started at 1,500 officers and 40,000 men, with 14,000 horses hauling 2,400 heavy wagons stretched over 30 miles of road. Supplies of food and fodder, at 130 tons per corps per day, were consumed quickly. German corps towed excellent field guns in 24 batteries of six guns each, and four more of four heavy tubes each. Above each corps flew six biplane scouts.[68] It was an impressive mass, yet things went wrong right away. Men dropped out of the march from heat exhaustion or with hobbled feet from tramping too far in heavy nailed boots. Horses fell out from heat and colic, saddle sores and split hooves from bad shoes of a different sort. Germans stole what they needed or wanted from civilians, committed atrocities along the way, and reeked from infrequent washing. Millions of men and horses defecated all along the routes. Just like the *Grande Armée* did while marching to Moscow in 1812, the long *feldgrau* columns left greasy trails behind.

No one was even thinking of trenches. Five French armies were organized into corps of 40,000, each equipped with advanced 75 mm mobile guns designed for a war of movement. A French 75 had double the rate of fire of the equivalent German gun, at up to 1,000 rounds per day. German troops called them "black butchers." Americans would use them in France in 1918, borrowing from the French because the unready American Expeditionary Force (AEF) lacked modern guns, along with much else.[69] However, French armies traveled in 1914 without heavy artillery. The cavalry were still armed for shock attacks, with sabers and lances and short single-action carbines. Many of the horse soldiers still wore cuirasses. Even the infantry retained a bayonet-and-shock doctrine. Marshal Ferdinand Foch and other thinkers in the prewar "French School" were most interested in the role of moral force to compensate for numerical weakness. Before the war, French generals brooded on their inferior position and decided to emphasize the idea that moral factors in war would always trump the manpower superiority of the German enemy. Optimism about the role of "national spirit" and *élan* was a perfect complement to the new school of vitalism then storming the gates of French philosophy, including military thought.[70] Also obscuring what was about to happen, everyone fought with weapons whose power and effect were untested by war on this scale, from rapid-fire rifles such as the German Mauser and British Lee-Enfield to machine guns, rifle grenades and hand grenades, and a range of light and heavy horse-drawn artillery.

The German march timetable in France, inherited from Schlieffen, arose from a combination of fear of and contempt toward the Russian Army shared by many German officers. The Russians were believed to be unable to mobilize and deliver forces to threaten East Prussia for at least six weeks.[71] That was all the time there was to beat the French Army if a short-war scenario was to play out. With the French defeated the small British Expeditionary Force (BEF), which posed no significant military threat, must withdraw from the continent, leading Britain also to leave the war. With the Western powers beaten and the western borders of Germany secured, the bulk of the *Kaiserheer* could safely board a fine, purpose-built military rail net to be rushed eastward to stop the Russians from advancing too deeply into East Prussia. As noted, the plan ignored the vulnerability of Austria, leaving it to deal with the bulk of the Russian Army on its own. There was no genuine prewar coordination between the Habsburg AOK in Vienna and Moltke's General Headquarters or OHL (*Oberste Heeresleitung*). Austria was simply left to defend in the east against the largest army in Europe, which Conrad foolhardily planned to attack in Galicia, while Berlin sought complete victory on its own in France. In the event, there was panic in Germany as two Russian armies advanced toward East Prussia sooner than expected, requiring Moltke to pull out two corps from the western offensive to defend (or rather, to calm) the home front.

In the east, larger Russian armies moved south to batter the Austrians, rolling into Conrad's madly maneuvered and tardy forces in Galicia. Meanwhile, two other armies constituting a much smaller Russian force headed into East Prussia in a planned concentric advance on Königsberg. The Russian hope was to trap the Germans as Moltke hoped to trap the French. There were only small German forces available as the Russians advanced faster than expected. The situation was saved for Moltke by different rates of movement by the two Russian armies, personal jealousies between their generals, bad communications, a lack of radio security (Russians broadcast in the clear in plain language), and failure to deploy cavalry to scout for and screen the infantry. After an initial panicked reaction, those errors were taken advantage of by aggressive and superior German movement and concentration, leading to victories at Tannenberg (August 26–30) and the Masurian Lakes (September 9–14), terrible bloody defeats for the Russians but not decisive beyond local effects.[72] Tannenberg was later highly touted in part to supply the German propaganda machine, partly because it seemed to validate encirclement operations and the idea of mission tactics, in this case by Generals Paul von Hindenburg and Erich Ludendorff (and their highly capable staffs). It is a notable irony that the two opening German victories in 1914 were unplanned battles in the east, while a detailed plan intended to produce a great victory in France led to decisive defeat instead.

The five German armies on the move in the west swung deep through Belgium before turning into northern France. The original concept was to march around Paris, itself a giant fortress city: fourteen inner forts dating to before 1870 were ringed by 25 newer fortresses. Once past the capital, the German right wing would slam an iron door shut behind French armies earlier fixed and trapped along the frontiers. Standing in the way at first was the Belgium Army, with just 117,000 full-time regulars in six light infantry divisions and one cavalry division, but another 236,000 reservists called up during the summer mobilization. Most were assigned to Belgium's fixed defenses: *la position fortifiée de Liège,* a complex of 10 large and many smaller forts and connected field works. Liège fell after a hard pounding by modern siege guns. German 1st and 2nd Armies then led the right wing rushing through Belgium starting on August 16. Things went wrong for the Germans from the start, as they had for the French heading toward Moscow in 1812. Movement was slowed by too many troops, wagons and guns moving over too few roads as German logistics deteriorated rapidly once the armies moved past their railheads. On August 22, French 3rd and 4th Armies moving eastward from Paris clashed in the Ardennes with German 4th and 5th Armies. The two German armies were to serve as the hinges of the great revolving iron door, joining the right and left wings of Moltke's whole frontage. French casualties were especially heavy.[73] The main fight still lay ahead, along the Marne.

The story of the 120,000 man BEF was brave enough, but too often has departed from history into myth, a near fairy tale of superb professional defiance of masses of lesser German troops, of faint-hearted enemies and feckless allies, of hard-won victories by guts and better rifles. Turning initial defeat into outright myth, the tale of the BEF continues with a retreat for the ages, more glorious than many advances, all culminating in a heroic forced march leading to precisely timed intervention at Ypres in November that ensured Germany would never win the war. The facts are rather different.[74] The BEF moved slowly toward first contact, without the excuse of numbers clogging the roads. It ran into part of the oncoming mass on the German right wing and suffered a bad defeat at Mons (August 23–24). Then it took 8,000 more casualties at Le Cateau (August 26), the most by a British army in any battle since Waterloo a century before. Rather than establishing the superiority of British rifles and elite professionals, in both these sharp battles the BEF was outfought by a well-led and better equipped *Kaiserheer*. The "Old Contemptibles"[75] were of a kind with Louis-Napoléon's *grognards*, filled with courage but older and outdated in skills, weapons and experience. The BEF actually retreated pell-mell from Mons in what bordered on a rout. Its pullback was stopped only after intervention from the highest political levels in London, upon a plea from the French commander, General Joseph "Papa" Joffre (*le père Joffre*). The Old Contemptibles fought hard and marched harder but were badly led and poorly equipped. They would make a last stand at Ypres later in the fall. The great burden and successes for the British Army came later, along the Somme and then beyond during the second half of the war. The BEF was still a small unit, imperial force. By 1916 it would be a million-man army, still learning to conduct large operations. In 1918 it would be an innovative, breakthrough force. But the fight in 1914 was always between the French and Germans.[76]

The traditional view of Joffre was that he was narrow-mindedly devoted to the prewar cult of the offensive, to the idea of *élan vital* as the decisive factor in battle and war. The truth is more complex. It is true that Joffre was determined to attack, but not from a mystical belief in *élan vital*. He did not want his armies to be trapped as French armies had been trapped at Metz and Sedan in 1870. Like the Germans, and everyone else in 1914, he and the French officer corps were devoted to the ideal of quick war in which decision was reached by battle, in a collision of the main armies that responded to the Moltkean tactics of the Germans. A short war would also spare France the long-war and conscription disadvantage of its smaller population. This confluence of French and German short-war doctrine meant that a huge battle was nearly inevitable. That said, Joffre was more patient than either his now outdated reputation or the idea of *élan vital* suggests.[77] He concentrated at the northeast frontier in the first days, as directed in his prewar Plan XVII, crafted as chief of the *état-major* from 1911. Once there, he waited to discover German movements. By August 6, he had a covering force in place and was ready to attack, coordinating with a long-standing alliance agreement with Russia to send 800,000 tsarist troops into East Prussia 15 days after mobilizations began.

Joffre made his change in strategy clear in General Instructions No. 1, issued on August 8. He would send his main force not into the "lost provinces" of Alsace and Lorraine, but into central Belgium. Plan XVII was thereby abandoned. It was never much more than an intention to concentrate the armies along the borders, respecting Belgian neutrality while positioning to either drive into Alsace-Lorraine or pivot into Belgium. It was always less of a rigid plan than the Schlieffen-Moltke plans. Joffre would now drive into the advancing German center, which he expected to be weaker than it was and in a different place than it was, and fight a great battle. He also attacked on the extreme right into Alsace-Lorraine on August 14 (the same day as the Russian attack in East Prussia), but this was not the main French thrust. That came later in Belgium while the fierce Battles of the Frontiers were already underway.[78]

Moltke watched the armies move and the battles develop, his moods swinging wildly from sudden hope for obliteration of the French armies to despair over looming defeat. He was ebullient in mid-August, thinking he might achieve a new Cannae after all, against years of doubt and better judgment while studying war plans in peacetime. Despite the disruption of his plan already taking shape in the battles along the frontier, he still hoped to fix the bulk of the French Army in place against his anvil. He therefore counterattacked in Alsace-Lorraine on August 20, to tie down more French corps and hold them in place as the heavy right wing continued its long march south.

Joffre charged two armies into Belgium the next day, seeking contact and a fight. His position in Lorraine began to deteriorate, but he was confident in his (false) assumption that the Imperial German Army would not drive widely across Belgium. He expected its turn south to be sharper, closer to the frontiers, not far past Paris to the west. So he continued attacking as the weight of the *Kaiserheer* did precisely what he thought it would not, swing wide and deep across Belgium. He also did not realize that Moltke had already committed *Landwehr* reserves in his lead forces. The Germans were thus much stronger in the opening battles than Joffre expected. It was a major error, delaying realization that the mortal threat was on his left in the form of the German right wing, the hammer, swinging down from the north. He recovered well, however, shifting French armies leftward using a significant advantage of interior lines. He also pleaded with the HQ of the BEF, by this point a headquarters divided and bickering badly at the highest command level, to stop retreating from the mauling at Le Cateau and turn back to face the enemy.[79] ·

The BEF's slow move back north, which played a role in the outcome of the major battle about to take place, was thus part of a larger French improvisation of a strong defense then a counterattack along the Marne River. This was about to become the main fight of the whole campaign in the West in 1914. It took place along the line of the Marne during September 5–11, stretching from north of fortified Paris to the ancient Roman fortress town of Verdun. Two million Germans faced two million French and 100,000 British, as four German armies contended with four French armies and the BEF.[80] (This count includes German 1st Army and French 6th Army engaged along the River Ourcq, connected by combat and outcome to the six armies fighting along the River Marne.) In addition to being one of the most important battles of the 20th century, it was possibly the most decisive. It stopped the German advance and the Schlieffen-Moltke scheme, and thereby set the conditions for four years of trench war. It was principally a French and German affair, though the BEF played a role. Measuring how great a role provides a commentary more on us than the armies doing battle, if we take as the measure of a country's contribution the roll of its dead and wounded, especially in negative comparison to others. That said, at First Marne the BEF suffered 1,701 total casualties. That was fewer than in some individual French and German brigades.[81]

German armies were approaching Paris, so the French government departed for Bordeaux, as it would again (and thence on to Vichy) when the panzers pushed across France in 1940. General Joseph-Simon Galliéni was left in charge of the emptying capital and its garrison. The effects of the frontier battles were being felt on both sides, not just in extremely high casualties but also in physical wear, especially on the marching German corps just reaching the Marne. Most importantly, the planned German ratio of 3:1 attack superiority was gone. Moltke's right wing had started out already reduced from the Schlieffen ideal of 7:1. It was badly eroded on the march and in a series of small but wearing encounter battles along the way. That meant it was the French who were superior in number as the critical fight began. Joffre hastily configured a new army, designated as 6th Army, from reserves and the Paris garrison.[82] With Moltke's reserves pre-committed to the knockout blow, there was little German strength not already on the roads. It was all or nothing. The head of the hammer, 1st Army under General Alexander von Kluck, was in pursuit of battered and retreating French 5th Army when Kluck decided to turn southeast, doing so in order to complete a *Kessel* encirclement. General Karl von Bülow's 2nd Army was told to move southeast of Paris in echelon with Kluck's 1st Army. At this critical moment, dangerously poor communications and wider failures of military intelligence left Moltke out of touch as two of his armies on the right wing, 1st and 2nd, marched discretely away from his control and each other, farther with every step and hour. A gap opened where their wings should have touched, slowly widening under willful generals who failed to communicate with each other or inform Moltke's HQ.

Meanwhile, Joffre disengaged as many troops as he could from the frontiers, shifting left into a defense line north of Paris, assembling along the Marne. Already, some elements advanced to attack the still unsuspecting Kluck, whose march route was known to Joffre, but not Moltke, from maps captured on the body of a dead German staff officer. Other French units positioned to make blocking attacks against other German armies.[83] Joffre had seen the danger on his left and responded swiftly, abandoning prewar planning assumptions to react to what was in the field before him. He knew he needed every available soldier for the critical battle, including the adjunct of the BEF, which had retreated out of the fight. That was why he personally sought out and traveled to BEF HQ to plead with its commander, General Lord French, to stop retreating, turn and make ready to fight again. Under heavy political pressure from London, including a dressing down of the British commander by Lord Kitchener, the BEF finally turned as its generals meekly accepted chastisement and fresh orders.[84] Its 70,000 exhausted men marched back north past Crécy, site of former English martial glory. The Great Retreat of the Allied armies was over. Now came the greatest battle of the war.

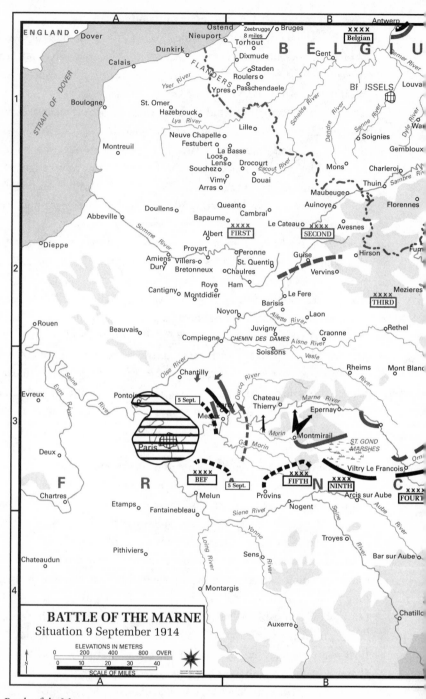

Battle of the Marne.

Courtesy of the Department of History, United States Military Academy at West Point. Redraw by George Chakvetadze.

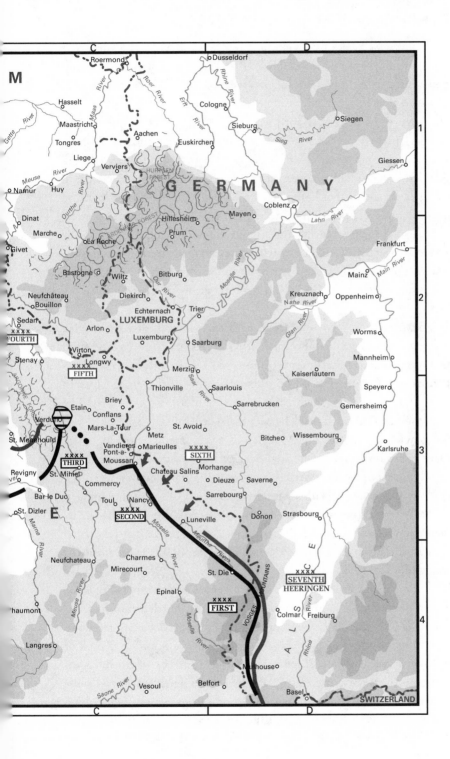

On September 3, the first Germans reached the Marne. Moltke was worried by rumors coming into OHL of British and even Russian landings to open a third front in Denmark. They were baseless, but distracting. He also realized that Joffre was massing to counterattack north of Paris, and that his own right wing was both weak and hanging. On September 4, he issued a directive that changed the whole war: to 6th and 7th Armies, fix and hold as many French corps as possible in Lorraine; to 4th and 5th Armies, keep attacking to fix more French in the Argonne woods; to the right flank, the former hammer, 1st and 2nd Armies under Kluck and Bülow, stop and hold position; to 3rd Army, also on the right, support 1st and 2nd Armies as opportunity and strength of opposition dictates.[85] The *Kaiserheer* was, in short, told to stop in place and ready to *receive* a massive blow from the French—exactly the opposite of what it had hoped to do, and what years of thinking and operational planning proposed it must do, in France.

The next day, the French attacked with their scratch 6th Army: *bleu* and *feldgrau* masses crashed into each other in a corps vs. corps level fight 25 miles north of Paris. Sixth Army comprised 80,000 men of the Paris garrison, reservists and other second-line troops, a just-off-the-boats Algerian division, and a corps detached from 3rd Army; in all, 150,000 men. The number included 3,000 moved by General Galliéni on September 7–8 in 600 black-and-red Renault Model AG1 taxis (meters running there and back). Not nothing, but hardly the *Taxi de la Marne* ("Battle of the Taxis") that clever propaganda of the day, and popular memory ever after, asserted saved France in its most vital hour of need.[86] It was more important that all these ragtag units were hastily assembled into a strike force by Galliéni and rushed north ahead of the arrival of more substantial French forces. Kluck had no idea the new French 6th Army was there until the blow landed.

The main attack was launched on September 7. Over the following days, nearly 1 million French and 70,000 from the BEF hurtled into 750,000 Germans, as some 49 Allied infantry and 8 cavalry divisions faced 46 German infantry and 7 cavalry divisions. Few if any units were at peak or paper strength on either side. A confusion of orders sent two of Kluck's corps marching north to the Ourcq River to try to trap French 5th Army, while Bülow withdrew three more corps 10 miles to a defensive position behind the waters of the Petit Morin. Since OHL was not fully informed, the net result of these and other independent moves was to widen to 20 miles the gap between the separating wings of German 1st and 2nd Armies. They fought discretely, as a result. Meanwhile, the BEF continued its slow march (25 miles in three days, against little opposition) into the widening gap. It helped, but the basic structure of First Marne was a brilliant pivot by Joffre and other French generals, swinging 6th Army, 5th Army, 9th Army and 4th Army around a strong anchor of 3rd Army at Verdun. Two other French armies, 2nd Army and 1st Army, defended the Alsace-Lorraine frontier.

French corps defended against Kluck but attacked Bülow's exposed right wing, where some French troops refused to accept an offered surrender of nearly 500 Germans, who were shot. Germans had also massacred prisoners, and inconvenient civilians, during their August march through Belgium into northern France. Bülow's flank was turned just as the BEF arrived in the gap at dusk, alongside French troops pressing home that day's attacks. That night, Bülow pulled back even farther, widening the gap between two German armies to 30 miles. Over this critical day and night, Moltke entered the first stage of what became a complete mental and moral breakdown. As his plan stalled and then fell apart, he knew the worst nightmare for the *Kaiserheer* and for Germany was coming true. The war was already a slaughter that must henceforth descend into a raw killing contest that could well consume the nation, and certainly its ambition.[87]

That night a full division from German 3rd Army launched an attack against a French division asleep across the Somme, striking after 3:00 a.m. They had been pounded all day by French 75s. Lacking mobile artillery to reply, their commander ordered a night bayonet assault. Men were told to unload rifles, pocket breechblocks, and fix bayonets. Officers assembled and herded the ranks as if it were Leipzig or Waterloo, though no one ever attacked with empty guns at night on those killing fields. After wading across the Somme in the dark, the charge went in to the sudden sound of bugles and beaten drums.[88] More French died than Germans in the hand-to-hand fighting that ensued, thousands in all. The next day, this local advance was stopped for lack of food and reinforcements. It meant nothing beyond glorious anachronism, if shoving a Mauser M1898 sawback bayonet into a waking man's chest or gut can be considered glorious.

The crisis of the battle came in the yawning gap between German 1st and 2nd Armies where 70,000 exhausted troops of the BEF at last arrived in four sluggish columns, all worn out by poor leaders who had made them march 600 miles since the war began. The British advance into the gap was also slowed by effective German rearguard actions. Finally, however, the BEF was in the right place, along with the French, to threaten to do real damage to the Germans. A major clash was avoided because the threat of Allied troops in the gap between two German armies proved enough. Bülow issued a terse retreat order, without consulting OHL, and pulled back with a light cavalry screen behind. That withdrawal forced Kluck to pull out as well over the next two days, heading for the Aisne River. Moltke sent an emissary around the various army HQs on September 9. Lieutenant-Colonel Richard Hentsch then confirmed to army commanders a general retreat order issued by Moltke's HQ on September 10. The *Kaiserheer* pulled back from the Marne in reasonably good order, not stopping until it reached the Aisne. Then it chose the best high ground, and started to dig. A tired Allied pursuit caught up after the Germans stopped retreating and turned face. Efforts to rush an attack against the German line failed against determined defense of the first shallow trenches that now appeared. These soon reached the Atlantic, as repeated efforts to flank also failed in the so-called "race to the sea." Until there were no more flanks. Until 1918.

The *Kaiserheer* was just 20 miles from Paris when it turned away. Many men saw the city's nightglow, in a time before heavy bombers forced city blackouts. For years they argued over and lamented receiving the stop and then retreat orders. A generation later, their sons would recall spires atop onion-domed churches seen in the distant outskirts of Moscow in December 1941, and never again. Germans lamented that failure, too. Much lamentation was coming to Germany. The soldiers of 1914 later claimed they could have won in France that summer and autumn, and perhaps they might have. Fighting has a dynamic all its own, and no battle is truly decided before it's fought, or very few. Still, the German idea was high-risk and most unlikely to succeed whether Moltke reinforced the right wing or not. At any number of points the fight along the frontiers, and then along the Marne, might have turned out differently than it did. Had that happened, had the *Kaiserheer* won in 1914, no doubt military history shelves would be lined with books proclaiming that Schlieffen had been a genius, and that the younger Moltke far surpassed his uncle as a mover of armies and as a modern great captain. Instead, the Germans lost in a catastrophe almost as mad as Austria's, and Moltke suffered a collapse. Like Louis-Napoléon outside Metz in 1870, he lost all personal drive and confidence and was useless as a leader thereafter. He may even have had a stroke. In any case, he was forced to resign on September 14. Falkenhayn replaced him, writing in private with his usual coldness: "Schlieffen's notes are at an end and therefore also Moltke's wits."[89]

The change in commanders was not announced to the public in Germany for four months, until January 1915. It was withheld to hide from Germans the full measure of the defeat along the Marne. Bethmann Hollweg and other civilian authorities in Berlin, like the OHL and generals in command of all the losing armies, systematically lied about their defeat in France and about the number of casualties taken.[90] Lying about losing, lying about what it meant for the war effort, denying defeat and the real reasons for it, would become a major legacy of the high command of the *Kaiserheer*. After 1918, military lies would poison hope for political change in Weimar Germany and German reconciliation in Europe, as well as for fundamental military lessons learned by the German officer corps. Already in 1914, blame for the defeat began that would wreck German postwar democracy, as the *Kaiserheer* shifted responsibility to any and all but its own officers and men.[91] Erich Ludendorff, an enemy of Weimar democracy from the start in 1919, and a key ally of Hitler in Bavaria in the 1920s, blamed the defeat on hidden machinations of Freemasons and Jews. Not rigid prewar thinking and planning, too reliant on impossible logistics; not disobedient and delinquent generals; not worn-out, over-marched armies with too many green reservists; not tactics always untethered from strategy; not even the powerful and flexible French resistance that should have been respected. After 1945, in Nuremberg testimony and in memoirs, another group of German generals would similarly exonerate themselves from all responsibility for a lost war and for their many crimes.

***

THERE WOULD BE a Second Marne in the summer of 1918. Just as in a war of spades and shells, barbed wire and frustrated offense, without flanks or movement, there would be a Second Champagne, a Third Ypres, and a Twelfth Isonzo. The great fight now called First Marne was, for all that later war and mass killing, a genuinely decisive battle. Though not in a way either the French or Germans intended, with both armies embarking on the campaign looking to win the whole war all at once. Its immediate effect was to keep Italy out of the war, and in the longer term, outside the Central Powers alliance with Germany. The *Regio Esercito* and government in Rome watched the mighty *Kaiserheer* lose and decided against keeping a prewar commitment to Germany. In 1915 Italy would be bribed to switch sides, joining the Entente in exchange for secret promises of territory (*Italia irredenta*), at Austrian expense. It made little difference. The southern front could not determine the victory or defeat of the major belligerents. Its main effect would be to accelerate the decimation of the Italian and Habsburg armies, and by extension speed up the wearing out of troops and resources on both sides in the west. By 1917, losses in futile fighting in the Alps would drain the Western Allies and Germans alike, drawing down the human reserves on the Western Front as each side was compelled to prop up a failing ally fighting in the mountains for a few acres of alpine meadow and miles of rock.

More importantly, First Marne was a decisive *defensive* victory by the French Army. It prevented France from losing the war and stopped Germany from winning it right at the beginning, and therein lies its enormous significance in shaping the basic contour of the Great War. Marshal Ferdinand Foch put it this way in his memoirs, published in 1931: "We had not gained a great victory over the enemy, but we had prevented him from gaining one over us."[92] Defeat of German hopes for the complete destruction of French military resistance in a single stroke meant that France would keep fighting, that the French nation would resist in arms as long as it could, as long as there were German boots still on French soil. Failure thus committed Germany to an extended fight in a war not just of armies but of peoples, against the aroused determination of France and the growing armed might of Britain, including also until the end of 1917 the vast empire of Russia. And Italy, and many small nations attached to or beholding to the Western Allies. And before the end, even the indifferent United States. First Marne meant the war would go on until the exhaustion of nearly all the major participants and the fatal cracking open of several: Austria, Germany, Russia and the Ottoman Empire.

It overthrew a century of military theory about winning short wars via designed and carefully executed battles of annihilation, in the Frederickian and Napoleonic style and speed and manner. It sparked a renewed theoretical and professional military interest in strategies of attrition as a way to win modern industrial wars against other Great Powers. One appalled and angry observer, H. M. Tomlinson, wrote a few years after the war ended, pointing to trenches that appeared along the Aisne in the aftermath of First Marne: "The whole library of military science and history was as obsolete by the end of November 1914 as the runes of witchcraft."[93] Not everyone agreed. Germans brooded on how close they thought they had come to victory at First Marne, remembered the church spires of Paris, and clung to strategic-victory-by-battle dogma into World War II. Only too late did German generals understand that was beyond their and Germany's ability.[94]

Even as the *Kaiserheer* began to retreat, Bethmann Hollweg's staff drew up a list of explicit war aims that appeared to some later historians to prove gross aggression from the start in Berlin's thinking and war planning. The "September Program," as Bethmann Hollweg's hasty memorandum is known, called for serial annexations of borderlands to Germany, the reduction of Belgium to vassal status and France's renunciation of its status as a Great Power. That would shift the focus of the war and future geopolitical struggle to the main enemy, Britain. After the war, Germany was to dominate Europe "in west and east for all imaginable time." Not even its own allies were safe from Berlin's insistence on complete domination, for the September Program added that it would be necessary to use armed force to compel Austria-Hungary into a *Mitteleuropa* under German rule. In a separate portent of German actions in a later war, the Kaiser called for the expulsion of non-Germans living in Alsace-Lorraine and all new areas to be annexed.[95] It seemed a first draft of permanent military, political and economic hegemony; a calculated and brutal outline for Germany's elevation by war to *Weltmacht*.

The September Program was never actually official cabinet policy and was not a true blueprint for a postwar diktat. It was a first draft of a different idea, representing the brutal realization of Germany's profound and self-inflicted isolation in the midst of a now desperate *Weltkrieg* that had no end in sight. Berlin's war policy had just cut Germany off from all world markets. Bethmann Hollweg knew that just to survive as a Great Power, Germany must build a *Mitteleuropa* empire from territory and resources all around it, not in Africa or Asia as it tried belatedly and with only limited success before the war. It was a fantasy, for the most part, a first pass at adjusting to the new geostrategic realities of the long war of endurance Germany had trapped itself within. Yet such ideas and hubris did not emerge from air. They were laced through German thinking, like a virus. Expansion and dominance over Europe was always a logical conclusion in pursuit of *Weltpolitik* and *Weltmacht*, once a world war of Germany's making blocked its expansion and trade and its access to vital resources outside Europe. Isolation and aggression became reinforcing, self-fulfilling prophecy, whirling inside a military cul-de-sac.

Annihilation of Strategy

IN THE OPENING campaign of World War I in the west, Germans and French each sought to fight a climactic war-winning battle. They did so because each feared that failing to win a short war meant falling into and losing a long one. The French advanced into Belgium looking to fight it out because of an offensive-minded doctrine that spoke in part to fear of being disadvantaged by a chronic demographic shortfall. Their thrust missed the main German strength advancing across Belgium farther west. The *Kaiserheer* struck with its reserves already deployed because Berlin feared that a grand coalition would suffocate it with men and war matériel if it did not win right away. Moltke's right-wing hammer wheeled wider than Joffre expected through Belgium and thereby missed the main strength of the French Army, which was not where Schlieffen predicted it would be or Moltke hoped it would be. Joffre knew better than to be trapped rushing into Alsace-Lorraine, his back to Belgium when it was so full of Germans. When strength finally met strength along the Marne, the armies mauled each other in the same old ways, and some new ones. The French won, decisively, but no one annihilated anyone. It was worse for the Germans.[1] A short war for them meant a more limited war they just might win. A long war meant a peoples' war they feared they would surely lose. A war of nations. Total war. And not just against France. Too many British died at German hands at Mons. Too many Russians fell at Tannenberg. National passions were engaged. National honor was at stake. Moral commitment to further fighting and to revenge was in the air.

The *Kaiserheer* had moved first in early August. It was also the first army to stop and dig in once all hope to win fast on the Western Front was done. On November 8, Falkenhayn told the kaiser that the war in Flanders had simply stopped moving: "The barbed wire cannot be crossed."[2] Henceforth, Germany faced what it most feared, war on two fronts against a grand coalition that outmatched it in almost every key measure. The outcome on the

Marne thus gave both sides what neither wanted but the Central Powers could least afford, a war of dreary yet deadly monotony fought from inside trenches that got deeper and more elaborate, dugouts and bunkers that became more permanent. A war of constant trickling attrition, of slow grinding down of men and matériel in a kind of permanent low-level battle called trench warfare; punctuated by massive offensives that mostly went nowhere, except back into the trenches with fewer men than they started with, but also fewer men on the other side. Nations brought up to venerate the ideal of battle learned to live with attrition, then to embrace it as a war-winning method. In the years of fighting that lay ahead they would search for new ways to accelerate its effects by engaging more guns, more gas, more mines, more men.

Trench systems filled with ordinary men who seemed to grow more like each other and less like the civilians they left behind, although they hated each other well enough to kill each other by the millions. Ordinary enlisted were known to the French as *poilus* ("hairy ones"), to the Germans as *Landser* (private), to the British as Tommies. They had names for each other, too, as in *les boches* ("cabbage heads"), as the French called Germans. "Ivans" faced "Fritzes" in trenches and combat in the East. Other curious names were heard in the Alps and Balkans, Galicia and the Carpathian snows, and across the Middle East. In 1918 American "doughboys" arrived, and were greeted by Canadians and West Indians, Muslims from India and *tirailleurs* from West Africa, all already there for years. Greeted, too, by ANZACS from another hemisphere, young Australians and New Zealanders very far from home, fighting someone else's war. Lives at the fronts were lived huddled under howling shells and whistling bullets and with hissing gas. Life for any of these ordinary men in extraordinary circumstances could end over a tinned breakfast in death by a sniper, on a night patrol, from harassing shells, artillery storms, or poison gas. Every few months, there was another great outbreak of intense mass killing, as one side rose "over the top" of their trench to come stumbling across a no man's land of shell pits and wire and pre-sited kill zones for the machine guns on another major offensive, until the other side stopped the attack and went back the other way in counterattack. On and on it went.

By the end of the Battles of the Frontiers and First Marne, of Tannenberg and the Masurian Lakes, and a dozen fights in Galicia and Serbia, by the end of 1914 it was clear the war would be far longer and much harder than anyone foresaw. Mobility had broken down and would take years to restore. Logistical systems failed everywhere. Men and armies all dug deeper to get below the hurtling shells and chittering machine guns.[3] Then everyone looked for old and new ways to dig the other mole army out and kill it. That is not to say the generals gave up on movement. They never did. They just did not know how to restart it. Or, more accurately, once they restarted it they could not keep it going. Over the next three years nearly every tactic and offensive failed, leading to greater loss of life until some decided grimly that attrition was the way to win after all.

Before armies could move again they needed to create flanks, and that meant somehow punching holes in the enemy's lines. The search for the critical breakthrough was underway, as everyone still thought mostly in terms of offense. The OHL (*Oberste Heeresleitung*) looked to regroup its armies in the west (*Westheer*) for a new offensive in 1915, after losing 100,000 men in a desperate last ditch effort at First Ypres in October–November 1914. Nor was it the Allies' job to sit in place. It was instead to drive the Germans out of France and Belgium. They *had* to attack in 1915. The problem was the lack of flanks, which disappeared into forts that literally dipped into the Atlantic on one end and rode up Alpine slopes on the other. In between, 440 miles of trenches gouged out clay and chalk and rich black earth, cut through thick woods and even moved underground though linked limestone caverns with little no man's lands down the middle. This was positional war, a vast siege of millions. A fight with spades and entrenchments, with barbed wire and fortifications; the mobilization of entire nations for total war without respite.

Now that they were all in a long war together, no one was ready. Britain did not have the men, and no one else had the matériel. Everyone was forced to scramble, demobilizing skilled workers back to factories to make shells and engines and rifles. Many factories had to shut down in August because skilled workers were mobilized to fight what all expected to be a short war. The damage to civilian economies was immense. Lost wages and postponed purchases hit every business, from corner shops to restaurants to paper mills to the garment industry. It had to be reversed. Now the nations would not just take up arms but enlist farmers and riveters and arc welders as well. It was a war of spades and wire and rifles and firing shells at the front, but also a war of sowing and harvests and industry and commerce and making shells behind the lines. Above all, it was about the shells.

Peoples' war meant that millions of women were militarized as well as mobilized, right from the start in auxiliary volunteer organizations, later with some coercion. Rationing boards were set up, production studies made, massive expansions of government war powers passed in country after country. There was censorship of all kinds, serious and silly, threatening and tyrannical. Arrests of dissenters real and imagined took place everywhere,

British trench at the Somme (1916).
Courtesy of Wikimedia Creative Commons.

including in the democracies. The Allies only slowly learned to tap into their biggest advantage: three world-girdling empires thick with people and economic resources, connected by the oceanic sea lanes guarded by the Allied navies or over land routes guarded by the tsar's legions across multiple time zones. All that was before more aggressive policies coming out of Berlin threatened to bring the United States into the war in 1915, and did so in fact in 1917. Not counting imperial populations in India and Africa that were also partly mobilized, the Allies in 1915 had 260 million people to 120 million of the Central Powers, and 60 percent more national income. In private, Lloyd George spoke confidently of the latter as early as September 1914, of winning the war with "silver bullets."[4]

Germany had planned meticulously for a short war, but not at all for a long one. It had to improvise everything, immediately. So a strange order went out on September 10, 1914, the same day OHL told its generals to stop their armies all along the Marne, to turn them away from Paris and the onrushing Allies. On the day that Germany's leaders admitted they were in it for the long haul, the first order recognizing the new reality was sent to the field armies from the Prussian War Ministry. It said to scavenge everything, even from corpses: "Cavalrymen were to be buried only in their 'underwear and pants,' with boots, tunics, and equipment gathered for reuse. Dead and wounded infantrymen were to be stripped of all ammunition and weapons . . . Castings from artillery shells, broken machine guns, shattered artillery pieces, caissons, and harnesses [off dead horses] were to be gathered up. All parts of downed aircraft and Zeppelins likewise were to be retrieved."[5] A little later on the home fronts, rationing started to bite harder as governments looked ahead to winters with partly lost harvests and markets shut down or shortage-ridden from mutual blockades. Before the war ended, starvation would return to parts of Europe, principally hitting civilians. Jean de Bloch would be proven right. In conditions of stalemate and scarcity the armies would eat before the peoples did.

In the spring and summer of 1915 the *Kaiserheer* launched a wholesale re-organization of its defensive doctrine in the west, moving to a complex inter-locked trench system, employing carefully sited flanking positions and prac-ticing pre-set counterbarrages. It built wherever possible on reverse slopes of the high ground it had chosen in 1914, to protect infantry and bunkers from Allied artillery. Initially, its heavy first-line tactics fared poorly against Allied infantry attacks supported by artillery, so it scrambled to develop more flexi-ble defenses, shifting men out of the first trench (main battle line), redeploy-ing most into second trenches, then massing in a third trench in a defense-in-depth designed to absorb breakthroughs and then to counterattack. This system recognized Germany's need to avoid excessive casualties by thinning numbers in the first line, then counterattacking from a more thickly manned second line and later from a heavily defended third line.[6] Defending in depth reduced casualties but also promised a slower war, and that way Germany could never win. Already Allied production overmatched it, pouring not just out of the factories in Britain and France but into Europe from the world-wide French and British Empires, as well as from the still neutral United States. An alternative was to try to win in the east instead of the west, where it had failed in 1914. OHL would shift its offensive efforts back and forth in the years ahead, west (1914) to east (1915) to west (1916) to east (1917) to west (1918), in the search for some way out of the two-front war. It did not find one until the collapse of Russia in 1917 gave the OHL some hope that it might defeat the Western Allies with its last effort in 1918.

The French Army also developed new trench warfare tactics during 1915, including its own comparably complex defense-in-depth trench system. In both the German and French cases, the new systems backstopped an offen-sive policy. That is, they were meant to reduce casualties in certain locales and improve overall defense against enemy breakthroughs, but did so partly so that more troops could concentrate elsewhere to attack. At the strategic level, the French Army's offensive tactics shifted from blunt attempts at direct breakthrough (*percée*) to deliberate attrition (*grignotage*), or as Joffre inimitably phrased it, "nibbling away" at German strength to take back France in small bites. The destruction of Germany's armies remained the paramount goal, but the Allies took territory only in a step-by-step approach, no longer driven to reclaim every inch of sacred soil with even more sacred blood lost in all-out offensive operations.[7] Besides, building up the means to win at total war took time, especially in laggard Britain.

Fighting slowed in the first months of 1915 as artillery in all armies was retarded by an across-the-board shell shortage. Batteries started to hoard shells, as individual guns were reduced to just five or ten rounds per day, sometimes to just one, defeating the design and purpose of rapid-fire, self-recoiling modern guns. Shell manufacture during Prussia's 19th century wars was 7,000 per week. By 1915 each army needed 20 times that production *per day*. Different kinds of shells were also needed once trenches appeared: not fragmentary or shrapnel from light mobile guns, but high explosives from heavies and mortars, to penetrate down to dugouts and cut apart fields of barbed wire before the infantry crossed over in an attack. Shortages were felt first in France but were worst overall in Russia, where the shell crisis was compounded by other shortages of critical war supplies. Out of five million Russian soldiers in uniform in early 1915 just 1.2 million had a rifle, partly due to failures to deliver by several British and American suppliers.[8] Overwhelmed by German artillery and forced into a broad retreat from Poland in mid-1915 (a withdrawal which would not be reversed until the Red Army returned to Poland in 1944), one Russian general sighed: "Germans expend metal, we expend life."[9]

Britain was forced to change its entire army structure, not just that of its forces in the field. By the end of First Ypres (October 19–November 22, 1914), where the BEF made its best showing of the whole 1914 campaign, its original cadres were all but destroyed. Kitchener would recruit Britain's first-ever million-man conscript army, not least with the intention that once everyone else's armies were worn out Britain's reserves would be intact and it must therefore dominate both the war and the peace.[10] Training on such a scale took time, however. The French Army would have to hold while Britain armed for land war, an aspect of military power it had largely ignored before 1914 while concentrating budgets and interest in the naval arms race with Germany. Manpower demand led to lowering of height and health standards, including formation of whole "bantam" units of very short men. The British

Western Front, 1915–1916.

Courtesy of the Department of History, United States Military Academy at West Point.

Army was not alone in that standard shift. High casualties forced the French and German armies to enlist physically and mentally substandard soldiers. Australians, Canadians and Americans were on average often noticeably larger men than their European counterparts, especially later in the war.[11] However shorter than ideal some men and units were, from 1916 Germans learned that Schlieffen's short-war dismissal of Britain's likely contribution to decision in the land war had been fatally wrong. Germans destroyed the small BEF in First Ypres, but by 1918 they would face 25 replacement corps in a completely remade British Army.

***

OVER THE NEXT four years a steel storm reshaped landscapes on a scale that befuddles memory and imagination even now. It remade into vast kill zones the gentle poppy meadows of Flanders and the warm green fields of France. It tore apart the vales of Galicia and plowed a crop of corpses into the plains of western Russia. It ripped showers of stone splinters from the mountainsides down onto flinty battlefields in the Carpathians and the Isonzo valley of the high Alps. It choked the Drina and Danube, the Vistula and Somme with human flotsam and jetsam as total war was waged by whole peoples, not just armies and navies. Wide zigzag wounds slashed the face of Europe for 440 miles from the Atlantic to the Alps. The trenches were twice as long on the Eastern Front, though discontinuous. Shorter trenches blocked mountain passes or cut across fields in the Balkans and on the Austro-Italian front. The mature systems were miles wide on each side of no man's land, in parallels of three or more lines of a defense-in-depth, backing men away from the reach of artillery. Rear lines were crammed with troops waiting to stop a petering breakthrough as it lost momentum and outran its artillery, then to counterattack. Front lines wound through millions of craters whose wound scars are still there in unnaturally roiled and pitted landscapes, somewhat gentled with erosion and soft grasses and passed time.

Leviathans did it, mauling each other with high explosives and armies of digging mole-men. Fighting zones were connected to rear areas by thousands of communications and supply trenches, roughly angled away from the zig-zags. For another hundred miles or so deep rear areas were engaged, hinterlands beyond that. Aircraft flew over a surface clotted with the moral purpose and physical exertion of contending nations. Much of the suffering on the Western Front was crowded into a compact zone between Verdun and Flanders, as long sections saw only intermittent low-intensity combat. Quiet sectors were farther south, where terrain widened no man's land and reduced contact, and lesser strategic objectives lowered imperatives to attack. Men still killed and died in these sections and suffered all the indignities of the trenches, though in a slower blur of night raids, harassment shelling, patrols and sniping.

Behind the fighting lines the land was crisscrossed and traced with military roads and railways; with long earthworks, endless rows of pine barracks, fortified canals; with bunkers, depots, tank parks, hospitals and cemeteries; with R&R camps and brothels. Everything was serviced by seaside docks and busy ports that brought men to fight, women to nurse, food and war matériel from all over the world. It took 100,000 cooks to feed upwards of two million men on the Western Front alone, every day, despite frontline troops eating cold food such as tinned bully beef, hard cheese and harder biscuits.[12] Coastlines bristled with shipyards, with convoys unloading and bases for U-boats, fragile little ships that took the war down into a cold and unforgiving third dimension. Merchants zigged and zagged across whole oceans as escorts circled, looking for signs of the silent grey wolves below, as the powers searched for decision by strangulation at sea once the initial land battle failed them.

World War I was filled with inventive new barbarisms. H. G. Wells was proven right, Norman Angell was not: there was war in the sky. In September 1914, during the decisive battle along the Marne, unarmed scouts made sketches of observations or just mental notes reported when they landed. A few took up hand-held cameras. Then it was realized that scout planes had advantages of distant observation unequaled in the history of war as they followed the retreating German armies, told Allied generals exactly where they were, and guided in attacks and artillery. Once all movement stopped and the first shallow trenches reached the Alps and also touched the Belgian coast, there was an impassable barrier to any movement behind enemy lines by spies or cavalry, historically the sources of combat intelligence. War swelled up into a fourth dimension, where observation balloons floated like anchored manatees behind the trenches, oddly graceful in obesity until hauled frantically down or bursting into flame with men tumbling out of baskets, not wearing parachutes, jumping to escape the flames. Fixed-wing scouts soon became critical to all sides, their cameras the keen eyes of the big guns, of mapmakers and operations planners.[13]

Fighters went up to hunt the balloons and scouts, then to ward off each other. The blue filled with twisting dogfights of canvas and wood and mad machine-gun chatter. It streaked with white and black pufferies of collapsing observation balloons and trailing oily smokes from plunging planes and burning men. On the ground and belowground were the uniformed hordes digging like demented mice or moles into muddy earth or clay or chalk, hiding from plunging shells that always fell more accurately after the planes passed over. Airships and fixed-wing bombers brought the war to cities next, to Liège and Paris and more systematically to London, and to cities just over the frontiers of Germany.[14] Londoners went into the Underground to wait out the bombs, as they would again 25 years later. Aircraft bombed and strafed the armies, too. Hundreds of fields of aircraft in neat squadron rows grew in range, speed and number with each passing month during 52 months of all-out war.

Below the Flying Circuses and *escadrilles* pastures were pitted and pocked by shells that fell in Perseid-like bombardments on both sides, for days without stopping. Crater fields formed to shape a lunar face as suffering of the countryside joined the suffering of soldiers as in no prior war. Corpses were unburied, chopped by shelling, turned into crater stews of rot and disrespect. Trees disappeared, grass ceased to grow, churned and meaty soil and air stank of putrefaction. It reeked of poison, too, as pea-green mustard gas and other heavier-than-air death gases crept into craters and trenches searching for men to choke. Blister agents attacked skin and sight, gas corroded the tissue of lungs, nerve agents destroyed the central nervous system and left men flopping like caught trout in a boat until they died. Gas masks were handed out, so vomit agents were added to the shells to make men pull off the masks and inhale the poisons.[15] In 1916 young J. R. R. Tolkien served on the Somme. He saw death, of course, and woundings and trauma. He felt an intense companionship with his own band of brothers that he later imbued into his epic *Fellowship of the Ring*. He saw drowned faces with open eyes looking up beside duckboard as he walked past, through a lifeless land of rot and clanking metal monsters that tore up nature, where the air was tinged with a smear of poison. He thought it all evil. Years later he wrote about it. He called it Mordor.

Poets found different voices than the eager boyishness of Rupert Brooke: the righteous anger about civilian hypocrisy of Siegfried Sassoon, the cynical detachment of Robert Graves, the religious-toned personal tragedies of Wilfred Owen.[16] Or no meaning at all, later in Dadaism. Artists, too, found new subjects. The famous put them on evocative canvas and etchings that hang in galleries still.[17] More ordinary artists among the troops sculpted unknown statues that stand today overgrown and crumbled in an Ardennes wood, made of surplus German cement. Others carved chapels in caves, or pornographic sculptures one or two caves over. Or just their names and home cities. Most men did not find poetry or high art or gods in the trenches, standing there alongside the handful of famous artists and poets whose works filter dead perceptions and blot out the voices of the millions. Not meaning to, perhaps, yet doing so when taken to speak for a whole people or a generation. Ordinary men found their own meaning, or none at all, in the trenches. We chance missing their wider experience if we perceive the war mainly through the sights and words of a handful of artists and poets.

For the vast majority, those whose nameless place resides in history inside some drear statistic, it was not about all that. Not at all a storybook war from boy's adventure tales of flags and heroes, or finding a "red badge of courage" and manhood under fire.[18] Or cursing about it later in Latin and Greek or soft pastels. It was about savage killing: fighting with fists, knives, spades, grenades and flamethrowers; more distant killing with poison gases, bombs and shells or strafing; and little wars against animals, lice and fearless corpse rats fat from easy food. It was about mutism and trauma, daily fears and night terrors. *Samogon* dripping from a Russian still, wine looted from French and Italian vineyards. Hot food, then maybe furtive sex behind the lines. Comforting a pal or burying him, and long-distance love and breakups in handwritten letters. Above all, it was an experience of mass anonymous death. The first million by the end of 1914. Nine million before it ended in 1918, or more. There are different ways to count.

What met a generation of schoolboys raised on heroic stories of Marlborough, Frederick and Napoleon was not glory but hard death in ways old and new. Cold death from a sniper while tangled and frantic on jags of barbed wire invented by far-off ranchers to hem in cattle. Hot death as liquid flame gushed over a man to light him up like a Roman candle. Slick greasy death as a sawtooth bayonet snicked easily into a gut. Gurgling death, throat ripped out or jaw torn away by a machine-gun bullet, unable to cry for aid. Lonely death at the bottom of a shallow crater filled with yellow rainwater and piss, and bits of horse and human flesh upturned and minced by the last bombardment. Instant death as a boy turned into a mush of pink pulp and red mist when a high-explosive shell landed a foot away, one drop in a steel rain that fell for days and nights on end. Fumbling death from mustard gas or worse, much worse chemicals as the war went on.[19] So much death that tens of millions gagged down every meal inside a sweet-sick odor of putrefying horse and human flesh. It was a war of night raids, mud and cold, trench foot, trench mouth, trench fever and trench coats; of wristwatches instead of fobs; of *souvenirs* replacing keepsakes, after so much time spent by English-speaking troops in France or Flanders; of troglodyte living in clay dugouts or

chalky caves, pursued even belowground by the sounds of fury. It meant loading with shovels into a coal sack an indeterminate mush of flesh and cloth
that five minutes ago was a childhood friend. French called men killed this
way *viande à canon* ("cannon meat").

New marvels took wing and wheel, efficient killing machines out of industry like the world never saw before. On a scale never heard or seen before. Not
the fluttering of fletches sounding like a passing flock of doves as arrow storms
fell on Agincourt. Not the occasional boom of cannon at Castillon or even
the steadier roar at Königgrätz. Instead, a cacophony of screaming shells and
thudding explosions. A permanent battle that drove some men mad inside the
moment, running from the parabolic screeching as tens of millions of cased
high explosives hurtled in from miles away over days and nights. There was
unmitigated stress from constant combat exposure not over a few hours or
days of battle, as in past wars, but for months at a time. It was not, as once
thought, shells that produced what was at first called shell shock. It was the
extreme and sustained stress that induced deep trauma in everyone if they
stayed in it too long. At the worst: mutism, uncontrollable crying, catatonic
fits, self-mutilation, convulsions, nonstop shaking, profound fear of loud
noises, fugue states or total loss of personal identity and memory, fatalism,
loss of survival instinct, suicide. Silent traumas were clung to inside a howling
storm of war, insulating from the insane crowd, but also separating men in
combat from their families and societies.[20] Though not all. Not even most.

The vast majority somehow endured, got up the next day, ate bad food,
made macabre jokes, went on patrol, took a watch on the firing step and followed officer orders even if they disagreed. They griped and grumbled but
were also proud of their service and country. Their nations endured for and
with them.[21] Soldiers in all the armies stayed and dug, stood and fought, went
on leaves and always came back. They grew harder, more lethal and skilled.
Armies and men adjusted to the end of mobile battle with its immense casualties. They learned to live in comparative safety in the trenches, some with
derision for reduced and limited attack objectives. Not all were Paul Baumers,
sinking into traumatized loss and solitude until all went quiet with death on
the Eastern or Southern or Western fronts. They may have shared a sense
of common suffering, but that does not mean they felt they were the same
as men in the other uniform. Ernst Jünger spoke for many with his ashen
vitalism, his embrace of nationalist war and images of the front fighter as a
moral hero overcoming industrial power. More perhaps than did Erich Maria
Remarque with his haunting antiheroes, broken by combat, and his interna-
tionalist pacifism.[22] If we forget the soldiers' commitment to their nations

making total war, pass over in discomfort their silent moral agreement to endure the unendurable and to do the unspeakable, we do not see or understand their war. We corrupt it into ours.

***

VERDUN WAS THE longest battle in history, lasting from February 21 to December 18, 1916. Over 1.7 million French rotated into the fight at Verdun, against 700,000 Germans. It was started by Falkenhayn to test a new way of war Germans had long feared as inevitably fatal to them but now turned against the Allies: attrition not in place of the ideal of annihilation, but as a form of obliteration by different means. Falkenhayn proposed to make the French Army bleed itself white by inducing it to attack en masse into his waiting artillery, into a *Blutmühle* ("blood mill") consuming such numbers that France must be knocked out of the war. Then Britain would be forced out, too, unwilling to fight on alone and in any case unable to sustain the continuous front. Flanks would return, with opportunities for German operational genius in a war of resumed movement.

Put more clinically, Falkenhayn meant to decimate the Allied manpower reserve by provoking an immense counterattack, then defending against it with massed artillery before launching his own war-winning offensive once the Allied line was thinned. Offense always lost more numbers than defense. He did not care if the counterattack came at Verdun or the Somme or in Champagne. He would stop it, then commit his reserves to break a weakened Allied front. He never really gave up on the old idea of a decisive battle of encirclement leading to total victory. He meant to use bloodletting as the preliminary to revival of German maneuver and encirclement tactics, to push on to victories of a more traditional sort.[23] After winning in the west, he thought, Germany could negotiate an end to the war from a position of strength. However, others were not so ready to settle short of Germany's original war aims, or the expanded aims as framed by Bethmann Hollweg in September 1914. It is also hard to imagine that a victory at Verdun might temper ambitions as Falkenhayn said. There were powerful men in the *Kaiserheer*, Hindenburg and Ludendorff not least among them, who intended not to negotiate but to use victory to carve a *Mitteleuropa* empire from conquered Slav lands. To make the Second Reich into a true world power. They dreamed of a great victory on the Western Front in 1916 mainly to free armies to move east to crush Russia, too.

Falkenhayn thought the French would defend all-out the passes down to the Meuse at Verdun, sometimes called the "Thermopylae of France."

He would wear out the French Army, which he expected to charge like a wild boar onto the spear of his waiting artillery. He meant to defeat the French before new British corps assembling on the Somme mounted a relief offensive. He codenamed his plan Operation *Judgment* (*Gericht*). It relied on provoking French honor into making an all-out counterattack, leading to destruction of the French Army by massed artillery. The model was Second Champagne (*Herbstschlacht* or the "Autumn Battle") that ended on November 6, 1915. There, the French took exceptionally high casualties from German heavy artillery, which broke their offensive. Falkenhayn once again turned to the guns to destroy an enemy he could not maneuver around. He meant his infantry to attack only to provoke a massive counterattack. However, as so often in German military history, disobedient generals in the field had other ideas. Where Falkenhayn intended only to take a line of eastern hills to better position his artillery for the coming slaughter of the French, German 5th Army's commander planned a full infantry assault, which would lead to much higher German losses over a long and brutal fight.

Assault troops rested in concrete bunkers (*Stollen*), protected from shells but 1,000 yards back from the French trenches, not the 100–200 yards of Allied attacks. It was a calculated risk. Significant first-wave casualties were expected as troops traversed farther in the open under fire, though it was thought a saturation barrage would keep losses down. Awaiting their arrival was the strongest fortress complex in the world, on paper. Verdun's hills mushroomed with forts—some Roman, some designed for Louis XIV by Vauban, some late 19th century, modernized with steel and concrete and earthworks. Yet it was mostly a hollow defense. Verdun was a quiet sector, so there was little or no daily French reconnaissance, few telephone lines and too little barbed wire. Most forts were stripped of guns and isolated, without communications linking them.[24] Military intelligence also failed. Alsatian deserters reported the German build-up, but were ignored. If an attack was imminent, where were the jump-off trenches the Allies always used? Nor did anyone ask why steeples were disappearing on the other side, the reason being to confuse counter-battery fire adjustment. Paris and London believed the *Kaiserheer* would attack Russia in 1916, and were busy preparing their own offensives: the French in the spring; the British and Russians in the summer; the Italians in the Alps. The Allied plan for 1916 was to bring pressure and casualties on all sides of Germany at once. Instead, the Germans struck first and unexpectedly.

Not everything went in favor of the Germans. Fifth Army was ready on February 12, but it snowed for a week, hampering the artillery sighting that was critical to the whole battle concept. Infantry waited in frigid conditions, in dugouts filled with runoff and ice. The delay was critical. French military intelligence now realized a fight was coming, and Paris reinforced with three full divisions, raising the defense to three corps in and around the salient. Then the snow stopped. Falkenhayn had massed 1,201 big guns, the most to that point in history. He had ready another 200 heavy short-range mortars. The guns looked down three-sided firing lines into a salient packed with enemy troops, while the shell crisis of early 1915 was long since past. Good rail lines on the German side (though not the French) kept ammunition coming. This was to be a victory not by maneuver but hard pounding with steel and high explosives. Falkenhayn expected casualties to be low in the three attacking corps, not knowing that his generals would disobey his orders within hours or days and overcommit the infantry. His best laid schemes had already gone awry in any case. Thanks to a little February snow, the French were alert, reinforced and waiting.

At 7:15 a.m. on February 21, 1916, a steel storm broke over the French. Shells weighing as much as 1,700 pounds flew from huge 380mm cannon some 12–15 miles away, in great parabolic arcs, appearing as black dots that got bigger as they fell out of the sky onto the town and rear areas and cascaded onto the frontline trenches. Only the long-range guns fired to start, marching a barrage of exploding dirt and flame and hot shrapnel showering onto French trenches and forts and the town. By 9:00 a.m. communications to the first trench were cut. During a firing pause, stunned men in robin blue staggered out of the dugouts into strange quiet. Hidden guns were waiting for this moment. Heavy short-range mortars lobbed bombs into stunned infantry. Long-range guns shifted onto targets in the rear, as more infantry assembled. The thunderous roll of over 1,400 cannon went on all day, reaching a crescendo from 4:00 to 5:00 p.m. French guns replied, but many batteries were knocked out by precise opening fire. Other French gunners were forced to huddle for protection against incoming gas shells.[25] Survivors watched in horror as countrymen vanished into a violent squall of exploding steel and dirty snow. Germans cheered as French trenches disappeared beneath a boiling roll of acrid smoke, illuminated from inside by brilliant flashes followed by thunderclaps. Witnesses said it was like a great storm, a line squall churning along the ground. Only there were tens of thousands of men inside. In one half-mile sector just 50 survivors remained from 1,000 men who breakfasted together six hours before. Dead and wounded were everywhere. Bodies or just entrails hung inside torn uniforms in branches of burned-out trees.

In late afternoon, German infantry probes touched the first trench, infiltrating more than assaulting. It was mostly empty of resistance, whole sectors abandoned by the living or full of dead. At 5 p.m. the artillery stopped. In fading February light and hard cold, the infantry attack started. Confident nothing could have lived through the barrage, 80,000 *Feldgrauen* moved forward, farther ranks upright in close order heading for the shattered French line. A long, grey tidal surge, rank upon rank. Storm troopers and combat engineers used acetylene torches to cut any unbroken wire, then grenades and bayonets to finish the last dazed defenders. Shattered French units resisted hand-to-hand with bayonets, grenades and sharpened spades. The onslaught came from elements of three German corps led by elite assault troops. They flanked clusters of cut-off French, eight flamethrower companies spurting liquid fire along zigs and zags and down inside bunkers. It was a terror weapon. Men ran in panic from the flames, toward the second line. Germans turned their own machine guns around to fire into the exposed backs of running men.

The first trench fell inside 30 minutes in A Sector. The second line as well. Reports were sent back to army HQ saying all the French were dead. However, B and C Sectors resisted, fighting out of unbroken woods and fixed machine-gun positions. Only a winter night stopped the killing. It snowed again, gently blanketing immobile wounded slowly bleeding out as the cold prolonged the process. The next morning isolated defenders counterattacked. That only cost more lives. One company of 120 brave French were led forward by a lieutenant with sword held up as if he was Ney at Borodino or Waterloo. They met a storm of steel hail from machine guns and Mauser rifles to pale memories of Prussian rapid-fire with needle-guns at Königgrätz or French chassepots and *mitrailleuses* at Gravelotte.[26] In just minutes, the attack was reduced to lost memories in blue, all killed to no purpose but a boy's childish vanity.

They stopped running from the flamethrowers as snipers shot out the fuel tanks, turning German carriers into human torches with their own weapon. More resistance came from isolated teams of machine guns in broken villages and small forts. Just a few held up whole sections of the great grey wave, until their ammo ran out and the Germans killed them. Over a hard day's night, thousands more wounded froze or bled out all alone, just the second night of 10 months to come of all-out fighting around Verdun. Before it ended 300 days later, three-fourths of the French Army cycled through the battle, marking its *poilus* with shared suffering and France with a memory of terrible national resolve. Ten square miles saw a density of death unmatched by any other World War I battle, unmatched also by Omaha Beach on D-Day or the sands of Iwo Jima or the slopes of Monte Cassino. In 1942 they would call Stalingrad the "Russian Verdun."

Falkenhayn wanted one thing: defensive bloodbath by artillery. His generals moved instead like moths to the flame of battle. They attacked all-out with the infantry, wanting to take the fortresses and flatten the Verdun salient, not sit in a half-moon and fill it with attacking French killed by distant German guns. Falkenhayn's changed operational doctrine had not permeated or persuaded the senior officer corps to abandon its old habit of seeking direct overthrow of the enemy in battle.[27] On the third day, German infantry surged forward. Only now more French batteries were in range, while German guns had trouble moving over the craters they had made earlier. The mobile artillery struggled and fell behind the infantry assault. On the fifth day, Germans reached the outer defenses of Forts Douaumont and Vaux. A tragicomedy ensued when not a shot was fired in defense of Douaumont, as Brandenburger Pioneers (special forces engineers) simply climbed inside a window above the dry moat. Psychologically, it was a key moment. Church bells rang out in Berlin as a national holiday was declared. France was dismayed yet grew grimmer. Some French units resisted to the last man, buying time to rush reserves to the killing fields from all over France. Joffre wanted to withdraw to behind the Meuse, but civilians in Paris said no. Not one inch of sacred soil was to be surrendered. Whatever the cost, it was decided that Verdun must not fall. A place of quiet neglect since the frontier battles of 1914 became the focus of national honor and all-in effort. And so the French Army swallowed Falkenhayn's poison bait. He was going to get his sustained bloodletting, though not in the way he expected or the *Kaiserheer* could long sustain. Already the French had lost 24,000 men in just five days. It would have been a good start for the Germans, except they lost 25,000.[28]

The stage was set for 10 months of carnage at Verdun as the French Army showed the fighting spirit Falkenhayn had counted on to press it in a blood mill. Fresh divisions were hurled into the fight, a seawall of *bleu*-clad bodies to hold back a surging *Feldgrauen* tide. Within days, 200,000 more men were on the way to Verdun, raising the French commitment to nine corps. General Henri-Philippe Pétain was sent to take command. He did not believe in attrition, in fighting raw material power with the bodies of men. He believed in firepower, in artillery. A month earlier, the French Army had issued a directive: "One does not fight matériel with men."[29] So Pétain summoned every gun France could spare from other fronts to come to Verdun to kill Germans, also shifting batteries to a high enfilade position now that German infantry

was massed inside the salient, against Falkenhayn's intentions.[30] Pétain repaired morale with hot food and rapid rotation on short combat leaves out of
the front line, in a constant flow of reserves and rested men. Concern for the
poilus endeared him to the nation. Later, in his dotage as president of Vichy,
his mind and judgment drifted and he collaborated too closely with Nazi occupiers. Not in 1916 at Verdun, where he famously promised France: *On ne
passe pas!* ("They shall not pass!"). It became the signature slogan of French
Army and national defiance of Germany for the rest of the war.

Now began the hard fighting. German attacks with gas and flamethrowers and massed infantry. French counterattacks. Again and again, war without end. The French packed into the 10-square-mile pocket reached half a
million, along with 170,000 horses. Nearly as many Germans arrived on the
other side. Women of both nations worked double shifts making shells, regular and gas-filled, to kill each other's husbands and sons. Munitions work
was a vital part of the war effort and understood as such. It morally entangled
women along with fighting men and made them explicit targets for bombing and attempted starvation by naval blockade. As the shells arrived on the
battlefield, a psychological dynamic took hold. Commanders knew attacks
stood little chance of success but feared that ceasing to attack would cast a
pall over their troops. No one fought for ground, except tactically to take a
fort or woods needed for the next attack. It was all about national prestige
now. The ancient motive of fighting for honor was not removed from war in
the modern world. It was central at Verdun, and indeed the whole of World
War I.[31]

German tactics changed in the midst of battle. *Trommelfeuer* (artillery
bombardment) gave way to infantry assault under generals who attacked
without regard for casualties.[32] The OHL thus drained its reserves, fed into
the *Kessel* fight Falkenhayn started at Verdun to erode French reserves.
Germans started to talk ominously of the *Maasmühle*: the mill on the Meuse
that ground down their men and divisions. It ruined Falkenhayn's plan, for
even if fatal bleeding of the French Army's strategic reserve made it vulnerable to a German offensive, simultaneous bleeding of the German reserve
meant there were no troops available to make the attack. German inferiority
in numbers relative to France and its Allies, already obvious before the war,
only worsened with every passing month. So there was rising talk from generals that the numbers didn't matter. They convinced themselves that their
troops were morally, indeed spiritually, superior as fighting men. After the
war, OHL Operations Officer Gerhard Tappen wrote, "the worth of the individual German soldier was so much greater than the enemy that numbers

alone could not be decisive."[33] It is another signature sign of the short-war delusion when spiritual or moral factors are upheld over weakness in troop numbers or industrial matériel. Confederates did it in the American Civil War ("one good Reb is worth five damn Yankees"). Germans would do it again in World War II. Japanese did it in all wars from 1895 to 1945. Even if it was true to start with, high morale was never decisive in the end. Matériel and manpower exhausted, then crushed, the weaker power.

The key to French success at Verdun was resupply. Fresh corps, food and shells, fodder and horses, everything traveled the last 50 miles on a single-track railway or by light trucks on a narrow second-class road, though one quickly widened to handle more traffic. The internal combustion engine came of age and went to war at Verdun as trucks rolled night and day. At the height of the effort, 6,000 trucks and cars arrived at the terminus every 24 hours, or one every 14 seconds. Discipline was ruthlessly enforced on a no-stops lifeline French called the *Voie Sacrée*—the Holy Road. For ten months it was the pulsing jugular of the French Army: cut it and France would bleed to death. German air power proved not up to the job, as not one bridge over the Meuse was bombed, and the trucks and trains rolled on.[34] Verdun was all about logistics. The Germans missed the point, and the bridges. French air power, on the other hand, played a key role. Once air superiority was established over the battlefield the accuracy of massed artillery (nearly 3,000 French guns by June) markedly improved. German infantry packed into the salient by too-ambitious generals died deaths by shellfire that Falkenhayn had intended for the French.

Fighting swayed back and forth over the same broken terrain, churned to mud and craters by thousands of guns. The same ruins changed hands time and again as assaults washed up to the pitted walls of Douaumont and Vaux and lesser forts, and over key hills like Le Mort-Homme ("Dead Man"), Termite Hill, Côte 265 and Côte 304. Fighting over the hills lasted until May. Hundreds died at Verdun in an hour or a day, replaced by thousands pouring in from all across France and Germany, some as young as 16. They fought with hand grenades from hole to hole, not even really in trenches anymore. Those had been obliterated by the shelling. One day, in a fight that changed nothing, Germany lost 2,400 men, roughly the same count as U.S. dead on D-Day in 1944. Yet where the Allies grabbed a bit of Europe that bloody day and never let go, that many lives spent at Verdun in 1916 bought Germany exactly nothing. Attrition looked an awful lot like annihilation up close, with dead from both sides mixed and minced in the same mud. One French journalist noted of the fighting at Verdun: "Nothing there resembles a proper battle."[35]

This was the Lost Generation, one of many down the annals of war. They were ripped from their lives and fed into combat, torn from the lives of women who bore them or who loved them or whom they loved. Boys' lives were spent like pennies on bitter fruit by pitiless old men, consumed by the Moloch of War, fed into its maw by the ambition and vanity of nations. Among the wounded and captured at Verdun was French Captain Charles de Gaulle. Among the Germans who fought there was young Lieutenant Erwin Rommel. Less famous in later life were millers, carpenters, poets, poultry keepers, bourgeois, workers, schoolteachers in uniform and their students, atheists and devout, and the great majority consisting of plain countryfolk, befuddled peasants whose lives disappeared under pounding by French 75s and German *Trommelfeuer.*

Horses also died. On a single day, 7,000 horses were killed by French guns, 97 by one big shell burst. Many thousands were killed at Verdun, screaming with gaping shrapnel wounds or keeled over from gas, unable to take cover upon hearing the whistle of a falling shell or take heed of a shouted warning or dive into a crater or trench like their drovers. They were too big for shrapnel to miss. Gas masks were made for them from feed bags, but that hardly helped. They were buried in big pits and covered in lime. All life disappeared. No tree stood, no grass grew, no bird sang. Few buildings survived shelling. Poison death hung in the air along with the constant stink of putrefaction. Trying to bury a man often got two more killed. So bodies were rolled into shell craters where more shells halved and quartered them. It was a soldier's battle now. Generals mattered little. Corporals, sergeants and captains mattered more. So did hot soup, which runners carried under shell and sniper fire. For the French a cheap red wine ration, known as *pinard,* was crucial. Runners strapped flasks of it to their legs, delivering even if killed. *Merci. Vive le mort!*

***

AS FRENCH FOUGHT Germans to a standstill over 10 months at Verdun, other Allied armies attacked the Germans on other fronts. The idea was the same as Falkenhayn's, but more strategic than merely operational. First, wear out the German reserve by inflicting (and thus, also taking) high casualties, then try to break through weakened lines to finish the war in the traditional way, by moving, encircling and doing great harm to newly exposed flanks.[36] Italians attacked along the Isonzo front five times in 1916 alone, putting as much strain as they could on the armies of the Central Powers. Fighting scoured the Balkans and Romania and Bulgaria, too.[37] Ottoman and British armies fought in the Middle East in 1916. Cavalry and camel formations advanced or fell back along ancient roads to Jerusalem and Damascus in a war of movement that attracted world attention, mainly by contrast to the stalemated immobility in Europe.[38] Germans also fought a small war in East Africa in 1916, attacking the Allies' imperial periphery.[39] The Russians stunned the Central Powers with their greatest offensive of the war. Starting on June 4, the Brusilov Offensive smashed half the Habsburg army in just 10 days and broke the rest into demoralized fragments held together only by German troops and generals.[40] Europe was drowning in war in 1916. Strange new machines fought each other in its skies, bombed and strafed the ground. Mechanical behemoths crawled in its fields, sinking into mud. Navies starved whole nations with blockade and counterblockade, on and under the seas. Armies killed thousands daily. Everyone and everything was connected to the war.

On June 24, the Allies hit the Germans at the Somme with a massive barrage by 3,300 cannon plus 1,400 trench mortars and naval guns. The barrage lasted a week, hurling over 2.5 million shells onto the German line, though too many were shrapnel that exploded on the surface while leaving bunkers and the Germans inside mostly unharmed. Worse, fully one-third of the British shells failed to explode at all. After seven days of this, British troops went over the top, and lost 19,240 killed and 37,646 wounded on just the first day, July 1, 1916. This was the nadir and culmination of two years of industrial war with no prior experience as guide. However hard the lessons, the British did learn from the Somme and a second slaughter at Passchendaele, and other lessons at Cambrai and Arras. British performance was dramatically improved by late 1917, and superior by 1918.[41] However, the cost of learning was shocking and immense.

Lots of Germans died at the Somme as well. Falkenhayn refused to yield ground and threw in what was left of the *Westheer* reserve. Outnumbered on all fronts, he clung to a brittle doctrine of comparing casualties. "The first principle of position warfare," he said, "must be not to surrender a foot of ground and when ground is lost to throw in even the last man in an immediate counter-attack." Falkenhayn thus did at the Somme what he wanted the French Army to do at Verdun—the *Ausblutung* ("bleeding out") of his own reserves by clinging to every bit of ground. His subcommanders all agreed with this approach. Still, they were startled by the scale and intensity of the matériel battle and by troop losses. Each arriving German division at the Somme was used up within two weeks, putting even more pressure on strained reserves than the slow drain caused by the months longer but less intense fighting at Verdun.[42]

Continuing to fight at Verdun cut the French Army contribution to the Somme offensive from 40 divisions to just 14. Still, over the next four months the equivalent of 166 Allied divisions assaulted 147 divisions of the *Westheer*, an army Falkenhayn now called Germany's "iron wall," not its "iron fist" as it was known earlier in the war. The change from offensive to defensive metaphor was striking. Nor was it just matériel advantages that made the difference. The Allies were also outfighting the Germans in an all-arms battle. If the Somme was not quite a bloody victory for the British Army, it was a significant Allied strategic success in that it wore down German reserves and morale.[43] Britain would raise additional corps and attack again in 1917, but Germany did not have such strength left. Despite the experience of 1914–1915 in Flanders, despite defense-in-depth and an experimental doctrine of attrition-by-artillery at Verdun, the *Kaiserheer* was incapable of sustaining a war of men and matériel on this scale. It suffered 430,000 casualties at the Somme alone, piled atop more butchers' bills from Verdun, the Isonzo front in Italy and the Brusilov Offensive on the Eastern Front.

When the last German attack stalled at Verdun in July, the *Kaiserheer* had nothing left. By August the OHL had only one division in reserve. Falkenhayn went over to defense, only with Germans in the exposed position flailed by French guns on the heights around. He was fired as Chief of Staff on August 29, replaced by the eastern generals, Hindenburg and Ludendorff. The French then went on offense at Verdun, grinding at lost ground, nibbling into the German position month after month. Douaumont was retaken in October, Fort Vaux on November 2. This time, hardly anyone cheered. It ended in December in mutual exhaustion. It was worse than a major battle lost. Along with the Allied relief offensive on the Somme, which was far stronger than Falkenhayn expected, Verdun was a watershed. Casualties at Verdun alone were 337,000 Germans to 377,000 French.[44] Trading men at close to 1:1 was not the calculus Falkenhayn had expected or the *Kaiserheer* could afford. Intended to bleed France to death, the longest fight of 1916 severely hemorrhaged Germany as well. Yet Verdun was only one of many battles that accelerated the wearing out of armies on all sides that crimson year, Germany's most of all.

Verdun was a victory for France, but a Pyrrhic one for the French Army. Mutinies broke out in April 1917 that left it incapable of resuming offensive actions until mid-1918.[45] Luckily, the *Kaiserheer* had so damaged itself it could not take advantage. It was also nearly worn out, with mere boys called up along with cadres of unhealthy and substandard men. It was stretched over too many fronts. As hundreds of thousands of French and Germans died at Verdun, more French and British and Germans bled each other at the Somme, Russians and Germans perished by bushels in the east, and more Germans died fighting Italians in the Isonzo Valley. Germany had only so much blood and reserves of fighting men, and too many enemies. Rather than seek terms as hope of military victory faded into positional fighting, under the hidden dictatorship of Hindenburg and Ludendorff Germany committed everything. There would be no more costly offensives like Verdun, at least not just to look for a limited advantage to get a better chair at the peace conference. No more proposals for minor adjustments to the international order and Germany's status within it. Henceforth it was total war for *Weltmacht oder Niedergang* ("world power or ruin")[46] The eastern generals returned to seeking total victory by direct military means, by sweeping campaigns and envelopments to match Tannenberg and the Masurian Lakes. Hindenburg remained certain even after the war was lost and over that the only way to win had been to stay on offense.[47]

Berlin looked to any means to further this end, including at sea. Stalemate was achieved there, too, as the anticlimactic standoff at Jutland (May 31–June 1, 1916) meant the idea of fighting a decisive naval battle was taken off the table. Some German thinkers had contemplated *Staatskaperei* ("state-approved piracy") before World War I, but the idea was obliterated by Tirpitz's battle-fleet planning. That meant surface ships capable of commerce raiding were too few, too harried by Allied navies, or already sunk, taking away another option.[48] However, the global grain harvest in 1916 was very poor. The German high command hoped that U-boats could take advantage and worsen its effects, bringing starvation to the Allies and cutting Britain off from essential food and fuel.[49]

The urgency of the U-boat plan was established by Admiral Henning von Holtzendorff in a memorandum on December 22, 1916, two weeks after the end of the fight at Verdun: "The war requires a decision before autumn 1917, lest it should end in the mutual exhaustion of all parties and thus be a disaster for us ... If we succeed in breaking England's backbone, the war will immediately be decided in our favor." As for the United States: "Fear of a diplomatic rupture should not lead us to recoil from making use at the decisive moment of a weapon that promises victory for us."[50] A month later the decision was made to resume unrestricted submarine warfare, to strangle Britain with U-boats before American belligerence so tipped the balance of forces that Germany could not win. The United States declared war on April 6. Again, Berlin's policies guaranteed that it would face too many powerful enemies all at once. Again, Germans must win fast and win everything or lose everything in a war of exhaustion: knock out Russia in 1917, defeat France and starve Britain, all before the Americans arrived in sufficient numbers to make a real difference on the Western Front.

Germans managed the first part, knocking Russia out of the war. The tattered end of the 1916 Brusilov Offensive had radicalized many soldiers and tipped them toward mutiny in March 1917, when the tsar abdicated in the first of two revolutions in which his shattered army and soldiers played a major role. Russia was clearly defeated by midsummer, after suffering yet more casualties and mutinous reaction in the ill-advised and failed July or Kerensky Offensive (July 1–16, 1917).[51] Large numbers of soldiers began to refuse orders. Whole units threw down arms. Desertion and disobedience of officers worsened daily. This disintegration of the Russian Army greatly contributed to the Bolshevik Revolution in November that further opened the east to deep German advances. The Russian Army was effectively removed from the Allied order of battle by the end of 1917. This was due to Russian military collapse rather than operational superiority by the Germans, though that is not how smug German staff officers saw it, reported it at OHL, or remembered it later when contemplating a second invasion of Russia in 1941. In the absence of resistance, German armies continued to advance deep into western Russia, until the Bolsheviks finally agreed to an armistice in December. When negotiations stalled in January, they resumed the advance. That forced the Bolsheviks to accept harsh terms at Brest-Litovsk on March 3, 1918.[52] A conqueror's peace ceded to Germany (with smaller bits to Austria) all of Russian Poland and Lithuania, as well as Riga. Ukraine, Finland, Estonia and the rest of Latvia were declared independent states under German military and political protection. Smaller territories went to Romania and the Ottomans. That was 400,000 square miles and 45 million people, about half of European Russia. Also stripped was 50 percent of Russian industry, 90 percent of the broken empire's coal, and all its gold reserves. This crushing settlement was set aside only because Germany lost the war to the Western Allies later that year.

Acting as a hidden military dictatorship, Hindenburg and Ludendorff hardened everything—domestic politics and German war aims.[53] They also reversed the order of the Schlieffen idea, lurching the main military effort back to the east in 1917, aiming to knock Russia out, then return and win in the west in 1918. OHL thus again succumbed to the temptation of offense, to the allure of the next and sure-to-be-decisive campaign that first pulled the *Kaiserheer* westward in 1914, then east in 1915, west in 1916, east again in 1917, and finally back west in 1918, until total military defeat came. The one

Russian trench on Eastern Front (1917).
Courtesy of Wikimedia Creative Commons.

break in the ring of fire in 1916 came from Romania's entry on the Allied side in August, as Bucharest declared war in expectation of rapid and easy victory (who did not?). Instead, in just two months Romania suffered counterinvasion and occupation by two armies comprising units from all four Central Powers, then loss of control of its war effort to Russia.[54] Rather than end the war as the Allies hoped, by tipping the scales against Germany while it was already under all-around attack, Romania's defeat gave Berlin access to food stocks it desperately needed to extend its own military effort into 1918.

It was not just Berlin where views hardened. In France and Britain by election, in Russia by tsarist appointment, fiercer governments took power everywhere from 1916 with promises to pursue the war to a hard finish. The Entente powers matched hardening in Berlin with secret treaties to reduce Austria and break apart the Ottoman Empire, even a wild promise to give Constantinople to Russia. Second Rome (Orthodox Byzantium) was to be absorbed by Third Rome (Orthodox Moscow), in fulfilment of an old Muscovite geopolitical and religious ambition. Then tsarist Russia itself fell apart, into civil war and the hands of revolutionaries who turned violently on all Orthodoxy. Views hardened in Washington, too. Into early 1917, Americans still traded with and scolded everyone. While standing militarily on the sidelines, President Woodrow Wilson too self-righteously called for a "peace without victors" in a war trending toward total in ends and means. Once the United States entered the war that April, it would of course fight for a complete military victory. Afterward, Wilson presided over a victor's peace forced on defeated Germany at the Paris Conference in 1919. That was normal state behavior, once you strip away the self-deluding and high-minded rhetoric: seek to win a war once you are in it, then lock down your victory in the treaty to follow. Even so, none of the Allies contemplated such a diktat as Germany imposed on Russia in March 1918, radicalized war aims far beyond those of 1914 welded into the Treaty of Brest-Litovsk.

Everyone's war aims had changed with lost blood and treasure, as they always do, expanding to make the promised end justify all the past, present and future sacrifice. No one could stop. In some cases, their own peoples might hang them for having gotten into the war if the politicians and generals tried to get out short of victory. The threat of revolution kept conservative elites in several old empires struggling on well past where reason alone might suggest negotiating an end to fighting. Only the new Austrian Emperor, Karl I, tried to negotiate an exit, and he was blocked and humiliated by Conrad, his own government, and the officer class on which the dynasty relied. Political elites could not stop the runaway peoples' war they had started under the short-war delusion of 1914. Nor were they wrong to see their class privileges at stake, even their personal survival. Total war meant total victory or total defeat, and once they were in it they knew that. Why not fight on, then, if all was to be lost otherwise? So fight on they did, and lost everything anyway. As a result of defeat, the Habsburg, Hohenzollern, Ottoman and Romanov dynasties all would be overthrown. The Romanovs would all be killed.

Americans did not arrive in France in large numbers until early 1918. As the doughboys marched briskly down the gangplanks they came without modern artillery and other equipment. The Allies were happy to see them nonetheless, and stepped up to supply what Americans lacked. Out of earshot, some called the new arrival a "beggar army," as it remained dependent on Britain and France for much of its artillery, aircraft, gas, food and horses to the end of the war. Still, just getting oversize American divisions to France, then building out and running a huge supply organization over thousands of miles of sea, was a real contribution. Command of the American Expeditionary Force (AEF) by General John Pershing was another matter. He still clung not just to prewar tactical views but to discredited 19th-century views. He argued that marksmanship and the AEF's old model rifles were a match for German machine guns, insisting also on premature training for a resumption of open warfare, rather than learning how to fight from trenches. The big U.S. Army divisions absorbed heavy casualties as a result.[55]

It is another baleful testament to the appealing power of battle that so late into World War I the arriving Americans insisted on making mass frontal attacks. These were carried out against Allied advice, in the spirit of *élan vital* and prideful conviction that Americans could win fast where the European armies were bogged down. Besides aimed rifle-fire nonsense from Pershing, other American generals underappreciated the role of gas weapons. As a result, AEF soldiers suffered much higher percentages of gas casualties than other Allied troops in the final battles of 1918.[56] A major study persuasively demonstrates that AEF command failures at St. Mihiel and Meuse-Argonne mean it was mass, not combat skill, that was the main American contribution to Allied victory.[57] As one million Americans relieved French armies that summer, the French moved north to prop up the BEF, which was taking heavy casualties in the first two of five German offensives. In addition to sheer numbers of opposing French, German morale suffered from knowledge that more Americans were on the way, some jauntily singing that they were come to France to "pay our debt to Lafayette."[58]

***

AT THE START of 1917 Germany was falling far behind the Allied powers in war production of all kinds, but especially of aircraft, artillery tubes, and the new and battle-changing tanks. Britain and France therefore pulled ahead that year in developing combined arms tactics with aircraft and tank support for infantry looking to exploit a breakthrough and keep moving, deep into the enemy's rear areas. In contrast, German corps lacked enough spotter aircraft to properly coordinate even counterbattery fire, while their artillerymen were too often killed by their own defective guns as well as by their Allied counterparts. Old tubes wore out rifling, reducing accuracy or developed micro-cracks, lethally lowering safety. Munitions and fuse quality also declined.[59] Things only grew worse over another year of fighting, as ever greater disparity of supply began to affect troop morale.

Reformed command and a turn to defensive doctrines and practices along the Western Front looked to preserve German forces and just hold the line there during 1917, while Ludendorff and Hindenburg took other armies on offense in the east in a bid to win by a climactic mobile battle against the Russian Army. Despite success in Russia as the tsarist regime collapsed into a crisis of morale and revolution, by 1918 the *Kaiserheer* was probably capable only of prolonging the war in the west, even while rushing troops to the Western Front from the now quieted Eastern Front. Nevertheless, rather than defend a still strategically forward position and negotiate terms, Germany would try to win in the spring and summer with more massive offensives, preempting the impact of arriving American reinforcements on the Allied side. It would prove too little far too late, an effort to rescue a failed initial strategy that had led to defeat at First Marne and trench warfare ever after. Even so, the pull of the decisive battle *still* drew German military imagination onto operational offense, beyond any reasonable hope of strategic success.

The Allies felt it, too, the differing pull of the desire to win and the growing weight of losing so many men each time they tried. The Nivelle Offensive (April 1–24, 1917) ended in another blunted failure to break through, provoking mutinies in several divisions of the French Army. The troops did not run, but they refused to attack. It took Pétain many months to repair the damage, in time for the major battles of 1918. The British took up the slack despite their grim experience at Passchendaele, or Third Ypres, from October to November 1917. To many ordinary British soldiers who fought once more in the Ypres salient, and to Prime Minister Lloyd George and others who watched them do it and were appalled, it seemed just more bloody-minded, worn-out failure by unimaginative leaders in the field. Siegfried Sassoon wrote of it:

"I died in Hell—
(They called it Passchendaele). My wound was slight,
And I was hobbling back; and then a shell
Burst slick upon the duck-boards; so I fell
Into the bottomless mud, and lost the light."[60]

General Douglas Haig later claimed Third Ypres had a great impact on the *Kaiserheer*, delivering essential wearing down of its reserves. While it is true that hard battlefield lessons learned there and other places in 1917 helped shape Allied victory a year later, such talk about the relative effects of mass dying did not inspire fighting men or assure their worried families and government that the generals knew what they were doing.

Everyone tested new breakout tactics in 1917. Since the Allies had more resources, they did it better. Poison gas was always meant to restore movement to the battlefield, a role in which it failed; then it deteriorated into just another means of killing. Whereas tanks eventually worked to restore mobility, gas only added horror and suffering to soldiers' daily lives during harassing shelling, or in a preliminary bombardment. Still, it was available in large quantities, so both sides used it to the end of the war. Allied superiority in tanks and aircraft was a far more important technological advantage. Tanks provided a critical mass of mobile firepower once the Allies figured out how to maximize them in keeping a breakthrough going, while air superiority gave them advantages of target-spotting and long-range indirect artillery fire. Scouting from the air resumed critical importance as the armies rose out of the trenches and began to move again in 1918, with aircraft also advancing to tactical bombing and ground-strafing roles.

Heading into the final offensives of 1918, the British Army developed innovative small unit tactics that employed enhanced firepower with Lewis guns, rifle grenades and mortars. This allowed platoon-sized units to fight their way ahead, supported where possible by armored cars and lighter and faster Whippet tanks. The French Army also performed much better in 1918, as it recovered from the mutinies and morale crisis brought on by the Nivelle Offensive.[61] For three years the British and French had fought parallel wars, a prideful practice contributing to repeated operational failure. Finally, they agreed to fight under a unified supreme command. Victory was achieved only after they forged this more effective fighting partnership, after years of command friction and minimal cooperation.[62] That allowed huge advantages in war production, population, logistics and mechanization finally to be brought to bear under the able command of Ferdinand Foch. A unified command, superior production and improved logistics (with an increasing shift from horse power to motorized and mechanized transport), advanced the Allies toward victory in 1918. By then, the German armed forces were all but worn out, and severely outgunned and outnumbered.[63] In 1918 the number of troops in leading combat units were easily exceeded by those in the logistical tails of Allied armies. Again, the *Kaiserheer* could not compete. It was stretched on all fronts, and from the end of 1917 it faced stiffening competition for recruits from German domestic industry.[64]

Germany was also losing the war at the level of technology and basic production. World War I began as two key technological shifts were under way. First, mechanization of weapons accelerated the firepower revolution that began in the 19th century, greatly increasing killing ranges and lethality and thereby reinforcing already impressive advantages of defense in positional war. At the same time, human and animal muscle power was giving way to machine power. Under the pressures of wartime spending and innovation, this led in the last two years of the war to restoration of mobility in Allied armies by tank, tractor, truck and aircraft. What tipped the technological balance to the Allies further and faster was better wartime management. The Germans failed to match that organizational skill, in what was also a hugely uneven war of matériel. By 1918 the Allies integrated new technologies in innovative combined arms doctrine, better training and a unified command. The results were a late-war surge in the size and confidence of British Army operations, in particular. American divisions poured into France and started to learn how to fight in new ways. The French Army reemerged from refitting after the mutinies of 1917 into a revival in morale and high performance in combat. Even with the Russian Army knocked out of the war, all this gathering Western Allied strength was too much for increasingly ragged German troops and armies.

On the other hand, the Germans had an offensive system developed by, and informally named for, General Oskar von Hutier. His infiltration tactics were developed on the Eastern Front, then brought to the Western Front in 1918.[65] They rejected Allied-style frontal assaults after long artillery preparation in favor of shorter bombardments and attacks led by *Sturmtruppen* ("assault troops"). Instead of rifles, elite lead infantry used close-assault weapons (grenades, flamethrowers, pistols) to infiltrate through, rather than try to storm over, opposing trenches. They bypassed strongpoints under orders to maintain momentum of attack, pressing deep into rear positions to sow panic and confusion, and to disrupt communications and delay reinforcement. They left heavy bunkers and machine gun nests behind for the regular infantry that followed to isolate and take care of. These assault tactics proved quite successful, but they were not enough.

By 1918 everyone knew how to break through enemy trenches, whether by Hutier tactics, innovative British Army small unit tactics or French combined arms assaults with tanks and aircraft.[66] The key difference was that Allied armies and generals now had the numbers and resources to make their technological innovations and tactical systems work on a war-winning and not just battle-winning scale. Germans did not. As a despondent Paul Baumer notes in *All Quiet on the Western Front*: "For every one German plane there come at least five English and American. For one hungry, wretched German soldier come five of the enemy, fresh and fit. For one German army loaf there are fifty tins of canned beef over there. We are not beaten, for as soldiers we are better and more experienced: we are simply crushed and driven back by overwhelming superior forces."[67] Except they were *not* superior soldiers to the Allies in 1918, and the whole German Army was about to be beaten thoroughly and decisively in a return of the war of movement.

It helped the Allies greatly that Ludendorff attacked. It was what German generals and governments always did in hopeless situations, to try to salvage an impossible problem of their own making with an operational tour de force divorced from real strategic purpose. They would do it again from the first day of the next war, blundering to early strange victories that surprised even them before staggering to certain defeat that surprised almost no one. In the last campaigns of World War I, Ludendorff's political ascendancy and military primacy was a great burden. So, too, was the disconnected concept his operations repeated and typified. His pretentiously titled "grand operational scheme" for 1918 in the west comprised five major *Kaiserschlacht* spring and summer offensives. These achieved initial breakthrough and restored limited movement, but without a strategic goal and to no higher end, because they lacked objectives beyond the merely local and tactical. He created no fresh military facts that might either decide the war for Germany by winning it or ease terms in peace negotiations when it lost. The assaults penetrated the enemy's trenches and pushed back Allied armies, but to no larger purpose. Behind them lay only a vain hope that some follow-on opportunity might develop that could then be exploited to make more gains, still without a guiding strategic direction or result. Such lack of connection between operations and strategy expressed all that was wrong with the German war effort from the very start, and with the silent dictatorship of the generals at the end. What made this last effort truly fantastical was that Ludendorff still clung to belief in total victory. His only conception of peace was world power status for

Germany achieved via his own operational virtuosity, and that of German armies. When he was done, the *Landser* he led so badly held more territory in France yet were farther than ever from victory. Overextended and fought out, facing overwhelming enemy numbers, their morale finally cracked and they broke.

The tale is quickly told. Ludendorff identified and attacked the British Army as the main *Schwerpunkt* ("focus of effort") of his first two offensives, badly damaging the British before French reinforcements shored up the broken sector. In turn, French support to the British was made possible by Americans taking over French sectors in the Argonne. Ludendorff decided he needed to cut off that supply of support before finishing the British, so he switched to attack the French in his next two offensives. It was a major error that dispersed effort to no effect and let the severely battered British Army recover. His fifth offensive, the last ever made by the *Kaiserheer*, so completely lacked focus it ended after just four days.[68] Germany had spent all its reserves of men, morale and matériel, and was left in a worse strategic position. Taking more territory only created more miles of trench to defend with fewer men, while putting casualty-reduced corps into several vulnerable salients now subjected to Allied attack from three sides. Failure also demoralized soldiers whose will began to falter as they faced larger and better-armed Allied counteroffensives from midsummer, and an endless vista of reinforcement.[69]

In contrast, Foch coordinated follow-on Allied counteroffensives that began on July 18 and succeeded far beyond anticipation, regaining strategic initiative for the Allies and leading directly to victory by November. A much recovered French Army resumed its lead place in the Allied order of battle and as the principal instrument of German defeat in World War I. Over the course of the war the French Army did most of the Allied fighting and dying, and the French economy produced a good portion of overall Allied war matériel. France now provided operational and strategic direction to all other Allies, while American, British and Commonwealth armies accepted Foch as supreme commander as he ordered preparation for multiple assaults on Germany's last armies. His war-winning leadership made full use of overwhelming matériel and troop advantages to win by what might be called grand attrition, to end the war of *longue durée* by engaging and wearing out the German enemy at an accelerated rate.[70] All senior commanders (except the supremely self-confident Haig) were ready for another long winter and year or two more of combat. Instead, Foch provided the direction and leadership needed to win in 1918, a year earlier than expected, by collapsing the

German salients left naked to defeat by Ludendorff's feckless offensives.[71] When the salients broke, so did morale.

Ludendorff was a doctrinal Luddite who led the *Kaiserheer* to irredeemable defeat and then lied about it to his last days, throwing his name and support to Hitler and the Nazis, who also purveyed the "stab-in-the-back" myth after the war that denied Germany's military defeat in 1918. Foch was no Luddite, clinging to comparably outdated French doctrine. He evolved from a prewar belief in *élan vital* and aggressive offense in almost any circumstance. He learned to reduce casualties through a more technological and methodological attack in 1918.[72] Verdun taught him and the French Army that firepower could be substituted for bodies, but also that competitive killing could be turned back on the Germans in ways French theorists never thought possible before 1914, when they worried over France's permanent demographic disadvantage.[73] Nor did Foch "wait for the Americans and the tanks," as Pétain once reputedly said. Even Pétain didn't wait. French generals instead retrained the *poilus* in combined arms tactics and mobile operations. As fresh infantry arrived ill-equipped from across the Atlantic, they also supplied the Americans with heavy weapons and specialist troops and advisers, sometimes at the expense of their own divisions. Then they handed over chunks of the trench line in the Argonne and Ardennes forests, shifting corps north and west to relieve the British Army from its hard pounding. It was a true Allied effort.

The last Allied campaigns were marked by a compromise between the old step-by-step approach and blunter breakthrough tactics using tanks and aircraft. It was crucial that the new combined arms methods accepted attrition as an inescapable part of modern war, necessary to victory. But now mass casualties were encased in a revival of maneuver made possible by new weapons, better command and control, and genuine Allied cooperation from the tactical to the high command level. Allied armies ended the war with winning campaigns of open maneuver facilitated by wireless communications, better tactics and more mobile and lethal weapons, from gas to light tanks to better bombs and shells.[74] Thus, the first big American attack went in at Cantigny (May 28–31) well supported by French flamethrower troops, heavy tanks, aircraft and artillery.[75] Allied success did not take place in isolation from German exhaustion. A dynamic interaction of opposites accelerated Allied advances and German military collapse past what either side anticipated when the summer fighting began. The quick and catastrophic collapse of the *Kaiserheer* surprised everyone from Allied commanders and governments to ordinary German soldiers, many of whom *never* accepted that they lost the war.

Allied victory in 1918 was not, as Paul Baumer believed, only a triumph of technology and war matériel over German inadequacy in both. It also resulted from British tactical innovation, French tenacity in holding the lion's share of the front for years, and the margin of victory in troop numbers provided by late-arriving Americans. France mobilized at least 8.5 million men from a population of just 38 million. They died at a rate close to 900 per day over 1,560 days of war, for a total of 1.4 million killed and nearly 4 million more wounded. (Equivalent American casualties would have been 14 million from a population of 110 million.) The British started by sending a small expeditionary force rather than an army to France in 1914. By 1918 the British Army had raised millions of men, but was still outnumbered 5:9 by French troops in the field. When fighting stopped that November the AEF was still arriving, training and cooperating most closely with the French Army, including in several attacks against German salients.[76] The AEF was just approaching full fighting capability when the war abruptly ended. In sum, fighting on the Western Front was from start to end mainly a clash of Franco-German armies, with important British and Commonwealth forces in support. Late-arriving American resources and manpower helped to tip the final balance in a true Allied effort and victory over a tattered and by the end also ill-led enemy.[77] The debt owed to French resolve is enormous. That said, all the Allies, including also Canadians and Indians and ANZACs and many others, fought bravely and paid a high price in blood and treasure.

Germany's soldiers also fought bravely and well, but Germany lost World War I at all levels. Soon after the Armistice of November 11, 1918, its men started walking back to their homes. They were not done fighting even so. Some joined the *Freikorps* ("Free Corps"), private armies of veterans or right-wing militia that fought on the eastern border against a revived Poland. All were told they had not lost the *Weltkrieg*, and many believed it. This was the *Dolchstoss* myth, that German fighting men were not defeated but were "stabbed in the back" by socialists and Jews who took down the Reich and set up Weimar, by the "November criminals," as Hitler called these mythical traitors. Nor did the Armistice end fighting elsewhere. For years afterward an arc of violence flared down the western frontiers of the old Russian empire, from Finland to the Baltic states, Poland, Ukraine and Azerbaijan. From there war continued across the Middle East, where the Ottomans had been defeated, a second collapsing empire leaving former provinces to scramble and fight new masters and each other in bloody quarrels over where to draw disputed borders and how or whether to legitimize successor regimes.[78] It happened again after World War II, as hidden fighting continued in the western Soviet Union and in Yugoslavia, resumed openly in Greece, and in China on an immense scale, scoured Southeast Asia, and broke out in India as more overseas empires cracked and shattered from their great military effort or defeat in Europe. The two world wars broke so much of the old order that they were not easily or quickly ended even after total defeat was twice visited on the principal aggressor, Germany.

The common view that the mass armies that crashed into each other in the summer and fall of 1914 failed to learn anything in the years of trench fighting after that is wrong. The war was not just a tale of working class lions and *Landser* and *poilus* in the trenches badly served by donkey or Junker or *château* generals. The first open-field battles were indeed catastrophic, seeing the highest casualty rates of the entire 52-month war. They were fought in the case of Habsburg armies by massed infantry forced to fight with 19th-century close-order tactics that led to their abject slaughter.[79] However, other than Conrad, who mishandled Habsburg armies right to the end, generals did not forever lack the vision or intelligence to adapt once their prewar tactics failed or were stalemated.

The response by all major armies was to adapt to the reality of trench warfare by developing new and effective combat doctrine and deploying into formidable defense-in-depth in fighting, fire support and logistics systems.[80] This was a considerable success for officer class adaptation to *defensive* warfare that is perhaps too often overshadowed by a fixed attention to failed offense, to restoring movement to battle. As movement expired with disappearance of any flanks in late 1914, except in the east, soldiers dug to get under the machine guns and shrapnel, then the High Commands gave them the tools to dig deeper and farther back, defending themselves with wire and a depth of trench systems that attackers could not easily penetrate or exploit. It also happened because the armies of Europe had histories of positional war dating to the 17th century and quickly fell back on these traditions and methods. In an odd way, it was also because in some sense they all saw it coming. All the belligerent armies of 1914 foresaw some form of trench warfare (fighting from field fortifications) awaiting them if their short-war plans failed, as every single one did.[81] That is precisely why the generals and even more their governments succumbed to the quick-war illusion in the first place. It was always a desperate hope over likely reality.

German armies in France and Flanders only looked upright at the end to veterans who felt themselves unbeaten, still standing in foreign fields. In

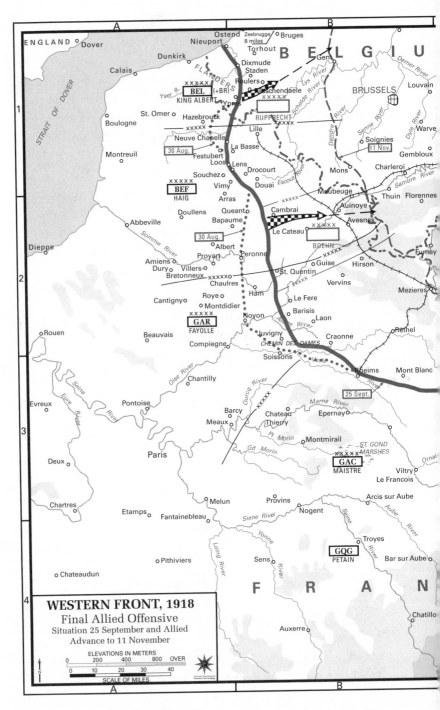

Western Front, 100 Days Campaign, 1918.

Courtesy of the Department of History, United States Military Academy at West Point. Redraw
by George Chakvetadze.

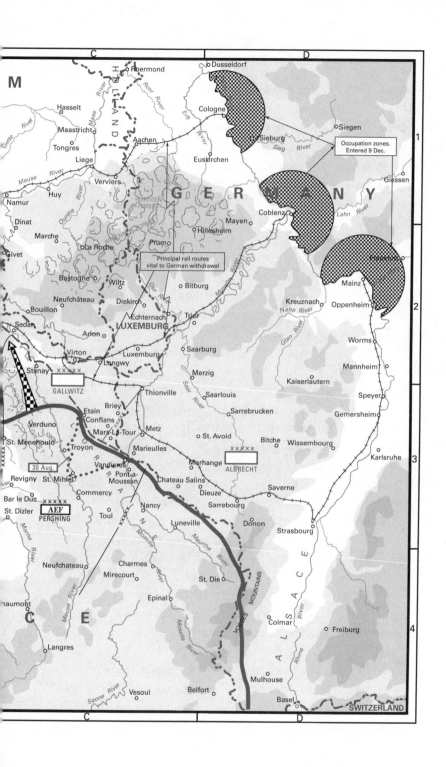

fact, the *Kaiserheer* was finished, later Ludendorff or *Freikorps* and *Dolchstoss* denials notwithstanding. Morale had collapsed, and with it most military effort, taking the form of a hidden military strike in German field armies over the last months of the war.[82] It was not that German troops were in a mood for mutiny or revolution. They were simply worn out and wanted to stop fighting, wanted peace in whatever form that might take. German soldiers did more for longer than probably any other army could have achieved. They won many battles. But they lost even more, and nearly all the important ones. They were exhausted by a war of numbers and matériel their country could never match, over so long a period that their enemies overcame an initial German tactical advantage designed for a short war, to defeat them up and down the full spectrum of combat and total war. German leaders did not deserve the service and loyalty they received from the ordinary *Landser*. Worse, no basic lesson was learned. The last futile offensives lost by the *Kaiserheer* pointed to the way successor German armies would also lose World War II in the end, in basic separation of vaunted tactical and operational dexterity from any guiding strategy to win a war against an enemy that overmatched them in numbers and matériel from the start.

Before it was over in 1918 the main Austrian and Russian armies also fell apart, as did the principal Italian army before recovering with Allied help. The U.S. Army had exactly the opposite experience. It was learning to discard outdated ideas rooted in its small 19th-century wars, and how to fight in the new total-war way, when the fighting ended just before its newly acquired battle skill could be put into full effect. The British Army was shattered twice, at Mons in 1914 and by the first two spring *Kaiserschlacht* offensives. However, in 1918 it had the real strength to recover and then join the Allied attack, fighting to victory in its final or Hundred Days campaign (July 18– November 11). Even so, the British Army was buckled just below the surface when the Armistice bells rang out.[83] Germany's great nemesis, the French Army, also staggered home to victory. Its long ranks of enduring *poilus* were nearly done in as they crossed the finish line on Armistice Day, exhausted like marathon runners in a high midsummer's race and heat.[84] For all that, the proud *poilus* and their nation had won the war, and they knew it.

Now they had to watch as politicians wasted the peace. The statesmen who met in Paris left the Great War's key question unanswered in the treaties they made, so that a second and more terrible war had to be fought, full of worse horrors than poison gas and troglodyte trenches, with more science and industry turned to destruction, more mass killing and learned hate. The incomplete outcome of what H. G. Wells had hoped in 1914 would be "the war that will end war" led instead to a second world war 20 years later.[85] The politicians and diplomats who gathered at Paris to craft peace and redraw the borders of broken empires and emergent nations abjectly failed. They did not frame what was a total military defeat of Imperial Germany achieved by Allied armies in ways the German people would accept and German leaders could endorse. Instead, the verdict of defeat that should have been delivered to Germans was dismissed, vacated by lack of clarity in the settlement and by the grand lies the generals and other German leaders told about the depth of their nation's and army's defeat, and their own responsibility for it. That meant World War I was completely indecisive on the only issue that truly mattered: Germany's voluntary or coerced willingness to curtail an ambition to dominance and to *Weltmacht,* to accept a more limited place in the extant international system. The Allies would not make the same mistake in 1945, once forced by German ambition and aggression to do it all over again at a much higher cost. To bring the fact of a second utter and crushing military defeat home, to persuade Germans to forgo war as an instrument of national greatness, their cities would be deliberately and methodically incinerated, their *Heimat* invaded, truncated, divided and occupied for nearly half a century.

13

Annihilation of Nations

THE ARTIFICIAL THUNDER heard along the horizon stopped in 1918, but what came afterward was not peace. Marshall Foch predicted in 1919 that the Treaty of Versailles signed by the Allies and Germany would be no more than "an armistice for twenty years."[1] He was exactly right. So was Charles de Gaulle, who later identified the two world wars as the Thirty Years' War of the 20th century. The ambition to *Weltmacht* of Germany's leaders was the keystone in the arch of total war that started in 1914 and in a real sense did not end until 1945. Once again, German leaders drew short-war lessons from their early victories at the expense of understanding the long-war lessons of their defeats. A terrible price would have to be paid by Allied populations for failure of their diplomats to secure the victory of their generals and soldiers, and by Germans for refusing to recognize the measure and magnitude of their defeat.[2] A second world war, truly total in the means and objectives of mass destruction, would have to be fought to render war's decision on Germany's excessive national ambition. To bring about its ruin.

Nearly all the little nations that managed to stay neutral in 1914 would be dragged in this time. Hitler annexed Austria and the Sudetenland from Czechoslovakia in 1938, without any shooting and with full Italian, British and French acquiescence. Then he invaded the rest of broken Czechoslovakia in early 1939. Finally the West stiffened, but it was too late to prevent the Nazis partnering with the Soviets to invade and partition Poland and divide and occupy the Baltic states that September and October. Over the next few months the Soviet Union attacked and annexed parts of Finland. It took more territory from Romania, and threatened several other small states. Germany invaded Denmark and Norway, with covert Soviet assistance, in April 1940. Next came invasions—all on the same day, May 10, 1940—of Luxemburg, the Netherlands, Belgium and France. Panzers rolled into Greece, and shattered Yugoslavia in April 1941. With the British in full retreat from Greece, *Fallschirmjäger* (German paratroopers) fell on Crete and drove the last

British troops off the continent altogether, their fourth evacuation in a year. Hitler and his lesser fascist allies controlled or occupied all of Europe, from the Atlantic to the Vistula, from the Baltic to the Mediterranean. His southern flank secured, Hitler readied to turn his forces east.

The war's cause and center was always Nazi Germany's radicalized ambition, but other aggressors moved to take advantage of the defeat of France and the weakening of Britain in 1940. Italy invaded the East African colonies of Kenya, Somaliland and Sudan as the war spread along the configuration of French and British colonies to East and West Africa, as well as along the world sea lanes to the Indian Ocean and the coastline of the Americas. Free French forces secured a toehold in West Africa and turned north, even as Italians contested with British and Commonwealth forces across East Africa. More Axis armies marauded over North Africa, as far east as Algeria and as far west as Egypt, threatening the Suez Canal. A pro-Axis coup in Iraq led to British intervention to stop a German takeover, while Free French troops invaded next-door Syria. Japan took the chance to move south out of its bases in China into French Indochina, positioning for the bigger strikes to come at the end of 1941. Its already strained relations with the United States were severely damaged, their deterioration accelerating toward war.

Half a world on fire, yet these were all peripheral actions, as was made clear when the whole center of the war shifted in the middle of 1941 as Hitler sent the Wehrmacht (the renamed German military)[3] and other Axis armies into the Soviet Union. Thereafter, the center of gravity of World War II and the main theater of fighting and decision moved to the bloodlands of central Europe and western Soviet Union. Italy, Finland, Bulgaria, Romania and Hungary were enticed or coerced into the fight that quickly engulfed and overran Belorussia, Ukraine and the Caucasus. No one could stay out, or not for long. Invasion, submission and collaboration, but also local and opportunistic aggression, overcame more states as the war spread to new regions and reached new depths of savagery.[4] It took on a special viciousness and murderous quality not seen even in the Great War, beyond benighted places like Armenia, as the conquerors began to implement extraordinary measures of race identification, separation, starvation and extermination.

A separate war in Asia started by the Japanese invasion of China in 1937 pulled in most of the smaller Asian nations before it ended in 1945. However, the China War, or Second Sino-Japanese War, was not initially linked to the war in Europe despite Japan's joining the Axis with Italy and Germany. It was the Pearl Harbor attack on December 7, 1941, and other attacks on British holdings in Hong Kong and Malaya, that altered the nature of the war in Asia, spreading Japanese forces from China into the Pacific Ocean. As importantly, it linked what had been a regional war in Asia strategically to the war in Europe when Germany and Italy declared war on the United States four days later.[5] Discrete Asian and European wars thereafter joined as a true world war, connected by American bridges over the Atlantic and Pacific Oceans made of an outpouring of war matériel, aircraft, armies and fleets. Japan followed up its initial successes by invading Burma, Malaya, the Dutch East Indies and the Philippines in the first months of 1942, also occupying far-flung island chains across the central and south Pacific. By the end of the year, however, Japan was pushed back into a perimeter defense, with only occasional offensive forays after that inside Burma and China. Parallel campaigns were fought by Japan and its enemies across the Pacific and in China and Burma until the end in 1945.

***

IN THE AFTERMATH of the shattering of the old order, brutalized societies replaced discarded or failed civilizations as criminal gangs heading radical political parties took power in several major capitals, first Moscow in 1918, then Rome in 1922 and Berlin in 1933. Lesser criminal gangs held power in lesser capitals, with political violence associated with radical mass parties nearly endemic. Vicious new secular ideologies celebrated state terror enforced by terror police, moving on to institutionalized mass murder and, both before and during the next war, to multiple class, ethnic and religious genocides. Bizarre new cults of personality upheld the warlords Hitler and Stalin as tyrant-generals. Even the more decent of the major belligerents would escalate from slaughtering youths in uniform in World War I to slaughtering "enemy civilians" in World War II, employing that signature term of the plunge into a lawless war where everyone on the far side of a gun or bombsight was deemed a potential and legitimate target. Before it ended, all Great Powers descended into totality of means in a much larger war fought to decide not just where to redraw borders or to exchange provinces among empires, but whether entire peoples would be destroyed and disappear from history and the world. World War II killed not 10 million, as did World War I, but 65 million or more in a war of unbridled exterminations. It was an absolute war of the peoples, with destruction and calculated mass murder unprecedented in scale and means.

All the major belligerents in World War II returned to starvation as a major instrument of policy and of their war effort, whether by naval blockades or direct food confiscations. The war led to malnutrition and starvation across much of Europe and Asia, including millions of dead from a famine in Bengal and another in Henan.[6] There was the Hunger Winter in the Netherlands, cannibalism in Leningrad and more in rural China. The Germans carried out a planned starvation of three million Red Army prisoners in 1941–1942, and millions more whom the Nazis deemed "useless eaters" and therefore refused to feed in a score of occupied countries. That was the prelude to forced clearances of unwanted populations, itself the prelude to postwar plans to colonize conquered and depopulated lands with racially verified ethnic Germans (*Volksdeutsche*). The final plan was for vast eugenically managed slave holdings ruled by a baronial class drawn from the top ranks of the Nazi Party and Wehrmacht, partitioning whole countries emptied by starvation or more active extermination of their prewar and historic peoples. It was the most radical set of final aims in the history of war.

Already during the war, slavery unto death came to Axis-occupied Europe. This was Hitler's real war, the war against peoples, which he believed in more than the war of borders and empires. He believed above all in *Rassenkrieg* (race war) in pursuit of a social and racial agenda so radical that concentration camps were set up specifically for children and women, and others for Roma and Jews. *Einsatzgruppen* (Special Task Forces) sent out as death battalions began the killings immediately, in Poland and later in the Soviet Union. Their tally of murders was surpassed by industrial-scale, purpose-built death camps of the Shoah, once the decision for total genocide was made. Smaller genocides of other minority peoples took place from the Baltic to the Caucasus. Too often overlooked are the abattoirs of Stalin's Gulag and a half-dozen little holocausts inside the Soviet Union by means of mass deportation and executions by the NKVD of whole "suspect minorities." More ideological-ethnic killing in Yugoslavia was partly covered over by partisan and civil wars. That was also true in Ukraine, Poland, Southeast Asia and China, and sundry other places that fell under Axis invasion and occupation or into vicious local civil wars fought inside World War II.

Surrendered soldiers were often killed outright, or during death marches or in prison camps or in forced labor battalions. Whole captive armies from France (1940) and Italy (1943) were deported to Germany, kept there as hostages against the behavior of their home countries. POWs were used as forced laborers by Imperial Japan and Nazi Germany. Axis prisoners were abused on a large-scale by the Soviet Union, where some Germans and Japanese were held for as long as a decade after the war. Terror police or uniformed party thugs and murderers were ubiquitous: Gestapo, Iron Guard, *squadristi*, OVRA, *Ustaše, Milice*, Arrow Cross, *Kempeitai*, NKVD, and others. The

Rape of Nanjing was a milestone in massacres of prisoners and civilians by the Japanese Army, marking a trail of atrocities that stretched across China, and later from Malaya to Manila. On the Bataan Death March and the "railway of death" the end for Allied POWs came slowly from daily beatings and starvation, or suddenly with beheadings and bayonets. Worse death marches of POWs and death camp inmates and hundreds of thousands of civilians took place in Hungary and Prussia and elsewhere just before the end.[7]

It cannot be seriously argued that there was moral equivalence between the two opposing alliances. However, it is essential to understand that a general deterioration in standards of wartime behavior did take place. Indiscriminate war at sea began on the first day, with a U-boat sinking of a passenger liner. It was continued by Axis and Allied navies alike, as part of mutual efforts at national blockades intended not just to interrupt commerce but to induce mass privation and starvation. "Butcher and bolt" commando raids came from the Allied side, while a deepening cult of death drove expanded suicide tactics and worse atrocities by the Axis. Several armies carried out mass shootings of tens of thousands of their own troops, the Red Army continuing to do so after the war ended when it recovered POWs who surrendered during the first year of the German invasion. Many men who somehow survived for years in Nazi prison camps were liberated only to be arrested and shot in Soviet camps, or confined for more years of forced labor. Indiscriminate war from the air also began on the first day, with the bombing of Polish cities and strafing of refugee columns. Before the war ended there was universal embrace of policies of terror bombing stretching from Poland to Stalingrad, from Dresden to Tokyo and Nagasaki. Civilians were not just killed as collateral damage in precision attacks that went awry, they were deliberately targeted in "morale bombing." By the end, Western Allied crews and policy destroyed 120 cities in Germany and 62 more in Japan, as firestorms reduced buildings and people to ash under incendiaries seeded by the air forces of the democratic nations. Barbarism gripped all the world. For a dread moment civilization stopped, untenable and unaffordable until the brutal fight was won.

***

THE FEARED SCENARIO of the interwar years in France was a militarily revived Germany with weakened neighbors on its southern and eastern frontiers and a strong but isolated France left alone to confront Berlin's revanchist intentions. Among the Great Powers in the war-winning coalition of 1914–1918, from 1923 only France struggled to contain Germany. It was abandoned in that critical effort by now isolationist former allies, as Britain,

Russia and the United States all withdrew into their own affairs in the 1920s. Fortification of its border as an enhancer of terrain effects and as a force-multiplier of the defenders inside made perfect sense. Forts would push German armies away from direct invasion via Alsace-Lorraine, forcing them to the far flanks. Since the Alps were impassable by huge modern armies, the Germans would be channeled north into the Low Countries, onto the old Schlieffen route, where this time they would be halted among the Belgian forests and Dutch polders by a powerful Allied strike force. If the *Westheer*, the German army on the Western Front, tried a surprise attack via the more direct route, border forts would at least delay it while France mobilized. Finally, fortification would permit a bolder strategy of concentration of the best and most mobile divisions for counterattacking into Belgium.

Fortifying the frontiers also took into account a crucial demographic inferiority that would be exacerbated by the coming "hollow years" (*années creuses*, or *classes creuses*) of 1914–1918. Starting in 1933, recruitment into the French Army would shrink dramatically due to missing sons from 1914–1918, when the French birthrate fell by almost 50 percent. Fortified defense took fewer men than field armies, and fewer men were on the way. Major fortification was proposed by Joffre and Pétain in the 1920s, but opposed by young mobile-warfare advocates such as Charles de Gaulle and many Third Republic politicians. Finally, the debate ended and the Maginot Line was built. Named for Minister of War André Maginot, who had been wounded at Verdun in 1916, it was constructed in phases between 1930 and 1939. The main fortifications on the northeast frontier with Germany included 22 large (mostly underground) fortresses and garrisons and 36 smaller ones. All were connected by lines of blockhouses, bunkers, hardened machine-gun nests, and connective rail lines. It was a reprise of the *Ne Plus Ultra* and of the trenches of 1914–1918, all in one. However, the Great Depression reduced plans to build the expensive armored strike force that was an essential component of the Maginot Line strategic concept.[8]

In France there was no longer any belief in a decisive battle of the sort Joffre went looking for in Belgium in August 1914, before fighting in more desperate circumstances but to success along the Marne. Offense was not in France's interest as a satisfied and status quo power. It was also beyond France's military abilities. Germany had too great an advantage in numbers, the Soviets were deep into radical isolationism and closed to a revival of the old Franco-Russian entente, and the British had disarmed on land back to pre-1914 levels and were perpetually several years away from rebuilding the million-man armies of 1916 to 1918 that were crucial to Allied victory. British alliance was assumed, given the geopolitical realities of the continent in the 1930s, but not formally assured by treaty. Nor could Americans be counted on to help defend international order against challenges from the fascist states, as they had pulled all troops out of Europe in the early 1920s and drew even farther back from all international security commitments when the Depression widened and deepened. France was pretty much left on its own as Hitler came to power and set out to revive German military capability to fit his expansive ambitions.

Paris planned a strong defense force of 90 divisions, supplemented by 12 Belgian divisions. Then it fortified its Alsatian frontier, not to hunker in fear but to free mobile armored and mechanized units to concentrate in a strike force farther north. The French Army was looking for something like a replay of the victory at First Marne, only it meant to hold along its own frontiers so that its best units could fight next time elsewhere than on the soil of France. Rather than any quick-war delusions, during the 1930s French planners anticipated a long war against a revived Germany. They knew they would need to tap into the resources of both the French and British Empires, and a larger alliance beyond that. They planned to mobilize for slow victory after withstanding the *furia Germanica* of a direct assault by the Wehrmacht.[9] The French Army believed it must hold at the start while waiting, again, for a small symbolic BEF to grow into a powerful multimillion-man British Army, backed by industrial mobilization of the world's foremost empire. Once the sounds of war and invasion forced cooperation with Paris by Brussels, mobility would be the key to quickly deploying from behind neutral Belgium's southern border with France to its border with Germany. Let Germans batter *their* army against a strong and fortified defense. The Maginot Line would hold as the strong right flank while mobile French armies, heavy in modern aircraft, tanks and artillery, moved speedily into Belgium. In two years or less, according to the planners, the Western Allies would face a Wehrmacht that would be badly weakened by blockade and bombing of its strategic assets and war factories. Meanwhile, geared-up Allied war economies would greatly outproduce Germany's and supply more advanced weapons to millions of fully trained conscripts from two world-straddling empires. At that point, the Allies would be ready to emerge from positional defenses on the Belgian and French frontiers and go on offense into Germany, where they would win the war.[10]

In sum, by the mid-1930s the French Army planned to repeat the supreme effort that led to Allied victory in 1918. It would ensure the main battles were in Belgium rather than France, but otherwise would stand and hold against the full German onslaught as it did the first time, largely unaided in the opening battles. It would buy the time it needed to complete economic and social mobilization, actualizing as real military power the latent potential of the French nation and Empire, while hoping for the same from the British Empire. Yes, Germany would not be idle. Its armed forces must grow as well. However, there was real confidence in Paris (and later, in London) that the Allies were inherently the stronger side in a future war of exhaustion with Germany, as they had proved to be last time, when Lloyd George's vaunted silver bullets indeed paid for lead ones on the path to victory. Once their nations and empires were fully in arms, economies and science and peoples all mobilized, Allied power would surely prove decisive over Germany. Although constrained by domestic divisions and the budget constraints of the Great Depression throughout the 1930s, France had a good plan for collective defense against a rearmed and vengeful Germany. If only its old allies cooperated.

Secret talks were held after Belgium returned to formal neutrality in 1936, alternately hopeful and deluded that legal neutrality might spare it a repeat of German invasion. Left on the wrong side of French defenses by this change was a vital region of Flanders ports, steel mills and coal mines needed for *une guerre de longue durée*. Paris planned to fight the long fight, and that meant Belgium and its industries and resources must be defended, no matter how myopic policy became in Brussels. That required a mobile strike force to move fast into Belgium as soon as the next war started, to a forward defense position along the Dyle River. To that end, France hoped to steadily strengthen an Allied strike force of mechanized and motorized corps, notably asking Britain to add to its armored divisions. It was hoped the British would concentrate spending on mechanizing and armoring its BEF divisions to add to the mobility and striking power of a unified Allied force. However, without the strains and incentives of war to encourage cooperation, old habits of weak coordination between Paris and London returned, made worse by disagreement over how to respond to Italian aggression in the Mediterranean. It was not clear whether opposing Italy would deter Mussolini from aggression or drive him closer to Hitler. The choice made was to appease Fascist Italy and Nazi Germany both, in a bid to buy time to build up Allied strength. Mussolini drifted away anyway, from a fatal attraction to Hitler.[11]

For years, French defense planning was hampered by the fact British politicians refused to make a forward commitment of the BEF or sign a treaty of alliance with France. Instead, under a policy called "limited liability," successive British governments held down continental commitments while

Adolf Hitler in Paris with Albert Speer (left) and Arno Breker (right) in 1940.
Courtesy of Wikimedia Creative Commons.

pursuing appeasement of Nazi Germany.[12] Only the war scare leading to the
Munich Conference in September 1938 changed the calculus. Any chance of
salvation by an anti-Hitler coup, which was a real possibility, passed when
the Munich deal undercut opposition inside the Wehrmacht. It also gave
Hitler the chance to remove disloyal generals, before they removed him

out of fear he would get Germany into a war for which it was not ready. He moved swiftly after Munich to assume direct authority over the Wehrmacht, sacking or reassigning dozens of generals and creating an *Oberkommando der Wehrmacht* (High Command of the Armed Forces), or OKW, which he headed personally. His dictatorship was now militarized as well as complete. A few brave and honorable men in the Wehrmacht still hoped for and plotted a coup that would follow an arrest or assassination of Hitler, though the outcome of Munich ended the last serious chance of that before the July 20, 1944, *Valkyrie* plot came close to killing him.

After Munich, things moved fast outside Germany as well. Stalin shifted from military autarchy and isolationism to active partnership in Hitler's aggression, and ultimately to shared partition of Eastern Europe by force and formal agreement. With war on the horizon, Britain rushed its air and land rearmament programs and sped up ground force preparations to join France in a long fight.[13] Britain proclaimed its firm military commitment to France on February 6, 1939, by which time Western Allied public opinion had also turned to favor armed resistance to Hitler. German invasion of the rump of Czechoslovakia on March 15 confirmed the decision. Next, Hitler demanded the surrender of Danzig, facing Poland with potential invasion thrusts from three sides: the Oder-Neisse line in the west, Pomerania in the north and occupied Slovakia in the south. In the event, Poland would be invaded from a fourth side as well when Soviet armies pushed in from the east in mid-September. In a belated attempt at deterrence, Allied governments gave public guarantees to fight if Poland was attacked by Germany. Unlike the calm and unsuspecting summer of 1914, over the summer of 1939 the air thickened with threats on all sides and with the rising likelihood of another Great Power war.

Britain had focused prewar spending on naval readiness for a long war at sea. From 1938 it spent more on Royal Air Force (RAF) fighter defense, with some bomber capacity, to ward German bombers from its cities. This would pay off after the fall of France in 1940, as the RAF defended Britain's skies and the Royal Navy deterred the *Kriegsmarine* from attempting a cross-Channel invasion. In time, the Royal Navy would protect vital convoys while the RAF developed a heavy bomber capability to bring merciless war to German cities and civilians. On land, however, things were more spare. Britain did not introduce conscription (National Service) until Hitler marched into what remained of Czechoslovakia in March 1939. Limited conscription passed that April. Rushing pell-mell toward war and years behind in readying its armies, Britain's leaders presumed reliance on French infantry and armor mass while they mobilized a mobile Field Force. The full British Army was not expected to be outfitted for offense into Germany until well into 1941.[14] When the Wehrmacht attacked in the west on May 10, 1940, just ten Territorial Army divisions were deployed with the BEF in France.

Nevertheless, in the months after the Munich Conference confidence that they would ultimately win a future war helped push London and Paris away from appeasement and into direct confrontation with Nazi Germany. A hardening in government policy was accompanied by real determination of Western publics to support military measures to stop Hitler's continuing aggression. Nor did Western militaries cower in fear of Nazi armed might. British and French leaders instead committed to repeating the slow path to victory of 1914–1918, and undertook realistic economic and military planning for a war they intended to win by strategic attrition.[15] The Allies would start with fortified and forward defense, absorb the Wehrmacht's opening aggressive blows (and those of the *Regio Esercito*, if Italy kept its Axis commitment to Germany). They would go over to offense later, but only from a position of maximum strength at a favorable time of their choosing. It was a realistic strategy to win, rooted in shared experience in the last war, that accepted that victory could only come with endurance over time. The fact that this strategy failed at the outset with the surprise defeat of France speaks not to a gross failure of Allied vision or competence at war but to the contingency of war, and to a remarkable string of luck Hitler and his generals enjoyed. Gambler's luck. The kind that exhilarates at first but runs out and collapses into disaster for those who cannot put down the iron dice, but just keep doubling down and rolling.

In Germany after 1918 military memories were distorted by a false sense of how close to victory planners and generals thought they had come at First Marne in 1914, and again at Second Marne in 1918. Berlin's unabated geostrategic ambition, given a rabid Nazi twist from January 1933, faced the same dilemma as before: insufficient resources for a long war of matériel, against too many enemies on too many fronts. Some generals had learned from losing. At the most senior levels of the Wehrmacht from 1935 there were those who feared that Hitler would lead Germany into a premature war against the West. However, many others thought that with new weapons— tanks and aircraft linked by radio—and improved mobile warfare doctrine, they could win next time. They looked to the movement phase in 1914 and again in 1918 and decided that mobility was normal warfare, while the longer midwar period of positional stalemate (*Stellungskrieg*) was the true anomaly. Trenches simply did not interest most German officers. Aggressors could not win from a trench. They needed to go over or around them somehow, to get to the decisive battle once again. They were convinced that they had come so close to victory in 1914 that they should start the next war as they had the last one, seeking victory by means of a "lightning campaign." German planners called this *Bewegungskrieg* ("maneuver warfare"). It was Western writers who later dubbed it blitzkrieg ("lightning war"). By whatever name, it was a vision of restored operational virtuosity, of a supposed special German talent for fast and adaptive warfare. That gave hope to the Wehrmacht that it would ride its panzers to a stunning victory in a short war, or rather over a series of short wars against Germany's usual multitude of enemies.[16]

General Staff planners recognized that modern war had moved beyond resolution by a single battle of annihilation (*Vernichtungsschlacht*). Instead, they would undertake a series of cauldron battles, strung together in a war of annihilation (*Vernichtungskrieg*) that would void Germany's insurmountable deficits in resources, war production and population. This fixation on a singular military method, the skilled operations and mobile tactics of maneuver warfare, sprang from persistent geopolitical weakness which called for radical military solutions, not ordinary ones. Secondly, it reflected generations of determination to break the so-called iron ring hemming in German ambitions to empire, regardless of chance or cost. Lastly, it represented a decided lack of political and military imagination. For two centuries Prussian-German thinking was marked by short-war illusions and attendant denial of the material obstacles to Great Power and then *Weltmacht* status. Nazi political and military culture were on the extreme end of this spectrum, additionally saturated with new and wilder racial fantasies that included quasi-military fantasisms about the triumph of fascist will over Western armies and decadence, and the innate superiority of German fighting men as springing from *völkisch* destiny.

Long before Hitler took power in 1933, the postwar German Army (called the *Reichswehr* until 1935) was planning for a future war to overturn the verdict of Versailles on Germany's role in Europe. Led by General Hans von Seeckt, a shadow General Staff was disguised as an administrative office (*Truppenamt*). It trained staff officers by another name in key operations theory, held staff rides and conducted war games. The *Reichswehr* resisted disarmament under treaty rules in the early 1920s by training in secret with the Red Army inside Soviet territory, as the two revisionist opponents of the 1919 settlement found common ground in opposition to the West and the postwar order. Germans designed or experimented with formally forbidden weapons, including tanks, at Kazan on the Volga. Some officers would return there as senior Wehrmacht commanders leading armored formations in 1942. A constricted navy worked on forbidden U-boats and drew up plans for one day laying down battleship keels and launching aircraft carriers. A forbidden air force worked with gliders for pilot training, laying a skills foundation and recruitment base for the later Luftwaffe. The military sponsored civilian flying clubs and endorsed *Hitlerjugend* (Hitler Youth) training of boys in map-reading, hiking, close order drill, marksmanship, leadership and other military skills.

Seeckt returned to mobility as the key to the next land war, insisting that the goal of all operations "will be to achieve a decision with highly mobile, highly capable forces, before the masses [of the enemy's armies] have even begun to move."[17] This assumption of beating slower armies into the field proved wrong about the Russian Army in 1914. This time would be different, Seeckt thought, because Germans would have panzers (*Panzerkampfwagen*) integrated into an all-arms attack linked by radio to driving and superior command will. The Allies had outbuilt and outfought the Germans with tanks and aircraft in 1917–1918. However, losers in war nearly always learn from defeat better lessons than winners take away from victory. So while every major army worked on armored warfare, the Germans placed the greatest emphasis on mechanized combined arms attack. They were matched only by the Red Army's concept of "deep battle," combined arms doctrine aiming at deep penetrations into the enemy's flanks and rear areas by mechanized and airborne forces, interrupting resupply and communications and paralyzing any response to encirclement by Soviet armored corps.[18]

Germans went beyond concentration of tanks as an attack mass to create a new kind of combined arms force: the panzer division (later expanded to panzer corps and panzer groups or armies). Tanks were supported by *Panzergrenadiere* (mechanized infantry) in half-tracks that could keep up off-road, and by independent reconnaissance units and mechanized artillery. A panzer division also had its own supply and bridging engineers. It could move fast to envelop an enemy unit, close an encirclement, then hold with its own infantry and artillery against counterattack. It was supported by integrated and coordinated tactical air power, easily and directly linked by command radio not just in the platoon leader's tank, as in the Red Army and most other armies, but in *every* vehicle. A panzer division was not just a lot of tanks attacking en masse ahead of or in support of infantry; it was designed as the instrument of a doctrine of total destruction of the enemy.[19] Panzers would bring everything to *Bewegungskrieg*, to swift campaigns and the resulting cauldron battles, that German officers had long dreamed of: penetration of crustal defenses, mobility to the flanks, advanced officer initiative, encirclement to total victory over less mobile and less capable enemy formations.

The way World War I ended suggested to all the planners that trench warfare was over, that mobility was restored to battle. With tanks, radio and aircraft, slow war was not necessarily the permanent condition of war among coalitions of Great Powers. Maybe by restoring maneuver to battle, genius and decision could also be restored? After all, shifts in technology and tactics seen in 1918 continued in the interwar years. Tanks and field artillery became more powerful, mobile and numerous. Infantry armies would have heavy fire support in attack as well as defense in the next war. They would have radios and swarms of swift aircraft as scouts and flying artillery, in the form of tactical bombers. German planners put faith in the revolutionary capabilities of tanks and aircraft; fascist ideologues, convinced their movement was the leading edge of modernity, added veneration of the new machines and doctrine. The war of motors, the internal combustion engine come of age, would break the stalemate of the war of spades. It would permit quick and decisive victories by protecting and empowering infantry beyond the railheads where German armies had broken down in the western battles of 1914. When the war came, from 1939 into 1941 German panzer forces would enjoy spectacular successes. Until their advantage was matched by armor and manpower on the other side, and the power of decision in a world war returned to superior ability to produce and deploy war matériel (*Materialschlacht*). Once defenders were no longer surprised by panzer thrusts and learned to respond with mines, artillery and planes, deployed in a strategic defense-in-depth and overwhelming quantities, the panzers would bog down and be systematically destroyed.[20] But first came giddy successes in Poland and France, and briefly in Russia.

Pursuit of an *idée fixe,* of the ideal of swift operational victory, was essential to the soul of the German way of war, a continuation of old ambition by other means. For Germany once again lacked the resources to win a war of matériel against the French and British Empires or the Soviet Union. Its planners knew it, and yet the militarized anarchy that was Nazi Germany meant they plunged into war anyway, despite knowing that German steel and oil production were wholly inadequate to the style of panzer war proposed by the generals and endorsed by Hitler. Rather than slowing aggression, this basic weakness added incentive to win fast, to seize vital resources to expand and enable the Wehrmacht to win the next war, then the next—or lose it all gambling on strategic outcomes won at the operational level. This was signature German practice before Adolf Hitler, the greatest military gambler of modern history, became *der Führer* (supreme leader). But in another way the departure from past practice was enormous, and harder to explain. An army that for decades sought to avoid people's war as the worst kind of fighting for Germany fully embraced a fanatical devotee of total war at its most extreme ideal of destruction. Hitler wanted territorial gains for Germany and access to military resources nearly as a second-level goal. He wanted war, as early as 1938, mostly for reasons of Nazi race ideology. He believed in war, seeing it as a positive social, moral and racial good. It was the mechanism that sorted out those few peoples racially fit to survive from the weak and inferior who must physically perish. To this strange man the officer corps swore a personal loyalty oath, then eagerly followed him into war against a grand coalition of Great Powers, and thence to Germany's and their own ruination.

Germany had no grand strategy in either world war, no plan to win beyond belief in the opening campaign, thereafter shading into vagaries. Its political leaders, military thinkers and generals in 1939 had studied battle history and their own recent and direct experience of modern war and behaved and acted, to recall a telling phrase of Napoleon, as "absolute strangers to strategy." Nazi ideologues claimed to have found in the racial and spiritual superiority of Germany's soldiers and the *Volk* that produced them a way around material inferiority. The "triumph of the will" was a central ideal of Nazism and key feature in fascist propaganda and Hitlerian fantasies. Not so for most General Staff officers and field generals. The officer corps instead relied on a different delusion, a core faith in their own professional skill, looking to operational dexterity and to improvisation as the way to avoid entanglement in a war of matériel they knew Germany could not win. Opportunities for success through cascading battles and campaigns of savage destruction would present themselves as a result of superior skill, not a triumph of will or race. This, too, was a delusion of innate German superiority, though of a different and older sort.

Besides, a crushingly fast war was the only option as long as Hitler insisted on radically revising the balance of power to make a new world order with Nazi Germany as the European hegemon and, at the wildest edge of his fantasy, the sole world power. Wehrmacht operational planning thus proceeded disconnected from basic strategic considerations or sound linkage to long-term economic management or war production. Believing in the short war was necessary to consider war at all, for rational analysis warned that military and geopolitical odds were always against Germany's hegemonic ambitions in either world war. Even so, hard men in Berlin gambled for world power so repeatedly and so recklessly that they ensured ruin by bringing into coalition

Expansion of Nazi Germany, 1933–1939.
Courtesy of the Department of History, United States Military Academy at West Point.
Redrawn by George Chakvetadze.

all the Great Powers around Germany, which after 1941 were united on stopping excessive German ambition if on nothing else. What remained was the
terrible how, all the heroics and horror of years of total war inflicted on the
world for a second time in a generation in a brutal stab for *Weltmacht* that
never stood much chance of succeeding.

The one thing German planners recognized was that a second naked challenge to international order must force an anti-German coalition into existence, meaning the only way to win was again to take out at least one major
opponent right at the start.[21] This operational ideal of *Vernichtungskrieg*
took on an additional and far more sinister meaning, as explained by Hitler
in person to hundreds of senior officers just before they invaded Poland
on September 1, 1939. He told his commanders bluntly, in his infamous
Obersalzberg speech on August 22, that he intended an absolute war from
the first day, against civilians as well as the Polish military. He demanded his
armies wage a war of extermination of such extreme cultural ambition and violence that once started it must end in his and Nazi Germany's total triumph
or total ruin. He said that the war he wanted meant not just obliteration of

the Polish Army but also of whole classes of people whom he designated as fit only for cultural and ultimately physical extermination. No objections were raised. Some senior officers went back to their headquarters and issued their own explicit extermination and murder orders.[22] The next day Hitler scored a diplomatic triumph with the Nazi-Soviet Pact, which ensured that the Wehrmacht would not face war with Great Powers on either flank. At least not yet. There would be time enough for Hitler and his willing generals to make that colossal error, too.

More immediately, Hitler miscalculated over Poland. He thought he was starting a small war against the Poles alone in 1939—a war of extermination of race enemies, to be sure, but a limited war in terms of the wider European and international system. Germany was well shy of the military strength needed to win a larger conflict when Hitler gambled by attacking Poland on September 1, and was stunned when Britain and France declared war two days later. He thought he had found their mettle wanting at and after Munich, that they would not fight him over Poland. He embraced war anyway, believing it was essential to *Rassenkampf,* the social Darwinian "race struggle" he saw at the core of all politics, domestic and foreign. He also needed Poland's resources to ready Germany to wage the next war, then the next and the next, escalating to larger enemies and bigger wars for dominance. His aggression was serial, his hate unslakable, his appetite for conquest incapable of satisfaction. He laid it all out in a manuscript that went beyond *Mein Kampf* in outlining foreign policy goals, which therefore remained unpublished in his lifetime. It made clear that race war and war more generally was always the black heart of his nihilism.[23]

***

IN 1939 STALIN was eager to ally the Soviet Union with Hitler and Nazi Germany in joint and serial aggressions against Poland and the other small states of Eastern Europe. The Nazi-Soviet Pact of August 23 codified a brutal spheres of influence agreement, paling in comparison the 1807 Tilsit agreement dividing Europe between the Russian and French Empires.[24] Warsaw hastened to complete a mobilization it had started late, in order to keep war workers in factories and laborers on farms during the vital harvest season. Poles also feared provoking Germany. That did not matter. Hitler did not need to be provoked to war. He craved it. In fact, months earlier he had ordered the OKW to draw up plans for invading Poland code-named *Fall Weiss,* or "Case White." In a portent of how poor Axis coordination would be throughout the entire war, Benito Mussolini was told of the pending attack only on August 24. Asked to contribute Italian troops, *Il Duce* recoiled from an act of aggression that might launch a Europe-wide war against Britain and France for which Fascist Italy was wholly unprepared. Hitler was surprised, and postponed the attack for several days. Meanwhile, Britain and France reaffirmed their military commitments to Poland. Now, any invasion must surely start a general war.

Not even that stopped Hitler. After losing his main ally and confirming that two Great Power empires were lined up against Nazi Germany, he ordered *Fall Weiss* to proceed. It was the German way, not just his. When surrounded and outnumbered, go on offense, break the iron ring of enemies to make at least one border secure by putting German troops on both sides. Yet it was also a product of his personal delusion about Allied readiness to fight. An ultimatum from London arrived, warning that if he did not withdraw from Poland by September 3 war would be declared on Germany, followed by the same ultimatum from Paris. Hitler was visibly stunned. After minutes of silence he turned to his Foreign Minister Joachim von Ribbentrop and asked, "What now?" Some of the leading figures in Germany's military knew what was coming, even if most of the generals embraced war with personal and professional enthusiasm. In private, head of the *Abwehr* (military intelligence), Admiral Wilhelm Canaris wrote: *"Finis Germania."*

Overnight on August 31, a *Schutzstaffel* (SS) special operations squad staged a border incident to give Hitler a domestic propaganda pretext for war. Hitler always feared the home front more than the enemy, a legacy of his view of the 1918 "stab in the back" of German soldiers by the "November traitors." Eight SS men dressed in stolen Polish Army uniforms secured by Canaris—whose wider doubts did not prevent participation. Under cover of dark, they staged a false-flag attack on Gleiwitz radio station on the German side of the Silesian border. They were supposed to make a broadcast, but the signal was so weak it was heard by very few, if anyone. In typically brutal SS fashion, they left murdered prisoners on display for photographers from Josef Goebbels' Ministry of Propaganda. The plot was framed by Reinhard Heydrich, rising regime star and protégé of Heinrich Himmler, head of the SS. Later infamous as the "Butcher of Prague," Heydrich headed *Einsatzgruppen* death commandos, chaired the Wannsee Conference on *Endlösung* ("the final solution"), and oversaw plans for the construction of Auschwitz and the other death camps. The war thus began in lies and murder, as Germans would wage it from first to last. By 1945 six million Poles, including three million Polish Jews, would be killed out of a prewar population of under 40 million.

Poles were not just outnumbered and outmaneuvered. It was also crucial that their main forces were deployed in a perimeter defense they could not hold, instead of a defense-in-depth. Bad dispositions were dictated by unfavorable geography but also by nationalist demands in a country only recently sovereign, where all soil was sacred and must be defended. Polish nationalism thus contributed to a frontier hard-shell defense that did not match Poland's military capabilities. The Polish Army was so stretched around the borders that it would be breached on three sides, including a southern front created by the destruction of Czechoslovakia at Munich and afterward. That was an act of naked aggression in which Poland foolhardily participated, taking a small piece of the spoils. The Poles also faced a virtually insoluble operational problem of defending exposed Danzig and the narrow neck of the Polish Corridor, a vulnerable territorial strip that was bequeathed to Poland as a political construct of the Paris Peace Conference in 1919.

At dawn on September 1, 1939, the first shots of the war boomed from an old *Kriegsmarine* cruiser that pounded the small Danzig garrison. It had entered the harbor days earlier on a supposedly friendly visit. Luftwaffe Heinkels and Stuka dive bombers screeched over the border, terrorizing civilian refugees with bombs and strafing while also covering driving penetrations by the panzers which also crossed at dawn. Over 1.5 million Germans in 60 divisions poured over the borders, led by five panzer divisions with over 300 tanks apiece, supported by elite *Panzergrenadiere* and four divisions of motorized infantry. Two army groups crossed in the north and south, aiming for concentric encirclements of Polish armies. A third attacked eastward, to fix the main enemy forces as the pincers closed behand. The Polish air force had just 313 planes, half of them bombers, and most of its fighters were obsolete. It was outnumbered by the Luftwaffe 5:1 in modern aircraft. In the first hours many Polish planes were destroyed on the ground or by superior German pilots in better aircraft. After just days, the few Polish planes left could do little to stop waves of Stukas and ME-109s bombing and strafing retreating infantry and civilians. Bigger Do-17 and He-111 bombers indiscriminately terror-bombed Warsaw to try to compel submission by the national government.[25]

The Wehrmacht faced 1.3 million Poles in underequipped units, still only partially mobilized. Poles were outnumbered in armored vehicles 15:1. They fielded 11 cavalry brigades but just two mechanized brigades equipped with obsolete tankettes (very light, undergunned and underarmored tanks). These and other light armor, greatly inferior to the onrushing panzer columns, were pounded and pushed aside by panzers and mobile guns or blown apart by Stukas. Some Polish infantry divisions were still assembling as the German spearheads struck. They were rushed into battle piecemeal, and destroyed one after another. Panzers broke through the frontier defense in several places, green defenders overwhelmed by fast-moving tanks and mechanized infantry, strafed in assembly areas by an unchecked and powerful air force built for just this role of tactical support of fast-moving ground forces. Very soon, the panzers were free to race across perfect tank country, flat and unobstructed by heavy forest or wide rivers or canals.

The *Fall Weiss* operational plan was an experiment in armored movement intended to win fast to avoid a positional stalemate or *Stellungskrieg*. It was tried out against Poland in 1939, but really meant for future use against the old enemies of World War I. In the first hours, General Heinz Guderian led XIX Corps south from Pomerania into the Polish Corridor, making an infantry river crossing in rubber boats to secure bridges for the tanks. By the end of the day two Polish infantry divisions were trapped. Two days later they were destroyed. Once the panzers broke through they rolled across open country at speeds that astonished the military and political worlds, even those who already believed in tanks as the future of mobile warfare. Hardened panzer spearheads proved unstoppable, leading in strong shafts comprised of follow-on leg infantry. It was an effective new style of mobile and mechanized war that distinguished German armies for the next two years. However, the oft-cited story that utterly obsolete Polish lancers charged modern German tanks is a myth. There were no cavalry charges made against panzers, although there was a fight between cavalry and armored cars that found and shot up an exposed Polish mounted brigade.[26]

The full operational design unfolded over the next two weeks. Outermost panzer thrusts on the northern and southern flanks were intended as a concentric attack to envelop the main Polish Army forces along the frontiers, west of Warsaw. The plan was to pinch off all avenues of retreat into central and eastern Poland, while slamming into several trapped Polish armies with the main German strength arriving from due west. Army Group South thus struck northward from German-occupied Slovakia. Army Group North linked Pomerania and East Prussia by crossing the Polish Corridor to isolate Danzig, then drove south to close the pincers west of the capital. It was repeatedly counterattacked by the Poles as it moved, but continued to advance.[27] The heaviest attack came from the west, across the Oder–Neisse river line in a drive east directly toward Warsaw, but really intended to contact, fix and hold the Polish armies for the northern and southern pincers to envelop, cut off, then crush back against the center. The center position was the declared *Schwerpunkt*, site of the decisive cauldron battle to come.[28]

Seven Polish armies concentrated in the west and center, exposed to encirclement by the armored pincers which met at the base of the Polish Corridor within three days. After the pincers joined the Germans sent reconnaissance-in-force units to drive on Warsaw from September 6–10. The only significant reverse for the panzers took place at the Bzura River (or Kutno), where German 8th Army was counterattacked on September 9 by Poznań Army, forcing a withdrawal of 10 miles that pulled 8th Army away from its approach to Warsaw. However, Poznań Army was itself forced to reverse course on September 14 by a penetrating attack by German 10th Army, with strong support from flights of Stukas and ME-109s. Then the lid was slammed on the whole western *Kessel* and triumphant German armies proceeded to destroy the Polish forces inside it.

Poles expected Allied help in the form of immediate bombing of targets in western Germany and a French offensive along the Rhine, earlier agreed to start no later than two weeks after a German attack began (timing was based on the French mobilization schedule). There is no evidence that France or Britain seriously contemplated offensive ground action during the battle on the other side of Germany. Recognizing that nothing could be done to save Poland, they decided that the best course was to continue their build-up and training for the defensive war they expected to fight for 18–24 months, while softening up Germany by a bombing campaign and winning at sea. The naval war was the one area outside Poland where the war seemed deadly serious from the first day, not least because Winston Churchill was recalled to government to serve as First Lord of the Admiralty. He immediately brought determined energy to the hunt for German commerce raiders. Also, the first controversial U-boat sinking of a civilian passenger ship, SS *Athenia*, took place after just a few hours on September 1.[29]

What the Allies saw as prudent realism on their part most Poles naturally saw as betrayal, as they fell under the long dark night of Nazi occupation. The deeper meaning of inactivity along the Rhine was *not* Allied betrayal, however. It was evidence that they were pursuing a long-war strategy. The campaign in Poland was correctly seen in Paris and London as the opening shot in a far bigger war. It would be foolhardy to leave strong fixed defenses built along the French frontier to make what could never be more than a symbolic attack into the Rhineland. This was a time for build-up of weapons systems and new divisions and armies, for training green conscripts while waiting for the balance of forces to shift in Allied favor. Also the idea of bombing was put on hold out of fear of retaliation to no larger purpose. The British dropped leaflets on the Ruhr instead, even as Germans decided it was a real war after all and shot down RAF planes. The "sitzkrieg" (or Phoney War or *drôle de guerre*), as this period of military inactivity was mockingly called, stretched out until a disastrous Anglo-French peripheral expedition to Norway met a German invasion arriving there at the same time in April 1940.[30]

The real betrayal came on the eastern Polish border. On September 17, Stalin declared Poland had "ceased to exist" and sent Red Army corps slashing over its eastern border to meet the Germans at a prearranged line drawn in a secret codicil to the Nazi-Soviet Pact.[31] The Soviet invasion was so late the Red Army entered eastern Poland while the bulk of the Polish Army was already defeated or surrounded by German armies in the west and center of the country. Small but fierce fights still took place. Assaulted on all sides, the Poles fought for 10 days more around Warsaw, which remained under German air and artillery attack until its garrison surrendered on September 27. The remnants of the Polish Army formally submitted on October 5, though many men crossed into Romania rather than surrender. Berlin and Moscow demanded that the Western Allies recognize the new order made by naked force in Central and Eastern Europe.

German losses in the month-long Polish campaign were 700 tanks, 8,100 killed and 32,000 wounded. The Red Army lost 2,600 killed, wounded or missing in briefer action. The Poles lost 70,000 killed and 130,000 wounded on all fronts, with 420,000 prisoners taken by the Germans and 240,000 falling into Soviet hands. Wehrmacht combat momentum carried some units well east of Warsaw, but they pulled back to the prearranged partition line from September 20 to 26. Guderian personally handed over Brest-Litovsk to the Red Army, site of the German diktat to the Bolsheviks in 1918. These brutal arrangements and joint invasion confirmed that the Nazi-Soviet Pact was really a de facto alliance of aggression, and that the Soviet Union had moved into the Axis camp against the West. Poland also demonstrated that for the rest of the war obliteration of opposition at all levels in occupied countries was the main goal and method of German and Soviet political leaders: the total destruction of armies was to be a mere prelude to annihilation of historic states and peoples. Thus the Polish state was jointly declared extinct and the killings of the peoples picked up pace.

This was not World War I. From the very first day of World War II, killing extended far past soldiers and losses went beyond territory or resources, reaching to extermination and physical elimination and national extinction. On the German side of the partition line, roving *Einsatzgruppen* death battalions killed Polish Jews and political and cultural leaders. On the other side, NKVD killers did much the same, rounding up and shooting those deemed capable of leading future resistance to Stalin, though excepting specific targeting of Jews. Mutually agreed deportations of minority ethnic groups were then carried out across the Nazi-Soviet boundaries. Deported *into* German-occupied Poland were *Volksdeutsche*, ethnic Germans removed from the Baltic states annexed by the Soviet Union, who joined other "settlers" arriving voluntarily from Germany itself.[32] Over the next months, Soviets shipped Poles, Balts and other now "internal" deportees from annexed territories to the Gulag. Germans filled urban ghettos with Jews herded and harried from the countryside and smaller towns, while ordinary *Landser* as well as Waffen SS and extraordinary *Einsatzgruppen* death battalions killed Jews and Roma and others with impunity and increasing cruelty. The racial sorting and re-seeding of a Nazi empire to come had begun.

Two totalitarian regimes and their terror police, the Gestapo and NKVD, among the most sinister organizations in all history, cooperated in forced divisions and transfers of the populations of several small countries. They forcibly removed or just killed anyone deemed not worthy of care or survival, with entire national homelands declared extinct and erased from the map. These deportations and killings were the first of many and much larger forced population movements that would follow, including in 1945 millions of German civilians expelled from eastern lands their forebears lived in for centuries. At the end of the last war, Woodrow Wilson had proposed to move borders to fit populations ("self-determination of nations and peoples"). In this new war, entire nationalities and historic minorities would be moved, or just murdered, to fit borders set by nothing more elevated than military force majeure. Even after Hitler was dead it continued, as the Western Allies and Soviet Union agreed to rearrange certain demographic facts on the ground in eastern and central Europe, then redrew national boundaries around them, shifting Poland westward and truncating what was once East Prussia and other parts of Germany. It was a brutal war started by Germans and conducted by their armed forces and political and other police with unparalleled cruelty and violence, for which Germany paid a historic price when it lost.

The war for Poland was over by the first week of October, but not active fighting by hundreds of thousands of Poles. After the Axis attack on the Soviet Union in 1941 tens of thousands of Polish prisoners were freed by Stalin to join all-Polish Red Army divisions fighting on the Eastern Front. Others were allowed to join the British Army fighting in the Middle East, joining units formed by other Poles who made their way to the West earlier from Romania. A Polish government-in-exile was established in Paris, moving to London when Paris fell in June 1940. Polish brigades and divisions joined Allied armies to fight in France in 1940, the Middle East in 1941–1942, Italy in 1943, France again in 1944, and into Germany itself in 1945. After the war they were refused permission to return to their homeland by Stalin, as a restored Poland was taken over by a communist regime propped up by the presence of the Red Army and NKVD. Not rising to fight were 22,000 Polish army officers captured by the Red Army in 1939 who were murdered by the NKVD in early 1940 at various sites inside the Soviet Union, the most infamous of which was in Katyn Forest outside Smolensk. More Poles died in the Home Army resistance against German occupation, during the Warsaw Ghetto uprising in 1943 and Warsaw Uprisings in 1944. Others died at the hands of Gestapo torturers and executioners and in concentration camps and death camps. Six million in all.

Germany had finally won a short war, but only against Poland. It destroyed an isolated minor power, a barley state trapped between the grinding mill-stones of Nazi Germany and the Soviet Union. The war Hitler started with the Western Allies would not be a short war. London and Paris were right, Hitler and his generals were wrong. Poland was the opening battle in a total war just barely under way, one that would be decided by vast mobilizations of whole nations for a war of the peoples the like of which had never been seen or attempted in history. Not even Hitler controlled the pace, and he would lose ever more control as the great fight swirled away from any one country's ability to direct or stop. Nazi Germany had started a war for Poland that became a war for Europe, then a world war. Its chances of winning dimmed at a basic level of build-up by all the Great Powers for a deeper war, even as its generals and panzers won their brightest victories.

It was Stalin who made the next move by attacking another quiet little country. Finland resisted the Soviet invasion at the end of 1939 surprisingly well, inflicting real damage on the first Red Army columns to cross its border. However, when the Soviet offensive was blocked the Stavka sent in 21 more infantry divisions supported by heavy artillery and air assets. Unlike the first battles of blunt and bloody frontal Red Army assaults, the new divisions were told to fight the smaller Finnish Army (*Maavoimat*) in a war of deliberate wearing rather than fancy maneuver. It was a sign of things to come, though not in the way that Hitler and other German observers misread it at the time. Yes, the enormous Red Army showed grave combat incompetence to start, but then it demonstrated that it and Stalin would accept however many casualties were necessary to prevail. [33] And it had a great many divisions in reserve, nearly twice as many as German intelligence had counted. This response to initial defeat said much about what war would be like on the Eastern Front, presaging that the Germans were preparing to fight the decisive campaigns of World War II in gross ignorance of their enemy and in a way nearly fore-doomed to failure: aiming for a quick knock-out blow against a regime with territorial and strategic depth, and latent military power, that blunted oper-ational finesse.

The Wehrmacht was impressed by the panzers in Poland and added more tank divisions to its armies as a top priority, readying to fight future lightning campaigns with bigger panzer armies and more powerful tanks. Meanwhile, all its major enemies were instead preparing their economies and armed forces to wage longer wars of material and human attrition. The Western Allies were for the moment hunkered behind fixed defenses but were in fact confidently waiting to be attacked, while the Red Army already showed a ca-pacity for slow positional fighting, the *Stellungskrieg* that so worried German planners. The whole leadership of the regime, from top Nazi Party and gov-ernment officials to the OKW and generals and the officer corps in the field, was committed to an ideal of war by maneuver leading to annihilation in great cauldron battles. Moreover, everyone thought they had the perfect in-strument to achieve this in the panzer corps and panzer armies. Of course, all of Germany's enemies would build tanks and field armored divisions, too, far more than German industry or recruitment reserves could keep up with even before the United States joined the ranks of Berlin's many mortal en-emies. All were or would become determined not just to defeat Germany a second time but to invade and crush Nazism in its homeland. Before all that unfolded, however, a strange victory by the panzers over the French Army reinforced misleading lessons of the war in Poland, and dogmatic German officer belief in short and lively campaigns as the epitome of a winning way in modern war.

***

IN 1940 FRANCE suffered one of the worst defeats in modern military his-tory as the heir to the French Army that stood fast and defeated the *Kaiserheer* from 1914 to 1918 was broken in a few weeks. Nearly 1.5 million prisoners were subsequently taken as hostages to Germany, where they remained to 1945. France never recovered its standing among the Allies or its prewar Great Power status and influence. This dramatic and strange defeat (*l'étrange défaite*), as historian Marc Bloch called it in wartime notes before he was shot by the Gestapo, came as a great surprise to everyone inside and outside France.[34] The British and French Empires were confident of victory because they were richer and more advanced than Nazi Germany, and had beaten

Imperial Germany through shared effort and sacrifice. One of the heroes of First Marne, General Maurice Gamelin, boasted just four months before the German invasion and devastation of the French Army that he hoped Hitler would do the Western Allies the favor of attacking. Foolhardy, but also an expression of confidence in an Allied policy of strategic defense, and in the balance of military forces and wider imbalance of power girding the Western empires. Hitler's regime boasted, too, of a Nazi economic miracle coming out of the Depression, but it had actually struggled to retool and rearm under a prestige-project economy that loomed near bankruptcy by 1938. It needed the Czech annexation and looted gold reserves just to keep going. Then the Nazis made a war to effectively steal Poland. France was another matter, and Hitler and his generals knew it.

Neither Hitler nor the German generals had a blitzkrieg concept at the start of World War II. What they shared was a loathing for trenches, along with a view resting atop two centuries of Prussian tradition of officers improvising aggressive operations in search of cauldron battles. Dismissing military intellectuality, Ludendorff once referred to the essence of German tactics as "punch a hole and see what develops." They did several times in the last years of World War I and got little result. They did it again in 1940. German success in the assault on France was *not* due to brilliant planning by the General Staff but to adjustments made on the fly, more than once over the objections of the High Command. In fact, senior planning staff vehemently objected to the plan Hitler finally adopted, fearing it could lead to catastrophe on the Ardennes roads right at the start of the operation. Actual successes, propaganda made at the time about operational brilliance, and postwar theoretical infatuation with *Auftragstaktik* has obscured the larger fact that there was a stumbling quality to Wehrmacht operations in France that went unnoticed until recently. Buried under a genius for deceit by the German generals and widespread awe at the outcome of defeat of a Great Power in just weeks was the fact that the destruction of the French Army in 1940 surprised everyone in the Wehrmacht, too.[35]

In 1940 the Wehrmacht was still only partly modern. It did not have enough tanks or half-tracks or trucks to move the bulk of its troops at speed to battle. A minority of infantry was mechanized or motorized, while most walked into France at the same pace as their fathers in 1914. Logistics was overwhelmingly animal-powered. Ammo carts, ambulances, field kitchens, food and fodder wagons were pulled by horses, as if it was 1914 or 1870 or even 1756. Clips from old newsreels inserted into documentaries that show tanks and mechanized infantry as the essential images of blitzkrieg recall

Nazi propaganda purposes and distort modern memory. They were mostly shot by Goebbels' or Wehrmacht film crews with the direct intent to frame a "National Socialist way of war," to fortify claims to a new fascist *élan vital* and to supreme modernism. Along with the direct psychological impact of actual swift victory, these images endure to imbue blitzkrieg and German armies with a reputation for doctrinal brilliance and advanced tactical rigor they do not fully deserve. German generals did not, in fact, plan a full-scale *Vernichtungsschlacht* in 1940 as they did in 1914. The end game was still total victory, but there was no Schlieffen-like certainty or plan how to achieve this. The fall of France in 1940 was not a triumph of planning or some brilliant new operational idea. It truly was a strange defeat for the French Army and a strange victory for German arms.[36]

The original *Fall Gelb* (Case Yellow) German plan for war in the West in 1940 was far more limited than 1914, or the plan that Hitler eventually adopted. OKW initially proposed not to conquer France but to wound and clear the French Army from north of the Somme, so that the Wehrmacht could occupy the Low Countries and northern France. That limited achievement would give the Luftwaffe close bases to terror-bomb British cities, perhaps even compel British submission to German dominance in Europe without having to cross an army over the Channel against ferocious RAF and especially Royal Navy resistance. However, this first ground operations plan was amended when Hitler spoke to General Erich von Manstein. He was persuaded to alter the main armored thrust, to relocate it from Army Group B in the north to Army Group A farther south, moving through the Ardennes to a position behind the main Allied armies, which would almost certainly head into Belgium. The all-or-nothing character of Manstein's *Sichelschnitt* ("sickle cut") amendment appealed to Hitler's core gambler's instincts and to the more aggressive panzer generals, but it was opposed by more traditional staff and careful operations officers at OKW. Nevertheless, the main armored strength *was* repositioned on Hitler's intervention, to strike into France through the Ardennes forest near Sedan.

Hitler would follow his old *Weltkrieg* commander's crude model, thrusting with the tanks to "punch a hole and see what develops," improvising along the way after that.[37] It worked in Poland, after all, where the Wehrmacht punched several big holes then enveloped the Poles. France was not Poland, however. The relevant borders were hilly and wooded. Roads through the Ardennes were narrow and few, so that the panzer columns must crawl at first while exposed to air attack and potentially be easily blocked from passage onto the flat plain of northern France. It was high-risk. The panzers might even be bottled up in the woods, trapped on the wrong side of the Meuse and decimated. As diversionary attacks hit the Netherlands and Belgium, five panzer and three motorized divisions would poke steel snouts into the woods then rumble along forest roads that were in places only one tank wide. Meanwhile, the main Allied armies moving into Belgium would meet only a diversion made in enough strength to look serious, and a lesser diversion in the Netherlands to hold Allied attention away from the Ardennes.[38]

On paper the combatants looked equal. Military experts thought the French had the best army in Europe, unit for unit, tank for tank, gun for gun. The *Armée de l'Air* was a formidable air force, too, although it was in the midst of a changeover in core aircraft and lacked enough modern types. Still, when paired with the RAF, the Allies were a match for the Luftwaffe. On the ground they had one-third more tanks at 3,500 in all, many of heavier makes than the majority of German panzers, which numbered just 2,300. The bigger problem was armored warfare doctrine. French ideas about "methodical battle" rested on central command of the tanks, heavy firepower stressed as the decisive factor over movement, and close infantry support provided by the tanks rather than concentrating armor in assault formations. German panzer corps stressed speed of leading armored wedges over firepower and decentralized initiative taken by commanders. It was to be cautious and managed battle vs. dash and improvisation, a contest in which many senior Allied commanders also had too rigid views or too jealous personalities.[39]

In secret military talks with Belgium that continued into 1940, it was agreed that the best French armored divisions (*divisions cuirassées*) and the BEF would advance to forward defensive positions in Belgium, but not until *after* a German attack began.[40] The Allies were confident in their stopping power once battle was joined, hence they agreed to move their best armored and mobile divisions to the Dyle Line to straddle what they thought would be the direction of the main German attack.[41] The top Allied divisions thus would be in exactly the wrong place when the panzers crossed the Meuse a week sooner than expected. Even that surprise might have been blunted if Allied armored and mobile forces had been held in an operational reserve, waiting and ready to react to enemy movement. Instead, they were committed to the wrong place by Alliance diplomacy, and by a small neutral's fearful illusions which held the Allied strike force at the wrong border until Germany decided to start the fighting. The policy conceded space and timing and all initiative to the Germans long before the big battle would begin.

Reality fell out of Belgian and Dutch skies early on May 10 and, at last, frontier guards on the Belgium border lifted crossing bars to allow Allied forces to move toward the Dyle Line. *Fallschirmjäger* and glider troops landed ahead of Army Group B, which advanced at speed. Their assault captured two bridges across the Albert Canal, breaching a key defense and letting the panzer diversion roll into Belgium ahead of schedule. Most shockingly, just 80 glider-borne engineers took the great fortress complex of Eben-Emael, thought capable of withstanding the fiercest bombardment and itself inflicting huge punishment on any invader. The engineers landed on the roof, achieving complete surprise, then rappelled down the walls to penetrate the interior by climbing through the fort's gunports. Once inside they blocked air vents and killed or otherwise suppressed the defenders with fixed explosive charges and flamethrowers, holding on until regular German infantry reached the complex in large numbers. Eben-Emael surrendered on just the second day. It was Douaumont all over again, but which much greater consequences.

Allied intelligence did not yet recognize the threat heading through the forests above Sedan. High Command was fixed instead on a persuasively large diversionary attack into Belgium and its own move to the Dyle Line, as well as on French 7th Army heading into the Netherlands to support the Dutch. On May 10, *Fallschirmjäger* had seized airfields around The Hague for Ju-52 transports carrying German 22nd Airlanding Division. They were stoutly resisted, with the Luftwaffe losing 80 percent of its total air transport capacity. The Dutch fought hard and retook most of the airfields, proving not for the last time that paratroops were extremely vulnerable to rapid counterattack as badly isolated groups of surrounded *Fallschirmjäger* took heavy casualties. However, German 18th Army raced into the Zeeland peninsula ahead of French 7th Army, which was allowed to enter by the Dutch too late and too far away from critical fighting zones to staunch the German assault. Dutch defenders broke dams to flood the polders before the advancing Germans, channeling the ground columns onto dike roads. But that traditional defense did not stop more airborne who dropped behind, taking key bridges and holding them for elite special forces (*Brandenburgers*) riding armored trains, leading tanks and motorized infantry over the border. Several trains were destroyed by the Dutch, but one crossed successfully at Gennep to enable German ground forces to link with airborne troops holding key bridges over the Maas and several major canals. Some crossings were made swiftly by the Germans in 1940 over the same rivers and canals that Allied armies would struggle or fail to take or hold four years later, in a premature and aborted attempt to liberate the Netherlands in September 1944.

Maas Line and Peel Line fixed defenses counted on by the Dutch were breached and abandoned on the first day. The deeper Ijssel Line was penetrated within two days as the Royal Netherland Army (*Koninklijke Landmacht*) retreated toward an inner sanctuary of waterlines and fortifications protecting Dordrecht, Utrecht, Haarlem and Amsterdam in a *Vesting Holland* ("Fortress Holland"). Water defenses were activated by Dutch forces that withdrew from Brabant, their line of retreat forcing them away from French 7th Army. German 18th Army moved fast over difficult terrain crisscrossed with rivers and canals, racing past hard defenses famous for breaking the momentum of invading armies in the past. As Dutch defenses crumbled the attackers struck a critical psychological blow on May 14 with merciless bombardment of Rotterdam by the Luftwaffe. Terror bombing and threats of destruction of Utrecht and other Dutch cities from the air had the desired effect, as the Dutch asked for a ceasefire the next day.

The double feint in force into the Low Countries reinforced Allied belief that was where the main battlefield would be, so they kept their best forces moving at speed into Belgium even as the first panzers poked out of the woods to reach the Meuse above Sedan. The Germans were more lucky than good in facing light opposition while traversing the forest. In the Ardennes there were huge traffic jams of tanks and trucks strung out for miles in three long columns. Some tanks literally crushed Belgian bicycle troops and French light cavalry who tried to stop them. However, towed artillery fell far behind the lead tanks as they reached the Meuse on May 13. The decisive battle of the campaign would be fought near Sedan, a name redolent with the odor of French defeat in 1870 and now the site of a second catastrophe for the French Army in 1940.

The German river assault nearly ended in disaster before it really got going, as machine guns held up the long panzer columns on the wrong side of the Meuse by shooting apart rubber boats full of engineers and assault infantry trying for a bridgehead over the river. Six times on May 13, Guderian's XIX Panzer Corps failed to cross against French resistance, with heavy infantry losses. It took two days of hard fighting to cross, and discovery of an undefended fish weir that French engineers failed to blow. German infantry crossed over the weir to set up a perimeter defense while engineers hastily built a load-holding pontoon bridge. Then the tanks crossed. A precarious two-mile bridgehead was widened to five in Verdun-like hand-to-hand fighting. Hitler became frightened by this early and unexpected success and, along with most of the senior officers at OKW, held back from taking chances to exploit the situation. OKW staff officers and generals on the ground argued

Campaign in the West, 1940.

Courtesy of the Department of History, United States Military Academy at West Point. Redraw
by George Chakvetadze.

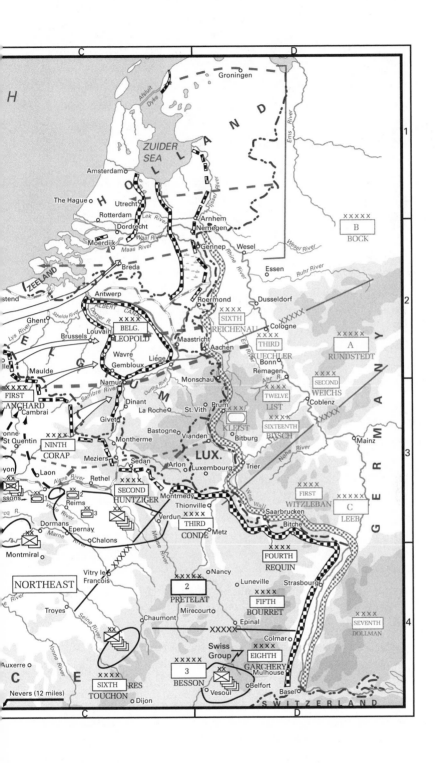

vehemently over what to do next and where to go with the tanks. Finally, several generals disobeyed orders and broke out on their own. Guderian's tanks poured into the narrow bridgehead between Sedan and Dinant. Some French infantry panicked but other units fought well. The old story of panzers boldly blowing through weak reservists according to a grand master plan, of German competence and martial superiority and French defeatism and military decadence, is so much myth.[42] It is more true that the Germans were lucky in the sequence of events leading to the Meuse crossing, where many French troops fought hard, as their casualty lists prove past doubt.

It was more a lack of mines rather than a lack of courage that let the panzers through. Panzer Corps Reinhard and Panzer Corps Hoth broke through separately, while Panzer Corps Hoepner attacked the Dyle Line in Belgium as a continuing diversion.[43] Throughout the key fight, many French infantry divisions were left holding the Maginot Line, unengaged or only lightly sparring with German troops across the way. Gamelin ordered more divisions from the reserve to reinforce at Sedan, but only scheduled them to arrive over the week of May 14–21. Nor did he yet recall the mobile forces from the Netherlands or Belgium. He was paced to the last war, and focused on the wrong front, as the panzer generals at the Meuse stole the initiative. Linear defenses on the west bank in front of Sedan cracked as the panzers got through a crustal defense and sped off onto the northern plain.

Guderian pulled away with 800 tanks and all his *Panzergrenadiere* but without waiting for follow-on leg infantry, as the French High Command thought he must. The breakthroughs included General Erwin Rommel's 7th Panzer Division, called the "Ghost Division" due to its uncertain whereabouts and habit of moving without authorization.[44] Finally, Allied HQs grew profoundly alarmed. The growing depth of armored penetration and the strength of attacking forces in the Ardennes were revealed in stunning reports of *Westheer* armor in places far forward from where Allied intelligence thought the panzers should or could be, and in much greater strength. Clearly, the main attack was developing in the south, not in Belgium as Allied planners thought. The first German tanks reached Cambrai on May 18, sending long columns of steel ahead to reach for the coast. Now the depth and position of the armor thrusts caused real panic in field HQs and Allied capitals.

Allied forces in Belgium were ordered to stop advancing toward the Dyle Line, to instead turn back to northern France where the main panzer strength had appeared, with German leg infantry huffing up behind. The turnaround to the west was made in place, meaning that the heavy combat elements were left at the rear of wrong-facing columns, the slowest transports at the head blocking the path of the combat units struggling to reach the main battle. Meanwhile, three panzer corps raced across northern France to the Atlantic to cut off all Allied forces in Belgium. Some moved so rapidly and far ahead of follow-on infantry that OKH and some of the generals in the field worried that an Allied counterattack into an exposed flank would break the infantry shaft below the steel panzer spear tip, trapping the German armor instead of retreating Allies. OKH knew that its armored columns were overextended and exposed to being cut off themselves, but after debate let them continue. In a screaming, ranting panic, Hitler intervened, issuing the first of two "Halt Orders" during the campaign. Confronted by generals at OKW who now wanted to push on to the coast anyway, he relented. He was also disobeyed in the field. The generals at the head of the tank columns were already lying and ignoring both OKH and Hitler. Their disobedience, not a brilliant master plan, ultimately led to French and British forces caught north of the panzer penetration being diverted to Channel ports to evacuate out of a closing trap.

As Guderian moved he discarded all but minimal protection of exposed flanks. Ordered to conduct a reconnaissance in force, he "scouted" ahead with an entire armored corps, lying to OKH with false reports of his position. Not only did he suffer no dire consequences, he was later rewarded and promoted for success. Rommel behaved similarly with Ghost Division, ignoring halt orders and pressing on to the coast. No Allied general in 1940, and few ever in the war, would attempt such independent action or get away with it. As Karl-Heinz Frieser, the leading historian of the 1940 blitzkrieg conclusively demonstrates in a major revisionist work, Guderian and Rommel were more lucky than good in this phase of the battle for France. They also benefited from weak leadership by Gamelin, slow Allied response times, a failed French counterattack into an exposed flank denuded of protective infantry left behind at the Meuse, and more failed counterattacks hindered by millions of refugees fleeing in panic along the same roads.[45]

The first big tank-to-tank battle of World War II was fought when Rommel's Ghost Division met French 1st Armored. Another even bigger fight pitted 240 heavy tanks of the French Cavalry Corps against swarms of lighter tanks from Panzer Corps Hoepner, supported by Stukas and fighters of the Luftwaffe. In that tank-to-tank battle the French lost 100 tanks but knocked out 160 panzers.[46] German tank-busting with Stuka dive-bombers proved tactically ineffective, but dive-bombing and strafing civilians and infantry columns as a psychological weapon rather more so, adding to a growing sense of panic and confusion. Charles de Gaulle's 4th Armored counterattacked on May 17 in an effort to disrupt Guderian's supply columns, but the weight of the *Westheer* armored thrust was too great to be stopped by such a localized effort. Reinforcing breakthrough success, OKW redeployed two panzer corps from Belgium freed from the diversion in force when the Allies turned around, raising the German armored force in France to nine panzer divisions and four motorized divisions. Swift-moving lead elements drove for the coast between Arras and the Somme, rolling right over or past the blood-soaked battlefields of the last generation's war at Mons, Arras, Ypres and other loathed places of positional carnage. General Franz Halder on the General Staff wanted to turn south, perhaps to revisit the aborted Schlieffen plan with panzers. Hitler overrode him, still worried about the exposed flank of the armored advance to the sea. Instead, he wanted all armor to stop to let German leg infantry catch up. The argument was fierce.[47]

The generals were arguing on the Allied side, too, while some politicians were already panicked. Gamelin was sacked on May 18 and replaced by General Maxime Weygand, recalled from colonial service in Syria. British armor attacked into Rommel's position near Arras on May 21, but the assault was blunted. When the first German boots dipped in the Atlantic after midnight most of the best outfitted and well-trained Allied troops were cut off in Belgium. French armies farther south massing to defend Paris from an expected German thrust were left mostly naked of armor. OKW and Hitler helped the Allies at this moment by halting Guderian's tanks. Hitler was dizzy with the unexpected success of *Fall Gelb* but, as often the case when facing a major choice, he was also nearly paralyzed by indecision. He feared a spectacular defeat instead, should the Allies counterattack in force and cut off his panzers. In fact, the Allied armies were incapable of making an effective counterattack other than locally. Hitler had another, nonmilitary reason for halting the armored columns. He wanted to reestablish personal command authority over OKW and all his disobedient field generals. He sacrificed complete and immediate destruction of the trapped Allied armies to that internal political goal.[48]

Allied retreat to the coast was made chaotic by mixing with the remnants of the Belgian Army and waves of 11 million panicked civilians. The latter clogged the roads with horse-drawn carts filled with household treasures, often with pregnant women or small children or aged parents riding on top. The refugee and troop columns were strafed and harried by ME-109s and bombed by Stukas. Below the panzer columns, the bulk of the French infantry tried to form a new defense line in the open country north of Paris. British Commander John Gort on May 24 gave the order to the BEF to retreat from

Arras toward Dunkirk, while the Royal Navy prepared Dover for evacuation.[49] The decision caused an uproar in Allied councils and was received as a severe breach of trust. Many French accused the British of abandonment.

There was still some talk in London of fighting on in France, of transshipping evacuated troops not to Britain but to southern French ports and then marching back to reinforce the new defense line forming north of Paris. Belgium surrendered on May 28, leaving the BEF and tens of thousands of French troops stranded in an enclave around Dunkirk. *Westheer* armored and mechanized units harried and pursued the retreating and subsequently trapped Allied armies. Fortunately for the BEF, Hitler and OKW ordered the tanks to stop and refit. Already, they were looking south to the coming battle with the remainder of the French Army, to its complete destruction. The panzer halt along with hard perimeter fighting around Dunkirk allowed 240,000 men of the BEF and 120,000 French and Belgians to sealift to Britain over several days and nights. Close fighter cover kept the Luftwaffe at bay as Allied troops left the shores of France without their vehicles, guns, tanks, and in many cases their rifles or their boots, left on the beach as they waded out to ships' boats or to one of the many little civilian ships that came across to help.[50]

A narrow and traditional explanation of French defeat in 1940 was that it all came down to tanks, and that French tanks were unequal to the panzers. That was simply not true, as tank for tank many of French tanks were in fact superior. The role of armored warfare doctrine was a different matter. There, the Germans were ahead of the Allies, though not as much as the victory made it seem. An alternative explanation focused on sheer ineptitude by Gamelin and other generals, arguing that France's strange defeat was a result of bad generalship, not poor troops or tanks or numbers.[51] Most wrongheaded of all, for many years the idea persisted that France was defeated due to moral decadence and deep social divisions, not for military reasons; that it was suffused with prewar defeatism as symbolized by the Maginot Line, a malaise that made the French Army unready and unwilling to fight.[52] In fact, the French Army did not hunker in defeatism behind fortifications. But nor did it plan for war as armored aggression or develop an offensive doctrine to match that of the Nazis and Wehrmacht.

France was a defensive power uninterested in aggressive war before 1940. That greatly influenced its armored doctrine, its decision to fortify the frontiers, and its posture of receiving rather than delivering the opening offensive blows at the start of what seemed sure to be another long war.[53] It would stand at the Maginot Line but also make a mobile forward defense.

A powerful armored strike force, replete with motorized infantry and artillery, would meet and stop onrushing Germans invading through Belgium and the Netherlands.[54] It was a reasoned and reasonable strategy. It just didn't work. Robert Doughty, leading historian of the French Army in the two world wars, argues that it lost in 1940 also because it prepared to fight the wrong way. It looked to wage "carefully controlled and methodical battles that were precisely the type of battles Germany intended to avoid. Under the pressure of war France simply could not respond to the type of fighting [the Wehrmacht pursued.]"[55] It did not help that Britain once again provided only a smallish army to aid France in the first campaign. It should be recalled, however, that the French Army was not wedded to permanent defense. Its strong armored divisions were meant to take war to the enemy once the British were fully mobilized, too.

In addition to British weakness at the start of the war, Allied strategy was also handicapped by prewar diplomacy. Belgian and Dutch delusions of survivable neutrality led to those neutrals' failing to coordinate defense policy with each other or the larger Western powers. Belgium's refusal to permit Allied forces to cross its territory prior to the opening shots of a German attack played a critical role in the defeat of 1940, ensuring that the most mobile Allied infantry divisions and nearly all their best armor were still moving toward the Dyle Line when three panzer corps broke over the Meuse at Sedan and raced for the coast behind them. Wehrmacht operations staff similarly used a small-scale invasion of the Dutch homeland to deceive the Allies as to the direction of the main panzer thrust, which was directly into France via the Ardennes. After a brave but confused and disconnected defense, the Dutch were compelled to surrender to superior mobile forces and ruthless threats of terror bombing of their most ancient cities.[56]

The Germans had a superior operations doctrine rather than a superior army in 1940, but that alone is not enough to explain their victory. It was also crucial that Allied armies were in the wrong place and that Gamelin and others were too slow to react to the fast-moving panzer corps as they broke over the Meuse and raced from Sedan to the sea. As unsatisfying as it may be to those who like military history to be tied up in taut causal chains, another key explanation is a series of accidents and contingent errors that allowed German generals to take advantage of what doctrinal and technological superiorities they did have: improvisation, speed, and tactical radio linking all arms from tanks to aircraft. The French Army was beaten by a concentration of German skill, but also by German luck; by superior doctrine and mission tactics improvisations, but also by the usual mix of fogged and bad decisions, and by the combat accidents and shifts in momentum that mark all battle. Only in this case, the iron dice turned up sixes repeatedly for just one side.[57]

The end in France came quickly. The government left Paris for Bordeaux, as it had in 1914. A largely infantry defense line was shored up with small packets of remaining armor, but the Germans easily punched a hole in the thin crust, bypassing strongpoints and racing into the center and south of France. Italy attacked in the Alps on June 10, a jackal come to feed off the lion's kill. Except the French Army in the south was still very much alive, so that the *Regio Esercito* was bloodied in the mountain passes. Two days later Germans paraded down the Champs Elysées, goose-stepping under Napoleon's triumphal arch even as Rommel set an armored speed record in the south, advancing with his tanks 160 miles in one day. Other divisions reached Grenoble or swung east to capture Maginot Line forts and garrisons from the rear. Guderian turned east into Alsace during the third week of June, trapping 500,000 French troops. De Gaulle and others who could left to fight on from overseas. Most of the nation turned to the hero of Verdun, Philippe Pétain, to save them again, this time by agreeing to terms and later by serving as president of the Vichy government. An armistice was signed at Compiègne on June 22, in Hitler's presence and in the same railway carriage where the Armistice of November 11, 1918, had been signed that the German leader so despised.

By the end of 1940 it seemed to most observers like Nazi Germany had won the war. Ahead for the French lay humiliation, occupation, collaboration and resistance as a long bleak night fell over France, and therefore also Europe. Ahead for Britain lay four years of war outside Europe before its troops again set foot on French soil, and nearly a year more after that before a partly revived France joined Britain and other Allied forces in the liberation of the western half of Europe. Germans were prepared to fight in a dynamic new way that let them win fast with panzers in Poland in 1939 and even more remarkably in France and the Low Countries in 1940. But they were not at all prepared for the longer war they faced after that. Or the vastly expanded and deeper war their continued aggression brought down upon Germany and Europe with the invasion of the Soviet Union. As bleak as things looked from Paris and London in 1940, in Berlin what lay ahead was total defeat and utter ruin.

14

Annihilation of Mercy

THE DEFEAT OF the French Army in 1940 changed the whole trajectory of World War II. Many at the time thought Hitler had won the war, that the world must adjust to a Nazi new order in Europe. All continental states were by then either allied to Nazi Germany, under occupation, or formally neutral but fast readjusting their diplomacy to account for Nazi hegemony. Sweden became more accommodative on economic issues while retaining a posture of stiff and well-armed neutrality. Finland looked to Germany for arms and a potential alliance to recover territory it had just lost to the Soviet Union. The smaller countries of eastern and central Europe shifted into the Axis or sought to remain formally neutral but overtly appease Hitler in other ways large and small, with favorable trade agreements and diplomatic recognition of his conquests, or by breaking ties with his enemies. Some adjusted domestic policy to mimic fascist values, to adapt to demands made by their own increasingly assertive fascist movements. An arc of pressure for change took shape especially along the southern borders of Nazi-occupied Europe.

Contrary to a postwar boast to have kept Spain out of the war and thus spared it destruction, General Francisco Franco wanted to join the Axis and take Spain to war to share in the easy spoils of Nazi conquests. He was less imprudent than Mussolini, who committed Italy without guarantees and was given little, but just as eager as Stalin, who acquired eastern Poland and the three Baltic states at a fraction of the cost to Germany of conquering western Poland. Franco wanted to pick off vulnerable French colonies in Africa. However, he could not come to terms with Hitler on the price of Spain's entry. Hitler and Franco met at Hendaye on the Spanish-French border on October 23, 1940, where clashing policies, interests and personalities all grated. Franco demanded financing for Spanish rearmament and weapons and other direct military assistance, but mostly he wanted French Morocco, which Mussolini also coveted. Hitler wanted to keep the French collaborationist government in Vichy quiet and to keep Fascist Italy in line, and so resisted transferring

Morocco to Franco. He also wanted bases in Spanish colonies for use in future operations in Africa and against Britain, and eventually the United States. They discussed jointly assaulting Gibraltar, but never did. Franco's interest in entering the war abated sharply from December 1942, after Allied landings were made in North Africa.[1]

Larger countries sped up their preparations for war, either alongside Hitler or against him. Mussolini recalculated his chances of waging *guerra parallela* ("parallel war") to take advantage of French defeat and British weakness. Where once he had dismissed Hitler as "a muddle-headed fellow," he grew both jealous and nearly euphoric in his admiration for the German dictator's military successes. He thought Hitler's gains provided Italy an opportunity to expand its own empire in tandem, that the hinge of history had turned away from the aging nations and old empires to favor what he saw as the younger and more virile fascist nations. Ideological themes and ever more impulsive behavior displaced his early profound cynicism and governing pragmatism. He went all-in, attacking France in June 1940. The French Army was already beaten north of Paris, but still held and bloodied the Italians in the Alps. Undeterred by the severe military weakness revealed in the short campaign in France, Mussolini became increasingly angered that Hitler did not take into account or accept Italian interests and ambitions in the Balkans. He determined to launch another parallel war in the Mediterranean, to keep up with German gains. He ordered an invasion of Greece on October 28, 1940, without consulting his ally in Berlin. Once again, ill-prepared and poorly commanded Italian troops lost badly, this time to a minor power that expelled the Italians and chased them back into Albania. This fiasco drew small British forces into the Balkans on the eve of the German invasion of the Soviet Union. That greatly angered Hitler.

The German leader wanted quiet on what he saw as his southern flank as he planned Operation *Barbarossa*. Originally set for November 1940, it was postponed to May 15, 1941, then postponed again to June 22. In the interim, before launching the largest invasion in the history of war, Hitler first sent troops into Greece to rescue his Italian ally from humiliation, and then into Yugoslavia when a coup brought a pro-British government to power in Belgrade. Germany and Italy jointly invaded on April 6, 1941. Yugoslavia's 1.2 million strong army offered almost no effective resistance, crumbling into component ethnic units in just 11 days (April 6–17). Croats and Slovenes declared independence and made separate peaces from the Serbs and Bosnians, as the country broke apart along with the army. It quickly fell into a set of vicious ethnic and religious civil wars in which some factions allied with the fascist powers and held the capitals and other cities, while partisan groups lined up with the Soviet Union or with Britain. Internal fighting continued all through World War II, and past the general peace in 1945.

Similarly, Hitler committed to shore up Italian defeats in the desert campaigns of 1941 to 1943, dispatching the compact *Afrika Korps* and larger forces to Tunisia later on. Mussolini consistently overestimated the capabilities of the Italian armed forces, which suffered from poor and outdated equipment and low morale. Some elite units fought as well as any other nation's at the local level, but the strategic outcome was ever-mounting Italian defeat. Compounding all other errors, Mussolini recklessly declared war on the Soviet Union in mid-1941, joining the *Barbarossa* campaign. He would eventually send more Italian troops to fight in Russia than in Italy's own imperial wars against the British in Africa. He joined Hitler again in declaring war on the United States in December 1941, a decision deeply unpopular with millions of Italians with ties to America. In 1943 he would be removed from power, leaving Italy divided and occupied as German troops arrived in force and numbers from the north while the Allies invaded from the south. To the end in 1945, Italy was riven by civil war and fought over by other peoples' armies.

Aggressive militarists in Japan also succumbed to the temptation to take advantage of the defeat of France and humiliation of Britain, where expulsion from Europe in four evacuations (Norway, France, Greece and Crete) forced the British to husband naval and air resources close to home, first in expectation of a possible German invasion then against Luftwaffe bombing. Japanese leaders still argued over the future direction of their imperial aggression but after Nazi Germany's victories in Europe they increasingly looked south toward vulnerable Western colonies. They also turned away from the Red Army colossus that bloodied the Japanese Army in a sharp battle in August 1939, in an undeclared little border war at Nomonhan (Khalkin Gol) along the border between Manchuria and Mongolia. Japan saw low-hanging colonial fruits of empires whose metropolitan centers were occupied or directly threatened by its partner in Berlin. It moved one army into French Indochina and positioned others for later attacks into the Dutch East Indies, Malaya, Hong Kong, Singapore, Burma and Bengal. The key decision came on July 27, 1940, just five weeks after the armistice was signed in France. The Imperial Japanese Army agreed on a strategy that abjured *hokushin* ("northern advance") in favor of accepting a version of the Navy's proposals for *nanshin* ("southern advance"). In return, the Imperial Japanese Navy dropped opposition to the army's demand that Japan formally join the Axis alliance, which it did on September 27th.

Britain was not just expelled from Europe, it was partly disarmed in 1940, its land forces build-up was set back many months by all the lost guns and equipment left behind during the retreat and on the beaches around Dunkirk. What Churchill dubbed the Battle of Britain began almost immediately, as the Luftwaffe relocated to bases in occupied France and fought the RAF over the Channel through June and July. The fight in the air was elevated to a pre-invasion level with a massive attack against southern England's RAF airfields starting in mid-August. In the autumn, the Luftwaffe bombed London and other urban centers, the RAF bombed Berlin, and the war of the cities began in earnest. The question of whether London should ask for terms from Berlin was discussed by the War Cabinet, which decided that Hitler would never keep any terms he agreed. Britain would fight on. It had no operations plan or means to win at first, now that its long-war strategy of alliance with France was shredded. But it would fight to keep the war going until the Soviets and Americans finally realized the mortal danger posed by Nazi Germany and entered the war to enable Britain to win as part of a grand coalition. Expecting invasion any morning during the summer of 1940, Britain shipped its gold reserves and foreign securities to Canada, from where it could buy American weapons and fight on if invaded. That signaled to the Empire, and to the United States, a determination to continue the war even if the island of Great Britain itself fell entirely under the Nazi jackboot. Before it was over, the British Army would raise and equip 2.2 million conscripts and 700,000 volunteers. Yet an army of that strength and training lay years in the future in 1940.[2]

Britain avoided German invasion—loosely and incompletely planned as Operation *Seelöwe*, or Sea Lion—by winning in the air over London and the Channel, and even more importantly because of the weakness of the *Kriegsmarine* and the strength of the Royal Navy's determined ability to intercept any invasion fleet. Had the invasion been assayed, it is certain that scenes of spectacular and probably even suicidal Royal Navy defense would have been seen in the Channel, and from the RAF in the air above it. Instead, during the fall and winter of 1940 to 1941 Britain's cities endured the Blitz. This terror bombing was conducted by an ill-prepared enemy air force with no real strategic bombing capacity, that lost too many planes to sustain the effort. Disappointed by the Luftwaffe and repeatedly put off by an unwilling *Kriegsmarine*, by September Hitler turned to planning a great attack on the Soviet Union by which he hoped to deny Britain its last possible continental ally and force London's acceptance of Nazi hegemony in Europe; and to gain territory and food supplies to expand his racial empire in the east. His commitment of always overstretched Luftwaffe resources to a much larger war in the east allowed Britain the time it needed to rearm and recover. Thereafter, it served as protector of the vital sea lanes, a thousand-mile-long platform for punishing Anglo-American air raids against German cities and war production, and ultimately as the staging ground and main support base for a decisive Allied invasion of Hitler's vaunted but vulnerable *Festung Europa* ("Fortress Europe").

In the meantime, fighting on the periphery of the Axis empires ensued as London pursued a policy of weakening and breaking off their outer edges. Britain sought to lop off Germany's minor allies and Italy's outer colonies, as well as foment subversion and armed resistance within Axis-occupied Europe, even as RAF Bomber Command hit hard at Germany's industrial and population heartland. Bombing would harass and weaken Nazi Germany while Britain accrued fresh allies, not least to swell land armies capable of invading Europe, which the British did not possess and could not raise alone. India would provide millions, with lesser contingents coming from all over the Empire, supported also by fragments of the shattered French Empire led by de Gaulle. Keep fighting, hold on and build up, do what can be done until tens of millions more joined the fight as Red Army *krasnoarmeitsy* and American GIs finally went to war against Germany. Only then, at some distant and as yet undetermined date, would a main assault be made by British forces back into Europe and on to Germany, with strong Allied ground forces alongside sufficient for Britain to win with this grand strategy of patient yet persistent war on the Nazi periphery.

However, events on the ground forced the premature commitment of limited resources pell-mell to defense of yet more small victims of Axis aggression that clung to neutrality until the last minute, begging for military aid only after their borders were breached by the *Regio Esercito* or Wehrmacht. The British were thus drawn into the morally noble but strategically losing Balkan campaign from 1940 to 1941, starting with the Italian invasion of Greece, then politically though not militarily into Yugoslavia. The Greeks fought better than the divided Yugoslavs but could not hold despite rushed British reinforcement. Fleeing the Balkans, defeated British forces and remnants of the Greek Army were evacuated by ship. Germans followed them to Crete with a stunning air assault by *Fallschirmjäger* and glider troops that took the main airport, then drove the British off the island. Another battle lost, another evacuation, this time to Egypt. As Churchill had already warned on June 4, 1940, about the Dunkirk departures from France, "Wars are not won by evacuations."[3]

In the United States, Franklin Roosevelt also shifted policy to adjust to the fall of France. FDR knew that with the French Army removed from the Allied order of battle, the U.S. Army might have to take its place at some point if Nazi Germany was to be stopped. It was never his preference, but it might have to become his policy. He dissembled about his intentions to the public until safely reelected for a third term in November 1940. Then he became more open and honest about readying the country for a possible war.[4] There was a long way to go. On September 1, 1939, the United States fielded only the seventeenth largest army in the world, after Romania. By 1945, American armed forces as a whole would be expanded by 3,500 percent. The U.S. Army jumped from under 200,000 men in the 1930s to over 8.3 million on active duty at the end of the war, with over sixteen million men and women serving in uniform in all. More than 3,000 overseas bases and supply and support depots would be added as well.[5] At sea, the U.S. Navy (USN) would out build all other navies combined until at war's end it deployed over 1,000 warships (all types), while its shipyards also produced huge numbers of cargo ships, troop carriers and tankers.

Along with anti-isolationists in Congress, Roosevelt began by pushing through a series of military expansions depicted as homeland defense and preparedness measures, starting with massive naval appropriations. More provocatively, he provided naval escort to convoys as far into the Atlantic as Iceland, in highly unusual "Neutrality Patrols" that put U.S. Navy warships in the path of German torpedoes. He negotiated destroyers-for-bases exchanges with Britain and provided Lend-Lease aid to Britain and China, and eventually also to the Soviet Union when Hitler broke his alliance with Stalin. He successfully repealed restrictive Neutrality Acts passed by an earlier, more isolationist Congress, and ordered progressively more harmful and severe sanctions against Japan. He persuaded Congress to introduce national conscription (Selective Service), which put 10 million American men in uniform by 1945.

With the United States still neutral in August 1941, FDR signed the Atlantic Charter with Churchill, making a declaration of what amounted to shared war aims which called openly for defeat of Nazi Germany and all its pernicious doctrines and ideas. The U.S. Navy lost the four-stacker destroyer USS *Reuben James*, along with 115 of its 160 officers and crew, to a U-boat attack on a convoy in the Atlantic on October 31, 1941. That was five weeks *before* Pearl Harbor.[6] War finally came in the Pacific with Japan's attack on December 7. Germany's and Italy's declarations of war four days later pulled the United States into the European war as well. The country was able to hit the ground running in war production and training, certainly more so than in 1917, in good measure due to FDR's prewar efforts.[7] December 5–11, 1941 was the critical week that changed the world and the world war. The Red Army counterattacked at Moscow on December 5, Pearl Harbor was hit two days later, and the German and Italian declarations of war against the United States on December 11 bridged the oceanic gulfs between separate Asian and European wars.

Stalin also needed to adjust policy in response to the unanticipated removal of the French Army from the ranks of Germany's enemies. The Stavka increased the pace of modernization and expansion of Red Army armored capabilities, even as Stalin renewed overt appeasement of Hitler. He needed more time, among other things to repair the damage done to Red Army leadership cadres in 1937 to 1938 during the *Yezhovshchina* or great purge, the bloodbath named for Nikolai I. Yezhov, head of the NKVD from 1936 to 1938. Before Yezhov was shot, when Stalin purged the purgers, he and the NKVD interrogated and savaged the officer corps. Arrests and killings continued well after Yezhov's execution, under Stalin's old crony Marshal Kliment Voroshilov. Systematic murders of Red Army and Red Army Air Force (VVS) officers did not end until early 1941. The principal victims were associated with Leon Trotsky's command dating to the Russian Civil War of 1918 to 1921, especially in the old cavalry arm (*Konarmiy*) that dominated senior leadership.

Out of 700 senior officers ranked brigade commander or above in 1937, over 400 were eliminated by 1941, including three out of five marshals, 18 top commanders, and 90 Military District commanders. Of this group, the most important and forward-looking military thinker and reformer was Marshal Mikhail Tukhachevsky. Also purged were officers who saw action in the Spanish Civil War from 1936 to 1939. Others were killed for varied causes, or none. By official count, 48,773 officers from 1937 to 1939 were purged, with special concentration on the VVS. About 11,000 officers were reinstated in 1940. More would be whisked from prisons or forced labor camps in 1941, reinstated and sent to the front where Soviet officers were dying in bushels daily in desperate combat during the first months of invasion. Officer suicides rose from 1939 to 1941, notably among younger officers who lived in dread of the consequences of promotion. Yet the purge also cleared the path to the top for highly talented mid-level officers, generals who made their mark in battle against the Wehrmacht and operations officers who planned and executed some of the greatest offensives of World War II. That was an important shift, although the rise of younger talent came about in spite of Stalin, not thanks to him.[8]

As damaging as the purge was on one level, it was not the primary cause of Soviet weakness and military inefficiencies on the eve of war.[9] In 1936 the new head of ordnance, G. I. Kulik (later executed by Stalin), opposed issuing automatic weapons to Soviet troops until their utility was demonstrated three years later in the snow and forests of Karelia during the Finnish-Soviet War. Kulik also issued orders to engineer larger-caliber anti-tank and anti-aircraft guns to match what he suspected were forthcoming German weapons. That led to a complete halt in gun production during the transition period. When the Germans attacked using smaller calibers of tanks and self-propelled guns than Kulik feared, the Red Army would be left short of very effective 45 mm and 76 mm anti-tank guns. A few military Luddites even fantasized about rebuilding the Red Army into an all-infantry force supported by horse-drawn carts, in opposition to the armored warfare and deep battle concepts championed by more modern officers purged with Tukhachevsky.

Along with inept high-ranking officers and ideologues the Red Army had more fundamental problems, such as slow logistics arising from too few miles of rail and very poor roads. Most railways ran city to city, not to the fighting zones. That forced reliance on horsepower and oxcart, in a country of vast open space. It meant that deployment by rail tended to be final, while little horizontal movement was possible after a division or corps arrived in place.[10] Another issue was the incompleteness of the doctrine of deep battle, toward which reforms and reassignments aimed but were not completed in time. That doctrine assumed the Red Army would fight the next war beyond the western borders of the Soviet Union, when it would not actually do so until 1944. As important to early defeat was the fact that when the war began the Red Army was caught having only partly implemented changes in its doctrine and basic training. It was still in transition to new rifle divisions and tank corps and reorganizing into tank armies and army groups (which the Red Army called "Fronts"). Officers in 1941 lacked command and staff experience with their own formations, let alone in leading a modern division, army or army group in desperate defense against a dynamic foe. The result would be mangled operations, with new and obsolete tank models often deployed in overlarge and unwieldy formations that had to be broken up and reorganized even in the midst of fighting enormous battles during the second half of 1941.

The short-term reduction in Soviet military effectiveness was dramatic, as was exposed in the bloody failure of Red Army assaults on the Mannerheim Line of fixed fortifications early in the Finnish-Soviet war in 1939. Both sides in the coming German-Soviet war looked to the Winter War to assess the strength of the Red Army in a future contest with the Wehrmacht. In

Finland, Soviet loss rates compared to the highest rates suffered by tsarist armies during the worst battles of World War I. Casualties in a 105-day invasion of a small neighbor were 131,476 dead, 264,908 wounded, 132,213 *hors de combat* from frostbite, and 5,846 captured by the Finns. That was 60 percent of the 900,000 troops engaged, whereas the Finnish Army lost 22,430 dead, 43,357 wounded and 837 captured. The immediate response from Moscow was not to seek the lessons of failure and try to correct them. It was punitive arrests of soldiers' families, exemplary executions at the front, and the use of blocking detachments to shoot any soldiers who retreated. In short, all the usual NKVD tactics and habits of Stalinist terror were used to move men into combat through fear, which was the only motivation the regime could conceive.[11] Yet beneath surface reports of Soviet military ineptitude reaching Berlin a deeper truth was that conscripts with poor morale, high indiscipline and high desertion rates *were* whipped into combat and to victory by an effective system of state terror. Brutal? It certainly was. Militarily wasteful and incompetent? Perhaps, but also cruelly and stoically successful, and a real warning of Red Army strategic depth that the Wehrmacht should have observed and better heeded.[12]

Stalin made more mistakes, such as moving Soviet frontier armies forward from an old defensive position called the Stalin Line, to lock in annexed territories in Poland and the Baltic with occupying forces that were, in consequence, deployed in unfinished defenses. He probably hoped that all the Western powers, regarded as inevitable enemies of the Soviet idea and state, might still do mortal combat with each other. At least until France fell. It is difficult still to know what the invariably mendacious and taciturn Stalin hoped or thought. In stark contrast, Hitler's thoughts tumbled out of him in such volume and so many repetitions he often exposed his own lies.[13] The Stavka also worked into 1941 on more aggressive plans, essentially for a preemptive strike against Nazi Germany. Controversy arose among historians many years later over these so-called "Icebreaker" plans, before settling on a consensus that Zhukov proposed only limited preemption in 1941, out of rising desperation about the threat posed by the Wehrmacht.[14] Zhukov's idea was for a large-scale spoiling attack, not aggressive war. However, the Red Army was incapable of making such an attack or, as events proved that summer, of holding in a strong positional defense at the frontiers. In any case, he was overruled by Stalin in favor of continued appeasement right up to the eve of invasion. Even so, Zhukov did not later blame everything on Stalin's obstinacy and political and strategic blindness. He also conceded that the Red Army indeed failed to anticipate the full striking power of the

Wehrmacht, and that "this was the primary factor that determined our losses in the initial period of the war."[15]

The General Staff in Berlin concluded from its study of the first part of the Winter War that defeating the huge Red Army would prove to be an easy task: "Russian 'mass' is no match for an army with modern equipment and superior leadership."[16] Missing was awareness or appreciation of the Soviet capacity to endure casualties (an average of 5,086 per day in Finland), and above all the ruthless willingness of the Stavka and Stalin to order the kind of brutal war that produced them. Staff officers also failed to realize that severe morale problems in the Red Army were overcome by sheer force and terror against Soviet troops, later softened by effective propaganda portraying the war as a preventive defense of the Motherland.[17] If German leaders had known the real strength shown by the Red Army, might they have reconsidered whether the Soviet Union was susceptible to defeat in the lightning campaign they planned? There is little evidence that they did or would have. They do not appear to have expected what actually happened, that the Wehrmacht would bog down in a protracted war of insufficient manpower and matériel, lurching from campaign to campaign to the middle of 1943 in an ever more futile search for operational victory to escape from the combat trap they fitted to themselves. Fewer if any foresaw falling back all the way to Berlin from 1943 to 1945, which would force a return to defensive skills learned in the trenches of World War I. There is nothing in Hitler's behavior to suggest he would have stopped, or anything in Wehrmacht thinking either, regardless of what intelligence said about the Red Army. German military planning was always based in short-war thinking, coming down to little more than "punch a hole and see what develops." That's what the panzers were for.

German planners studied the outcomes in Poland and France and decided they held in their hands the Philosopher' Stone of victory in war, and certainly over the Soviet Union. It was their new style of tank and combined arms destruction, an armored *Kessel*. Panzers would be the force-multiplier, the instrument of encirclement and decision over superior enemy numbers and resources. Panzer divisions brought together the force and speed of combined arms with uniquely German command skills and mission tactics, in ways that made the tanks unstoppable. This seemed confirmed for a third time in the 11-day war in Yugoslavia, where the panzers led a combined-arms assault that smashed a million-man army to pieces. Enemy divisions and corps dissolved before the thrusting steel columns, to collapse backward and inward into defeat. Hitler and the OKW confidently expected to do it all over again in Russia, albeit on a much greater scale and with more malicious race-struggle purpose and methods. The two most ambitious dictatorships of modern times were about to clash in the bloodiest war ever fought. *Barbarossa* was set to be the greatest invasion ever attempted, on a scale never tried before: four million men and thousands of tanks and aircraft were poised that summer to cross the borders of the Soviet Union, to usher in the triumph of German will and race superiority and display a national and even biological genius for war. It instead proved to be the most spectacular gamble and gravest miscalculation in the history of war.

***

BARBAROSSA SIMPLY COULD not have taken place without short-war thinking dominating the deep military culture of the Wehrmacht and the political culture and ideology of the Nazi regime it served. A year before, Hitler said to his planners and generals that invasion "achieves its purpose only if the Russian state can be shattered to its roots in one blow." In his governing campaign directive of December 18, 1940, he declared the goal and their job was "to crush Soviet Russia in a rapid campaign" by "bold armored thrusts."[18] He was so certain the panzers would win fast that even while OKW staff officers were still planning *Barbarossa* he ordered a production switch to make more landing craft during the second half of 1941. Once the panzers finished off the Red Army in short order as expected, he would need boats to cross his tanks over the Channel to defeat Britain and win the war in 1942. Many officers agreed with this assessment of German chances in Russia. Some gleefully thought they would destroy the whole Red Army in just four weeks.[19]

It started well, almost exactly as planned, with breakthroughs by the panzers at the borders leading into a sequence of cauldron fights trapping forward-deployed Soviet armies and whole army groups, fixed in place and destroyed. After just three weeks, Hitler grew so euphoric he considered a partial demobilization and ordered some war factories to change over to producing civilian goods. The Germans won several more Leuthens and Ulms, and a new Cannae of their most vivid martial dreams when they took 665,000 prisoners at Kiev. There, over the objections of some of his generals, Hitler turned large panzer columns away from Army Group Center's thrust toward Moscow to instead win a massive victory in the south. Army Group North cut off and besieged Leningrad on three sides, aided by the Finns. Other panzer columns penetrated hundreds of miles, capturing millions of Soviet prisoners while killing 1.5 million Red Army soldiers over the first six months of the Russo-German war.[20] Yet the Soviet regime did not collapse, the Red Army did not cease fighting, and the Germans did not win.

One reason was that a lot of Germans died, too, in the cauldron fights. Panzers and halftracks started to wear out and break down. Infantry morale flagged despite the victories, drooped from too much death and too many wounds even in victory, and from distance and constant fighting, and still more distance to walk in order to fight some more. The lightning campaign ended long before propaganda newsreels said. It ended before Hitler and the generals conceded that it had. New research shows it was stopped at Smolensk, with the brutal reduction of Army Group Center as it reduced the Yelnya Bulge of Red Army resistance from July 23 to August 21.[21] A month had passed, that was all, since the panzers started the war of motors rolling eastward. A month of dash and destruction and envelopments, and then it slowed and stopped. There would be renewed dashes, even more envelopments and mass surrenders, but the "smooth period" of panzer column advances was over.

Already the panzers were so worn-out they were incapable of winning the campaign, let alone the war. Logistics neglected or earlier denied meant that catastrophic failure quickly loomed instead.[22] David Stahel, widely regarded as the leading scholar of the *Barbarossa* campaign, aptly describes the whole German effort as "delusion as operative discourse."[23] Generals and Nazi ideologues alike had overlooked basic logistical realities and a mismatch between their limited military resources and unlimited military goals. They set out to conquer the Soviet Union with a German Army (and weak allied armies) that grew smaller from battle losses from the first hours and days. Within six weeks the Wehrmacht was locked into a war of brutal physical erosion, although its generals and as yet unbeaten soldiers still thought in short-war terms of encirclement battles and campaigns of sweeping tank advances reaching hundreds more miles deeper into Russia. Always grasping for a final victory that eluded them, over an enemy that was learning better how to fight and stop them, using space and scorched earth, anti-tank guns and Molotov cocktails and raw infantry courage. The western Soviet Union was several times larger than France. It was nearly 18 times the size of Poland (2.1 million square miles to just 120,000), where cocky panzer generals first waged the new armored war and persuaded themselves it and they could win anywhere. Senior generals now thought of First Marne instead. Their great fear was of stopping short of victory before Moscow, as they had stopped as younger men in front of Paris in 1914. They were right to be afraid, right to be haunted by visions of other peoples' well-defended capitals.

German generals proved early in Russia that, despite a lingering reputation even today for brilliance with tanks and field maneuvers, they had no special genius for war even at the operational level. Their triple thrust into the Soviet Union that midsummer must rank alongside the Schlieffen plan for foolhardy hubris and logistical unreality leading to catastrophic outcome. *Barbarossa* was in fact one of the worst planned, most chaotically mismanaged, most disastrous offensive campaigns in the history of modern warfare. With an economy and people unprepared for protracted war and the short-war gamble a quickly proven failure, Germany was immediately forced into a war of all-out material and human destruction against an empire with twice its population, greater military and economic resources, and at least comparable inner strength as a savagely brutal police and terror state. It was not huge space, or winter weather, or Hitler's interference with their supposed brilliance that beat the German generals and armies in Russia. It was shallow battle plans and worse logistical preparation heading into that space and weather, under that leader, whom they chose to follow.

It was also ferocious Red Army defenders who beat the Germans, who learned how to fight back, reorganized for total war, and defended without pity or mercy against a merciless invading army. German imperial ambition was stopped on one side of Europe by naval and air weaknesses and consequent inability to project military power across the Channel in the face of fierce British resistance. Germans were stopped on the other side by their weakness on land, which was only disguised by the early successes of the panzers but was revealed in their consequent inability to project military power far enough into the strategic depth of the Soviet Union to reach its vitals. Behind this double military failure lay racial and cultural arrogance, overconfidence and short-war thinking. How else could one consider, conceive, and then actually invade the largest land empire in the world except with an utter lack of strategic definition matched to real military capabilities?

Why do so while still engaged in a war against the largest sea empire in the world, also gathering its strength in the air war and attacking on land where it could, at the margins where Germany could not easily reinforce? Britain had a superior scientific and industrial base at home and open access to American and world resources via control of the sea lanes. Germany was cribbed and confined to trade with poorly and similarly blockaded local economies, and tied also to handicapping alliances with weak Italy and smaller powers in Central Europe. Campaign dexterity in Poland, good skill and good fortune in France, a divided and demoralized enemy army in Yugoslavia, none of that prepared the Wehrmacht to wage modern industrial total war. Königgrätz had reinforced quick-war illusions before the fateful plunge by Imperial Germany into protracted war in 1914. Early victories in World War II similarly reinforced ill-founded conclusions of an inherent operational superiority of the professional officer corps and Wehrmacht more generally over all enemies, even of invincibility. They braced a dangerous set of military and leadership and ideological concoctions that led directly to disaster in the east.

A few, but only a very few, saw what they had done much sooner than the rest. Most would not see it until the end of 1942 or even mid-1943. However, already in July 1941, just weeks into the *Barbarossa* campaign in Russia, the Chief of Staff of the German Army High Command (*Oberkommando des Heeres*, or OKH) had severe doubts. General Franz Halder was one of the principal architects of the Wehrmacht's abject obeisance to Hitler, going back to 1938. He cooperated and helped plan Hitler's serial aggressions, culminating in *Barbarossa*. Yet one day in July he confessed to his diary: "We have underestimated the Russian colossus, which has consciously prepared for war with all the effort that a totalitarian state can muster."[24] It was too late, and too reminiscent of Bethmann Hollweg's expression of worry on the morning he helped start the Great War. Even as Halder confessed his doubts, the panzer columns were already plunging deeper into the Soviet Union in forward-rolling self-immolation. It was total war for total ends unimagined in 1914. It would bring Nazi Germany to total defeat.

In the critical *Typhoon* operation, the drive on Moscow that began on September 30, the inherent instability of the mismatch between German operational and strategic goals led to fast shifts in priority targets, moving divisions and corps hundreds of miles from first deployments to then fight with insufficient resources along too many axes of advance. Expecting to easily surprise, disrupt and overwhelm the Red Army in another series of penetrations and sweeping envelopments right out of General Staff exercises, the Wehrmacht was itself reduced by persistent hard fighting, its losses made worse by brutal occupation policies and gross failures of transportation and logistical preparation.[25] With nearly all available men of military age already in uniform but its economy not yet fully mobilized, Germany was unable to make up the immense losses it suffered over the first six months in Russia. The tsarist Brusilov Offensive of 1916 had shown that when Russian armies were properly led they had real striking power. Germans were right to fear the Russian steamroller in 1914, wrong to hold the Red Army in contempt in 1941. Now they paid the price of that arrogance in blood, lost tanks and grinding defeat.

Germans were not done with phantasm yet, for hubris died hard among leading Nazis and the officer corps. Hitler wrongly extrapolated Red Army casualties to eight million by early November, concluding that the war was clearly and already won: "No army in the world, including the Russian, can recover from that." Evan Mawdsley, a leading scholar of the war in the east, puts it succinctly: "Wishful thinking about the battle of annihilation was replaced by wishful thinking about the war of attrition."[26] *Barbarossa* was replete with the usual German errors. This time there was also an astonishing failure of military intelligence which both exaggerated enemy casualties and missed the right numbers and types of tanks and aircraft in the Soviet order of battle, while grossly underestimating Red Army strength in rifle and tank divisions. The estimates were off the mark by wide margins, by 2:1 or more. Put another way, the Red Army was twice as large as German military intelligence thought at the start of the campaign in July, giving it vast reserves the Wehrmacht could never match. In the same month that Hitler privately proclaimed victory, while themselves trekking into the unknown on the road to Moscow many Wehrmacht officers reread Caulaincourt's 1812 diary chronicling the march of the *Grande Armée*.[27] The German Army narrowly avoided the same fate during its hasty retreat through howling snow in mid-December 1941, leaving shattered panzers and guns behind as the French had left broken carts and caissons: 4,200 lost or damaged tanks, 35,000 trucks, half a million dead horses and lots of *feldgrau* corpses, some mutilated by partisans just as Russians had mutilated French.[28]

German production never made up these huge losses. *Barbarossa-Typhoon* was for that reason and others the decisive campaign in the decisive theater of World War II. It had immense consequences for every participant in the war, and even those yet to join the fight. It put an end to Germany's *Weltmacht* ambition by forcing a contest of matériel so deep and prolonged the *Ostheer* finally just stopped, then was forced to retreat. A campaign was rushed into by planners faced with Hitler's demands to accelerate the war's timetable, so they resorted to all the old and unreliable tricks. The result was hubristic and horrifying all at once. *Barbarossa* was callous and callow in its brutal calculations of the desirability of total destruction of military and civilian targets alike, in seeking a war of annihilation (*Vernichtungskrieg*) in both the older military sense and the new Hitlerian sense of merciless genocide. It was haphazard and hasty in conception, and hugely undersupplied due to neglect of basic logistics and transportation in its execution. It endured chaotically independent generals, but without finding the good outcomes obtained largely by initiative married to chance in the campaign in France. Yet it was similarly thrusting and fast and typically German-officer professional in its purposeful striking at the flanks seeking envelopment, in its violence and goal of absolute battlefield triumph and overthrow of the enemy (*Niederwerfungsstrategie*). It was at the same time the culmination and defeat of a national style of war-making dating back to Frederick II.[29] It led directly to long-war defeat, as his "short and lively" wars had nearly done; as Schlieffen's and Moltke's *Vernichtungskrieg* plans had done in 1914; as now Hitler's and Halder's did in December 1941, and after. Mission orders and officer independence also ended, as Hitler sacked some of his best generals and took direct command of operations.

From the first day of *Barbarossa* exceptional destruction of the Wehrmacht began, until the offensive came to a grinding halt and futile defeat in the snow in front of Moscow. On December 5, the Red Army counterattacked and drove the Germans back. At a strategic level, the war was lost that same week in early December 1941. For in yet another fit of catastrophic gambler's hubris Hitler declared war on the United States six days later. Lost, but not even close to over. Most of the killing, destruction and horror lay ahead as the Wehrmacht learned that its early victories in Poland, France, the Balkans and initially also in western Russia were in fact aberrations; that the deeper tendency of modern Great Power wars was to arc toward decision by exhaustion, to move from short-war illusions to long-war attrition. The Polish and Yugoslav campaigns were won against small and isolated countries. Allied armies in France were unequal in combat power and effectiveness only due to poor dispositions and weak command. Over the rest of the long war to come, the Wehrmacht fell back to combat equality, and then to vast inferiority. Better anti-tank weapons took out the panzers while Germany's many enemies moved to full war production and coordinated an assault across all its borders and skies at once.

***

IN 1942 HITLER recognized that he needed vital resources to fight for years into the future, so he attacked south toward Kharkov and the Caucasus looking to secure food supplies and oil. Army Group South had thin reserves when it was ordered to undertake Operation *Blau* (Blue) in phases, with *Blau I* a drive to the Don starting in late June. Hitler strongly reinforced but still could only send the panzers to attack along a single axis, not the ambitious broad front and three axes of penetration made by the tanks in 1941. Army Group South was opposed by nine Soviet armies, but still reached Voronezh on the upper Don, and the Soviet extreme right flank, on July 6. Then the

Germans swung south, carrying out a classic series of rolling flank attacks while also bringing pressure to bear toward defenses on the middle Don. The result was one of the worst Soviet defeats of the whole war, as a yawning hole was ripped open and nearly 400,000 men and over 2,400 tanks were lost. However, no *Kessel* was created by the panzers, for the countryside was too open and the Red Army was learning how to retreat to avoid the pincers.

Blau II (later renamed *Clausewitz*) was planned as a rapid drive over the Donbass to take Rostov, which the lead tanks reached on July 23. Rather than assault a heavily defended city they crossed the Don farther north, then encircled Rostov from the east. Another triumph, it seemed. Hitler and OKH next divided Army Group South into Army Groups A and B. *Blau* split into two widely separated advances, incapable of mutual support. Illusory opportunity to inflict crushing damage on the Red Army, but more the lack of any governing strategy, induced Hitler to lurch from one goal to the next, shifting armies almost whimsically to reach for new objectives. Army Group A was sent onward into the Caucasus, reaching for the critical oil fields at Baku, which had drawn Hitler's eye away from Moscow and Leningrad in the first place. Its failed drive to the oil fields lasted from July 25 to December 31, 1942. Then came a spring fighting retreat through the mountain snows, nothing truly accomplished except to raise the casualty lists on both sides, in a contest of numbers that Stalin was willing to engage and the Germans would surely lose over time.[30]

Meanwhile, Army Group B started out as a mere auxiliary operation to cover the flank of the more critical effort to seize the minerals of the Caucasus. Then it trapped Soviet 62nd Army in the great Don bend in mid-August and crossed on August 21, opening a clear road to the Volga over perfect tank terrain.[31] Temptation called, and so the Germans drove on to Stalingrad. The attack entered the city and provoked months of the bitterest urban fighting perhaps of the entire war. However, German momentum petered out in the second week of November after meeting desperate resistance all autumn. Discipline was hard on both sides. On July 28, Stalin issued *Order #227* that demanded *Ni shagu nazad!* ("Not one step backward!"). NKVD blocking detachments and Red Army generals ensured that it was ruthlessly enforced at Stalingrad, and many other places. In a brilliant operation guided by General Georgi Zhukov, the most important figure in the Red Army in World War II, second only to Stalin, the Soviets struck back with overwhelming force on November 19. In this counteroffensive the Red Army displayed new skill in fighting and resupplying on the move as it hit with six armies, three on either side of two hard-pressed Soviet armies still fighting in and around the smashed streets and buildings of the "Russian Verdun." The Red Army also launched a diversionary and holding attack against Army Group North, at the Rzhev bulge. At the time there were 2.5 times as many Soviet troops and tanks and 50 percent again as many combat aircraft facing Army Group Center than facing spread-out Army Group South.

The counteroffensive at Stalingrad sliced right through 3rd Romanian Army sitting north of the city, advancing 100 miles before turning south to half-encircle German 6th Army and other Axis forces. On the southern flank, the other arm of the Soviet encirclement struck two days later, cutting through 4th Romanian Army deep into the Kalmyk steppe and the city rear area. Fleets of Soviet tanks and mobile infantry engaged that the *Abwehr* did not even suspect existed. Red Army armored columns and fast-moving infantry gobbled huge chunks of territory while leaving German strongpoints undigested and isolated in the rear, to be reduced later by follow-on troops. The pincers met at Kalach on the Don on November 23, catching all 6th Army inside. The Red Army called its maneuver a *kotel*, an encirclement. In any language, it was a *Kessel* in reverse.

Field Marshal Erich von Manstein was hurriedly recalled from the Caucasus and ordered to break through to the city with a scratch-formed Army Group Don, a hodgepodge of German, Romanian, Italian and Hungarian divisions. The commander of 6th Army, General Friedrich von Paulus, asked his *Führer* for permission to fight westward to link with Manstein, and was told to stay put and fight. Hermann Göring, head of the Luftwaffe, boasted that his planes could resupply 6th Army. They failed, miserably. It wasn't just the winter weather, it was a fundamental lack of suitable transport aircraft or enough aircraft. Frostbite and hypothermia overtook both sides, and civilians still trapped in the gutted city. Freezing, hungry, surrounded Axis troops were hard pressed as the siege closed around them. Outside the perimeter, Manstein's scratch force moved in relief on December 10. Within four days it ran into a counterstorm, as the Stavka loosed another counteroffensive to try to set a second set of deep pincers, looking to complete a double encirclement of all Axis forces within the Stalingrad battle zone. Russians attacked in numbers of infantry and new tanks and aircraft that astonished woefully undersupplied Axis armies. They quickly smashed through underequipped and demoralized Romanian, Hungarian and Italian armies, which surrendered, precipitating political crises in their home countries. Rapid advances by armored and motorized units stretched out 200 miles west of the city, threatening to trap all Manstein's Army Group Don. He pulled away, out of the closing pincer trap, halting all efforts to reach 6th Army on December 24, then reversing his line of march. The relief effort was over. Fighting, freezing, and dying inside Stalingrad went on for several more weeks.[32]

As the last airfields available to 6th Army were overrun, the last Luftwaffe aircraft to leave the tightening noose abandoned German wounded amidst scenes of decadence and total collapse of military discipline, descending into *sauve qui peut* acts of desperation. Inside the city, Red Army storm groups retook several key strongpoints on December 3, then pressed the attack street by street, house by house, even in the sewers. On January 10, the last assault began. Trapped and frozen Germans surrendered or were slaughtered in place. Just 110,000 survivors lived to see Paulus surrender on January 31. The captured enemy were marched down the banks of the Volga past singing Red Army divisions. Loaded into railway cars, they were shipped off to prison camps. A broadcast from Hitler's *Wolfsschanze* ("Wolf's Lair") HQ in the Rastenberg Forest proclaimed that "the sacrifice of the army, bulwark of a historical European mission, was not in vain."

But it was, all of it. None of the aims of *Blau* were achieved. Nazi Germany did not gain access to Baku's oil or the food stocks of southern Russia, nor could Hitler deny those resources to the Soviet Union. Worse, the Soviet war economy recovered during 1942 and began outproducing Germany's still underachieving production. That was also true of British war production, and the United States was now fully engaged in the war against Germany. Hitler turned on his generals. Heads rolled on angry orders issued from the *Wolfsschanze* as he flailed in the face of insurmountable material obstacles. Among the field marshals he sacked were Wilhelm List, Fedor von Bock and Franz Halder. The OKH fell more firmly under control of the more fawning Alfred Jodl and Wilhelm Keitel, and thus the whims and impulses of Hitler. The final change came a few months later.

The failure of both thrusts in *Blau* came from making each probe too weak, a problem of insufficient military resources and erratic leadership that would only worsen over time. Neither branching of *Blau* had any real objective other than to try to force a local Soviet military crisis. They led instead to a frustrating defeat in the Caucasus and to disaster on the Volga. Both setbacks sprang from a repetition of Ludendorff's admission that German tactical genius really came down to "punch a hole and see what develops." The Wehrmacht was still superior to its enemy in maneuver battle, although the Red Army was getting better at that, too, along with static defensive fighting. Yet *Blau* also demonstrated that military intelligence was persistently inadequate and that Germany's top political and military leadership was strategically inept. Germans had torn through Soviet defenses to reach the Don and the Volga and cut deep into the Caucasus. They encircled and destroyed whole armies and took vast swaths of territory. Then once more German armies outran their logistical systems, both in the Caucasus and at the Volga.

The Soviet counteroffensive around the breakwater of destroyed Stalingrad wrecked three Axis armies, while follow-on operations nearly trapped Army Group Don as well. It was clear by January 1943, even to Hitler and the OKH, that the Wehrmacht had suffered a strategic and not just an operational defeat. The Axis order of battle was left shorn of 50 division-equivalents of officers and men. Missing, too, were irreplaceable stocks of tanks and guns, trucks and wreckers (panzer recovery vehicles). Twenty-two Axis divisions, or rather their surviving elements, had surrendered to an enemy held in racial and martial contempt barely 18 months prior. German 6th Army and Romanian 3rd and 4th Armies were simply gone. German 4th Panzer Army was also bloodied and mauled, a remnant of its former self and combat power. The Luftwaffe was exposed as an ill-led shell of what it had been, with almost no supply capacity left and no long-range bombing capability. It had fighters for defense, but little more. Even paltry gains in the Caucasus would be surrendered in the spring, in order to pull out of another looming trap.

In mid-1943 the direction of the war reversed for good when four German armies and the bulk of German panzer forces lost at Kursk (July 5–23, 1943), the largest and most elaborate battle on the Eastern Front. Defeat for the *Ostheer* came in part from the failure of a remarkably unimaginative General Staff battle plan. It called for a blunt offensive into the teeth of an exception-ally well-prepared defense of a Soviet salient which projected 100 miles deep into German lines. The attack pincers were set to strike at the most obvious places imaginable: the hinges of the salient, precisely where Red Army gener-als suspected and prepared to defend in depth. Soviet intelligence knew de-tails of the German timetable and battle plans and met the oncoming panzer thrusts with well-hidden tank and air formations. Once again the operation was led by Georgi Zhukov, now a Marshal of the Soviet Union. He deployed his armies in dense fields designed to absorb and bog down the German assault in its earliest stages. Stalin and the Stavka had finally recognized a deep truth about the war, that it would be won only by attrition that wore down the *Ostheer*. Only then could a decisive thrust be made with dynamic Soviet tank armies and air superiority into the vitals of the *Ostheer* and then into Nazi Germany itself, in modified application of Soviet prewar thinking about "deep battle" operations.

Zhukov laid out a deep set of seven defensive belts at Kursk that absorbed the panzer blows, halted them, then smashed the panzer thrusts in both north and south. Where was the vaunted German operational art at Kursk? [33] Matched by superior Red Army defensive tactics, by minefields and tank-killing artillery and infantry. There was much courage on both sides and lots of killing and dying and the greatest tank battle in the history of war at Prokhorovka, where over 5,000 tanks and other armored vehicles engaged. [34] Despite regaining a technical advantage at Kursk with its Panthers and Tigers, Germany was being outproduced in tanks in such huge quantities by the Soviet Union and Western Allies that it never recovered its relative position from the losses of combat power in men and war machines it suffered in the summer of 1943. The accepted price of victory by Moscow was massive Soviet casualties and lost equipment. Some 3.5 million troops in total fought at and around the Kursk salient, nearly half the 8.5 million then positioned along a 1,500-mile-long Eastern Front. There followed a series of cascading Soviet offensives that, with pauses, continued until total victory in 1945. [35] During the fighting at Kursk word arrived in Berlin of landings by Western armies in Sicily. Hitler was forced to call a halt to the last strategic offensive by the *Ostheer* in order to strip away air and other assets needed for immediate defense in the West. Accelerating destruction on all fronts stripped the Wehrmacht of its offensive capability. It was forced onto permanent strategic defense, making only local counterattacks after July 1943.

German armies with fewer panzers and less air support every month dug deep into static defenses in the forested north around Leningrad and down the main fighting zones held by Army Group Center in the Vyazma-Bryansk region. Trench warfare was back, only in a discontinuous line and at strategic depths exceeding 100 miles or more. OKH shifted its remaining panzers into ad hoc battle groups which had to be widely dispersed for counterattack rather than attack roles after Kursk. Henceforth, the *Ostheer* tried to hold the long Eastern Front always with too few men and tanks and guns, with too few *Luftflotten* (air fleets) and infantry divisions, against an enemy who grew stronger every month in all things. German industry therefore shifted to defense, much later than it should have, to producing more anti-aircraft and anti-tank weapons, more assault guns and heavier tanks that sacrificed mobility to weight of armor and firepower, all necessary to support city fighting rather than open-field battle by swift panzer armies. The *Ostheer* was forced to shift from early-war blitzkrieg to what became late-war *Stellungskrieg.*

On the other side of Europe amphibious invasion loomed, threatening a similarly underequipped and indeed worse off *Westheer* that was readying to receive the return to France and the Low Countries of the Western Allies, now including the Americans and additional well-equipped Polish, Free French and Commonwealth forces. Contested retreat became the late-war German norm, not advancing to victory after victory with panzers in the lead position. Retreat from the Caucasus and southern Soviet Union. Retreat across the North African desert, pursued by British 8th Army after an Axis thrust toward Suez in mid-1942 also failed. The Wehrmacht had tasted its first big defeats at El Alamein and then Stalingrad. Two more armies would surrender to the Western Allies in Tunisia in the spring, even before the definitive turn at Kursk. It was all coming apart.[36]

The "breathing space" Hitler spoke of in 1942, the quiet time he believed he had between his declaration of war on the United States and the time Americans fully entered the war against Germany, was wasted and gone. The first American armies were already closing around the last Axis armies in North Africa at the start of 1943. The U.S. Army in the European theater was a virgin force but was learning fast, in the company of larger and more veteran British and Commonwealth forces that were at last well-armed, well-led, and made up of battle-tested and confident armored and infantry divisions. Western armies would next invade Germany's main ally Italy, from liberated south Mediterranean shores. With the Battle of the Atlantic against the U-boats effectively won just a few months into 1943, the Western Allies began building toward the main invasion of Germany through France and the Low Countries, stockpiling vast amounts of war matériel and millions of fighting men on bases in Britain. Fleets of bombers arrived in Germany's skies as a portent of what was coming, the USAAF bombing by day and the RAF pounding at night. Germany's cities were burning, one after the other. Allied heavy bomber fleets would destroy 120 German cities by 1945, some by deliberate firestorm.

Hitler's effort to build strength through an Axis coalition to match the United Nations Alliance failed. The bulk of the Romanian Army was destroyed at Stalingrad, while the Italians folded in Africa and grew dispirited on the Eastern Front. By mid-1943 Nazi Germany's minor allies were shredded of troops. Those who were left were poorly armed and morally uncommitted, of little aid to the Nazi cause beyond collaboration in the *Rassenkrieg*: the trains to the death camps were running fully loaded. Otherwise, the smaller Axis peoples were war-weary, their once confident fascist elites looking to get out before the vengeance of the Western Allies and the Red Army rode over the borders in massed tank formations the like of which Hitler's panzer generals hardly dreamed of controlling. The Western Allies were in southern Italy by

September, while the Soviets seized all initiative on the Eastern Front after Kursk. Three world empires were aroused and in arms against Nazi Germany, determined to destroy Hitlerism and German military power for generations to come. Any grand strategy Berlin thought it had was done. Any hope for *Weltmacht* gone. All that the German armed forces could do for the rest of the war was delay their inevitable retreat to the battered and bombed *Heimat* and their own final defeat and destruction. All that German civilians could do was watch their homes and cities turned to rubble all around them, watch their armies lose and their menfolk die. For all this Hitler blamed the Jews. The more Germans died and the closer Nazi defeat approached the more the killing machine of the Shoah accelerated its death rate, too.[37]

***

GERMANS NEVER CONSIDERED Russia unconquerable, having conquered it in 1918. Yet they neglected all the blood lost in the war of matériel that took place before that, from 1914 to 1917, before the tsar's army broke. So they dressed up enthrallment with battle as the quick campaign and sought decisive victory by panzer. From 1943, all they managed to accomplish by fighting every day was to stave off defeat to a different tomorrow. The once mighty *Ostheer* had been nearly victoried to death in western Russia in 1941, then again in its foolhardy advances to the Caucasus and Stalingrad in 1942. It was already severely wounded in the south when 6th Army reached the Volga and the inner city at Stalingrad and stopped moving east. After Kursk the whole *Ostheer* was seriously wounded and staggering, as it began the long retreat that ended in the ruins of Berlin in 1945. The paradox is that aircraft and tank and gun production for all major powers increased into 1944, forced enlistments swelled newly-formed divisions, armies and army groups, and the greatest amount of killing lay ahead. Germany was strategically defeated by 1943, but not yet beaten in the field in east or west. Most casualties of the war, military and civilian, still lay in the future. Especially along the Eastern Front.

The killing rate soared as two totalitarian empires grappled in a democracy of destruction and death. Until just a few months before the end of the war nearly all fighting on the Eastern Front still took place on Soviet soil. In the flat and treeless steppelands of the south fighting was more fluid, with far-reaching penetrations and envelopments still possible for a war of panzers. Sometimes panzers pushed locally eastward, but then big Red Army offensives moved the front always farther west. In the Pripet Marshes, partisans fought SS death battalions making kill-all sweeps through the swamps. Farther north, tank movement was inhibited by World War I–style trenches and earthworks. In the thick forests around Bryansk and Leningrad a war of siege and position visited with ghosts of Verdun and Ypres and the old war of spades. Germans, Russians and Finns also fought above the Arctic Circle, chipping into frozen ground with picks, fighting over ice lakes under pale white nights or in perpetual dark, trampling tundra flowers and mosses under boots and rolling tank treads during short summer days. Railways and truck convoys carried the living to the ice front along with millions of tons of equipment and shells. Horse-drawn carts and sledges took dead and wounded back to the rear, broken bodies still in Russian winter white or summer brown or in German and Finnish *feldgrau*. Young men who never dreamed they might see, let alone die in, such a clean and well-lighted place fell, as Voltaire said of an earlier frostbitten war, contending "over a few acres of snow."[38] And from hate. And pride of nations. And hard ideologies of relentless modernity. And macabre cults of acidly murderous personality.

The initial German advantage of surprise in 1941, compounded by Soviet internal instability and hostility to the regime in non-Russian frontier provinces, gave the *Ostheer* stunning opening victories—but only for a month or two, when the smooth and clear-cut winning stopped. Within six months it all evaporated into blood and smoke as the Red Army's fighting retreat wore down the Germans. *Barbarossa-Typhoon* also broke too many Red Army divisions, so that raw replacement armies in 1942 were badly mauled. Still, ordinary Russians learned how to fight better. From the end of 1942 they had more and better weapons to fight with. Core ethnic Russian units fought hard for nationalist reasons as the Red Army retreated out of the non-Russian western provinces into Russia itself. By 1943 Red Army divisions were of higher quality than in 1941, their troops and leaders knew how to counter German tactics, and morale was recovered. Soviet generals were better, too. Early favorites and old *Konarmiia* cronies of Stalin were fired or promoted into the Stavka, giving way to a new generation. Stalin showed some capacity for leadership and learning that tracked in reverse Hitler's hardening to experience and advice. He gave more rein to his best generals, while Hitler increasingly made the most minute decisions himself. Germany also lost, and the Soviet Union won, because the Red Army fought as part of an overpowering anti-German coalition of Great Powers, just as tsarist Russia did not beat Napoleon alone but as part of the Grand Alliance of 1813–1815. Nazi Germany was overmatched from 1943, attacked from all sides, and in the end also outfought by a coalition whose armies learned to blunt the initially novel

Wehrmacht tactics, whose efficacy wore out over time along with the reduced panzer armies.

Russia was not Poland or France. Not in size, or latent or actual military strength. Not in its Roman-like strategic space and depth of resources. Nor was it at all like France in the sheer savagery of Nazi repression and race and occupation policies, and the consequent ferocity of the irregular peoples' wars that came to characterize Soviet and other resistance in the East.[39] In addition, there was the vast destruction caused by the more traditional uniformed war, by the trenches and assaults, tanks and artillery, large moving armies and huge army groups that tore apart cities and countryside alike. As important as these differences, maybe more so, was the fact that neither the Nazis nor the Wehrmacht had any idea how to fight or win this different kind of war, a contest of deep moral and material resources at a scale and a duration for which they had not planned and which they could not control or limit once it began. The Nazis had only a murderous race theory that provoked more enemies into arms and deepened all the peoples' wars the more ideologues in Berlin and SS cadres in the field sought to implement Nazism in practice in occupied lands. They had only a crude leadership principle (*Führerprinzip*), which concentrated too much power of decision in too few hands, and into the wrong and frequently inept hands, more so as the war continued into 1944 and 1945 As the war went ever more badly for German armies and *Landser*, Nazis would turn to apportioning blame for defeat in dismissals and executions of German officers and then of ordinary soldiers.

Officers of the Wehrmacht had their vaunted mission tactics freedom and initial confidence in General Staff operations planning, but what they knew about war had been learned on smaller battlefields against more limited enemies. They rejected their own experience and skill at *Stellungskrieg* displayed from 1915 to 1918, yet proposed no war-winning plan or strategy for fighting deep inside Russia against an enemy which would not quit or surrender, and grew ever stronger as the *Ostheer* weakened with first battle contact, and ever more so from the end of 1941. Nazi Germany lacked the economy and population capable of mobilizing for total war to defeat the Soviet Union, which was organized for total war on the other side well before 1941. Nazis and the Wehrmacht, and by the end the distinction grew blurred, lacked the resources to match the hubris of their ambition. Their actions forced into being an otherwise unlikely grand coalition of three hugely powerful yet dissimilar empires—American, British and Russian—along with many smaller but contributing nations from Australia to India to Canada and Brazil. The Wehrmacht believed it had restored decisiveness to battle, thinking that was enough to restore decisiveness to short and lively wars through battle. It was not. Raw, coarse, brutal attrition remained the cruel, demanding and deciding god of modern industrial war. And so the terrible sacrificing on the altars of national and leadership vanity went on.

Barbarossa on the Soviet side was a story of blindness to danger and then blundering by Stalin, of military catastrophe following catastrophe and the worst casualties suffered in military history. Also a tale of astonishing recovery and resistance, and one of the greatest feats of heroic endurance of all time.[40] On the German side it was a story of extreme hubris, inadequate then broken logistics, hectic scrambling, shattered triumphalist illusions, and savage murder on an unheard-of scale. It must be asked, why did Hitler undertake to do it? Why were his generals so eager to go along with his war, that reached not just for the complete destruction of the Red Army but for the physical annihilation of whole peoples? Hitler did it out of an extreme ideological commitment that underlay his entire approach to war. His whole world-view and understanding of history was written in perverse, faux-biological theories of *Rassenkampf*, race struggle, and *Rassenkrieg*, race war. These were crackpot notions rising out of the miasma of social Darwinism that passed for systematic thinking in Nazi Party circles. Crude ideas of war and survival, of fighting as above economics, of race as the basis of power permeated *Mein Kampf* and Hitler's then unpublished second book, and all his speech, public and private. We know what Hitler wanted. So did his generals at the time.[41]

The generals shared more elements of this worldview than they later admitted, ranging from Hitler's fairly typical short-war thinking to conceit in their own special ability to wage fast campaigns like no other army. They were seduced by the idea of decisive battle, war of the ideal type seen at Cannae, Leuthen and Ulm. It led them into a catastrophic and total defeat that left Germany and their reputations in smoking ruins. It was at one level the culmination of generations of national risk-taking and ambition, of a Prussian-German military style of fast maneuver that ignored logistical constraints, was barely cognizant of intelligence on the enemy, indulged disobedient generals cocky about their abilities to improvise success on the fly, and above all lacked any overall guiding strategy or political restraint. Wehrmacht officers brought their own intellectual baggage and blinders to the gambler's table, their reliance on *Niederwerfungsstrategie* (literally "overthrow strategy") and *Vernichtungskrieg*, the ideal campaign and war of annihilation. Those terrible iron dice had been carried around by General Staff officers ever since they were first rolled by the elder Moltke to defeat Austria in 1866 and France in 1870. They were rolled again in 1914, and led to disaster. Thrown yet again in 1939 and 1940, they brought qualified successes. In 1941 this blinkered thinking was all that German planners could conceive, taking on the greatest military opponent in their history. *Longue durée* total-war realities, of the kind that drove more realistic Western Allied and Soviet planning and procurement decisions, were pushed aside in favor of the virtuoso general's art, pushed out of mind while making lightning dashes with the panzers and Luftwaffe. This highly constricted military imagination held sway in place of any real strategic concept. Somehow, operational skill would present further opportunities for victory. All the generals needed do to win was to punch another hole and keep winning.

It was all achingly familiar, a national or German way of war centered on old traditions of situational training, officer initiative and mission tactics, maneuver warfare, shock attacks, and aiming for surprise at the operational level, but without a war-winning strategic concept or cocoon beyond the first winning campaign or two.[42] Confidence born of their small victory of 1939 and strange victory of 1940 led to another bout of profound conceit at the start of *Barbarossa* in mid-1941. The belief that they could and would win fast brought two more years of all-or-nothing armored thrusts, staking all on diminishing operational returns inside an insoluble strategic dilemma, until Hitler and his generals were stopped at Stalingrad and Kursk, two immense accelerants of destruction in the east added to large defeats at Alamein and Tunisia. Nor was it just Nazis and officers. Intellectuals and cultural leaders were in on the great war gambles, too, committed to them over decades. Not just rough gambles with Germany's destiny, but with all Europe's, and by extension in an age of world empires, gambles with all the world. Historian Otto Hintze wrote during World War I: "If worse comes to worst, we shall let ourselves be buried beneath the ruins of European civilization."[43] Thirty years later, Germans who read him and thought much the same thing made it come true.

The German armed forces were a broad but not blank canvas on which the amateur artist and warlord brooding in Berlin painted his designs. Nazi ideas spread through the German military, contributing to massacres and atrocities that attended military operations everywhere all through the war: at sea, on land, from the air. The Luftwaffe was thoroughly nazified. The Kriegsmarine less so, although the U-boat service was, under Admiral Karl Dönitz, Hitler's successor and the last *Führer* in May 1945.[44] Spontaneous racial and related killings took place in Poland in 1939 and France in 1940, including massacres of black soldiers in the French Army, when *Westheer* troops murdered 1,000–3,000 captured Africans (*tirailleurs sénégalais* and Berbers). The killings were stoked by prewar hate in the ideological ambience of the *Hitlerjugend,* then nazified training of soldiers. But they also tapped into much older atrocity stories about *Schwarzen,* or "blacks," and lurid tales of facing *tirailleurs* in 1870 and 1914. There were also wild legends of a so-called Black Horror carried out by foreign troops in the Rhineland in 1918.[45] The facts and the motivations of widespread *Landser* participation in atrocities, massacres, murder of prisoners of war and acts of genocide are today all well documented.[46] Most men did not commit such horrific war crimes or participate in genocide out of fear of their superiors in the *Heer* or retaliation by the Nazi regime if they refused, for there was little to no punishment meted out in cases where decent men in *feldgrau* in fact refused to kill civilians or prisoners. Though it was not universal, an almost analgesic murder system and expectation of routine participation in atrocity was widespread across both the Wehrmacht and Waffen SS.

Rather than restrain this behavior, many German officers who did not consider themselves to be Nazis nonetheless embraced Nazi race goals, including exterminationist policies and practices in whole or part. Wehrmacht officers, not just Waffen SS or the callous killers of the *Einsatzgruppen*, implemented Hitler's so-called "commissar order" in 1941, to murder all captured Soviet political officers (commissars and lower-ranked *politruks*). Executions were carried out by all 13 German armies and 44 corps during the *Barbarossa* campaign. Millions of Red Army prisoners of war—the direct responsibility of the Wehrmacht, not the SS or rear area Nazi Gauleiters (governors)—were deliberately starved or left to die from exposure over the winter of 1941–1942. By German count, over 10,000 died on average every day over the first seven months of the war in the east.[47] The guiding aim and attitude of the generals was to be rid of millions of "useless eaters," POWs or civilians incapable of work who competed with German soldiers for food taken from the local populations, also left to starve and freeze as callow youths in *feldgrau* took their winter clothing and meager shelters, driving families into nights of snow. Depopulation by murder and starvation was a prerequisite to the *Ostheer* living off the lands it conquered. It was also prerequisite to planned ethnic German resettlement of what the Nazis called "racially cleansed" territories. The claim that Wehrmacht officers acted as a professional military aloof from Nazi politics and genocide was a grand lie, purveyed by the generals in their Nuremberg testimony and in their memoirs.[48]

The Wehrmacht was not the *Kaiserheer.* Its privates, NCOs and officers got right down in the blood and mud to kill prisoners or civilians routinely and on a massive scale. Sometimes it was instrumental, to secure a rear area or in reprisal for the least resistance. Or they did it just because they could. The worst had no reason to fear punishment from above should they indulge their most savage and cruel desires. German officers did not punish men for that.[49] Food shortages caused by occupation policy that disincentivized agriculture with total harvest confiscations added more unrest and death in military rear areas. Forced labor programs and deportations also provoked young people to run away or join partisan units. As the partisan bands grew in size and capability more savagery ensued. German HQs often designated unarmed and helpless runaways as "bandits," making them legitimate military targets. Nearly unquestioning compliance with Hitler's directive for mercilessly "combating banditry" (*Bandenbekämpfung*) provided thin justification for open massacres of civilians of all ages, especially Jews. Ferocious manhunts were part of a larger elimination program, joining slave labor (*Erfassung*, or "registration [of persons to hard labor]") and full genocide (*Endlösung der Judenfrage*, or "final solution of the Jewish question").[50] Contributing in the deep background was the Moltkean heritage of the harsh Prussian response to peoples' war in France in 1870, still a critical memory among officers that set up a perception that all partisan activity was criminal and hence justly subject to merciless military punishment. In World War II that included setting up designated kill-all zones and sweeping them for suspected bandits.

It was all enormously counterproductive to German exploitation of conquered lands, which was a central war aim. Extreme murderous repression in the east provoked ever greater passive resistance, then economic noncooperation, and ultimately some form of armed resistance. That made the occupied bloodlands of eastern and central Europe less valuable to the German war effort as well as less governable by SS and Wehrmacht overseers. As resistance of all kinds spread, rear areas behind the combat zones drew off scarce and desperately needed troops and frontline resources to carry out genocide and confiscations and labor roundups.[51] Most occupied territory thus produced diminishing economic returns just as these became ever more vital to the German war effort. The perpetrators did not care. They could not think or act differently, being who they were, where they were, with such power over life and death of millions. Resistance therefore increased reprisals and elevated the sadistic cruelty of fresh atrocities, leading to more resistance. Where other populations caught up in fighting in the last war had embraced a community of suffering in its wake but rejected war, the Nazis inculcated in Germans, not just in German soldiers, a community of battle that spoke of shared glory inside the destructiveness of war.[52] And for the Nazis, war was the essential tool of *Rassenkampf*.

The generals later tried to shift all blame for defeat and for their war crimes onto Hitler and other Nazis. Yet from the start they cleaved to a military culture that enabled his extreme exercise of strategic and ultimately also operational authority, and his wars of extermination against unarmed peoples as well as armies. With rare exceptions of principled disobedience, most German officers obeyed Hitler to his last days in the bunker in burned-out Berlin, even as he stripped them of final military authority within the Wehrmacht. Officers were like uniformed Fausts, losing bits of soul inch by inch in a dread bargain they had made by accepting Hitler's supremacy in the 1930s, merely in return for panzers and primacy of place among the beneficiaries of the Nazi revolution and war state. They accepted Hitler as their *Führer*, doing so personally and by oath to his spoken name. They did it despite his military ignorance and lack of training beyond trench running as a courier and corporal in the last war. They claimed they were bound to do so by their loyalty oath, but they were oath-bound to Weimar, too, and easily broke their word to that young and struggling democracy that might have kept Nazism at bay.[53]

Officers followed Hitler into destruction not from misplaced honor but from lack of it, and because they agreed with most of his goals for Germany and even with his extreme methods. General Staff officers and field commanders at the highest levels shared many elements of the Nazi worldview: anticommunism, antipacifism, vicious anti-Semitism. Above all, they agreed to rearmament and militarization of German society in the 1930s as a necessary step on the path back to aggressive and expansionist war and their old dream of serving in the military of a true *Weltmacht*. Exterminationist policies were tied directly to Hitler's ecstatic sense of impending total victory over the Soviet Union in 1941, then to blood vengeance for losing the war after that. They knew it, and they agreed to help him carry out his genocidal program, some ordering the killings with real enthusiasm. He told them before he started in 1939 that the purpose of his wars was *Rassenkrieg*, the wholesale destruction of entire and ancient peoples of Europe. They did not object. It was the whole point of the war. His war and theirs.

With a few principled exceptions—notably General Ludwig Beck, Major General Hans Oster, Major-General Henning von Tresckow and Admiral Wilhelm Canaris—nearly all senior officers were willing and even eager conspirators in the Nazi serial aggressions. Many were keen participants in regime atrocities and war crimes carried out in their command areas.[54] Too many officers shared Hitler's basic political and race views, including his ambition for a "racially purified" national community (*Volk*) erected through war as a dominant land empire in the east. Not all, but certainly most. The circle of senior officers who resisted war crimes was somewhat wider than the very narrow group who were active resisters willing to kill Hitler and displace the Nazi regime. There were several officers who protested against war crimes without ever joining the active resistance, such as the plot that led to the failed *Valkyrie* assassination and coup attempt on July 20, 1944. Within the officer corps there was a wide spectrum between direct participation in mass murder programs and principled opposition to them, a range of responses at all ranks: outright participation in criminal murders, reluctant acquiescence, personal indifference, modest opposition and, most rarely, covert or overt resistance.[55]

In the field, many commanders cooperated not just willingly but eagerly with the brutal *Einsatzgruppen* mobile murder brigades in their zones of responsibility and with Nazi food policy in occupied territories that they knew meant starvation of innocent millions.[56] Some took secret bribes from Hitler. All expected to be rewarded once they won the war, up to grants of immense baronial estates carved from dead countries with enslaved survivors to work their lands. They rallied to Hitler after every assassination failure by more principled colleagues with far more character and courage than they ever felt or showed. They rigidly believed that war demanded unity of political and

Einsatzgruppen in Ukraine (1942).

military command in one set of hands: Frederick's, Napoleon's, Moltke's, now Hitler's.[57] They accepted him as a latter-day *König-Feldherr*—their supreme commander and Germany's warlord. He would blend operations and policy as Frederick had, make politics and war as a seamless whole. Officers proud of their own military professionalism hence followed into a second *Weltkrieg* a rank amateur, a *böhmischer Gefreite* in Hindenburg's words, a mere "Bohemian corporal." They did so to Germany's moral and military ruin and their own—an officer corps of *feldgrau* Fausts stripped of soul and emptied of honor. Too often, because of their postwar lies, in histories of the war their professional feats of arms and technical skill are exaggerated or just recounted without this being said.

The *Ostheer* both advanced into and murdered its way to defeat in the east. The coarse ideological and racial nature of Nazi Germany's war made it much harder to win, and harder to exploit the spoils of war to make war pay for itself. Anti-Soviet populations that greeted forward German units as liberators, with offerings of bread and salt, quickly learned how wrong they were. Only Hitler could have made Stalin preferable by comparison in these captive nations, a cold and forbidding leader who had already killed millions of his own people by mass starvation, deportations, and in the Gulag. Hitler never saw the connection between prosecution of race war and losing the war of armies, for his war *was* the race war. Stalin at least recognized the potential of partisan warfare that broke out spontaneously against Nazi occupation across the western Soviet Union. He sent in officers and advisers to organize it and air-dropped weapons and supplies to exploit it militarily, though he also sent spies and secret police and assassins to control it, and later to eliminate it as a rival to his returning authority in 1944 and 1945. Partisans provided intelligence, sabotage of German logistics and killing of stragglers over a vast area. They tied down occupation troops and made a significant contribution to occupation woes, if less to *Ostheer* losses.[58] There was little to no comparable effort behind the lines against the Red Army, though a different Germany following a different occupation policy might well have supported one and benefited from local hatred of Soviet power.

Hitler saw the war in the east in purely ideological terms of his radical utopian vision of *Rassenkrieg,* as a cleansing racial struggle for territory and food in lands he viewed as empty of worthy souls and lives. Although the Nazis knew nothing of DNA, whose confirmed discovery did not come until 1953 when Nazism was in embers and ruin, their central war aim was nothing less than rewriting the human genome. Hitler's race war aimed at the military defeat of enemy armies only as prelude to physical elimination of whole peoples and classes, of Jews and Bolsheviks, Slavic intellectuals and cultural leaders, males of military age. All were to disappear from history and biology and the world, to be followed over years of occupation and resettlement by tens of millions more Slavs killed or expelled to clear a contiguous land empire settled by the racially vetted and purified German *Volk*. Then Germany would have the resource base and security of food supply, with which Hitler was obsessed, needed to ascend to world power. Insofar as the Nazis assimilated Clausewitz at all, which was not deeply, they revised him to say that annihilation of enemies in war (expanded to domestic enemies as well as foreign, civilian as well as military) was not the instrument or continuation of policy but its completion. The purpose of all war and policy for the Nazi regime was absolute destruction of enemy armies and of race enemies. Mass murder was built in from the outset, essential to the scheme. In all this Hitler and his Nazi cadres had wide support among Germany's leading political, military, scientific and economic elites.[59]

The fact that across the frontlines was the other great mass murderer of the 20th century, Josef Stalin, made the Eastern Front meat grinder even worse for the armies and peoples caught in its crimson gears. Millions in the western Soviet Union were killed in place in their homes and villages as industrial war rose over them as defeat of the German plan for a quick and easy victory in 1941 became protracted and total war. In addition to ethnic Poles, Jews, Ukrainians and Russians, millions of ordinary Armenians, Georgians, Kazakhs, Siberians, Uzbeks, Yakuts, and a dozen more minorities pulled into uniform or war factories from the Caucasus and across Siberia and elsewhere, were drowned in a tsunami of violence. Waves of suffering rolled over the grass oceans of the steppe lands, crashed into burning northern forests, inundated gutted and ashen cities. Deepening loyalty to one's own community was induced by shared suffering, but matched by terrible savagery toward the enemy as barbarism crept into every peoples' response during a filthy contest without limits.[60] Millions of men and women were determined to survive it as civilized people anyway. They resisted nihilism as day resists night, losing as often as they won but rising again and fighting back as Soviet military losses alone reached 10 million and 17 million more Soviet civilians died in killing fields unequaled in the history of war.[61]

As Nazi Germany started to run out of fighting men it called up specialist workers previously exempted for service in key war industries. To replace them, it imported millions of slaves and other forced laborers from all occupied lands. By mid-1944 some 5.6 million foreign workers were brought into Germany to clean its streets of rubble, sew its soldiers' uniforms, build its weapons: prisoners of war (French, Italian, Polish and Russian); Ukrainian slave girls sent into middle-class homes and to middling farms; even Jews, technically forbidden to set foot in the Reich but reprieved for a few months more to work to death in hidden German factories, malnourished and ill-treated, beaten or hanged for the most minor offenses against camp rules.[62] Many thousands lived and slaved underground at Nordhausen in the Harz mountains in Saxony, in a concentration camp codenamed DORA (*Mittelbau KL*). They worked on, but sometimes sabotaged, the last Hitlerian fantasies, his *Wunderwaffen* ("wonder weapons"), rockets and jets that would steal victory from the ash pile Nazism made of Germany and Europe.

Russian POWs were put to work in growing numbers in Wehrmacht field divisions as "Hiwis" (*Hilfswillige* or *Hilfsfreiwillige*), military auxiliaries or "volunteer helpers" assigned to shrinking combat units in desperate need of laborers so that all the Germans could fight instead. They were abused and despised, but did it in return for a little food or just not being shot.[63] Some served under arms in the anti-Soviet "Vlasov's Army" or as *Osttruppen* in "eastern brigades." They were shot whenever captured by the Red Army, as many thousands of Hiwis were after Stalingrad and more later in the war. Others were shot after the war ended. They were interrogated in German POW or work camps by Stalin's agents, grim men from SMERSH ("Death to Spies"), the military counterintelligence agency. They were condemned, deported to Siberia or ordered executed immediately for the treason of having surrendered in 1941 or 1942.[64] Hitler was right when he said in January 1943: "In this war there will not be the victors and the defeated, only the survivors and the destroyed."[65]

***

THE WEHRMACHT AND Nazi regime both proved incapable of matching tactics and operations to a war-winning strategy. Instead, they increasingly relied on what amounted to military superstitions about their claimed historical and professional superiority. This time, they also incorporated spurious racial perversions promising to overcome material inferiorities with the moral force and triumph of fascist will, a racial and ideological conceit militarily embodied in the Waffen SS. At first these units were disdained by Wehrmacht commanders, but soon the generals clamored for SS Panzer divisions to be attached to their armies, knowing they were better equipped and better motivated, fanatic fighters who were often more reliable than regular divisions. More ruthless also in pursuit of the *Rassenkrieg*. It was radical but also familiar, this call upon the moral factor in war that is so often the last resort of the materially overmatched. A related fantasy flowing from the need for fighting men led to Hitler's (and Himmler's) meetings with Muslim dissenters from the Soviet Union and colonies of the Western empires. Hitler was a vague though grossly ill-informed admirer of Islam, which he did not differentiate by country or region but instead regarded as a marker of one of the strongest of the "martial races" in history. The idea some in the SS proposed was to arrange a Nazi alliance with "the Islamic world," to somehow mobilize to the German cause millions of Muslims in India, the Middle East, the Balkans, and the southern Soviet Union. It led to a few thousand Muslims fighting in brigades of the Waffen SS and Wehrmacht, for local or personal reasons, but it had no strategic consequences of any kind.[66] On to the next fantasy.

As the war turned to decision by inexorable erosion of men and matériel after Kursk, Hitler relied more often on his personal experience of fighting in the trenches in World War I. He turned away from the military professionals who still urged more fluid attacks with the panzers, more unbridled *Bewegungskrieg*. He was a corporal back then, with no strategic eye or experience. Still, he disdained advice from OKW and an officer corps he always despised. This turn to instinct and limited experience led him to major errors of overly rigid defense that hastened defeat on both major fronts, later giving the generals a chance to say he ruined their war. All along, sycophants in his military court had encouraged belief in his military genius and his claims to be a geostrategic visionary. He was more usually, although not always, a tactical blunderer who increasingly refused to make reasoned retreats that might save entire corps and armies from encirclement and destruction, to let them fight another day. There was no national decision-making body to correct his errors, no equivalent to the Soviet GKO or the War Cabinet in Britain or the Joint Chiefs in Washington, let alone the Combined Chiefs of Staff (CCS) shared by the leaders of the Western Allies. Kowtowing generals at OKW like Keitel and Jodl might query an order, but never challenged him institutionally. It was another major flaw in the German way of war. Nevertheless, the generals must also shoulder a great deal of blame for the defeats. They were far less competent, let alone brilliant, than their self-image, self-serving postwar lies and self-crafted reputation say. They always wanted to do the only thing they knew, pursue limited operations seeking to resolve insoluble grand-war problems they had created by servicing military fantasies, Hitler's and their own. Long after conditions dictated defense, they still sought quick offensives with the panzer armies, struggling against suffocation by attrition like feral cats in a closing burlap sack.

In mid-1944 the Soviets and the Western Allies released massive and well-equipped army groups into offense, approaching Germany along multiple axes of advance simultaneously. Under the onslaught, the Wehrmacht quickly and progressively demodernized. Even panzer divisions, the pride of the new German military theory and key to early success, grew reliant on horse transport. In a far cry from the half-tracks still shown today in boastful newsreels made by Josef Goebbels, panzergrenadier battalions were issued bicycles to try to keep up with the tanks.[67] Maybe another "Miracle of the House of Brandenburg" might save Hitler's Germany, as once a stroke of fortune saved Frederick and Prussia? Even Hitler sometimes thought this, dreaming of escape from defeat through the deaths of Stalin or Churchill or FDR. Others agreed that a leadership death might change the course of the war, but these brave men failed to kill Hitler at his eastern HQ in the *Valkyrie* coup attempt on July 20, 1944. After the July Plot and Hitler's furious blood purge of the officer corps that followed, senior commands went to more loyal generals and even some overt Nazis, such as Field Marshal Walter Model. He was at least a militarily competent loyalist. Others were not, as when Himmler was briefly given a field command in 1945. To the last days of the regime Nazi leaders never let on even to each other, let alone to the German public, that the war was unwinnable and that defeat loomed at any hour. Instead, they ratcheted up propaganda, further nazified social organizations, and increased direct coercion inside Germany. Hitler's best biographer, Ian Kershaw, affirms that Hitler "had no exit strategy from the war."[68] Neither did the Allies, other than Germany's unconditional surrender and destruction of the Nazis. There was no going back, no negotiations to be made. It was a fight to the absolute finish on both sides.

Losing the war of motors and matériel almost from the first day was basic to Germany's defeat in 1945. Nazi managers made only a minor effort to organize the economy for a protracted war before 1939. Partly that was due to wishful thinking, but also because Hitler wanted a high level of civilian production in order to damp down internal unrest, which was how he (falsely) thought the last war had been lost in 1918. Most importantly for unpreparedness, Hitler provoked a fight with the Western Allies over Poland years before he expected to have to wage a long war, and well before the German economy was readied to sustain one. As late as April 1941, seven million howitzer shells could not be finished for lack of high explosive and propellant, while only 50 assault guns were turned out monthly. For all the admiring talk then and since about panzers, it is notable that German tank production did not peak until 1944, and then only at the expense of the Luftwaffe and U-boats in a great three-way rivalry for limited steel and skilled workers.[69] Obsolete tank chassis were welded under bigger main guns to make ad hoc anti-tank and other field weapons, while Western Allied industries produced tens of thousands of new assault guns and well-designed anti-tank guns as well as tanks. Even the severely war-damaged Soviet economy outproduced Germany's from 1943.[70]

Although the United States was still neutral until December 1941, it was already building out immense war industries far beyond what the Axis powers could match even in combination. Americans built nearly 68,000 tanks during World War II, and many more armored vehicles from half-tracks to armored cars to tank destroyers. The Soviet Union built 80,000 T-34s and light and heavy tanks. The British built many thousands of armored vehicles from light and heavy tanks to armored cars. Smaller economies like Canada also contributed to logistical swamping of the Axis by superior war production.[71] Even with captured vehicle and armaments production capability in occupied countries, Germany could not keep pace. Overall, German industry built just 46,000 armored vehicles. Many were late-war StuGs (*Sturmgeschütz*) and other assault guns designed for city fighting, mounted on obsolete tank chassis. Fewer than 2,000 panzers were the famously powerful and heavily armored Tiger Is or IIs. German war industry suffered as much or more from gross mismanagement under inept and frequently corrupt Nazi bosses as it did from shortages and supply and transport bottlenecks.

The Germans similarly fell far behind their enemies when it came to producing combat aircraft and air transport capability. In 1939 the entire U.S. aircraft industry had produced just 6,000 planes. From 1940 to 1945 the United States built 300,000 military aircraft, even though it sharply cut back production in 1944 as by then it had a surplus. In the same time frame, Britain added more than 130,000 military aircraft, including big heavy bombers that Germany did not attempt to match. The USSR built almost 160,000 military aircraft by the end of the war. German production of aircraft from 1939 to 1945 was under 120,000. Its ally Japan built just 76,000 planes, while Italy produced a paltry 13,253 military aircraft of all types in the years 1939 to 1943, when Mussolini was toppled.[72] German war production was handicapped by an effective naval blockade from 1939, compelling it to find substitutes for certain critical minerals and for fuel of all sorts. It was also subject to constant and heavy Allied bombing from 1943, which forced a shift to underground factories and dispersed manufacture. More targeted bombing in 1944 severely hampered fighter aircraft and coal oil production, and wrecked the rail net.

Even so, at the height of Nazi territorial expansion in mid-1942 Berlin had access to continental resources that should have allowed Germans to compete militarily much better and longer than they did. Instead, the Nazis mismanaged their war economy and so brutally repressed occupied peoples of their new empire that they guaranteed gross economic inefficiencies and hard resistance to efficient exploitation. Wars were launched to secure to Nazi Germany the resources to make more wars, then Hitler's inept regime utterly failed to exploit its opportunities. It turned to expropriation and forced and slave labor, while the Gestapo and SS squandered the good will of colonized peoples who might have greeted Germans as liberators from Soviet tyranny but were turned to resistance instead. On the other side, the Soviet Union and the Western Allies all made maximum use of their scientific, engineering, agricultural, transportation and production capabilities to overwhelm the Axis with the quality and quantity of their war effort.

Victory and defeat did not just come from comparative industrial capacity. It was not just about initiative-crushing and superior Allied firepower on the ground and from the sky, a final victory guaranteed by sheer numbers of planes and tanks and troops and war matériel. It was not simply an inevitable outcome of winning the war of motors, as the rank materialist Stalin said it must be. It also took superior foresight, leadership, wartime planning and strategic management. In all those areas the Nazis came up short, too. Very often, the Wehrmacht was also out thought or deceived by Western and Soviet intelligence in ways that had a major impact on the conduct and outcome of the war. German generals and troops were also outfought as the war continued, sometimes by numerically inferior Allied forces, as in the defensive battle at Mortain in Normandy and the better-known Ardennes campaign ("Battle of the Bulge"), and in other engagements on the Eastern Front.[73] By the end of the war most of the armies still waging it were far superior in combat skill to the place they had started, whether that had been as volunteer forces or mass armies of green conscripts with inadequate weapons. They were all better at managing larger units and battle, and quite efficient killing machines. Except for the Wehrmacht, which had only a fraction left of its original combat power, mobility and skill. Other armies were tired, eroded and nearing exhaustion; the Germans were broken.

Germany's war effort was further held back by extreme racism. Jews, Poles and other people of talent were banned from research, management and the universities. Many traveled abroad to join advanced Allied war research programs instead, including the Manhattan Project and various intelligence services. As for misogyny, even homeland emergency services did not mass-deploy women until 1941, long after all other major belligerents used women in war work and as uniformed auxiliaries. Nazi exterminationist ideology on race never relented, but the Nazis did give way concerning women as the strain of total war shifted views about the roles of women everywhere: 500,000 women were in the Wehrmacht in some capacity by 1945, while another million served in *Flakwaffenhelferinnen*, or anti-aircraft crews.[74] Even so, more was done sooner to bring women into vital war work in all the Western countries and by the Soviet Union, where a sharp shortage of men due to high casualties provided an additional spur to recruitment. Some 900,000 women served in the Red Army, with female conscription initiated in 1942. Perhaps 520,000 Soviet women fought in frontline units ranging from day bombers to night fighter pilots to tankers (drivers, loaders and gunners). More served as snipers, machine gunners, demolition troops, combat engineers, even infantry in grim "Women's Battalions of Death" that were modeled on Bolshevik originals of 1917 and the Russian Civil War. Another 200,000 served as combat medics and hundreds of thousands in rear areas and in anti-aircraft units. Millions more women did essential war work in factories and on farms, some literally pulling plows in harness to replace horses, oxen and tractors gone to the fronts to haul guns to better kill Germans.[75]

From the start, the British showed they intended to fight however long it took. Their peripheral approach of attacking Germany's minor allies and outer territories was a form of strategic attrition, undertaken while still without major allies in 1940–1941. The main idea was to weaken Germany internally with bombing while choking off external links via naval blockade; to use Britain's amphibious capability but severely limited land forces to chop off extensions and lesser Nazi allies (Italy and Vichy France, starting in their colonial empires), before landing main battle forces in France at a later date.[76] By late 1942 Britain had the armies, the allies and the specialty ships and aircraft to do this effectively. British forces won campaigns in East and North Africa while bombing German industry and cities and securing the convoy routes, bringing the resources and soldiers of the Empire and the Americas to fight Germany. Hitler played directly into this traditional British naval strategy by barracking large garrisons in nonvital promontories of German conquest and occupation. He also reinforced failure each time his Italian ally got into trouble in theaters of operations that were not critical to the final outcome, such as North Africa and the Balkans. German garrisons were therefore isolated from the main fighting, left too long or trapped at the end in Greece, Yugoslavia, Norway, arctic Finland and northern Italy.[77] The

Eisenhower inspects a Tiger II (1944).

difference was that the British had a strategy in engaging on the periphery of the main theater, while Hitler had only fantasies and gave in to his impulses.

With all Germany's enemies fully armed for all-out war, Josef Goebbels went public in February 1943 with a regime call for total war that elicited excited endorsement from a nazified and stamping crowd: "Do you want total war? Do you want it? . . . More total and more radical than we can imagine it today? . . . Let the slogan be: Now, people rise up and let the storm break loose!" A fine and dramatic slogan to rouse a Nazi crowd in Berlin, but total war was actually the Wehrmacht's worst nightmare. It could not win a long war, and certainly not against three Great Powers backed by all the population and industrial resources of their continental or overseas empires. Not when each of them was already what Nazi Germany aspired to be, a *Weltmacht*. Stalin stated the obvious when he heard what Goebbels said: the speech was an admission by the German leadership that their vaunted blitzkrieg had failed.[78] That year, the Western Allies brought total war to Germany in a way it could not send back at them, with firestorms and thousand-plane raids over its cities in a merciless Combined Bomber Offensive that lasted almost to the end in 1945. In mid-1944, all its enemies launched coordinated, concentric assaults with millions of troops attacking from all directions at once. Phantasm became nightmare.

Rather than fighting and winning the serial and progressively larger wars he boasted that he would, by 1942 Hitler ensured that Nazi Germany was at war with the three largest industrial and world powers at the same time: Great Britain, the Soviet Union and the United States. Strategically, it no longer mattered that France had been knocked out of the war in 1940 and that all of continental Europe was occupied and cowering under the Gestapo and SS occupation. Germans were overstretched fighting in Africa, under the oceans, in the skies over their cities, in northern Italy, in the Balkans, against partisans scattered across occupied Europe, and above all against the immense Red Army down the length of the western Soviet Union. Their only allies were weak and collapsing Italy; distant, weak and losing Japan; and a handful of small European satellite states whose armies were never modern or were already smashed and surrendered by the middle of 1943, just as the United Nations surged toward peak war production and skill.

It was even worse than that. Germany's alliance with Japan was never more than an alliance in name, and even Mussolini started and fought parallel wars with little shared intelligence and no strategic coordination whatever with Berlin. Axis alliance members shared little trade and did almost no joint research or economic or campaign planning. They did not even inform each

Big Three at Teheran (1943).
Courtesy of Wikimedia Creative Commons.

other about decisions to start whole new fronts or wars. Mussolini did not tell Hitler before he invaded Albania and later Greece. Germany did not warn Japan it would sign the Nazi-Soviet Pact while Japanese and Red Army forces were still battling at Nomonhan along the Mongolian-Manchurian border. Berlin did not tell Tokyo that the Wehrmacht would launch *Barbarossa*.[79] It was no way to run a war, or win it. The Western Allies' military and intelligence cooperation was not always smooth but overall was outstanding, including setting up the Combined Chiefs of Staff and Combined Bomber Offensive. Cooperation with the Soviet Union was far less than with each other, but there were several wartime summits, some highly limited intelligence warnings (one way, to Moscow), and real strategic-level coordination of overall attack timing and long-term plans, including hitting Germany from two sides at once in 1944.

Japan fought against much smaller contingents of Western military forces in Southeast Asia and the Pacific, yet it made no declaration of war on Germany's main enemy in the Soviet Union. Nor did Stalin declare war on Japan, the active enemy of his Western allies from December 1941. Not until three months after the surrender of Germany and two days after the atomic bombing of Hiroshima. Stalin repeatedly called for a second front in the West against Germany while the Red Army fought a massive and initially desperate but also one-front war against Germany until May 9, 1945, then a brief one-front war against dispirited and reduced Japanese forces on the Asian mainland from August 8, 1945. It was Britain and the United States which waged multi-continent wars (Africa, Asia and Europe), along with the war at sea and major commitments of resources to bring war to Germany's skies. Even at the height of its military power and conquests Germany could not even reach its armies across the narrow waters of the Channel to get at Britain. British and American fleets crossed two immense oceans to bring millions of ground forces and supporting naval and air war assets to fight Germans, Italians and Japanese on widely separated continents. Against this assembled coalition, surrounding Nazi Germany with a ring of iron and self-fulfilling prophesy, nowhere did Germans steer the direction of the war from 1943. The next year, invasion and combat on each of two fronts consumed Hitler's land armies at levels of destruction and death that exceeded the highest rates of the worst fighting of World War I.

***

AFTER THE PERIOD of uninterrupted German victories from 1939 to 1941 ended in front of Moscow, into 1942 technical proficiency and open spaces in the Soviet steppe and North African desert flats allowed panzer magic to swing a few more battles Germany's way. Though not in the forested north of Russia or in the narrow neck of land blocked by Montgomery with mines and artillery at El Alamein, before he counterattacked and destroyed Rommel's tanks and the Italian infantry. The panzers moved across the southern steppe to Stalingrad smoothly enough, but had much more trouble in the Caucasus and in the mountains of Tunisia, then in Sicily and Italy in 1943. Terrain mattered very much to panzer success or failure. So did cities, as Stalingrad showed. Tanks were easy targets in cities, which choked their lanes and blocked their firing lines. And for much of the second half of World War II, the fighting would move into cities. The other thing that stopped the panzers was the courage, tenacity, and tactical learning by Red Army and Western Allied soldiers. They now had better anti-tank weapons and improved doctrine, and so the initial German armored and tactical advantages passed.

The Red Army caught up to then surpassed the Wehrmacht in tank warfare capability and slashed into German positions and numbers, never sufficient in the first place. Western Allied armies did the same, so that on all fronts German panzer forces and armies were whittled to nubs. They were reduced by local German victories as much as by defeats. That is the nature of matériel war. No one battle or named defeat was decisive in a war-winning sense: not Stalingrad, El Alamein or Bizerta, not even Kursk.[80] Instead, each great battle accelerated the wearing out of Germany's armed forces and reserves, steepening the arc of attrition until all strategic initiative shifted to the Allies, inside Soviet territory then in eastern Europe, at sea and in the air. Highly aggressive panzer generals like Manstein and Ewald von Kleist proposed more maneuver warfare in the east, hoping to win fresh decisive battles in stretched campaigns where no one fight could ever decide the outcome. Theirs was an increasingly desperate effort to liberate from the tyranny of the enemy's matériel war the panzer idea and armies built for blitzkrieg and mission tactics initiative. They still wanted to achieve crushing decisions with their few remaining tanks, but were trapped and crushed by overwhelming Soviet forces instead.[81]

Comparatively high German military skill from 1939 to 1942 made the war's outcome and balance of forces seem more even than it was, but only at the start. From 1943 to the end, Western Allied and Soviet weight of war matériel matched to learned skills revealed that the German idea of decisive battle as a way to win a world war had always been a mirage. Fighting was hard and losses heavy as the Red Army crossed its 1940 borders to fight for the first time on foreign soil. Soviet tankers in T-34s and KV-2s drove around static

German positions, more troops and supplies accompanying in Lend-Lease trucks, all speeding past the steel bones of thousands of Red Army tanks lost in 1941 and 1942. One must not repeat the blitzkrieg myth in reverse, however, for the Red Army was still heavily dependent on horses. It would travel all the way to Berlin with many tens of thousands of horses, and camels as well. It hit bluntly with massed armor and infantry in assaulting tank armies that came on in waves, sustaining huge losses but unstoppable all the same. The British and Americans used more methodical armored tactics and air power to attrit the last panzers and infantry they faced in France and in the forest zone along the Rhine, then inside western Germany. They reached victory not with lighting jabs to mimic blitzkrieg but with heavy metal and firepower that spared the lives of their troops while tearing open Tigers and Panzer IVs to kill the crews inside.

Hitler had refused most ambitious plans after Kursk, recognizing before many of his generals did that the time of fancy offensive maneuvering with tanks was over. The panzers thereafter counterattacked only. Far from a war-winning instrument of decision via offensive blitzkrieg, panzers shifted into a critical firefighter role as conflagrations of Soviet armies engulfed the *Ostheer* in one sector after another in 1944, then broke though its almost immobile defenses everywhere in 1945. Much the same happened in the west, where the *Westheer* was broken into isolated fragments during the last year of the war. Luftwaffe Field Marshal Albert Kesselring maximized terrain in a ground command role to fight defensive battles in Italy that slowed and bled but did not stop the Western Allies. Gerd von Rundstedt and Erwin Rommel argued over how to meet an inevitable invasion of France and northwest Europe, and failed to agree or to stop it when it came. Now was the time for thousands of Sherman and Churchill tanks to swarm around an enemy so bereft of air power he could safely move his panzers and motorized troops only at night.

It is doubtful that Hitler ever had a war-winning military strategy. Without any vision or guiding purpose beyond the hate of race war, he changed operational objectives erratically and too often. The pattern became more macabre and absurd over the last year of fighting, as the so-called Third Reich crumbled all around yet no one dared to question his decisions, especially after he survived the *Valkyrie* assassination attempt. Reverting to World War I–style static defense, he refused to yield any ground and lost it all, defending everything and so defending nothing, as Frederick once said. Hitler declared a defensive line along the Dnieper as Germany's new *Ostwall*, or "East Wall." With his usual fantasist conceit, he ordered construction of an impenetrable barrier of field fortifications 1,000 miles long, to run from the Gulf of Finland to the Sea of Azov. A few fieldworks were prepared along a route that followed natural river barriers, giving the idea some defensive value, but it was mostly fantasy and hardly held up the Red Army five months later. More imaginary walls and "fortresses" were proclaimed but never built, some no more than markers on a map in Hitler's command bunker, others made of inadequate clusters of guns and infantry told to never retreat. They were invariably cut off and wiped out by the Russians. Nazi Germany hunkered down like a wounded porcupine under Allied and Soviet assault, too late to save the empire won in 1939–1941 and fatally mismanaged every day after that. As imagined fortress positions crumbled in the east, so too shoreline defenses grandiosely named *Festung Europa* were broken though by brave men on D-Day (June 6, 1944) and in weeks of fighting that followed.[82] Inland, a nearly 400-mile "West Wall" following the old *Siegfriedstellung* or Siegfried Line of the 1930s was not solid either, despite extensive use of forced laborers and valued materials to build it. Western troops would breach it easily and pour into Germany in 1945.[83]

The last months of the war were total in ways never seen before or since, on the ground and in the air over Germany. Hitler pulled his last garrisons out of the Balkans, but unaccountably left others uselessly in Norway as Germany burned. Western armies slogged north of Rome to reach south Germany only just before the end, but the Germans in France were shattered in August 1944. Their remnants regrouped in the Netherlands and in the forests along the banks of the Rhine. Army Group Center also effectively ceased to exist in August 1944, when the Red Army's Operation *Bagration* bashed right through it in Belarus. Other Soviet army groups smashed into Romania and Poland and pummeled into East Prussia and Saxony and Austria.[84] The Wehrmacht faced concentric envelopment not of one of its armies or army groups, the limit of what it had achieved with its vaunted panzer doctrine and armies, but of the entire nation.[85] It was strategic encirclement on a war-winning scale to dwarf anything conceived by Napoleon or Moltke or Schlieffen, far beyond the capability of *Barbarossa*: millions of men and thousands of tanks were poised to cross all of Germany's borders, stabbing it from all sides so that there could be no doubt who won this war and who lost.

German soldiers of the *Westheer* still put up tough resistance in the Huertgen Forrest and other defensive fights, before Hitler wasted last reserves in an utterly useless counteroffensive in the Ardennes ("Battle of the Bulge"). Overwhelmed on all sides, the Germans attacked. It was all they knew. With no objective gained or even gainable, they drove the last panzers westward through the Ardennes in 1944 and were stopped—out of guns, out of planes, out of tanks, and literally out of gas. The last units were destroyed in 1945 in isolated pockets that resisted inside western and southern Germany. With even more futility, Germans attacked for the very last time into Hungary in March 1945, their last offensive of any kind in World War II. Air supremacy fixed the last panzers in place and destroyed them, freezing all movement until remnant German forces were trapped in pockets along with terrified refugee civilians, on the Courland Peninsula and all down the Rhine. Scenes of despair and destruction in these last places of German resistance defy description. Both the *Westheer* and the *Ostheer* were utterly shattered and destroyed, the latter in more vicious and bloody fighting that recalled and repaid what it did in Russia.

Soviet, American, British and Commonwealth forces had more trucks, half-tracks and tanks, guns and planes. More of everything. They rode around hapless Germans too often left fixed in positions both thankless and tankless even in designated panzer divisions. German tactics were well known, deflected and defeated by Allied armies on every front: Italy, France, Belarus, Poland, Hungary, then in Germany itself. The last Wehrmacht attacks in the battle-scarred Ardennes and in Hungary were near-parodies of blitzkrieg, relying on captured fuel stocks to move the panzers at all. *Bewegungskrieg* had advanced from triumph to tragedy to end in farce and total defeat. The conquest of southern and western Germany saw no major battles, just the crushing weight of superior Allied forces and grinding smaller-scale combat against broken or trapped remnants of shattered German armies, corps and divisions. Defeat came with a thousand cuts: small fights, not huge battles, but cumulatively decisive actions all the same. No last battles came close to the scale and intensity of Stalingrad or Kursk or Falaise in Normandy, where so many panzers died. Even the Red Army assault in the bloody Battle of Berlin was more of an anaconda crushing of the last fanatic resistance than a set-piece fight of modern armies poised to do battle as if at Waterloo.[86]

Over the endgame of World War II the Wehrmacht lost all the battles, all its armies and all its honor in the moral and physical rubble it had made of Germany and much of Europe. Neither Hitler nor his generals knew what to do, so they fought on and on. The price of fantasy was total destruction. During the last year of carnage Nazi Germany's war effort was beyond management or repair, as broken and battered panzer armies and retreating infantry grew less mobile, less effective, less dangerous to the world. It should not be forgotten that behind the *feldgrau* and steel shield the officer corps provided Hitler, the SS death machine erected by the Nazi state continued mass murder programs to exterminate millions more innocent civilians.

Drawn-out defense put German civilians through the heaviest Allied bombing and firestorm campaign of the whole war. There was also wilder nazification of the home front as defeat approached, with roaming gangs of Nazi Party thugs in brownshirt uniforms hanging accused deserter soldiers from lampposts as the revolution consumed the children it once coddled in the Hitler Youth.

Grim men in red-striped General Staff trousers in Berlin and the grey-clad generals leading what was left of the German armies who caused all this had been there a generation earlier, as young officers during another lost world war. They had deluded themselves in the 1920s and 1930s about the true causes of that first defeat, and persuaded themselves that they could win the next time. Lacking the imagination to do more than try essentially the same thing as in 1914, they lost a second *Weltkrieg*. Attacks from all sides strained Wehrmacht armor and human reserves past the breaking point, collapsing all German armies inward or overrunning them during the first five months of 1945. Forward units of several immense Soviet and Western Allied army groups met on a bombed out bridge at Torgau on April 25, 1945. Hitler killed himself in Berlin five days later, but Nazi and Waffen-SS fanatics fought on for another week after that, until the German unconditional surrender on May 8 to the Western Allies and May 9 to the Soviet Union.

World War II was so big, so fundamentally attritional, not even the Allies could do it all. By late 1944 they, too, strained for replacements under the weight of effort and casualties, and the moral and psychological stress of years of making total war. The Americans had gambled on a smaller army than they really needed, one at the end suffering reduced combat effectiveness from casualties and insufficient replacements. Britain and Canada were exhausted of suitable men, fielding tired and undermanned and thus less aggressive divisions in 1945. The British Army was forced to cannibalize some of its divisions just to keep the rest going. Some Red Army conscripts still went to war without boots, shuffling along beside the horse-carts. But at the end, Germans were often without food, fuel or ammunition, as production virtually ceased and what was produced could not be moved. German soldiers knew too well what they had done in Russia to expect mercy to arrive from the east, and so fought harder in that direction. As the Red Army entered Berlin and other towns and cities, the revenge was indeed pitiless.[87]

Unable or unwilling to increase pressure on the ground with infantry and tank attacks that cost lives on their side, even as the great encirclement closed the Western Allies increased the pace of destruction of German cities from the air. Succumbing to the logic of total war, Western air forces had long since drifted from precision bombing and avoiding noncombatant targeting. From 1943 they sent the bombers to deliberately target civilians and general morale. In 1945 they used almost uncontested air power, as air war historian Tami Biddle puts it, "in its most unbounded and unconstricted form, in a bid to keep the European war from dragging on into 1946."[88] To finish the fight and make the point last in German memories, they embraced the full measure of total war. General George C. Marshall told the press that historical precedent and old rules for terminating wars no longer applied. There was instead a "compelling necessity to plan and make provisions for the waging of war not only until the armies of the enemy are strategically defeated but until these forces are *actually annihilated*."[89] General Henry "Hap" Arnold concurred: "We must not get soft. War must be destructive, and to a certain extent inhuman and ruthless."[90] Thousand-plane raids brought war without mercy to civilians, to drive home that they must never again permit their leaders to choose war. Nazism and Weltmacht dreams drifted into history along with acrid black smoke rising over city after city, while in the east overrun autobahns were lined with burning panzer hulks and tens of thousands of *feldgrau* corpses from Courland to Dresden to Berlin. Civilization stopped to let brutality and barbarism do its necessary work. The same would be done to Japan.

Annihilation at Sea

THE ALLURE OF battle was not confined to Europe. Japanese military and civilian leaders also succumbed to a fatal attraction to proposals for quick victories over vastly superior foes. If anything, they did so more wildly than Germans, indulging spectacular delusions of rapid decision in opening campaigns against more powerful enemies they could never hope to defeat in protracted wars. From shortly after the Meiji Restoration of 1868, the *Nihon Teikoku Kaigun* (Imperial Japanese Navy, or Kaigun or IJN) and *Nihon Teikoku Rikugun* (Imperial Japanese Army, or Rikugun or IJA) operated at the center of Japan's rise in global prestige and presence. Through it all, including the wars, the two services refused to cooperate in framing a single coherent strategy while always competing ferociously for resources, budget allocations, and primacy in national policy and war.[1] No civilian government could correct their military assumptions or fix their divergent and rebellious behavior. Disobedience came not just at the top, but throughout junior officer ranks as well, moving along horizontal rather than vertical lines of loyalty. On the other hand, Japan's drive to wars of empire was not solely military. Imperial ideology was broadly shared by civilian and military elites who agreed to constant expansion to gain economic resources and world-power rank. Why reverse imperial achievements made even without proper authority by disobedient rebels outside Japan? Building out the Empire was always a one-way street where rebels acted knowing that gains they made at the periphery would be approved by the center.[2] The result was a cascade of aggressions, each tripping over the last until imperial overreach brought the whole endeavor back to Japan's shores as the calamity of strategic bombing and total war defeat.

The Kaigun modernized and expanded from the 1890s, the first decade of Japan's active seeking of overseas empire by war. From the start it emphasized ship quality over quantity, as well as an aggressive combat doctrine of first-strike and seeking a decisive sea battle as the culmination of all training, doctrine and procurement.[3] This orientation toward climactic battle expressed some internal cultural and political origins, but mainly it was an attempt to compensate with an initial knockout blow for persistent inferiority as measured against rival navies, starting with Qing China's. In 1895 Kaigun officers were more cautious than their Rikugun counterparts heading into the First Sino-Japanese War (or Japan-Qing War, or War of Jiawu). The conflict was ostensibly fought over the independence of Korea, but was in fact rooted in Japan's modernization and the challenge that posed to a Chinese-centered power system in north Asia that was cracking under pressure from extra-regional Great Powers. The Kaigun's main task was to secure supply routes and support amphibious landings. However, an emerging battle doctrine of ferocious attack, of audacity matched to firepower, was tested as an overconfident Qing fleet made challenge in the Yellow Sea, off the mouth of the Yalu River.

The *Beiyang* (Qing Northern Seas Fleet) was one of four Chinese fleets that operated separately, without any central command or modern controls. It was also a hodgepodge assembly without homogeneity in ship designs. Some were older ironclads or otherwise lightly armed and armored. Its battleships were big and German- or British-built, but old and quite odd ducks. They had heavy armor but woefully outdated short-barrel guns that fired in arcs so restricted that they dictated fighting in short lines. Chinese battle doctrine did not really rise to fleet-to-fleet action instructions. *Beiyang* captains were trained to fight in pairs, with the pairs in turn formed into parallel lines. Weaker ships brought up the rear of each line, more for their protection than to add firepower to the line of battleships. The majority of Japanese warships had been built in Britain or France. They were twice as fast as the Chinese battleships. Also, their smaller but rapid-firing guns had a 6:1 fire superiority rate. Nevertheless, *Beiyang*'s overall gun-size advantage gave its captains confidence as they steamed to the Yalu to find and face down the upstart Kaigun.[4] Under pressure to win fast at sea to enable land operations, Admiral Itō Yūkō took a 10-ship *Rengō Kantai* (Combined Fleet) into the Yellow Sea looking for battle.

He soon met the 10-ship *Beiyang*, under Admiral Ding Ruchang, passing the mouth of the Yalu late in the morning of September 17, 1894. Spotting smokes rising over the horizon, the admirals steamed for one another but in different formations. The Chinese were ill-formed in ragged parallel lines, whereas Itō made one column of two squadrons. Ding opened fire at 5,000 meters, beyond the range of his short guns. Itō held all fire as his ships closed

Battle of the Yalu River (1894).
Courtesy of Wikimedia Creative Commons.

range at twice the speed of the Chinese line. At a precise signal, the Japanese column split into two, a faster flying squadron steaming ahead of the main squadron. The flying squadron then turned for the Qing right flank, its modern cruisers intent on sinking the weakest Chinese ships, then curling around the end of the line to rake other ships. Itō fired at 3,600 meters, but thick armor on the battleships repelled all lighter Japanese ordnance. While no shells penetrated to harm the hulls, crew losses were heavy as shrapnel and high explosive impacts hit all over decks and superstructures. A mêlée ensued, with close-in firing of all calibers by both sides. There were also attempts at cruiser-to-cruiser rammings. As smoke enveloped the fleets, hundreds died in anonymous agony in oil and fire, in steam or salt water. Now came hard pounding by the main battle lines as rapid-fire Japanese guns raked Chinese battleship superstructures while 12-inch shells crashed into ships in reply. The Japanese entered the fight believing that superior speed and tactics would defeat superior guns on the Chinese ships. They were right. While Itō's fleet suffered damage and losses, five Qing warships were sunk as the Chinese fought handicapped by slower speeds and a poorly conceived parallel-pairs formation. The rest fled under fire. Some were also out of ammunition.[5] Everyone everywhere read the decisive outcome as saying that Japan was now a player in Asia, a rising power to one day contend with China for regional primacy.

The Kaigun also acquired its first overseas bases late in the war with China, giving it a postwar maritime direction in direct competition with the Rikugun's idea of *hokushin* ("northward advance") to Siberia and northern

China. The Battle of the Yalu River was the first major step in the Kaigun's alternate preference for *nanshin* ("southward advance"), which would make use of its new amphibious and blue water capabilities. Henceforth, the Kaigun looked to surmount its origins as a regional coast guard, demanding higher budget allocations sufficient to convert it into a world-class navy. It wanted bigger and more modern ships capable of true ocean cruising, and an enhanced political role as counterweight to the Rikugun's interest in expansion on the mainland. Literally adding fuel to that intense debate, the Japanese economy began converting from coal to dependence on oil. Since oil was a basic resource that Japan was forced to import over the water, the change brought a new naval imperative to secure unassailable overseas market access and fuel oil supplies. Victory at the Yalu also confirmed the Kaigun tactical ideal of a fleet built for knockout, decisive action against a materially superior force. The idea was captured in a series of doctrinal and tactical slogans: *ka o motte shū o sei-su* ("using a few to conquer many"), *kenteki hissen* "fight the enemy on sight") and *nikuhaku-hitchū* ("press closely, strike home"). Two leading scholars of the Kaigun note that these vague mantras were as much psychological as tactical, forming a semi-mystical approach to combat that dominated Japanese naval outlook over the next half century.[6]

Pressure for quick victory at sea also arose at the start of the Russo-Japanese War. This time it led to a badly botched operation: a surprise assault on the Russian Pacific Squadron, anchored without pickets and under full inner harbor and peacetime lighting at Port Arthur (Lüshunkou). Admiral Heihachirō Tōgō's destroyers attacked during the frigid night of February 8–9, 1904. They achieved complete surprise, but then the attack dissolved into confusion born of indiscipline by Japanese captains. Eager destroyers charged the inner harbor singly or in pairs, one of which collided before firing salvos at anchored Russian ships whose officers and crews were mostly onshore. It should have been a massacre. Instead, the destroyers fled the harbor and bolted for their home base in Korea, without even making after-action reports on the fight to Tōgō. They had in fact scored damage on two battleships and a cruiser, though nothing critical or fatal.

Tōgō shelled the harbor from his capital ships the next day, until the Russians came out to drive him away. He then set up a long-distance blockade from his main base in Korea, mainly using cruisers and destroyers. It was an exhausting exercise, given the need for ships of the day to constantly recoal. They did it on station, a filthy and difficult task. Over the coming weeks and months more torpedo attacks were made by Japanese destroyers. All came to naught. Tōgō several times bombarded the port from his battleships, but more usually was busy with his main task of supporting land operations else-where. He turned next to blockships, thrice failing to jam the outer harbor with sunken hulks. Finally, a field of sea mines worked. A Russian battleship hit one of the mines and blew up in the outer harbor as it came out to do battle. The powerful mine and follow-on explosions killed most of its crew and Admiral Stepan Makarov, commander of the Russian Pacific Squadron. One mine changed the course of the war, even if a single ship's smoke rising over Port Arthur's outer harbor was a far cry from the decisive sea battle that naval officers wanted.[7]

Leaderless, the rest of the Russian Pacific Squadron came out of Port Arthur to make a run for Vladivostok. Tōgō intercepted, forcing the Battle of the Yellow Sea (August 10). It was a chase and running fight right from the start, as the Russian intention was simply to get away, not to engage in a fleet action. The critical moment came when the flagship *Tsesarevich* lost steering, and the Russian Pacific Squadron lost its replacement admiral, when several hits wrecked the flagship's bridge. Once again, accurate and rapid Japanese fire demonstrated that naval shells did not have to penetrate plate armor (none in fact did) to knock out larger capital ships. *Tsesarevich* circled uncontrollably, as *Bismarck* would in the Atlantic in 1941 before she sank, except that *Bismarck* was alone that day. *Tsesarevich* was leading a whole squadron, follow-on ships loyally mimicking its maneuvers ("hold-ing to its wake and grain"). As the big battleship curled back into its own line its confused movements quickly proved contagious. The whole Russian battle line simply came apart, leaderless and eager to flee, each ship on its own. Ships ran, most trying to get back into Port Arthur but some scatter-ing to neutral ports, under Japanese pursuit fire that added more death and damage and humiliation to the Russian defeat. Only nightfall saved a worse disaster. As it was, two battleships were gone, along with six of eight cruisers and 13 of 25 destroyers.

Russian ships based out of Vladivostok did better in the months that fol-lowed, raiding the Japanese coast and sinking several troop transports filled with conscripts. Not the Russian Pacific Squadron, however. The main battle fleet in Pacific waters was done, beaten at sea and then finished off from the landward side when Rikugun troops attacked Port Arthur, approaching the port overland. They came over and down surrounding hills to make massed, almost suicidal charges that were repelled by Russian infantry, machine guns and artillery, with huge loss of life. Japanese reports later described the initial ground battle as *shizan kekka* ("a mountain of bodies and a river of blood").[8] However, ensconced in the heights after the infantry was repelled, heavy artillery systematically destroyed much of the inner harbor and sank the warships anchored below. Losing a squadron of warships to a land attack, a fleet lost to an army, was one more humiliation in a war full of humbling of Russia. Far worse lay ahead.

The Russian Baltic Fleet, renamed Second Pacific Squadron, was ordered to steam to the Sea of Japan, over 18,000 miles away, going the long way around the tip of Africa.[9] It departed on October 2, 1904, arriving off Japan after months of death and misery and mutiny among raw conscript sailors along the way. Then it was decimated at the Tsushima Strait by the waiting Japanese on May 27–28, 1905. Everything went wrong right from the start, for this most benighted fleet since the Invincible Armada left Lisbon to sail to Calais, thence around Scotland and Ireland to return to Spain having achieved nothing for god or king or country except an epic of suffering. One problem was coal. Russia had no coaling stations en route and Britain would not permit sales or supply to the enemy of its Japanese ally (Britain and Japan had signed an alliance in 1902, aimed in part at Russia). The fleet needed a half million tons of coal, so it took as much as it could with it as it left port. It was piled everywhere: on the decks, under bunks, inside gun turrets. Coal dust choked filthy men into daily misery, and still it was not enough. Fortunately, Kaiser Wilhelm stepped forward to tweak the nose of the British lion. He offered his Russian cousin colliers to help get the Baltic warships to Asia. Second Pacific Squadron thus steamed under Admiral Zinovy Rozhestvensky with four new-class battleships and three older ones, four new and three older cruisers, nine destroyers, a repair ship, a hospital ship, German colliers and some tugs. After all three squadrons joined in Annam, 42 ships in all made a combined eight-month voyage to Japan.

The crews were nervous from the moment the fleet left port to steam down the coast of Western Europe. Rumors of Japanese destroyers and torpedo boats in the North Sea led to a shooting incident in the foggy Dodger Bank the night of October 21–22, when one ship signaled falsely but frantically that it was under attack. Russians shot up several fishing trawlers, thinking they were Japanese torpedo boats closing to attack. A crisis with Britain was averted by issuing an apology and agreeing to international arbitration, eventually making compensation to the families of the dead. In the interim, British cruisers angrily and showily shadowed the contrite Russians past Gibraltar to Tangier. There, the fleet divided. Its bigger ships could not use the Suez Canal, so they steamed around Africa, without proper sea charts so far from cold Russian waters. They ran into a hurricane next, as they rounded the Cape of Good Hope. The squadrons rejoined at Madagascar, where the fleet spent the next 77 days waiting on a third group that did not catch up until Annam in French Indochina, where the fleet lingered another 33 days.

While in Madagascar, the crews learned that Port Arthur had surrendered. They also heard about Bloody Sunday (January 22, 1905) back in St. Petersburg, where 1,000 entirely peaceful demonstrators had been massacred in front of the Winter Palace, shot or trampled as they tried to petition the tsar about basic working conditions and suffrage rights. The 1905 Revolution was underway, but these sailors were miserably stuck off the southeast coast of Africa, far from home and families caught up in the turmoil in Russia. They were headed to a war that seemed already lost, in far-off waters none had ever seen. The captains lifted anchor anyway. The fleet headed around India and turned north for Indochina. While this farce of a mission steamed in filth and heat and seeming futility across the Indian Ocean to Annam, more ships arrived via Suez. On board this Third Pacific Squadron were 1,400 men who had mutinied before leaving Russia in February. They brought real discord and brooding revolutionary ideas with them.[10]

Tropical diseases added to the coal dust, bad food, incompetent officers and dull weeks spent at sea, causing widespread depression and suicides. After recoaling, the combined squadrons steamed from Annam to Singapore, slinking into harbor on April 8. Japanese spies counted the ships and reported their poor condition to Admiral Tōgō. The Russians heard that heavy land fighting was under way in Manchuria, and that revolution at home was unraveling into anarchy that was paralyzing the tsarist regime and war effort. Crews were sick, surly and demoralized. Some were in a murderous and mutinous mood. Captains quarreled. More than half a year had passed since leaving to do battle, and yet the crews remained poorly trained and unskilled in gunnery. They hardly practiced shooting or battlespeed maneuvers in order to save ammunition and coal. Meanwhile, Tōgō's men were practicing, repairing, training, waiting. Kaigun ships gleamed with newness and spit and polish and hard discipline. All guns were primed, crews rested and well-trained. Confidence was high.

In a traditional line of battle fight between major navies, each ship in a warfleet steamed in column by squadron while "holding to the wake or grain" of the flagship or its squadron leader. Any ship that fell out of station for any reason was under standing orders to rejoin the battle line with as much alacrity as its captain and crew and engines could muster. This tactic avoided battles that deteriorated into severely damaging, because unpredictable, pell-mell poundings with big guns (in 1904, also by torpedoes). Navies were hugely expensive to build and maintain. Rather like 17th-century armies, the main incentive was therefore to avoid a mêlée marked by ship-to-ship actions. Individual captains were told to cleave to their guiding admiral's purpose and instructions, which was often just to preserve his fleet. The advantage of line fighting was that it maximized the firepower of broadside gunnery by every ship in the fleet as it passed the enemy line. However, the tactic limited initiative by captains and squadrons, and was criticized for militating against strategic decision in war at sea. In too many linear battles, said the critics, damage was done to individual ships and lives were lost, but fleets survived and no real decision was ever achieved. The ideal was instead to break the line, as Nelson did so spectacularly at Trafalgar. The perfect maneuver was to "cross the T" at one end of the enemy line or to break into the line, raking ships on either side at close range. That was what Nelson did at Trafalgar, achieving an overwhelming victory that dominated naval thinking everywhere 100 years later, the way Cannae or Ulm haunted the imaginations of a thousand generals bound to make war on land and forever in search of some way to enfilade a flank. The captains of the confident Japanese fleet steaming out to engage the weary Russians had visions of Trafalgar in their heads. They would come close enough.

The Russians had to steam right past the Japanese in order to reach Vladivostok. At 3:30 a.m. on May 27, 1905, a Japanese fast cruiser spotted an old, slow Russian ship bringing up the tail of the column. The cruiser captain flashed a signal to Tōgō, waiting in a nearby bay. The Russians were moving through the Tsushima Strait in three divisions: new battleships in the van, older and slower battleships in the second division, and mostly useless because outdated and outclassed ships in the rear division. They were pursued by four Japanese cruisers, waiting and watching as Tōgō steamed out to do sea combat with the rest of the battlefleet: four battleships, 11 cruisers, and a swarm of fast destroyers and torpedo boats. First contact with the Russian line was lost in the mist but picked up again after 6:00 a.m. as Tōgō steamed on board *Mikasa* into the Tsushima Strait to intercept and win a Trafalgar for Japan. Playing the warrior-poet, he signaled: "Today the sky is bright but the waves are high."

The Russians had more big guns in total and hence an edge in total weight of fire and distant fire, but Japanese ships and guns were faster and their crews more skilled. The chase lasted hours. At 1:55 p.m. Tōgō ordered the fleet to battlespeed and unfurled a "Z" flag, sending an arranged signal to all his captains. He was fully conscious of world naval history, so he deliberately echoed Nelson at Trafalgar: "The fate of the empire rests upon this one battle; let every man do his utmost."[11] In fact, the fate of the Empire of Japan would not be decided by any *one* battle, not even one so spectacular and one-sided as this one would prove to be. Modern war was already beyond singular decisive battles, even if the opportunity was more nearly still there at sea than on land, because at sea there is no place to retreat and reform, only depths to drown ships and men. Yet war must have its romance, of the man and the moment. That is why memory of Tōgō's signal at Tsushima Strait, both within the Kaigun and by the nation of Japan over the following decades and in later wars, says more about the allure of battle than about the truth of battle— about the appeal of decisive combat as a means of the weak overthrowing the strong, the lower overturning the higher, the hard physical overcome by the spiritual. Not about strategic realities on a misty spring day off Kyushu and Honshu, or in the decades and wars that followed.

The Russian ships were still overloaded with coal, whereas Tōgō had dumped his excess overboard to increase battle speed. A badly led, demoralized and at least partially outdated Russian fleet was heading into disaster at the hands of a highly competent, well-trained, more adept Imperial Japanese Navy. Yet, as nearly always in battle and war, chance far more than supposed genius played a hand. Tōgō's plan was to attack with his big ships' guns by day then send his little torpedo boats in at night for close action. During the chase, however, he saw that the Russians were much farther into the Strait than earlier reported and might escape before his smaller ships could attack. He therefore turned his whole line to intercept, each big warship turning in succession to his wake. His admirers say it was his idea from the start to "cross the T" of the Russian battle line with this brilliant move, by turning bravely into its guns, taking heavier initial fire to achieve the ultimately superior firing position. Yet it seems more likely that Tōgō was just surprised to find the enemy fleet where it was and simply reacted to it, boldly and with aggressive choice, certainly skillfully, but not by forethought or design or genius. After closing the range, at 6,400 meters his broadside guns opened fire.

The much slower Russians were still scrambling ineptly to form a single line of battle, some ships even stopping engines to avoid collisions. The fleets came into parallel, and hammering by the big guns began. *Mikasa* was hit over and over, but overall superior Japanese gunnery made up for having fewer big guns. Many hits were scored by Tōgō's well-practiced crews. The Russians scored, too, at least in the first half hour. After that, smoke, fear and confusion disrupted all gunnery. Fighting went on all day, with two Russian battleships and several cruisers mauled in exchange for lesser damage to Tōgō's faster and more nimble ships, which outscored 2:1 in hits. Put another way, about five or fewer of each 100 shells the Russians fired hit Tōgō's ships, while 10 or fewer of every 100 incoming hit the mark. Japanese shells were also much more explosive, by a factor of four. They did not penetrate armor but they burned hotter, setting ships on fire. The keys to the outcome were the superior construction and design of Tōgō s individual ships, their homogeneity of design and tactics acting together as a fleet, and their high speed and fine handling in tight combat turns and battle maneuvers.[12] Finally, where Russian crews were poorly trained and the fleet incompetently led, Japanese had both luck and competence with them, two essential ingredients for victory in battle and success in war. That is why, although the Russians began with an advantage of 41:17 in long-range 12-inch guns, the higher Japanese rates of fire with smaller guns and superior maneuverability and more accurate gunnery by better trained crews overcame it.

To men underneath the steel storms engulfing the ships these numbers did not matter. Shells indifferent to life or character or nationality smashed into decks and turrets to set sailors, gun turrets and superstructures on fire. As ranges closed between the battle lines smaller calibers were brought to bear, rapid and voluminous fire pouring into the Russians especially, whose returned fire lessened as their line became more disorderly and command and control lapsed or was interrupted. Steel deck plates buckled, airbursts showered white-hot metal splinters onto crews working the ships or guns, liquid fire spurted from high-explosive shells to burn everything—ammo, steel, flesh. As the Russians turned away from the storm, at 3:10 p.m. the *Oslyabya* rolled over and sank, the first modern battleship lost to enemy action. It was not the last. The *Suvorov* lost steering and did circles inside her own acrid black smoke. She went down at 7:00 p.m., finished off by a hard-charging Japanese torpedo boat. In the evening gloom, surviving ships circled without knowing their bearings or their place in the line; isolated in private panic, inside a battle smog, with men feeling the burned-out adrenalin of combat stress.

Paint burned and curled off the ships, as did all hemp ropes and ship's boats and any exterior wood on railings or doors or decks. Coal scattered over the Russian decks and interior holds caught fire, burning red and adding to the choking, thick black air. Incoming hot metal showers wrecked steering gear and cut communication voice pipes running from bridges to gun turrets and engine rooms. Animals tethered to decks as live meat, as well as crew and lashed cargo, were blasted overboard by direct shell impacts. Funnels, masts and turrets were smashed or bent, put out of action. Explosions rocked magazines and engine rooms, filling interiors with sounds of fury and barbecue odors. Fire control was knocked out, forcing crews to flood against flames threatening to reach the magazines and explode whole ships. Everywhere, dying and dead men. Other men terribly burned or wounded, sprawled over jagged and ruptured deck plate or behind torn bulkheads. Still the mighty shells from the battleships whistled down, in great parabolic arcs, smacking into ships with sheer weight and force before exploding. Leveling a bit now in trajectory as the fleets drew nearer and into mêlée and flatter close-range fire, and the danse macabre flashing and glinting and burning on the water became a slaughter.

More and more shells arced in from Japanese cruisers and destroyers, thudding into fat slowing targets. Exploding against shattered steel, cracking hulls, slicking broken bridges and buckled decks with oil and water and blood. Deep inside ships, terrified men heard the pounding going on overhead, felt the shudders of their own big guns firing back, rolling and roiling the ship; heard them stop as turrets were knocked out; struggled to breathe in blinding, choking smoke from burning coal and clouds of cordite as ventilation fans were smashed. The air belowdecks filled with burning odors, of oil and men and metal. Boilers ruptured with gushes of high-pressure steam, to send scalded, hairless, faceless men floundering, flesh falling off the bone. Such wounded were beyond any hope, except relief from agony in the release of death. Slabs of hot shrapnel cleaved off other men's limbs or impaled them. Nothing could be done to help these wounded, screaming and pleading inside a steel and explosive storm. Others went overboard, thrown by blast effect of the shells or jumping into the sea. They flailed inside oil fires burning all around atop the waves, scorching ship's boats and floundering men dying of fire and water all at once.

It was not over yet. Two Japanese squadrons steamed in separate circles around the confused Russian ships. When they closed the circle, the Russians were back in line and steaming hard north to escape, *Borodino* leading. The Japanese put on a burst of speed and the battle lines drew parallel. Again heavy gunnery was exchanged. *Alexander III*, already badly wounded, capsized and sank at 6:50 p.m., taking her crew with her. Twenty minutes later, *Borodino's* magazine was hit and she blew apart. Ahead waited a line of Tōgō's torpedo boats, just visible as horizon dots. Most Russian ships turned south, steaming hard for port. Japanese destroyers attacked them in the dark, target ships illuminated for their torpedoes by burning oil and stricken comrade vessels. One squadron of little ships was led by Suzuki Kantarō, who would be prime minister of Japan during the 1945 surrender. He sank *Suvorov* a few hours earlier. Now his fast, low-profile boats closed to suicidal ranges before loosing torpedoes and laying strings of mines. The battleship *Navarin* hit a spread of mines laid before her course and sank. The battleship *Sisoi Veliky* was hit and sank the next day. All other Russian ships scattered, putting on flank speed if they still could. Most steamed north for Vladivostok, but some headed into neutral ports and were interned. Five capital ships were surrounded by Tōgō's faster and now triumphant fleet, and were shown mercy at last. They surrendered. Smaller ships surrendered later, or were sunk or scuttled by harder captains.[13]

The Russians lost 4,800 men killed, thousands more wounded, 6,000 prisoners, and 34 out of 38 ships engaged. Another 1,900 crew were interned. Japanese loses were 110 killed and three torpedo boats, with some damage large or small to various ships. The whole Russian fleet was smashed in an utter, incomprehensible defeat. In terms of lopsided outcome, Tsushima Strait was on a par with Lepanto in 1571. Except that Tsushima was more decisive in the war that hosted it. That was because of what was going on politically in Russia and strategically in the land war in Manchuria. The tsarist regime was profoundly embarrassed and shaken and under domestic siege, while the war on land had been stalemated for months at levels of loss neither side anticipated nor could sustain. The main Russian Army strength was too far away and perhaps too politically unreliable to bring to bear against Japan, while the Japanese were in turn stunned by the level of casualties, which forced them to dramatically extend conscription and age-cohort call-ups. With the war straining both sides desperately on land, the one-sided loss at sea tipped the balance, delivering the decisive blow against Russian prestige and morale. It also gave enough success in the other direction to allow Tokyo to conceal its heavy land losses and desperate finances, and proclaim victory. In short, both sides used the battle as an opportunity to make the formal peace each desperately needed.

Tsushima Strait was one of the most complete tactical victories in naval history, also ranking with Lepanto and Trafalgar in terms of one-sidedness and destruction of an enemy fleet. In terms of Japanese naval culture, however, it was one of the worst things that could have happened to the Imperial Japanese Navy. For 40 years this victory would be cited as confirming a rigid doctrine of decisive battle at sea, an idea whose time was already past as a war-winning strategy. Observing at Tōgō's side at Tsushima Strait was a young naval officer, Isoroku Yamamoto. Later, he went to Harvard and attended the Washington Naval Conference in 1921–1922, traveling the country and learning about the future enemy in detail as few Japanese leaders ever did. On December 7, 1941, he would be in a battleship trailing the carriers, directing the attack on the U.S. Pacific Fleet anchored at Pearl Harbor, an attack initially codenamed "Operation Z" to honor Tōgō's victory in the Tsushima Strait. Yamamoto, too, would seek a knockout blow, albeit by the new means of naval aviation. Then he would lead the carriers to strategic defeat at the Battle of Midway in June 1942, again seeking the culminating sea battle naval officers dreamed of for decades but never achieved. At Midway and Leyte Gulf and elsewhere, many brave Japanese would do "their utmost" time and again, as the fate of their Empire was decided not by a single battle but overwhelming enemy numbers at sea and superior forces on land, in a protracted contest they started but could never really hope to win. The seeds of future catastrophe were already there in 1905, sprouting with naval victories over China and Russia into the great hubris of total war in the Pacific four decades later.

***

LIKE THE NAVY, the Imperial Japanese Army emerged out of the complex nation-building processes of the Meiji Restoration. During the *Boshin Senso* (Boshin Civil War) of 1868–1869 and then the samurai revolt in the Satsuma Rebellion (1877), the emergent army displayed and encouraged a mixed samurai-commoner culture that would mark the Rikugun to the end of World War II. The original blend was reinforced as Meiji reform and then conscription led to middle-class and other commoner professional soldiers displacing most of the old volunteer samurai. Successive central governments inculcated professionalism and a sense of national service, consciously centered on a new emperor cult that was elaborated and deepened over time in an effort to provide a unifying national vision.[14] This effort was not always successful, however, at the top or across horizontal lines of lingering and often far more powerful clan loyalty. The Rikugun looked modern as it headed off to war with China and then Russia, but it was run by an officer corps still divided into traditional factions along lines of pre-Meiji regional and clan identities. Many lines of horizontal loyalty exceeded the vertical (leading to the High Command and the emperor) in ways that encouraged a culture of disobedience among lower-ranked officers to higher civil and even military authority. In short, the old local loyalties to clan and onetime lordship remained powerful, no matter that men put on the Western-style uniform of the modernizing Japanese nation and state. This deep trait in Rikugun military culture would turn catastrophic in the 1930s, when sub-loyalties led to independent actions by lower-ranking officers that pulled Japan into war in China without Tokyo's initial consent.[15]

Beyond issues of fractured loyalty, the forming military culture of the Rikugun was complex and multi-sourced in other ways, a mix of imported

European influences and adopted and adapted Japanese traditions. Tactical doctrine, modern discipline and field training were imported from France and later from Germany. That reinforced an imperial cult indoctrination calling for strict obedience to military orders and hierarchical authority theoretically flowing down from an emperor-god. However, a reflexive disobedience and ferocious warrior spirit were displayed by samurai against the national army during the Satsuma Rebellion. This contributed to a parallel culture of disobedience that grew more important over time, as real and faux samurai intangibles were imported into the Rikugun by reformers keen to tap into moral and spiritual forces to make up for Japan's persistent material shortcomings. Most notably added was a tradition of fighting to the death no matter how hopeless the odds, a moral ideal that ostensibly tapped into ancient samurai traditions. German instructors played a role in this. They stressed to trainees the importance of extreme aggressiveness and offensive spirit in battle, neglecting logistics well beyond what was common even in triumphalist Germany at the time.[16] However, this influence should not be exaggerated. The Meiji army showed far more reasoned and tactical prudence than the Rikugun would in World War II. The irrational death cult that came later was present from the start but not yet rooted. It competed with rational and more modern military notions both imported and learned later in combat. Overemphasis on what was called "spiritual education" that led to death cult behavior in the Rikugun in its last two decades dates more to a disastrous partial implementation of military reforms in the 1920s.[17]

Back in the 1890s, the Rikugun was less concerned with martial spiritualism than with building out basic military infrastructure, including railways that arrived at Hiroshima in western Japan and were thus convenient either for homeland defense or quick overseas deployment to the mainland. The first test of the reformed Rikugun and new infrastructure came in Korea in 1894 against Qing armies, on paper a much greater force, just as the *Beiyang* appeared superior to the Combined Fleet before they met in combat. Certain that the Chinese would not put up a real fight, Japan's generals planned for a very short war: no winter clothing for the troops, no real medical service, minimal logistics support and an invasion plan challenging China's vast reserves of military power with untested divisions totaling just 120,000 men. Japanese campaign planning bore all the usual markers of material shortcomings signaling a turn to fast-war illusions. Fortunately for the Japanese, the Qing regime was in turmoil, its army divided into ethnic and regional factions and lacking overall central command. As weak and ill-prepared as the Rikugun would prove to be once it arrived on the mainland, the Chinese were even worse off.[18]

The Imperial Japanese Army that set off to fight Qing China was conspicuously modern in weapons and appearance. Japanese conscripts carried then current single-shot rifles and wore European-style black jackets and kepis. They were trained to drill and march and fight like European units. They looked like, and were intended to be, modern soldiers rather than feudal samurai. To further make the point, Japanese officers carried French swords, not traditional samurai *katana*.[19] Everything else that came later in the Rikugun's history was there in embryo from the start: operational reliance on the decisive battle to keep war short and lively in the German style, with almost no strategic overlay; arrogant planning that assumed too much would be gained too easily, and that the enemy was unworthy and inferior in fighting capacity and lacked warrior spirituality; interservice rivalry that reached dysfunctional levels that seriously hampered field operations; disobedient generals to make German mission tactics deviations pale by comparison. Coming also were brutal and frequent massacres of prisoners and civilians.

The Rikugun was intent on maintaining political primacy over the Kaigun at home, but to reach and operate in Korea it needed transport and protection of its supply lines against the Qing Navy. It could not really move, therefore, until after the Battle of the Yalu River wrecked the *Beiyang* fleet. Already, the officer corps displayed two unfortunate pre-battle habits that lasted to 1945: failure or refusal to integrate civilian concerns and wider political interests in operational planning, and deliberate exclusion of the Kaigun from planning even amphibious operations and the required sea supply to follow after the armies landed. Partly, this ignoring of civilian authority and naval capability stemmed from the imported apolitical pose of the German Great General Staff, and its related indifference to the *Kriegsmarine*. An exaggerated level of interservice disdain was adopted into Rikugun culture along with Imperial German training and weapons and fighting doctrine. However, it also arose from the assertion of local loyalties to the clans and opposition to *any* central authority, in an unruly military culture dating to the decade of civil turmoil after the Meiji Restoration. The result was an extreme level of hostility toward the Kaigun that never abated.

Stemming from chronic lack of interservice cooperation and little to no joint planning, there were no troop transports to carry the Rikugun over the water. An island nation set out to wage an overseas war without troopships or cargo vessels. It was a warning sign of gross inadequacy and poor planning that would persist in Japan's later and larger wars. Improvising, troops and supplies were carried to Korea in chartered mail packet ships and a few hastily purchased foreign vessels. As the Kaigun had not yet defeated the *Beiyang* fleet, a landing close to Beijing was too risky. First Army was landed at Inchon and told to march on Beijing via Korea instead, while Second Army screened its advance by occupying the Liáodōng Peninsula. The Rikugun might look and march like a modern army, but few outside observers thought that China could be defeated by the upstart island nation that landed so few troops in mid-June 1904.

Facing massive but internally divided and mismanaged Qing armies and reserves, Japan's generals did not lack confidence or ambition. They were planning far more than a limited Korean campaign. Reflecting the military theory of the day in Europe and the wider spirit of the times that would soon make a cult of celebrating *élan vital*, the Rikugun sought a decisive battle on land by all-out offensive action. They hoped to provoke a singular battle and thereby destroy the Qing armies the way their German instructors had destroyed French armies at Metz and Sedan a quarter century earlier. Their new Sedan, their imitative Cannae, would be fought on the Zhili plain of China. Certain that one fight would decide the whole war, they set out to march there and achieve triumph. It was high ambition, given their raggedy force in Korea and the weak logistics system behind it. The supply problems started right away. Rikugun logistics were so poor that marching troops slaughtered and ate the oxen pulling their supply and ammo carts. It was the need for food that sent First Army plunging forward toward Pyongyang, with promises from HQ that basic supplies would follow and that if not, the Chinese had vast stores just waiting to be captured. German armies were told something similar in the Ardennes in 1944, sent to fight ahead to capture fuel needed by the panzers just to make the next objective on a headquarters map. In mid-September, hungry Japanese arrived and a small Qing garrison in Pyongyang was overcome in a sharp corps-level fight. Its remnant withdrew to the Yalu, to take up a more defensible position and await the next Japanese move.[20]

In the interim, the naval victory at the Yalu River allowed the landing of Second Army in the Liáodōng Peninsula. It took Port Arthur in November, leading to a massacre of surrendered Chinese. Tokyo made the same excuses it would about Nanjing in 1937—that Chinese soldiers refused to surrender or hid in mufti. Farther north, the advance by First Army into China broke down in massive logistics failure despite recruiting 150,000 desperately poor local laborers. In lieu of uniforms they wore peasant bamboo hats and had unit numbers painted on their clothes. Many thousands froze to death

First Sino-Japanese War (1894).
Courtesy of Wikimedia Creative Commons

or died of camp disease; others deserted.[21] Everything began to fall apart, from basic logistics to food and medicine, followed by troop morale. First Army next ran into heavy casualties from Chinese infantry fire when it attempted regulation fire-and-advance rifle charges, made in dense formations that were no longer suited to modern defensive firepower wielded even by demoralized Chinese troops. Lack of a proper medical corps and commissariat wore out troop morale. Conscripts also lacked incentive to fight and some threw away their weapons. The lesson drawn later was that conscripts must be drilled better, must learn that willpower and moral factors and superior Japanese spirituality could overcome the worst physical hardship.[22] It was a lesson that ensured much suffering by Japanese troops in later campaigns and longer wars.

General Yamagata Aritomo, commander of First Army, was quite ill. Nevertheless, he decided on his own to advance on Mukden without waiting for authorization or support from Imperial General Headquarters (IGHQ), the oversight body that nominally coordinated between the services and supposedly managed the war effort as a unified whole. He moved First Army away from its supply base to start a winter campaign in frigid Manchuria in December, showing reckless disregard for the troops. Poor health soon sent him back to Hiroshima, but First Army kept going over frozen roads. It had almost no supply following from Pyongyang. His men lacked winter clothing. Some wore only straw sandals. "Coolies" wearing painted numbers on peasant shirts and hats in ad hoc logistics units were of course much worse off. More died or deserted as the winter march continued. Frostbite started to knock men out of the ranks as First Army arrived in Manchuria. Only the evident combat inferiority and worse supply conditions of the opposing Chinese armies prevented disaster.

Liáodōng and Korea were under Japanese occupation, but the decisive battle on the Zhili plain eluded the Rikugun's grasp and capabilities. And now the war plan changed. IGHQ sent Second Army to take from the rear a large Chinese naval base at Weihaiwei on the Shandong Peninsula. With the Kaigun blockading from the other side, the port surrendered in February after a three-week siege. First Army then won the Battle of Yinkou in Manchuria on March 5, 1895. An amphibious landing at Haichow north of Shanghai along with the capture of the Pescadores near Taiwan, both in late March, was the final straw for China. The Treaty of Shimonoseki followed on April 17, releasing Korea from Qing control and ceding Liáodōng to Japan. However, the settlement would not stand. Russia, France and Britain intervened to force Tokyo to give back Liáodōng. This national humiliation at Western hands was never forgotten or forgiven, not even when Japan agreed to provide one-third of the international force that intervened in China's Boxer Rebellion a few years later.[23] Animosity toward Russia ran especially high.

***

THE BATTLES OF the 1904–1905 Russo-Japanese War revealed much of what was to come in Europe during the Great War a decade later, even if the right lessons were drawn by very few: industrial slaughter as mass infantry armies ran into new military technologies that stymied and stalemated movement; millions forced into trenches by machine guns and rapid-fire artillery; denial of decision until the armies were nearly worn out by casualties and moral strain, the *Kaiserheer* most of all. Planning for war began in Tokyo in 1900, looking to win by a quick victory of the Moltkean sort over a much larger and established Great Power. The decision was made at an Imperial Conference on February 4, 1904. The idea was to win decisively at Mukden before the ponderous Russians could bring in reinforcements, which IGHQ thought would take six to eight months. Japanese troops were better equipped this time. Newly dressed in khaki, they carried a five-round rifle, were backed by the latest German field guns, and had boots in place of sandals. Russia was a far more formidable enemy than China, but once again the officer corps did not lack confidence.

This was the first war in which modern armies on both sides deployed machine guns and rapid-fire artillery. The immense casualties that resulted shocked all observers, starting with the first big and portentous fight at Nanshan (May 24–26, 1904). It took place at the narrow neck of the Liáodōng Peninsula, after First Army had advanced from Inchon to push a minor Russian force back across the Yalu. Three divisions of Second Army advancing in dense columns were cut down at Nanshan at rates beyond anything anticipated by the IGHQ, stopped by the entrenched Russians and intense defensive fire. Some 16,000 Japanese fell in frontal assaults at Port Arthur next (August 19), with 23,000 more casualties suffered at Liáoyáng (August 25–September 3). Propagandists eager to deceive the public as to troop morale and fighting spirit depicted these disastrous assaults not as tactical errors leading to appalling casualties but as meritorious examples of spiritual and moral superiority, calling the men who made them *nikudan* ("human-bullets" or literally, "bullets made of flesh").[24] The outline of a fateful pattern was set, though not yet locked in stone, within the Imperial Japanese Army and in its presentation of combat deaths to the Japanese public. Casualties would only go up along with claims of glorious death and rising expectations of ultimate sacrifice by ordinary soldiers, in this war and in all Japan's wars to follow.

The Russians counterattacked at Liáoyáng in October, ensuring that tens of thousands more young men died on both sides, slaughtered by machine guns and rapid-fire rifles and artillery. Almost 60,000 casualties were taken by the Japanese alone. These were unheard of numbers, speaking to the firepower revolution in military technology that continued through the second half of the 19th century to produce true machine guns, self-recoil and rapid-fire steel guns, and more powerful explosive shells. In Russia, the publication of long death lists sent large and angry crowds into the streets, adding more fervor to ongoing revolutionary protests over food shortages and opposition to the war, raising doubts about the ineptitude of the tsarist regime waging it with Russia's sons. In Japan, newspapers hid casualties and predicted that a new Sedan was just within reach.[25] What came next more presaged the abattoir of the armies at Verdun.

The worst of the fighting was at Mukden (Shenyang), where before the war the Rikugun had confidently believed it would win in an all-out battle. Instead, siege-like combat lasted from February 22 to March 10. Mukden was another bloodbath, pitting 300,000 Russians behind earthworks and ramparts against 200,000 Japanese. When it was over and the Japanese occupied the city, over 160,000 men from both sides were casualties in the frozen Manchurian mud. The wounded were left in the care of two armies whose medical establishments were primitive and overwhelmed. The slow dying went on for weeks afterward. As Russia collapsed in on itself with the full weight of the 1905 Revolution, Japan declared it had won a great victory. It did, but later that May at Tsushima Strait rather than Mukden. Japan was actually lucky to escape the war so soon, its smaller armed forces nearly as mauled and bloodied on land as Russia's inept navy was bloodied and beaten on the water. As talks commenced in Portsmouth under an offer of American mediation, Russia was collapsing out of war into revolution, as it would again in 1917. Japan looked to be in better shape, but it was in fact running out of men and war matériel—as it would again, catastrophically, in 1945.

The lies by the elites began in Tokyo, as did the censorship and military myth-making. The same lies were told for the next 40 years by generals, admirals, daily newspapers, governments and cultural leaders, right to end of Empire in atomic smoke and ash. First they denied the scale of casualties, then they denied they were tragic, then they said they were glorious. It was the start of a cult of celebrated, ritualized, officially approved death for the state and the emperor. Reaching deeply into legends, literature and folk traditions, an ideological and state-appropriated *bushidō* code was artificially crafted, then upheld to soldiers and sailors as the highest moral and military ideal. Repatriated prisoners were screened, interrogated, then shamed and shunned in their home villages and towns. An official ideology of the "Yamato race," of ethnic and cultural superiority, was purveyed that centered on the emperor cult and the supposed racial purity and uniqueness of an island people, sanctified by Shinto rites and blood sacrifice of martyrs interred at the Yasukuni Shrine. Military mysticism and superstition were floated in the form of idealized stories of blood sacrifice and "human bullets" and "war gods" that pretended to be rooted in samurai history and traditional Japanese values but were largely a fabrication of the modern state and armed forces.[26]

Did the officer corps learn the lessons of Mukden? Not at all. In keeping with the pre–World War I emphasis of militaries on *élan vital*, but without the excuse of not having direct experience of defensive firepower that held in Europe (outside Russia) to 1914, Japanese officers concluded that it was superior *seishin* ("national spirit") that had won the war over a far mightier foe. Strategists drafted more plans for future decisive victories by double envelopment modeled on idealizations of Königgrätz or Sedan. They did not think about Mukden-like slaughters except for self-assurances that they would avoid them by operational skill and fast-moving battles. All of that ignored an inability to actually envelop Russian armies in any battles during the fighting in Manchuria. Oleg Benesch explains how the Rikugun thereafter invented the "way of the samurai" to bolster its elevation of spiritual warfare over material war, in which it would probably always be deficient: "Infantry was the decisive arm in combat, the spirit of the attack the basis of warfare, and hand-to-hand combat the decisive factor in battle."[27] Emphasis was actually placed on infantry assault with bayonets, as if it was still 1745 and *maréchal* Saxe was in command. It hadn't worked then, either. Nonetheless, infantry were told to advance even when lacking artillery support, in order to maintain attack momentum. Sheer ferocity of attack would make up for lack of firepower and the enemy's entrenchments.

This effort to shift from firepower back to hand-to-hand fighting values came at the very moment the firepower revolution culminated in a massive shift of combat power from offense to defense. The declared reason was an asserted belief in the spiritual superiority of the Japanese soldier, his intangible moral qualities and by extension, the moral superiority of all Japan celebrated in the new Meiji nationalism. Undergirding that faith, however, was classic compensation by short-war thinking: in the absence of real material strength, patriotism and moral qualities will surmount our enemy's immense manpower and matériel advantages. Japan thus retained the option of aggressive war as a viable instrument of national advancement and colonial and imperial acquisitions of new territories and resources. It could defeat much larger enemies because the Japanese were morally better, man for man, soldier to soldier, nation to nation. The national army of the Meiji represented a turn away from the samurai toward modernity. The Rikugun added back an element of anti-modern, not just premodern, military culture. It would serve Japan or at least the officer corps in the short run. In time, however, it would lead to total defeat.

Exhausted, bled out and exposed on land even if spectacularly victorious at sea, and thus far less successful militarily than the elites allowed the Japanese people to know, Japan nevertheless gained much from the external wars of the Meiji period. Two military victories in ten years against larger, more powerful neighbors brought the end of Chinese-style insecurity relative to the West, and the creation or at least the beginning of the Meiji ideal of *fukoku kyōhei* ("rich nation, strong army").[28] International prestige came with a 1902 alliance with the principal world and naval superpower, Great Britain, then seeming defeat of another Great Power in tsarist Russia. Japan also gained an imperial colony in Korea and another in Taiwan and the Pescadores, spurring the domestic economy with expropriated overseas food and servile labor. All this turned Japanese elites and policy outward, to continuing aggressive expansion and the one-way path to overseas empire.

***

MILITARY VICTORIES, HOWEVER qualified, against two larger powers in ten years burnished Japan's world status while diminishing both China and Russia. Success at sea elevated the Kaigun to an essential instrument of Imperial advance, even as it also left a legacy of victory by singular engagement that guided naval theory and procurement right through World War II. Over the decades that followed, the national inheritance of Trafalgar-like victories at the Yalu River and Tsushima Strait was augmented by imported naval theory. Permeating the Kaigun, as was the case with most navies, were ideas of naval warfare purveyed by Alfred Thayer Mahan, an American strategist and the key naval thinker of the day. Mahan wrote enormously influential books on the idea of sea power which he conceived as counterparts to Jomini's works on land warfare.[29] He argued that the dominant powers were not land empires but naval powers with strings of overseas bases and markets, which took advantage of the efficiency and uninterrupted advantages of oceanic transport. Just as Jomini downplayed the importance of technological changes for land warfare, Mahan maintained that advances in weaponry and armor at sea had not altered the basic principles of naval strategy, that naval warfare remained constant and that dominant power was linked to command of the seas and their great trade routes and overseas markets (trade protection and interdiction). Again like Jomini on land, when it came to open war Mahan emphasized the need for concentrating forces at sea to deliver stunning, decisive blows at critical junctures.

There was some thinking about more drawn-out naval warfare in corners of the Kaigun, but overall it remained tied to an all-consuming Mahanian idea of a major sea battle against its next likely enemy. That "budgetary enemy" (a term used in negotiations with the Rikugun) was named in 1905 as the U.S. Navy, in an analysis that identified future war opponents by capabilities rather than strategic posture or actual military intentions. Rather than arm for long-term strategies of convoy and *guerre de course* by surface raiders and submarines, most thinking focused on the battlefleet as the instrument of decision by climactic battle.[30] In the 1923 Imperial Defense Policy the U.S. Navy was elevated to the "hypothetical enemy," against whom future war was all but inevitable. The result was naval procurement policies and rigid combat doctrine that over several decades looked ahead to a climactic surface battle against the far more powerful American navy, to the neglect of all else.

In the decisive sea battle concept, small surface ships and submarines would wage preliminary *zengen sakusen* actions ("progressive reduction operations") against the U.S. Pacific Fleet, to reduce enemy ship numbers and even gunnery odds before the main fleets of battleships met to decide the issue.[31] Night-fighting exercises by smaller ships and submarines, which later gave the Japanese unintended but real advantages in convoy interception actions off Guadalcanal, focused on reduction or support operations to prepare for the critical action between the main fleets. The point was to whittle down the U.S. Navy main battlefleet as it steamed toward Japan, too confident in its superiority, and to clear the way to a conclusive daytime battleship fight called the *yokuchō kantai kessen* ("decisive fleet battle the morning after"). That was the hour and day when the Kaigun would steam to victory over the USN. It would destroy the American fleet with its qualitative superiority in gunnery, for even though it expected to have fewer battleships each of these would be superior in design and crewed by spiritually superior fighting crews.[32] So, attrition yes, but only to set up annihilation of the U.S. fleet.

A deep source of this persistently offensive thinking was an indigenous, older military culture of ferocious attack when facing superior forces. This hearkened to land warfare traditions evident in Rikugun tactics as well, such as stress on thrusting small groups of warrior-soldiers against the heart of any enemy position, to overcome it with superior virtue. This underlying culture of combat ferocity led directly to such overt doctrines as fierce attack by torpedo boats, submarines as attack adjuncts to the battlefleet rather than commerce raiders, and deliberate design of destroyers as all-out attack platforms armed with up to a dozen torpedo tubes.[33] That was not like Western-style destroyers. They were designed as fleet pickets or convoy escorts and protectors, or as sub hunters (hunter-killers or attack boats) and mainstays of anti-submarine warfare (ASW). Unfortunately for the Kaigun, this battleship and decisive battle legacy was framed as doctrine right at the effective end of the big gun era, then locked in by victory over Russia. That left doctrine, planning and procurement policy looking to a great sea battle decided by fleets of all big-gun battleships just as more vital threats were emerging from technologies of submarines and naval air power. The effect, felt by other major navies as well but not to the same degree, was to render obsolete the dogmatic Kaigun mantra of victory by *taikan kyohōshugi* ("big ships, big guns"). While all major navies still laid down battleship keels into World War II, despite growing doubts everywhere among naval air power advocates about battleship utility, the Kaigun went farther than any other major navy in cleaving to a doctrine of climactic battle to be won by superior big-gun ships.

Although the Kaigun looked to the U.S. Navy as its future antagonist, before the mid-to-late 1930s it could point to little by way of an actual clash of national interests with the United States that might be worthy of resolution by war. One effect of decades of tunnel vision, from 1905, about the

USN as the main future enemy was to undercut wider political and diplomatic approaches to geopolitical conflicts. It made it easier to set aside non-
violent means of moving Japan into the inner community of major trading
nations and Great Powers. As importantly, long-term planning to fight the
U.S. Pacific Fleet underwrote budgetary claims in the annual competition
for funds with the Rikugun, a factor not to be underestimated as a driver of
policy and war. In internal bargaining, navy leaders insisted it was essential to
match 70 percent of USN tonnage and gun capability. There was real anger
when, for wider political reasons, tighter limits were agreed to by Japan's leaders at the Washington Naval Conference in 1922. Treaties held the Kaigun to
a 60 percent capital warship ratio relative to the USN.[34] During the "Treaty
Era" from 1922 to 1936, naval officers divided into an anti-treaty faction that
wanted no limits at all on capital ships and those accepting legal limits as long
as Japan pursued unfettered and imaginative construction of nonregulated
classes, especially heavy cruisers.[35]

The U.S. Navy was also dominated into the mid-1930s by Mahanian
precepts of decisive sea battle, although it also experimented with three-
dimensional fleet concepts (naval air, surface and submarine) that it would
rapidly develop once war began.[36] Early war plans called for a knockout battle
in the Central Pacific, to be decided as in dominant Japanese thinking by a
battleship gunnery duel fought after luring the enemy's carriers into a trap
and destroying them. This victory would relieve the Philippines while opening the way to defeat Japan either by naval blockade or invasion. Ascendant
into the mid-1930s in U.S. Navy debates were "thrusters." This key group
wanted an initial main fleet "thrust across the Pacific" leading to a major
battle, rather than a slower, methodical offensive. However, by 1935 a more
cautious faction settled on a strategy that accepted the loss of the Philippines
at the outset of a war with Japan (although the U.S. Army did not), while
postponing a Central Pacific fleet vs. fleet battle to some later date.[37]

This parallel in battle focus by key factions in the two Pacific naval powers
contrasted greatly with disdain for such a strategy in the Royal Navy, which
spent much more time and energy on logistics and industrial leadership as
sources of strategic sea power. That largely reflected the absence of a German
or Italian battlefleet capable or willing to fight toe to toe against it.[38] In the
event, Italy's *Regia Marina* would be caught by surprise by Mussolini's impetuous haste to join the jackal's feast in France. That meant that war came
too soon for the Italian fleet, some three years before its planned refurbish-
ment of older capital ships and launch of more modern ones. The *Regia
Marina* would thus decline to seek a major battle when Mussolini took

Italy into naval war in the Atlantic and Mediterranean in 1940. Thereafter, it fought a largely successful but limited defensive campaign, frustrating Anglo-American hopes to more quickly clear Fascist Italy's warships from the vital convoy lanes of the Mediterranean.[39] In the 1920s Soviet doctrine held that decisive sea battle was a chimera. The *Voenno-morskoi Flot SSSR* rejected Mahanian theory in an era it said was dominated by submarines and carriers, which it saw as "unblockable." That changed overnight with Stalin's order to build prestige-incurring battleships and the NKVD's dispatch of adherents of the old view into graves or the GULAG during the great purge of 1937–1938. Battleship keels were laid to take command of nearby seas, but the big ships were still unfinished when war came and could not be completed after that. Soviet shipbuilding was physically dislocated when the Germans overran or blockaded key yards and ports in the Black Sea, while the land war diverted steel and skilled workers into priority tank, aircraft and artillery production.[40]

That left the Kaigun clinging to dogma born of a battle theory based in study of 18th- and 19th-century wars, reinforced by its own early history. Its officers insisted on building ships to engage in fleet battle as the essence and ultimate determinant of all naval warfare. It became another article of faith, and the allure of naval battle, that the quality of Japanese ships, weapons and sailor training would trump American quantity.[41] This was comparable to German military superstition about the war-winning capabilities of panzers and panzer generals, an entrenched belief in a narrow technical and tactical solution to a self-created strategic dilemma. In both cases, the scenario could only hold if the next war was short and decisive. There would be no fallback plan if it was not; no taking account of long-war probabilities and the requirements of a war of naval attrition. The most honest planners and officers knew that Japan could never hope to win such a war, that when facing the U.S. Navy and war capacity it was win fast or lose everything.

The short naval war delusion took hold in Japan at all levels, not just in spite of but *because* of its known scientific, economic, industrial and military weakness relative to the anticipated or "hypothetical enemy." Japanese admirals did not plan a long war deluded that they could win. They planned what they desperately hoped would be a short naval war, deluded that they *might* win, while knowing that was the only kind of war in which they stood even a gambler's chance. This belief in victory at the outset over what must become in the longer term far more powerful surface fleets and naval air forces was psychologically, institutionally and doctrinally essential to the imperial policy Tokyo and the Kaigun pursued. It was believe in the short war or give up the entire imperial project, and that was an option no one in Japanese leadership, military or civilian, could even begin to imagine. They would have to be forced to abandon their vision of empire acquired by aggressive expansionist war. War was coming. Fire and ruin lay ahead.

From 1936 Japan declined to renew the naval limitations agreed by treaty at Washington in 1922, and announced that it would build capital ships beyond the expired treaty limits. That breakout from legal restraints satisfied the fire-eaters who wanted no restrictions, but of course it also freed and spurred the U.S. Navy and Congress to do the same. Washington first accelerated and then moved past a catch-up shipbuilding program begun in 1934, initiating post-treaty naval appropriations that stunned Japanese budget and naval planners. This crash program was guaranteed to overwhelm Kaigun capabilities and render its doctrine and training for the decisive sea battle nearly useless. U.S. naval construction promised to push Japan in just a few years below the old 60 percent treaty limit, down to just 30 percent by 1944. Japanese doctrine required the battlefleet to be at no less than 70 percent when it engaged in the decisive action. The raw numbers were staggering. Where the 1934 catch-up already called for 102 new warships by 1942, in 1938 Congress approved a 20 percent increase in tonnage, plus 1,000 more naval aircraft and upgrades and modernization of all older ships. Japan now faced something of Imperial Germany's pre-1914 dilemma: go to war soon with the odds very long, or wait until they became impossible. Like Berlin in 1914, Tokyo chose war.

Unable to lay down hulls or even modernize older ships at the same pace as the United States, from 1937 Japanese admirals looked to technology to narrow the gap by commissioning a class of superbattleships, starting with *Yamato* and *Musashi*. These secretly built vessels were meant for one role: destroying lesser American battleships in a fleet action. With 18-inch guns unmatched by any other battleship in the world, their sole purpose was to outgun and outrange anything the USN could put to sea for many years to come, new appropriations or not.[42] Against swelling ship numbers, only superships could bring victory. In a frantic search for a technical fix that bespoke rising desperation, plans were made for seven more superbattleships to be armed with even bigger 19.6-inch guns. This was pure fantasy. Japan's limited steel mills and shipyards were at full capacity, struggling to meet existing capital warship programs while failing miserably to produce anywhere near enough tankers and auxiliaries.[43] Quality versus quantity was not an inherently irrational concept or ambition facing a more numerous enemy, but too little quality against so much quantity was, because none of the seven additional superships were finished while the U.S. Navy expanded to breath-taking levels. Yet few Japanese in the Kaigun or government ever reconsidered the wisdom of fighting the Americans at all.

The 1940 defeat of France changed the course of World War II in Asia almost as much as it did in Europe, for Germany's victory fatally weakened the British, French and Dutch defense of their colonies in Southeast Asia. This new fact enticed Japan to finally choose which direction of conquest it would follow. Overland to the north of its bases in Manchuria and China it faced the tested military power of the Soviet Union. The generals were far more wary of the Red Army after being bloodied at Lake Khasan (or Changkufeng, July 29–August 11, 1938), then battered by Soviet armored divisions in support of Mongolian forces at Nomonhan (or Khalkin Gol), in an undeclared border war that started in June and culminated in major combat from August 20 to September 16, 1939.[44] In mid-1940 the road looked much easier heading south, over the water, where Japan might pick off barely defended and highly valuable colonies of European countries already occupied by its Nazi ally or, like Britain, fearing it soon would be. Southward the main problem was the United States, which had a major air base and a small army in the Philippines, while its Pacific Fleet had recently redeployed from San Diego to Hawaii.

The navy had tugged where it could toward *nanshin* from 1937 to 1940, seizing enclaves and bases on the south China coast, taking Hainan Island and the Spratlys, positioning for future wars of conquest across Southeast Asia. Well before relations between the governments in Tokyo and Washington eroded past repair, the Kaigun was partially mobilizing for the war it hoped to see in the Pacific.[45] Its advocacy of the southern advance was secured when the Rikugun at last agreed that the southern way held more opportunity than the road north. The *hokushin* advance guaranteed total war against a proven and fearsome enemy, where the *nanshin* advance offered at least a gambler's chance at quick victory. Moreover, capturing weakly defended southern colonies would bring the oil and other critical resources the army also needed for its war in China, as well as for a future war it hoped to wage against the Soviet Union.[46]

Choosing the *nanshin* advance to the south grew more urgent when, also in response to the fall of France in May–June 1940, the U.S. Congress hurriedly passed the Two-Ocean Navy Act in July. Its scale once again staggered the Japanese. Admiral Harold Stark, Chief of Naval Operations, testified to Congress that the new appropriation sought by the U.S. Navy would allow it build an additional seven fast battleships (more capable than older models of keeping up with carriers), 18 aircraft carriers, 3,000 naval aircraft, 27 cruisers, 115 destroyers and 43 submarines. That was over and above 130 warships then under construction from earlier appropriations and 358 in commission. It was an increase of 70 percent USN base strength.[47] The object lesson was that if one's resource base resembled that of Blefuscu, well matched in war only against Lilliput, one should not play at iron dice with an aroused Gulliver. It was too late. Japan's elites were already committed, too far down the imperial path to turn back short of war. Japan would not give up its empire and return to second-tier status, as from late 1940 Franklin Roosevelt would essentially insist it must do. It would accept war before conceding its ambition.

***

IF JAPAN MUST fight, it preferred to attack. If it must attack, it needed surprise. The Kaigun could not win if the opening campaign of the war against the United States was anything less than spectacularly short and truly decisive, a dim prospect at best. Its leaders and planners could not see past the initial advantage of a surprise attack that did fundamental damage to the U.S. Pacific Fleet lying at anchor in an exposed and reachable harbor in Hawaii. If they did look to initial failure or beyond a first success, they saw inevitable naval losses and an inability to make them up, while the U.S. Navy recovered past its original strength. They struck anyway. Accept war or decline. Attack first and hard or lose later, slowly but inexorably. It had come to this, as it had come to Germany in 1914. *Weltmacht oder Niedergang* was not an Imperial Japanese slogan, but the essence of that hugely destructive idea was there in the core military thinking in Tokyo nonetheless.

In a febrile prewar mood from 1940, Kaigun negotiators turned to the proposition of war against the United States as a new chip against the army in negotiations over budget allocations. The Rikugun *must* give a larger share of the budget to the Kaigun. After all, the navy would need more of everything to defeat the Americans and thereafter secure control of conquered colonies. Of these, the oil fields of the Dutch East Indies were the greatest prize among resources made essential by progressive tightening of American sanctions in 1940, then FDR's total cutoff of oil exports in 1941. The Kaigun's fatal attraction to the oil of Southeast Asia, and four decades of seeing the U.S. Navy as its natural enemy and the Pacific as a natural theater for Japan's imperial expansion, were principal causes of taking the *nanshin* path to war. A search for economic security was about to become a war for primacy in a resource-rich imperial zone taken by force.[48] Taking would not be the same as holding on, however. The first was within Japan's reach in 1940 due to the tectonic shifts caused by Nazi victories in Europe, but the second ambition would prove far beyond its grasp far more quickly than even the most pessimistic of Japanese foresaw.

The army was deep into stalemate in China, a war it could not win or finish but would not abandon. It had broad support to continue, for if Japanese elites both military and civilian agreed on anything it was that Japan never gave up gains already made. The die was cast when the Rikugun moved unopposed into northern Indochina on September 22, 1940. Japan joined the Axis alliance five days later, on September 27. With occupied Vichy unable to defend Paris, let alone Hanoi and the rest of Tonkin, Tokyo thought it was better to get there before the Germans did. Hitler was in fact hardly interested in Indochina or capable of taking it, yet Japanese leaders understood well enough that, fellow member of the Axis or not, there was no honor or trust among thieves of whole countries.[49] Over the winter the two services argued about where and how fast to move next on the southern road. The army proposed a lightning strike to take Malaya and the Dutch East Indies, confident of avoiding war with the Americans. The navy demurred, asking for more time and resources. The fateful choice was made in July 1941, when troops moved from Tonkin into southern Indochina (Annam, Cochin China and Cambodia).

Naval exercises conducted in April 1940 had shown that the main prize of the oil fields of the Dutch East Indies could not be seized and held without going to war against both Britain and the United States. The admirals advised IGHQ and the government that they could win, but not if such a war lasted beyond 18 months, given the critical need of battleships for oil. Not reported to the civilian government or to the Rikugun was that it took cheating by umpires in several war games to ensure victory over the Americans.[50] Across the Pacific, similar fleet exercises by the USN showed quite the opposite result. They revealed great potential for damage by submarine and naval air power against the Kaigun.[51] The occupation of French Indochina went ahead that autumn anyway, and gave both Japanese services forward air bases for a further and wider advance into Southeast Asia. The price was high. Roosevelt was already profoundly hostile to Tokyo's ambition and policies, and now he saw Japan as little different from its aggressive fascist allies in Europe. It was a member of the Axis, after all, and behaving similarly toward all its neighbors. Relations with Washington grew more embittered during 1941 as FDR insisted not only that Japan abandon its pursuit of empire in Southeast Asia by pulling out of Indochina, but that it must also leave China.

There followed a series of progressively crippling U.S. sanctions ranging from scrap metal to essential minerals, and finally oil.

Cut off from American oil and with no more than an 18-month supply in reserve for major military operations, naval leaders urged war sooner rather than later. At an Imperial Liaison Conference in October 1941, Chief of Staff Admiral Osami Nagamo exclaimed: "The Navy is consuming 400 tons of oil an hour. The situation is urgent. We want it decided one way or the other quickly."[52] This self-generated crisis led to unusual interservice and government unity centered on evocation of extreme national spirit, and an attendant drive into war as both honorable and necessary. The decision was broad and collective, concurred with by most civilian and military leaders. Even Emperor Hirohito feared another junior officer coup attempt should Japan back down.[53] The decision to attack Pearl Harbor and British and Dutch colonies in Asia was not made from ignorance of the deep strength of the foe, as once thought, but with knowledge if not understanding of superior U.S. capabilities. That awareness was provided to decision-makers in Tokyo by a desperately anxious admiral-ambassador in Washington, Nomura Kichisaburō.[54]

The leadership of Japan united in an astonishing conclusion, that the solution to the stalemate in China was to launch whole new wars against Britain and the United States in Southeast Asia and the Pacific. Japan hoped to stun the Western powers into ending supply of the *Guomindang* via the Burma Road, while securing the vital oil (and rubber and rice) it needed to maintain an overstretched empire and carry on the war. On this as on most things, Tokyo had no real intelligence as to how its foes would respond.[55] It simply proposed to force acceptance of its hegemony over Asia by expelling colonial powers in a faux crusade against colonialism, made in order to grab those same colonies. It all came down to having overreached in China and now refusing to abandon gains in the face of American resistance. The only course through the maze was to hit the United States hard and fast, to force it to accede to Japan's regional dominance. The whole idea was a high-risk gamble that even if attacked, Americans would not want to send their sons to die in unheard-of places just to restore other peoples' empires. Despite decades of war planning and considering their "hypothetical enemy" across the wide Pacific, Japan's leaders did not foresee that the United States would hurl armies and fleets of ships and planes at them in steel and fire tsunamis. Filled with nationalist pride but also trepidation, they decided to start a war that was both preventable and unwinnable.[56]

The Rikugun understood it could not fight the U.S. Army on equal terms, not least because the bulk of its forces were bogged down in China. It planned to hunker behind a fortified perimeter to which the navy would deliver its men, there to fortify and hold out on island after island in a manner that must raise assault costs to the attacking Americans, and thereby deter any direct Allied challenge to the more important colonies to be seized in Southeast Asia. Whatever it and the navy together seized by amphibious operations, the Rikugun would hold with ferocious spirit. It might lose the outer shell, but it would secure the colonial prizes closer to the home islands, while also protecting earlier gains in China. In contrast, the Kaigun was cocky about its chances in battle with the U.S. Navy. Only tactical doubts were indulged or allowed. Then Yamamoto proposed a major change to a decades-old plan to lure the Pacific Fleet west, attriting it all along the way with "progressive reduction operations" before fighting a winning fleet action. He laid out an alternate plan to attack the Pacific Fleet first with concentrated naval air power, while it lay at anchor at Pearl Harbor.[57] It seemed to some to be a radical departure from all prior doctrine, accepting a shift from big guns to the striking power of carriers. Even so, it incorporated and spoke to the usual desperate illusions and reliance on a single battle, not at Pearl Harbor but afterward, once the American fleet was sharply reduced in combat power. Actually, in the Hawaii attack Yamamoto was mainly using carriers as a substitute force to reduce the U.S. battle line before the truly decisive engagement.

While Yamamoto thought the war was a long-odds gamble, at least his plan would protect the home islands and guard the flank of the *nanshin* advance into 1942. He also thought that striking a hard blow against the Pacific Fleet might give Japan a year or so to consolidate conquests and fortify its new outer defense perimeter.[58] Other senior officers remained deeply skeptical of abandoning the original reduction operations and battleship engagement plan. They only accepted Yamamoto's alternative when he threatened to resign, and only while also formally reiterating that the final objective of all naval action was to defeat the U.S. Navy in a fleet-to-fleet action after luring it closer to Japan following the attack on Pearl Harbor.[59] In the end, many senior admirals supported the attack plan because they agreed it would chip away at the enemy's battle line prior to the climactic fight they had planned for all their professional lives, and now expected to see.[60] And so the orders were given and the fleet steamed, and the air over Hawaii filled with desperation and war planes.

Except for the USS *Arizona*, which blew up, and the USS *Oklahoma*, which turtled, the United States suffered only temporary loss of its older battleships at Pearl Harbor on December 7, 1941. All other damaged battleships were sunk in too-shallow harbor waters, and therefore later raised, repaired, and returned to service. Other than the tragedy of lives lost, it almost did not matter what damage was done to the slow U.S. battleships. What Pearl Harbor really settled was the old argument inside the USN between the big-gun faction and naval aviation advocates. By sidelining old and slower battleships but leaving the carrier force intact, the Japanese attack ultimately turned the USN into a carrier task force navy in the Pacific. The advance toward Japan therefore would be made in increments under the protection of naval and island-based air power, rather than a single fleet thrust with battleships as once proposed. Worse for Japan, its leaders falsely assumed they could wage a limited war on the periphery of enemy power in the Pacific, as when Japan had fought on China's periphery in Korea in 1895 and on tsarist Russia's periphery in Manchuria in 1904–1905. The United States did not see it that way. Having been attacked, it would not be stopped by an oceanic peripheral defense or early losses. The United States military was going to Japan.

Faced with an enemy ready to wage a wearing campaign as well as total war at sea and later, by air, Japan's admirals possessed a narrow appreciation of the new all-out character of naval warfare and war more generally. They therefore rejected the traditional alternative of weaker navies, a war of raids on ports and commerce that avoided fleet-to-fleet actions. Such a conflict was without honor. Battle was all. Even attacking naval supply operations was seen as contrary to their warrior tradition. They wasted a real opportunity. The Kaigun had a diverse fleet of submarines, including the world's largest and most advanced submersibles, armed with the world's best torpedo in 1941. Yet its admirals disdained using these fine weapons to scour shipping along the American coast or to attack troop convoys off Australia or shipping around India, except sporadically and always half-heartedly. Instead, submarines were assigned to long-distance attack missions to reduce U.S. capital warship numbers before the still longed-for climactic battle that must be fought to win the Pacific War. Built to intercept 21-knot USN battleships, they were immediately confronted by much faster carriers, a result paradoxically flowing from Japanese success in damaging old battleships at Pearl Harbor.

Kaigun submarines performed poorly at Hawaii and the Battles of the Coral Sea (May 3–8, 1942) and Midway (June 4–5, 1942). Then they were forced into a supply role for which they were not designed or intended when heavy and protracted fighting broke out unexpectedly on Guadalcanal

(August 7, 1942 to February 7, 1943). After that, the admirals refused to release submarines to make *guerre de course* because they would not abandon
the idea of an elusive fleet battle in which submarines would play a role against
American battleships. That delusion lasted deep into 1944, by which time it
was too late to do much at all with the paltry number of submarines left to
Japan.[61] Despite hoarding these to do battle, all though the war the force was
also diluted by dispersing individual boats on frantic scouting missions, to
shell the coast of Oregon to no discernible purpose, to evacuate or supply cut-
off island garrisons, to sit off ports and monitor traffic, even to transport gasoline for sea planes.[62] Where the USN early switched to commerce-raiding
or anti-supply roles for its submarines, insistence on keeping submarines attached to the battle line of the Combined Fleet long past any hope of actually arranging a climactic battle only ensured that prewar doctrine devolved
almost into wartime pathology.

For the same reason, the Japanese built superior destroyers designed not
for convoy escort or even fleet protection but to launch torpedo attacks that
would make *nikuhaku hitchû* ("press closely, strike home") attacks against the
big ships in the U.S. battle line.[63] Blind to the role of their own submarines as
potential commerce raiders, Kaigun admirals largely ignored ASW weapons
development and training along with the possibility that the enemy might
send submarines to sink Japanese merchant shipping, and specially target a
tanker fleet that was inadequate even before the start of the war. After a slow
start for American submarines, that is exactly what happened. The U.S. Navy
pursued all-out submarine warfare, employing its force in the most successful and ruthless *guerre de course* in the history of submarines.[64] Meanwhile,
Japanese destroyers were seldom nearby to protect the targeted merchant
marine and critical tanker fleet.

Planners also focused naval aviation—fleet carriers, seaplanes, and island-
based air groups of fighters and bombers—on wearing down USN numbers
prior to a final decision to be exacted by the superbattleships, whose construction they were forced to cancel for want of steel and shipyard capacity.
The tactical idea was drearily familiar: gradually overcome enemy superiority by *yōgeki sakusen* ("interceptive operations"). The decisive sea fight would
follow, probably off the Philippines. This was not a strategy of attrition as
understood by any other navy. It was always foreplay to the main fleet battle.
It took to the end of 1942 for planners to bow to wartime reality and deem
it necessary to convert limited shipbuilding capacity away from superbattleships to replace carrier losses, thereby also accepting the demonstrated
domination of naval aviation over big guns. The unfinished hull of *Shinano*,

a *Yamato*-class superbattleship laid down in 1940, was thereafter converted into the largest carrier of the war. It took three years to finish the job, due to scarcity of supplies and skilled labor and the paucity of Japan's shipyard capacity. Then *Shinano* was sunk with heavy loss of life by an American submarine in late November 1944, days after its commissioning and still without any planes on its deck.[65] By then, true pathology was coming to dominate all Japanese military operations and tactics. A cult of death gripped the Empire's sea, land and air forces ever harder the more hopeless things became and the closer total war approached the home islands.

16

Annihilation of Illusions

FOR DECADES, RIKUGUN war plans focused on an entirely different future enemy than the one the Kaigun contemplated: tsarist Russia before World War I and the Soviet Union thereafter. A fundamental disjuncture opened between the services that was never corrected, continuing right to the eve of war in 1940. Naval officers prepared to fight the United States while army officers readied to fight the Soviet Union. There were efforts to resolve the issue, but they actually made things worse while also revealing the near limitless recklessness of the prewar elites, civilian as well as military. For example, as early as 1918 an official Imperial policy signed by the emperor settled on a typical compromise that decided nothing: the armed forces should prepare to fight *both* Russia and America. China was also there to be exploited, as it collapsed into warlordism and civil war. Throughout the 1920s and 1930s Japan thus prepared for war against a potential coalition of China, the Soviet Union and the United States. Daunting, yes, but said to be winnable because at the outset the Rikugun would wage a lightning war in China and thus secure the resources it needed to fight off the Soviets and Americans.[1] In the end, Japan got it all, but not as expected: a grinding ground war in China, a slow-rolling naval and air war against the United States, and a blitzkrieg-like assault not against but by the Red Army in 1945.

Japan's elites were suffused with military and imperial illusions, from fast war to the racial superiority of the Yamato race to superior spiritual qualities of their fighting men that would surely overcome severe deficiencies in matériel. Once war started its military would become progressively radicalized as defeat approached, inculcating devotion to an emperor cult that at its extreme demanded fighting to the death in a manner asked by no other army in Europe or Asia. In return, soldiers and sailors were told they were past moral reproach by Japanese civilians, and certainly by any foreigners who came under their control. Taught that surrender was dishonorable, many came to hold it in utter contempt, at the cost of their own lives or the lives of prisoners of war. Disregard for empathy or pity for civilians and prisoners, encouraged by racialized imperial and military culture, led straight to atrocity in well-lit places like Nanjing and along the railway of death. Yet when it was all over, it was Japanese illusions of superiority and ambitions to empire that were utterly annihilated.

***

NOT ALL JAPANESE succumbed to the same illusions. In 1916 General Tanaka Giichi chaired a committee of 25 officers studying war as it was unfolding in Europe. He could not accept that the attritional nature of modern war as revealed in the trenches meant that Japan faced impossible odds against its effort to build an empire in Asia. He knew that Japan's strength was always insufficient to challenge the Western colonial powers directly. He drew two conclusions that would keep open the chance for acquiring empire by war. Acknowledging that World War I showed the day of short cabinet wars was done, he said Japan must have economic independence for a future drawn-out war. That meant it needed unfettered control of resources in Manchuria and China, because in any future war among industrial nations endurance, not *seishin* spirit or superior *élan vital*, must decide the outcome. His solution to trench warfare that must sap Japan's already minimal strength was not to abjure war but to launch it sooner, against weak Asian neighbors, in a bid to make Japan strong enough to fight European powers in the future. However, a more dominant group venerated German prewar doctrine even after its defeat in 1914 and Germany's defeat in 1918. They clung to the belief that there was only one way for Japan to overcome its weak position, as there had been for Germany: win fast at the beginning or not at all. Flirting with total war analysis and planning only confirmed that prospects in any long war were insurmountable for Japan, so again and again its military leaders returned to the idea of the win-or-lose-all battle. Warning images of other people's trenches were pushed aside by imperial temptations and cultural imperatives.

In the 1920s debate continued between a reform faction on the General Staff that wanted a modern firepower army ready for a slow war of matériel and traditionalists who believed in *seishin* spiritual superiority and an opening and war-winning battle. In 1927 the traditionalists, admirers of Schlieffen, rewrote the infantry combat and command manual to stress that moral factors and offensive spirit were always decisive in war—all evidence of their own lifetimes to the contrary notwithstanding. Then Ishiwara Kanji, a young staff officer in the Kwantung Army and a key plotter of expansionist war by

Japan, provoked the military action that led to the invasion of Manchuria in 1931. Ishiwara was a millenarian religious fanatic but also an important strategic theorist. He argued, like Giichi, that Japan's wars must be decided in the same way other modern wars were decided, by a great and lasting contest of population and war matériel among nations and empires. He believed the takeover of Manchuria would provide the resources needed to compete with Russia and the United States, but only if Japan was also remade into a one-party state embodying a unified national spirit under a regime guiding economic mobilization for total war.[2]

Ishiwara was influential in his actions leading Japan into war for resources in Manchuria but not persuasive about the larger issue of the kind of protracted future war Japan must wage against more powerful enemies. Some colleagues wanted centralized and planned industrialization to lay the foundation for total war mobilization down the road, to create economic and strategic depth for Japan to allow it to compete as an equal among the Great Powers. That was happening in the Soviet Union, where starting in the 1920s Stalin was force-building a war-state that would in fact survive a Schlieffen-like attempt at rapid invasion and defeat. That's what existed in the sprawling if latent resource bases of the British Empire and the United States, but not in semi-industrialized and resource-poor Japan. However, too many factions pulled policy in mutually contradictory directions, until one faction or another decided on immediate action over debate and pulled all of Japan farther down the one-way street of military commitments to expanded overseas empire.

Many young officers who agreed that Japan needed to widen its resource base did not understand Ishiwara's long-war reasoning. They were mainly interested in the production of weapons, right away.[3] They wanted only the products of war factories without the effort of building the deeper economy needed to sustain a future total war. They did not believe in total war, in attrition as a path to victory or just as the revealed reality of modern Great Power conflicts. They were military romantics, and some were military spiritualists, who rejected the triumph of *Materialschlacht* over moral strength, and who still believed in all-out battle and victory through reliance on warrior virtues such as ferocity in attack. By 1936 this *seishin* faction was back on top of policy and imperial strategy turned back to delusion. It was actually proposed in the joint Imperial Defense Policy that Japan could fight and defeat the Soviet Union and the United States simultaneously, winning fast wars against each, one on land and the other at sea.[4] When disobedient and impatient junior officers started an unnecessary war in China the next year, Japan headed into a quagmire it could not exit and toward a total war it was never ready to fight. That was the draw the imagination of battle exercised for weaker states devoted to becoming more powerful in the mid-20th century: it twisted reality, denied experience, blended political ambition and desire with military and imperial delusion. Then the choice was made.

The one area of interservice agreement throughout this period was on an overriding principle of *Tosui-ken*, the idea that the emperor exercised supreme command and strategic direction. That meant effective service autonomy in practice, because authority over the military could never be surrendered to civilians in the central government if it resided legitimately in the emperor alone. Moreover, there was no policy coordinating body with power to enforce shared resources or decide strategy. IGHQ was too weak to impose centralized military control on the rival services, let alone dictate a unified grand strategy they both must follow. Imperial Liaison Conferences, which began in 1937 as Japan plunged into the China quagmire, prepared paper compromises rather than real guidance. Critical differences over the direction of national policy and war planning represented more than normal interservice politics and wrangling, as found in other countries and militaries. They formed a fundamental divide over grand strategy, over the whole purpose and design of the overseas imperial project pursued since the 1890s. The rivalry of the Rikugun and Kaigun remained the central fact of Japanese politics and diplomacy and military adventurism, and a source of chronic strategic confusion leading by 1941 to fighting several big wars all at once.

All that was smoothed over in the Imperial Defense Policy approved by the emperor in June 1936, a compromise reiterating that the Rikugun should prepare for war against the Red Army in Siberia while the Kaigun readied for war with the U.S. Navy in the Pacific. Actually coordinating grand strategy would mean the two services must accept differential budget allocations. Instead, each pursued its own interests, always trying to maximize its share of the budget to do so. At a critical moment when the old international order was unraveling everywhere, that meant radical departure from an older one-enemy-at-a-time wisdom to instead pursue a divided policy against very different enemies, with no central direction to war planning. It also meant the list of military ambitions kept growing, since there was no way to restrain either service from adding its own new mission and objectives. Hence, in 1937 it was agreed to plan for war against China as well as the United States and Soviet Union. That was not an informed national decision so much as a reaction to Sino-Japanese relations deteriorating, and separate and disobedient army factions agitating for invasion. With strategic caution abandoned on land, the

Japanese Objectives in Asia, December 1941.

Courtesy of the Department of History, United States Military Academy at West Point.

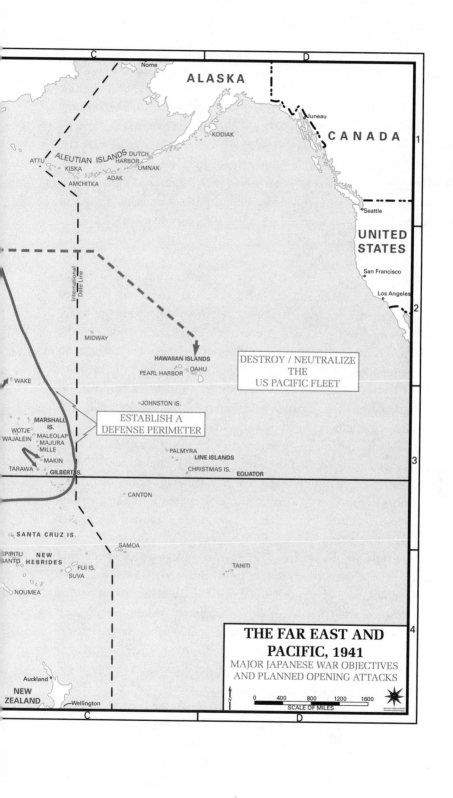

THE FAR EAST AND
PACIFIC, 1941

MAJOR JAPANESE WAR OBJECTIVES
AND PLANNED OPENING ATTACKS

0   400   800   1200   1600
SCALE OF MILES

Kaigun cast a cold eye on Royal Navy assets at Singapore, thereby adding the British Empire to the list as a *fourth* likely enemy. This was reckless hubris of a kind rarely seen. It was not rational in any serious sense. It was politically and institutionally driven, existing in a theoretical and operational bubble outside any strategic plan or even idea. What it meant in practice was that Japan's military prepared (procured weapons, trained) to fight two separate wars, the navy's and the army's, against the United States and the Soviet Union when it did not have the resources to wage either. Then it invaded China instead in 1937, as rising nationalism threatened imperial gains on the mainland and local officers decided to take action without higher consultation.[5]

***

THE IDEA OF beating two Great Powers in simultaneous quick wars was risible, especially as the Rikugun was in fact prepared to fight only backward and weak Chinese armies. It armed down, literally employing inferior weapons, to the less modern level of its actual Chinese opponent and not up to the modern weapons standards of its potential Soviet and American enemies. So deep was contempt for China's weakness that neither side in the *hokushin* vs. *nanshin* debate factored into their arguments a real-world hardening of Chinese nationalism. That attitude led to more ill-advised aggression, beginning with rogue officers in Manchuria who provoked the Marco Polo (Lugouqiao) Bridge confrontation with local Chinese forces on July 7, 1937, leading to what Japanese called the *Shina jihen* ("China Incident"). Shots were fired out of the dark near a bridge over a tributary of the Hai River. Japanese troops of the North China Garrison Army were in the area, enforcing extraterritorial treaty rights. A single Japanese private went missing for two hours, but otherwise no one was hurt. However, officers on the spot were determined to take advantage of the situation. An apology was demanded and the Chinese were instructed to withdraw from other key bridges, opening the road to potential conquest of northern China. The Chinese garrison refused to move.[6] Japanese and Chinese troops clashed the next morning as a local squabble escalated into a war crisis. Local units had long hoped for a pretext to invade, and this minor incident provided it. The rest of the Rikugun went along, approving the invasion of northern China. Nationalist China would no longer accept humiliation at the hands of Japan, and moved to fully mobilize. Rikugun leaders were aware of the *Yezhovshchina* blood purge of the Red Army then underway and thought Moscow's terrible distraction might be Tokyo's great opportunity, not just to expand into China but also possibly for war with the Soviet Union. Reinforcements were sent from Korea and three fresh divisions from Japan on July 25. Two days later the Japanese attacked into China in force, starting the Second Sino-Japanese War.

The culture of disobedience had once again hijacked the whole dynamic of Japanese policy.[7] On the other hand, the invasion of China took place within a context of ongoing imperial expansion that was embraced by many military and government leaders, and thus was endorsed within days at all levels of the Rikugun and by senior figures in the civilian government. Military disobedience was less important than empire. Recent research suggests an even more complex scenario may have played out. Key civilian leaders, notably Prime Minister Konoe Fumimaro and later Prime Minister Hiranuma Kiichirō, may have supported engagement in China in order to forestall what they saw as an even more reckless impulse by the ultranationalist *Kōdōha* (Imperial Way) faction within the Rikugun, which was eager to attack the Soviet Union. In addition, they were concerned to check influence of the *Tōseiha* (Control Faction) that demanded closer ties with the European fascist states. Working with new archival sources, Andrew Levidis suggests that "one of the principal considerations" in the Cabinet decision to back military engagement in China was fear that "if hostilities were too rapidly terminated . . . the restored Imperial Way faction would push for the redeployment of these divisions north to Manchuria in preparation for war with the Soviet Union."[8] War with China was deemed less threatening than the Rikugun's urge to fight the Soviet Union.

Against an enemy with more strategic depth than they could handle, the Japanese fought in China as the Germans would fight in Russia four years later, lurching from mobile operation to operation without a real strategic connection or plan to win the war. Japanese also pursued such appalling occupation policies that intensified national resistance was guaranteed. Casualties were immense on the Chinese side, but also and right from the start far beyond what was expected by the Japanese in their own ranks. Again presaging German experience, territory and cities fell to the invaders, but to escape total destruction Chinese armies withdrew deeper into the southwest and the interior of a country big beyond Japanese ken or experience. And so the war went on, and casualties mounted to levels we still cannot accurately count today on the Chinese side. The cruelty of this war was also comparable to the later German invasion of the bloodlands of Europe. Generals and soldiers behaved very often in an unrestrained, even bestially murderous manner. Advancing Japanese armies did not at first bother to take prisoners or killed them after surrender, just as they had during the First Sino-Japanese War. It only got worse. As in other protracted wars, the more Japanese soldiers died in battles or at the hands of Chinese the deeper the frustration of strategic quagmire became, and the harsher and harder Japan's terms became to end it.

Hard war began right away. General Chiang Kai-shek (Jiang Jieshi) was warlord and dictator, head of China's *Guomindang* (National People's Party) and its attendant army. He decided to open a second front 600 miles to the southeast at Shanghai. The fight engaged 750,000 Chinese against 250,000 Japanese over three months, starting in mid-August. By the end of November over 40,000 Japanese and at least 200,000 Chinese were killed. An amphibious landing on November 5 threatened the Chinese divisions with encirclement, forcing a westward withdrawal and Japanese advance. That in turn set the stage for the Rape of Nanjing, a seven-week serial atrocity beginning in December. It was the worst massacre and pillaging of its kind during the war, with perhaps 200,000 Chinese butchered (the numbers remain notoriously controversial).[9] It was far from the last atrocity perpetrated by Japanese forces in China.

The idea of mediation by the German ambassador was discussed in Tokyo even as the killing was underway in Nanjing, but was dismissed. Instead, in January 1938 Japan rejected all third party calls for mediation and terminated all future relations with Chiang Kai-shek's Nationalist government. It would follow a hardline policy, possibly because top civilian leaders feared that if the widening but still limited war in China was ended too soon, by negotiations, the Imperial Way faction in the Rikugun would push to attack the Soviet Union instead, plunging Japan into full-scale war with a major world power.[10] In the event, the war in China only deepened as fierce and determined resistance continued and mounting Japanese casualties created a moral and political commitment to a quagmire that became harder to reverse with each overseas death. Tokyo set up collaborationist and puppet regimes in several occupied Chinese regions. This signal of a clear long-term intention to partition and thereby dominate China provoked deeper resistance, guaranteeing that the war would go on even as the scale and depth of fighting eluded Japanese control.[11] Meanwhile, overconfident field generals disdainful of central command kept pushing inland, stretching an over-tasked and perpetually inadequate logistics system beyond its capability. Again like the German thinkers and trainers who originally mentored them, they disdained logistics. That was not something that should concern the warrior class of a warrior people. Without changing any strategic considerations by new and often unauthorized operations, they took more casualties and thereby forced more militarization and mobilization for total war by all Japanese society.

In March 1938, the Chinese stunned the Japanese when two columns were smashed into retreat by *Guomindang* forces, with large-scale losses. More heavy fighting followed around Xuzhou, where the Chinese lost whole divisions but the main armies once again survived.[12] The Japanese were forced to change to a policy of territorial occupations rather than attempting to defeat the *Guomindang* in the field by always seeking and fighting more battles. It was a recognition that the war was going to last a long time. During the preliminary to next major campaign, for Wuhan, Chiang Kai-shek showed just how ruthlessly he and the *Guomindang* would fight back. To slow down two divisions of advancing Japanese he broke the dikes on the Yellow River, flooding three provinces and killing nearly 1 million Chinese civilians while creating 3.9 million refugees.[13] The flooding held off the Japanese for a few months, until the waters subsided and the advance resumed along the flooded riverbanks with the help of barges and gunboats.

Astonishingly, even while mired in this deepening war in China the Japanese generals dreamed about the war they really wanted, northward on the *hokushin* road against the Red Army. In the middle of a major land war that was already deviating from predicted duration and casualties, reckless officers in the *Guandong* ("East of the Barrier") Army on the Soviet border engaged in heavy fighting with the Red Army. Once again, they acted without central authority. The combat reached division and corps levels into August. Fighting would be even more severe at Nomonhan a year later, when the Red Army in support of Mongolian forces bloodied the Japanese just before the Nazis and Soviets concluded their nonaggression pact and invaded Poland.[14] The next two years of Japanese politics and statecraft was marked by strengthening ties to the European fascist states through the Anti-Comintern Pact, political and bureaucratic mobilization of all Japanese society for war, and changing foreign policy in response to shifts in the fortunes of war in Europe and in relations with the United States.

Meanwhile, the fighting in China continued. Japanese armies advanced astride the Yangzi River into encounter battles near Wuhan that pitted 300,000 Japanese troops against 1 million Chinese. Rikugun divisions were too far from their bases during this series of Wuhan battles, which marked the limits of Japanese logistics capabilities and strategic penetration. The Rikugun was forced by the strategic depth of China, and by profound national resistance, into a makeshift strategy of small garrisons and larger raids. That meant using lesser-quality conscripts in fixed positions to hold on to initial gains won along the coast and interior penetrations that followed river or railway lines. Now came wearing, constant casualties as Britain and the

United States fed in supplies to Chiang Kai-shek's armies in southern China via Hong Kong and the Burma Road.[15] The Japanese killed far more Chinese, but their own casualties were so high they forced a move away from the official tactics of spirited infantry assaults to an emphasis on speed and mobility in response to Chinese attacks, even though the Rikugun lacked the modern means of mechanized warfare to carry out this tactical shift.

Japan's military policy was reckless rather than bold and imaginative, overextending military commitments that chased prior commitments, thinning resources without offering a solution or strategic purpose or proposed end. Local offensive followed offensive, some by the *Guomindang*, more by the Rikugun. The fighting shifted forward fighting lines but did not break the strategic stalemate after 1941, as more Allied war matériel flowed in to prop up Chiang Kai-shek's armies and kill Japanese while also tying down the bulk of the Rikugun's divisions in China. More befuddled conscripts arrived to hold the lines and small garrisons, but were used on offense only to strike opportunistically against an enemy whose territory had proven much too large to conquer and who was protected also by membership in a rising Great Power coalition created by Japan's own actions from late 1941. There was some movement, but battles are best understood in this period as episodes of accelerated attrition. All were individually indecisive, but cumulatively and strategically they wore out the armies on both sides in a contest of endurance as much or more than military skill. Because Japan sought permanent partition and lasting dominion, Nationalist armies in the south and much smaller numbers of Communist guerrillas in the northwest resisted fiercely, while key international players intervened to tie down Japanese forces and keep China intact. All the while, more modern American and Allied air forces and armies island-hopped across the Pacific, intending to bomb and invade the increasingly exposed Japanese home islands.[16]

Nevertheless, into 1944 the senior officer corps in both the Rikugun and Kaigun stayed intoxicated with the idea of tactical and operational success as directly fungible into strategic victory in nested wars in Asia: a civil war in China waged inside a regional Asian war started by Japan, fought within the larger world war that now extended across the Pacific.[17] On the mainland, only the fact that it was fighting inferior Chinese armies, far too often led by corrupt generals, prevented the Rikugun's collapse from shoddy logistics and larger strategic failures. In the Pacific War, extraordinary effort in an impossible endeavor was asked of ordinary Japanese in uniform. Clearly losing in the Pacific and well on the way to total defeat outside China by the end of 1943, 500,000 troops undertook the largest and longest campaign in Rikugun history from April 1944 to February 1945. In an operation codenamed *Ichigō* (Number One), the Imperial Japanese Army drove down the central coast, smashing *Guomindang* forces in its way, then turned inland and headed for Chiang Kai-shek's main base and headquarters at Chóngqìng.

The principal Japanese objectives were to cut all supplies to Chóngqìng, push back American bomber bases in southern China out of range of the home islands, and force the *Guomindang* to end the China War. The Japanese also needed to clear a land route for their forces cutoff in French Indochina, where their garrison no longer could be supplied by sea due to great losses suffered by their merchant marine, both to American submarines and naval air power. Initially, the Japanese enjoyed offensive success not seen since 1937–1938, including in central Henan province where a rapid encirclement was effected by Japanese tanks in newly deployed armored divisions. In May, the Japanese occupied large swaths of south central China. In June, they drove toward Indochina in three connected operations (*Togo-1, Togo-2,* and *Togo-3*). This supreme effort ended in yet more China lying beyond the reach and control of the Rikugun, just as there was always more Russia ahead of the *Ostheer* no matter how much territory the panzers rolled across. The 1944 offensives into southern China never really had a chance to extricate Japan from the overall defeat that was clearly on the way.[18] Rage and frustration swelled into a scorched-earth ferocity and the renewal of what Chinese called *Sānguāng Zhèngcè* and Japanese later dubbed the *Sankō Sakusen* or Three Alls order, first issued in 1940: "Burn All. Loot All. Kill All." Rage was not victory.

Nor could anything save the Japanese in Burma, where some troops went into final battles without weapons against revived and better officered and armed British and Indian Army divisions. Unarmed Japanese were told to follow and take rifles from their dead, just as some Russian infantry were told to do in 1915 and again in 1941. Burma saw guerrilla war, major and deep deployments of special forces by the British, long campaigns of jungle treks leading to sieges, and the total disintegration of Japanese 15th army at Imphal and Kohima. The last campaign was marked by more rank and insubordinate disobedience by Japanese generals, some of the worst yet most predictable logistical failures of the entire war, and immense suffering of ordinary soldiers on a failed retreat to the Irrawaddy River that amounted to a self-inflicted death march. A complete breakdown in Japanese command, supplies and morale permitted Western armies to push deep into Burma in early 1945. The last months in theater for the Japanese were truly catastrophic. Remnants of a broken army and smashed divisions, beyond supply or hope, tried to fight their way out but only suffered enormous loss of life. Some units lost 60 to 90 percent of their men.[19]

***

IN THE END it was the loss of Japan's other nested war, in the Pacific, that decided and ended the China War and led to the surrender and evacuation of all Japanese forces in Asia.[20] Japan's leaders had made the decision to fight the United States in 1941 in high confidence that the armed forces were primed, ready and well-supplied. In fact, the Kaigun took a desperate gamble that was blunted inside six months, while the Rikugun had no real strategy for war in the Pacific, having planned to fight the Red Army for decades while actually fighting in China for several years before Pearl Harbor. Instead, there were vague plans to seize Indian Ocean bases to cut off Britain from its overseas empire while Nazi Germany strangled it on its home islands. With Britain out of the war, it was reasoned, *Guomindang* armies in southern China would be cut off from outside supply and must collapse. At that point, Washington would surely agree to negotiate acceptance of Tokyo's domination of Asia. Autarkic, powerful Imperial Japan would emerge as a *Machtstaat*. That all depended on being able to use the captive resources of Southeast Asia to wage protracted war in China and the Pacific. However, Japanese planners had wildly miscalculated how quickly they could exploit Southeast Asia's raw materials, not least due to a lack of merchant cargo shipping and tanker capacity to bring those vital resources to Japan. And that was before the shipping lanes became infested with U.S. Navy submarines and roving naval air power.[21] Unready and unable to fight for very long itself, Japan counted on the unwillingness of the United States to fight at all once it was presented with the accomplished facts of Japan's brilliant opening victories. Americans would quail before Japan's demonstrated *seishin* character. The superior spiritual would defeat mere matériel. It was all a grand illusion.

As strained as that imagined scenario was, it was the one chance to permit Japan to avoid total defeat and retain its empire. Strike at Britain together with Nazi Germany in the first year, while Americans were weak because still reeling from Pearl Harbor. In the year or so that attack bought before the Americans sallied in force into the Pacific, fortify an outer perimeter defense that would deter any counteroffensive by raising costs and casualties. Had Japanese leaders delayed the decision for war for two more weeks they would have seen the Wehrmacht stopped and then thrown back in front of Moscow. It is possible that would have changed their calculus that Germany was winning, that they must strike before the U.S. Navy became too powerful and the opportunities in Southeast Asia disappeared. Possible, but not probable. There was no going back, no real way to reverse their commitment to war and empire. In the event, Japanese leaders moved from exultation straight to euphoria over a string of victories during the months following Pearl Harbor, by which time they should have realized that their Nazi ally was bogging down militarily in Russia in much the same way they were already tied down in China.

Despite decades of Kaigun planning for a singular naval engagement there would be no decisive sea battle decided by "big ships, big guns." Americans never committed the greater part of their fleet to a decisive contest, as Japan needed them to do. The Kaigun thus never got the critical victory that it planned and needed. It only got Pearl Harbor. That partial success mostly accelerated an U.S. Navy shift in procurement and tactical directions in which it was already leaning, away from battleships to aircraft carriers as its main strike weapon. [22] Moreover, American shipbuilding capacity was so great the United States continued to build all classes of warships all through the war. Until Japanese admirals lost almost every asset in two desperate surface battles in the Philippine Sea in 1944, they continued to believe in a naval war of sharp offensives and singular battles. They never accepted the decisiveness of attritional war even when they were mired in it. Their war was all a frenzied catastrophe.

The preeminent historians of the Kaigun, David Evans and Mark Peattie, state the case exactly. The naval high command and the naval officer corps as a whole "neither understood nor prepared for *war* at all. Rather, it believed in and prepared for *battle* . . . the single, annihilating surface victory, fought essentially on the navy's terms and intended to force the enemy to his knees.... [This] created a fighting force that was both one-dimensional and brittle."[23] And therefore, the Kaigun was fairly quickly beaten at all levels, as combat power and performance were progressively reduced. Thus, a superb cadre of about 800 highly skilled aviators ("sea eagles"), more experienced than any other carrier pilot force in the world in 1941, was sent into combat again and again trying to land a knockout blow against U.S. carriers. But too few had been trained before the war, and they were unsupported by an effective pilot replacement or training scheme during the war. Starting with the first sea battles and losses, Kaigun pilot skills entered irreversible decline. In contrast, the U.S. Navy rotated pilots and crews into rear area training programs from 1938, where they flew an expanded fleet of training planes produced even at the expense of combat aircraft. This system steadily raised the experience and expertise of the whole naval air arm. The Japanese tried to catch up from 1941, which was far too late.[24] After that, the U.S. also built faster and better naval aircraft in huge numbers, and many dozens of carriers to bring destruction to Japan's remaining fleets and in fast carrier raids also to its overseas bases.

Compounding the pilot shortage in what quickly became a carrier war in the Pacific was a chronic shortage of oil and refined fuels. Japan's tanker fleet was undersized to begin with and made more vulnerable by refusal to use smaller warships to escort convoys, since the admirals wanted all destroyers kept with the battlefleet for the big show to come. Small tankers steaming alone became a prime target for USN submarines and later, naval air attack. Losses were irreplaceable. Only *four* new tankers were built by Japan over the entire war, so limited was shipbuilding capacity. Over the last 15 months of World War II only 9 percent of Japanese tankers made it through the submarine and air gauntlets. The response of the two services to the catastrophe of the loss of the tanker fleet was to lie to each other about their respective oil reserves and to conceal stocks. All this incompetence and lack of preparation and wartime self-deceit and mutual lying, despite one of the main reasons for going to war in 1941 being to secure access to oil from the Dutch East Indies. As a result, from 1943 the Kaigun suffered a crisis of depleted fuel reserves and shortages that limited basic training, undercutting the quality of already poor pilots and the number of air and sea patrols that could be undertaken. By 1945, what was left of the battlefleet was restricted to waters close to the sources of fuel and under short air cover. Desperate methods were resorted to that bespoke a catastrophic lack of Kaigun capability and deeper strategic planning, such as carrying drum oil on battleships and experimenting with potato gasoline that competed with the dwindling domestic food supply.[25]

Other overseas resources for which Tokyo went to war were similarly underexploited. Japan before the war was as dependent on its merchant marine as Great Britain, but during the war it could not replace losses to prowling submarines. From late 1944 it lost more ships to air patrols operating from the Philippines. Still more losses came from huge fields of mines laid in the sea lanes around Japan by submarines and aircraft in the honestly named Operation *Starvation*, a five-part USN program to eliminate all shipping around the home islands.[26] Late in the war Japan was forced to reduce warship production to favor cargo ships, but it did not have a fraction of the shipbuilding capacity of the United States that did so much to help Britain survive the U-boat threat, while also carrying American land and air power across two oceans. In a real sense, Japan had lost what might be called the battle of the shipyards before the war began.[27] Then it lost the battle of ships, failing even to coordinate its own land-sea operations out of service rivalry or to seriously interrupt enemy operations out of misuse of its small warship assets. Thus, when the Rikugun made a major if belated effort to secure South China Sea coastal links to Southeast Asian resources in 1944, the Kaigun had already lost control of the adjacent sea lanes. That made the bloody land fighting pointless.[28]

From 1941 to 1945 the Kaigun converted or built just 15 carriers, mainly smaller seaplane types. Some were launched late in the war when there were no aircraft or trained pilots to equip them in their designed role. By 1945 Japan lost 334 warships and hundreds more auxiliaries. Over the course of the war, U.S. warship production exceeded that of all other navies combined. The U.S. Navy in 1945 put to sea over 1,000 warships, including 141 carriers (all types) and many tens of thousands of warplanes, supported by 232 submarines and swarms of auxiliaries: troopships, transports, oilers, hospital ships and others.[29] The gap in the merchant marine was even greater. By August 1945, Japan's merchant fleet was reduced to 1.5 from 6 million tons, the tanker fleet was gone, the Kaigun was a ghost fleet emptied of combat power, and the home economy was starved of all key metals and any fuel oil to run industry. Over the last six months, Japan's adversaries swarmed around its shores with so many naval assets that submarines were ordered to sink tiny fishing boats in a target-depleted theater, even after some USN captains objected to such orders on humane grounds. Gun film records show USN fighters flying from fast carrier strike forces strafing any moving vehicle, and even lone cyclists and harmless beach walkers. The U.S. Navy submarine and air blockade by 1945 shared with the USAAF air campaign over Japan's cities a characteristic of massively effective destruction never imagined before the war by the Japanese, or even by the Americans who achieved it. Allied capacity for, and campaigns of, total destruction were still expanding when the war mercifully ended.[30]

There was no need to wait until 1945 to measure Japanese planning and strategic inadequacy. The first year of fighting revealed how badly prepared Japan was for any kind of war, short or long, on land or at sea or in the air. For example, because the Kaigun expected the U.S. Navy to steam across the Pacific to fight the decisive sea battle near the Philippines, its own ships were designed for high-speed combat not long-distance operations. No at-sea replenishment and refueling system was even experimented with until just before the war began. When it was finally deployed, it was primitive compared to the extraordinary USN underway-supply capacity.[31] Even naval shells and aviation ordnance ran short as the war lengthened, a problem that became endemic and critical in the latter years. Production was exacerbated by strains on private companies caused by conscription of too many skilled workers taken as replacement infantry into the unexpected casualty mill of the war in China.

It was a problem experienced across all Japanese war production. Capacity was further limited by a premodern and almost cottage-industry approach even in the aircraft industry. Home island transportation and distribution nets were rudimentary, slowing further with fuel shortages and scattering more widely under pressures of bombing in 1945. Americans were producing and moving vast amounts of industrial war matériel over two oceans. Inside Japan, supplies of finished goods such as crated fighters had to be moved by oxcart. Japan also lost the technology race early, as its prewar scientific base was always too small and during the war was too poorly mobilized to keep pace with Allied advances in metal alloys, engines and weapons. By 1944, swarms of superior enemy fighters and bombers flown by much better trained pilots outgunned and outperformed diminishing numbers of inferior Japanese planes and barely trained pilots. Even accounting for the lion's share of U.S. war production flowing across the Atlantic to the war against Germany, the lopsided statistics fill whole ledgers. The United States produced 61 tons of explosive to every one by Japan; it built 5.83 million gross tons of shipping to just 600,000; it mobilized 16.4 million men to 9.1 million Japanese; it fielded 88,000 tanks to just 2,515 for the Rikugun.[32] It is an accountancy of hopeless as well as needless war and suffering brought to Asia and the Pacific by expansionists and militarists who could not turn back on the one-way street to empire they started down in 1895.

***

ANGUISH AND DESTRUCTION was in the end brought to the Japanese people as a whole. Failure to anticipate basic logistics needs in a war that lasted beyond the first battle or first year brought terrible suffering to ordinary Japanese in uniform and to civilians. It started with isolated island garrisons tormented by starvation and disease. The Kaigun could not resupply these garrisons but refused to evacuate, insisting even when the Rikugun did not that the outer islands of a declared Pacific defense zone must not be lost. The year Yamamoto and the naval air arm purchased with the qualified victory at Pearl Harbor was squandered as the Kaigun ignored island garrison calls for building materials, heavy construction equipment, and the skilled labor battalions needed to fortify defenses in the newly acquired territories. Japan seized an island "Outer Defense Perimeter" stretching 14,200 miles (22,800 km). From such hubris came a logistical nightmare, a war of distances the

Kaigun could not service and the Rikugun could not hold. Indeed, battle-seeking admirals hardly even tried. They failed to minimally protect or provision dropped-off army garrisons or their own *Rikusentai* marines. Instead, they burned though massive amounts of oil in a futile attempt to force and fight a decisive fleet action, in repeated operations ranging from the Indian Ocean to the Aleutians.

Lacking materials, right down to such basic items as bulldozers and cement, Japanese soldiers and marines left stranded on sparse Pacific outposts were forced to build everything by hand, including their own rudimentary housing. *Setsueitai* (construction units) utilized soldier-workers but also forced laborers from Taiwan and Korea, working under Japanese engineers or just low-ranking officers. Few defensive works were completed on the islands of the Outer Defense Perimeter when Allied (American and Australian) amphibious forces counterattacked starting in 1942, far more swiftly and massively than Japanese intelligence had predicted or the defenders could handle.[33] Also stranded on the perimeter islands, non-Japanese laborers were forced to serve in combat whenever a base was attacked. They had exceptionally low morale and were near-useless in firefights in which they had no stake except personal survival. In the confusion of combat, they could be killed by Japanese unwilling to surrender or Americans or Australians who did not distinguish them from regular Japanese troops. Isolation only deepened as the merchant marine went to the bottom nearly entire by war's end and cut-off garrisons were forced to feed themselves, supplied at best by submarines with no design or carry capacity to do the job. Supplies did not get in, wounded and sick men did not get out. The contrast with USN supply services and with Seabees swarming over Guadalcanal, and every other liberated island after that, could not have been greater. The suffering of cutoff Japanese garrisons became chronic and extreme as more were bypassed and left to starve in the Allied island-hopping campaign of 1943–1945.

Rikugun generals were hardly more realistic than the admirals. At war in China, they agreed to war with Britain and the United States while still planning their most desired war, against the Soviet Union. Swift victories in their initial Hundred Days campaign seemed to suggest they had been right about the superiority of Japanese troops compared to Western forces manning colonial outposts in Asia. The Rikugun enjoyed uninterrupted advances from December 1941 through April 1942: Hong Kong, Malaya, Singapore, Burma, the Dutch East Indies, half the huge island of New Guinea, sundry South Pacific island chains. IGHQ planners chortled at how smoothly invasion fleets carrying Japanese divisions moved, and how swiftly Western and local military opposition was overcome as the colonies fell one after another.[34] Next came phase two: consolidation of strategic island points from which any American counterattack must proceed, and elimination of the American bases and presence in the Philippines. That archipelago was lightly defended, and its loss had been anticipated and accepted by War Department planners. Still, once again reflecting a lack of interservice consultation, Manila fell too quickly for the battleship fleets to assemble and fight the decisive sea battle longed for by Kaigun officers. Instead, carriers emerged immediately as the critical ship type on both sides in battles in the Coral Sea in May and at Midway in June.

Midway was planned by the Kaigun but came as a surprise to the Rikugun, which soon found itself fighting in the long polar night in the Aleutians as a result of a diversion attack on Attu and Kiska that turned into a protracted winter campaign.[35] At Attu, the army lost its first complete unit of the war. It also set a terrible precedent, for before making a final suicide attack the unit doctor killed all men too badly wounded to join in. He reportedly did it in order to preserve Imperial honor. It was more faux *bushidō,* acts of cold murder celebrated in domestic propaganda as *Attu gyokusai* ("glorious death"). Japanese were told Midway was a great victory, not that their navy lost four fleet carriers there and many irreplaceable pilots. To maintain the lie, veterans of the defeat were physically segregated and isolated upon returning to Japan. The calamity of Midway (and Attu) was compounded by a months-long, bloody slogging toward defeat on Guadalcanal straddling the end of 1942 and start of 1943.[36] In less than a year, Japan's war was already breaking down. Or rather, it was converted into a losing naval and amphibious fight in the Pacific. That added further strain to the stalemated ground war in China it had hoped to win by attacking over the water to end Allied supply of the *Guomindang* and to obtain vital resources crucial to sustaining its military effort.

Violating its own doctrine, the Kaigun failed to concentrate its ships for a knockout blow while it enjoyed temporary but clear superiority after Pearl Harbor. Instead, a series of costly carrier battles (and lack of cement and interest) left the Outer Defensive Perimeter unfinished, with Australia and Hawaii still available to Japan's enemies as jumping-off stations for deep Southern and Central Pacific counteroffensives.[37] Within just six months, the Kaigun started its descent into a progressively less effective force while the U.S. Navy learned as it rose to dominance over Japan at sea. It started in the Solomons at the end of 1942, after the Japanese first won a series of small-ship night surface actions. The United States then marshaled enormous industrial, economic and intellectual resources that stopped the Japanese advance (with major and far too often forgotten assistance by Australia). Ahead of schedule, the United States launched an overwhelming counteroffensive in the South Pacific. Its huge strength then permitted a second thrust toward Japan through the Central Pacific, starting from the Gilbert Islands, all this while deploying 80 percent of non-naval military assets to Europe and expending a smaller proportion of GDP than any other major belligerent in World War II. British and Indian Army units also regrouped, reequipped and attacked into Burma in 1943. Meanwhile, the infantry war in China continued to grind on.[38]

The Japanese were stunned. IGHQ had always been afraid of American productive capacity, hence its battle-winning obsession, but it did not foresee just how aggressive the American response would be. Nor how fast the United States would build new and better ships and aircraft to escort and transport army and marine divisions to attack the island defense perimeter, break through it, and begin *twin* drives toward the home islands. The balance of naval and air forces shifted fast and irrevocably with combat casualties, poorly used and isolated Japanese assets, and increased production of American ships and planes. As naval historian Mark Peattie explains, "the United States launched against the overextended Japanese a type of sea power so revolutionary and so massively armed and equipped that the Japanese navy was unprepared to respond at any level—strategic, operational, or tactical."[39] By the end of 1943 the Empire of Japan's most desperate hour approached, leaping over or bounding through almost pathetic island outposts in the Pacific. Japan had parked many tens of thousands of its sons in indefensible outer perimeter locations without adequate means of defense. It demanded that they fight to the death for the Empire, to inflict insupportable casualties on the enemy to deter him from attacking all the way to Japan. Then the military abandoned them to disease, starvation, and enemy harassment or assault. Japan's home islands would soon be under direct threat from the air and invasion by sea. An ill-made, fixed defensive strategy had been hollowed and broken in under two years.

Japan's leaders turned yet again to the idea of the decisive battle as an escape from the reality of attrition. Both services sought to force the issue with increasingly desperate lunges and tactics, trying to change *something* in the cascade of military misfortune. They must break American will to continue the twin offensives toward the home islands or lose their honor and the war. The only way to do that, it was thought and agreed, was by major battles, one at sea and the other on land. ASW patrols, convoy escort, all other defensive naval activities were sacrificed to the chimera of the single battle against American will to continue the war and determination to invade the home islands. Warships of all sizes and classes concentrated for a supreme effort. The Rikugun girded, too. Its men fought to the last on island after island to drive home to Westerners the future cost of an invasion. They called it *shukketsu* ("bleeding").[40] In the end, this effort worked only in a perverse and unexpected way. Once the United States developed the air and later also atomic assets to stand off and pound Japan's home islands into rubble or submission, its leaders among the Joint Chiefs and especially in the U.S. Navy started to reconsider whether a costly invasion was necessary.

Everywhere, Japan was in retreat. Everywhere, its sons made the enemy fight hard. Japan's defeat was not all about succumbing to superior numbers of tanks and aircraft and ships, better weapons and more of them, though it largely was. Allied troops got tougher, too. Forced to fight hand-to-hand in desperate small-unit combat against dug-in and fanatic Japanese defenders, they did so ruthlessly and well, on island after island, amphibious assault after assault. On Saipan (June 15–July 9, 1944), there played out the full, demented tragedy as even civilian women hurled their children and then themselves off what are today called "Suicide Bluff" and "Banzai Cliff." Whole families who hesitated were shot down or grenaded by watching Japanese officers. The fight for the island then ended in a raggedy death charge by over 3,000 men, including ambulatory wounded, diseased and emaciated soldiers hobbling out of sickbeds to shout *Tennō Heika Banzai!* ("Long live the Emperor!"). All senior officers committed *seppuku,* led by Admiral Chuichi Nagumo, who had steered the carriers at Pearl Harbor and Midway but had fallen out of favor and sea command by 1944. Nearly the whole Saipan garrison of 30,000 was wiped out, then celebrated in home-front propaganda as *nikudan*—a garrison of "human bullets" infused with proper *seishin* spirit and devotion to death, like those who fell at Liáoyáng or Mukden in 1904 and 1905.[41]

General William Slim, who was in command of British XIV Army, comprised of Indian Army and British and Commonwealth troops and special forces in Burma, put it this way about the Japanese enemy the Allies faced: "He fought and he marched till he died. If five hundred Japanese were ordered to hold a position, we had to kill four hundred and ninety-five before it was ours—and then the last five killed themselves."[42] It was only a slight exaggeration, heading into 1945. It also masks in tough, grudging praise for the enemy's courage the rank stupidity and wastage of his unimaginative, hold-at-all-costs positional tactics and the mentality of his officer corps. For when the faux samurai of the Imperial Japanese Army met modern firepower in combat in Southeast Asia and the Pacific, the faux samurai and his men disappeared into blood and body parts.

IGHQ mapped out and declared an Absolute National Defense Sphere, an inner strategic zone where all-out defense would take place along an inner security perimeter comprising Burma, Malaya, western New Guinea, the Dutch East Indies, Carolines, Marianas and Kuriles. Territory held by Japanese forces outside the sphere was considered strategically expendable, useful only to delay the enemy's advance to the vital core of Japan's empire. Some army officers protested this wasteful strategy, preferring to fall back to big islands such as the Philippines or Taiwan, to meet the Allies in more regular combat with big units. But by then the Kaigun lacked sea transport to supply even small isolated garrisons, let alone to pull them out or move to a major stand on the Philippines or Taiwan. So everyone just fought on, in place. It was the British and Australians and Americans who chose where and when to fight, as well as whether to fight at all or if they would instead hop over isolated garrisons.

Things were going very badly for the Axis by the middle of 1944. Fascist Italy was knocked out of the war and Nazi Germany's so-called *Festung Europa* was breached on both ends. But little changed in Tokyo. On July 24, with some of Hitler's generals hanging on piano wire from meat hooks after trying to kill him four days earlier, IGHQ issued a new directive. Without a hint of self-consciousness or irony, it was called *Shō-go* ("Operation *Victory*"). It proposed to retrench from the defense perimeter, already breached in any case from Burma to the Marianas, to return to its original decisive battle concept. The Rikugun was to commit 70 percent of all its remaining assets to this singular effort, leaving just 30 percent to hold its positions in China, across Southeast Asia and in the Pacific. *Shukketsu* was over. Instead of bleeding the enemy slowly as he advanced, the Rikugun committed to again seek victory by a single great battle. It identified four possible areas where it might yet win such a victory: the Philippines, Taiwan, the home islands (excluding Hokkaido) and Hokkaido (excluding the other home islands). It was more rank delusion, well past when there was any possible excuse for it.

This most extreme form, perhaps ever, of the temptation to battle as an escape from a strategic cul-de-sac of the generals' own making ensured that the war would end for Japan in absolute destruction. Although that is not how Japanese leaders saw it at the time. They said that Allied stamina would fail first, because decadent Western powers did not have the moral character to finish the fight, that their reliance on matériel hid a fatal cultural and spiritual weakness. Their peoples could not absorb casualties the way the unique

Yamato race could, in a *seishin* devotion of sacrifice. New tactical manuals were written and issued to the troops. They called for all-out, fanatic fighting on any islands that remained while the main forces gathered for the final and winning battle. They insisted on no surrenders, demanding glorious death in the run-up to the final battle. *Shō-go* thus guaranteed catastrophic losses on land and at sea, and the destruction of Japan's cities in 1945. Literally to the last day of the war—after both atomic bombs fell and the Red Army attacked in overwhelming force on the mainland—IGHQ and the War Cabinet kept shifting the location of this elusive miracle of arms that would redeem all their losses and all the suffering of the Japanese people. As the enemy advanced toward the home islands *Shō-go*, too, was moved ever closer to Japan, then to the home islands themselves. Faith in deliverance by battle was not allowed to waver. Tragically, it grew more fanatic and absurd and morally vulgar as the end neared.

What was left of the Combined Fleet sallied out in desperate last throws of war dice, only to suffer ruinous and unrecoverable losses of naval air assets at the Battle of the Philippine Sea (June 19–20, 1944), or "Great Marianas Turkey Shoot" as American sailors and pilots called it, comparing stiff Japanese flight patterns and inexperienced pilots to infamously dull-witted birds back home. Hundreds of aircraft were destroyed along with the ill-trained young men who flew them. Kaigun commanders committed everything they had left at Leyte Gulf (October 23–26, 1944), including making the first *Tokkō* ("special attack") or *kamikaze* ("divine wind") suicide attacks on Allied ships. They lost nearly 1,600 aircraft in these two climactic battles waged over the Philippine Sea. Leyte was so complex a naval battle with so many interacting twists of good fortune and bad decisions that it might have had a different outcome with a few changes of luck or command. Yet even had the Japanese prevailed initially, it is difficult to see any result beyond a delay in the final destruction of the Kaigun followed by a successful landing and liberation of the Philippines.

As it was, after losing at Leyte the Kaigun was rendered incapable of offensive action. Its last carriers had few or no planes or trained aviators, and its capital warships and escorts were thus left without air protection in what was overwhelmingly a naval air war in its final stages. It could no longer even defend itself, let alone project power to challenge enemy fleets and outposts as it once did. It could not interdict the huge invasion fleets everyone knew would be coming soon to the home islands, except with the most desperate measures of suicide attacks by ill-fated pilots and later, similar failed attempts by its greatest ships.[43] Its major assets went down singly or in batches, starting with the superbattleship *Musashi* sunk at Leyte, followed by the converted carrier *Shinano* that November. With all collapsing, on January 20, 1945, Kaigun and Rikugun rivals agreed *for the first time* on a single and joint operations plan. Fitting the moment and mood, they called for all-out suicide attacks to defend the home islands. Again with no irony recognized or intended, IGHQ code-named the proposed action *Ketsu-gō* ("Operation Decisive").[44]

Meanwhile, despite huge disparities in men and matériel accruing to the Americans and their Filipino allies, Luzon's rough terrain allowed the undermanned and ill-supplied Japanese under General Tomoyuki Yamashita to fight a determined defensive action on Bataan through February 1945, then wage large-scale mountain war to the end of the war. Engulfed in a rising death cult, Japanese troops ran amok in Manila in a reprise of earlier city massacres. More casualties among civilians in the city accrued from misdirected American artillery and bombing. On Iwo Jima, dug-in and well-led Japanese defenders hurt the U.S. Marines badly, thereby firming rather than eroding American resolve.[45] Brutally and to no real purpose, defense continued against grimly hardened Australians in forgotten campaigns against abandoned garrisons on Borneo and New Guinea, where at the surrender just 10,000 ragged, starving survivors of Japanese 18th Army were left alive out of a strong garrison of 140,000.[46] Death on land, at sea, in the air. Always death, and more death. Not glorious at all, in fact. More nihilistic: thin, fanatic, futile, fatalist.

***

THE PACIFIC WAR is often described as a race war, with the racism ascribed principally to Westerners.[47] While it is certainly true that racism was present throughout, the charge is false on two counts. It mistakes as a fundamental cause of fighting what was mostly surface expression of combat rage, and it fails to see the same effects on both sides. In fact, while Americans dehumanized Japanese in combat talk and propaganda images, Westerners were demonized by Japanese in much the same way.[48] Cruelty and atrocity came from the unforgiving brutality of combat against an enemy too often prepared to fight to the death. Yet even facing the death cult behavior of *kamikaze* attacks, USN intelligence officers left records that are unmarked by any cultural, let alone racial, stereotypes about Japanese.[49] If censure is to be apportioned by historians decades removed from the emotion of total war, one should perhaps start by noting that the Rikugun murdered tens of thousands of Western POWs and hundreds of thousands of Asian prisoners, often systematically. American, Australian and British armies did no such thing, even if there were occasional murders and mistreatment of helpless Japanese. Then there was the extreme horror of Unit 731.[50] A war without mercy was indeed fought in the Pacific, but so it was in China and Europe as well. There was little mercy left anywhere in the world by 1945.

Of course racism was present in the Pacific theater. There was cheap racist language on both sides. There always is. This is one of the epiphenomena of combat, tangential to the truly important facts and outcomes in war. Westerners also spoke of "Italian sloth" and "Teutonic efficiency," not from racism but as a lazy mental shorthand. Racism does not explain why the war in the Pacific was fought or how. Mostly, it is the war that explains the racism. During the fight, and because of the fight, hate grew on both sides. A magma of combat hate swelled with ferocious fighting at Shanghai and Wuhan, erupting beneath the Nanjing Massacre, broken Yellow River dams, refusal to take Chinese prisoners, murder of those already held. It was there in the Bataan death march and massacres in Hong Kong and Singapore, in wartime mistreatment of occupied populations and in late-war wanton brutality in Manila and a dozen cities in China. It flowed with atrocity stories leaking from POW camps and the railway of death, and in letters home from scared frontline troops facing enemy soldiers just a grenade toss away. Soon Japanese were pictured in cheap Western propaganda as monkey-men and savages and racist terms salted the speech of marines, headline writers, politicians, and comic books for children. It happened in reverse, too. Japanese routinely portrayed Westerners as blue demons from old folk tales, with claws and fangs and inhuman blue skin. They portrayed the British as monkey-men, as half-apes or part swine. So did the British during World War I about Germans, drawn in newspapers as ape-rapists of virgins and drooling brutes with hatchets in one hand and *Pickelhaube* above. There was rather a lot of social Darwinism in the air before and during the world wars.

Hate is the conjoined twin of war. Older and more primal than any racism that bubbled up in the Pacific. Hate flowed over Europe in the Wars of Religion, and people burned. It rose as republican ferocity exploded out of France from 1794 and with reactionary determination to preserve the ancien régime at almost any cost, extending to crush far more gentle revolutions years after the Republic was gone and Napoleon sulked in exile on St. Helena. It burned Moscow down rather than give it to the French to sleep in, then surged to Paris to restore a fat Bourbon king no one wanted back, twice. Carnivorous rage turned Spaniards as savage against isolated French garrisons as Japanese and Australians turned on each other in New Guinea.

All wars saw murders of prisoners and civilians, most with no issue of race involved. Rage scorched paths of destruction over the havoc radius of passing armies. It marked off savage people's wars with guerrilla crimes and retaliations in country after country. It sent Cossacks riding down straggler boys to murder and mutilate in the red snow, French in 1812, Germans 130 years later. It came out of war, born joined to brutality as war slipped the leash that only ever loosely holds it back.

It came from fear of being shot or bayoneted at Verdun, or captured and mutilated by a Soviet partisan, or murdered by a roving SS death commando. From being 18 or 20, far from home, ashamed over crying in your slit trench every night, embarrassed by loss of bowel control. From lying under a barrage during another accursed Isonzo battle or charging a sleeping French division over the Somme with bayonet and unloaded Mauser. From seeing a buddy step on a landmine on Guadalcanal or disappear into a pink mist at El Alamein or Okinawa. Or watching a mate die from a sniper's bullet while hung up on the wire at Ypres or on the ash at Iwo Jima, or charging the Russian machine guns at Mukden, or sick with typhus in a prison camp, or doing forced labor down a Honshu mine. It came from hedge-fright because you thought *tirailleurs* or snipers were hiding behind every haystook or down the next cellar, so you tossed in a grenade as you passed by and heard a family scream. It came from scrambling with 10,000 other prisoners for "a bit of potato, please," looking up as a callous camp guard tossed scraps into a surge of starving men.

One did not need racial differences in either world war for hate to arise from combat, to lead to rage and murder. Canadians murdered Germans in the trenches of World War I after a rumor spread that one of theirs had been crucified with bayonets at Ypres. True or not, some believed it and retaliated with brutish cruelty. This is regrettable but also fairly commonplace. Combat, not propaganda images or comics or editorials or training films, is what made young men in the Pacific refuse to take prisoners unless ordered (though the incidence is much exaggerated). Too many Japanese had killed their captors with hidden grenades or fake surrenders for fresh arrivals to take chances. So innocent Japanese died, as murders and war's mayhem mounted. Combat led on the other side to sadistic humiliation and brutal mistreatment of Chinese and Allied POWs, to beatings and beheadings, to death marches and slave labor camps, to killing American POWs at the end of the war rather than letting them be liberated. Hundreds were burned, shot or bayoneted.

Japanese were taught that they were *shido minzoku*, a superior and "leading nation." The idea was not truly malevolent until the 1930s, or at least did not preclude cooperation with other nations. It did hold that Japan had achieved a perfect synthesis between East and West and thus should play a special role in leading East Asia toward progress, freedom from colonial powers, and a cultural renaissance. During the march to war, then during war, the idea took on a darker meaning. Other Asians were portrayed as backward, like children needing to be led to the bright uplands of the Greater East Asia Co-Prosperity Sphere. That was to be a closed trading system and imperial power bloc that Japan would establish by war, oversee and exploit. Japanese propagandists said that "Asia is for Asians," when they really intended for it to be divided among the victorious Japanese, and not even all of them. It justified selling opium to Chinese but banning it for their own troops. It justified forced prostitution and gambling to finance the *Guandong* Army, and 300,000 women held in rape camps as so-called *ianfu* (comfort women). Or killing all police and young men in Nanjing, then raping and killing the women. It led to beatings, beheadings, forced labor, starvation, massacres, bayonet practice on live prisoners, Unit 731 vivisections, and the Three Alls order. It justified whatever the Imperial Japanese Army needed to do or wanted to do.

We need a wider view of all this hate and rage in the Pacific War. We need to recall that Soviets and Germans dehumanized and horribly tortured and mutilated each other, too. That civilians were killed with huge cruelty in immense numbers on the Eastern Front in Europe. That the democracies killed Germans from the air without mercy from 1943 to the end of the war. Killing is an unnatural act. It is hard to get most men to do it. It must be made to seem less than murder by reducing the humanity of the enemy. You must make the enemy seem subhuman in order to get your armed teenagers to kill his armed teenagers. This is normal in war, which always excuses one's own barbarism while preserving belief that while we fight with honor and high idealism the enemy does not. In such a whirl of wartime hate, it hardly seems important that as men kill other men they indulge in petty racial name-calling. Focusing on hot racist language in World War II is almost trite. It certainly misses the more important point of deeper hate. Did Americans hate Japanese? Yes, of course. They were a deadly, skilled and dangerous enemy. The reverse was also true. Japanese learned to hate Americans, all the more as defeat approached and terrible things were done from the air. It would be quite odd if enemies in war did not hate. Yet, few Western soldiers hated Japanese before they first met and faced brave sons of Japan in combat, as was also true in reverse.[51]

Whatever role race played in combat and atrocity during the Pacific War, it must be stressed that it was the war in Europe that was a race war at its very core, right to its origin in Germany. The Nazis even had a name for it: *Rassenkrieg*. It was in Europe, not Asia, where whole peoples were marked for extermination under spurious racist theories and sex between "lesser races" and "higher races" was made a hanging offense. It was in Europe that millions died simply because of who they were, for innocent weakness in the face of armed power and profane ideology. It was in Europe that death battalions roamed from the first day to the last, and death marches crisscrossed a continent; that all belligerents tried to starve out the others. It was in Europe that the Western Allies and the Soviets each killed far more German civilians than Japanese civilians were killed from a much larger population. It was in Europe that the central war aim of the principal aggressor was a spurious biological New Order to be carved into the world with chisels of mass murder, genocidal exterminations by gas and bullet, tens of millions starved and others sterilized, all leading to postwar human breeding programs and vast continents of slavery.

***

ALLIED LAND FORCES overmatched anything Japan could field. Then came VE-Day (May 8, 1945), releasing millions of Allied and Soviet reinforcements from Europe if need be. In the face of this looming and hopeless reality, Japanese generals still insisted on a final and radical *seishin* operation, a supposed *Ketsu-gō* battle on the home islands. This was the climax of a pervasive cult of death that guided the brutal behavior of the officer corps and parts of the civilian government at the end. It was not the desire of most ordinary Japanese who were trapped, soldier and civilian, by the *seishin* assertions and arrogance of their national elites. Suicide tactics were ordered at every level, not just by *kamikaze* pilots. There were to be more massed *banzai* charges; more suicide infantry crouched low inside little dug-out "octopus pots" as on Iwo Jima, waiting to blow up themselves and a passing Sherman; more *kaiten* ("human torpedoes") and death's men in mini-submarines; *Ohka* (piloted jet-bombs) rocketing down at invasion ships; *fukuryu* (suicide divers) ready to blow up themselves and passing landing craft from underneath, in the shallows of the home islands. Japan's proclaimed Absolute National Defense Sphere was breached on and under the sea, on land and in the air. Only the home islands remained. Stripped of allies, hope and defenses, and facing absolute destruction, the military said to fight on.

At Okinawa (April 1–June 21, 1945), thousands of *kamikaze* along with a handful of *Ohka* attacked the invasion fleets in suicide waves.[52] The last super-battleship went down on April 7, as *Yamato* made what amounted to a suicide diversion run. The pride of the Kaigun, an immense temple of steel bearing the name of the whole nation, was sent as a mere decoy to draw off U.S. naval air power so that *kamikaze* could reach the enemy fleet and carriers. The flagship of a big-gun fleet and idea was swarmed by hundreds of aircraft from a surplus of carriers, bombers biting like gnats until it disappeared inside a massive explosion along with 2,498 crew. In the land battle, many Japanese ignored the suffering of islanders. They mistreated Okinawans, killed them as spies or just nuisances, and made no effort to protect them as they became trapped in the middle of the biggest ground fight of the Pacific War. Rikugun officers knew they would lose but were glad to bleed the Americans a little longer, to gain time to bring more divisions back from China to fight the apocalyptic battle, moved on paper by IGHQ to Kyushu. No one in 1937 or 1941 could or did imagine any of that.

It was said with contempt that Americans relied too much on firepower, as if their material superiority was the same thing as spiritual inferiority. As if being stronger and better and far more efficient at making and winning at war was not the right and proper role of soldiers, of armies and navies, only a base thing to be despised by true warriors who could think of no other end than personal suicide amidst the ongoing immolation of their defeated nation, as fire fell from skies filled with enemy bombers. Western soldiers were weak, afraid of hand-to-hand fighting with Japanese. On the home islands they would meet the glory of total national defense, animated by *seishin*. They would be stopped by *ichioku gyokusai*, 100 million defenders ready "to die gallantly as a jewel shatters." That was the last slogan and moral demand, for 100 million *gyokusai* given the promise of beautiful death in battle. They were to die for a higher value, akin to dying for *patria* in the Roman case, out of loyalty to the emperor and to the transcendental value of the whole nation.[53] In fact, Japanese soldiers on Okinawa started to surrender in unheard-of numbers while Japanese civilians on the home islands were nearing their breaking point from hunger, city bombing and fear of invasion.[54]

Kamikaze were a grave threat to the invasion fleets, though not to the outcome of the invasion. Operating "inside a wilderness of mirrors," as T. S. Eliot wrote in a different context, Japanese intelligence exaggerated the number and quality of enemy ships sunk by the suicide attacks off the coast of Okinawa, claiming many carriers and battleships.[55] Wild battle allure gripped Admiral Ukagi Matome, commander of Fifth Air Fleet, who thought his suiciders were wiping out the entire invasion fleet to win the definitive battle for Japan. They did damage aplenty, sinking 47 warships and killing 5,000 sailors, posing the single greatest threat to the U.S. Navy in its history. Yet there were so many more ships in the fleet and in follow-on fleets to come that invasion was unstoppable by Japanese force. Ukagi's optimism did not survive the battle. He admitted to his diary: "From now on our air strength doesn't permit us to carry out more than air guerrilla warfare . . . We have been following the road to defeat."[56] Nor was it just Americans off Japan's shores anymore. The British Pacific Fleet readied to support British and Commonwealth troops in the coming Allied invasion of the home islands. It was the largest fleet ever sent to sea in the history of the Royal Navy, so redundant in capabilities that one ship was happily converted into an underway brewery.[57] The Red Army was also stirring toward massive force in Manchuria and northern China, timed to three months after the defeat of Nazi Germany. And in the midsummer skies over Japan's cities rafts of B-29s flew nearly unmolested, sowing a whirlwind of fire and death and black rain.

***

DURING 1944–1945, THE hardest lessons of total war fell out of the sky as the Western Allies brought ruthlessness and grim determination to strategic bombing campaigns, first over Nazi Germany, then to Imperial Japan. They completed the systematic destruction of 120 cities in Germany and reduced 62 more Japanese cities, the last two by atomic fire. Bombing did not start out as a principal terror weapon targeting "enemy civilians," as the civil populations in the Axis countries soon came to be called, though that is where it ended up. It began as a military effort to reduce the enemy's war production by attacking key industries in deep rear areas. However, killing civilians from the air as a modern and even commonplace practice was there from the start of bombing as far back as September 1914, in Allied and German raids made with planes and bombs that looked like toys by the standards of World War II.[58] In 1945, bombing city targets was the culmination of a rare but decided short-war delusion peculiar to Western air forces, and some politicians. An old vision from H. G. Wells and a dream of air power theorists of the 1920s combined to hurl immense fleets of Allied strategic bombers into enemy skies as a strategic and hoped-for war-winning weapon. One perhaps sufficient to avoid repeating the terrible Allied battle casualties of the Great War.

After World War I most observers were impressed not by what bombing did but by what it might yet do. Air-power theorists proposed targeting war-making industry deep in the enemy's strategic rear with flocks of strategic bombers, a singular weapon that could fly right over the terrible trenches to drop ordnance on the factories that armed and equipped fighting men, that clothed and housed and fed the armies. The main attraction was prac-tical. Bombers were very good at destruction. But there was a moral compo-nent from the start: revulsion for trench warfare and the slaughter of youths in uniform. It would be more moral, it was said by advocates of air power, to target industries in the enemy's strategic hinterlands than to send huge armies of conscripts to attack each other out of trenches. Bombing seemed to promise a way to break the stalemate. It appealed to all types of powers but to the democracies most of all, societies with governments more sensitive to the political price of mass casualties and in a defensive crouch heading into World War II. Bombing was also more cost-effective as an interwar deterrent threat than arming and equipping million-man conscript armies, which ap-pealed to democratic politicians as the Great Depression bit hard and long.

Between the world wars, radical ideas about bombers were widespread but only two air forces devoted serious resources to developing the aircraft and related technologies necessary: the RAF and USAAF. They championed strategic bombers as offering "the knockout blow," a war-winning weapon beyond compare. Italians developed air theory but lacked industry to match. Germans, French, Soviets and Japanese chose to build tactical bombers to support field armies and navies instead. Only Britain and the United States also planned fleets of strategic bombers, building out in the case of the RAF directly on Great War experience. These plans accelerated as Germany and Japan terror-bombed small-power cities in the late 1930s, starting with Guernica in the Basque country in Spain, which the Luftwaffe bombed in April 1937. Japan hit Shanghai that August. China was not a small country, but in 1937 it was a weak and divided power with no air capacity to strike back at Japan. Next came Warsaw in September 1939 and Rotterdam in May 1940. Results were mixed. Bombing did not win in Spain; Poland was crushed by German tanks with Luftwaffe aid; the Dutch surrendered to air terror, but also to the swiftness of panzers; China endured.

Strategic bombing was about attrition. Germans and Japanese hated at-trition. As weaker powers they thought principally in terms of short deci-sive wars, of the "triumph of the will" and of *seishin*, of special national and warrior virtue triumphing over superior material forces. They were entirely willing to terror-bomb, but lacked the capacity to do it on a grand scale. Nazi Germany proved that during its failed bombing campaign over Britain in 1940–1941, and Japan proved it with merely intermittent bombing of Chinese cities that remained limited because it lacked the planes and funds, not the ill intention. Mostly, the Axis powers were short-term thinkers, and bombing was a long-term weapon. They believed in conquering armies, and so built tactical not strategic aircraft and air forces to support their ground forces. Japan built additionally to supply naval air power needs as protection for its battlefleet. Germany and Japan intended to take and occupy territory, to win on the ground. Britain and the United States had no such territorial ambitions, and lots of water between them and the panzers. They could afford to stand off and obliterate from a distance.

Luftwaffe bombing of British cities in 1940 did nothing to win the war for Germany but much to loosen British moral inhibitions and inculcate a popular desire for payback, provoking the British to retaliate by bombing German cities. They probably would have done it anyway. Britain was strong at sea and in the air but near helpless on land in 1940. It needed time to raise, train, arm and equip millions of conscript soldiers, and millions more from across the Empire. It also needed to show occupied Europe and skeptical (and then still neutral) Americans that the British Empire was committed to fighting against Nazism for the long haul. Bombing did all that. The RAF could badly hurt Nazi Germany from the air, perhaps even decisively, it was thought. And so the planes were built, elite crews were trained to hit precision economic and military targets, and an extremely heavy investment in bombers and talent headed over the Channel to pound Germany.

Then the results were assessed in a devastating report in August 1941, which suggested that RAF bombing in ways that tried to spare German civilians was utterly ineffective in hurting the German war economy. Too many things got in the way of accurately hitting intended targets: bad weather and reduced visibility, especially in winter; poor navigation aids; inaccurate bombs and bombsights; no long-range fighter escort, and hence heavy losses to increasingly sophisticated German air defenses, from radar-guided antiaircraft artillery to night fighters reaching all the way in and back from the French coast, thickening over Germany. Fully one-third of RAF bombers failed to reach their designated target zones, while just one in five put bombs within five miles of the intended target.[59] The conclusion was obvious. RAF crews were dying, and costly aircraft were falling from the sky over Germany, principally to crater the countryside. It had to change. Britain had invested too much effort and treasure and lives in the air war to accept such meager results.

Bomb patterns must widen. If the only way to hit a factory was to bomb all around it, to bomb the area where it was located, that must be done. The greased moral slope thus led to what the RAF called "area bombing," and to looser definitions of acceptable targeting that widened to large urban areas in order to knock out or burn down factories inside. What of civilian workers living nearby? Acceptable collateral damage. Besides, they were not really in-nocent because they were helping the Nazi war effort. German war work was dispersing and moving underground in any case, so Churchill spoke of "de-housing" workers to slow production. What about their families? Deaths of innocents were regrettable but acceptable and necessary. Besides, they were Germans. And Germans started it. The first moral duty of the British and Allied governments was to protect their own people by winning the war, any way they could. Bombing looked to some like it might even do it all on its own.

There was no stopping now. It was logical and moral to target war workers and burn their homes and neighborhoods. The best way to do that was to target cities for massive destruction, to wipe out workers and housing stock (usefully also inflicting a massive internal refugee problem on Germany), destroy transportation nets, public facilities, everything of value. Nothing was of more value to the enemy than his people's will to continue the war, to resist. That was targeted next. The RAF called it "morale bombing." Hitler's Minister for Propaganda, Josef Goebbels, standing underneath and looking out over the rubble of Hamburg and Berlin and a hundred other cities, called it terror-bombing and whipped up storms of hate and vengeance against the air crews that did it.[60] Germans largely agreed with Goebbels. Gestapo and local authorities had to protect shot-down *Terrorflieger* ("terror flyers") whom incited mobs wanted to murder.[61] They also blamed *Reichsmarschall* Göring and his Luftwaffe and turned on Nazi Party officials, sometimes tear-ing off their Party badges and beating them in the streets while local police just stood and watched.[62]

In mid-1943 the Allies took the gloves off. All-out bombing was approved at the highest levels: prime minister, president, the Combined Chiefs of Staff. Churchill wrote as early as July 1940 of his belief in bombers: "There is one thing that will bring . . . [Hitler] down, and that is an absolutely devastating, *exterminating* attack by very heavy bombers from this country upon the Nazi homeland."[63] Roosevelt was a believer, too. He educated a crowd of eager youths in 1941: "Across both oceans, on the oceans, and above the oceans the struggle is one of armed forces, with the ghastly result of destruction and slaughter on a scale unparalleled in modern history. It had to be so. Against naked force the only possible defense is naked force. The aggressor makes the rules for such a war; the defenders have no alternative but matching de-struction with destruction, slaughter with greater slaughter."[64] The publics approved of bombing, demanded more bombing. Immense resources were in-vested in building bigger, better aircraft that could fly longer to more distant targets with larger bombs.

By 1943 the Western Allies finally had the means to make total war from the air. They unleashed it as the Combined Bomber Offensive (CBO) approved at the Casablanca Conference (January 14–24, 1943). The Combined Chiefs agreed that the USAAF would bomb by day while RAF Bomber Command conducted area bombing of Germany by night. The Casablanca Directive for the CBO combined all threads of thinking about the functions of strategic bombing: destruction of enemy transportation and communications nets, retardation of war production, and conscious and deliberate suppression of civilian morale. Within the overall strategic directive given to the Western Allied air forces was a list of primary objectives, by priority: U-boat pens, the German aircraft industry, transportation and communications targets, and synthetic oil facilities and oil fields. This directive papered over Allied tensions between those intent on morale bombing to win the war and those who still saw bombing's contribution as precision wrecking of enemy production and preparing for a ground invasion with targeted strikes.

The head of RAF Bomber Command, Air Marshall Arthur Harris, interpreted the order as allowing the morale bombing he preferred. He wrote a candid internal memo that October: "The aim of the Combined Bomber Offensive ... is the destruction of German cities, the killing of German workers and the disruption of civilized community life throughout Germany. It should be emphasized that the destruction of houses, public utilities, transport and lives; the creation of a refugee problem on an unprecedented scale; and the breakdown of morale both at home and at the battle fronts by fear of extended and intensified bombing are accepted and intended aims of bombing policy. They are not by-products of attempts to hit factories."[65] The Allies believed that killing the citizens of Axis countries would ultimately spare lives in the Allied countries, principally by avoiding a repetition of the awful casualties of the ground war from 1914–1918. When it was over, 120 German cities were gutted, struck off a CBO master target-list one by one. Refugees fanned out in disturbed pond circles of retold horror and woe, spreading shock and despair across the Reich.

It began with a series of air battles and raids during 1943 which Harris argued would be decisive. They were not. The first was fought in the smog-filled skies above the Ruhr Valley, starting on March 5. Over the next four months bombers pounded Ruhr cities and industries, taking heavy casualties over the most heavily defended territory in Germany. Nuremberg, Essen, Dortmund, Duisburg and Düsseldorf were attacked multiple times. Bochum, Oberhausen and smaller cities were also hit, at a cost of 1,000 Allied

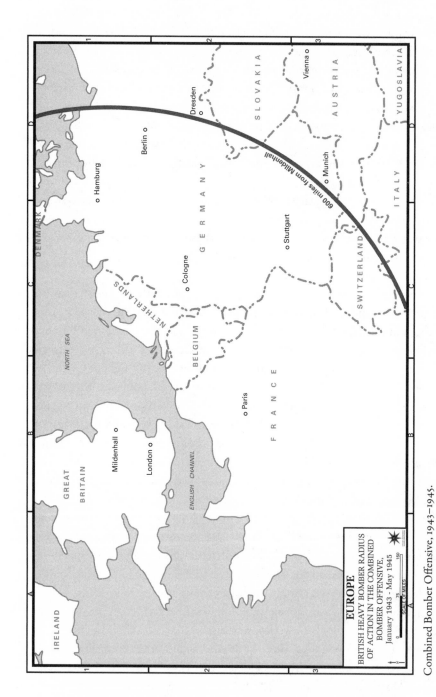

Combined Bomber Offensive, 1943–1945.

Courtesy of the Department of History, United States Military Academy at West Point. Redrawn by George Chakvetadze.

aircraft lost over the whole Ruhr campaign. While heavy damage was done and much loss of German life incurred, the Ruhr continued to produce critical coal resources for the Nazi war economy. Undeterred by limited results, Harris ordered the bombing of more cities, including Cologne.

A series of four great raids by 3,000 heavy bombers carried out the new raids, lasting until August 2, 1943. The first saw nearly 800 bombers arrive over Hamburg at midnight on July 24 and 25, in an operation codenamed *Gomorrah*: the Allies knew what they were doing. More raids followed, American by day and British by night. On July 27–28, the RAF sent in 700 bombers. A quarter of a million buildings, with a total frontage of 133 miles, disappeared into high-explosive blooms and incendiary fires. It was the first-ever artificial firestorm, a tall funnel of flame that reached 800° Celsius. Its hurricane-force vortex sucked in more fuel: smashed buildings and dead and living people. Pedestrians were turned into torches as 44,000 died and 125,000 were hurt, many burned alive or crushed under fallen buildings. Hundreds of thousands were left stunned and homeless.[66] Still the big bombers came, droning in hundred-mile columns overhead, returning to bomb the homeless and the rubble. Hamburg's shipyard stopped building U-boats, all war production declined, many tens of thousands of refugees scattered across Germany, and hot vengeance felt warm in the gut in all the Allied countries. *Gomorrah* was deemed a huge success.

At the first Québec Conference (August 17–24, 1943), official emphasis on morale bombing was dropped in favor of attacking clearly listed, high-value targets prior to invasion. Among these, the highest priority was smashing the Luftwaffe's fighter force. U.S. 8th Air Force attempted two precision raids on the critical and heavily defended fighter and ball-bearing works at Schweinfurt, with a companion raid against Regensburg (August 17 and October 14, 1943). The Schweinfurt raids were a turning point in the air war. Out of 376 American bombers that made the first raid, 147 never saw their home airfields again. The second was even more disastrous, with 60 bombers shot down and 142 badly damaged out of an attacking force of 291. The USAAF was chastened in its belief in precision bombing and the ability of heavy bombers to defend themselves. It did not try to hit Schweinfurt again until February 1944. The focus of RAF Bomber Command remained city bombing, turning next to Berlin through the winter of 1943–1944. The Americans, having reconsidered the wisdom of daylight precision attacks that cost so much, joined the RAF in taking the war to Berlin. The RAF and USAAF carried out coordinated thousand-bomber raids against the city, dropping bombs from Germany's roof into Berlin's cellars, subways and suburbs. In that sprawling city the Allies failed to make a firestorm and suffered serious losses, over 500 bombers and 5,000 crew. The raids shredded what was left of Göring's reputation inside top Nazi circles. They successfully rendered 450,000 Berliners homeless, but the Allies judged them a costly failure and moved on to attack cities less well-defended than Hitler's capital.

An official focus in the first half of 1944 on reducing German fighter production and luring existing fighters up to be destroyed was preparation for the coming D-Day landings and *Overlord* campaign. It was made possible by the advent of long-range American fighters. P-51 Mustangs equipped with drop tanks, capable of escorting bombers deep into Germany, turned the air war permanently in favor of the Allies. Rising confidence and air dominance led to a "Big Week" operation, a massive six-day campaign (February 20–25, 1944) code-named *Argument*. It was carried out by the U.S. 8th, 9th, and 15th Army Air Forces based in Britain and Italy, and by RAF Bomber Command. Over 6,150 bombers were involved in a week-long assault on Luftwaffe fighter factories and bases. The Allies lost 411 aircraft but set back fighter production for months, while also attriting existing pilots and planes to establish air supremacy over the landing zones in France and beyond. Thereafter, German pilot skills were noticeably lessened and kill ratios climbed with each raid. With long-range escorts available, even Bomber Command began carrying out more daylight raids.

With air supremacy established and Allied and Soviet armies on Germany's borders, the real destruction began—city after city, by firestorm wherever possible, if good weather and the combustibles were right. The Allies had so many bombers some older models were stuffed with ordinance, flown toward Germany and bailed out by crews, to crash into urban areas without any pretense of precision whatsoever. They were a kind of Hellburner dropped from the sky. Other raids were flown as bait to draw up fighters to be destroyed by better Allied planes and pilots. The climax, though not the end of it, came at Dresden on February 13–15, 1945. The Wehrmacht was collapsing on all fronts but not quite dead, while Dresden had not yet been heavily bombed. It was a major rail and road center, packed with refugees fleeing the advancing Red Army. In part, the Allied plan was to create a massive refugee crisis that would clog roads and slow German military maneuver and reinforcement, to help the Soviet advance. It began with 20 pathfinders swinging in on illuminator missions, darting low to mark the target with colored smokes and indicator fires. Within 30 minutes the city center twinkled and tall streamers of green, red and yellow smokes rose up. Next came 500 RAF Lancasters, dropping high explosives and incendiaries. They were unusually accurate due to air supremacy and perfect or "Churchill" weather. Thousands of heavy high-explosive bombs landed smack on the city center, some burrowing into rubble with time delay fuses set to later kill firemen and medics and rescuers. Then the fire-starters set it all alight.

The pattern bombing worked. Hundreds of little fires merged into a great firestorm, until shearing walls of flame like the eye-wall of a hurricane whipped around, but faster even than a Category Five storm—over 200 mph, with temperatures exceeding 800° Celsius. Dresden had few bomb shelters, just makeshift tunnels connecting old cellars. These became death traps as fire snakes slithered down, following flowing air and people, coiling over huddling clusters of refugees. Clouds of odorless carbon monoxide also sought the underground, poisoning thousands more. They died the best deaths that night, silent and painless. The next day, 300 American B-17s arrived. At 100 miles they saw an immense column of acrid black smoke but no city. So they bombed the smoke. For three days the bombers came in long streams, eager to hit the best-marked target of the war. Nearby Allied POWs were forced to clear the charred corpses and rubble. Among them was a very young Kurt Vonnegut, whose postwar novel *Slaughterhouse-Five* perhaps did more to obscure than explain the dread event by turning the fantastically real into satirical fantasy.

Bombing for psychological effect of the sort Harris consistently promoted was one thing, and remains subject to sharp and trenchant criticism on both moral grounds and for failure to achieve what was promised. Strategic bombing overall was another matter. There is a strong argument to be made that for all the horror it led to, and the disapprobation that has followed ever since, Allied bombing contributed a great deal to final victory over Germany. By 1945 the bombers would destroy Germany's transportation systems and demolish most vital war industries, especially oil supply and refining, and effectively end fighter production. Then Allied and Soviet tactical air power pinned the last German armies to the ground, forbidding movement and paralyzing local and operational reactions. Neither Germany nor Japan could by the end of their respective wars move military supplies, complete production or deploy weapons and divisions as they wanted, even inside their homelands.[67]

***

CITY BOMBING OVER Germany continued into April 1945, by which time few targets were left. By then, B-29 bombers were already busy ruining Japan. Officially and publicly, the target of the Very Long Range (VLR) bombing offensive was Japan's war economy. Just as over Germany, however, where the decision to bomb cities indiscriminately and for primary psychological effect was made in 1943, industrial targets in Japan could only be hit with saturation or area bombing. Over Germany, the operational shift was inexorable to targeting cities, as was the moral shift from accepting civilian casualties to bombing civilians deliberately to produce morale and psychological and refugee effects. So, too, over Japan. The real target of the B-29s, the target of all winning war, was not just the enemy's physical ability to resist but even more the enemy's will to resist.[68] Only this was total war, in which whole populations were declared to be the enemy, with no holds barred as to means or limits to destruction. It was the democracies that did it, which says much about the morally sloped nature of all modern warfare. It happened over Germany first, where clearly military resistance not difference of race from the Allies was the issue. So, too, over Japan, where bombing was about winning and not race. The atomic bombs were intended for German cities, too, but Germany quit the war in May 1945 while Japan fought on.

Japan's leaders spoke in private of as many as 20 million dead when invasion came, and did not flinch from demanding that their suffering people should meet that price, only to lose a long-since hopeless war in the end, regardless of final sacrifice. On the Allied side, purpose-built intercontinental B-29s reached for Japan from Saipan at a time when total war logic and morality was already accepted policy by otherwise decent leaders and nations, who believed they had to do anything to win the war and end its destruction as soon as possible.[69] It must be said clearly. Indiscriminate and ruthless desolation of Japanese cities was not due to Western racism, as is far too often recklessly and falsely charged. It rose out of new military capability, numbed moral sensibility, and a raw will to end and win the worst, bloodiest war in history. That iron was not just present in 10 Downing Street and the White House. By 1945 it stretched from Yorkshire and Dover across to Maine and California, and from Vancouver to Canberra and Auckland. Almost without exception, bombing was hugely popular. Everywhere, it was believed bombing would spare the lives of Allied soldiers, that it was necessary to win, and that it was righteous retribution against the aggressor Axis states.

The Japanese fought relentlessly into 1945 in bloody battles on New Guinea and dozens of islands and atolls scattered over the vast spaces of the Pacific. Burma was a jungle hell for both sides. The New Georgia campaign in the Central Solomons was but one of many fierce engagements with scattered Japanese garrisons that remained highly motivated late into the war. Australians faced a hard fight in New Britain against 70,000 Japanese from

1943 into 1945. The fanatical defenses of tiny island specks on the routes to
Tokyo fed deep fears of the high cost of invasion, as Japan's leaders fully intended they should; deterrence of home island invasion by inflicting fear of
mass casualties was the only semblance of strategy they ever had. At Tarawa
(November 21–23, 1943) from a garrison of 4,600 just 17 Japanese soldiers
were taken alive. On Kwajalein (January 30–February 5, 1944), out of 7,900
only 105 survived. At Eniwetok (February 17–23, 1944), just 66 Japanese and
Korean prisoners were taken as the rest of the garrison perished. At Biak (May
27–June 20, 1944), from a force of 10,000 men a few hundred lived to surrender, many taken only when too hurt to kill themselves or their captors at the
end. Leaders of democratic peoples fearful of taking heavy casualties chose
to bomb Japan's cities in hope to prevent losses among their own troops.[70]
It was an easy moral choice at the time. They did it over Germany, too, over
a much longer period and with higher civilian casualties. The problem was
that Japan was much harder to reach than Germany, where the bombers flew
from Britain and from liberated Italy. Initial USAAF efforts to bomb Japan
with B-29 raids from India were disappointing, even before refueling sites
in China were pushed out of range by the *Shō-go* offensive. However, once
Saipan was taken the Japanese home islands came within round-trip range
of the B-29s.

The chosen instrument of destruction and yes, also retribution, was fire.
Professors at leading American universities studied Japan's building materials and the layouts of its cities and noted densely packed worker houses
made largely of wood and paper (German cities had more stone buildings).
They tested the combustibility of these materials, studied optimal bomb
patterns, and calculated the proper ratio of incendiaries to high explosive required to create self-sustaining holocausts of fire. They learned how to make
firestorms to consume Imperial Japan's cities, housing stock, hospitals and
railyards, factories and workers, above all its will to resist. Bombers would
roast Japanese morale until it crackled and broke. The Allies were entirely
clear-eyed about this.

The B-29s arrived over Tokyo on March 9–10, 1945, to carry out what remains the single most lethal and destructive act in the history of war, greater
than the atomic bombs. Japanese lack of resources for air defense, and lack
of defensive-mindedness going back to before the war, meant that the B-29s
flew over an almost open and undefended city. So they came in low, stripped
of guns, ammunition and gunners. That added 3,000 pounds of extra incendiaries to each aircraft. They flew in single file, conserving fuel and ensuring that their bombs landed in compact patterns designed to make Tokyo's

buildings into shattered fuel for a self-feeding firestorm they meant to leave behind. USAAF command formally approved the mission's intention of killing large numbers of civilians. So did the Joint Chiefs. So did Franklin Roosevelt. The B-29s were built to do it. The crews all knew it, too: civilians as targets were explicitly listed in their flight orders.[71]

The first sign was a low drone of engines in the night: pathfinders flying ahead of the bomber stream, looping in crisscross patterns to mark the drop zone. Snapping sounds came next as thousands of marker flares burst into brightly colored rings. Families came out and gathered on hillsides to watch the show in the city bowl below. Children cried out excitedly at the sight of tens of thousands of little fairy lights in the distance, for it is a dirty, secret truth about war that it is full of horror but often also beautiful and exciting, like fire itself. Next came the main force, 279 B-29s carrying napalm and high explosive. They dropped their loads neatly inside the marked rings. Within 15 minutes, a cold winter night became unbearably hot. Geysers of liquid flame erupted from 300,000 incendiary casings, dancing yellow, white, green and blue. The smell of petroleum was everywhere as napalm gushed and ignited. Cracking and snapping sounds as timbers and walls of houses gave way. Survivors recalled intense radiant heat and heavy thuds as buildings collapsed. Everywhere, sharp sounds of rippling flame and crackling wood and sizzling human and animal fat, roast meat smells and rushing hot winds carrying away unheard screams. A thousand fires jumped from roof to roof, violently mating until a single vortex churned over Tokyo. The B-29s had done it: they made a firestorm. Just two planes were lost in exchange for sixteen square miles of destroyed city as Tokyo burned uncontrollably for 10 hours. Rising ash turned snow black as it fell—the first of 62 Japanese cities where black rain washed over rubble and ruin and hundreds of thousands of dead and burned civilians in 1945. Inside the hurricane of flame, 250,000 buildings burned along with 83,973 dead, with another 41,000 severely injured. One million civilians were rendered homeless, left without shelter or hope. It was more casualties than in any military action in the history of war.[72] At least, so far.

What was it like inside the firestorm? A huge funnel of flame jumped over all firebreaks, ravenous for fuel, finding it in still more buildings, cars, trams, people and dogs. A tsunami of fire moved over the gently sloped city, pushing superheated vapor downslope that incinerated flesh without touching, igniting air inside lungs like a pyroclastic flow racing down Mount Fuji. They died on fire or insensate from heat; hacking and choking from smoke; silently from carbon monoxide poisoning as the whirling walls of flame stole the city's oxygen and exhaled poison gases. They ran with hair and clothes aflame. Infants on mothers' backs were found charred when the mothers stopped running and checked. People ran to open spaces and died anyway, the heat was so intense, the air so robbed of oxygen. They crowded into canals and died there, boiled to death. In Tokyo Bay, thousands managed to escape the flames but drowned when the tide came in. The "all-clear of aircraft" siren sounded at 5:00 a.m., but Tokyo burned all day. Bodies were carted off on corrugated iron sheets to temples or parks, for cremation. Those already charcoal lumps were picked up in buckets and buried in pits: 70,000 dead were faceless, unidentifiable.[73]

The system worked. So the B-29s were sent back to set Japan afire. Two days after the Tokyo raid they hit Nagoya. Osaka burned the next day, and Kobe four days later. Yokohama was torched, and dozens more cities into midsummer. The Japanese would have done the same, as they showed over Shanghai and other cities in China. But they lacked the capability to reach their enemy's cities with intercontinental bombers. Just as surely, they would have dropped atomic bombs on their enemies, if their research programs had not all failed to deliver that capability to their government and the military. All the Japanese could manage to send over the Pacific was thousands of *fu-go*, hot-air balloons made of paper (including by schoolgirls mobilized for total war), loaded with incendiaries and bombs and carried on the jet

Aftermath of Tokyo Firestorm (1945).
Courtesy of Wikimedia Creative Commons.

stream across the Pacific. Provoked to research this means of retaliation by the Doolittle Raid of April 1942, *fu-go* floated over the ocean into the spring of 1945. Only 630 are known to have landed out of 9,000 sent over. Their targeting was just as ineffective, and completely indiscriminate. They were intended principally as a terror weapon to raise morale in Japan while also causing panic and inflicting some economic damage on the United States (and Canada). They landed as far east as Iowa and from Alaska to northern Mexico. Only one managed to kill anybody. Outside Bly, Oregon, four curious schoolchildren and their teacher died when they mishandled a *fu-go* landed on the ground.[74]

To their credit, Americans dropped leaflets in advance telling Japanese to run from their cities. Millions did. War production fell 75 percent as urban workers fled. Morale plummeted, too. *Kempeitai* military police reported rising unrest and anger at the government. Elites began to worry that if it continued, revolution might come to Japan as it came to Russia in 1905 and 1917, erupting out of war and defeat.[75] Workers refused to work. Millions walked into the countryside to escape the bombing and look for food, perhaps in a village where they had once lived in peace before Japan's leaders took half of Asia into war—all for the vanity of the Kaigun and Rikugun and militarist civilian elites, not even for the vanity of the nation. Some in the War Cabinet wanted to end it, to ask for terms. Others called for *nikudan* attacks and suicide tactics and *ichioku gyokusai*, for 100 million to die as broken jewels. For such leaders the war had become a cult of death, a shroud to drape over a whole nation. There is no other way to understand it.[76]

Allied invasion of Kyushu, the first of two necessary invasions of the home islands, was set for November 1. In Tokyo, a defense order of June 6 said to prepare to meet the invaders on the beaches, to fight along the shores with all-out special attacks by suicide troops infused with *seishin* fervor. At 200 miles out, the invasion convoy was to be met by mass suicide attacks from *kaiten* and mini-subs, by *Ohka* and 4,000 *kamikaze*. Along the shoreline, *fukuryu* would blow up themselves and landing craft from below. Cave-hidden artillery would pound any Allied infantry struggling to reach the shore, demoralized by the defenders' virtuous ferocity. Perhaps 50 percent of all invaders would perish by that point. Then masses of Japanese troops, including *Guandong* divisions fresh from Manchuria, would strike in continuous human waves. Nothing was to get in the way of killing the attackers. Japanese wounded were not to be carried away but left where they fell: "Tending to comrades cannot be condoned." The enemy would never leave the shoreline, but if he did, mobile reserves would finish him off. Interior roads were torn apart to force Shermans into fields where suicide squads waited to attack each tank. Every officer and solider was under explicit orders to undertake suicide attacks. Two weeks later came a follow-up directive intercepted by Allied intelligence, warning of what awaited: "The battle will be literally the decisive battle—a fight to the finish . . . air and sea forces must annihilate the Allied invading forces at sea. Ground forces must . . . overwhelm and annihilate the enemy at the coast."[77] And so the atomic bombs fell. And so the last illusion was annihilated.

In a distant desert, Manhattan Project scientists had conducted the first ever atomic test (Trinity) on July 16, 1945. At the Potsdam conference (July 17–August 2, 1945), Harry Truman told Stalin. Along with Britain and China, the United States issued a warning to Japan of what was coming. In retrospect, it was not so clear on the day as perhaps Truman thought or as it might have been. Moral issues relating to the atomic bombs seem more stark to later observers than they did at the time, in the firestorm heat of total war from the air. Allied intelligence had already identified at least 625,000 troops in southern Kyushu in 14 field divisions, all under threat of death by courts martial if they tried to surrender. In fact, 900,000 men awaited in Sixteenth Area Army defending Kyushu.[78] The Rikugun was still expanding its strength in the home islands to meet the invasions, importing troops from the mainland and rousting conscripts. Thus there followed two atomic attacks, on Hiroshima on August 6 and Nagasaki on August 9. It was not a hard decision to use the bomb, given where the air war had already been, with no restraints at all remaining in the war on any side.

After decades of controversy, a clear preponderance of evidence affirms that the atomic bombs were dropped primarily to end the war as quickly as possible, and that they in fact did so. The shock effect of the bombs was enhanced by a massive Red Army assault into Manchuria and northern China that began between the bombings, on August 8.[79] Rikugun generals had planned and hoped for war with the Red Army for decades. Yet when the red storm finally broke in the north, they and their armies in Manchuria and north China were hopelessly outfought and offered scant resistance. In fairness, many local divisions were replacements for better *Guandong* army units sent to Kyushu. Some 600,000 surrendered. A number of them would never see Japan again, retained in Siberia as forced laborers the same way some German prisoners were held in the western Soviet Union until after Stalin died in 1953.[80] *Kempeitai* worry and reports about social revolution building across the country shook the government, even as it considered how to respond to the bombings and Soviet assault, which had the character of an

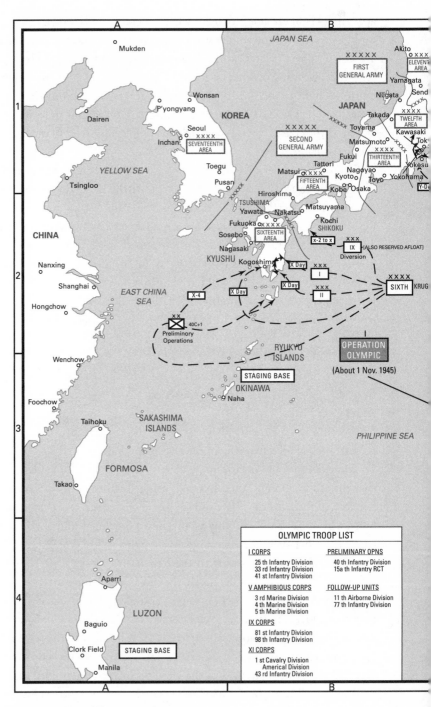

Operation *Downfall* invasion of Japan, 1945.

Courtesy of the Department of History, United States Military Academy at West Point. Redraw by George Chakvetadze.

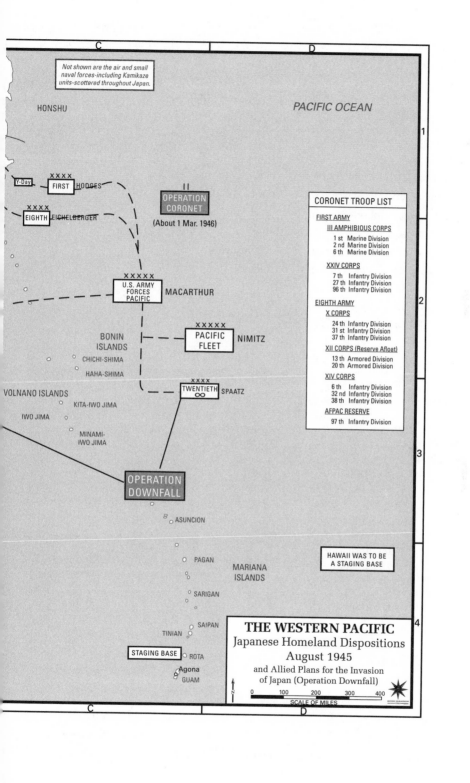

Not shown are the air and small naval forces-including Kamikaze units-scattered throughout Japan.

HONSHU

PACIFIC OCEAN

Y-Day — XXXX FIRST HODGES

OPERATION CORONET

(About 1 Mar. 1946)

XXXX EIGHTH EICHELBERGER

XXXXX U.S. ARMY FORCES PACIFIC MACARTHUR

BONIN ISLANDS
CHICHI-SHIMA
HAHA-SHIMA

XXXXX PACIFIC FLEET NIMITZ

VOLNANO ISLANDS
KITA-IWO JIMA
IWO JIMA
MINAMI-IWO JIMA

XXXX TWENTIETH ∞ SPAATZ

OPERATION DOWNFALL

ASUNCION

PAGAN

MARIANA ISLANDS

HAWAII WAS TO BE A STAGING BASE

SARIGAN

SAIPAN
TINIAN

STAGING BASE ROTA
Agona
GUAM

CORONET TROOP LIST

FIRST ARMY
  III AMPHIBIOUS CORPS
    1 st Marine Division
    2 nd Marine Division
    6 th Marine Division

  XXIV CORPS
    7 th Infantry Division
    27 th Infantry Division
    96 th Infantry Division

EIGHTH ARMY
  X CORPS
    24 th Infantry Division
    31 st Infantry Division
    37 th Infantry Division

  XII CORPS (Reserve Afloat)
    13 th Armored Division
    20 th Armored Division

  XIV CORPS
    6 th Infantry Division
    32 nd Infantry Division
    38 th Infantry Division

AFPAC RESERVE
    97 th Infantry Division

THE WESTERN PACIFIC
Japanese Homeland Dispositions
August 1945
and Allied Plans for the Invasion of Japan (Operation Downfall)

0   100   200   300   400
SCALE OF MILES

armored blitzkrieg.[81] They wondered whether *kokutai,* the underpinnings of the Imperial state, could survive many more days of war.

Japan was defeated, completely and decisively. Still it did not surrender. Truman was deeply affected by initial reports of high casualties and ordered that no more atomic bombs were to be dropped unless he specifically authorized it. However, he also ordered that conventional attacks continue at their "present intensity." The next atomic bomb would become available on August 21. It could always be used on a third city after that. Or during the invasion, when at least seven atomic bombs should be ready to blast defenders off the beaches and clear a route through any forces that remained in place inland.[82] Perhaps if the atomic bombings had been limited to such clear military use they would today carry less opprobrium from the living, so far removed from total war, who sit in comfortable judgment on a dead generation in countries that are guarded by ICBM nuclear deterrents. The moral Rubicon had been crossed long before August 6 and 9, 1945. Then and for the future.

In the week that followed Nagasaki, U.S. aircraft crossed the skies of Japan dropping leaflets onto burned-out cities revealing the content of surrender talks that the Japanese government refused to tell its people were even underway. The Allies backed away from their demand for unconditional surrender to allow Japan to retain at least the outer forms of *kokutai,* of the emperor system. All the while fearing a coup by fanatic officers would follow this revelation the War Cabinet met to discuss surrender. It stalemated, delivering up a 3:3 vote, half wanting to surrender but the other three *still* arguing for Armageddon, for *ichioku gyokusai,* for millions of shattered jewel deaths. Facing social upheaval and a possible end to his dynasty and the imperial system, though not from any discernible compassion for his suffering people or for humanity's sake, Hirohito broke the tie. Imperial Japan bowed before the Allies, agreeing to terms on August 15. Having supported a Nazi alliance and at the very least standing by during years of an ever more fanatic approach to foreign policy and to war, Hirohito recorded his first public statement while hidden inside a bomb shelter in his palace compound. Before it was broadcast, young officers steeped in a culture of disobedience tried to intercept the recording to stop its being heard by the Japanese people (*Kyūjō Jiken* or "Kyūjō Incident"), but they failed. Several of the young rebels then committed suicide.

In his *Gyokuon-hōsō* ("Jewel Voice Broadcast"), delivered in courtly Japanese that few common people understood, Hirohito never admitted an iota of responsibility for himself or for the serial aggressive wars initiated by the Japanese military. Instead, he deflected all blame from his person and from Japan, proclaiming that war had been declared only in self-defense, apologizing not to Japan's victims but solely to its collaborationist puppets for failing to complete a shared mission of "emancipation of East Asia." He said he was proud that the war had secured "the structure of the Imperial State," airily proclaiming that all Japanese must now "endure the unendurable."[83] As if they had not done so already. Edward Drea aptly concludes that Hirohito "valued the imperial institution more than his people, his army, and his empire."[84] When they heard the speech rebroadcast to Rikugun units across Asia, some officers anticipating fighting on chose to commit suicide. Others murdered their last Allied prisoners of war. Japan's representatives signed the formal instrument of surrender on the deck of the USS *Missouri* in Tokyo Bay on September 2. A little farther out sat immense Allied war fleets the like of which no one in Japan had ever imagined their enemies could produce, let alone anchor just off the emperor's sacred shores.

Both before and throughout World War II, at multiple junctures, Japan had different choices available than the ones its leaders actually made, including how to conduct the fight and how to behave toward occupied peoples and captive soldiers. It even had a choice about when and how to end its catastrophically losing war, to halt a rain of fire curtaining its home islands like a descended aurora. Its leaders chose to fight into atomic destruction instead. In that sense, they shared with and echoed what Hitler said of his own choice not to surrender his nihilism, not to give up even the ruins of Nazi Germany until the Red Army was barely a long grenade toss away and he finally shot himself, how he would fight on "until five minutes past midnight." And so the slaughter had gone on across Asia, too, long past any hope for Japanese military success. It fell from the air, it rolled over land and on and under the seas. More millions were murdered, more cities disappeared under pillars of fire, more skeletal men fought to their last for the vanity of brutal officers and empires, and had to be dug out by other scared men with tanks and bombs and flamethrowers. War without mercy.

Conclusion

HOW TO WIN decisively in war is the aspiration of all professional military, and a main subject of concern to those who study war. Yet it is the single hardest thing to do, to translate combat into achievement of an important strategic and political goal that the other side is forced to recognize and accept when the war is over. Starting in the Renaissance, European intellectuals—followed only much later by experimenting generals commanding real armies—looked to classical models of decisive battle as the elusive alchemist secret, the key to transmuting princely ambition and will into lasting success in politics through war. This book has argued that military intellectuals afterward moved too far in that direction, ultimately to the Clausewitzian ideal of climactic battle as the culmination of all operations, and to generals of genius as the instrument of perfect war. It has tried to show instead that attrition was good, if you were a defensive power and not an aggressor in a hurry to win before the balance of forces and a new grand coalition formed in anger and took up arms to stop you. If you were an aggressor, especially if starting from a markedly inferior material position, if you were Frederick or Napoleon or either Moltke or Nazi Germany or Imperial Japan, you despised and feared attrition by coalition and would strike first, do anything to avoid it from the outset. You also convinced yourself that you *could* avoid it, that your special tactical or operational skill, your iron will or *élan vital* or race superiority or *sensei* spiritual strength, made you superior in war even to far more powerful enemies. You would triumph over matériel.

Sometimes aggressors won. They found a chink in a *trace italienne* bastion or learned how to maneuver armies around stone borders. They isolated enemies to defeat them one by one, or for a short time eluded high social and fiscal costs to win and change the face of war. They ignored human costs and immense expense that created barriers to decision, diminishing the utility of war for settling disputes among social and political elites. They sought to break free of the straightjacket of stone and of ever-improving defensive rates of fire to reach the Elysian Fields of victory with mobile armies, there to destroy their enemy in a single day or a single campaign of decision. Most could not achieve this or never tried, but history endorsed those who could, even if they did so by luck as much as skill, even if they lost everything in the end. As long as their losing was innovative or artful.

Ignored and belittled were the many more successful generals who fought to a stalemate, because defense and not aggression was their mandate. History, or at least historians, favored the bold and heroic few over the plodding many who made war within the limits of stone and cannon, of slow fortification and long sieges. Who did not seek to impose their will with the lives of other men on fortified Lines or miles upon miles of barbed wire and trenches and artillery. Who let some other general waste an army and spend a sovereign's treasure battering at the ramparts until his men's spirit broke or the nation's blood and treasure were spent. Even the failed heroic beat defense every time in traditional military history. Prussia is wrecked, yet Frederick is the greatest of Germans. France is in ruins, but an age is named for Louis or the genius of Napoleon.

The allure of battle would matter little had not the long wars it led to altered the course of world history in conflicts of prolonged destruction and suffering, in wars revealed and waged as contests of logistics and endurance that lasted many years or even many decades. Marlborough is touted even today as the greatest of all English generals and a key reinventor of decisive battle, yet he was distrusted by the Dutch for killing so many of their men to so little purpose and fired as well from command of British armies, to clear a path to a negotiated peace. Why recall the sins and errors of Old Fritz in Berlin when the cynical young Frederick was so deft and *decisive* on the battlefield? Stand and admire the passing comet of war called Napoleon, who steered the surging *levée en masse* and Revolutionary armies out from France to conquer all of Europe, revealing that he was so in love with war he could not stop and lost it all again. Twice. Yes, but it was *glorious*.

Napoleon was undeniably the greatest of the horse-and-musket generals. He was also the last, which is more important. War changed under him even as he waged it. He was unmatched until other generals and armies caught up and France wore out because he never knew when to stop, even in victory. Napoleon's example distorted much later generalship and understanding of modern war, evoking varying attempts to capture and bottle his purported genius, ranging from condensed abstract "principles of war" to campaign studies by General Staff officers. His personal virtuosity did much damage to later understanding even by historians of the role of strategic attrition in the defeat of France in 1814, and hence of the impossibility of lasting victory by more virtuosity in 1815. Yet what really mattered in the end, what shaped the outcomes of victory and defeat, was state mobilization of mass armies everywhere, and nearly all alike. More important in the history of war than his career and battlefield tactics is that the *levée en masse* locked in the dominance of mass infantry armies of conscripts over professionals, while also giving them new motivation to fight for the state and against foreign armies that looked and fought just about the same before a generation of war was done. Yet history and popular imagination fix on Napoleon, framed in divine gold by Clausewitz in a flush of youthful idolatry he never quite gave up, almost as gilded as in heroic oils by the court painter David.

A cult of battle overtook thinking about the conduct of war, to reshape the modern military imagination. Perversely, it was shared Enlightenment and Romantic idealization of genius, in this case of military genius, that portended the newly aggressive spirit. About few other areas of human endeavor besides the random walk of war is the word "genius" used so cheaply and commonly.[1] Storied and thrilling exploits of celebrity generals call across time and borders with an intense allure that few resist. Records of tactical magnificence seem to validate belief that the battlefield is the ultimate arena of creativity, that splendid place where genius is revealed and triumphs just when it matters most. It deploys regiments with an oblique march or a panzer thrust or a *coup d'oeil* that chooses perfect ground and finds the open flank and attacks. Even if such genius on horseback fails, its effort is celebrated as artistic and worthy; a solitary creative will orchestrating a symphony of order out of the chaos and cacophony of combat while lesser men fall, flee or fail. Battle is portrayed as the final arena of will and power, where a rare few of surpassing talent master a murder-brimmed hour that signifies and changes everything: opening or closing the great gates of empire from the gilt imperial ambitions of the Kremlin to the supposed jihad dreams of the Sublime Porte, from the cold Protestant snows of Sweden to the Hall of Mirrors reflecting Louis XIV's vanity at Versailles to the yawning, burned-out gate at Hougoumont that marked the end of Napoleon's career. This is nonsense on stilts, but its allure abides nonetheless.

Looked at more objectively, the modern great captains were indeed unique and unconventional commanders. But their tactical dexterity is overly celebrated above more careful and less famous generals who waged positional warfare. Still today the great names are hailed as visionaries. Some were genuine innovators and scored impressive battlefield victories. Yet they all failed to overcome the suffocating limitations of logistics or new defensive technologies. The novelty and utility of their early tactics were exposed; their armies, too, wore out from too much war and expense and bloodletting. Maurits prepared for battle and was stymied by stone walls and an enemy military culture that wisely stayed behind them; Gustavus led the fight from the front and was killed; Marlborough lost his last battle and was dismissed; Frederick was saved from destruction and loss of Prussia itself only by *fortuna;* Napoleon lost everything as he had won it, making endless war for its own sake, with no final goal in sight.

Battle-seeking as a heroic ideal was embedded in the history of the Napoleonic Wars and then in the work of Jomini and Clausewitz and others, who elevated the normal allure of battle to a level of pseudoscientific dogma. Across the 19th century, what came to be known as the battle of annihilation, and nothing less, was said to promise decisive victory, given the short time available before an underlying balance of power raised an opposing coalition against even a genius on horseback. War was said to demand supreme talent in the saddle, genius embodied in a general, or caught like a sunbeam in purity of distilled doctrine, or seated around a General Staff planning map. It required studying and emulating the great captains, depicted in Platonic-ideal terms by long dusty ranks of 19th-century historians who focused on campaign tactics and generalship in battle and little else, certainly not the deeper social determinants of victory and defeat. The ideal of the decisive engagement was enshrined after 1815 in the operational thinking of victorious enemies even more surely than it was in the defeated and constrained French Army.

Two tragically contradictory trends—attritional reality versus idealized battle—were obscured by Prussian success in the Wars of German Unification. Moltke's stunning victories were more near-run and complex, and chance-filled, than was understood at the time. Despite his warnings not to try to replicate them, everybody tried, notably his direct successors. The lessons of the Crimea and American Civil War, pointing in a different direction, were ignored in the flush and fear of Prussian quick success. Not even the touted German genius for the war of movement could hold back the peoples from the event horizon of attrition. For attrition was coming, built into modern war at the Great Power level at least by coalition balances of power and population and shared military technology, by the rifle and artillery firepower revolutions, by mass conscript armies and raw secular ideologies and bureaucratic capacity to mobilize whole nations for total war.

As states grew more capable of economic and bureaucratic management of large armies and resources, the stakes grew higher. Militaries added industrial technologies to already strong defenses, to their ability to smash offense with firepower. Assault by massed infantry became a slaughter nearly every time it was tried, even as all the Great Powers grew capable of mobilizing millions of fighting men. New nightmares of logistics presented that not even the Prussian Great General Staff could solve despite decades of planning. Nevertheless, the alternative of unheroic attrition offended moral, aesthetic and historical sensitivities. Worse, it gave no hope to aggressors that war was still available as a continuation of their ambition by other means. Generals and publics raised on legends of the great captains and victories old and new wanted decisive battles above all else.

The cult of the offensive before World War I took hold of military imaginations just as a threefold revolution crowned. Defensive firepower continued to increase, ensuring defense had the advantage over massed attacks; conscript armies, pulling latent reserves of whole nations and empires into war from the outset, continued to expand until they fielded tens of millions; and strong and nearly permanent diplomatic alliances made it impossible to isolate and defeat one Great Power at a time, as had been done in 1866 and 1870 but even Moltke warned could not be done again. These changes reached their culmination in two total wars in the first half of the 20th century, both started by German leaders who succumbed to the short-war delusion *because* they knew they could not win through to *Weltmacht* any other way, not in the face of huge material disadvantage. The greatest, most casualty-strewn battles in the history of war proved mostly just accelerants of attrition from 1914. Yet battle-centric thinking survived even the holocaust of the trenches. The leaders of Nazi Germany and Imperial Japan did it all over again, bringing on total war the like of which was never imagined before, and rates of attrition in a second world war that exceeded those of the first, adding in vast civilian deaths as well.

Short-war thinking informed both Imperial German insecurities before 1914 and fascist exhalations leading into World War II. It infused military superstitions in Japan as well, centered on reassurance that unique spiritual qualities rooted in a special culture and warrior ethos could overmatch several superior enemies, even if they were challenged all at once. A fast strike looking to shatter the enemy's main force was the siren call compelling both these weaker powers. It was their weakness that made the short-war idea appeal so powerfully to Germans and Japanese, who told themselves they were strong but could not supply an answer to the most basic question posed by their decisions to make war: what will you do if your onset plans fail and the war goes big and long? In a fast-war scenario, an opening victory rendered all further strategy unnecessary, so they never gave strategy the time or attention they paid to tactics. The rub was that failure at the start left them vulnerable, floundering as to what to do next. Armies were exposed at the end of overstretched supply lines facing more numerous, undefeated and now aroused enemies in long wars for which neither Germany nor Japan had prepared. The choice was unacceptable retreat or advance and try again. Punch another hole and see what develops. Give in to the allure of annihilation a second time, and a third. Advance deeper into quagmires of attrition until no more advance was possible, then stop. And lose everything in annihilations that became indistinguishable from nihilism.

Allied material superiority did not win either of the world wars by itself. Fire and steel, muscle and bone, were not autonomous of good generals and political leadership, not separate either from soldier courage, forbearance and ruthless will to win. Allied victory was not inevitable in World War I (as Russia's defeat shows) or World War II (as France's defeat shows), only highly probable. It was still essential that tens of millions of ordinary people, soldiers and civilians alike, sacrificed so much to defeat the most rigid and obtuse regime in Europe by 1918 and the most vile regime in history by 1945. What material and population superiority gave the Allies (including the Soviet Union) was the time they needed to learn how to fight, then the managed resources needed to finish the fight. Superiority in troops and matériel still had to be matched to tactics, leadership and force management, and to soldiers' courage and civilian sacrifice. It was, nevertheless, matériel that provided the buffer of delayed defeat, then the resources leading to victory as hard lessons were gleaned and mass armies learned how to fight by fighting.

We may agree or not that some wars were necessary and just. Even when we do, we must keep our eyes open to the grim reality that victory was usually achieved by grinding attrition and mass slaughter. That outcomes were seldom subject to individual heroics or the machinations of command genius. Modern wars among the Great Powers were not won by better character or brilliant command, although intelligent leaders and the solid character of soldiers and the armies they composed were as important as they always are in combat and war. Intelligence, doctrine, quality of political and military leaders, morale of troops, economic and social underpinnings of mass production, core logistics and the uncertain course of fighting were all factors in shaping the outcomes of the major wars. Hence war's uncertainty and high-risk allure to gambler states.

Attrition can seem to mock soldiers' virtue, as they face anonymous death from morally indifferent long-distance weapons. Industrial war can look like reduction into carnage in which the gods are always on the side of the big economies and the biggest battalions. Yet we ought not to infer that the mass bloodshed of modern wars was always pointless, that huge casualties were always a useless tragedy. War is not ever and always a mere deceit employed by pernicious elites and old men to lure youth into vain combat without meaning, leaving them deluded and then dead on some foreign field, though it can be, and has been far too often. Courage and loyalty mattered to soldiers in all armies, at the very least. We must not be so callow or callous as to dismiss what they did in combat as irrelevant when facing the almighty firepower of modern industrial war.

Individual character counted for much in early modern war, in keeping a tight pike or musket formation, holding a thin red or blue or all-black line. It mattered when soldiers in a long firing rank, watching a white puffery erupt across a green field at an enemy's cannon row, did not know where a whistling shell was going to land. It may be that such moral character and forbearance counted even more in an age of industrialized war. The good officer and his well-motivated and trained soldiers were essential to combat effectiveness, especially when no one saw as they stood alone against incoming death or maiming in a far corner of the battlefield. Isolated courage that will never be witnessed or known or recorded is almost certainly the hardest type.

Although I have argued that valor in modern warfare was seldom determinative, exceptional physical and moral courage was often in evidence on both sides in many modern battles, from the smallest skirmishes to the largest clash of whole army groups. It was seen in small unrecorded firefights at the squad, platoon or company levels, as well as in division and corps-sized assaults. It was there in advances knee-deep in salt surf under heavy fire, over a hundred different beaches; and yes, also behind barking machine guns facing a human wave upright and crossing no man's land. It was found in enduring the indescribable suffering of a bitter winter, tending dying comrades; while huddling under a saturation barrage waiting to emerge to face long lines of enemy in *bleu* or *feldgrau*. It was there in lone cockpits over London in 1940, standing at the guns at Borodino, walking in rank with fusils shouldered up the greasy slope at Fontenoy, facing chattering machine guns at bloody Mukden. We see real meaning in a moment of combat or personal courage or endurance, later in a memoir of the trenches or Iwo Jima or the Huertgen Forrest or at Bryansk. We know it as men and boys straining against the call of instinct to run, crossing instead over a killing zone in a hundred different wars, to close and fight hand-to-hand with other terribly frightened men and boys in different colored uniforms. Such courage still counts. The experiences and sacrifices of soldiers at Shiloh or the Marne or Kharkov or Juno Beach were not mean, small or morally useless acts. Attrition by battle or by bombing does not annihilate all moral and human meaning.

The problem with conclusions that claim to know the lessons of history is that history teaches so many different lessons. It is next to impossible to know which apply to contemporary events, about which perception and knowledge are necessarily thickly veiled. One is therefore as likely as not to apply the wrong lessons from history, while making entirely original mistakes. That said, the main lessons to be drawn from this survey are ancient yet fundamental. First, beware the vanity of nations and the hubris of leaders, civilian and military; but perhaps civilian most of all. There is grave danger to youth forced into uniform by the hurried ambitions of old men who never wore one, never smelled cordite wafting overhead or knelt by a dying comrade. Also from those who did, but who lost the wars of their youth and grew grim and determined to try again. There is nothing particularly original in those observations, except to say that vanity is original with each generation that makes war.

Second, always be deeply skeptical of short-war plans and promises of easy victory, for they shall surely go awry as combat commences and descends into chaos, and an intelligent and determined enemy refuses to accept the initial verdict. Let us be rid as well of all claims to genius of the greatest generals and of the whole idea of genius in war, whether of the fawning nationalist sort or Clausewitz's more refined version. It is no more than a form of armchair idolatry divorced from real explanation of preparation and supporting resources and skill, which then meets with chance in battle. Claims to genius distance our understanding from war's immense complexity and contingency, which are its greater truths. The best field captains react better and more quickly to war's essential confusion (the fog of war) than others, but no one truly commands or ever controls such a complex and dynamic thing as battle, let alone war. Assertion of genius separate us from war's wider and shared character, and from its suffering. It upholds the imagined heroic over the brutally horrific, however just the cause and necessary the war may be or might have been. Its celebration by national partisans and historians, who are too often one and the same, obscures the stumbling even of the greatest generals and the grim endurance of soldiers. Let us be done with all that, with talk and poses and lies about genius in war.

What of the future? The idea of decisive battle will always be more alluring than winning by attrition—morally and aesthetically; to generals and theorists, and to publics hungry for war news. Yet exhaustion of the enemy

has in modern times more usually achieved political ends in big wars fought
among the Great Powers, which suggests that more humility is needed. For
there is an almost ineluctable propensity in war to error, to blundering from
early brilliance into carnage and slow exhaustion by bleeding out armies and
nations. Thus, cabinet wars fought to limited ends with limited means by
cruelly rational monarchs were displaced not by more nimble generals who
knew how to reach decision through battle, but by even longer and more destructive wars of attrition; by *guerre à outrance* as aroused nations struggled
for a generation then on to exhaustion, the armies wrestling until one weary
sumo *rikishi* at last collapsed just before all the others did. As it has happened
before, it should not surprise us if it happens again. Not today or tomorrow,
perhaps, but in the continuing history of endless war that lies ahead.

Technologies and societies changed constantly over past centuries, alter-
ing the armies and navies they sent away to war. Those who did not recognize these changes, a difficult thing to do while they were happening, were
more likely to fail in war because they resorted to what they knew best: how
to fight the last one. It was even worse to fight according to a theoretical
model of supposed eternal principles of war that were always mere snapshots
of a peculiar time and place that no longer obtained. The same was true for
overreliance on initially superior fighting spirit to defeat an enemy's greater
material resources and numbers. When believed in by leaders of states such
myths shaded into military mysticism, and plunged into war-losing error
in the expectation of winning quickly. Cities that took 1,000 years to build
were destroyed in a month of combat, in a day of bombing, or in an atomic
minute. The assumption that the moral factor would be decisive in modern
war helped lead to that calamity. Then it seemed to die in a buzz saw of industrial combat, in campaigns fought over years to grinding ends with armies
of tens of millions, with blockading navies, strategic bombers, endurance of
mass casualties. By 1945 there could be no illusion about spiritual factors, as
total war ushered in killing and destruction on a global scale hitherto unimagined and unforeseen. Or so it was said.

Did it really stop, much as we might want to believe that it did? A number
of lengthy, post-1945 conflicts suggest not. Highly motivated opponents
facing modern armies made up with new forms of ruthless nationalist or religious *élan* what they lacked in numbers and war matériel, or the latter was
supplied to them by outside powers that fought wars of attrition by proxy.
That was true in some measure from Algeria to Vietnam in the 1960s, in
Afghanistan against the Soviets in the 1980s and NATO after that, and in
Iraq since 2003. In the second half of the 20th century and the first decades of

an already bloody and conflict-ridden 21st century, new patterns of war have emerged that are very different from the past. Long and brutal wars since 1945 were decided—or were not decided, but continued over decades and continue still—more by will and moral endurance by the weaker side than by raw military power to commit destruction by the physically stronger party. Drawn-out peoples' wars emerged as the dominant form of armed conflict after 1945.

War evolves. Total war seems for now to have slipped back into history, ushered off the stage of policy choices by strategic ICBMs that can deliver complete annihilation even of the mightiest of the Great Powers in under an hour. The balance of terror, of mutual nuclear threat, waits in silos and under arctic ice in silent submarines, however little unwary publics are conscious of that fact since the end of the Cold War lessened their worry but not the capabilities of nuclear states. Tactical even more than strategic nuclear weapons appear to make all-out war by immense conscript armies unnecessary and unwinnable, robbing conventional war as it developed to 1945 among the major states of the power of decision. They also give a dark new meaning to the idea of short war. It would be another mistake, however, to assume that this pattern will be permanent or that the world has seen the last of total war just because the next one might turn out to be the last war ever. We walk the knife edge always between misunderstood lessons of wars past and new mistakes waiting to be made by the next generation, which will not remember real war and might think it would like to try it. That, too, has happened before.

Has the phenomenon of the allure of battle ended in our own time? There are a legion of examples that say no. Among the more salient, Saddam Hussein rushed Iraq to war with Iran in September 1980, intending to take advantage of the chaotic Iranian Revolution to seize limited territorial goals but in fact commencing a large-scale conflict that lasted almost eight years, to August 1988. His invasion of neighboring Kuwait just two years later on August 2, 1990, led to international intervention and enforcement of no-fly zones and routine bombings by several foreign air forces that lasted to 1998. In 2001, NATO intervened in Afghanistan to overthrow the Taliban. It did, yet is still fighting there. In 2003, the United States led a truncated coalition in an invasion of Iraq expected to defeat the eroded and second-rate Iraqi Army quickly and decisively. It did, but a long war against regime elements and Islamist radicals was not formally declared over until 2011, when in fact it still was not. A widening and worsening civil war between Shi'a and Sunni continued for years after that. Thirteen years on, there is no end in sight as this is written. Related conflict shattered Syria and spilled across the greater Middle East into the Arabian peninsula and North Africa. And elsewhere?

In September 2015, Indian Army Chief General Dalbir Singh Suhag declared that his forces were fully prepared for the "swift, short nature of future wars." Pakistan Army Chief General Raheel Sharif boasted back: "Our armed forces stand fully capable to defeat all sorts of external aggression . . . short or long."[2] So the illusion abides. So the next war looms.

Notes

INTRODUCTION

1. A concise summary of this tradition is Yuval Noah Harari, "The Concept of 'Decisive Battles' in World History," *Journal of World History* 18/3 (2007): pp. 251–266.
2. "Operations" refers to command and movement of large units—in the period considered in much of this book, divisions, corps, armies and army groups. In essence, tactics are how one wins battles, operations are how one wins campaigns, and strategy is how one wins wars.
3. Wilfred Owen, "Dulce et Decorum Est" (March 1918).
4. Rupert Brooke, "The Dead" (April 1915).
5. For example, Stephen Ambrose, *D-Day: June 6, 1944: The Climactic Battle of World War II* (New York: Touchstone, 1994).
6. Michael Howard, "When Are Wars Decisive?" *Survival* 41/1 (1999): p. 130.
7. Victor Davis Hanson, *Carnage and Culture: Landmark Battles in the Rise of Western Power* (New York: Doubleday, 2001): p. 8.
8. Michael Howard, "The Use and Abuse of Military History," *Parameters* XI/1 (1981): pp. 9–14; John Whiteclay Chambers, "The New Military History: Myth and Reality," *Journal of Military History* 55/3 (1991): pp. 395–406; Peter Paret, "The New Military History," *Parameters* XXI (1991): pp. 10–18; Roger Spiller, "Military History and Its Fictions," *Journal of Military History* 70/4 (2006): pp. 1081–1097.
9. J. Boone Bartholomees, "The Issue of Attrition," *Parameters* (2010): pp. 5–19. The classic debate was framed by Hans Delbrück, *The Dawn of Modern Warfare: History of the Art of War*, Vol. 4 (Lincoln: University of Nebraska Press, 1990), and Basil Liddell Hart, *Strategy: The Indirect Approach*, 4th ed. (London: Faber, 1967). The literature on the debate is now vast.
10. Russell Weigley, *The Age of Battles: The Quest for Decisive Warfare from Breitenfeld to Waterloo* (Bloomington: Indiana University Press, 1991): pp. xii–xvi.
11. A recent example of the genre is Paul Davis, *Masters of the Battlefield: Great Commanders from the Classical Age to the Napoleonic Era* (New York: Oxford University Press, 2013).
12. Anonymous. Originally, a 13th-century German proverb. It became famous in English mainly about the unhorsing of Richard III at the Battle of Bosworth Field (August 22, 1485), the last major battle of the Wars of the Roses. In 2013 the king's hacked, stabbed and beaten scoliotic bones were discovered buried under a parking lot, a paved-over former churchyard. The remains were reinterred at Leicester Cathedral in 2015.
13. On the influence of Napoleon on generals of World War I, see Lorenzo Crowell, "The Illusion of the Decisive Napoleonic Victory," *Defense Analysis* 4/4 (1988): pp. 329–346.
14. For example, Bevin Alexander, *How Great Generals Win* (New York: Norton, 2002).
15. Victor Davis Hanson argues for a problematically unique and virtuously lethal Western tradition of linear battle in *The Western Way of War: Battle in Classical Greece*, 2nd ed. (Berkeley: University of California Press, 2009), and more ambitiously in *Carnage and Culture: Landmark Battles in the Rise of Western Power* (New York: Doubleday, 2001) and "The Western Way of War," *Australian Army Journal* 2/1 (2004): pp. 157–164.

16. See Carter Malkasian, *A History of Modern Wars of Attrition* (Westport: Praeger, 2002): pp. 1–6. Steven Biddle makes the argument for "force employment" over "mass" as the key determinant in modern battles, but concedes that his argument pertains to battle rather than to war: *Military Power: Explaining Victory and Defeat in Modern Battle* (Princeton: Princeton University Press, 2006).

17. The leading work is Robert Citino, *The German Way of War: From the Thirty Years' War to the Third Reich* (Lawrence: University Press of Kansas, 2005).

18. Stephen Van Evera, "The Cult of the Offensive and the Origins of the First World War," *International Security* 9 (1984): pp. 58–107; Antulio Echevarria, "The 'Cult of the Offensive' Revisited: Confronting Technological Change Before the Great War." *Journal of Strategic Studies* 25/1 (2002): pp. 199–214.

CHAPTER 1

1. Widely read 19th- and 20th-century examples include Edward Creasy, *Fifteen Decisive Battles of the World: From Marathon to Waterloo* (London: Bentley, 1851); Thomas Knox, *Decisive Battles Since Waterloo* (New York: Putnam's Sons, 1887); Nugent Robinson, *A History of the World with All its Great Sensations*, 2 vols. (New York: Collier, 1887); Frederick Whitton, *Decisive Battles of Modern Times* (New York: Houghton-Mifflin, 1923); J. F. C. Fuller, *A Military History of the Western World*, 3 vols. (New York: Funk & Wagnalls, 1954–1956); and Fletcher Pratt, *Battles that Changed History* (Garden City, NY: Hanover House, 1956).

2. For example, Paul Cartledge, *Thermopylae: The Battle that Changed the World* (New York: Knopf Doubleday, 2007). Two noted historians of World War II posit that in military history "above all, one can trace the outcome to specific battles and incidents that gave rise to larger results." Williamson Murray and Allan R. Millet, *A War to Be Won: Fighting the Second World War* (Cambridge: Harvard University Press, 2000): p. 304. There are refreshing contrasts to the "decisive battle that changed everything" argument and genre, recently including Theodore Corbett's contrarian study, *No Turning Point: The Saratoga Campaign in Perspective* (Norman: University of Oklahoma Press, 2012), and John D. Grainger, *The Battle of Yorktown, 1781: A Reassessment* (Woodbridge: Boydell. 2005). A scholarly collection that goes well beyond battle narrative to discuss social, religious and ideological contexts is Ariane Boltanski, et al., eds., *Du fait d'armes au combat idéologique XIe-XIXe siècle* (Rennes: Presses Universitaires de Rennes, 2015)

3. Among recent examples are Joseph Dahmus, *Seven Decisive Battles of the Middle Ages* (Chicago: Nelson-Hall, 1983); David Eggenberger, *An Encyclopedia of Battles: Accounts of Over 1,560 Battles from 1479 B.C. to the Present* (New York: Dover, 1985); Robert Mantran, *Les grandes dates de l'Islam* (Paris: Larousse, 1990); H. Verma and Amrit Verma, *Decisive Battles of India Through the Ages* (Campbell: GIP, 1994); Richard Gabriel and Donald Boose, *Great Battles of Antiquity* (Westport: Greenwood, 1994); Paul Davis, *100 Decisive Battles: From Ancient Times to the Present* (Oxford: Oxford University Press, 2001); Richard Holmes and Martin Evans, *A Guide to Battles: Decisive Conflicts in History* (Oxford: Oxford University Press, 2009); Mir Bahmanyar, *Vanquished: Crushing Defeats from Ancient Rome to the 21st Century* (Oxford: Osprey, 2009); Christer Jorgensen, editor, *Great Battles: Decisive Conflicts that Have Shaped History* (New York: Parragon, 2007); Jim Lacey and Williamson Murray, *Moment of Battle: The Twenty Clashes That Changed the World* (New York: Bantam, 2013); G. B. Malleson, *The Decisive Battles of India from 1746 to 1849* (New Delhi: Asian Educational Services, 2007; facsimile reprint of the new edition, London: Reeves & Turner, 1914; originally published 1883); Bryn Hammond, *El Alamein: The Battle that Turned the Tide of the Second World War* (Oxford: Osprey, 2012); Robert Lyman, *Kohima: The Battle that Saved India* (Oxford: Osprey, 2012); Geoffrey Roberts, *Victory at Stalingrad: The Battle that Changed History* (London: Longman, 2002); and Richard Overy, *A History of War in 100 Battles* (New York and Oxford: Oxford University Press, 2014). The motif is prominent in popular films such as *Decisive Battles of the Ancient World* (History Channel: 2004), *Frontier: The Decisive Battles of the Old Northwest* (History Channel, 2000), and *Decisive Battles of World War II* (Cannon Vision, 2013).

4. Hanson, *Carnage and Culture*: pp. 168–169 and passim. John Lynn provides a concise and compelling critique in *Battle: A History of Combat and Culture* (Boulder, CO: Westview Press, 2003): pp. 13–27. Also see John France, "Close Order and Close Quarter: The Culture of Combat in the West," *International History Review* 27-3 (2005): pp. 498–517. An intriguing rebuttal of prior descriptions of hoplite war is Christopher Matthew, *A Storm of Spears: Understanding the Greek Hoplite at War* (Philadelphia: Casemate, 2012): pp. 1–16, 127–128. Peter Krentz also offers a different view of hoplite warfare, weapons and tactics in *The Battle of Marathon* (New Haven: Yale University Press, 2010): pp. 51–60, 143–143, 157–159.

5. Herodotus, *The Histories* (New York: Penguin, 2003). Herodotus has been criticized for gullible invention and writing fiction rather than history. For one thing, the gods continued to play a fundamental causal role in his explanations. On the other hand, Thucydides did not treat the gods as relevant to the issue of causation. I am grateful to Loren J. Samons for this contrast.

6. Ibid., pp. 563–585, and passim.

7. J. A. S. Evans, "Herodotus and the Battle of Marathon," *Historia: Zeitschrift für Alte Geschichte* 42/3 (1993): pp. 279–307; Krentz, *Marathon*: pp. 137–160, 172–174.

8. Such broad decisiveness of Marathon is reiterated in Alan Lloyd, *Marathon: The Crucial Battle That Created Western Democracy* (London: Souvenir Press, 2005); and Richard Billows, *Marathon: The Battle That Changed Western Civilization* (New York: Overlook Press, 2010). On Marathon's more specific place, see J. F. Lazenby, *The Peloponnesian War: A Military Study* (London: Routledge, 2004): p. 43. Many popular histories make comparable claims about other ancient fights. For example, Barry Strauss, *The Battle of Salamis: The Naval Encounter that Saved Greece—and Western Civilization* (New York: Simon & Schuster, 2005).

9. Again, I am grateful to Loren J. Samons for this insight.

10. For more balanced views of the role of battle vs. logistics and other factors in Greek warfare, see Robin Lane Fox, *Alexander the Great* (London: Penguin Books, 2004); idem, *The Long March: Xenophon and the Ten Thousand* (New Haven: Yale University Press, 2004); John Lee, *A Greek Army on the March: Soldiers and Survival in Xenophon's Anabasis* (Cambridge: Cambridge University Press, 2007); Archer Jones, *Art of War in the Western World* (New York: Oxford University Press, 1987): pp. 1–26, 65–70.

11. Yozan Mosig and Imene Belhassen, "Revision and Reconstruction in the Punic Wars: Cannae Revisited," *International Journal of the Humanities* 4.2 (2006): pp. 103–110; and J. F. Lazenby, *Hannibal's War: A Military History of the Second Punic War* (Norman: University of Oklahoma Press, 1998): pp. 77–85.

12. The practice of frenzied appeasement of Roman gods with human sacrifice continued for years after Cannae. Eve Macdonald, *Hannibal: A Hellenistic Life* (New Haven: Yale University Press, 2015): p. 188.

13. Alvin H. Bernstein, "Strategy of a Warrior-State: Rome and the Wars Against Carthage, 264–201 B.C.," in Williamson Murray et al., editors, *The Making of Strategy: Rulers, States, and War* (Cambridge: University of Cambridge Press, 1994): p. 78; Lazenby, *Hannibal's War*: pp. 29–86.

14. As discussed below, Cannae obsessed Prussian and German military thinkers and war-planning into the 19th and 20th centuries. It continues to be written about extensively today. Mark Healy, *The Battle of Cannae: Hannibal's Greatest Victory* (Oxford: Osprey, 2000); Robert O'Connell, *Ghosts of Cannae: Hannibal and the Darkest Hour of the Roman Republic* (New York: Random, 2010); Richard A. Gabriel, *Scipio Africanus: Rome's Greatest General* (Washington: Potomac, 2008): pp. 25–54; Adrian Goldsworthy, *Cannae: Hannibal's Greatest Victory* (New Haven: Phoenix, 2007). Goldsworthy doubts that the Fabian strategy achieved victory, but also criticizes Hannibal for assuming that his great tactical victory at Cannae was enough to bring Rome to terms. A "face of battle" account of the nature of fighting is Gregory Daly, *Cannae: The Experience of Battle in the Second Punic War* (London: Routledge, 2002).

15. An outlier is Yozan Mosig and Imene Belhassen, "Revision and Reconstruction in the Second Punic War: Zama—Whose Victory?" *International Journal of the Humanities* 5.9 (2007): pp. 175–186. More reliable are Lazenby, *Hannibal's War*: pp. 219–225, and Macdonald, *Hannibal*: pp. 198–217.

16. Trevor Dupuy, *Understanding Defeat* (New York: Paragon, 1990): pp. 10–11. See instead Gabriel, *Scipio Africanus*: pp. 175–197.

17. Ibid., pp. 83–174; Bernstein, "Warrior-State," pp. 56–84; Lazenby, *Hannibal's War*: pp. 87–232; Adrian Goldsworthy, *The Punic Wars* (London: Cassell, 2001): pp. 197–221; 222–244; idem, *The Fall of Carthage* (London: Cassell, 2007).

18. Alfred von Schlieffen, "Cannae Studies," reprinted in Robert T. Foley, editor, *Alfred von Schlieffen's Military Writings* (London: Frank Cass, 2002): pp. 208–218. On the linkage of Cannae to Schlieffen's promotion of a unique "German way of war" he tied to Sedan in 1870, see Andrew Loren Jones, "Debating Cannae: Delbrück, Schlieffen, and the Great War" (2014), Electronic Theses and Dissertations, Paper 2387, http://dc.etsu.edu/etd/2387.

19. Julius Caesar, *The Conquest of Gaul* (London: Penguin Classics, rev. ed., 1983); Michael Sage, *Roman Conquests: Gaul* (London: Pen and Sword, 2012); Jones, *Art of War*: pp. 72–79.

20. The dominant account of the defeat was Tacitus, *Annals of Imperial Rome* (London: Penguin Classics, 1996): pp. 61–89; it was also treated in Ovid, *Tristia* ("Lamentations"). A modern revival in the decisive-battle genre is Peter Wells, *The Battle that Stopped Rome* (New York: Norton, 2003). Wells incorporates fresh and important archeological discoveries from 1987, though that does not validate his claim in the Preface that Teutoburger Wald was "perhaps the most decisive battle in European history."

21. Creasy, *Fifteen Decisive Battles*: pp. 115–140; German nationalist view of the Teutoburger Wald as the "sister of Cannae" quoted at p. 137. Also see Fuller, *Military History*, Vol. I: pp. 239–253.

22. "Roman Military Disasters and their Consequences," Special Issue, *Classical World* 96/4 (2003).

23. Bernstein, "Strategy of a Warrior-State," especially pp. 60–68. It is also true that Rome's armies were capable of great internal as well as outward brutality and, especially in the eastern empire, often performed the critical task of occupation and suppression rather than protection of the populace. Benjamin Isaac, *The Limits of Empire: The Roman Army in the East* (Oxford: Oxford University Press, 1990, 2004): pp. 80–87; 101–160. On logistics, see the masterful work by Jonathan Roth, *Logistics of the Roman Army at War* (Leiden: Brill, 1998), especially pp. 279–328; also Jones, *Art of War*: pp. 26–91. More generally, Philip Sabin, editor, *Cambridge History of Greek and Roman Warfare*, Vol. 2: *Rome from the Late Republic to the Late Empire* (New York and Cambridge: Cambridge University Press, 2008).

24. Note to author by Loren J. Samons, March 18, 2016.

25. G. Halsall, "Movers and Shakers: The Barbarians and the Fall of Rome," *Early Medieval Europe* 8 (1999): pp. 131–145; Martin Goodman, *Roman World* (New York: Routledge, 2012): pp. 89–170; Thomas Burns, *Rome and the Barbarians, 100 B.C.–400 A.D.* (Baltimore: John Hopkins University Press, 2009): pp. 248–373; Edward Luttwak, *Grand Strategy of the Roman Empire* (Baltimore: Johns Hopkins University Press, 1976): pp. 127–190; Adrian Goldsworthy, *Roman Army at War 100 BC–AD 200* (Oxford: Oxford University Press, 1998): pp. 39–75, 163–170; idem, *How Rome Fell: Death of a Superpower* (New Haven: Yale University Press, 2009): pp. 283–415; Ramsey MacMullen, *Corruption and the Decline of Rome* (New Haven: Yale University Press, 1988): pp. 171–177, 199–208; M. J. Nicasle, *Twilight of the Empire* (Amsterdam: Geiben, 1998); Walter Goffart, *Rome's Fall and After* (London: Hambledon, 2003); A. D. Lee, *War in Late Antiquity* (Malden: Blackwell, 2007).

26. Charles Oman, *A History of the Art of War in the Middle Ages: 378–1278* (Ithaca: Cornell University Press, 1953): pp. 41–62; Hans Delbrück, *History of the Art of War*, Vol. 3: *Medieval Warfare* (Lincoln: University of Nebraska Press, 1990): pp. 13–92; Ferdinand Lot, *Art militaire et les armées au moyen âge en Europe et dans le Proche Orient* (Paris: Payot, 1946): passim; J. F. Verbruggen, *The Art of Warfare in Western Europe during the Middle Ages from the Eight Century to 1340*, 2nd ed. (Woodbridge: Boydell, 1997): pp. 204–275. The old view that medieval troops, both mounted and missile, up to c.1200 "functioned more as individuals than groups" survives in Jones' *Art of War*: pp. 92–147. Quoted at p. 144.

27. Wood, *Merovingian Kingdoms*; Philippe Contamine, "La fondation de *Regnum Francorum*," in Contamine, editor, *Histoire militaire de la France*, Vol. 1 (Paris: Press Universitaires de France, 1992–1994): pp. 5–18; Kelly DeVries and Robert Smith, *Medieval Military Technology*, 2nd ed. (Toronto: University of Toronto Press, 2012): pp. 99–114. Jan Wilhelm Honig ascribes the error in part to the 19th-century influence of Clausewitz and basic misunderstanding of medieval

conventions that regulated strategy: "Reappraising Late Medieval Strategy," *War in History* 19/2 (2012): pp. 123–132.

28. Philippe Contamine, *Guerre, état et société à la fin du moyen âge* (Paris: Presses Universitaires de France, 1972). Cited here from the English version, *War in the Middle Ages* (Oxford: Blackwell, 1984): pp. 1–29.

29. Important correctives to the older view include Bernard Bachrach, *Merovingian Military Organization* (Minneapolis: University of Minnesota Press, 1972); Patrick Geary, *Before France and Germany: The Creation and Transformation of the Merovingian World* (Oxford: Oxford University Press, 1988): pp. 3–76; Ian Wood, *Merovingian Kingdoms, 450–751* (London: Longman, 1994); Peter Heather, *The Goths* (Oxford: Blackwell, 1997); Michael Kulikowski, *Rome's Gothic Wars* (Cambridge: Cambridge University Press, 2007); Timothy Reuter, "Carolingian and Ottonian Warfare," in Maurice Keen, editor, *Medieval Warfare: A History* (Oxford: Oxford University Press, 1999): pp. 13–35; Roger Collins, *Early Medieval Europe, 300–1000*, 3rd ed. (New York: Palgrave 2010): pp. 31–113; 151–172.

30. Theodore Mommsen, "Petrarch's Conception of the Dark Ages," *Speculum* 17/2 (April 1942): pp. 226–242. The key 19th-century text in Renaissance studies is Jacob Burkhardt, *Civilization of the Renaissance in Italy* (New York: Modern Library, 2002), originally published 1860. In it, he celebrated a sharp break from a fading medieval world which he broadly dismissed as profoundly superstitious and debasing.

31. The claim that Charlemagne (*Carolus Magnus*) deserved to be counted as one of the great captains of military history was controversial then and since. For example, Philippe Wolff, *The Awakening of Europe* (Harmondsworth: Penguin, 1968): p. 18.

32. A condensed version of the older view of medieval cultural and military decline survives in Wolff, *Awakening of Europe*: pp. 15–35. An important alternate is Contamine, *War in the Middle Ages*: pp. 1–2 and passim. The updated view is found in the most recent research on the period, such as Leif Inge, *Siege Warfare and Military Organization in the Successor States 400–800* (Leiden: Brill, 2013): pp. 149–189, 234–255.

33. Clifford Rogers argues that the English *chevauchée* was battle-seeking, not battle-avoiding, in "Edward III and the Dialectics of Strategy, 1327–1360," *Transactions of the Royal Historical Society* 4 (1994): pp. 83–102. On other modes of medieval warfare, see Ivy Corfis and Michael Wolfe, editors, *The Medieval City Under Siege* (Woodbridge: Boydell, 1999); Kagay and Villalon, *Circle of War*: pp. 33–44; Christopher Allmand, "War and the Non-Combatant in the Middle Ages," in Keen, *Medieval Warfare*: pp. 253–272; Clifford Rogers, "By Fire and Sword: *Bellum hostile* and Civilians in the Hundred Years' War," in Clifford Rodgers and Mark Grimsley, editors, *Civilians in the Path of War* (Lincoln: University of Nebraska Press, 2002): pp. 33–78; Strickland, *War and Chivalry*: pp. 204–229.

34. On Oman's period belief in decisive battle, see Azar Gat, *A History of Military Thought from the Enlightenment to the Cold War* (Oxford: Oxford University Press, 2001): p. 6.

35. Oman, *War in the Middle Ages*, especially Chapter 4, in which he argues for the primitiveness of "feudal" armies and warfare. A similar argument is made in H. J. Hewitt, *The Black Prince's Expedition of 1335–1357* (Manchester: University of Manchester Press, 1958). Reinforcing Oman's depiction of military primitiveness were Hans Delbrück's *Barbarian Invasions*: pp. 13–9, and Ferdinand Lot, *Art militaire et les armées au moyen âge en Europe et dans le Proche Orient* (Paris: Payot, 1946). Correction began with J. F. Verbruggen's identification that knights actually fought as cavalry, in groups and not singly: *Art of Warfare*: pp. 19–109. Also see David Bachrach, "Early Ottonian Warfare," *Journal of Military History* 75 (2011): pp. 393–409; Contamine, "La fondation de *Regnum Francorum*," pp. 5–18; DeVries and Smith, *Medieval Military Technology*, loc. cit.; and Clifford Rodgers, *War Cruel and Sharp: English Strategy under Edward III, 1327–1360* (Woodbridge: Boydell, 2000).

36. Henry J. Webb, "Prisoners of War in the Middle Ages," *Military Affairs* 12/1 (1948): pp. 46–49; Delbrück, *Medieval Warfare*: pp. 429–543. Much modern scholarship corrects this view. See John France, "Recent Writing on Medieval Warfare," *Journal of Military History* 65 (2001): pp. 441–473.

37. See note 44, below.

38. Tours-Poitiers is traditionally dated to 732. Richard Holmes and Martin Evans follow modern research in dating it to either 733 or 734, in *Oxford Guide to Battles* (Oxford: Oxford University Press, 2006): p. 43.

39. Edward Gibbon, *Decline and Fall of the Roman Empire* (London: Penguin Classics, 1994): Chapter 52.

40. Ranke, *History of the Reformation in Germany* (1844): Vol. 1, Chapter 5; Creasy, *Fifteen Decisive Battles*: pp. 157–169; Delbrück, *History of the Art of War: The Barbarian Invasions*: pp. 14, 441; Dahmus, *Seven Decisive Battles*: p. 8 and passim. On visual memory, see Charles de Steuben's impressively romantic *Bataille de Poitiers en octobre 732*, painted in 1837. The core thesis on the shift to heavy cavalry was developed by German medievalist Heinrich Brunner, though its suddenness was challenged by Charles Oman, Hans Delbrück and others. See Kelly DeVries, *Medieval Military Technology* (Peterborough: Broadview, 1992): pp. 95–110. The old thesis of a sudden advent of Frankish heavy cavalry did not survive a decisive critique by Bernard Bachrach, "Charles Martel, Shock Combat, the Stirrup and Feudalism," *Studies in Medieval and Renaissance History* 7 (1970): pp. 47–75.

41. David Motadel, *Islam and Nazi Germany's War* (Cambridge: Belknap Press, 2014): p. 65.

42. William Watson, "Battle of Tours-Poitiers Revisited," *Providence: Studies in Western Civilization* 2/1 (1993); Charles Bowlus, "Two Carolingian Campaigns Reconsidered," *Military Affairs* 48/3 (1984): pp. 121–125; John France, "Military History of the Carolingian Period," *Revue Belge d'Histoire Militaire* 26 (1985): pp. 81–99. Bernard Bachrach dissents, portraying Charles Martel's attack on the Muslim camp at Poitiers as demonstrating a complex and sophisticated Carolingian military system that sustained large armies and went beyond Roman military manuals and practices, citing the fact that Carolingians had their own military manuals that included topics such as scouting: *Early Carolingian Warfare: Prelude to Empire* (Philadelphia: University of Pennsylvania Press, 2011): pp. 26–32, 170–177, 182–188.

43. Robert Cowley and Geoffrey Parker, editors, *Reader's Companion to Military History* (New York: Houghton Mifflin, 2001): p. xiii.

44. For example, in 1991 a foreign policy analyst lamented that "massive Islamic immigration into France" after World War II may have "reversed Charles Martel's victory in 732 at the battle of Tours." William Lind, "Defending Western Culture," *Foreign Policy* 84 (1991): p. 42. In 2001, Victor Davis Hanson wrote in a nearly desperate defense of his fraying "Western way of war" thesis, which holds that war in the West shares a continuous heritage with the classical experience and linear-civic modes of fighting: "what is clear is that Poitiers marked a general continuance of the successful Western defense of Europe." *Carnage and Culture*: pp. 166–167. One military historian charges Hanson with radical reductionism about all military history from the fall of Rome to the 16th century, forced through the prism of the battle of Tours-Poitiers. France, "Culture of Combat," quoted at p. 501, referencing Hanson's *Why the West Has Won*.

45. A counterpoint that deals with battle as strategy is John Hosler, *Henry II: A Medieval Soldier at War, 1147–1189* (Leiden: Brill, 2007): pp. 125–194; also idem, *The Warfare of Henry II: 1149–1189* (Wilmington: University of Delaware Press, 2005).

46. Idem, *Henry II*: pp. 103–124; John France, *Western Warfare in the Age of the Crusades* (Ithaca: Cornell University Press, 1999): pp. 66–86; J. F. Verbruggen, *Art of Warfare*: pp. 276–350; Kelly DeVries, *Infantry Warfare in the Early 14th Century: Discipline, Tactics, and Technology* (Woodbridge: Boydell, 2000); Contamine, *War in the Middle Ages*: pp. 126–172; Matthew Bennett et al., editors, *Fighting Techniques of the Medieval World, 500–1500* (London: St. Martin's, 2006): pp. 6–65; Honig, "Reappraising Late Medieval Strategy," pp. 132–151; David Caldwell, "Scottish Spearmen, 1298–1314: An Answer to Cavalry," *War in History* 19/3 (2012): pp. 267–289.

47. An evocative depiction of the strategic purposes of riding out on *chevauchée* is John Lynn, *Battle*: pp. 73–109. That anything was achieved more than using takings from plunder, ransom and confiscations to pay for more war is disputed by M. Postan, "The Costs of the Hundred Years' War," *Past & Present* 27 (1964): pp. 34–53. On conventions and practices of this type of "war against the land," see Strickland, *War and Chivalry*: pp. 258–290. On the wider practice of ransom as a private activity rather than state action, see Rémy Ambühl, *Prisoners of War in the Hundred Years War: Ransom Culture in the Late Middle Ages* (New York: Cambridge University Press, 2013).

48. Helen Nicholson, *Medieval Warfare* (New York: Palgrave 2004): pp. 13–38; Geary, *Before France and Germany*: pp. 3–76; Wood, *Merovingian Kingdoms*: pp. 203–220; Bachrach, *Merovingian Organization*: pp. 113–130; Heather, *Goths*, op. cit.; Reuter, "Carolingian and Ottonian Warfare," in Collins, *Early Medieval Europe*: pp. 99–132.

49. Richard Jones, "Fortifications and Sieges in Western Europe," in Keen, *Medieval Warfare*: pp. 163–185; Rogers, *Medieval Warfare*, Vol. 3: pp. 264–270; Contamine, *War in the Middle Ages*: pp. 101–114; Jim Bradbury, *The Medieval Siege* (Woodbridge: Boydell, 1992); DeVries and Smith, *Medieval Military Technology*: pp. 187–282; André Chatelain, *Architecture militaire médiévale* (Paris: l'Union REMPART, 1970); Raymond Ritter, *L'architecture militaire du Moyen Age* (Paris: Fayard,1974); Bennett, *Fighting Techniques*: pp. 170–209.

50. Contamine, *War in the Middle Ages*: pp. 228–237; 250–259.

51. Norman Housley, "European Warfare, *c.*1200–1320," in Keen, *Medieval Warfare*: pp. 113–135; Michael Howard, *War in European History*, rev. ed. (Oxford: Oxford University Press, 2009): pp. 1–19; Reuter, "Carolingian and Ottonian Warfare," pp. 13–35; Delbrück, *Medieval Warfare*: pp. 93–223. On the difficulty of distinguishing endemic social violence from what might be more properly called warfare, see selected essays in Richard Kaeuper, editor, *Violence in Medieval Society* (Woodbridge: Boydell, 2000). On political complexities, see France, *Western Warfare*: pp. 39–52. On hard physical limits, see John Pryor, editor, *Logistics of Warfare in the Age of the Crusades* (Burlington: Ashgate, 2006). On war in broad cultural contexts, see Corinne Saunders et al., editors, *Writing War: Medieval Literary Responses to Warfare* (London: D. S. Brewer, 2004); Matthew Strickland, *War and Chivalry: The Conduct and Perception of War in England and Normandy, 1066–1217* (Cambridge: Cambridge University Press, 1996); and Kagay and Villalon, *Circle of War*, op. cit.

52. Howard, *War in European History*: pp. 1–19; Norman Housley, "European Warfare, *c.*1200–1320," in Keen, *Medieval Warfare*: pp. 113–135; Delbrück, *Medieval Warfare*: pp. 93–223; Contamine, *War in the Middle Ages*: pp. 30–64.

53. Sam Zeno Conedera, *Ecclesiastical Knights: The Military Orders in Castile, 1150-1330* (New York: Fordham University Press, 2015); Joseph F. O'Callaghan, *Reconquest and Crusade in Medieval Spain* (Philadelphia: University of Pennsylvania Press, 2004): pp. 124–151; Desmond Seward, *Monks of War: The Military Religious Orders* (London: Methuen, 1972): pp. 143–204; and Part III, David Kagay and L. J. A. Villalon, editors, *Crusaders, Condottieri, and Cannon: Medieval Warfare in Societies Around the Mediterranean* (Leiden: Brill, 2003): pp. 175–238.

54. Seward, *Monks of War*: pp. 95–142; Eric Christiansen, *The Northern Crusades, 1100–1525* (Minneapolis: University of Minnesota Press, 1980); Alan Forey, *Military Orders from the 12th to the Early 14th Centuries* (New York: Palgrave 1991). For a more sympathetic view, see William Urban, *Teutonic Knights: A Military History* (Barnsley: Greenhill, 2006).

55. The classic study was Steven Runciman's *A History of the Crusades*, 3 volumes (Cambridge: Cambridge University Press, 1951–1954). An unsentimental work by Christopher Tyerman is *God's War: A New History of the Crusades* (Cambridge: Belknap, 2006); see also idem, *The Debate on the Crusades* (Manchester: Manchester University Press, 2011). Shorter works include Hans Mayer, *The Crusades*, 2nd ed. (Oxford: Oxford University Press, 1988), and Jonathon Riley-Smith, *Crusades*, 2nd ed. (New Haven: Yale University Press, 2005). More specialized studies are Zsolt Hunyadi and Jozsef Laszlovszky, editors, *The Crusades and the Military Orders* (Budapest: Central European University Press, 2011), and Carole Hillenbrand, *The Crusades: Islamic Perspectives* (Edinburgh: Edinburgh University Press, 1999). On logistics, see Christopher Tyerman, *How to Plan a Crusade: Reason and Religious War in the Middle Ages* (Oxford: Allen Lane, 2015).

56. On military aspects, see Jonathan Sumption, *The Albigensian Crusade* (London: Faber, 1978). On the local social conditions and religious views that underlay the Cathar rebellion, see Emmanuel Le Roy Ladurie, *Autour de Montaillou, un village occitan* (Castelnaud-la-Chapelle: L'Hydre, 2001), and idem, *Histoire du Languedoc* (Paris: Presses Universitaires de France, 1974). On conventions of chivalry concerning ransom, prisoners and combat in siege and battle, see Strickland, *War and Chivalry*: pp. 132–229, and Craig Taylor, *Chivalry and the Ideals of Knighthood in France* (Cambridge: Cambridge University Press, 2013).

57. In general, Guelphs supported the popes while Ghibellines supported autonomy for the Hohenstaufen dynasty and more political latitude for Holy Roman Emperors, but each party was in fact a complex alliance of rival lords, free cities and feuding great families that also defended regional territorial bases. Long after the political contest over the authority of popes vs. emperors ended, the factions divided further and fought on for their own material and territorial or other interests. See Louis Green, "Changes in the Nature of War in Early 14th Century Tuscany," *War & Society* 1/1 (1983): pp. 1–24. On Dante Alighieri's angry views, see Anthony K. Cassell, "Dante in the Eye of the Storm," in *The Monarchia Controversy* (Catholic University of America Press, 2004): pp. 23–49.

58. Peter Purton, *A History of the Late Medieval Siege* (Woodbridge: Boydell, 2010); Geoffrey Hindley, *Medieval Siege and Siegecraft* (Barnsley: Pen & Sword, 2009).

59. Niccolò Machiavelli, *The Art of War* (Chicago: University of Chicago Press, 2003): passim; Felix Gilbert, "Machiavelli: The Renaissance of the Art of War," in Peter Paret, editor, *Makers of Modern Strategy from Machiavelli to the Nuclear Age* (Princeton: Princeton University Press, 1986): pp. 11–31; John R. Hale, *War and Society in Renaissance Europe, 1450–1620* (Baltimore: Johns Hopkins University Press, 1998): passim.

60. Inter alia, Clifford Rogers, "The Military Revolutions of the Hundred Years' War," *Journal of Military History* 57/2 (1993): pp. 241–278; Maurice Keen, "Changing Scene: Guns, Gunpowder, and Permanent Armies," in *Medieval Warfare*: pp. 273–292; John Stone, "Technology, Society, and the Infantry Revolution of the 14th Century," *Journal of Military History* 68/2 (2004): pp. 361–380; Anne Curry and Michael Hughes, editors, *Arms, Armies, and Fortifications in the Hundred Years War* (Woodbridge: Boydell 1994); David Simpkin, *The English Aristocracy at War* (Woodbridge: Boydell 2008): pp. 183–190; Frank Tallett, *War and Society in Early Modern Europe, 1495–1715* (London: Routledge, 1992): pp. 21–23. A markedly different view is that of Jeremy Black, *War and Technology* (Bloomington: Indiana University Press, 2013): pp. 71–100. Also see Howard, *War in European History*: pp. 33–34; Verbruggen, *Art of Warfare*: pp. 111–275; DeVries, *Infantry Warfare*: pp. 23–31; 65–85; 191–199.

61. On the new emphasis on battle in 14th-century warfare, see DeVries, *Infantry Warfare*: pp. 1–8 and passim, and Nicholson, *Medieval Warfare*: pp. 113–143.

62. John Keegan, *The Face of Battle* (New York: Viking Press, 1976): pp. 108–113; Anne Curry, *Agincourt: A New History* (Stroud: Tempus, 2005): pp. 235–268, 291–297.

63. Bert Hall, *Weapons and Warfare in Renaissance Europe* (Baltimore: Johns Hopkins, 1997): pp. 41–66; 105–155; Contamine, *War in the Middle Ages*: pp. 74–89; 126–172; Bennett, *Fighting Techniques*: pp. 66–129; Andrew Ayton and J. L. Price, "The Military Revolution from a Medieval Perspective," in idem, editors, *The Medieval Military Revolution* (London: IB Tauris, 1995): pp. 1–22; Stone, "Technology," p. 377.

64. Verbruggen, *The Battle of the Golden Spurs: Courtrai, 11 July 1302* (Woodbridge: Boydell, 2002).

65. A tight tactical discussion is Jones, *Art of War*: pp. 154–161. On initial English successes through superior tactics, see Desmond Seward, *The Hundred Years' War: The English in France, 1337–1453* (London: Penguin, 1978): pp. 41–76; Jonathan Sumption, *The Hundred Years' War*, Vol. 1: *Trial by Battle* (Philadelphia: University of Pennsylvania Press, 1991): pp. 319–410; 455–534; and Philippe Contamine, *La guerre de Cent Ans*, 9th ed. (Paris: Presses Universitaires de France, 2010): pp. 22–45; and Jones, *Art of War*: pp. 161–168.

66. Adrian Bell and Anne Curry, *The Soldier Experience in the Fourteenth Century* (New York: Boydell, 2011); Kelly DeVries, "The Question of Medieval Military Professionalism," in Michael Neiberg, editor, *Arms and the Man* (Leiden: Brill, 2011): pp. 113–130.

CHAPTER 2

1. Some challenge the idea that the Hundred Years' War can be understood as a single conflict rather than serial wars. See the fine trilogy by L. J. Villalon and Donald Kagay, editors, *The Hundred Years War* (Leiden: Brill, 2005, 2008, 2013). Still, it is treated here as a complex yet strategically unified struggle, with lulls and distinct phases, but unified nonetheless. Well-regarded general histories

include Christopher Allmand, *The Hundred Years' War* (Cambridge: Cambridge University Press, 1988); Contamine, *La guerre de Cent Ans*; Anne Curry, *Hundred Years' War, 1337–1453*, 2nd ed. (New York: Palgrave 2003); Jean Favier, *La Guerre de Cent Ans* (Paris: Fayard, 1980). On interactions of military and social affairs, see Richard Kaeuper, *War, Justice and Public Order: England and France in the Later Middle Ages* (Oxford: Oxford University Press, 1988), and Wright, *Knights and Peasants*.

2. Michael Maller, "Mercenaries," in Keen, *Medieval Warfare*: pp. 209–229; Steven Gunn, "War and the Emergence of the State," in Frank Tallett and D. J. B. Trim, editors, *European Warfare, 1350–1750* (Cambridge: Cambridge University Press, 2010): pp. 50–73; John Bell Henneman, "The Military Class and the French Monarchy in the Late Middle Ages," *American Historical Review* 83/4 (1978): pp. 946–965. More generally, see George Duby, *The Chivalrous Society* (London: Arnold, 1977): pp. 94–111, 134–148.

3. David Simpkin, *The English Aristocracy at War: From the Welsh Wars of Edward I to the Battle of Bannockburn* (Woodbridge: Boydell, 2008): pp. 183–190; Seward, *The English in France, 1337–1453*: pp. 19–102; 127–152; Marilyn Livingstone and Morgen Witzel, *The Road to Crécy: The English Invasion of France, 1346* (London: Taylor & Francis, 2005). On "war against the land" and conventions of chivalry and attrition, see Strickland, *War and Chivalry*: pp. 258–290.

4. Clifford Rogers argues that English *chevauchées* were intended to force battle: "Edward III and the Dialectics of Strategy, 1327–1360," *Transactions of the Royal Historical Society* 6/4 (1994): pp. 83–102. He revisits the thesis in "To Make an End to the War by Battle," in *War Cruel and Sharp*. Intended or not, a major battle was indeed the outcome of the great *chevauchée* by the Black Prince, leading to the Battle of Poitiers. Also see "To Make Chevauchées and Harm His Enemies: Three Campaigns of Early 1356," in ibid; and Lynn, *Battle*: pp. 73–110.

5. Seward, *The English in France*: pp. 41–76; Sumption, *Trial by Battle*: pp. 319–410; 455–534; Contamine, *La guerre de Cent Ans*: pp. 22–45. On logistics and finance, see H. J. Hewitt, *Organization of War Under Edward III, 1338–1362* (Manchester: Manchester University Press, 1966): pp. 28–92; 180–186.

6. Maller, "Mercenaries": pp. 209–229; M. Warner, "Chivalry in Action," *Nottingham Medieval Studies* 42 (1998): pp. 146–173; Nicholas Wright, "Ransoms of Non-combatants During the Hundred Years War," *Journal of Medieval History* 17/4 (1991): pp. 323–332; idem, *Knights and Peasants*: pp. 80–116. A dated but classic work is Siméon Luce, *Histoire de Bertrand du Guesclin et de son époque* (Paris: Hachette, 1876).

7. Contamine, *La guerre de Cent Ans*: pp. 46–71; Seward, *The English in France*: pp. 103–126; Sumption, *Hundred Years' War*, Vol. 3: *Divided Houses*: pp. 18–280.

8. More generally, see Laurence W. Marvin, "Atrocity and Massacre in the High and Late Middle Ages," in Philip G. Dwyer and Lyndall Ryan, editors, *Theatres of Violence: Massacre, Mass Killing and Atrocity throughout History* (New York: Berghahn Books, 2012): pp. 50–62.

9. Jonathan Sumption takes his grand history of the war up to 1422 in *The Hundred Years' War*, Vol 4: *Cursed Kings* (2015).

10. Seward, *The English in France*: pp. 127–152; Nicholas Wright, "Ransoms of Non-combatants During the Hundred Years War," *Journal of Medieval History* 17/4 (1991): pp. 323–332; idem, *Knights and Peasants: The Hundred Years' War in the French Countryside* (Woodbridge: Boydell, 1998): pp. 80–116; Jones, *Art of War*: pp. 169–173. On Agincourt, see Alfred H. Burne, *The Agincourt War* (Westport: Greenwood, 1976); Keegan, *Face of Battle*: pp. 78–116; Curry, *Agincourt*.

11. William Shakespeare, *Henry V* (1599); Winston Churchill, *A History of the English Speaking Peoples*, Volume I: *The Birth of Britain* (Cassel, 1956–1958).

12. "In achyncourt feld he fauth manly, throw grace of god most mervelowsly, he had both feld and vyctory . . . *Deo gracias Anglia, redde pro victoria!*" ("England give thanks to God for victory!"). *Agincourt Carol* (n.d.).

13. Curry, *Hundred Years' War*: pp. 73–82; 86–90; Seward, *The English in France*: pp. 153–212; Kelly DeVries, *Joan of Arc: A Military Leader* (Stroud: History Press, 2011); J. Glénisson, editor, *Jeanne d'Arc, une époque, un rayonnement* (Paris: Editions du Centre national de la recherche scientifique, 1982); Bonnie Wheeler and Charles Wood, editors, *Fresh Verdicts on Joan of Arc* (New York: Routledge, 1996).

14. Contamine, *La guerre de Cent Ans*: pp. 80–99.

15. Henneman, "The Military Class and the French Monarchy": pp. 946–965; Steven Gunn, "War and the Emergence of the State," in Tallett and Trim, *European Warfare*: pp. 50–73; P. S. Lewis, editor, *The Recovery of France in the 15th Century* (London: Macmillan, 1971); Clifford Rogers, "Military Revolutions of the Hundred Years' War," *Journal of Military History* 57/2 (1993): pp. 241–278; Seward, *The English in France*: pp. 233–252.

16. Michael Hicks, *Wars of the Roses* (New Haven: Yale University Press, 2012). Formigny ended the longbow's reputation for superiority. Its last significant action was in the Wars of the Roses, with an occasional flurry of inconsequential appearances after that. DeVries and Smith, *Medieval Military Technology*: p. 39; Stone, op. cit. p. 371.

17. Seward, *The English in France*: pp. 253–262.

18. Kelly DeVries, "Castillon," in idem et al., editors, *Battles that Changed Warfare* (New York: Metro, 2008): pp. 78–87.

19. Contamine, *La Guerre de Cent Ans*: pp. 100–106; P. S. Lewis, editor, *The Recovery of France in the 15th Century* (London: Macmillan, 1971): passim; Contamine, *La Guerre de Cent Ans*: pp. 107–123.

20. On Byzantine military policy, logistics and war finance, see Edward Luttwak, *The Grand Strategy of the Byzantine Empire* (Cambridge: Belknap, 2009). A classic, controversial argument for the critical role of Byzantium for the Latin West is Henri Pirenne, *Medieval Cities: Their Origins and the Revival of Trade* (Princeton: Princeton University Press, 1925, reprinted 2014), and other works. A very different argument is that of Molly Greene, *A Shared World: Christians and Muslims in the Early Modern Mediterranean* (Princeton: Princeton University Press, 2010).

21. On Ottoman military capacities, but also constraints, on operations in this period, see Rhoads Murphey, "Ottoman Military Organization in Southwestern Europe, 1420–1720," in Tallett and Trim, *European Warfare*: pp. 135–158; idem, *Ottoman Warfare, 1500–1700* (London: UCL, 1999); Virginia Aksan, "Ottoman War and Warfare, 1453–1812," in Jeremy Black, editor, *War in the Early Modern World, 1450–1815* (Boulder, CO: Westview, 1999): pp. 147–175.

22. On Renaissance cultural responses to Islam, see Thomas Arnold, *The Renaissance at War* (New York: Smithsonian, 2006): pp. 122–155; Nancy Bisaha, *Creating East and West: Renaissance Humanists and the Ottoman Turks* (Philadelphia: University of Pennsylvania Press, 2004); Margaret Meserve, *Empires of Islam in Renaissance Historical Thought* (Cambridge: Harvard University Press, 2008); Philippides and Hanak, *Fall of Constantinople in 1453*: pp. 3–290; and Robert Schwoebel, *Shadow of the Crescent: The Renaissance Image of the Turk, 1453–1517* (New York: Palgrave 1969). On the general reaction and import, see Michael Angold, *Fall of Constantinople to the Ottomans* (New York: Routledge, 2014): pp. 1–24 and passim.

23. Franz Babinger, *Mehmed the Conqueror and His Time* (Princeton: Princeton University Press, 1978): pp. 64–100, 215–268; 347–408; Kelly DeVries, "Lack of a Western European Military Response to the Ottoman Invasions of Eastern Europe," *Journal of Military History* 63/3 (1999): pp. 539–559; John Guilmartin, "Ideology and Conflict: The Wars of the Ottoman Empire, 1453–1606," *Journal of Interdisciplinary History* 18/4 (1988): pp. 721–747; and Brian Davies, editor, *Warfare in Eastern Europe, 1500–1800* (Leiden: Brill, 2012).

24. On the greater sophistication and power of the Ottoman state and military compared to any state in Europe in this period, see Gábor Ágoston, *Guns for the Sultan: Military Power and the Weapons Industry in the Ottoman Empire* (New York: Cambridge University Press, 2005): pp. 190–206 and passim, and Rhoads Murphey, *Ottoman Warfare, 1500–1700* (London: UCL Press, 1999): pp. 13–64, 105–114.

25. Constantinople had been sacked once before, but without its walls being breached. Attacked twice in 1204 by Latin knights of the Fourth Crusade, it was captured on the second attempt in a confusion of complex misunderstandings, broken contracts, mob violence and internal disunion over the murder of Emperor Alexios IV. Its walls were scaled and holed by hand, not breached by trebuchet or other bombardment. After a Byzantine resurgence, the Latins were driven out in 1262. Donald Queller, *Fourth Crusade: The Conquest of Constantinople, 1201–1204* (Philadelphia: University of Pennsylvania Press, 1997); Thomas Madden, "Vows and Contracts in the Fourth Crusade," *International History Review* 15/3 (1993): pp. 441–468; Stephen Turnbull, *Walls of Constantinople*

(Oxford: Osprey, 2004): pp. 47–57; Susan Wise Bauer, *History of the Renaissance World* (New York: W. W. Norton, 2013): pp. 673–682.

26. Marios Philippides and Walter Hanak, *The Siege and the Fall of Constantinople in 1453: Historiography, Topography, and Military Studies* (Burlington: Ashgate, 2012): pp. 291–568.

27. Really big guns were given distinctive *noms de guerre*. The "King's Daughter" was a famous English bombard. "Mons Meg," weighing 15,000 pounds of iron, was the prize piece in Burgundy's impressive and widely admired arsenal. "Mad Margot" (*Dulle Griete*) resided in Ghent, while "Chriemhilde" served Nuremberg. The largest stone-throwing bombard ever built was the "Tsar Cannon" (*Tsar'-pushka*), built in Moscow in 1586.

28. Alternatively, "Cutter of the Strait." On Ottoman artillery more generally in this period, see Gábor Ágoston, "Ottoman Artillery and European Military Technology in the Fifteenth and Seventeenth Centuries,"*Acta Orientalia Academiae Scientiarum Hungaricae*. Vol. 47, No. 1/2 (1994), pp. 15-48.

29. Steven Runciman, *The Fall of Constantinople: 1453* (Cambridge: Cambridge University Press, 1965, reprinted 2012): pp. 73–85, 133–144. Runciman supersedes a 1903 classic on the great siege by Edwin Pears. Also see Michael Antonucci, "Siege Without Reprieve," *Military History* 9/1 (April 1992), and Philippides and Hanak, *Siege and Fall of Constantinople*: pp. 359–428. Of literary and polemical interest is the classic though jaundiced account by Edward Gibbon, "End of the Roman Empire," in *Decline and Fall of the Roman Empire* (1783).

30. So-called berserkers sometimes suffered casualties as high as 90 percent.

31. Runciman, *Fall of Constantinople*: pp. 100–122; Philippides and Hanak, *Siege and Fall of Constantinople*: pp. 429–546.

32. Antonucci, "Siege Without Reprieve"; Runciman, *Fall of Constantinople*: pp. 133–159.

33. It has long been the practice of conquerors to erect their temple and triumphant god upon the ruins and altars of the defeated enemy's faith, proof that his weaker gods had failed. In Jerusalem the Temple Mount was similarly converted, and remains a contested site to the present time. Hindu temples were destroyed and replaced by Aurangzeb; Aztec temples rose above the conquered city-states of their enemies, and today lie under Catholic cathedrals and churches erected by the conquistadors. Taliban in Afghanistan infamously destroyed the great 6th-century Buddhas of Bamiyan statues in 2001. In Iraq in 2015, Sunni radicals from ISIS ("Islamic State") blew up or tore down centuries-old Shia mosques and Christian churches alike. And so it goes, once and future wars of religion contesting over whose side the gods are on, if any, in war and history.

34. On Ottoman capacity to move and supply armies and on siegecraft, see Murphey, *Ottoman Warfare*: pp. 65–104, 115–121.

35. Nancy Bisaha, *Creating East and West: Renaissance Humanists and the Ottoman Turks* (Philadelphia: University of Pennsylvania Press, 2004): pp. 60–69, 125–132; Margaret Meserve, *Empires of Islam in Renaissance Historical Thought* (Cambridge: Harvard University Press, 2008) pp. 30–34, 65–67, 74–75, 95–99.

36. Meserve, *Empires of Islam*: pp. 1–5; Ágoston, *Guns for the Sultan*, passim; Murphey, *Ottoman Warfare*: pp. 13–64, 105–114.

37. Ottoman armies overran Greece, Serbia and Bosnia by 1466. They wrested Euboea from Venice in 1470 and landed troops at Otranto in 1480. DeVries, "Lack of a Military Response": pp. 539–559; John Guilmartin, "Ideology and Conflict: The Wars of the Ottoman Empire, 1453–1606," *Journal of Interdisciplinary History* 18/4 (1988): pp. 721–747. This slow-motion invasion involved much frontier fighting, often by irregulars on both sides, but few outright battles: Mezokeresztes was the only major field-battle of the long war (1593–1606) with the Habsburgs. Günhan Börekçi, "A Contribution to the Military Revolution Debate: The Janissaries Use of Volley Fire during the Long Ottoman-Habsburg War of 1593–1606 and the Problem of Origins," *Acta Orientalia* 59/4 (2006): pp. 424–429.

38. Andrew Hess, "The Ottoman Conquest of Egypt (1517) and the Beginning of the Sixteenth-Century World War," *International Journal of Middle East Studies* 4/1 (1973): p. 57. On the varied and often strange Renaissance responses to news of the fall of Constantinople, see Terence Spencer, "Turks and Trojans in the Renaissance," *Modern Language Review* 47/3 (1952): pp. 330–333; Arnold, *The Renaissance at War*: pp. 122–155; Angold, *Fall of Constantinople*: pp. 1–24 and passim.

39. Linda T. Darlin, "The Renaissance and the Middle East," in Guido Rugierro, editor, *A Companion to the Worlds of the Renaissance* (Oxford: Blackwell, 2002): pp. 55–69.

40. John Hale, "Early Development of the Bastion: An Italian Chronology, 1450–1534," in John Hale et al., editors, *Europe in the Late Middle Ages* (Evanston: Northwestern University Press, 1965): pp. 466–494; Christopher Duffy, *Siege Warfare: The Fortress in the Early Modern World 1494–1660* (New York: Routledge, 1979): pp. 8–42. On the old-style fortifications, see A. Châtelain, *Architecture militaire médiévale* (Paris: l'Union Repart, 1970); B. H. St. J. O'Neil, *Castle and Cannon: A Study of Early Artillery Fortifications in England* (New York: Praeger, 1960); Ritter, *L'architecture militaire médiévale*; Richard L. Jones, "Fortifications and Sieges," in Keen, *Medieval Warfare*: pp. 163–185.

41. Meserve, *Empires of Islam*: pp. 5–6.

42. A fascinating study of military imagery from Italy to Germany and Flanders is John R. Hale, *Artists and War in the Renaissance* (New Haven: Yale University Press, 1990). More generally, see Bisaha, *East and West*: 174–187, and Meserve, *Empires of Islam*: pp. 238–244.

43. DeVries, "Ottoman Invasions," pp. 554-555; Stephen Christensen, "European-Ottoman Military Acculturation in the Late Middle Ages," in B. P. McGuire, editor, *War and Peace in the Middle Ages* (Copenhagen: Reitzel, 1987): pp. 227-251.

CHAPTER 3

1. J. R. Hale demonstrated that the origins of the *trace italienne* date to around 1450. The complex full or geometrical artillery fortress was perfected in Italy between 1500 and 1515 and was widespread in final form by 1530. Hale, "Early Bastion," pp. 466–494. Also see Howard, *War in European History*: pp. 35–37; Jones, *Art of War*: pp. 194–195.

2. For example, the French artillery fortress guarding the mouth of the St. Lawrence River at Louisbourg, Nova Scotia. It was built between 1720 and 1740.

3. Much debate about the timing, locale and nature of the early modern "revolution in military affairs," if there even was one, revolves around the impact of the *trace italienne* and the full-bastioned artillery fortress on the composition of armies. Inter alia, see John A. Lynn, "The *trace italienne* and the Growth of Armies: The French Case," *Journal of Military History* 55/3 (1991): pp. 297–330, and Geoffrey Parker, *The Military Revolution: Military Innovation and the Rise of the West, 1500–1800* (Cambridge: Cambridge University Press, 1988): pp. 169–171.

4. On the experience of siege vs. battle in early modern warfare, see Tallett, *War and Society*: pp. 44–49.

5. On the medieval idea of defeat in battle as a measure of God's just punishment (*peccatis exigentibus*), see Kelly DeVries, "God and Defeat in Medieval Warfare," in D. Kagay and L. J. A. Villalon, editors, *The Circle of War in the Middle Ages* (Woodbridge: Boydell, 1998): pp. 87–100.

6. Azar Gat, *A History of Military Thought from the Enlightenment to the Cold War* (Oxford: Oxford University Press, 2001): pp. 1–11; "The New Caesars," Arnold, *Renaissance at War*: pp. 102–121; and see Chapters 4 and 5 in Felix Gilbert, *Machiavelli and Guicciardini* (Princeton: Princeton University Press, 1965).

7. On Vegetius and Machiavelli, see Christopher Allmand, *The De Re Militari of Vegetius: Reception, Transmission, and Legacy of a Roman Text in the Middle Ages* (Cambridge: Cambridge University Press, 2011): pp. 1–3, 139–147. On the medieval legacy, see ibid., pp. 251–328; Nicholson *Medieval Warfare*: pp. 13–20, 135–142; Bernard Bachrach, "The Practical Use of Vegetius's *De Re Militari* in the Early Middle Ages," *The Historian* 21/7 (1985): pp. 239–255; and Philippe Richardot, *Végèce et la culture militaire au Moyen Âge* (Paris: Economica, 1998).

8. Allmand, *The De Re Militari*: p. 7.

9. Ibid. pp. 3–7.

10. Howard, *War in European History*: pp. 25–27.

11. Allmand, *The De Re Militari*: pp. 17–46. On the long evolution of military contractors and the efforts of princes and states to control them, see Jeff Fynn-Paul, *War, Entrepreneurs and the State in Europe and the Mediterranean, 1300–1800* (Leiden: Brill, 2014).

12. Allmand, *The De Re Militari*: pp. 314–320. Machiavelli, *Discourses*, Book I, Chapter 21 and Book II, Chapter 20, and *The Art of War*, Book I. Refuting Machiavelli's depiction of condottieri is Michael Mallet, *Mercenaries and Their Masters: Warfare in Renaissance Italy* (Barnsley: Pen and Sword, 2009); and idem and John R. Hale, *The Military Organization of a Renaissance State: Venice, c.1400–1617* (Cambridge: Cambridge University Press, 1984): pp. 181–198; 313–336. Also see John R. Hale, *Machiavelli and Renaissance Italy* (New York: Macmillan, 1960).

13. An uncritical, ideologically-driven and celebratory view of the virtue of battle, arguing for inherent superiority of armies of crusading Western citizen-soldiers effecting "a brilliant burst of democratic frenzy . . . meeting and smashing tactically any enemy army that stands in its way," is Victor Davis Hanson, *Soul of Battle* (New York: Anchor, 1999). Quoted at p. 116.

14. Machiavelli's inaccurate depiction of condottieri survived for centuries, as did his broad disdain for military medievalism. In the battle-worshiping 19th century, the influential medievalist Charles Oman echoed Machiavelli's caricatured disdain for condottieri and similarly elevated battle over all other desirable modes of fighting. Oman, *Art of War*: pp. 283–312. The image of condottieri as feckless was not corrected until historian Hans Delbrück opened a debate with German planners in the wake of World War I over whether Germany would be best served in the next war by a "strategy of exhaustion" (*Ermattungsstrategie*), involving the attrition of supplies and enemy will to fight on, or a "strategy of annihilation" (*Vernichtungsstrategie*), actively seeking destruction of the enemy's main army in a single decisive battle or over a campaign. The German General Staff was not impressed or much interested in his histories. A concise discussion of their famous but sterile dispute is Citino, *German Way of War*: pp. 63–66.

15. *Discourses*, Book III, Chapter 11; Hale, *War and Society in Renaissance Europe*: pp. 75–126, 209–254. Hale eschews campaign and battle history in favor of military social history, focusing on cultural factors, morale, finance and the effects of fortification on politics. Also see William P. Caferro, "Warfare and Economy in Renaissance Italy, 1350–1450," *Journal of Interdisciplinary History* 39/2 (Autumn 2008): pp. 167–209. On hardships of daily life and death in early modern armies (especially on medicine and mortality), see Tallett, *War and Society*: pp. 105–147. A survey of theoretical interests is Thomas Arnold, "Violence and Warfare in the Renaissance World," in Guido Rugierro, editor, *A Companion to the Worlds of the Renaissance* (Oxford: Blackwell, 2002): pp. 460–474.

16. Gat, *History of Military Thought*: pp. 3–4; Machiavelli, *Discourses*, Book I, Chapter 21 and Book II, Chapter 20, and *The Art of War*, Book I. More accurate portraits are in Geoffrey Trease, *Condottieri, Soldiers of Fortune* (New York: Holt, Rinehart and Winston, 1971), and Mallett, *Mercenaries and their Masters*: pp. 51ff.

17. Machiavelli, *Art of War*, Book I; Gilbert, "Machiavelli," pp. 11–31; Gat, *Military Thought*: p. 5. On the Swiss, see "The New Legions," in Arnold, *Renaissance at War*: pp. 68–101.

18. Hale, *War and Society in Renaissance Europe*: pp. 13–45. A comparable but less protracted round of city-state fighting was the War of the Cities (1454–1466). Leading cities of Prussia (Danzig, Elbing and Thorn), later joined by 16 other towns and the Junkers, formed the *Preussische Bund*. The ensuing war engaged militias, armies of Poles, Tatars and the waning Teutonic Knights. More generally, see Tom Scott, "Turning Swiss: Cities and Empire, 1450–1550," *German History* 4/1 (1987): pp. 95–101.

19. Charles V abdicated in installments: as Holy Roman Emperor in 1555, in favor of his brother Ferdinand; in Spain in 1556, in favor of his son Philip II. He retired to a monastery in Estremadura, where he died in profound melancholia two years later. Martyn Rady, *Emperor Charles V* (London: Taylor & Francis, 1988): pp. 89–93; James Tracy, *Emperor Charles V, Impresario of War* (Cambridge: Cambridge University Press, 2002): p. 5, 269.

20. Quoted in Howard, *War in European History*: p. 23.

21. The classic work is Garrett Mattingly, *Renaissance Diplomacy* (Boston: Houghton-Mifflin, 1955).

22. Michael Mallet and Christine Shaw, *The Italian Wars, 1494–1559* (New York: Routledge, 2014). Also see J. R. Hale, *Renaissance War Studies* (1983); F. L. Taylor, *The Art of War in Italy 1494–1529* (Cambridge: Cambridge University Press, 2010); and Jones, *Art of War*: pp. 182–194.

23. R. J. Knecht, *Francis I* (Cambridge: Cambridge University Press, 1982): pp. 42–51.

24. On pike square tactics, see Jones, *Art of War*: pp. 175–178, and Gerry Embleton and Douglas Miller, *The Swiss at War, 1300–1500* (Oxford: Osprey, 1979): passim.

25. Knecht, *Francis*: pp. 44–51; idem, *Renaissance Warrior and Patron: The Reign of Francis I* (Cambridge: Cambridge University Press, 1994): pp. 62–87.

26. Fernando González De León, "Spanish Military Power and the Military Revolution," in Geoff Mortimer, editor, *Early Modern Military History, 1450–1815* (New York: Palgrave, 2004): pp. 25–42.

27. On origins, see Robert Frost, *The Northern Wars: War, State and Society in Northeastern Europe, 1558–1721* (New York: Routledge, 2000): pp. 23–43; Karin Friedrich, *The Other Prussia: Royal Prussia, Poland and Liberty, 1559–1772* (Cambridge: Cambridge University Press, 2000): pp. 121–146; 171–188; Norman Davies, *God's Playground: A History of Poland*, Vol. 1 (New York: Columbia University Press, 1981): pp. 116–124; 134–148; Robert Crummey, *The Formation of Muscovy, 1304–1613* (New York: Routledge, 1987): pp. 205–233.

28. Richard Dunn, *The Age of Religious Wars, 1559–1715* (New York: Norton, 1979); Olaf Asbach and Peter Schröder, editors, *Ashgate Research Companion to the Thirty Years' War* (Burlington: Ashgate, 2014); and relevant entries in Cathal J. Nolan, *Age of the Wars of Religion*, 2 volumes (Westport: Greenwood, 2006).

29. See below and Joachim Whaley, *Germany and the Holy Roman Empire*: Vol. 1 (Oxford: Oxford University Press, 2013): pp. 619–631; Derek Croxton and Anuschka Tischer, *The Peace of Westphalia: A Historical Dictionary* (Westport: Greenwood, 2001).

30. Frost, *Northern Wars*: pp. 226–300; Stewart Oakley, *War and Peace in the Baltic, 1560–1790* (New York: Routledge, 1992): pp. 104–120; Peter Englund, *The Battle that Shook Europe: Poltava and the Birth of the Russian Empire* (London: IB Tauris, 2013): pp. 35–52, 240–252; "Battle of Pultowa," in Creasy, *Fifteen Decisive Battles*: pp. 168–176.

31. Denis Crouzet, *Les guerriers de Dieu: La violence au temps des troubles de religion, vers 1525–vers 1610* (Seyssel: Champ Vallon, 2005); James Wood, *The King's Army: Warfare, Soldiers and Society during the Wars of Religion in France, 1562–76* (Cambridge: Cambridge University Press, 1996); Henry Heller, *Iron and Blood: Civil Wars in Sixteenth-Century France* (Montreal: McGill-Queen's, 1991); Mack P. Holt, *French Wars of Religion, 1562–1629* (Cambridge: Cambridge University Press, 2005); Robert Knecht, *The French Civil Wars, 1562–1598* (New York: Routledge, 2014); Barbara Diefendorf, *Beneath the Cross: Catholics and Huguenots in Sixteenth-Century Paris* (Oxford: Oxford University Press, 1991).

32. Margaret of Parma (1522–1586) was the illegitimate daughter of Charles V, Holy Roman Emperor, and through their father also half-sister of Philip II. Regent of the Netherlands from 1559–1567, her impolitic remarks fed the mood of rebellion, most famously her dismissing Dutch nobles presenting a petition of grievances as "beggars" (*gueux*), a name that stuck. She warned Philip against the savage repression later carried out by his generals. He did not listen.

33. John Guilmartin, *Gunpowder and Galleys: Changing Technology and Mediterranean Warfare at Sea in the Sixteenth Century* (Cambridge: Cambridge University Press, 2003): pp. 235–268. J. F. C. Fuller's assessment of the strategic outcome of Lepanto is highly partisan and hence different: *Military History*, Vol. 2: pp. 1–40.

34. Leading works include Henry Kamen, *Philip of Spain* (New Haven: Yale University Press, 1997); Geoffrey Parker, *The Grand Strategy of Philip II* (New Haven: Yale University Press, 1998); and Colin Martin and Geoffrey Parker, *The Spanish Armada* (Manchester: Manchester University Press, 1988). The classic telling of the Armada, outdated in certain conclusions, is Garrett Mattingly's *Armada* (New York: Houghton Mifflin, 1959).

35. Philip quoted in Geoffrey Parker, "Making of Strategy in Habsburg Spain: Philip II's 'Bid for Mastery,' 1556–1598,' in Murray: *Making Strategy*: p. 149. Paul Kennedy disputes that Philip II had hegemonic ambitions in *Rise and Fall of the Great Powers* (New York: Vintage, 1987): pp. 31–71. Geoffrey Parker points out that that is not how Spain's neighbors saw things at the time in "Bid for Mastery," pp. 115–150. On the origins of the Dutch revolt, see Jonathan Israel, *Dutch Republic: Its Rise, Greatness and Fall, 1477–1806* (Oxford: Clarendon, 1998): pp. 155–219.

36. On Spanish pay issues and mutinies, see Olaf van Nimwegen, *The Dutch Army and the Military Revolutions, 1588–1688* (Woodbridge: Boydell, 2010): pp. 21–84. More generally, see H. L. Zwitzer, "The Eighty Years' War," in Hoeven, *Exercise in Arms*: pp. 33–56; Paul Allen, *Philip III and the Pax Hispanica, 1598–1621* (New Haven: Yale University Press, 2000); Alastair Duke, *Reformation and Revolt in the Low Countries* (London: Hambledon, 1990); Jonathon Israel, *Conflicts of Empires: Spain, the Low Countries and the Struggle for World Supremacy, 1585–1713*

(London: Hambledon, 1997); idem, *The Dutch Republic and the Hispanic World, 1606–1661* (Oxford: Oxford University Press, 1982); Geoffrey Parker, *The Dutch Revolt* (Ithaca: Cornell University Press, 1977); Marco Van der Hoeven, editor, *Exercise of Arms: Warfare in the Netherlands, 1568–1648* (New York: Brill, 1997).

37. Ronald Asch, *The Thirty Years' War: The Holy Roman Empire and Europe, 1618–1648* (New York: St. Martin's, 1997); Geoffrey Parker, editor, *The Thirty Years' War* (New York: Routledge, 1993); Peter Wilson, *Europe's Tragedy: The Thirty Year's War* (Cambridge: Harvard University Press, 2011): pp. 8–11. Still useful, and arguing against Wilson's revisionism, is S. H. Steinberg, *The Thirty Years' War and the Conflict for European Hegemony, 1600–1660* (New York: Norton, 1966). On central issues of wartime diplomacy, see J. H. Elliott, *The Count-Duke of Olivares: The Statesman in an Age of Decline* (New Haven: Yale University Press, 1989): pp. 65–79, 359–408, 457–639; and David Parrott, *Richelieu's Army: War, Government and Society in France, 1624–1642* (Cambridge: Cambridge University Press, 2001): pp. 84–163.

38. Russia stayed out of the Thirty Years' War but saw localized religious fighting with a separate origin from the larger religious quarrels in Europe. For example, in 1648 "Morozov riots" roiled Moscow. These were outbursts of rabid and violent piety directed against boyar retainers of Tsar Alexis, who responded with a savage purge. The British Isles were more involved in the German war, not least as a recruiting base for mercenaries and confessional volunteers, but England was not a formal belligerent. It then descended into domestic crisis, army politics and civil war between king and Parliament. The Wars of the Three Kingdoms (or English Civil Wars) continued for several years after Westphalia, with a pronounced confessional flavoring to the fighting, especially in Ireland. James Wheeler, *Irish and British Wars, 1637–1654* (New York: Routledge, 2002): pp. 195–246.

39. "Peace of Westphalia," in Helfferich, *Documentary History*: pp. 252–273. The Peace of Westphalia refers to a set of discrete treaties named for the demilitarized Imperial cities where they were negotiated over several years: two Treaties of Münster and the Treaty of Osnabrück. The first Treaty of Münster (January 1648) ended the Eighty Years' War. Second Münster and Osnabrück (October 1648) framed the settlement of the Thirty Years' War. See Nolan, *Age of the Wars of Religion*, Vol. 1: pp. 931–936.

40. "Advice of Cardinal Richelieu of France," in Helfferich, *Documentary History*: pp. 151–152; Parrott, *Richelieu's Army*: pp. 399–504; Wilson, *Europe's Tragedy*: pp. 371–384, 464–465, 551–553; "War and *raison d'état*," J. H. Elliot, *Richelieu and Olivares* (Cambridge: Cambridge University Press, 1984). More generally, see William Church, *Richelieu and Reason of State* (Princeton: Princeton University Press, 1972); Michel Carmona, *Richelieu: L'ambition et le pouvoir* (Paris: Fayard, 1983); Joseph Bergin and Laurence Brockliss, editors, *Richelieu and His Age* (Oxford: Oxford University Press, 1992).

41. Holy Roman Emperors retained the old right in hereditary holdings. However, outside those lands the principle (though not always the practice) of general toleration was accepted from 1648. Confessional minorities within the Empire would be permitted to practice as they chose as long as they had done so in that area by the status quo year (*Normaljahr*) of the treaties, agreed after much jockeying debate as 1624. It was a hard peace to reach.

42. See "Imperial Instruction for the Peace Conference" and "Letter of Cardinal Mazarin to the French Plenipotentiaries," both reproduced in Helfferich, *Documentary History*: pp. 233–248; also see Wilson, *Europe's Tragedy*: pp. 671–747.

43. Innocent X, Papal bull *Zelo Domus Dei*, November 26, 1648.

44. Daniel Nexon, *The Struggle for Power in Early Modern Europe: Religious Conflict, Dynastic Empires, and International Change* (Princeton: Princeton University Press, 2009): pp. 265–288.

45. See the important collection edited by Olaf Asbach and Peter Schröder, *War, the State, and International Law in Seventeenth Century Europe* (Farnham: Ashgate, 2010).

CHAPTER 4

1. A later deviation from the kingly model was the New Model Army of Oliver Cromwell. However, a comparable pattern of professionalism, drill and discipline also characterized English armies from the mid-17th century. Henry Reece, *The Army in Cromwellian England, 1649–1660* (Oxford: Oxford University Press, 2013); Roger Manning, *An Apprenticeship in Arms: The Origins of the British Army, 1585–1702* (Oxford: Oxford University Press, 2006): pp. 430–444.

2. The role of naval finance and build-out in early modern state formation and social change is less well-developed in theoretical literature than perhaps it should be.

3. Michael Roberts, "Military Revolution, 1560–1660," in Clifford Rodgers, editor, *The Military Revolution Debate: Readings on the Military Transformation of Early Modern Europe* (Boulder, CO: Westview Press, 1995): pp. 13–36; "Paradigms," in ibid. pp. 37–116; Geoffrey Parker, *The Military Revolution: Military Innovation and the Rise of the West, 1500–1800* (Cambridge: Cambridge University Press, 1996): pp. 6–44; 155–176; idem, "Limits to Revolutions in Military Affairs," *Journal of Military History* 71/2 (2007): pp. 331–372; Brian Downing, *Military Revolution and Political Change* (Princeton: Princeton University Press, 1992). The idea was later stretched to include whole new areas and technologies not in the original theory. For example, Michael Paul, "Military Revolution in Russia, 1550–1682," *Journal of Military History* 68/1 (2004): pp. 9–46; Kaushik Roy, *Military Transition in Early Modern Asia, 1400–1750: Cavalry, Guns, Government and Ships* (New York: Bloomsbury, 2014); and Peter Lorge, *The Asian Military Revolution* (Cambridge: Cambridge University Press, 2008): pp. 154–175.

4. Tallett, *War and Society*: pp. 188–231; Kennedy, *Great Powers*: pp. 70–114; Hall, *Weapons and Warfare*: pp. 157–236; Clifford Rogers, "'As if a sun had risen': England's 14th Century RMA," in MacGregor Knox and Williamson Murray, editors, *Dynamics of Military Revolution, 1300–2050* (Cambridge, Cambridge University Press, 2001): pp. 15–34.

5. Jeremy Black, "A Military Revolution?" in Rodgers, *Military Revolution Debate*: pp. 95–116; idem, *Beyond the Military Revolution: War in the 17th Century World* (Basingstoke: Palgrave 2011): pp. 151–187; idem, *War in the 18th Century World* (Basingstoke: Palgrave, 2013): pp. 188–208.

6. A strong critique pointing to a teleological tendency in RMA literature is David Parrott, *The Business of War: Military Enterprise and Military Revolution in Early Modern Europe* (Cambridge: Cambridge University Press, 2012). Parrott deals with mercenaries and military contractors, or "the business of war" during the Thirty Years' War.

7. Stone, "Infantry Revolution of the 14th Century," op. cit. p. 364; Black, "A Military Revolution?": pp. 95–116.

8. Whatever the merits or flaws of the RMA thesis, the core idea of a military revolution importantly moves war back to the center of history in trying to explain the rise to dominance of the West. Perhaps one day the RMA will be widely accepted in the same sense that theories of other "revolutions" in science, industry and culture are regarded by historians as having shaped the world as we know it today. This valuable speculation is made by Guy Chet, "Teaching in the Shadow of the Military Revolution," *Journal of Military History* 78 (July 2014): pp. 1072–1073.

9. Most notably Justus Lipsius, a neo-stoic philosopher at Leiden whose work, *De Militia Romana* (1596), profoundly influenced Willem Lodewijk and Maurits of Nassau.

10. Günther Rothenberg, "'Military Revolution' of the 17th Century," in Paret, *Modern Strategy*: pp. 32–63; Nimwegen, *The Dutch Army*: pp. 85–116; Marjolein 't Hart, *The Dutch Wars of Independence* (New York: Routledge, 2014): pp. 37–57, 65–70, 92–96.

11. Delmer Brown, "The Impact of Firearms on Japanese Warfare, 1543–98." *Journal of Asian Studies* 7/3 (1948): pp. 236–253; Michael Richardson, "*Teppo* and *Sengoku*: The Arquebus in 16th Century Japan," *Concord Review* 1 (June 2011): pp. 187–210; Matthew Stavros, "Military Revolution in Early Modern Japan," *Japanese Studies* 33/3 (2013): pp. 243–261. Richardson argues against a tendency to exaggerate the impact of the arrival of Western firearms in Japan.

12. Börekçi, "Janissaries Use of Volley Fire": pp. 407–438; Gábor Ágoston, "Firearms and Military Adaptation: The Ottomans and the European Military Revolution, 1450–1800," *Journal of World History* 25/1 (2014): pp. 85–124; idem, *Guns for the Sultan: Military Power and the Weapons Industry in the Ottoman Empire* (Cambridge University Press, 2005): passim. Murphey, *Ottoman Warfare*: pp. 13–34, 65–104; Kenneth Chase, *Firearms: A Global History to 1700* (Cambridge: Cambridge University Press, 2003): pp. 56–140.

13. G. Perjés, "Army Provisioning, Logistics and Strategy in the Second Half of the 17th Century," *Acta Historica Academiae Scientarum Hungaricae* 16 (1970): pp. 1–51. On Dutch logistics, see Nimwegen, *The Dutch Army*: pp. 117–131, 361–377.

14. Jones, *Art of War*: pp. 214–220.

15. Geoffrey Parker, *The Army of Flanders and the Spanish Road, 1567–1659: The Logistics of Spanish Victory and Defeat in the Low Countries' Wars* (Cambridge: Cambridge University Press, 2004); Parrott, *Business of War*: pp. 139–195; John Childs, *Armies and War in Europe, 1648–1789* (Manchester: Manchester University Press, 1982): pp. 1–27.

16. Jones, *Art of War*: pp. 214–220; Creveld, *Supplying War*: pp. 5–16; F. Redlich, "Contributions in the Thirty Years' War," *Economic History Review* 12/2 (1959): pp. 247–254.

17. Contamine, *War in the Middle Ages*: pp. 200–207; 260–295; Bradbury, *Medieval Siege*: passim; Ivy Corfis and Michael Wolfe, editors, *The Medieval City Under Siege* (Woodbridge: Boydell, 1999): pp. 35–68.

18. Nimwegen, *Dutch Army*: pp. 85–116; Parker, "Limits to Revolutions."

19. John Lynn, *Women, Armies, and Warfare in Early Modern Europe* (Cambridge: Cambridge University Press, 2008).

20. O. van Nimwegen, "Maurits van Nassau and Siege Warfare, 1593–1597," in Hoeven, *Exercise in Arms*: pp. 113–132; Nimwegen, *The Dutch Army*: pp. 151–170.

21. Parker, "Limits to Revolutions"; Nimwegen, *Dutch Army*: pp. 171–188.

22. In 1619, Maurits had the head of the pro-truce party, Johan van Oldenbaarneveldt, executed for treason, ostensibly for seeking to reduce the influence of the army by raising more *waardgelder* (militia) units. Grotius was jailed but escaped in 1621 and went into exile, where he completed *De jura belli et pacis* in 1625. Ibid., pp. 196–206; Israel, *Dutch Republic*: pp. 399–449.

23. See the sequence of documents "The Defenestration of Prague," "Declaration of Elector Frederick V of the Palatinate," "Edict of Ferdinand II Annulling the Bohemian Election," "The Battle of White Mountain," and "Terrifying and Piteous News from Bohemia," in Tryntje Helfferich, editor, *The Thirty Years War: A Documentary History* (Cambridge: Hackett Publishing, 2009): pp. 14–57. Also see Wilson, *Europe's Tragedy*: pp. 3–12, 269–313.

24. Nimwegen, *Dutch Army*: pp. 207–216.

25. Jones, *Art of War*: pp. 221–223, 245–246.

26. Scots mercenaries home from the Thirty Years' War, most from service with the Swedish Army, used a version of "leather guns" to cover their crossing of the River Tyne in 1640. Irish armies tried to deploy ad hoc leather guns during the Wars of the Three Kingdoms, mostly to bad result. Irish soldiers either learned about them from service in Germany or from the Scots. Either way, it was not a successful example of technological diffusion.

27. Nils Ahnlund, *Gustavus Adolphus the Great* (New York: History Book Club, 1999): pp. 116–120.

28. A quick survey of cavalry spanning this period is John Ellis, *Cavalry: The History of Mounted Warfare* (Barnsley: Pen & Sword, 2004): pp. 77–108.

29. Ibid., pp. 81–84; Jones, *Art of War*: pp. 196–197.

30. Stuhm is also known as Honigfelde. On the war with Poland, see Roberts, *Profiles in Power*: pp. 46–58.

31. On "the great decision" by Gustavus to intervene in the Thirty Years' War, see ibid. pp. 59–72 and idem, "The Political Objectives of Gustavus Adolphus in Germany," *Transactions of the Royal Historical Society* 7 (1957): pp. 19–46. A contemporary account is "Gustavus Adolphus' Invasion of the Empire," in Helfferich, *Documentary History*: pp. 98–106. Wilson's views of motives and strategy differ sharply from interpretation that follows Michael Roberts, Gustavus Adolphus' eminent biographer and historian of the wars of Sweden's *Stormakstid* or "Great Power Period." Wilson, *Europe's Tragedy*: pp. 459–464.

32. Michael Roberts, *Profiles in Power: Gustavus Adolphus* (New York: Routledge, 2014): pp. 19–108.

33. A revisionist view, that Gustavus improvised not just his maps but also his strategy in Germany, is offered by Peter Wilson. He disputes larger imperial-economic motives, arguing instead that the need to keep the army content by making war in Germany pay its wages was a larger motive: *Europe's Tragedy*: pp. 461–464.

34. Roberts, *Profiles in Power*: pp. 109–126; Jones, *Art of War*: pp. 223–232.

35. A contemporary account is "The Sack of Magdeburg," in Helfferich, *Documentary History*: pp. 107–112.

36. Russell Weigley asserts that Breitenfeld marks the start of an "Age of Battles" lasting to 1815: *Age of Battles*: pp. xi–xii. That seems too arbitrary on both ends.

37. "The Battle of Breitenfeld," in Helfferich, *Documentary History*: pp. 113–117; Wilson, *Europe's Tragedy*: pp. 472–477; Weigley, *Age of Battle*: pp. 3–23; Wilson's figures differ slightly. Also, his relentless revisionism leads to cavalier dismissal of the tactical advantages bestowed by prewar reform of the Swedish Army. A closer military analysis is Jones, *Art of War*: pp. 232–237.

38. "Protestants Triumphant," "The Swedish Discipline," in Helfferich, *Documentary History*: pp. 118–136.

39. Jones, *Art of War*: pp. 237–241.

40. Weigley, *Age of Battles*: pp. 29–30.

41. Roberts, *Profiles in Power*: pp. 162–180; Weigley, *Age of Battles*: pp. 31–36.

42. "The Assassination of General Wallenstein," in Helfferich, *Documentary History*: pp. 144–147. More generally see Geoff Mortimer, *Wallenstein: Enigma of the Thirty Years' War* (Houndmills: Palgrave, 2010).

43. Wilson, *Europe's Tragedy*: pp. 786–806.

44. William Guthrie, *The Later Thirty Years' War* (Westport: Greenwood, 2003).

45. J. L. Price, "A State Dedicated to War? The Dutch Republic in the 17th Century," in Ayton, *Medieval Military Revolution*: pp. 183–200; David Parrott, "Strategy and Tactics in the Thirty Years' War: The 'Military Revolution,'" *Militaergeschichtliche Zeitschrift* 38/2 (1985): pp. 7–26; Barbara Donagan, "Halcyon Days and the Literature of War: England's Military Education Before 1642," *Past and Present* 147 (1995): pp. 65–100. Even Swedish horse partly reverted to caracole tactics as late as the 1680s, so that the new Swedish shock cavalry and old *Ritter* pistol tactics mixed in battle for decades. Polish *Pancerna* cavalry employed caracole to the end of the 17th century. Ellis, *Cavalry*: pp. 81–84; Jones, *Art of War*: pp. 196–197.

46. The change to the fusil, most famously the "Brown Bess," was made late in Britain due to long isolation from continental theory and practice; many English officers retained outdated aristocratic preferences for edged weapons later than elsewhere. Roger Manning, "Styles of Command in Seventeenth-Century English Armies," *Journal of Military History* 71/3 (2007): p. 698; Richard Holmes, *Redcoat: The British Soldier in the Age of Horse and Musket* (New York: Harper-Collins, 2001): pp. 32–46.

47. Jones, *Art of War*: pp. 268–272; Brent Nosworthy, *The Anatomy of Victory: Battle Tactics, 1689–1763* (New York: Hippocrene, 2000). A dubiously deterministic survey is N. A. Roberts, J. W. Brown, B. Hammett and P. D. F. Kingston, "A Detailed Study of the Effectiveness and Capabilities of 18th Century Musketry on the Battlefield," *Journal of Conflict Archaeology* 4 (2008): pp. 1–21.

CHAPTER 5

1. John A. Lynn coined the term "state commission army" to describe the evolution of this 18th-century form. "International Rivalry and Warfare, 1700–1815," in T. C. W. Blanning, editor, *The Short Oxford History of Europe: The 18th Century* (Oxford: Oxford University Press, 2001): pp. 178–217. On the French army, see his masterful *Giant of the Grande Siècle: The French Army 1610–1715* (Cambridge: Cambridge University Press, 1997). On officer aristocrats, David Bien, "The Army in the French Enlightenment: Reform, Reaction and Revolution," *Past & Present* 85 (1979): pp. 68–98. On Dutch reforms, Nimwegen, *Dutch Army*: pp. 301–324. On English practices, David Chandler, *Marlborough as Military Commander* (New York: Scribner's, 1973): pp. 62–77.

2. For the naval side, see Denver Brunsman, *The Evil Necessity: British Naval Impressment in the Eighteenth-Century Atlantic World* (Charlottesville: University of Virginia Press, 2013).

3. P. E. Kopperman, "'The Cheapest Pay': Alcohol Abuse in the Eighteenth-Century British Army," *Military History* 60 (1996): pp. 445–470; A. N. Gilbert, "Why Men Deserted from the Eighteenth-Century British Army," *Armed Forces and Society* 6 (1980): pp. 553–567; Christopher Duffy, *Military Experience in the Age of Reason* (Ware: Wordsworth, 1998): pp. 98–104, 166–167, 172–173.

4. Lynn, *Battle*: p. 129.

5. Idem, "Food, Funds and Fortresses: Resource Mobilization and Positional Warfare in the Campaigns of Louis XIV," in *Feeding Mars: Logistics in Western Warfare from the Middle Ages to the Present* (Boulder, CO: Westview Press, 1994): pp. 137–159.

6. Lynn, "Growth of Armies"; Christopher Duffy, *Fire and Stone: The Science of Fortress Warfare, 1660–1860* (Mechanicsburg: Stackpole, 1996); and idem, *Siege Warfare: The Fortress in the Early Modern World 1494–1660* (New York: Routledge, 1979).

7. Clausewitz, *On War*, Michael Howard and Peter Paret, editors (Princeton: Princeton University Press, 1976): Book IV/11 and Book VI/10–1: pp. 258–262, 393–403.

8. Marlborough had paid spies among French officers in opposing armies, and likely also inside no less than the *Conseil d'en haut*, advisory body to Louis XIV.

9. An accessible collection of Vauban's maps, plans and sketches, and useful guide to period siege practices, is Jean-Denis G. G. Lepage, *Vauban and the French Military under Louis XIV: An Illustrated History of Fortifications and Strategies* (Jefferson: McFarland, 2010).

10. Nimwegen, *Dutch Army*: pp. 132–145, 442–447, 456–459; John Lynn, "A Quest for Glory: The Formation of Strategy Under Louis XIV, 1661–1715," in Murray: *Making of Strategy*: pp. 192–194; Henry Guerlac, "Vauban: the Impact of Science on War," in Paret, *Modern Strategy*: pp. 64–90; John Hebbert and George Rothrock, *Soldier of France* (Oxford: Peter Lang, 1990): passim; Jamel Ostwald, *Vauban Under Siege: Engineering Efficiency and Martial Vigor in the War of the Spanish Succession* (Leiden: Brill, 2006): pp. 5–13; 46–91; 123–172; 215–308. Parker, *Military Revolution*: pp. 115–145.

11. Jānis Langins, *Conserving the Enlightenment: French Military Engineering from Vauban to the Revolution* (Cambridge: MIT Press, 2004); Ostwald, *Vauban under Siege*.

12. On the efficacy of siege warfare vs. sieges as a form of "abortive" warfare, see Jamel Ostwald, "Marlborough and Siege Warfare," in John Hattendorf et al., editors, *Marlborough: Soldier and Diplomat* (Rotterdam: Karawansaray, 2012): pp. 122–143.

13. Quoted in Christopher Duffy, *The Fortress in the Age of Vauban and Frederick the Great, 1660–1789* (London: Routledge & Keegan Paul, 1985): pp. 13–14.

14. Quoted in Chandler, *Art of Warfare*: p. 234.

15. John Lynn, *Giant of the Grande Siècle*: pp. 107–126, 550–551; Weigley, *Age of Battles*: pp. 50–51; Martin van Creveld, *Supplying War: Logistics from Wallenstein to Patton*, 2nd ed. (Cambridge: Cambridge University Press, 2004): pp. 5–16.

16. Jean Bérenger, *Turenne* (Paris: Fayard, 1987): Chapter 4: "Turenne et l'armée"; Lynn, "Glory," p. 192.

17. Jean-Philippe Cénant, "Le ravage du Palatinat: Politique de destruction, stratégie de cabinet et propagande au début de la guerre de la Ligue d'Augsbourg," *Revue historique* 2005/1 (n° 633): pp. 97–132.

18. On march practice and battle tactics, see Chandler, *Marlborough* (1973): pp. 77–93.

19. Jones, *Art of War*: pp. 267–319; Strachan, *European Armies*: pp. 23–37; Martin van Creveld, *Technology and War* (New York: Free Press, 1989): pp. 87–95.

20. Weigley, *Age of Battles*: pp. 37–43; John Childs, *Warfare in the Seventeenth Century* (Washington: Smithsonian, 2001): pp. 86–113; Peter Wilson, "European Warfare, 1450–1815," in Black, *War in the Early Modern World*: p. 196; Lynn, "Glory," p. 196.

21. Lynn, "Glory," pp. 178–204; idem, *The Wars of Louis XIV: 1667–1714* (Boulder, CO: Westview, 2003); Jeremy Black, *From Louis XIV to Napoleon: The Fate of a Great Power* (London: UCL Press, 1999): pp. 33–69. François Bluche, *Louis XIV* (London: Blackwell, 1990); Jöel Cornette, *Le Roi de guerre: Essai sur la souveraineté dans la France du Grand Siècle*, 3rd ed. (Paris: Payot, 2010); R. Hatton, *Louis XIV and Europe* (London: Macmillan, 1976); Andrew Lossky, *Louis XIV and the French Monarchy* (New Brunswick: Rutgers University Press, 1994).

22. Most notably, Jean-Baptiste Colbert, Henri de Turenne, Louis de Bourbon (*le Grand Condé*), Michel Le Tellier and his son, François Le Tellier (*marquis de Louvois*).

23. G. Rowlands, "Louis XIV, Aristocratic Power and the Elite Units of the French Army," *French History* 13/3 (1999): pp. 303–331.

24. Bluche, *Louis XIV*: pp. 241–263; J. R. Jones, *The Anglo-Dutch Wars of the Seventeenth Century* (London: Longman, 1996).

25. Louis did not pursue religious goals in his first Dutch War, but he tried to crush all dissent at home in preparation for his next one. Carl Ekberg, *The Failure of Louis XIV's Dutch War* (Chapel Hill: University of North Carolina Press, 1979); Paul Sonnino, *Louis XIV and the Origins of the Dutch War* (Cambridge: Cambridge University Press, 2003); idem, *"Plus royaliste que le pape,"* in David Onnekink, editor, *War and Religion After Westphalia, 1648–1713* (Farnham: Ashgate 2008): pp. 17–24. G. Satterfield, *Princes Posts and Partisans: The Army of Louis XIV and Partisan Warfare in the Netherlands, 1673–1678* (Leiden: Brill, 2003).

26. Lynn, "Glory," p. 203.

27. Bluche, *Louis XIV*: pp. 283–306, 419–458; Israel, *Dutch Republic*: pp. 807–862; James Scott Wheeler, *Making of a World Power: War and the Military Revolution in Seventeenth-Century England* (Stroud: Sutton, 1999); Manning, "Styles of Command," pp. 684, 698–699. On the impact of the Anglo-Dutch Brigade on English professionalism, see John Childs, *The Army, James II, and the Glorious Revolution* (Manchester: Manchester University Press, 1980): pp. 119–137.

28. Geoffrey Symcox, "Louis XIV and the Outbreak of the Nine Years War," in Ragnhild Hatton, editor, *Louis XIV and Europe* (New York: Macmillan, 1976): pp. 179–212; Lynn, *Wars of Louis XIV*: pp. 191–265.

29. Bluche, *Louis XIV*: pp. 513–539. A different view is that of Mark Thomson, who sees Louis' Spanish claims as reasonable, in "Louis XIV and the Origins of the War of the Spanish Succession," *Transactions of the Royal Historical Society*, 5th ser., 4 (1954): pp. 111–134. On the Dutch, see Israel, *Dutch Republic*: pp. 968–984.

30. Richard Holmes, *Marlborough: Britain's Greatest General* (New York: Harper-Collins, 2008): pp. 119–128, 151–153, 165–166, 467–474. Quoted at p. 3; Chandler, *Marlborough*: pp. 12–44; Corelli Barnett, *Marlborough* (London: Wordsworth, 1974): pp. 11–25.

31. Lynn, *Wars of Louis XIV*: pp. 24–27; Daniel Dessert, *Argent, pouvoir et société au Grand Siècle* (Paris: Fayard, 1984); John Brewer, *Sinews of Power: War, Money, and the English State, 1688–1783* (London: Unwin Hyman, 1989): pp. 73–108, 132–179; Martin Jones, "War and Economy in the Age of William III and Marlborough," *Parliamentary History* 9/1 (1990): pp. 212–214.

32. John Stapleton, "Marlborough, the Allies, and the Campaign in the Low Countries," in Hattendorf, *Marlborough*: pp. 144–171. For Marlborough's own views, see Henry Snyder, editor, *The Marlborough-Godolphin Correspondence*, 3 volumes (Oxford: Oxford University Press, 1975), and less directly David Chandler, editor, *Military Memoirs of Marlborough's Campaigns, 1702–1712* (Mechanicsburg: Stackpole, 1998). On relative Dutch and British commitments, see Jamel Ostwald, "The 'Decisive' Battle of Ramillies, 1706: Prerequisites for Decisiveness in Early Modern Warfare," *Journal of Military History* 64/3 (2000): p. 664n67.

33. On Marlborough's purported genius, see Carlton, *This Seat of Mars*: pp. 223–227. John Hattendorf raises the question but does not resolve it in "Courtier, Army Officer, Politician, and Diplomat," *Soldier and Diplomat*: pp. 38–102.

34. Holmes, *Britain's Greatest General*. Holmes's biography is filled with wistful Anglophilia and parallel and unfair portrayals of how French generals "scuttle away" from the shadow of the magnanimous English genius. Similarly, ordinary redcoats triumph but French blue and white coats run from lack of courage at p. 241, 294, and passim.

35. Holmes, *Britain's Greatest General*: pp. 438–481. A typical early nationalist view is Richard Kane's 1747 hagiography, *Campaigns of King William and the Duke of Marlborough, with Remarks on the Stratagems by Which Every Battle Was Won or Lost, from 1689 to 1712* (BiblioBazaar reprint, 2010). Winston Churchill, in *Marlborough: His Life and Times*, 4 volumes (1933–1938), went all in on the decisive character of his ancestor's battles, proclaiming them to have been "crashing blows in the field." He wrote it while in residence at Blenheim Palace.

36. Jaap Bruijn, "The Anglo-Dutch Navies in Marlborough's Wars," in *Soldier and Diplomat*: pp. 274–299. William Maltby, "Origins of a Global Strategy, England 1558–1713," in Murray, *Making Strategy*: pp. 151–177; Shinsuke Satsuma, *Britain and Colonial Maritime War in the Early Eighteenth Century* (Woodbridge: Boydell, 2013).

37. Michael Hochedlinger depicts Marlborough's relationship with Prince Eugene as critical to Allied success in blocking Louis XIV from hegemony in "Friendship and Realpolitik," *Soldier and Diplomat*: pp. 248–273.

38. In striking contrast, credit is duly given to others by Alan Gay in "John Churchill, Professional Soldiering, and the British Army, c1660–c1760," *Soldier and Diplomat*: pp. 103–121.

39. Overall see John B. Hattendorf, *England in the War of the Spanish Succession* (New York: Garland, 1987). On the wider war in Spain, see David Francis, *The First Peninsular War, 1702–1713* (New York: St. Martin's Press, 1975); Henry Kamen, *The War of Succession in Spain, 1700–15* (London: Weidenfeld & Nicolson, 1969). On domestic rebellion in France, specifically the "Revolt of the Camisards," see Roy McCullough, *Coercion, Conversion, and Counterinsurgency in Louis XIV's France* (Leiden: Brill, 2007): pp. 21–52; 181–242.

40. Will Stroock, "Marlborough's Art of War," *Strategy & Tactics* 238 (2006): pp. 6–17.

41. For comparison to a similar role of fortresses and strongpoint defense in the Baltic from 1700–1711, or the first half of the Great Northern War, see Bernard Kroener, " 'The only thing that could save the empire,' " in *Soldier and Diplomat*: pp. 216–247.

42. Jamel Ostwald, "Marlborough and Siege Warfare," in *Soldier and Diplomat*: pp. 122–143; Chandler, *Marlborough*: pp. 94–122; Barnett, *Marlborough*: pp. 28–36.

43. Holmes, *Britain's Greatest General*: pp. 211–214, 249.

44. J. B. Morton, "Sobieski and the Relief of Vienna," *New Blackfriars* 25 (1944): pp. 243–248, doi: 10.1111/j.1741-2005.1944.tb05698.x.

45. John Lynn, "How War Fed War," *Journal of Modern History* 65/2 (1993): pp. 132–140.

46. Holmes, *Britain's Greatest General*: pp. 258–269; Chandler, *Marlborough*: pp. 126–135, map at pp. 134–135; Barnett, *Marlborough*: pp. 86–103; Lynn, *Wars of Louis XIV*: pp. 286–288.

47. Holmes, *Britain's Greatest General*: pp. 272–276. David Chandler gives much lower numbers of dead and wounded in an older study, *Marlborough*: pp. 136–137.

48. Holmes, *Britain's Greatest General*: pp. 277–281.

49. Chandler, *Marlborough*: pp. 145–150.

50. Nosworthy, *Battle Tactics*: pp. 370–371.

51. Holmes disparages the courage of French soldiers at Blenheim in *Britain's Greatest General*: p. 294. It does not seem proper for historians to later query and belittle the courage of men under fire. How many professors would have stood fast in an 18th-century battle line?

52. Jones, *Art of War*: pp. 274–277; Barnett, *Marlborough*: pp. 104–121.

53. Holmes, *Britain's Greatest General*: p. 297.

54. Chandler, *Marlborough*: pp. 158–183.

55. Holmes, *Britain's Greatest General*: pp. 329–352; Lynn, *Wars of Louis XIV*: pp. 266–360. Marlborough quoted in Ostwald, "Ramillies," p. 675.

56. Chandler, *Marlborough*: pp. 201–222.

57. Holmes, *Britain's Greatest General*: pp. 353–406; Lynn, *Wars of Louis XIV*: pp. 319–321. A skeptical view of the "decisive" consequences of Ramillies is Ostwald, "Ramillies," pp. 665–677.

58. A long-standing argument over numbers is discussed in André Corvisier, *La Bataille de Malplaquet, 1709* (Paris: Economica, 1997): pp. 74–75.

59. Chandler, *Marlborough*: pp. 240–272; Lynn, *Wars of Louis XIV*: pp. 331–335.

60. Clément Oury, "Marlborough as an Enemy," in *Soldier and Diplomat*: pp. 192–215.

61. Bluche, *Louis XIV*: pp. 532–572; Lynn, *Wars of Louis XIV*: pp. 325–335.

62. Quoted in Lynn, *Wars of Louis XIV*: p. 335.

63. Holmes, *Britain's Greatest General*: p. 361.

64. Jonathan Swift, *The Conduct of the Allies* (Ann Arbor: University of Michigan Press, 1916).

65. Chandler, *Marlborough*: passim but especially pp. 300–331. Weigley argues that Marlborough restored decisiveness to battle, but not to war, in *Age of Battles*: pp. 74–78.

66. Ostwald, "Ramillies," pp. 653–654.

67. See Tony Claydon, "A European General in the English Press," in *Soldier and Diplomat*: pp. 300–319.

68. Chet, "Teaching the Military Revolution," pp. 1073–1074.

69. Allan Guy, "John Churchill, Professional Soldiering, and the British Army, c1660–c1760," in *Soldier and Diplomat*: pp. 103–121.

70. François Ziegler, *Villars: Le Centurion de Louis XIV* (Paris: Perrin, 1996); Claude Sturgill, *Marshal Villars and the War of the Spanish Succession* (Lexington: University of Kentucky Press, 1965). A rare English paean, redolent with old-fashioned admiration and praise for Villars' genius,

is William O'Connor Morris, "Villars," *English Historical Review* 8/29 (1893): pp. 61–79, available at http://www.jstor.org/stable/548315.

71. Lynn, *Wars of Louis XIV*: pp. 350–358.

72. One study argues that battles were more decisive in the British Isles between the 15th and 18th centuries than on the Continent, because of a heavier death toll. Yet it shows that only 15 percent of military deaths in the Wars of the Three Kingdoms came in battles *and* sieges, defined as "high-intensity combat." Over three times as many deaths resulted from chronic skirmishing and other "low-intensity combat," which suggests that diseases and hardships of camp life, and maneuvering without fighting set-piece battles, were far more wasting. Charles Carlton, *This Seat of Mars: War and the British Isles, 1485–1746* (New Haven: Yale University Press, 2011): pp. 96–110; 144–178; 237–265. Alternately, on attrition by "Fabian strategy" vs. "annihilation," see Stanley Carpenter, *Military Leadership in the British Civil Wars, 1642–1651* (New York: Frank Cass, 2005): p. 64, 87, 116, 148, 153. A traditional "decisive battles" treatment is Malcolm Wanklyn, *Decisive Battles of the English Civil Wars* (Barnsley: Pen & Sword, 2006).

73. Jeremy Black, *The Battle of Waterloo* (New York: Random House, 2010): p. 14. Robert Citino agrees, in *German Way of War*: pp. 34–36.

74. Voltaire's views on Louis XV's wars mainly followed French opinion. Émile Léonard, *L'Armée et ses problemes au XVIIIe siècle* (Paris: Libraire Plon, 1958): pp. 217–233.

75. Adrienne Hytier, "Les Philosophes et le problème de la guerre," *Studies on Voltaire and the Eighteenth Century* 127 (1974): pp. 243–258.

76. Antonio Torio, *Diderot et la Guerre* (Villeneuve: Presses Universitaires du Septentrion, 1995): passim. On Voltaire's different naiveté about war, see Armstrong Starkey, "To Encourage the Others: The *Philosophes* and the War," in Mark Danley and Patrick Speelman, editors, *The Seven Years' War: Global Views* (Leiden: Brill, 2013): pp. 23–46.

77. Armstrong Starkey, *War in the Age of the Enlightenment*: (Westport: Greenwood, 2003): pp. 10–20, 105–132.

78. Patrick Riley, "The Abbé de St. Pierre and Voltaire on Perpetual Peace in Europe," *World Affairs* 137/3 (1974–1975): pp. 186–194.

79. Starkey, "Philosophes," pp. 37–40.

80. Starkey, *War in the Enlightenment*: pp. 33–68.

81. Sara Eigen Figal, "When Brothers Are Enemies: Frederick the Great's 'Catechism for War,'" *Eighteenth-Century Studies* 43/1 (2009): pp. 21–36.

82. Gat, *Military Thought*: pp. 14–80. Tactics and military geometry as a favored topic and pastime of courtiers at p. 25.

83. David Parrott, "Cultures of Combat in the Ancien Régime: Linear Warfare, Noble Values, and Entrepreneurship," *International History Review* 27/3 (2005): pp. 518–533.

84. On Enlightenment fascination with genius, see Herbert Dieckmann, "Diderot's Conception of Genius," *Journal of the History of Ideas* 2/2 (1941): pp. 151–182.

85. Clausewitz, *On War*: pp. 134, 157–158.

86. Starkey, *War in the Enlightenment*: pp. 49–52; Maurice de Saxe, *Mes rêveries* (1732), translated as *My Reveries Upon the Art of War* (Harrisburg: Stackpole, 1985). On modern evaluations of Saxe as a general, see Jean-Pierre Bois, *Maurice de Saxe* (Paris: Fayard, 1992): passim, and Robert Quimby, *Background of Napoleonic Warfare: The Theory of Military Tactics in Eighteenth-century France* (New York: Ams Press, 1957): pp. 41–61.

87. Reed Browning, *The War of the Austrian Succession* (New York: St. Martin's, 1993): pp. 206–212. On Fontenoy and concepts of courage and forbearance in battle, see Lynn, *Battle*: pp. 111–114, 143–144. On British infantry tactics, see Holmes, *Redcoat*: pp. 32–33, 88–134, 201–205, 216–221.

88. Quoted in Starkey, *War in the Enlightenment*: p. 114.

89. Voltaire, *Henriade*, available at http://catalog.hathitrust.org/Record/006544585. See also Abbé de Prades, "Certitude," *Encyclopédie*, Vol. 2 (1752).

90. Browning, *War of the Austrian Succession*: p. 210; Starkey, *War in the Enlightenment*: pp. 116–120. Casualties from David Chandler, *The Art of Warfare in the Age of Marlborough* (Tunbridge Wells: Spellmount, 1997): p. 306. The most complete account is Jean-Pierre Bois, *Fontenoy, 1745: Louis XV, arbitre de l'Europe* (Paris: Economica, 1996).

91. Saxe, *Mes rêveries* (1732). Gat, *Military Thought*: pp. 34–35.

92. Voltaire reacted as a French patriot, delighting in the victory and publishing a paean to Louis XV and Saxe: *Poeme de Fontenoy* (1745). See John R. Iverson, "Voltaire, Fontenoy, and the Crisis of Celebratory Verse," *Studies in Eighteenth Century Culture* 28/1 (2010): pp. 207–228. On Voltaire's view of Fontenoy and wider contemporary reaction, see Starkey, *War in the Enlightenment*: pp. 105–132.

93. Quoted in Gat, *Military Thought*: p. 44.

94. These remarks extend modestly from John Lynn's discussion of cultural conceits of battle as high aesthetic, including peacock displays of aristocratic male sexuality, in *Battle*: pp. 111–144. On the period's "honor culture," see Starkey, *War in the Enlightenment*: pp. 69–103.

95. See the excellent commentary and prints in Theodore Rabb, *The Artist and the Warrior: Military History through the Eyes of the Masters* (New Haven: Yale University Press, 2011): pp. 83–118.

96. On David's images of Napoleon, see ibid., pp. 152–158.

CHAPTER 6

1. Alternatively, "I have often gone to war too lightly and pursued it for vanity's sake." Quoted in Bluche, *Louis XIV*: p. 221. Such neatly ironic moral summaries put in Louis' mouth could well be apocryphal.

2. *Grenzer* manned fortified villages, blockhouses and watchtowers along Austria's Karlstadt and Windische borders. In the Napoleonic Wars, they were retrained and used as regulars in line battalions. Günther Rothenberg, *The Austrian Military Border in Croatia, 1522–1747* (Urbana: University of Illinois Press, 1960); idem, "The Habsburg Army in the Napoleonic Wars," *Military Affairs* 37/1 (1973): pp. 1–5.

3. "Partisan," called in German *Parteigänger* or *Partisanen*, were irregular troops employed mainly by Habsburg Austria. They were mostly Croats, Serbs and Greeks who fought the Ottomans in the 16th–17th centuries along the *Militärgrenze* frontier between the Habsburg and Ottoman empires, where cross-border raids were almost a way of life. The modern meaning of irregular volunteers resisting foreign occupation deep behind established frontlines did not yet apply.

4. Holmes, *Redcoat*: pp. 15–16, 65, 183–192, 225–226; S. Reid and R. Hook, *British Redcoat, 1740–1793* (London: Osprey, 1996). A parliamentary commission decided on "Indian khakee" only in 1883. "The Colour of the Military Uniforms," *British Medical Journal* 1/1163 (April 14, 1883): p. 730, available at http://www.jstor.org/stable/25262857. The full switch to khaki came in 1902.

5. Daniel Hohrath, *Uniforms of the Prussian Army under Frederick the Great from 1740 to 1786* (Vienna: Militaria, 2012); Gueorguy Vilinbakhov et al., *Au service des Tsars: La garde impériale russe, de Pierre le Grand à la révolution d'Octobre* (Paris: Musée de l'Armée, 2010); Stephen Summerfield, *Austrian Seven Years' War Infantry and Engineers: Uniforms, Organization, and Equipment*, 2nd ed. (Huntingdon: Trotman, 2015).

6. W. Y. Carman, *British Military Uniforms from Contemporary Pictures, Henry VII to the Present Day* (London: Hill, 1957); Michael Barthorp, *British Infantry Uniforms since 1660* (Poole: Blandford, 1982).

7. For example, see Antoine-Jean Gros' 1807 mural *The Battle of Abukir, 25 July 1799*.

8. Peter H. Wilson, *German Armies: War and German Politics, 1648–1806* (London: Routledge, 1998): pp. 202–297. On 18th-century British Army recruitment, see Robert Johnson, "The Scum of Every Country," in Erik-Jan Zurcher, editor, *Fighting for a Living: A Comparative Study of Military Labour 1500–2000* (Amsterdam: Amsterdam University Press, 2014).

9. Christy Pichichero, "*Le Soldat Sensible*: Military Psychology and Social Egalitarianism in the Enlightenment French Army," *French Historical Studies* 31/4 (2008): pp. 553–580.

10. Stephen Conway, "The British Army, 'Military Europe,' and the American War of Independence," *William and Mary Quarterly* 67/1 (2010): pp. 69–100.

11. Matthew Spring, *With Zeal and Bayonets Only* (Norman: University of Oklahoma Press, 2008): pp. 169.

12. Voltaire, *Candide* (London: Penguin, 1947). Originally published in 1759 in France as *Candide, ou l'Optimisme.*

13. Spring, *With Zeal and Bayonets*: pp. 171–177; Duffy, *Military Experience*: pp. 26–65.

14. The key reformer was Jean-Baptiste de Gribeauval, from 1765. Frédéric Naulet, *L'Artillerie Française (1665–1765): Naissance d'une Arme* (Paris: Économica, 2002); Bruce McConachy, "The Roots of Artillery Doctrine: Napoleonic Artillery Tactics Reconsidered," *Journal of Military History* 65/3 (2001): pp. 618–621.

15. Lynn, *Battle*: pp. 122–123.

16. Duffy, *Military Experience*: pp. 140–197.

17. Ibid., pp. 216–219, 230–236.

18. Spring, *Zeal and Bayonets*: pp. 177–215; Nosworthy, *Anatomy of Victory*: pp. 29ff.; A. Balisch, "Infantry Battlefield Tactics in the Seventeenth and Eighteenth Centuries on the European and Turkish Theatres of War: The Austrian Response to Different Conditions," *Studies in History and Politics* 3 (1985): pp. 83–84; John Houlding, *Fit for Service: The Training of the British Army, 1715–1795* (Oxford: Clarendon, 1981); H. C. B. Rodgers, *The British Army of the Eighteenth Century* (London: Allan & Unwin, 1977); R. Ross, *From Flintlock to Rifle: Infantry Tactics, 1740–1866* (Cranbury: Associated University Presses, 1979).

19. Citino, *German Way of War*: p. 50.

20. The literature on naval warfare in this period is vast, but a very good starting place is Michael Palmer, "'The Soul's Right Hand': Command and Control in the Age of Fighting Sail, 1652–1827," *Journal of Military History* 61/4 (1997): pp. 679–705.

21. Duffy, *Military Experience*: pp. 204–206.

22. John Scott, "The Drum" (1782).

23. On the development of the cult of Frederick, see Tim Blanning, *Frederick the Great: King of Prussia* (New York: Random House, 2016): pp. 496–501.

24. Thomas Carlyle, *History of Friedrich the Second, called Frederick the Great*, 4 volumes (New York: Harper, 1864). An abridgment of the military sections is Cyril Ransome, editor, *Battles of Frederick the Great* (New York: Scribner's, 1892). A notable biography is Gerhard Ritter, *Frederick the Great: A Historical Profile* (London: Eyre & Spottiswoode, 1968). Ritter portrays Frederick as always seeking victory by battle, not baroque maneuvers. Also see Robert Asprey, *Frederick the Great: The Magnificent Enigma* (New York: Ticknor and Fields, 1986); David Fraser, *Frederick the Great: King of Prussia* (New York: Fromm, 2001). On strictly military affairs, see Christopher Duffy, *Frederick the Great: A Military Life* (New York: Routledge, 1985).

25. The idea of a "special path" arose from early explanations of German historical trends that supposedly led inexorably to the Nazi Revolution of 1933. *Sonderweg* or "wrong turn" arguments about the broad sweep of German history held that Nazism was the only possible outcome of centuries of history. Its adherents claimed that all great events, from the Lutheran Reformation to the rise of Brandenburg-Prussia to unification of Germany under Bismarck and Moltke, moved inexorably to the ascent to power of the Nazis. This is rejected by modern historians as crudely reductionist and ahistorical.

26. Frederick II, "The Sovereign and the Study of War" and "From the Pages of History," *Frederick the Great on the Art of War* (New York: De Capo, 1999): pp. 35–55, 213–257; Gat, *Military Thought*: pp. 58–60.

27. On Wellington and his troops, see Rory Muir, *Wellington: The Path to Victory* (New Haven: Yale University Press, 2013): pp. 533–536. French minister quoted in Lynn, *Battle*: p. 123.

28. An explanation and even apologia of Frederick's 1756 decision to attack Saxony as a preemptive strike, with Austria, France, Saxony and Russia all assumed to be readying to attack him anyway, is offered by Blanning, *Frederick the Great*: pp. 281–283.

29. The most recent biography to emphasize youthful scarring in Frederick's upbringing as lifelong motivator of his actions and policy is ibid., pp. 3–148.

30. Frederick II, *The Refutation of Machiavelli's Prince; Or, Anti-Machiavel* (Athens: Ohio University Press, 1981).

31. Denis Showalter notes that Frederick was conservative in domestic affairs, being especially reluctant to change the military establishment because the Prussian Army was the basis of the core

social contract that undergirded the state and his dynasty, a unifying bargain of army and monarchy wherein the Junkers accepted commissions and a free hand with serfs in exchange for absolutism. *Wars of Frederick the Great* (London: Longman, 1996): passim.

32. Robert Citino is persuasive that a Prussian fighting doctrine developed from this time that emphasized movement at the operations level (*Bewegungskrieg*): striking fast, staying fluid and ready to move to the next threatened front, and above all knocking out *some* enemy with a lightning blow (a strategy based on the campaign rather than a single, knockout "battle of annihilation"). *German Way of War*: p. 36, 52–53, and passim. Denis Showalter rejects the idea of consistent German supremacy in operational warfare dating to Frederick II in "Prussian-German Operational Art, 1740–1943," Olsen Andreas and Martin van Creveld, editors, *The Evolution of Operational Art from Napoleon to the Present* (Oxford: Oxford University Press, 2011): pp. 35–63. Basil Liddell Hart championed a parallel concept for Britain, but leading historians reject it at the strategic level. David French, *The British Way in Warfare, 1688–2000* (London: Unwin Hyman, 1990); Keith Nelson and Greg Kennedy, editors, *The British Way in Warfare: Power and the International System, 1856–1956* (Burlington: Ashgate, 2010). Unlike the major studies on Germany by Citino, neither of these works deals with much operations history.

33. Browning, *War of the Austrian Succession*: pp. 37–50.

34. Robert Pick, *Empress Maria Theresa; the Earlier Years, 1717–1757* (New York: Harper, 1966).

35. Along with chronic border skirmishing, Austria fought wars with the Ottoman Empire in 1663–1664, in the "Long War" of 1683–1699, and again in 1716–1718 and 1737–1739. During the "Long War" it also fought against Louis XIV in Italy, Spain and southern Germany.

36. See Michael Hochedlinger, *Austria's Wars of Emergence: War, State, and Society in the Habsburg Monarchy, 1683–1797* (New York: Longman, 2003); Christopher Duffy, *Army of Maria Theresa: The Armed Forces of Imperial Austria, 1740–1780* (London: David & Charles, 1977).

37. Quoted in review of Zbigniew Góralski, *Maria Teresa*, in *Polish Review* 45/2 (2000): p. 244.

38. On campaigns and battles, see Browning, *War of the Austrian Succession*: pp. 113–323; on diplomacy and politics, Matthew Anderson, *The War of the Austrian Succession, 1740–1748* (New York: Longman, 1995). Wide-angled views of Frederick are Duffy, *Frederick the Great,* and Asprey, *Frederick the Great*: pp. 139–262.

39. Gunnar Åselius, "Sweden and the Pomeranian War," in Danley, *Seven Years' War*: pp. 135–164; Oakley, *War and Peace in the Baltic*: pp. 129–156. On Russia's fiscal-military state after Peter I, see Carol Stevens, *Russia's Wars of Emergence, 1460–1730* (New York: Routledge, 2007): pp. 277–285; and before that, idem, *Soldiers on the Steppe: Army Reform and Social Change in Early Modern Russia* (DeKalb: Northern Illinois University Press, 1995).

40. Voltaire, *Candide*: p. 110. See Ian Steele, *Warpaths: Invasions of North America* (Oxford: Oxford University Press, 1994): pp. 175–247, and Michael Laramie, *The European Invasion of North America: Colonial Conflict Along the Hudson-Champlain Corridor, 1609–1760* (New York: ABC-Clio, 2012): pp151ff. Older but still useful is Howard Peckham, *The Colonial Wars, 1689–1762* (Chicago: University of Chicago Press, 1964).

41. Voltaire, "What Happened to Them at Surinam," *Candide*, Chapter 19: pp. 110–111.

42. Matt Schumann and Karl Schweizer, *Seven Years' War: A Transatlantic History* (New York: Routledge, 2008): pp. 4–44; Black, *Fate of a Great Power*: pp. 96–127.

43. Weigley, *Age of Battles*: p. 170.

44. Citino objects to using the term "oblique," but it has such an established place in the historical literature it is hard to replace. *German Way of War*: p. 51.

45. Dennis Showalter argues that Frederick was a defender of the international system, only wishing to change its structure by forcing Prussia's admission to the first rank of powers: *Wars of Frederick the Great:* p. 358. However, *forcing* change by aggressive war is referred to in diplomatic history and international relations parlance as the policy of a "revisionist" or even revolutionary power, not of a *defensive* or status quo state that accepts an existing and lawful diplomatic order and works within its agreed rules. To claim that Frederick was a defender of the international system of his day is to fall back into the language trap of Louis XIV's assertion of "defensive aggression."

46. Frederick II, "Anatomy of Battle," in Jay Luvaas, editor, *Frederick the Great on the Art of War* (New York: Da Capo, 1999): pp. 139–169.

47. Citino, *German Way of War*: pp. 38–51; Showalter, *Wars of Frederick the Great*: pp. 45–50; Franz Szabo, *The Seven Years' War in Europe, 1756–1763* (New York: Routledge, 2008): p. 5, 28, 67.

48. *Petite guerre* was known as *partizan* war in the Balkans, *kleine Krieg* ("small war") in Germany, and from the early 19th century as *guerrilla* ("small war"), from the Peninsular War in Spain (1808–1813). On this sometimes underappreciated aspect of 18th-century warfare, see Sandrine Picaud-Monnerat, *La petite guerre au XVIIIe siècle* (Paris: Economica, 2010).

49. The *Militärgrenze* (*vojna krajina* or *vojna granica*) or "military frontier" was established in 1527 by Ferdinand I as a zone of military obligation undertaken by Serbs and Bosnian Vlachs migrating away from the advance of the Ottoman Empire. He allowed them to settle and stay in return for protecting the frontier. Garrisons of local troops spared the Habsburg treasury while redirecting violent "bandit" energies back against the Ottomans. It was a band 20–60 miles wide and over 1,000 miles (1,600 km) long. During the 17th–18th centuries, it was measled with 90 fortresses, mostly rudimentary ones rather than full-bastioned artillery forts. It was guarded by *Grenzer*. See Rothenberg, *Military Border.*

50. Citino, *German Way of War*: p. 49–50.

51. Showalter, *Wars of Frederick the Great*: pp. 74–76.

52. Browning, *War of the Austrian Succession*: pp. 213–218; Citino, *German Way of War*: pp. 52–62; Weigley, *Age of Battles*: pp. 174–175.

53. Browning, *War of the Austrian Succession*: pp. 257–363.

54. Weigley, *Age of Battles*: pp. 176; Gat, *Military Thought*: p. 40.

55. Bismarck once said: "The whole of the Balkans is not worth the bones of a single Pomeranian grenadier." On the recovered bones of an actual Russian grenadier killed at Kunersdorf in the war Frederick provoked, see Grzegorz Podruczny, "Lone Grenadier: An Episode from the Battle of Kunersdorf, 12 August 1759," *Journal of Conflict Archaeology* 9/1 (2014): pp. 33–47.

56. Jürgen Luh, "Frederick the Great and the First World War," in Danley, *Seven Years' War*: pp. 1–22. Luh partly exonerates Frederick, saying every history of the war is wrong and that it really broke out on May 28, 1754, at Lake Erie (p. 3). It is a quixotic date and argument, especially as he later notes that Frederick was planning war all along but was unsure which side he would take, and that "Frederick started the war on the European continent" (p. 16). More reliable is Asprey, *Frederick the Great*: pp. 425–559.

57. Starkey, "Philosophes," pp. 23–24. On the many theaters of war 1756–1763, see the compelling collection Danley, *Seven Years' War*. On logistics, see Schumann and Schweizer, *Seven Years' War*: pp. 91–129. For one example of the influence of press and politics, see Mark Danley, "The British Political Press and Military Thought during the Seven Years' War," in idem, *Seven Years' War*: pp. 359–398. Quoted at p. 129.

58. Hamish Scott, "The Seven Years' War and Europe's *ancien régime*," *War in History* 18/4 (2011): pp. 429–430; Starkey, "Philosophes," p. 31; Citino, *German Way of War*: pp. 71. The definitive two-volume study of Austria and the war in Europe is Christopher Duffy, *Instrument of War: The Austrian Army in the Seven Years' War* (Chicago: Emperor's Press, 2000); idem, *Force of Arms: The Austrian Army in the Seven Years' War* (Chicago: Emperor's Press, 2008).

59. Michael Roberts, *The Age of Liberty: Sweden, 1756–1763* (Cambridge: Cambridge University Press, 1986): pp. 15–58, but especially 43–45; Patrik Winton, "Sweden and the Seven Years' War, 1756–1763: War, Debt, and Politics," *War in History* 19/1 (2012): pp. 5–31; Marian Füssel, "'*Féroces et barbares?*' Cossacks, Kalmyks and Russian Irregular Warfare during the Seven Years' War," in Danley, *Seven Years' War*: pp. 243–262.

60. Szabo, *Seven Years' War*: pp. 24–29.

61. Ibid., pp. 36–59; Citino, *German Way of War*: pp. 67–70. Delbrück was scathing about Frederick's performance at Kolin in *Art of War*, Vol. 4: p. 344.

62. Citino, *German Way of War*: pp. 72–75; Christopher Duffy, *Prussia's Glory: Rossbach and Leuthen, 1757* (Chicago: Emperor's Press, 2003): pp. 7–35.

63. Ibid., pp. 36–64.

64. Robert Citino ranks this movement and attack among "the greatest moments in the history of the horse arm." *German Way of War*: p. 79.

65. Ibid., pp. 78–81; Szabo, *Seven Years' War*: pp. 94–98; Showalter, *Wars of Frederick the Great*: pp. 177–192; Duffy, *Wars of Frederick the Great*: pp. 174–176; idem, *Military Life*: pp. 134–143; idem, *Prussia's Glory*: pp. 65–90; Asprey, *Frederick the Great*: pp. 464–473.

66. Citino *German Way of War*: pp. 83–90; Duffy, *Prussia's Glory*: pp. 138–175.

67. Szabo, *Seven Years' War*: pp. 159–169. On maneuvers after the battle: pp. 240–255.

68. A late-19th-century German print echoing the bloodless Enlightenment sensibility is *Prussian Infantry Advance at Leuthen* by Carl Röchling (1890). Russian painters remembered Zorndorf as a storm of war, as in *Battle of Zorndorf* (1852) by Alexander Kotzebue. Russian painted memory from the mid-19th century is not as often romantic or heroic. For example, Kotzebue's *Battle of Kunersdorf* (1848) is full of chaos, confusion and pathos.

69. Quoted in Citino, *German Way of War*: p. 99.

70. By the 1790s, horse artillery also supported infantry. Marquis de Lafayette called it "flying artillery." It was very expensive and not adopted by France until 1791. McConachy, "Napoleonic Artillery Tactics," p. 623.

71. Blanning, *Frederick the Great*: p. 256–258, quoted at pp. 257, 258.

72. On the building expense and hard logistics of this long war, see Schumann and Schweizer, *Seven Years War*: pp. 91–129.

73. Blanning, *Frederick the Great*: p. 282; and Szabo, *Seven Years' War*: pp. 48–98, passim, 313, 382.

74. Szabo, *Seven Years' War*: pp. 285–291, 312–335, 352–373; Duffy, *Army of Frederick the Great*: pp. 194–196, 235; Frederick II, "The New War of Positions," in Luvaas, *Frederick the Great on the Art of War*: pp. 263–305.

75. Szabo, *Seven Years War*: pp. 374–422.

76. Ibid., pp. 280–281.

77. Voltaire: "God is always on the side of the big battalions."

78. On Frederick as cornered predator and the military defeat of Prussia, see Szabo, *Seven Years' War*: pp. 203–255; 328–373. On his cult of admirers, see Blanning, *Frederick the Great*: pp. 496–501.

79. Citino, *German Way of War*: pp. xi–xii, and most insightfully pp. 64–66; also Peter Paret, "Clausewitz and Schlieffen as Interpreters of Frederick the Great," *Journal of Military History* 76/3 (2012): p. 837–845; Reed Browning, "New Views on the Silesian Wars," *Journal of Military History* 69/2 (2005): pp. 532–533.

80. On the depth of Frederick's gamble in 1756, see Szabo, *Seven Years' War*: pp. 36–88.

81. See Jonathan R. Dull, *The French Navy and American Independence: A Study of Arms and Diplomacy, 1774–1787* (Princeton University Press, 2015); Ronald Hoffman and Peter J. Albert, editors, *Diplomacy and Revolution: The Franco-American Alliance of 1778* (Washington: Historical Society, 1981); Jeremy Black, *Fighting for America: The Struggle for Mastery in North America, 1519–1871* (Bloomington: Indiana University Press, 2011): Chapters 7 and 8; idem, *Fate of a Great Power*: pp. 128–147.

CHAPTER 7

1. A surpassing biography is Philip Dwyer, *Napoleon: The Path to Power* (New Haven: Yale University Press, 2008) and *Napoleon: Citizen Emperor* (New Haven: Yale University Press, 2015). Also see Alan Schom, *Napoleon Bonaparte* (New York: Harper Collins, 1997), and Patrice Gueniffey, *Bonaparte, 1769–1802* (Cambridge: Belknap, 2015).

2. The literature on the causes of the French Revolution is immense. See for example the essays in Thomas Kaiser and Dale Van Kley, editors, *From Deficit to Deluge: Origins of the French Revolution* (Stanford: Stanford University Press, 2011).

3. For the perspective of international history, locating causes of the French Revolution in errors of diplomacy rather than domestic burdens and blunders, see Paul Schroeder, *The Transformation of European Politics, 1763–1848* (Oxford: Clarendon, 1994): pp. 1–52. Also T. W. C. Blanning, *The French Revolutionary Wars, 1787–1802* (New York: Hodder, 1996) and *Origins of the French Revolutionary Wars* (New York: Longman, 1986). Blanning argues that the war radicalized the Revolution rather than the reverse.

4. Timothy Tackett, "The Flight to Varennes and the Coming of the Terror," *Réflexions Historiques* 29/3, *Violence and the French Revolution* (Fall 2003): pp. 469–493.

5. Schroeder, *Transformation of European Politics*: pp. 53–99.

6. Famously assassinated in 1793 by the Girondin Charlotte Corday, for his role in the September Massacres. See the death portrait by Jacques-Louis David—7QGjl9R141MCBw at Google Cultural Institute.

7. Timothy Tackett, "Rumor and Revolution: The Case of the September Massacres," *French History and Civilization* (2011): pp. 54–64; Blanning, *Revolutionary Wars*: pp. 71–82.

8. Arno Mayer, *The Furies: Violence and Terror in the French and Russian Revolutions* (Princeton: Princeton University Press, 2000): pp. 171–226.

9. Alain Gérard, "La Vendée: Répression, ou terrorisme d'État?" *La Revue administrative* 60.360 (2007): pp. 574–577; I. A. Gérard, *"Par principe d'humanité": La Terreur et la Vendée* (Paris: Fayard, 1995); Mayer, *The Furies*: pp. 323–370; Hervé Coutau-Bégarie and Charles Doré, editors, *Histoire militaire des Guerres de Vendée* (Paris: Economica, 2010).

10. On the Terror, the army, and the war to 1794, see Owen Connelly, *Wars of the French Revolution and Napoleon, 1792–1815* (New York: Routledge, 2006): pp. 40–67.

11. Guns of the *système Gribeauval*, introduced by mid-18th century artillery reformer Lieutenant General Jean Baptiste Vaquette de Gribeauval, were standardized under a new production system that cast excellent but lighter and more mobile field cannon with good range. They were the best battle cannon of the era. René Chartrand, *Napoleon's Guns: 1792–1815*, Vol. I (Oxford: Osprey, 2003): pp. 3-14, 33-34, 44-45.

12. On skirmish tactics, see Paddy Griffith, *The Art of War of Revolutionary France, 1789–1802* (London: Greenhill, 1998): pp. 208, 214, 220–225. On cavalry, see Rory Muir, *Tactics and the Experience of Battle in the Age of Napoleon* (London: St. Edmundsbury, 1998): pp.105–139.

13. David Chandler portrays Napoleon as a genius in *Campaigns of Napoleon: The Mind and Method of History's Greatest Soldier* (New York: Macmillan, 1995): pp. 133–204. Although much more critical, Owen Connelly still uses "military genius" and "battlefield genius" in the opening two pages of *Blundering to Glory: Napoleon's Military Campaigns* (Wilmington: Scholarly Resource, 1984): pp. 1–2. An analytical middle ground is provided by Geoffrey Ellis, *The Napoleonic Empire*, 2nd ed. (London: MacMillan, 2003): pp. 73–80. Russell Weigley, ill-disposed to the idea of decisive battle or decisiveness in war in almost any circumstance, nonetheless admires Napoleon's technical art of war in *Age of Battles*: pp. 354–398. An older, denser study informed by direct command experience as a senior British officer in World War II is James Marshall-Cornwall, *Napoleon as Military Commander* (London: Penguin, 2002).

14. Quoted in Carter Malkasian, *A History of Modern Wars of Attrition* (Westport: Praeger, 2002): p. 3. Napoleon's focus is reminiscent of Isaiah Berlin's famous essay *The Hedgehog and the Fox* (Princeton: Princeton University Press, 2013).

15. For example, Bruno Colson grafts Napoleon's hodgepodge sayings and widely scattered thoughts onto Clausewitz's systematizing, even mimicking the eight-part structure of *On War* in idem., editor, *Napoleon on War* (Oxford: Oxford University Press, 2015). It is a poor fit.

16. Starkey, "Philosophes," p. 36, 43–45; R. R. Palmer, "Frederick the Great, Guibert, Bulow: From Dynastic to National War," in Paret, *Modern Strategy*: pp. 105–113; Linda Colley, "Whose Nation? Class and National Consciousness in Britain 1750–1830," *Past & Present* 113 (1986): pp. 97–117.

17. Lynn, *Battle*: pp. 183–188; Jordan R. Hayworth, "Evolution or Revolution on the Battlefield? The Army of the Sambre and Meuse in 1794," *War in History* 21/2 (2014): pp. 170–192.

18. A survey study is Marie-Cécile Thoral, *From Valmy to Waterloo: France at War, 1792–1815* (New York: Palgrave, 2011).

19. Bien, "Reform, Reaction and Revolution," pp. 68–98.

20. On political origins of the *levée*, see Scott Lytle, "Robespierre, Danton, and the *levée en masse*," *Journal of Modern History* 30/4 (1958): pp. 325–337; text available at http://tofindtheprinciples. blogspot.com/2010/08/23-august-1793-revolutionary-france.html and reprinted in John Lynn, *Bayonets of the Republic: Motivation and Tactics in the Army of Revolutionary France, 1791–1794* (Boulder, CO: Westview Press, 1996): p. 56.

21. On the complex origins of the *levée* decree in the wider struggle between Danton and Robespierre, see Lytle, "*Levée en masse*," pp. 325–337. On the *levée* as political and military tool of the state, see Wolfgang Kruse, "Revolutionary France and the Meanings of Levée en Masse," in Roger Chickering and Stig Förster, editors, *War in an Age of Revolution, 1775–1815* (Cambridge: Cambridge University Press, 2010): pp. 299–312. A case study of implementation at the local level is Annie Crépin, *Révolution et Armée Nouvelle en Seine-et-Marne, 1791–1797* (Paris: Editions du CTHS, 2008): pp. 121–135.

22. Alan Forrest, "*La patrie en danger*: The French Revolution and the First *Levée en masse*," in Daniel Moran and Arthur Waldron, editors, *The People in Arms: Military Myth and National Mobilization Since the French Revolution* (Cambridge: Cambridge University Press, 2003): pp. 18–19.

23. On artillery from casting to movement to tactics, see Kevin Kiley, *Artillery of the Napoleonic Wars* (London: Greenhill, 2004), and Ken Adler, *Engineering the Revolution: Arms and Enlightenment in France, 1763–1815* (Chicago: University of Chicago Press, 2010).

24. Günther Rothenberg, *The Art of Warfare in the Age of Napoleon* (Bloomington: Indiana University Press, 1978): p. 99. This was a more common occurrence in the Russian Army in 1917 and in the Red Army early in the Russian Civil War. Republican armies in the Spanish Civil War experienced similar issues with ideologically indoctrinated troops. On difficulty with discipline and training in an atmosphere of radical egalitarianism, see George Orwell, *Homage to Catalonia* (1938), especially Chapter 3.

25. Rothenberg, *Art of Warfare*: pp. 110–113; Maxime Weygand, *Histoire de l'armée française* (Paris: Flammarion, 1961): pp. 210–211; Hoffman Nickerson, *The Armed Horde, 1793–1939* (New York: Putnam, 1940): pp. 74–75; Blanning, *French Revolutionary Wars*: pp. 71–127; Griffith, *Art of War*: pp. 80–85, 175–187, 199–206, 212–217. French Marxist historians especially pointed to revolutionary *élan* as a sufficient explanation.

26. Key works are Jean-Paul Bertaud, *La Révolution armée: Les soldats-citoyens et la Révolution française* (Paris: Laffont, 1979); Lynn, *Bayonets of the Republic*; and as a synthesis, Connelly, *Wars of the French Revolution*. Also see Michael Hughes, *Forging Napoleon's Grande Armée: Motivation, Military Culture, and Masculinity in the French Army, 1800–1808* (New York: New York University Press, 2012): pp. 17–107.

27. Rafe Blaufarb, *The French Army, 1750–1820: Careers, Talent, Merit* (Manchester: Manchester University Press, 2003): pp. 133–193.

28. Lynn, *Bayonets of the Republic*: pp. 21–40, 163–184. Lynn's focus is the *Armée du Nord*, largest of 11 French frontier armies, but his penetrating conclusions have wider application.

29. Alan Forrest, *Conscripts and Deserters: The Army and French Society during the Revolution and Empire* (Oxford: Oxford University Press, 1989): pp. 43–73; 169–186.

30. Bertaud, *La Révolution armée*: p. 100, 191. The *levée* marked a dividing line for a century of fierce ideological, political and budgetary struggle between conservative proponents of professionalization and left-radical advocates of a citizen militia, of reliance on a conscript and republican army. Each side invoked 1793 as iconic to its warning or praise. The debate was critically important before the Franco-Prussian War of 1870–1871 and again before World War I.

31. Alan Forrest, " L'armée de l'an II: La levée en masse et la création d'un mythe républicain," *Annales Historiques de la Révolution française* 335.1 (2004): pp. 111–130; idem, "*La patrie en danger*": pp. 8–32. On generals and officers in the Napoleonic era, see Muir, *Tactics*: pp. 141–192. On revolutionary vs. conservative military cultures, see John Lynn, "Toward an Army of Honor: The Moral Evolution of the French Army, 1789–1815," *French Historical Studies* 16/1 (1989): p. 164. On Austria and the revolutionary challenge, see Charles Ingrao, *The Habsburg Monarchy, 1618–1815* (Cambridge: Cambridge University Press, 2000): pp. 220–241.

32. Bertaud, *La Révolution armée*: p. 217. Variegated figures in Lynn, *Bayonets of the Republic*: pp. 49–57.

33. Alan Forest, "The Logistics of Revolutionary War in France," in Chickering, *Age of Revolution*: pp. 177–196; Jacques Godechot, *Les institutions de la France sous la Révolution et l'Empire* (Paris: Presses Universitaires de France, 1968): pp. 361–363, 367; "Introduction," in Donald Stoker et al., editors, *Conscription in the Napoleonic Era* (Abingdon: Routledge, 2009): pp. 1–2; Frederick Schneid, editor, *Warfare in Europe, 1792–1815* (London: Ashgate, 2007): pp. xv–xvi. Britain did not carry nearly so great a land army burden. It used subsidies to instead hire

foreign armies and sustain alliances that balanced against France in land warfare, while the Royal Navy dominated at sea. Christopher Hall, *British Strategy in the Napoleonic War, 1803–1815* (Manchester: Manchester University Press, 1992); Martin Robson, *A History of the Royal Navy: The Napoleonic Wars* (New York: I. B. Tauris, 2014).

34. Connelly, *Blundering to Glory*: p. 84.

35. Lynn, *Bayonets of the Republic*: pp. 43–118; 163–260; 278–286; Bertaud, *La Révolution armée*, loc. cit.

36. Howard Brown, "Politics, Professionalism, and the Fate of Army Generals after Thermidor," *French Historical Studies* 19 (1995): pp. 132–152.

37. Peter Mezhiritsky, *On the Precipice: Red Army Leadership and the Road to Stalingrad, 1931–1942* (Solihull: Helion, 2012); Geoffrey Roberta, *Stalin's General* (New York: Random House, 2012).

38. On soldier understanding that this was not literally true, see Jean Morvan's *Le Soldat imperial* (Paris: Plon-Nourrit, 1904): pp. 435–443.

39. Connelly, *Blundering to Glory*: p. 152–153.

40. Jean-Paul Bertaud, *La Vie quotidienne des soldats de la Révolution, 1789–1799* (Paris: Hachette littérature, 1985): pp. 114–115; 290–292 and passim.

41. Morvan quoted in Lynn, "Army of Honor," p. 172.

42. Ibid., pp. 152–173. See also Owen Connelly, "A Critique of John Lynn's 'Toward an Army of Honor: The Moral Evolution of the French Army, 1789–1815,'" *French Historical Studies* 16/1 (1989): 174–179. Arguing against so clear a break from Robespierre's concept of *virtu* to Napoleon's inculcation of honor is John Elting, *Swords Around a Throne: Napoleon's Grande Armée* (New York: Da Capo, 1997). Also see Jean-Paul Bertaud, *Quand les enfants parlaient de gloire: L'armée au coeur de la France de Napoléon* (Paris: Aubier, 2006).

43. On the mythology of patriotic death in France, see Lynn, *Bayonets of the Republic*: pp. 173–176. On the new republican patriotism and its fighting myth and legacy, see Forrest, "Mythe Républicain," pp. 111–130.

44. Connelly, *Wars of the French Revolution*: pp 8–39.

45. A clear, concise discussion is Paddy Griffith, *Forward into Battle: Fighting Tactics from Waterloo to the Near Future* (Novato, CA: Presidio, 1990): pp. 12–49. Also see Brent Nosworthy, *With Muskets, Cannon and Sword: Battle Tactics of Napoleon and His Enemies* (London: Hippocrene, 1995).

46. Griffith notes that because musketry was less than decisive, columns took less accurate fire and fewer casualties than is often assumed. *Forward into Battle*: p. 37. On Napoleon's scrambling opportunism in the first Italian campaign, see Connelly, *Wars of the French Revolution*: pp. 77–96; Rothenberg, *Art of Warfare*: pp. 98–126. On later campaigns, see Frederick Schneid, *Napoleon's Italian Campaigns: 1805–1815* (Westport: Praeger, 2002).

47. Quoted in Lynn, *Battle*: p. 199.

48. The clearest, most concise critique of Napoleon's habit of "scrambling" recovery from setbacks and defeats as comprising the core of his warcraft is Connelly, *Blundering to Glory*: pp. 23–50, 77–92.

49. Gérard Bouan, *La premiere campagne d'Italie* (Paris: Économica, 2011).

50. Martin van Creveld, "Napoleon and the Dawn of Operational Warfare," in idem and John Olsen, editors, *The Evolution of Operational Art from Napoleon to the Present* (Oxford: Oxford University Press, 2011): pp. 9–34.

51. On Egypt, the strangest of Napoleon's campaigns, see Connelly, *Wars of the French Revolution*: pp. 51–62, and Chandler, *Campaigns of Napoleon*: Part IV, "Oriental Interlude." On Italy, see Blanning, *French Revolutionary Wars*: pp. 221–225; and Connelly, pp. 107–117.

52. See *Consecration of the Emperor* at http://louvre.fr.

53. Uncritical admiration of the patriotic sort, originally identified with *Grande Armée* veterans, became known as "chauvinism" after a (possibly fabled) fanatic named Nicolas Chauvin. The French original is even more revealing: "*idolatrie napoléonienne.*" *Oxford English Dictionary*.

54. See Joseph Clarke, "'Valor Knows Neither Age nor Sex': *Recueil des Actions Héroïques* and the Representation of Courage in Revolutionary France," *War in History* 20/1 (2013): pp. 50–75, and Peter Paret, *Imagined Battles: Reflections of War in European Art* (Chapel Hill: University of North Carolina Press, 1997).

55. A broader view is Robert L. Jackson, "Napoleon in Russian Literature," *Yale French Studies* 26, *The Myth of Napoleon* (1960): pp. 106–118.

56. In 1804, the young noble was kidnapped in Baden and shot for treason in France, condemned by a secret tribunal for a part in a planned Bourbon coup he never played in fact. It was an assassination by trial, to intimidate all Bourbons who hoped for a Restoration and to frighten with ruthlessness all Europe into accepting a new dynasty and the Empire that Napoleon was about to declare. It was not the only judicial murder of his reign, just the most infamous.

57. On propaganda, see David's images of Napoleon in Rabb, *The Artist and the Warrior*: pp. 152–158 and http://www.ngv.vic.gov.au/napoleon. Antoine-Jean Gros evokes Jeanne d'Arc in *Bonaparte sur le pont d'Arcole* (1801), while in *Bataille d'Aboukir* (1806) dying Mamluks in Egypt implore Napoleon's semi-divine mercy while French troops slaughter all around him.

58. Paul W. Schroeder, "Napoleon's Foreign Policy: A Criminal Enterprise," *Journal of Military History* 54/2 (1990): pp. 147–162. Also see Black, *Fate of a Great Power*: pp. 178–196; Alexander Grab, *Napoleon and the Transformation of Europe* (New York: Palgrave, 2003): pp. 19–33, 197–203.

59. David, *Napoleon crossing the Alps*, available at http://www.histoire-image.org/photo/zoom/ben11_david_001f.jpg.

60. Marie Louise, Empress of the French from 1810 to 1814 and mother of Napoléon François Bonaparte, styled by his father "King of Rome." Both left France for good in April 1814. She died in 1847. He died in 1832, at age 21.

61. Schroeder, "Criminal Enterprise," p. 155. Also see Frederick Kagan, *The End of the Old Order: Napoleon and Europe, 1801–1805* (New York: Da Capo, 2006).

62. Undeterred, Vincent Hawkins and T. N. Dupuy in "Napoleon in Victory and Defeat," in *Understanding Defeat*: pp. 93–118, report in sports-score style that out of 55 "major or significant battles . . . he won forty-eight, drew three, and lost four." As for the losses, including those of his last four campaigns in 1814, these can be attributed to the fact that Napoleon "got precious little help from the French populace." Yet he "demonstrated that his military genius had not dimmed." It seems *idolatrie napoléonienne* lived long after, among some military historians.

63. James Charleton, editor, *The Military Quotation Book* (New York: St. Martin's, 2013): p. 5. Connelly writes: "Napoleon was a military genius . . . His other critical advantages were his awesome energy; his ability to scramble; to make his men follow him, to hit again and again; and his ability to accept defeat . . . [He] also owed much to the ineptitude of his enemies and to luck . . . Finally he had superb subordinates." *Blundering to Victory*: p. 1.

64. Charles Esdaile, *Napoleon's Wars: An International History* (London: Penguin, 2007): pp. 154–208; Frederick Schneid, *Napoleon's Conquest of Europe: The War of the Third Coalition* (Westport: Praeger, 2005): pp. 37–62; Connelly, *Blundering to Glory*: pp. 80–82; David Gates, *The Napoleonic Wars, 1803–1815* (New York: Hodder, 1997): pp. 15–37; Chandler, *Campaigns of Napoleon*: pp. 381–442.

65. John Lynn too admiringly argues that it was on the slopes of the Pratzen at Austerlitz that "Napoleon achieved his masterpiece, and in doing so changed the European concept of battle itself." Even leaving aside the usual euphemistic analogy of battlefield slaughter to the "art of war," that conclusion surely goes much too far. *Battle*: pp. 179–180.

66. Schneid, *Napoleon's Conquest of Europe*: pp. 91–144; Esdaile, *Napoleon's Wars*: pp. 209–253. A detailed account is Christopher Duffy, *Austerlitz, 1805* (Hamden: Archon, 1977).

67. Connelly, *Wars of the French Revolution*: p. 128.

68. On diplomacy from Austerlitz to Tilsit, see Schroeder, *Transformation of European Politics*: pp. 287–323.

69. Narrative of the campaign in Chandler, *Campaigns of Napoleon*: pp. 443–508, and Gates, *Napoleonic Wars*: pp. 48–69. Napoleon quoted in Connelly, *Blundering to Glory*: p. 116. Also see the campaign reconstruction by a French officer based on after-action reports: Scott Bowden, translator, *Napoleon's Apogee: Pascal Bressonnet's Tactical Studies 1806: Saalfeld, Jena and Auerstädt* (Madison: Military History Press, 2009).

70. Entitled on the Louvre web site *The Compassionate Emperor*, www.louvre.fr. Also see David O'Brien, "Propaganda and the Republic of the Arts in Antoine-Jean Gros's *Napoléon Visiting the Battlefield of Eylau the Morning after the Battle*," *French Historical Studies* 26/2 *French History in*

the Visual Sphere (2003): pp. 281–314. On casualties, see Michel Roucaud, "La mort dans les armées napoléoniennes: Du combat au traumatisme," in Hervé Drévillon et al., editors, *Guerres et armées napoléoniennes: Nouveaux regards* (Paris: Ministère de la Défense-DMPA 2013).

71. Quoted in Connelly, *Blundering to Glory*: p. 110; Citino, *German Way of War*: pp. 120–127; Gates, *Napoleonic Wars*: pp. 69–82.

72. Chandler, *Campaigns of Napoleon*: pp. 559–584; Esdaile, *Napoleon's Wars*: pp. 282–287. On artillery tactics, see Muir, *Tactics*: pp. 29–50.

73. On diplomacy from Tilsit to 1812, see Schroeder, *Transformation of European Politics*: pp. 384–442.

CHAPTER 8

1. Dorothée Malfoy-Noël, "Le baptême du feu: Faire ses premières armes dans les armées napoléoniennes," and Vladimir Brnadić, "Gagner les cœurs et les esprits: Officiers et soldats illyriens de l'armée napoléonienne, 1809–1814," both in Natalie Petiteau, Jean-Marc Olivier and Sylvie Caucanas, editors, *Les Européens dans les guerres napoléoniennes* (Toulouse: Privat, 2012).

2. The classic works on life and death in Napoleon's armies are Marcel Baldet, *La Vie quotidienne dans les armées de Napoleon* (Paris: Hachette, 1964), and Maurice Choury, *Les Grognards et Napoleon* (Paris: Librairie académique Perrin, 1968). Choury sees most peasants in uniform as willingly embracing the Empire and fighting for its values.

3. Bruno Colson, *Le Général Rogniat, ingénieur et critique de Napoléon* (Paris: Economica, 2006): passim.

4. Nosworthy, *Battle Tactics*: pp. 174–181. Strachan, *European Armies*: pp. 51–52: Creveld, *Technology and War*: pp. 94–96. Arguing against this proposition is McConachy, "Napoleonic Artillery Tactics," pp. 617–640. "Napoleon had advocated winning battles at the lowest possible cost in human life: 'all my care will be to gain victory with the lowest possible shedding of blood. My soldiers are my children' . . . His letters immediately after Eylau [display] a sudden realization . . . of the costs of war." Quoted at pp. 638–639. It would be odd in the extreme if Eylau was the first time seeing the aftermath of a field of battle had the power to impress Napoleon's moral sensibility. It seems more likely he was worried principally about lost combat power and feigning the sentimentality.

5. "Introduction," in Donald Stoker et al., editors, *Conscription in the Napoleonic Era* (Abingdon: Routledge, 2009): pp. 1–4; André Corvisier, editor, *Histoire militaire de la France* (Paris: Presses Universitaires de France, 1992): pp. 238–244; Aurélien Lignereux, "Les Européens face à la conscription napoléonienne (1800–1814)," in Petiteau et al., *Les Européens dans les guerres napoléoniennes*: pp. 173–188.

6. Wilson, *German Armies*: pp. 298–330; Martin Kitchen, *A History of Modern Germany, 1800 to the Present*, 2nd ed. (London: Wiley-Blackwell, 2011): pp. 10–17.

7. Strachan, *European Armies*: pp. 8–33; Howard, *War in European History*: pp. 75–93; Larry Addington, *Patterns of War Since the Eighteenth Century* (Bloomington: Indiana University Press, 1994): pp. 19–44; Stoker, *Conscription*: p. 3; and Forrest, *Conscripts and Deserters*: pp. 43–73; 169–186.

8. On national patterns, see the essays by Harold Blanton on France, Dierk Walter on Prussia, Arthur Boerke on Austria, and Frederick Schneid on the general if temporary militarization of all of Europe in Stoker, *Conscription*; and Elise Wirtschafter, "The French Army 1789–1914: Volunteers, Pressed Soldiers and Conscripts," in Zurcher, *Fighting for a Living*.

9. Thomas Hippler, *Soldats et citoyens: Naissance du service militaire en France et en Prusse* (Paris: Presses universitaires de France, 2006). On Germany, Mark Hewitson, "Princes' Wars, Wars of the People, or Total War? Mass Armies and the Question of a Military Revolution in Germany," *War in History* 20 (2013): pp. 452–49, and Peter Paret, *The Cognitive Challenge of War: Prussia 1806* (Princeton: Princeton University Press, 2009). See Christina Moll-Murata and Ulrich Theobald, "Military Service and the Russian Social Order, 1649–1861," in Zurcher, *Fighting for a Living*.

10. Kevin Linch, *Britain and Wellington's Army: Recruitment, Society and Tradition, 1807–1815* (New York: Palgrave, 2011): pp. 3–35, 99–104, 144–145.

11. Blücher has a reputation as a blunt old hussar, a battle-axe to Napoleon's saber and Wellington's clever rapier of tactical possibilities. Michael Leggiere presents him as a highly effective coalition leader who came to aid, or even rescue, Wellington at Waterloo despite terrible Prussian losses two days earlier and the fact that Wellington did not relieve Blücher at Ligny (June 16, 1815). Michael V. Leggiere, *Blücher: Scourge of Napoleon* (Norman: University of Oklahoma Press, 2014).

12. Citino, *German Way of War*: p. 104, 110–119, 127–128; Gates, *Napoleonic Wars*: pp. 86–99; Esdaile, *Wars of Napoleon*: pp. 182–216.

13. Michael Leggiere *Napoleon and Berlin: The Franco-Prussian War in North Germany, 1813* (Norman: University of Oklahoma Press, 2002): pp. 57–58, 89–97, and passim.

14. For the long-term significance of this change, see Stephen Rogers, "August Gneisenau," in David Zabecki, editor, *Chief of Staff*, Vol. 1: *Napoleonic Wars to World War I* (Annapolis: Naval Institute Press, 2008): pp. 43–59. On officers and the General Staff in 1813, see Leggiere, *Napoleon and Berlin*: pp. 99–100, 130–133.

15. Michael V. Leggiere, *Napoleon and the Struggle for Germany: The Franco-Prussian War of 1913*, Vol. 1: *The War of Liberation, Spring 181,* and Vol 2: *The Defeat of Napoleon* (Cambridge: Cambridge University press, 2015).

16. Rothenburg, "Habsburg Army," pp. 3–4.

17. For example, see Jac Weller, *Wellington in the Peninsula, 1808–1814* (London: Kaye & Ward, 1969), and David Chandler, *Campaigns of Napoleon*, Chapters 16 and 92.

18. Griffith, *Forward into Battle*: p. 28. Also balanced is Muir, *Tactics and Experience of Battle*: pp. 51–104.

19. April 3, 1811, after a fight at Sabrugal. James Arnold, "A Reappraisal of Column Versus Line in the Peninsular War," *Journal of Military History* 68/2 (2004): pp. 535–552. Wellington quoted at p. 545. Arnold is persuasively critical of Chandler's and Weller's emphasis on British firepower, which he traces to earlier bad work by Charles Oman. The concise rejoinder "musket counting" is his.

20. Jean-Marc Lafon, "Des violeurs et meurtriers ordinaires? Les officiers et soldats napoléoniens en Espagne: Analyse du sac de Castro Urdiales (Cantabrie, 11 mai 1813)," in Petiteau et al., *Les Européens dans les guerres napoléoniennes*: pp. 149–170; Morvan, *Le soldat impérial*, Vol. 2: pp. 485–497.

21. Arnold, "Peninsular War," pp. 549–550. A strong revisionist work is Charles Esdaile, *Fighting Napoleon: Guerrillas, Bandits, and Adventurers in Spain* (New Haven: Yale University Press, 2004). He does not see the *guerilla* contribution in Spain as in any way strategic, whereas David Chandler attributes half of all French casualties to the irregulars, or about 50 every day, in "Regular and Irregular Warfare," *International History Review* 11/1 (1989): pp. 2–13.

22. On Goya, see www.museodelprado.es, especially *Los desastres de la guerra* (ca. 1812) and *El 2 de mayo de 1808 en Madrid*. On Goya's response to French cruelty, see Rabb, *Artist and the Warrior*: pp. 158–165.

23. Similar desperate measures occurred in German garrisons in the Balkans in the last years of World War II, where some units comprised one-armed or one-eyed veterans. Such men were normally invalided out of service, but by that point the Wehrmacht could not spare them.

24. Huw Davies, *Wellington's Wars: The Making of a Military Genius* (New Haven: Yale University Press, 2012): pp. 76–98.

25. A detailed battle history is Rory Muir, *Salamanca, 1812* (New Haven: Yale University Press, 2001).

26. Muir, *Path to Victory*: pp. 43–166, 92–94, 322–323, 366–369, 396–403; idem, "Wellington and the Peninsular War: The Ingredients of Victory," in *Inside Wellington's Peninsular Army, 1808–1814* (Barnsley: Pen & Sword, 2007); Davies, *Wellington's Wars*: pp. 140–213.

27. Arnold, "Peninsular War": p. 551. Also Muir et al., *Wellington's Peninsular Army* (Barnsley: Pen & Sword, 2007), and Connelly, *Wars of the French Revolution*: pp 142–154.

28. See Ian Robertson, *A Commanding Presence: Wellington in the Peninsula, 1808–1814: Logistics, Strategy, Survival* (Stroud: History Press, 2008).

29. Michael Broers, *Napoleon's Other War: Bandits, Rebels, and their Pursuers in the Age of Revolutions* (Oxford: Peter Lang, 2010): p. 1–18; 53–104; 129–180.

30. Esdaile, *Napoleon's Wars*: pp. 346–400. Like Paul Schroeder, Esdaile sees Napoleon as essentially an opportunist and warmonger.

31. An account of Wagram by a senior historian is Günther Rothenberg, *The Emperor's Last Victory: Napoleon and the Battle of Wagram* (London: Cassell, 2005). The definitive campaign history is John Gill's trilogy: *1809 Thunder on the Danube,* 3 volumes (Havertown: Casemate, 2009–2010). A shorter campaign narrative is Gates, *Napoleonic Wars*: pp. 109–146.

32. Gill, *Thunder on the Danube,* Vol. 3: p. 328, and passim.

33. Esdaile, *Napoleon's Wars*: pp. 110–153; Schroeder, *Transformation of European Politics*: pp. 177–230. Rich in detail on the wide social effects of a generation spent at war (1789-1815) is Jenny Uglow, *In These Times: Living in Britain through the Napoleonic Wars* (New York: Farrar, Straus and Giroux, 2014).

34. Blanning, *French Revolutionary Wars*: pp. 189–220; N. A. M. Roger, *The Command of the Ocean: A Naval History of Britain, 1649–1815* (New York: Norton, 2004): pp. 426–441; 528–574; Janet Macdonald, *British Navy's Victualling Board, 1793–1815* (Woodbridge: Boydell, 2012). On the deep roots of Royal Navy power and success over generations of war against France, see David Syrett, *Shipping and Military Power in the Seven Years' War: Sails of Victory* (Exeter: University of Exeter Press, 2008).

35. In a close blockade, ships did not return to port in winter but were provisioned at sea. On the 1793–1815 British blockade and Napoleon's countering Continental System, see Lance Davis and Stanley Engerman, *Naval Blockades in Peace and War: An Economic History Since 1750* (Cambridge: Cambridge University Press, 2006): pp. 25–52; also Macdonald, *Victualling Board*; Roger Knight and Martin Wilcox, *Sustaining the Fleet, 1793–1815: War, the British Navy, and the Contractor State* (Woodbridge: Boydell, 2010); and Roger Morriss, *Foundations of British Maritime Ascendancy: Resources, Logistics and the State* (Cambridge: Cambridge University Press, 2011).

36. Roger Knight, *Britain Against Napoleon: Organization of Victory, 1793–1815* (London: Allan Lane, 2013).

37. On the broad administrative context, see Katherine Aaslestad and Johan Joor, editors, *Revisiting Napoleon's Continental System* (Basingstoke: Palgrave Macmillan, 2015).

38. Napoleon said after his abdication in 1815, while in British custody: "Wherever wood can swim, there I am sure to find this flag of England." Remark attributed at Rochefort, July 1815, before boarding HMS *Bellerophon* as prisoner. Napoleon always referred to his British enemies as "English" and Britain as "England."

39. Hitler would come to the same conclusion in 1940, to attack the Soviet Union even though it was in de facto alliance with Nazi Germany at that time. Neither he nor Napoleon had a war-winning plan or strategy, merely operational ones. Neither man left himself any choice. Each gave in easily to wishful thinking and "decisive campaign" illusions. Yet it is also true that neither man *wanted* to make a different choice.

40. June 27, 1709, old style.

41. An indispensable account is Armand de Caulaincourt, *With Napoleon in Russia,* edited by Jean Hanoteau (New York: William Morrow, 1954). Also see Marie-Pierre Rey, "La grande armée dans la campagne de Russie," in Drévillon, *Guerres et armées napoléoniennes.*

42. Dominic Lieven, *Russia Against Napoleon* (London: Penguin, 2010). Lieven forever dethrones the myth that winter beat Napoleon, explaining the debacle of 1812 more in terms of active Russian efforts than French deficits, and certainly not the weather. A shorter account is David A. Bell, *The First Total War: Napoleon's Europe and the Birth of Warfare as We Know It* (New York: Houghton Mifflin, 2007): pp. 256–262. A strong critique of Bell's use of "total war" for this period is Michael Broers, "The Concept of 'Total War' in the Revolutionary-Napoleonic Period," *War in History* 15 (2008): pp. 247–268.

43. Connelly, *Blundering to Glory*: pp. 163–164. On pillaging, see Griffith, *Art of War*: pp. 51–62; David R. Stone, *A Military History of Russia* (Westport: Praeger, 2006): pp. 100–105.

44. Quoted in Lieven, *Russia Against Napoleon*: pp. 160–161.

45. Quoted in Connelly, *Blundering to Glory*: p. 167. A rich account of the battle performance of bitterly jealous Russian (and German) commanders of the tsar's army is Alexander Mikaberidze, *The Battle of Borodino* (Barnsley: Pen & Sword, 2007).

46. Lieven, *Russia Against Napoleon*: pp. 193–199.

47. Esdaile, *Napoleon's Wars*: pp. 476–478.

48. Quoted in Connelly, *Blundering to Glory*: p. 171.

49. On the burning of Moscow, see Caulaincourt, *With Napoleon in Russia*: pp. 112–119; Lieven, *Russia Against Napoleon*: pp. 213–214.

50. Quoted in Connelly, *Blundering to Glory*: p. 172.

51. http://www.bbc.co.uk/history/ancient/archaeology/napoleon_army_01.shtml.

52. Alexander Mikaberidze, *The Battle of the Berezina* (Barnsley: Pen & Sword, 2010).

53. Schroeder, *Transformation of European Politics*: pp. 445–582; Munro Price, *Napoleon: The End of Glory* (New York: Oxford University Press, 2014): pp. 5–88.

54. Ralph Ashby, *Napoleon Against Great Odds: The Emperor and the Defenders of France, 1814* (Westport: Praeger, 2010): pp. 169–176, 180–189.

55. Price, *End of Glory*: pp. 89–110; Muir, *Path to Victory*: pp. 537–589; Leggiere *Napoleon and Berlin*: pp. 256–277; Gates, *Napoleonic Wars*: pp. 221–254; Lieven, *Russia Against Napoleon*: pp. 437–459; Citino, *German Way of War*: pp. 137–138.

56. Connelly, *Blundering to Glory*: p. 193; Price, *End of Glory*: pp. 110–152.

57. On the 1815 call-up and guards, see Ashby, *Against Great Odds*: pp. 50–51, 79–86.

58. Esdaile, *Napoleon's Wars*: pp. 460–531; Lieven, *Russia Against Napoleon*: pp. 460–493; Ashby, *Against Great Odds*: pp. 124–125, 132–133, 137–139.

59. Price, *End of Glory*: pp. 218–231. A detailed campaign history is Michael Leggiere, *The Fall of Napoleon: The Allied Invasion of France* (Cambridge: Cambridge University Press, 2007): pp. 42–62, 534–554. More favorable to Napoleon is George Nafziger, *The End of Empire: Napoleon's 1814 Campaign* (Solihull: Helion, 2015): pp. 401–490. Also see Andrew Uffindell, *Napoleon 1814: The Defense of France* (Barnsley: Pen & Sword, 2009).

60. Schroeder, *Transformation of European Politics*: pp. 477–582; Esdaile, *Napoleon's Wars*: pp. 532–565.

61. Jacques Houdaille put the figure at 863,000 in "Pertes de l'armée de terre sous le premier Empire, d'après les registres matricules," *Population* 27 (January 1972): pp. 113–114; Gates says 916,000 in *Napoleonic Wars*: p. 271.

62. Connelly, *Blundering to Glory*: pp. 201–217; Esdaile, *Napoleon's Wars*: pp. 545–554. Again, the battle literature on Waterloo is vast. Recent studies include Jeremy Black, *Battle of Waterloo* (New York: Random, 2010); Alan Forrest, *Waterloo* (Oxford: Oxford University Press, 2015). Also see Carl von Clausewitz, *On Waterloo: Clausewitz, Wellington and the Campaign of 1815*, available at www.Clausewitz.com (2010), which reprints Wellington's 1842 memorandum written in response to Clausewitz and other critics at pp. 219–236.

63. He made the comment many years later, on November 2, 1831. Quoted in Philip Henry, *Notes of Conversations with the Duke of Wellington* (New York: Da Capo Press, 1973), originally published 1888.

64. Taking the opposite view is Lt. Colonel James Wasson, who sees a single-handedly made RMA in operations. *Innovator or Imitator: Napoleon's Operational Concepts and the Legacies of Bourcet and Guibert* (Fort Leavenworth: School of Advanced Military Studies, U.S. Army Command and General Staff College, 1998).

CHAPTER 9

1. Gat, *Military Thought*: p. 270–271; Michael Bonura, *Under the Shadow of Napoleon: French Influence on the American Way of Warfare from Independence to the Eve of World War II* (New York: New York University Press, 2012): pp. 11–40.

2. Peter Paret, "Clausewitz and the Nineteenth Century," in Michael Howard, editor, *Theory and Practice of War* (Bloomington: Indiana University Press, 1975): pp. 21–41; Jay Luvaas, "European Military Thought and Doctrine, 1870–1914," ibid., pp. 69–93; Stig Förster, "Facing 'Peoples' War': Moltke the Elder and Germany's Military Options After 1871," *Journal of Strategic Studies* 10/2 (1987): pp. 209–230; Foley, *Path to Verdun*: pp. 14–25, 34–37.

3. Gat argues that this approach to military study grew out of Kant's widely influential theory of art. *Military Thought*: pp. 143–148, 177–180, 197–198. Also see Citino, *German Way of War*: pp. xii–xiii. A very different view is Starkey, *War in the Enlightenment*: pp. 211–216.

4. Clausewitz, *Principles of War* (1812); this short work was a precursor to his later and greater study, *On War*. Available online at http://www.clausewitz.com/readings/Principles/index.htm.

5. Gat, *Military Thought*: p. 212.

6. Clausewitz, *On War*: Book VI, Chapter 30; Gat, *Military Thought*: pp. 201–216.

7. Foley, *Path to Verdun*: pp. 210–228; Hew Strachan, *Clausewitz's On War* (New York: Atlantic, 2007): pp. 106–146.

8. Gat, *Military Thought*: p. 310. On long-term Prussian cultural and political reactions to the French Revolution and how these related to midcentury policy, see William Carr, *Origins of the Wars of German Unification* (New York: Longman, 1991): pp. 1–33.

9. German military thought is portrayed as starkly rigid in Michael Kitchen, "Traditions of German Strategic Thought," *International History Review* 1–2 (1979): pp. 163–190. In contrast, almost reverential is Trevor Dupuy, *A Genius for War: The German Army and General Staff, 1807–1945* (New Jersey: Prentice-Hall, 1977). Scholarly and balanced are Gordon Craig, *The Politics of the Prussian Army* (Oxford: Clarendon Press, 1955); Arden Bucholz, *Moltke, Schlieffen, and Prussian War Planning* (Providence: Berg, 1991); Luvaas, "European Military Thought;" and Gat, *Military Thought*: pp. 314-381

10. Clausewitz, "On Genius," *On War*: Book IV, Chapter 2; Alfred von Schlieffen, "Cannae Studies," pp. 208–218; and see the luminously insightful discussion of Clausewitz and on his impact on 19th century German military thinking in Gat, *Military Thought*: pp. 108–265, 314–381.

11. The best single-volume study in English is Geoffrey Wawro, *The Austro-Prussian War: Austria's War with Prussia and Italy in 1866* (Cambridge: Cambridge University Press, 1997). Closely related in themes and high quality is idem, *Franco-Prussian War: The German Conquest of France in 1870–1871* (Cambridge: Cambridge University Press, 2005).

12. Howard, *War in European History*: p. 75–94, quoted at p. 94; Strachan, *European Armies*: pp. 8–33; Addington, *Patterns of War*: pp. 19–44; Frederick Schneid, "Napoleonic Conscription and the Militarization of Europe?" in Donald Stoker et al., editors, *Conscription in the Napoleonic Era* (Abingdon: Routledge, 2009): pp. 189–205.

13. Helmuth von Moltke, "The Nature of War," in Daniel Hughes, editor, *Moltke on the Art of War: Selected Writings* (Novato, CA: Presidio Press, 1995): p. 33. Foley, *Path to Verdun*: pp. 14–37; Howard, *War in European History*: p. 95.

14. Dennis Showalter, "The Retaming of Bellona: Prussia and the Institutionalization of the Napoleonic Legacy, 1815–1876," *Military Affairs* 44/2 (1980): pp. 57–63; Alfred Vagts, *A History of Militarism: Civilian and Military*, rev. ed. (Westport, CT: Greenwood, 1981): passim; Theodore Ropp, *War in the Modern World* (Baltimore: Johns Hopkins University Press, 1959): pp. 143–160; Howard, *War in European History*: pp. 94–115.

15. Denis Showalter, "Soldiers into Postmasters: The Electric Telegraph as an Instrument of Command in the Prussian Army," *Military Affairs* 37 (1973): pp. 48–52; Angela Fleming and John Hamilton, editors, *The Crimean War as Seen by Those Who Reported It* (New Orleans: Louisiana State University Press, 2009), originally published in 1856 as "Complete History of the Russian War." An older study is Lynn Marshall Case, *French Opinion on War and Diplomacy During the Second Empire* (Philadelphia: University of Pennsylvania Press, 1954).

16. Frederick Schneid, "A Well-Coordinated Affair: Franco-Piedmontese War Planning in 1859," *Journal of Military History* 76 (2012): pp. 395–425; Dennis Showalter, "Railroads, the Prussian Army, and the German Way of War in the Nineteenth Century," in T. G. Otte and Keith Neilson, editors, *Railways and International Politics: Paths of Empire, 1848–1945* (New York: Routledge, 2006): pp. 21–44. Showalter's earlier work superseded an original study by Edwin Pratt, *The Rise of Rail-Power in War and Conquest* (London: P. S. King, 1915).

17. Robert O'Connell, *Of Arms and Men: A History of War, Weapons and Aggression* (Oxford: Oxford University Press, 1990): pp. 189–211.

18. William Reid, *The Lore of Arms: A Concise History of Weaponry* (New York: Facts on File, 1976): pp. 149–150, 224–225; Strachan, *European Armies*: pp. 111–113.

19. Tolstoy served in Crimea as a young officer in 1854, an experience that turned him toward pacifism. British accounts are reprinted in Fleming and Hamilton, *The Crimean War*: pp. 98–168. On the soldier's experience, see Alastair Massie, *National Army Museum Book of the Crimean War: The Untold Stories* (London: Macmillan, 2004). On the long siege of Sebastopol, see Orlando Figes, *The Crimean War* (New York: Holt, 2011): pp. 345–410.

20. On origins, see David Goldfrank, *The Origins of the Crimean War* (New York: Routledge, 2013); Werner Mosse, *The European Powers and the German Question, 1848–1871* (New York: Octagon Books, 1969): pp. 49–79; David Wetzel, *The Crimean War: A Diplomatic History* (New York: Columbia University Press, 1986); Figes, *Crimean War*: pp. 1–129. On strategy, see Andrew Lambert, *The Crimean War: British Grand Strategy Against Russia, 1853–1856* (Farnham: Ashgate, 2011): pp. 113–128.

21. *Ubique, quo fas et gloria ducunt.*

22. Alfred Lord Tennyson, "The Charge of the Light Brigade" (1854). A broad and rich discussion is Holmes, *Redcoat*: pp. 234–243.

23. "They came on in the same old way and we defeated them in the same old way." Remark attributed to Wellington about the Allied victory at Waterloo. An overview written very much in the old "drums and trumpets" style is Robert Edgerton, *Death or Glory: The Legacy of the Crimean War* (Boulder, CO: Westview Press, 1999).

24. Chorus of a popular song dating to 1877, referring to the Crimean War from the point of view of a possible new war in the "Great Game" between Britain and Russia in Central Asia.

25. Winfried Baumgart, *The Crimean War, 1853–1856* (New York: Oxford University Press, 1999): pp. 61–90, 115–166, 203–216; L. G. Beskrovnyi, edited and translated by Gordon E. Smith, *The Russian Army and Fleet in the Nineteenth Century: Handbook of Armaments, Personnel and Policy* (Gulf Breeze: Academic International Press, 1996), originally published in Russian in 1958; René Guillemin, *La guerre de Crimée: Le Tsar de toutes les Russies face à l'Europe* (Paris: Editions France-Empire, 1981); Alain Gouttman, *La guerre de Crimée, 1853–1856* (Paris: SPM, 1995); Figes, *Crimean War*: pp. xviii–xix, 363, 371, 467, 483, 488–489; Baumgart, *Crimean War*: pp. 215–216; John Curtiss, *Russia's Crimean War* (Durham: Duke University Press, 1979).

26. Baumgart, *Crimean War*: pp. 211–213; Figes, *Crimean War*: pp. 355–356, 449; J. N. Westwood, *Endurance and Endeavor: Russian History, 1812–1992*, 4th ed. (Oxford: Oxford University Press, 1993): pp. 71–84, 93–97; "Reforms and Reactions," in Warren B. Walsh, editor, *Readings in Russian History*, Vol. 2 (Syracuse: Syracuse University Press, 1963): pp. 367–533.

27. A building arms race among sectarian Irish led to an arrested British Army mutiny in 1912 that distracted officers and elites before the start of World War I. There followed direct military engagement in Ireland during the Easter Rising of 1916 and the Anglo-Irish War after World War I. On the prewar crisis, see C. J. Bartlett, *Defence and Diplomacy: Britain and the Great Powers, 1815–1914* (Manchester: Manchester University Press, 1993): pp. 59–93.

28. On this complex era in internal German national and Europe-wide diplomatic history, see James J. Sheehan, *German History, 1770–1866* (Oxford: Clarendon Press, 1989): pp. 391–450, 588–729, 853–911; Mosse, *German Question*: pp. 129–145; and Carr, *Origins*: pp. 1–54.

29. Still valuable on the diplomacy of this period is A. J. P. Taylor, *The Struggle for Mastery in Europe, 1848–1914* (Oxford: Clarendon Press, 1954): pp. 99–125; idem, *Bismarck* (New York: Vintage, 1967): pp. 53–123. On Italy, see Frederick Schneid, *The French-Piedmontese Campaign of 1859* (Rome: Ufficio Storico, 2014). Also, Kitchen, *Modern Germany*: pp. 71–112.

30. Mosse, *German Question*: pp. 81–146. On the "good years" of the Second Empire in France, see Alain Plessis, *The Rise and Fall of the Second Empire, 1852–1871* (Cambridge: Cambridge University Press, 1985): pp. 58–151. A broad-ranging cultural critique is David Baguley, *Napoleon III and His Regime: An Extravaganza* (Baton Rouge: Louisiana University Press, 2000).

31. Speech to the Prussian Diet, September 30, 1862.

32. An overview is Kitchen, *Modern Germany*: pp. 113–138. A strong critique of Bismarck as a revolutionary statesman is Lothar Gall, *Bismarck: The White Revolutionary*, Vol. 1 (London: Allen and Unwin, 1986). Also sharply critical is Jonathan Steinberg, *Bismarck: A Life* (Oxford: Oxford University Press, 2011). More favorable is Otto Pflanze, "Realism and Idealism in Historical

Perspective: Otto von Bismarck," in Cathal J. Nolan, editor, *Ethics and Statecraft*, 2nd ed.: pp. 149–164.

33. See Brendan Simms, *The Struggle for Mastery in Germany 1779–1850* (New York: Palgrave, 1998).

34. Jay Luvaas, *Military Legacy of the Civil War: The European Inheritance* (Lawrence: University Press of Kansas, 1988): pp. 119–142; Citino, *German Way of War*: pp. 142–147; Weigley, *The American Way of War* (New York: Macmillan, 1973). pp. 59–91; Antulio Echevarria, *Reconsidering the American Way of War* (Washington: Georgetown University Press, 2014): pp. 32–46; Carol Reardon, *With a Sword in One Hand and Jomini in the Other* (Chapel Hill: University of North Carolina Press, 2012): pp. 17–54, 89–124, 137, and on the "cult of genius," pp. 55–88; Gat, *Military Thought*: pp. 284–292; Michael Bonura, *Under the Shadow of Napoleon* (New York: NYU Press, 2012): pp. 36–37 and passim.

35. Emory Thomas, *The Dogs of War: 1861* (New York: Oxford University Press, 2011): pp. 21–36; 46–48, 50–51, 78–79.

36. Joseph Harsh, *Confederate Tide Rising: Robert E. Lee and the Making of Southern Strategy, 1861–1862* (Kent: Kent State University Press, 1998): pp. 5–10.

37. A superb study is Donald Stoker, *The Grand Design: Strategy and the U.S. Civil War* (Oxford: Oxford University Press, 2010). On logistics, see James Huston, *Sinews of War: Army Logistics 1755–1953* (Washington: Office of the Chief of Military History, 1966): pp. 159–252.

38. The idea of a "rifle revolution" in the American Civil War appeared in John Mahon, "Civil War Infantry Assault Tactics," *Military Affairs* 25 (1961): pp. 57–68. It was widely accepted by historians at first, as in Grady McWhiney and Perry Jamieson, *Attack and Die: Civil War Military Tactics and the Southern Heritage* (Tuscaloosa: University of Alabama Press, 1982): pp. 48–68, and James MacPherson, *Ordeal by Fire* (New York: Knopf, 1982): pp. 193–195. A fundamental challenge to this older thesis argues that the rugged terrain of battlefields and parabolic trajectory of rifled bullets meant that close-order line tactics remained paramount and effective in the American war, resulting in most combat taking place at 100 yards or less for long periods of time. Volume of fire rather than rifled accuracy was what mattered, says Earl Hess in *The Rifle Musket in Civil War Combat: Reality and Myth* (Lawrence: University Press of Kansas, 2008): pp. 9–34, 85–120, 197–216; and idem, *Civil War Infantry Tactics: Combat and Small Unit Effectiveness* (Baton Rouge: Louisiana State University Press, 2015).

39. The main interest of Austria-Hungary in Italy was to prevent Italian unification under Piedmont, but it lacked the military power and diplomatic skill to do so. Geoffrey Wawro, "Austria versus the *Risorgimento*," *European Studies Quarterly* 26 (1996): pp. 7–29. On mobilization, see Showalter, *Railroads and Rifles*: pp. 3 6–37; 48.

40. Quoted in Strachan, *European Armies*: p. 73.

41. Daniel Hughes, "Introduction," in *Moltke on the Art of War*: pp. 5–6. Moltke quoted in Hajo Holborn, "The Prusso-German School: Moltke and the Rise of the General Staff," in Paret, *Modern Strategy*: p. 289.

42. Urlich Wengenroth, "Industry and Warfare in Prussia," in Stig Förster and Jörg Nagler, editors, *On the Road to Total War* (New York: Cambridge University Press, 1997): pp. 263–282. Bismarck preferred the terminology "state-nation" to "nation-state," arguing that what made a power was not common ethnicity or culture (*Kultur*) but political unity under a single sovereign. Pflanze, "Realism and Idealism."

43. Michael Howard, *Franco-Prussian War* (London: Routledge, 2001): pp. 18–28; Carr, *Origins*: pp. 34–88; Dierk Walter, "Roon, the Prussian Landwehr, and the Reorganization of 1859–1860," *War in History* 16/3 (2009): pp. 269–297; Manfred Messerschmidt, "Prussian Army from Reform to War," in Förster and Nagler, *Road to Total War*: pp. 263–282.

44. A. J. P. Taylor, *Bismarck: The Man and the Statesman* (New York: Vintage, 1967): p. 81.

45. Denis Showalter, *Wars of German Unification* (New York: Bloomsbury, 2004): pp. 88–200; Christopher Clark, *Iron Kingdom: The Rise and Downfall of Prussia, 1600–1947* (Cambridge: Belknap, 2006): pp. 518–531.

46. Mosse, *German Question*: pp. 146–252; Taylor, *Bismarck*: pp. 73–81; Wawro, *Austro-Prussian War*: pp. 40–44; Otto Pflanze, *Bismarck and the Development of Germany, 1815–1871*, Vol. 1 (Princeton: Princeton University Press, 1963): pp. 233–261; J. C. Clardy, "Austrian Foreign

Policy during the Schleswig-Holstein Crisis of 1864." *Diplomacy and Statecraft* 2 (July 1991): pp. 254–269; Showalter, *Wars of Unification*: pp. 123–200; Carr, *Origins*: pp. 89–135. A more personality-driven interpretation is David Wetzel, *A Duel of Giants: Bismarck, Napoleon III, and the Origins of the Franco-Prussian War* (Madison: University of Wisconsin Press, 2003).

47. Arthur Coumbe, "Operational Command in the Franco-Prussian War," *Parameters* 21/2 (1991): pp. 86–99. Moltke did not use the term "operations" in the modern sense. Nor did most German writing or thinking yet see operations as a discrete level of activity residing between strategy and tactics. However, the modern usage of "operational level" of war is ubiquitous in the historical and professional literature, as well as genuinely helpful.

48. Günther Rothenberg, "The Habsburg Army and the Nationality Problem in the Nineteenth Century, 1815–1914." *Austrian History Yearbook*: 3/1 (1967): pp. 70–87; Geoffrey Wawro, "Inside the Whale: The Tangled Finances of the Austrian Army, 1848–1866." *War in History* 3 (1966): pp. 42–65. A rich and still highly useful earlier study is Günther Rothenberg, *The Army of Francis Joseph* (West Lafayette: Purdue University Press, 1976).

49. On Moltke's freeing the Prussian Army of Jominian shackles and inculcation instead of the blood and iron spirit of the ideas of Clausewitz, Scharnhorst and Gneisenau, see Gat, *Military Thought*: pp. 310–341.

50. Wawro, *Austro-Prussian War*: pp. 24, 30–35; and idem, "An 'Army of Pigs': The Technical, Social, and Political Bases of Austrian Shock Tactics, 1859–1866," *Journal of Military History* 59 (1995): pp. 407–434.

51. Martin van Creveld, *Command in War* (Cambridge: Harvard University Press, 1985): pp. 103–147.

52. Clausewitz, *On War*: pp. 115–116, 119–121.

53. Howard, *Franco-Prussian War*: pp. 2–3; Showalter, "Railroads," pp. 21–44; idem, *Wars of Unification*: pp. 201–239; Carr, *Origin*: pp. 34–88; Clark, *Iron Kingdom*: pp. 531–535.

54. Moltke, "Importance of Railroads," and "Significance of Telegraphs," in *Moltke on the Art of War*: pp. 107–114.

55. Wawro, *Austro-Prussian War*: pp. 15–16; Holborn, "The Prusso-German School," pp. 281–295.

56. Citino, *German Way of War*: pp. 151–152.

57. John Shy, "Jomini," in Paret, *Modern Strategy*: pp. 143–185; Strachan, *European Armies*: pp. 60–75; Wawro, *Austro-Prussian War*: pp. 18–19; and Holborn, "Prusso-German School," pp. 287–288. Moltke's plans are reprinted in Helmuth von Moltke, *Moltke's Projects for the Campaign of 1866 Against Austria* (London: HMSO, 1907): pp. 3–32.

58. Wawro, *Austro-Prussian War*: pp. 52–65; Clark, *Iron Kingdom*: p. 536–537.

59. Pflanze, *Bismarck*, Vol. 1: pp. 262–365; Wawro, *Austro-Prussian War*: p. 20; Helmuth von Moltke, *Strategy, Its Theory and Application: The Wars for German Unification, 1866–1871* (Westport: Greenwood, 1971).

60. Gordon Craig, *The Battle of Königgrätz: Prussia's Victory over Austria, 1866* (Philadelphia: Lippincourt, 1964): pp. 1–25. Craig did not have access to important German archives and diaries that were rediscovered by Western scholars after the collapse of the Soviet Union. The new information enriches the surpassing study by Geoffrey Wawro, *Austro-Prussian War*: pp. 82–123.

61. Ibid., pp. 126–127.

62. Craig, *Königgrätz*: pp. 26-42, and Arthur Wagner, *The Campaign of Königgrätz* (Westport: Greenwood Press, 1972), reprint of 1889 original: pp. 36–68.

63. Logistics expert Martin van Creveld speculates that had the campaign lasted much longer, supply inadequacies must have seriously hampered Moltke's operations against Austria. Creveld, *Supplying War*: pp. 79–85. Moltke quoted at p. 81.

64. A dissenting view is Clark, *Iron Kingdom*: pp. 539–540.

65. Craig, *Königgrätz*: pp. 43–70; Creveld, *Command in War*: pp. 123–132; Wawro, *Austro-Prussian War*: pp. 124–180.

66. Quoted in ibid., p. 179. Emphasis in original.

67. Ibid., pp. 183–192. Quoted at p. 196. Emphasis in original.

68. Moltke, *Strategy*: pp. 52–54.

69. Craig, *Königgrätz*: pp. 81–89; Wawro, *Austro-Prussian War*: pp. 202–203. Wawro is scathing in criticism of Benedek.

70. Ibid., pp. 208–215.

71. Holborn, "Prusso-German School," p. 294; Wawro, *Austro-Prussian War*: pp. 238–273; Craig, *Königgrätz*: pp. 113–164; Creveld, *Command in War*: pp. 132–140.

72. Craig, *Königgrätz*: pp. 87–112; Wilhelm I quoted in Creveld, *Command in War*: pp. 137–138.

73. Quoted in Craig, *Königgrätz*: p. 111; and Wawro, *Austro-Prussian War*: p. 233. Emphasis in original.

74. Craig, *Königgrätz*: pp. 113–138; Wawro, *Austro-Prussian War*: pp. 242–247. Moltke quoted at p. 247.

75. Dozens of horses and 52 men were killed. A "Battery of the Dead" monument was erected by the Habsburgs in 1914. It is located at Chlum, now in the Czech Republic.

76. Ibid., pp. 250–262, quoted at p. 267.

77. Ibid., pp. 264–274.

78. Citino, *German Way of War*: p. 172.

79. Craig, *Königgrätz*: pp. 99, 113–164. Wawro makes this strongly revisionist but also persuasive criticism of Moltke's decision to attack a day prematurely, denying himself full envelopment. *Austro-Prussian War*: p. 273.

80. Robin Okey, *The Habsburg Monarchy 1765–1918: From Enlightenment to Eclipse* (New York: Palgrave 2000): pp. 157–190; Alan Sked, *The Decline and Fall of the Habsburg Empire, 1815–1918* (New York: Pearson, 2001): pp. 187–238; F. R. Bridge, *From Sadowa to Sarajevo* (London: Routledge, 1972): pp. 1–29; David Blackbourn, *History of Germany, 1780–1918*, 2nd ed. (New York: Wiley-Blackwell, 2003): pp. 171–203.

81. Mosse, *German Question*: pp. 253–290; Pflanze, *Bismarck*, Vol. 1: pp. 314–316, 401–405; Carr, *Origins*: pp. 136–143; Gordon Craig, *Germany 1866–1945* (New York: Oxford University Press, 1978): p. 1–21; Taylor, *Bismarck*: pp. 92–122; idem, *Struggle for Mastery in Europe*: pp. 201–254; Heinrich Friedjung, *The Struggle for Supremacy in Germany, 1859–1866* (London: MacMillan, 1935): pp. 300ff.

82. See, for example, Karl E. Meyer and Shareen Blair Brysac, *Tournament of Shadows: The Great Game and the Race for Empire in Central Asia* (Washington: Counterpoint, 1999).

CHAPTER 10

1. Mosse, *German Question*: pp. 81–146.

2. Carr, *Origins*: pp. 144–202; Showalter, *Wars of Unification*: pp. 285–313; Mosse, *German Question*: pp. 213–332; Pflanze, *Bismarck,* Vol. 1: pp. 419–457.

3. On the collapse of social and reform policies, culminating in a disastrous "Liberal Empire" experiment in 1869–1870, see Alain Plessis, *The Rise and Fall of the Second Empire, 1852–1871* (Cambridge: Cambridge University Press, 1985): pp. 152–167; also Roger Price, *The French Second Empire: An Anatomy of Political Power* (Cambridge: Cambridge University Press, 2005): pp. 255–404.

4. Original text and full context in Edmund Wright, editor, *A Dictionary of World History*, 2nd ed. (Oxford: Oxford University Press, 2007). On general causes of the war and Bismarck's specific duplicity regarding the Ems Dispatch, see Clark, *Iron Kingdom*: pp. 548–550; Taylor, *Bismarck*: pp. 92–122; idem, *Struggle for Mastery in Europe*: pp. 171–205; Wawro, *Franco-Prussian War*: pp. 16–40; Pflanze, *Bismarck,* Vol. 1: pp. 466–469.

5. Otto von Bismarck, Speech to the North German Confederation Reichstag, September 24, 1867; Moltke, "War and Peace," pp. 22–35; quoted at p. 22.

6. Strachan, *European Armies*: pp. 108–115; Wawro, *Franco-Prussian War*: pp. 41–64; Douglas Porch, *Army and Revolution: France, 1815–1848* (London: Routledge, 1974).

7. Eugène Carrias, *La pensée militaire française* (Paris: Presses Universitaires de France, 1960): pp. 232–235; William Serman, *Les origines des officiers français, 1848–1870* (Paris: Publications de la Sorbonne, 1979); Stéphane Audoin-Rouzeau, *1870: La France dans la guerre* (Paris: Armand Colin, 1989): pp. 87–91.

8. Plessis, *Second Empire*: pp. 1–11, 152–167; Price, *French Second Empire*: pp. 41–254; David Baguley, *Napoleon III and His Regime: An Extravaganza* (Baton Rouge: Louisiana University Press, 2000): pp. 118–148.

9. Howard, *Franco-Prussian War*: pp. 30–33; Richard Holmes, *The Road to Sedan: The French Army, 1866–1870* (London: Royal Historical Society, 1984): passim; Wawro, *Franco-Prussian War*: p. 42, 46.

10. Antulio Echevarria, "Helmut von Moltke," in Zabecki, *Chief of Staff*, Vol. 1: pp. 89–108; Dupuy, *Genius for War*: pp. 44–69, 89–109; Walter Görlitz, *History of the German General Staff, 1657– 1945* (New York: Praeger, 1957): passim; Dallas Irvine, "The French and Prussian General Staff Systems before 1870," *Journal of the American Military History Foundation* 2/4 (1938): pp. 192–203.

11. Arden Bucholz, *Moltke, Schlieffen, and Prussian War Planning* (New York: Berg, 1991): pp. 31–57; Wawro, *Franco-Prussian War*: pp. 49–50, 66–67; Richard Holmes, *Road to Sedan*: pp. 165–179; Thomas Adriance, *The Last Gaiter Button: A Study of the Mobilization and Concentration of the French Army in the War of 1870* (Westport: Greenwood Press, 1987): pp. 54–62; Howard, *Franco-Prussian War*: pp. 57–76; E. R. Rocolle, "Anatomie d'une mobilisation," *Revue historique des armées* 2 (1970): pp. 34–69.

12. Irvine, "French and Prussian Staff Systems," p. 192; Bertrand Taithe, *Citizenship and Wars: France in Turmoil, 1870–1871* (London: Taylor & Francis, 2001).

13. Holmes, *Road to Sedan*: pp. 229–231; Howard, *Franco-Prussian War*: p. 94, 96, 188; Wawro, *Franco-Prussian War*: pp. 155–156.

14. Moltke, "Independence of Subordinate Commanders," *Moltke on the Art of War*: pp. 132–133; Wawro, *Franco-Prussian War*: pp. 53–54.

15. Adriance, *Last Gaiter Button*: pp. 20–38; Howard, *Franco-Prussian War*: pp. 29–39; Arpad Kovacs, "French Military Institutions before the Franco-Prussian War," *American Historical Review* 51/2 (1946): pp. 217–235, and Richard Challener, *The French Theory of the Nation in Arms, 1866–1939* (New York: Columbia University Press, 1955): p. 13.

16. Helmuth von Moltke, *Moltke's Military Correspondence, 1870–1871*, Part I: *The War to the Battle of Sedan* (Oxford: Clarendon Press, 1923): pp. 28–33; Dennis Showalter, *Railroads and Rifles*: pp. 40– 51; Bucholz, *Prussian War Planning*: pp. 31–43; Hughes, "Introduction," *Moltke on the Art of War*: p. 14.

17. Wawro, *Franco-Prussian War*: pp. 41–42. The precise figure published by the Great General Staff was 1,183,389. Comparable figures of around 1.2 million are provided in Adriance, *Last Gaiter Button*: pp. 40–41, 63.

18. Moltke, "Infantry," "Cavalry," and "Field Artillery," in *Moltke on the Art of War*: pp. 161–166, 201–208.

19. Chassepot bullets were wrapped in linen rather than paper. All major militaries followed, with linen or brass cartridge ammunition after 1870: Reid, *Lore of Arms*: pp. 149–150, 224–225. Also see Strachan, *European Armies*: pp. 111–113.

20. Adriance, *Last Gaiter Button*: pp. 9–10; Barthélemy Palat, *Histoire de la guerre de 1870–1871* (Paris: Berger-Levrault, 1903–1908): Vol. 2: pp. 228–232; Wawro, *Franco-Prussian War*: p. 58.

21. The *Armée du Rhin* was slated to receive 1,037,555 rifles for its roughly 300,000 men. Adriance, *Last Gaiter Button*: p. 85.

22. Moltke, "Infantry and *Jäger*," in *Moltke on the Art of War*: pp. 201–208.

23. Moltke laid this out clearly in later writings. See his *Strategy, Its Theory and Application: The Wars for German Unification, 1866–1871* (Westport: Greenwood, 1971).

24. Moltke, "1869 Regulations for Large Unit Commanders," *Moltke on the Art of War*: pp. 171–224; Holborn, "Prusso-German School," pp. 281–295; Günter Rothenberg, "Moltke, Schlieffen, and the Doctrine of Strategic Envelopment," ibid., pp. 296–325; Strachan, *European Armies*: pp. 115– 116; Howard, *Franco-Prussian War*: pp. 93–182; Wawro, *Austro-Prussian War*: p. 287.

25. Ibid., pp. 65–84.

26. Ibid., pp. 74–76; Creveld, *Supplying War*: p. 86; Adriance, *Last Gaiter Button*: p. 83, 92–98; 104– 109; *La Guerre de 1870–1871*, Vol. 2: pp. 127–133; Palat, *Histoire de la guerre de 1870–1871*: pp. 158–160.

27. Douglas Fermer, *Three German Invasions of France: The Summer Campaigns of 1870–1914–1941* (Barnsley: Pen & Sword, 2013): Part I: "1870: The Débâcle."

28. Adriance: *Last Gaiter Button*: pp. 49–50.

29. Howard, *Franco-Prussian War*: pp. 45–47, 79, 85–87, 122–126; Adriance: *Last Gaiter Button*: pp. 120–127; Michel Cantal, *La Guerre de 1870* (Paris: Bordas, 1972).

30. Helmuth von Moltke, *The Franco-German War of 1870–1871* (New York: Harper, 1892): pp. 8–14.

31. Still the best short accounts of these frontier battles are Wawro, *Franco-Prussian War*: pp. 85–137, and Howard, *Franco-Prussian War*: pp. 85–138.

32. On cavalry's role in screening and reconnaissance in the 1870 campaign and lesser role in battles dominated by rapid-firing infantry on both sides, see David Dorondo, *Riders of the Apocalypse: German Cavalry and Modern Warfare, 1870–1945* (Annapolis: Naval Institute Press, 2012): Chapter 2.

33. This conclusion emerges clearly from the battle narrative offered in Wawro, *Franco-Prussian War*: pp. 121–137. On the key role of the German guns at Froeschwiller, see Howard, *Franco-Prussian War*: pp. 109–119.

34. Citino, *German Way of War*: p. 187.

35. Wawro, *Franco-Prussian War*: pp. 107–120; Howard, *Franco-Prussian War*: pp. 85–98. Prussian killed and wounded at Spicheren were double the French number, at over 5,000.

36. Wawro, *Franco-Prussian War*: pp. 130–131. Quoted at p. 131 and in Pflanze, *Bismarck*, Vol. 1: p. 483.

37. Isabel Hull, *Absolute Destruction: Military Culture and the Practices of War in Imperial Germany* (Ithaca: Cornell University Press, 2005): pp. 5–90; Raffael Scheck, "Killing of Black Soldiers from the French Army by the Wehrmacht in 1940," *German Studies Review* 28/33 (2005): pp. 595–606; idem, *Hitler's African Victims: The German Army Massacres of Black French Soldiers in 1940* (Cambridge: Cambridge University Press, 2008). More generally, Alan Kramer, *Dynamic of Destruction: Culture and Mass Killing in the First World War* (Oxford: Oxford University Press, 2007): pp. 31–68, 211–229.

38. Howard, *Franco-Prussian War*: pp. 120–121.

39. Ibid., pp. 122–147; Ropp, *War in the Modern World*: pp. 171–172. On the war and revolution, see Price, *French Second Empire*: Adriance: *Last Gaiter Button*: 128–132; Wawro, *Franco-Prussian War*: pp. 75–79.

40. Ibid., pp. 121–137.

41. Ibid., pp. 138–185. Moltke and Roon conversation at p. 160; Moltke, *Franco-German War of 1870–1871*: pp. 48–50; Bucholz, *German Wars*: pp. 139–184.

42. Moltke, "Gravelotte," in *Moltke on the Art of War*: p. 67; Wawro, *Franco-Prussian War*: pp. 164–185.

43. Quoted in Wawro, *Franco-Prussian War*: p. 169; Philip H. Sheridan, *Personal Memoirs of P. H. Sheridan* (New York: C. L. Webster, 1888), Vol. 2: Chapters 16 and 17; Adriance: *Last Gaiter Button*: p. 132.

44. Wawro, *Franco-Prussian War*: p. 174.

45. Howard, *Franco-Prussian War*: pp. 147–149, 163–164, 187–191, 228–229, 260–267.

46. Moltke, *Franco-German War of 1870–1871*: pp. 104–105; Wawro, *Franco-Prussian War*: pp. 244–245.

47. An overview that largely absolves Bazaine of responsibility for the defeat of 1870 is Edmond Ruby and Jean Regnauld, *Bazaine, coupable ou victime? A la lumière de documents nouveaux* (Paris: Peyronnet, 1960). Also see Maurice Beaumont, *Bazaine, les secrets d'un maréchal* (Paris: Imprimerie nationale, 1978): pp. 1811–1888.

48. Adriance: *Last Gaiter Button*: p. 133.

49. Wawro, *Franco-Prussian War*: p. 194.

50. Moltke, *Franco-German War of 1870–1871*: pp. 70–72, 84–88.

51. Howard, *Franco-Prussian War*: pp. 203–223; Wawro, *Franco-Prussian War*: 211–224; Sheridan, *Personal Memoirs*: Chapter 18; Frederick III, *Diaries of the Emperor Frederick during the Campaign of 1866 and 1870–1871* (London: Chapman & Hall, 1902): pp. 89–99.

52. Wawro, *Franco-Prussian War*: 227–228; Frederick III, *Diaries*: p. 99.

53. Wawro, *Franco-Prussian War*: pp. 240–253; Howard, *Franco-Prussian War*: pp. 258–268, 276–277.

54. Rupert Christianson, *Paris Babylon: The Story of the Paris Commune* (New York: Penguin, 1994): pp. 117–166; Stéphane Audoin-Rouzeau, "French Public Opinion in 1871 and the Emergence of Total War," in Förster and Nagler, *Road to Total War*: pp. 393–412; John Merriman, *Massacre: The Life and Death of the Paris Commune of 1871* (New Haven: Yale University Press, 2015).

55. Blum became the first socialist premier of France in 1936, long after coming to prominence during the Dreyfus Affair before World War I. Arrested by Vichy, he was imprisoned by the Nazis at Dachau. He survived the war.

56. Christianson, *Paris Babylon*: pp. 167–272; William Serman, "French Mobilization in 1870," in Förster and Nagler, *Road to Total War*: p. 283–294; Howard, *Franco-Prussian War*: pp. 233–256; On the politics of siege, see Jean Brunet-Moret, *Le Général Trochu, 1815–1896* (Paris: Editions Haussmann, 1955).

57. Ropp, *War in the Modern World*: p. 174; Wawro, *Franco-Prussian War*: pp. 237–238, 256–269, 288–290, 309–310; Howard, *Franco-Prussian War*: pp. 249–256, 374–391.

58. Moltke, "Rapid Decision," *Moltke on the Art of War*: pp. 125–126. He elided this struggle in "The Nature of War," then blamed it all in the French. Ibid., p. 24, 32–33.

59. Foley, *Path to Verdun*: pp. 18–20; Stig Förster, "Facing 'Peoples' War': Moltke the Elder and Germany's Military Options after 1871," *Journal of Strategic Studies* 10/2 (1987): pp. 213–214; Howard, *Franco-Prussian War*: p. 417, 436–437, 445; Hew Strachan, "From Cabinet War to Total War," in Roger Chickering and Stig Förster, editors, *Great War, Total War: Combat and Mobilization on the Western Front, 1914–1918* (Cambridge: Cambridge University Press, 2000): pp. 19–34.

60. Förster, "Facing Peoples' War," pp. 213–214; Foley, *Path to Verdun*: 20; Gerhard Ritter, *The Sword and the Scepter*, Vol. 1: *The Prussian Tradition, 1740–1890* (Coral Gables: University of Miami Press, 1969): pp. 219–223; Showalter, *Wars of German Unification*: pp. 314–340.

61. Taylor, *Struggle for Mastery in Europe*: pp. 212–227; Stig Förster, "The Prussian Triangle of Leadership in Face of Peoples' War," in idem and Nagler, *Road to Total War*: pp. 115–140. On civilian experience, see the rich cultural history by Rachel Chrastil, *The Siege of Strasbourg* (Cambridge: Harvard University Press, 2014), especially Chapters 3, 4, and 5, and idem, *Organizing for War: France, 1870–1914* (Baton Rouge: Louisiana State University Press, 2010): pp. 6–14, 21–24, 31–36, 45–48, 131–133.

62. Wawro, *Franco-Prussian War*: pp. 278–280; 287–290.

63. For connections between German atrocities in 1870 and 1914 (and 1940), see John Horne and Alan Kramer, *German Atrocities, 1914: A History of Denial* (New Haven: Yale University Press, 2001); also Jeff Lipkes, *Rehearsal: The German Army in Belgium, August 1914* (Leuven: Leuven University Press, 2007): pp. 543–574.

64. Wawro, *Franco-Prussian War*: pp. 276–298; Robert Tombs, "The Wars Against Paris," in Förster and Nagler, *Road to Total War*: pp. 541–564.

65. Pflanze, *Bismarck*, Vol. 1: pp. 490–504; Howard, *Franco-Prussian War*: pp. 432–456; Wawro, *Franco-Prussian War*: pp. 299–314; Craig, *Germany, 1866–1945*: pp. 27–37; Steinberg, *Bismarck*: pp. 258–311; Clark, *Iron Kingdom*: pp. 556–595; Carr, *Origins*: pp. 210–213; Mosse, *German Question*: pp. 333–358.

66. On the idea of a general "tactical crisis" and the German solution to it, see Antulio J. Echevarria, *After Clausewitz, German Military Thinkers Before the Great War* (Lawrence: University of Kansas Press, 2001): pp. 13–64; idem, "Heroic History and Vicarious War: Nineteenth-Century German Military History Writing," *The Historian* 59 (1997): pp. 573–590. Also see Strachan, *European Armies*: pp. 89–106.

67. Douglas Porch, *The March to the Marne: The French Army, 1871–1914* (Cambridge: Cambridge University Press, 1981): pp. 23–32; James Stone, "The War-in-Sight Crisis of 1875 Revisited," *Militärgeschichtliche Mitteilungen* 53 (1994): pp. 304–326.

68. Allan Mitchell, "'A Situation of Inferiority': French Military Reorganization after the Defeat of 1870," *American Historical Review* 86 (1981): pp. 49–62; idem, *Victors and Vanquished: The German Influence on Army and Church in France after 1870* (Chapel Hill: University of North Carolina Press, 1984): pp. 29–117.

69. Porch, *March to the Marne*: pp. 105–153, 213–254; Howard, "Men Against Fire," pp. 519–524; Maxime Weygand, *Histoire de l'armée française*: pp. 291–317; Joseph Revol, *Histoire de l'armée française* (Paris: Larousse, 1929): pp. 203–219; Gorce, *French Army*: pp. 1–61; Challener, *Nation in Arms*: pp. 32–79.

70. Foley, *Path to Verdun*: p. 16–23. Moltke quoted at p. 23. Also in Roger Chickering and Stig Förster, editors, *Anticipating Total War: The German and American Experiences* (Cambridge: Cambridge University Press, 1999): p. 347.

71. Studies that portray Moltke as a military genius include Rothenberg, "Doctrine of Strategic Envelopment"; Martin Kitchen, *A Military History of Germany* (Bloomington: Indiana University Press, 1971): passim; Bucholz, *Prussian War Planning*; idem, *Moltke and the German Wars, 1864–1871* (New York: Palgrave, 2001): pp. 50–76; Larry Addington, *The Blitzkrieg Era and the German General Staff, 1865–1941* (New Brunswick: Rutgers University Press, 1971). Dissenting are Dupuy, *Genius for War*: pp. 44–45, and Terence Zuber, *The Moltke Myth: Prussian War Planning, 1857–1871* (Lanham: University Press of America, 2008).

72. Moltke, "Victory the Main Point," pp. 128–129; Hughes, "Introduction," in ibid., pp. 12–19; Schlieffen, "Cannae Studies," in Foley, *Schlieffen's Military Writings*: pp. 208–218; Martin Kitchen, *The German Officer Corps, 1890–1914* (Oxford: Clarendon, 1968): pp. 96–114; idem, "German Strategic Thought," pp. 163–190; Wawro, *Austro-Prussian War*: p. 283; Snyder, *Ideology of the Offensive*: pp. 107–156; Michael Howard, "Men Against Fire: The Doctrine of the Offensive in 1914," in Paret, *Modern Strategy*: pp. 519–524.

73. Robert M. Citino, *The Path to Blitzkrieg: Doctrine and Training in the German Army, 1920–1939* (Boulder, CO: Lynne Reinner, 1998); idem, *Quest for Decisive Victory: From Stalemate to Blitzkrieg in Europe, 1899–1940* (Lawrence: University Press of Kansas, 2002): pp. 181–185, 281–282; Michael Geyer, "German Strategy in the Age of Machine Warfare, 1914–1945," in Paret, *Modern Strategy*: pp. 527–597.

74. Foley, *Path to Verdun*: pp. 4–5 and passim; Paul Jankowski, *Verdun* (New York: Oxford University Press, 2013).

75. William B. Yeats, "The Second Coming" (1919).

76. That was the view of Colmar von der Goltz, on Moltke's staff. Foley, *Path to Verdun*: pp. 25–30.

77. Förster, "Facing 'Peoples' War," pp. 209–230. Kitchen, *Military History of Germany*: pp. 138–144; Wawro, *Austro-Prussian War*: p. 288.

78. Gordon Craig, *The Politics of the Prussian Army* (Oxford: Clarendon Press, 1955): pp. 238–298; Ritter, *Sword and the Scepter*, Volume 1: pp. 193–206.

79. Stephen Van Evera, "The Cult of the Offensive and the Origins of the First World War," *International Security* 9 (1984): pp. 58–107; Jack Snyder, *Ideology of the Offensive: Military Decision-Making and the Disasters of 1914* (Ithaca: Cornell University Press, 1984). A contrary view is Antulio Echevarria, "The 'Cult of the Offensive' Revisited," *Journal of Strategic Studies* 25/1 (2002): pp. 199–214.

80. Pflanze, "Realism and Idealism," pp. 149–164; Wolfgang Schivelbusch, *The Culture of Defeat: On National Trauma, Mourning, and Recovery* (New York: Picador, 2004): pp. 103–188. On Bismarck's fall from power under Kaiser Wilhelm II, see Taylor, *Bismarck*: pp. 231–253.

81. This motif was present in much pre–World War I strategic rumination, already blending with social Darwinian biological imperatives for some that presage Nazism. For example, see the 1912 essay on Imperial Germany's geostrategic position by Friedrich von Bernhardi, *Unsere Zukunft: Ein Mahnwort an das deutsche Volk* [Our future: A word of warning to the German people] (Stuttgart: J. G. Cotta, 1912). Excerpted and translated as "The Inevitability of War," at www.germanhistorydocs.ghi-dc.org/sub_document.cfm?document_id=775.

CHAPTER 11

1. Jean de Bloch (Ivan Bliokh), *The Future of War in its Technical, Economic, and Political Relations: Is War Now Impossible?* (New York: Doubleday & McClure, 1899): pp. xii–xxxviii, 262–263, 356. Only the last volume of his six-volume Russian work was published in English. All six were published in France and Germany. See Grant Dawson, "Preventing 'A Great Moral Evil': Jean de Bloch's 'The Future of War' as Anti-Revolutionary Pacifism," *Journal of Contemporary History* 37/1 (2002): pp. 5–19. Critics dismissed his antimilitarism, asserting that "the moral factor" remained decisive over machine guns and artillery. See the 1901 review by Edward van Dyke Robinson,

Political Science Quarterly 16/2 (1901): pp. 338–341. Basil Liddell Hart praised Bloch in *The British Way in Warfare* (London: Faber & Faber, 1932): p. 123. On German thinking, see Echevarria, *After Clausewitz*: pp. 65–120.

2. Norman Angell, *The Great Illusion: A Study of the Military Power to National Advantage* (New York: G. P. Putnam's Sons, 1910).

3. Hew Strachan, *The First World War* (Oxford: Oxford University Press, 2001): pp. 64–102.

4. Robert Graves, *Goodbye to All That* (New York: Knopf, 1958): p. 67. Also see the Imperial War Museum podcast *Over by Christmas*, available at http://www.iwm.org.uk.

5. Michael Neiberg, *Dance of the Furies: Europe and the Outbreak of World War I* (Cambridge: Belknap, 2011): pp. 1–4, 117–120, 140–142, 150–166.

6. A subtle discussion is Strachan, *First World War*: pp. 103–162. On long-war popular consent, see Alexander Watson, *Ring of Steel: Germany and Austria-Hungary in World War I: The Peoples War* (New York: Allen Lane, 2014). For more personal accounts, see Stephan Kurt Westmann, *Surgeon with the Kaiser's Army* (Barnsley: Pen & Sword, 2014): pp. 3–40; Georges Blond, *The Marne* (London: Prion, 2002): pp. 13–14.

7. Rupert Brooke, "The Dead" (1914).

8. Earl Ziemke, "Annihilation, Attrition, and the Short War," *Parameters* 12/1 (1982): p. 24.

9. This thesis was made famous by Barbara Tuchman in *The Guns of August* (New York: Macmillan, 1962). Also see Christopher Clark, *The Sleepwalkers: How Europe Went to War in 1914* (New York: Harper, 2014).

10. The literature is vast. On diplomacy and origins, see the balanced anthology Richard Hamilton and Holger Herwig, editors, *The Origins of World War I* (Cambridge: Cambridge University Press. 2003), and Holger Afflerbach and David Stevenson, editors, *An Improbable War? The Outbreak of World War I and European Political Culture before 1914* (New York: Berghahn, 2007). Also see Margaret MacMillan, *The War that Ended Peace: The Road to 1914* (New York: Random House, 2013): pp. 28–55, 80–109, 142–211. On military and doctrinal origins in the key Central Powers, see Geoffrey Wawro, *A Mad Catastrophe: The Outbreak of World War I and the Collapse of the Habsburg Empire* (New York: Basic, 2014): pp. 1–120, and Citino, *German Way of War*: pp. 191–237. An outlier on Britain and the war is Niall Ferguson, *The Pity of War* (London: Penguin, 1999): Chapters 6 and 7.

11. On Austria and Germany, see Watson, *Ring of Steel*: pp. 53–103, 375–415.

12. A controversial thesis that is not widely accepted, that Russia sought war from 1912 over issues with and within the Ottoman Empire, forcing Germany to declare war, is Sean McMeekin, *The Russian Origins of the First World War* (Cambridge: Belknap, 2011).

13. On opposition to war in Britain as well as manipulation of intelligence by a small group of politicians and Foreign Office officials, see Douglas Newton, *The Darkest Days: The Truth Behind Britain's Rush to War, 1914* (London: Verso, 2014).

14. On diplomacy of these discrete choices, see Hamilton and Herwig, *Origins of World War I*: pp. 300–442, and the essays in idem, editors, *Decisions for War, 1914–1917* (Cambridge: Cambridge University Press, 2004). A masterful three-volume study is Jay Winter, editor, *The First World War* (Cambridge: Cambridge University Press, 2014). On the Ottomans, see Eugene Rogan, *The Fall of the Ottomans: The Great War in the Middle East* (New York: Basic Books, 2015): pp. 1–74.

15. On victory without battles in "small wars" before 1914, see Bruce Collins, "Defining Victory in Victorian Warfare, 1860–1882," *Journal of Military History* 77 (July 2013): pp. 895–929.

16. On the Ottomans and Balkan powers, see Michael Reynolds, *Shattering Empires: The Clash and Collapse of the Ottoman and Russia Empires, 1908–1918* (Cambridge: Cambridge University Press, 2011): pp. 1–106; Edward Erickson, *Defeat in Detail: The Ottoman Army in the Balkans, 1912–1913* (Westport: Praeger, 2003); Richard Hall, *The Balkan Wars, 1912–1913: Prelude to the First World War* (New York: Routledge, 2000); Samuel Williamson, *Austria-Hungary and the Origins of the First World War* (New York: St. Martins, 1991); Strachan, *First World War*: pp. 35–64; Sean McMeekin, *The Ottoman Endgame: War, Revolution, and the Making of the Modern Middle East, 1908–1923* (New York: Penguin, 2015): pp. 2–162.

17. Erickson, *Defeat in Detail*: pp. 1–36, 45–48; Hall, *Balkan Wars*: pp. 22–68; Sean McMeekin, *The Berlin-Baghdad Express: The Ottoman Empire and Germany's Bid for World Power* (Cambridge: Belknap Press, 2010): pp. 54–99.

18. Notably in two battles in the Çatalca (Chataldja) fortified lines just east of Istanbul. Erickson, *Defeat in Detail*: pp. 122–136, 251–292; Hall, *Balkan Wars*: pp. 32–38, 90–91.

19. Rogan, *Fall of the Ottomans*: pp. 75–242.

20. On Balkan lessons, see Nicholas Murray, *The Rocky Road to the Great War: The Evolution of Trench Warfare to 1914* (Washington: Potomac, 2013): pp. 171–210.

21. The principal book behind the controversy was Fritz Fischer, *Germany's Aims in the First World War* (London: Chatto & Windus, 1967). A concise summary of the main arguments in this crucial debate is *Journal of Contemporary History* 48/2, Special Issue, *The Fischer Controversy after 50 Years* (2013).

22. Wawro, *Mad Catastrophe*: pp. 383–385.

23. On antecedents to war in this region, see Mark Biondich, *The Balkans: Revolution, War, and Political Violence* (Oxford: Oxford University Press, 2011): pp. 1–94; Richard Hall, *Balkan Breakthrough* (Bloomington: Indiana University Press, 2010): pp. 1–35; Andrej Mitrović, *Serbia's Great War, 1914–1918* (London: Hurst, 2007): pp. 1–102; Glen Torrey, *The Romanian Battlefront in World War I* (Lawrence: University of Kansas Press, 2012): pp. 1–44.

24. On the Habsburg effort to use military culture to generate loyalty to the state, see Laurence Cole, *Military Culture and Popular Patriotism in Late Imperial Austria* (Oxford: Oxford University Press, 2014).

25. Wawro, *Mad Catastrophe*: passim; Lawrence Sondhaus, *Franz Conrad von Hötzendorf: Architect of the Apocalypse* (Boston: Brill, 2000): pp. 81–138. Wawro is scathing; Sondhaus less so, but still sees Conrad as failing at the strategic level.

26. Quoted in Wawro, *Mad Catastrophe*: p. 94.

27. Ibid., pp. xxiii, 1–13, 383–385. Quoted at p. 385.

28. Max Hastings, *Catastrophe 1914* (New York: Knopf, 2013): pp. 138–158.

29. Norman Stone, "Army and Society in the Habsburg Monarchy, 1900–1914," *Past and Present* 33 (1966): pp. 95–111; Geoffrey Wawro, "Morale in the Austro-Hungarian Army," in Peter Liddle and Hugh Cecil, editors, *Facing Armageddon: The First World War Experienced* (London: Pen & Sword, 1996): pp. 399–412.

30. Wawro, *Mad Catastrophe*: pp. 67–71, 121–168, 186–191; Hastings, *Catastrophe*: pp. 386–410; Stone, *Eastern Front*: pp. 70–91; Watson, *Ring of Steel*: pp. 104–159.

31. On Italy, see Mark Thomson, *The White War: Life and Death on the Italian Front, 1915–1919* (New York: Basic, 2008): pp. 294–327.

32. Sondhaus, *Conrad*: pp. 139–170; Wawro, *Mad Catastrophe* pp. 269–385.

33. Watson, *Ring of Steel*: pp. 514–556. On similar problems faced by all the armies and belligerent economies to some degree, see Allan Millet and Williamson Murray, *Military Effectiveness: The First World War* (Cambridge: Cambridge University Press, 2010): passim.

34. Wawro, *Mad Catastrophe*: pp. 372–385.

35. Strachan, *First World War*: pp. 1–35.

36. Jonathan Bailey, "Military History and the Pathology of Lessons Learned: The Russo-Japanese War," in Williamson Murray and Richard Sinnreich, editors, *The Past as Prologue: The Importance of History to the Military Profession* (Cambridge: Cambridge University Press, 2006): pp. 170–194; Echevarria, *After Clausewitz*: pp. 121–156.

37. An overview is Strachan, *European Armies*: pp. 59–74. On Russian reforms: Bruce Menning, *Bayonets Before Bullets: The Imperial Russian Army, 1861–1914* (Bloomington: Indiana University Press, 1992): pp. 6–86; Forrest A. Miller, *Dmitrii Miliutin and the Reform Era in Russia* (Charlotte: Vanderbilt University Press, 1968): pp. 196–200; David Schimmelpenninck van der Oye et al., *Reforming the Tsar's Army: Military Innovation in Imperial Russia from Peter the Great to the Revolution* (Cambridge: Cambridge University Press, 2011): pp. 11–55; John Steinberg, *All the Tsar's Men: Russia's General Staff and the Fate of Empire, 1898–1914* (Baltimore: Johns Hopkins University Press, 2010). On Russian fighting doctrine, see Jacob Kipp, "Tsarist and Soviet Operational Art, 1853–1991," in Creveld and Olsen, *Evolution of Operational Art*: pp. 64–85; Richard Harrison, *The Russian Way of War: Operational Art, 1900–1940* (Lawrence: University Press of Kansas, 2001): pp. 5–72.

38. On the politics of the French Army, see Porch, *March to the Marne*, and Paul-Marie de La Gorce, *The French Army: A Military-Political History* (London: Braziller, 1963). Also see relevant chapters

from Pierre Chalmin, *L'Officier français de 1815 à 1870* (Paris: Rivière, 1957) and Raoul Girardet, *La société militaire de 1815 à nos jours* (Paris: Perrin, 2001).

39. On Britain's prewar continental commitment, see the essays by William Philpott and Thomas Otte in Keith Neilson and Greg Kennedy, editors, *The British War of Warfare: Power and the International System, 1856–1956* (Farnham: Ashgate, 2010): pp. 83–100 and 301–324.

40. Tirpitz outmaneuvered the generals, cabinet and Reichstag in appropriations battles that threatened to limit his vision of a world-class battle fleet. During the war he took contradictory positions on decisive naval battle vs. *guerre de course* (commerce war) via surface raiders and U-boats. He was forced out in March 1916. Michael Epkenhans, *Tirpitz: Architect of the German High Seas Fleet* (Washington: Potomac, 2008): pp. 15–72; Keith Bird, "The Tirpitz Legacy," *Journal of Military History* 69/3 (2005): pp. 821–825.

41. Peter Schenk, "Germany: The Kriegsmarine," in Vincent P. O'Hara et al, editors, *On Seas Contested* (Annapolis, MD: Naval Institute Press, 2010); Patrick Kelley, *Tirpitz and the Imperial German Navy* (Bloomington: Indiana University Press, 2011): pp. 263–322; Roger Parkinson, *The Late Victorian Navy: The Pre-Dreadnought Era and the Origins of World War I* (Woodbridge, UK: Boydell, 2008).

42. On the long British struggle to incorporate citizen-soldiers, see Harold Raugh, *The British Army 1815–1914* (London: Ashgate, 2006), and Michael Ramsey, *Command and Cohesion: The Citizen Soldier and Minor Tactics in the British Army, 1870–1918* (Westport: Praeger, 2002).

43. Günther Rothenberg, *The Army of Francis Joseph* (West Lafayette: Purdue University Press, 1977): pp. 9ff.

44. Günther Rothenberg, "Moltke, Schlieffen, and the Doctrine of Strategic Envelopment," in Paret, *Makers of Modern Strategy*: pp. 296–325. Quoted at p. 296. Also see Lynn, *Battle*: pp. 212–213.

45. Schlieffen's "Cannae Studies" were not just about Cannae; they interpreted in light of Cannae all the major campaigns of Frederick, Napoleon and Moltke. Schlieffen, "Cannae Studies," in Foley, *Schlieffen's Military Writings*: pp. 208–218. On Königgrätz, quoted in Wawro, *Austro-Prussian War*: p. 271. Also see Peter Paret, "Clausewitz and Schlieffen as Interpreters of Frederick the Great," *Journal of Military History* 76/3 (2012): pp. 843–845.

46. "Memorandum of 1905: The Schlieffen Plan" and Schlieffen's "Addendum to the Memorandum, 1906," translated and reprinted in Foley, *Schlieffen's Military Writings*: pp. 163–177. Also see "Comments by Moltke on the Memorandum, c.1911" in ibid., pp. 178–182. Pioneering criticism was Gerhard Ritter, *The Schlieffen Plan* (London: Oswold Wolff, 1958).

47. An acrid debate erupted with Terence Zuber's "Schlieffen Plan Reconsidered," *War in History* 6/3 (1999): pp. 262–305, and *Inventing the Schlieffen Plan* (Oxford: Oxford University Press, 2002). Zuber claimed there was no Schlieffen Plan and no endorsement of annihilation as the goal of operations. Germany's Military History Research Office published *Der Schlieffenplan: Analysen und Dokumentedocuments*, including a copy misfiled for decades in the Freiburg archive, translated as Hans Ehlert et al., editors, *The Schlieffen Plan: International Perspectives on German Strategy for World War I* (Lexington: University of Kentucky Press, 2014). See especially the reprint of Gerhard Groß, "There Was a Schlieffen Plan." Also in *War in History* 15 (2010): pp. 389–421. Other essays deal with Russian, Austrian, French, Belgian and British planning. Key is the documentary Appendix: pp. 339–526.

48. Kitchen, *German Officer Corps*: pp. 64–71; Graydon Tunstall, *Planning for War Against Russia and Serbia* (Boulder: Social Science Monographs, 1993): pp. 33–39; Eric Dorn Brose, *The Kaiser's Army: The Politics of Military Technology in Germany During the Machine Age, 1870–1918* (Oxford: Oxford University Press, 2001): pp. 49, 73–77.

49. On Moltke's fear of long war, see Annika Mombauer, *Helmuth von Moltke and the Origins of the First World War* (Cambridge: Cambridge University Press, 2001): pp. 211, 285–287, and Stig Förster, "Facing 'Peoples' War': Moltke the Elder and Germany's Military Options After 1871," *Journal of Strategic Studies* 10/2 (1987): pp. 209–230.

50. Craig, *Prussian Army*: pp. 238–298. A subtle study of German thinking is Foley, *Path to Verdun*: pp. 1–81. Also see Echevarria, *After Clausewitz*: pp. 203–204.

51. Quoted in Holger Herwig, "Germany and the 'Short-War' Illusion: Toward a New Interpretation?" *Journal of Military History* 66/3 (2002): p. 688. On Moltke's views in 1912, see L. L. Farrar, *The Short-War Illusion: German Policy, Strategy & Domestic Affairs, August–December 1914* (Santa

Barbara: Clio, 1973): pp. 137–138. Also see Strachan, *First World War*: pp. 1005–1014; Roger Chickering, *Imperial Germany and the Great War, 1914–1918,* 3rd ed. (Cambridge: Cambridge University Press, 2014): pp. 18–23.

52. Herwig, "Germany and the 'Short-War' Illusion," p. 688.

53. Holger Herwig, *The Marne, 1914* (New York: Random House, 2009): pp. 3–29; Mombauer, *Moltke*: pp. 283–289; Foley, *Path to Verdun*: pp. 79–81; Tim Hadley, "Military Diplomacy in the Dual Alliance," *War in History* 17/3 (2010): pp. 294–312.

54. Annika Mombauer, "The Moltke Plan," in Ehlert, *Schlieffen Plan*: pp. 43–66; Robert Foley, "The Schlieffen Plan—A War Plan," in ibid., pp. 67–84.

55. This crucial question is raised by a leading historian of Germany in World War I, Holger Herwig, in "Germany and the 'Short-War' Illusion," p. 693.

56. Falkenhayn quoted August 1, 1914, in Herwig, *Marne*: p. 29.

57. Foley, *Path to Verdun*: pp. 5–6, 74–81.

58. Stig Förster, "Dreams and Nightmares: German Military Leadership and the Images of Future War, 1871–1914," in Chickering, *Anticipating Total War*: pp. 343–376.

59. In London, Winston Churchill used the same bracing metaphor of a coming storm of war. So did Henri Poincaré in France. John Stoessinger, *Why Nations Go to War*, 10th ed. (New York: Thompson Wadsworth, 2008): p. 3.

60. L. L. Farrar, *Short-War Illusion:* Bethmann-Hollweg quoted at p. 5.

61. Jehuda Wallach, *The Dogma of the Battle of Annihilation: The Theories of Clausewitz and Schlieffen and their Impact on the German Conduct of Two World Wars* (Westport, CT: Greenwood, 1986), originally published in German in 1967; Michael Geyer, "German Strategy in the Age of Machine Warfare, 1914–1945," in Paret, *Makers of Modern Strategy*: p. 531; Echevarria, *After Clausewitz*: pp. 94–120; Michael Handel, *Clausewitz and Modern Strategy* (London: Frank Cass, 1986): pp. 213–286; Strachan, "Clausewitz," pp. 370–372; Dennis Showalter, "German Grand Strategy: A Contradiction in Terms?" *Militärgeschichtliche Mitteilungen* 2 (1990): pp. 65–102; idem, "From Deterrence to Doomsday Machine: The German Way of War, 1890–1914," *Journal of Military History* 64 (2000): pp. 679–710; Addington, *The Blitzkrieg Era*: pp. 9–27; Denis Showalter, *Tannenberg: Clash of Empires* (Hamden: Archon, 1992): pp. 13–35.

62. Brose, *Kaiser's Army*: pp. 138–182.

63. Herwig, "Germany and the 'Short-War' Illusion," p. 688; Foley, *Path to Verdun*: pp. 59–81.

64. France would adopt a similar defense between the world wars, building and manning the Maginot Line at great expense. There was no more aggression left in France before either war.

65. Herwig, *Marne*: pp. 132–158; Dieter Storz, "This Trench and Fortress Warfare is Horrible," in Ehlert, *Schlieffen Plan*: pp. 137–188; Foley, *Path to Verdun*: p. 66.

66. See Frank Buchholz, et al., *The Great War Dawning: Germany and its Army at the Start of World War I* (Vienna: Verlag Militaria, 2013).

67. A consensus among Western military thinkers in 1914 was that cavalry was most useful as a supporting arm for screening and reconnaissance, with some utility as dismounted rifle infantry. See Dorondo, *Riders of the Apocalypse*: Chapter 3; Stephen Badsey, "The Boer War and British Cavalry Doctrine: A Reevaluation," *Journal of Military History* 71/1 (2007): pp. 75–97. A contrarian view is Gervase Phillips, "Who Shall Say That the Days of Cavalry Are Over?" *War in History* 18/1 (November 2011): pp. 5–32. On the late-war revival of cavalry, see Paddy Griffith, *Battle Tactics of the Western Front: The British Army's Art of Attack, 1916–1918* (New Haven: Yale University Press, 1994): pp. 159–162.

68. Herwig, *Marne*: p. 46.

69. Captain Harry Truman commanded an American battery of French 75s. One such gun now resides in the Harry S. Truman Library & Museum.

70. Ferdinand Foch, *Des principes de la guerre*, 4th ed. (Paris: Berger-Levrault, 1917); Stefan Possony and Étienne Mantoux, "Du Picq and Foch: The French School," in Edward Earle, editor, *Makers of Modern Strategy* (Princeton: Princeton University Press, 1943): pp. 206–233; Eugène Carrias, *La pensée militaire française* (Paris: Presses Universitaires de France, 1960): pp. 278–281; Gat, *Military Thought*: pp. 382–440. On early thinking about willpower in face of the new firepower, see the reprint of Ardant du Piq, *Battle Studies* (Mechanicsburg: Stackpole, 1987).

71. On prewar Russian planning, see Strachan, *First World War*: pp. 297–316.

72. Hastings, *Catastrophe*: pp. 258–285; Stone, *Eastern Front*: pp. 44–69; William Astore and Dennis Showalter, *Hindenburg* (Washington: Potomac, 2005): pp. 15–23; Citino, *German Way of War*: pp. 224–237.

73. Terrence Zuber credits superior German tactics for inflicting higher casualties in these encounter fights, though without ever questioning inferior German strategy, in *Battle of the Frontiers: Ardennes, 1914* (Stroud: Tempus, 2007).

74. A myth-breaking study is Peter Hart, *Fire and Movement: The British Expeditionary Force and the Campaign of 1914* (New York: Oxford University Press, 2015).

75. "Old Contemptibles" was a term proudly adopted by the BEF in response to a reported remark by Kaiser Wilhelm, probably apocryphal, that it was "a contemptible little army."

76. Hart, *Fire and Movement*: pp. 42–179.

77. Douglas Porch, "The Marne and After: A Reappraisal of French Strategy in the First World War," *Journal of Military History* 53/4 (1989): pp. 363–386; idem, "Clausewitz and the French," in Michael Handel, editor, *Clausewitz and Modern Strategy* (London: Frank Cass, 1986): pp. 287–302.

78. The seminal revision to an 80-year-old view of Joffre is Robert A. Doughty, "French Strategy in 1914: Joffre's Own," *Journal of Military History* 67/2 (2003): pp. 427–454, and idem, *Pyrrhic Victory: French Strategy and Operations in the Great War* (Cambridge: Harvard University Press, 2005): pp. 46–104.

79. Hart, *Fire and Movement*: pp. 156–162.

80. A concise summary is Strachan, *First World War*: pp. 242–280. On the BEF at the Marne, see Hart, *Fire and Movement*: pp. 180–197.

81. Herwig, *Marne*: pp. 153–155, 175–177, 182–183; Strachan, *First World War*: pp. 208–242; Hastings, *Catastrophe*: pp. 200–257, 340.

82. Herwig, *Marne*: pp. 219–224.

83. Hastings, *Catastrophe*: pp. 286–312.

84. Hart, *Fire and Movement*: pp. 180–186.

85. Strachan, *First World War*: pp. 254–256; Herwig, *Marne*: pp. 234–236.

86. A highly favorable account of Galliéni is Blond, *The Marne*: pp. 97–132. On the taxis: pp. 170–183.

87. Hastings, *Catastrophe*: pp.187–194; Blond, *The Marne*: pp. 208–219.

88. Herwig, *Marne*: pp. 257–258.

89. Falkenhayn quoted in Hastings, *Catastrophe*: p. 338.

90. Herwig, *Marne*: pp. xxiii–xix, 301–302.

91. Foley, *Path to Verdun*: pp. 56–57; Wallach, *Dogma*: pp. 87–93.

92. Ferdinand Foch, The *Memoirs of Marshal Foch* (London: William Heinemann, 1931): p. 200.

93. Quoted in Ziemke, "Annihilation" (1982): p. 23.

94. Robert T. Foley, "Preparing the German Army for the First World War," *War & Society* 22/2 (2004): pp. 1–25.

95. Wayne Thompson, "The September Program: Reflections on the Evidence," *Central European History* 11/4 (1978): pp. 348–354; Farrar, *Short-War Illusion*: pp. 22–33, 102–116.

CHAPTER 12

1. Farrar, *Short-War Illusion*: p. 15.

2. Quoted in Foley, *Path to Verdun*: p. 103.

3. See Ian Brown, *British Logistics on the Western Front: 1914–1919* (Westport: Praeger, 1998): pp. 41–74. On the general condition of infantry, see Griffith, *Battle Tactics*: pp. 47–64.

4. Wawro, *Mad Catastrophe*: pp. 372–373. On economic mobilization, see Chickering, *Great War, Total War;* Stone, *Eastern Front*: pp. 194–211; Leonard Smith et al., *France and the Great War, 1914–1818* (New York: Cambridge University Press, 2003): pp. 42–75; and Strachan, *First World War*: pp. 815–992.

5. Quoted in Herwig, *Marne*: pp. 303–304. On the shift in planning, see Farrar, *Short-War Illusion*: pp. 28–31. On reorganization, see Chickering, *Imperial Germany and the Great War*: pp. 32–50.

6. Foley, *Path to Verdun*: p. 163; Jean-Claude Laparra, *La machine à vaincre: De l'espoir à la désillusion; histoire de l'armée allemande 1914–1918* (Verdun: 14–18 Éditions, 2006): p. 121; Robin Prior and Trevor Wilson, *The Somme* (New Haven: Yale University Press, 2005): pp. 266–271; Jack Sheldon, *The German Army on the Somme, 1914–1916* (London: Pen & Sword, 2005): pp. 93ff.

7. Jonathan Krause, "The French Battle for Vimy Ridge, Spring 1915," *Journal of Military History* 77/1 (2013): 91–113. An alternative view is that of Anthony Clayton, *Paths of Glory: The French Army, 1914–1918* (London: Cassell, 2003). An outlier is John Mosier, *Myth of the Great War* (London: Profile, 2001). Also see Smith, *France and the Great War*: pp. 77–83, 113–145; Robert Ferrell, "What's in a Name? The Development of Strategies of Attrition on the Western Front, 1914–1918," *Historian* 68 (2006): pp. 722–746; Paul Harris and Sanders Marble, "The 'Step-by-Step' Approach: British Military Thought and Operational Method on the Western Front, 1915–1917," *War in History* 15 (2000): pp. 17–42.

8. Wawro, *Mad Catastrophe*: p. 57 and p. 424n55; Stone, *Eastern Front*: pp. 144–164.

9. Quoted in Foley, *Path to Verdun*: p. 149. On Habsburg and Russian Army travails in 1915, see Richard DiNardo, *Breakthrough: The Gorlice-Tarnów Campaign, 1915* (Santa Barbara: ABC-CLIO, 2010); Graydon Tunstall, *Blood on the Snow: The Carpathian Winter War of 1915* (Lawrence: University Press of Kansas, 2010).

10. Strachan, *First World War*: pp. 993–1005; Spencer Jones, *From Boer War to World War: Tactical Reform of the British Army, 1902–1914* (Norman: University of Oklahoma Press, 2012); Hastings, *Catastrophe*: pp. 463–496; David French, "The Meaning of Attrition, 1914–1916," *English Historical Review* 103 (1988): pp. 388–389.

11. Sanders Marble, editor, *Scraping the Barrel: The Military Use of Substandard Manpower, 1860–1960* (New York: Fordham University Press, 2012): pp. 5–131. The same downward shift in standards occurred again in World War II in all armies, including the U.S. Army. By 1944 American medical examiners passed men who had *no* teeth as fit for combat. Rick Atkinson, "Projecting American Power in the Second World War," *Journal of Military History* 80 (2016): p. 348.

12. Rachel Duffett, *The Stomach for Fighting: Food and the Soldiers of the Great War* (Manchester: Manchester University Press, 2012); Martin van Creveld, "World War I and the Revolution in Logistics," in Chickering and Förster, *Great War, Total War*: pp. 57–72; Peter Lummel, "Food Provisioning in the German Army in the First World War," in Ina Zweiniger-Bargielowska et al., editors, *Food and War in Twentieth-Century Europe* (Farnham: Ashgate, 2011): pp. 13–26. On late adjustment to the long war, see Brown, *British Logistics*: pp. 41–74.

13. Birger Stichelbaut and Piet Chielens, *The Great War Seen from the Air: In Flanders Fields, 1914–1918* (Brussels: Mercatorfonds, 2013); John Morrow, "The First World War, 1914–1919," in John Olsen, editor, *A History of Air Warfare* (Washington: Potomac, 2010): pp. 3–26.

14. Christian Geinitz, "The First Air War against Non-Combatants," in Chickering and Förster, *Great War, Total War*: pp. 207–226.

15. On gas effects, see Edgar Jones, "Terror Weapons: The British Experience of Gas and Its Treatment," *War in History* 21/3 (2014): pp. 355–375. For a German view of the Somme battle, see Westmann, *Surgeon with the Kaiser's Army*: pp. 69–85.

16. A critical study is Paul Fussell, *The Great War in Modern Memory* (Oxford: Oxford University Press, 2013).

17. Raphaëlle Branche, "De l'art dans les tranchées," *Vingtième Siècle: Revue d'histoire* 94 (2007): pp. 253–255; Rabb, *Artist and the Warrior*: pp. 182–198. Specifically on artists response to the trenches: pp. 182–183. Cave chapels and statues viewed by the author in a private photo collection. Also see Evan Hadingham, "The Hidden World of the Great War," National Geographic Society, available at http://ngm.nationalgeographic.com/2014/08/ww1-underground/hadingham-text.

18. See Henri Barbusse, *Le feu: Journal d'une escouade* (Paris: Flammarion 1917); published in English as *Under Fire: The Story of a Squad* (New York: E. P. Dutton, 1917).

19. For a wider view, see Michael Freemantle, *Gas! Gas! Quick, Boys! How Chemistry Changed the First World War* (Stroud, UK: Spellmount, 2012). On treating gas wounded, see the firsthand account by a German medic in Westmann, *Surgeon with the Kaiser's Army*: pp. 95–106.

20. Ted Bogacz, "War Neurosis and Cultural Change in England, 1914–22: The Work of the War Office Committee of Enquiry into 'Shell-Shock,'" *Journal of Contemporary History* 24/2 (1989): pp. 227–256.

21. Alexander Watson, *Enduring the Great War: Combat, Morale and Collapse in the German and British Armies, 1914–1918* (Cambridge: Cambridge University Press, 2009): pp. 140–183; Gary Sheffield, *Forgotten Victory: The First World War, Myths and Realities* (London: Headline, 2001): passim; Westmann, *Surgeon with the Kaiser's Army*: pp. 107–119.

22. Ernst Jünger, *Storm of Steel* (London: Penguin, 2004), first published in 1920; Erich Maria Remarque, *All Quiet on the Western Front* (New York: Ballantine, 1987), first published in 1929. Also see Herbert Sulzbach, *With the German Guns: Four Years on the Western Front* (Barnsley: Pen & Sword, 2003), and Jason Crouthamel, "Nervous Nazis: National Socialism and Memory of the First World War," *War & Society* 21/2 (2003): pp. 55–75.

23. Jankowski, *Verdun*: pp. 35–46.

24. Georges Blond, *Verdun* (London: White Lion, 1976): p. 30; Holger Afflerbach, "Planning Total War? Falkenhayn and the Battle of Verdun, 1916," in Chickering and Förster, *Great War, Total War*: pp. 113–131.

25. Jankowski, *Verdun*: pp. 12–13.

26. On the "storm of steel" facing any infantry out of the trenches and in the open, see Griffith, *Battle Tactics*: pp. 38–44.

27. Foley, *Path to Verdun*: pp. 212–215.

28. Ibid., pp. 219–220.

29. Quoted in Jankowski, *Verdun*: p. 109.

30. See Henri-Philippe Pétain, *Verdun* (London: Mathews & Marrot, 1930): passim.

31. On honor in modern war, see Howard, "When are Wars Decisive," pp. 127–128.

32. Foley, *Path to Verdun*: pp. 229–234.

33. Quoted in ibid., p. 185.

34. Jankowski, *Verdun*: pp. 72–73, 77.

35. Quoted in ibid., p. 84.

36. Hew Strachan, "Breaking the Deadlock," *MHQ: Quarterly Journal of Military History* 16 (2004): pp. 72–83; William Philpott, *Anglo-French Relations and Strategy on the Western Front 1914–1918* (London: Macmillan, 1996): pp. 112–128.

37. Michael Barrett, *Prelude to Blitzkrieg: The 1916 Austro-German Campaign in Rumania* (Bloomington: Indiana University Press, 2013): pp. 264–281.

38. Rogan, *Fall of the Ottomans*: pp. 243–310; Mcmeekan, *Ottoman Endgame*: pp. 247–314

39. Edward Erickson, *Ottoman Army Effectiveness in World War I* (New York: Routledge, 2007): pp. 61–117; John Grainger, *The Battle for Palestine* (New York: Boydell, 2006); Strachan, *First World War*: pp. 495–643.

40. Graydon Tunstall, "Austria-Hungary and the Brusilov Offensive of 1916," *The Historian* 70/1 (2008): pp. 30–53; Stone, *Eastern Front*: pp. 35–61, 232–263; Timothy Dowling, *The Brusilov Offensive* (Bloomington: Indiana University Press, 2008): pp. 62–134.

41. Brian Bond, *Britain's Two World Wars Against Germany* (New York: Cambridge University Press, 2014): pp. 125–143.

42. William Philpott, *Bloody Victory: The Sacrifice on the Somme and the Making of the Twentieth Century* (London: Little Brown, 2009): pp. 167–208; Keegan, *Face of Battle*: pp. 207–284. Falkenhayn quoted in Robert Foley, "Learning War's Lessons: The German Army and the Battle of the Somme 1916," *Journal of Military History* 75/2 (2011): p. 479.

43. Jankowski, *Verdun*: p. 99; Foley, "Learning War's Lessons," p. 480–482, 492, Falkenhayn quoted at p. 472; Philpott, *Bloody Victory*: pp. 207–289; Tim Travers, *The Killing Ground: The British Army, the Western Front and the Emergence of Modern Warfare* (London: Routledge, 1990): pp. 127–199; Gary Sheffield, *The Somme* (New Haven: Yale University Press, 2005); Prior and Wilson, *The Somme*: pp. 35–56, 112–118.

44. William Philpott, *War of Attrition: Fighting the First World War* (London: Overlook, 2014): p. 226.

45. Elizabeth Greenhalgh, *The French Army and the First World War* (Cambridge: Cambridge University press, 2014: pp. 170–270; Smith, *France and the Great War*: pp. 113–145; Robert Doughty, "How Did France Weather the Troubles of 1917?" and Michael Neiberg, "'What True Misery Is': France's Crisis of Morale 1917," in Peter Dennis and Jeffrey Grey, editors, *1917: Tactics, Training, and Technology* (Loftus: Australia Military History Publications, 2008): pp. 88–104, 105–124.

46. A contemporary perception of this idea of Germany's war aims is Nicholas Butler, "The Road to Durable Peace," *Advocate of Peace* 80/4 (April 1918): pp. 110–111. Also see Roger Chickering, "Sore Loser: Ludendorff's Total War," in idem and Stig Förster, editors, *The Shadows of Total War, 1919–1939* (New York: Cambridge University Press, 2003): pp. 151–178.

47. That was a central theme of Hindenburg's self-justifying memoir *Aus meinem Leben* ("Out of My Life"), published in 1920; it was republished in a heavily edited and abridged English version as *The Great War* (London: Greenhill, 2006).

48. Lisle Rose, *Power at Sea: The Age of Navalism, 1890–1918* (Columbia: University of Missouri Press, 2007): pp. 216–246; David Olivier, *German Naval Strategy 1856–1888: Forerunners of Tirpitz* (New York: Routledge, 2012): pp. 41–76; 130–189. Also see Lawrence Sondhaus, *Preparing for Weltpolitik: German Sea Power Before the Tirpitz Era* (Annapolis: Naval Institute Press, 1997).

49. On U-boat war from 1915 to 1918, see Rose, *Power at Sea*: pp. 247–292.

50. Memorandum translated and reproduced in Dirk Steffen, "The Holtzendorff Memorandum of 22 December 1916, and Germany's Declaration of Unrestricted U-boat Warfare," *Journal of Military History* 68/1 (2004): pp. 215–224. Germany's declared reason for resuming the practice was American war loans to the Allies.

51. Dowling, *Brusilov Offensive*: pp. 282–301; Joshua Sanborn, *Imperial Apocalypse: The Great War and the Destruction of the Russian Empire* (Oxford: Oxford University Press, 2014): pp. 171–204.

52. Translated text available at https://wwi.lib.byu.edu/index.php/The_Peace_Treaty_of_Brest-Litovsk

53. Martin Kitchen, *The Silent Dictatorship: The Politics of German High Command under Hindenburg and Ludendorff, 1916–1918* (London: Holmes & Meier, 1976). Also see Chickering, *Imperial Germany and the Great War*: pp. 66–153. A defense of this shift as a rational response to long war is Watson, *Ring of Steel*: pp. 464–465.

54. Barrett, *Prelude to Blitzkrieg*: pp. 1–31, 212–122, 280–281.

55. On the steep American combat learning curve, see Timothy Kutta, "The American Army in World War I," *Strategy & Tactics* 217 (2003): pp. 6–22, and Edward Coffman, *The War to End All Wars: The American Military Experience in World War I* (Lexington: University of Kentucky Press, 1998): pp. 121–186, 262–298.

56. Nick Lloyd, *Hundred Days: The Campaign that Ended World War I* (New York: Basic Books, 2014): pp. 115–132.

57. Robert Ferrell, *America's Deadliest Battle: Meuse-Argonne, 1918* (Lawrence: University Press of Kansas, 2007): pp. 112–147.

58. Music and lyrics at http://www.loc.gov/item/2014570675/.

59. Foley, "Lessons," p. 496.

60. Siegfried Sassoon, "Memorial Tablet" (October 1918).

61. Griffith, *Forward into Battle*: pp. 50–94; Williamson Murray, *Military Adaptation in War* (Cambridge: Cambridge University Press, 2011): pp. 74–118.

62. Tim Travers, *How the War Was Won: Command and Technology in the British Army on the Western Front, 1917–1918* (London: Routledge, 1992): pp. 11–109.

63. Elizabeth Greenhaigh, *Victory Through Coalition: Britain and France during the First World War* (Cambridge: Cambridge University Press, 2005): pp. 186–264; Travers, *How the War Was Won*: pp. 110–182; David Stevenson, *With Our Backs to the Wall: Victory and Defeat in 1918* (Cambridge: Belknap Press, 2011): pp. 222–243.

64. Brown, *British Logistics*: pp. 179–210; Martin Horn, *Britain, France, and the Financing of the First World War* (Montreal: McGill-Queen's University Press, 2002): pp. 28–56; Rachel Chrastil, *Organizing for War: France, 1870–1914* (Baton Rouge: Louisiana State University Press, 2010): pp. 112–126; Robert T. Foley, "The Other Side of the Wire: The German Army in 1917," in Dennis and Grey, *1917*: pp. 155–178. On France, see Rémy Porte, *La mobilisation industrielle, « premier front » de la Grande Guerre?* (Cahors: 14–18 Éditions, 2006). More generally, see Strachan, *First World War*: pp. 993–1113.

65. Griffith, *Forward into Battle*: pp. 100–101; Bruce Gudmundsson, *Stormtroop Tactics: Innovation in the German Army, 1914–1918* (New York: Praeger, 1988).

66. Tim Gale, *The French Army's Tank Force in the Great War* (Farnham: Ashgate, 2013): pp. 126–130.

67. Remarque, *All Quiet*: p. 286.

68. David Zabecki, *The German 1918 Offensives: A Case Study in the Operational Level of War* (New York: Routledge, 2006): pp. 73–76, 81–82, 324, 326–327; Ian Passingham, *The German Offensives of 1918: Last Desperate Gamble* (Barnsley: Pen & Sword, 2006); Martin Kitchen, *The German Offensives of 1918* (Stroud: Tempus, 2001). On Ludendorff and the General Staff, see Paul J. Rose in Zabecki, *Chief of Staff*, Vol. 1: pp. 109–122.

69. Lloyd, *Hundred Days*: pp. 71–73; 234–237; Zabecki, *1918 Offensives*: pp. 233–278.

70. That is the persuasive central thesis of the study by Doughty, *Pyrrhic Victory*.

71. Haig also believed it could be won in 1917. Each of his major campaign plans assumed at least the possibility of forcing a German collapse. Lloyd, *Hundred Days*: pp. 139–140; Harris, *Haig*: pp. 298–354; 485–517.

72. Elizabeth Greenhaigh, *Foch in Command* (Cambridge: Cambridge University Press, 2011): pp. 192-216, 263-494; idem, *Victory Through Coalition*: pp. 228-264.

73. Doughty, *Pyrrhic Victory*: pp. 250-310.

74. Griffith, *Battle Tactics*: pp. 101–176; Travers, *How the War Was Won*; Gary Sheffield and Dan Todman, editors, *Command and Control on the Western Front: The British Army's Experience, 1918–1918* (Staplehurst: History Press, 2004); Jonathon Boff, "Combined Arms during the Hundred Days Campaign," *War in History* 17 (2010): pp. 459–478; idem, *Winning and Losing on the Western Front: The British Third Army and the Defeat of Germany in 1918* (Cambridge: Cambridge University Press, 2012): pp. 74–159; Simon Robbins, *British Generalship on the Western Front 1914–1918: Defeat into Victory* (London: Frank Cass, 2005): pp. 83–131.

75. Alan Millett, *Well Planned and Splendidly Executed*, 2nd ed. (Chicago: Cantigny Foundation, 2013).

76. Jean-Bapiste Duroselle, *La Grande Guerre des Français* (Paris: Perrin, 1994): p. 7; Doughty, *Pyrrhic Victory*: p. 1–2; Krause, "Vimy Ridge," p. 92; Robert Bruce, *A Fraternity of Arms: America and France in the Great War* (Lawrence: University Press of Kansas, 2003): pp. 97ff.

77. These important points are made well in Boff, *Winning and Losing*: pp. 226–251.

78. Rogan, *Fall of the Ottomans*: pp. 311–384; David Fromkin, *A Peace to End All Peace: The Fall of the Ottoman Empire and the Creation of the Modern Middle East*, 2nd ed. (New York: Holt, 2009): pp. 415–568.

79. Steven Jackman, "Shoulder to Shoulder: Close Control and 'Old Prussian Drill' in German Offensive Infantry Tactics, 1871–1914," *Journal of Military History* 68/1 (2004): pp. 102–104.

80. A seminal study of German adaptation to trench warfare is Graeme C. Wynne, *If Germany Attacks: The Battle in Depth in the West* (Westport: Praeger, 1971), originally published in 1940. An important corrective to the older view is Foley, "Learning War's Lessons," pp. 471–504, and idem, "Dumb Donkeys or Cunning Foxes? Learning in the British and German Armies during the Great War," *International Affairs* 90/2 (2014): pp. 279–298.

81. That is the illuminating insight of Murray's *Rocky Road*: pp. 225–238 and passim.

82. Wilhelm Deist, "The Military Collapse of the German Empire: The Reality Behind the Stab-in-the-Back Myth," *War in History* 3 (April 1996): pp. 186–207. Also see Westmann, *Surgeon with the Kaiser's Army*: pp. 120–151.

83. Lloyd, *Hundred Days*: pp. 167–270. An important corrective to a tendency in British histories to credit the Hundred Days campaign with almost the whole of the Allied drive to victory, neglecting the huge role of the French Army, is Doughty, *Pyrrhic Victory*: pp. 405–507.

84. Ibid., pp. 504–512.

85. H. G. Wells, *The War that Will End War* (New York: Duffield, 1914). In electronic form at http://catalog.hathitrust.org/Record/000403366. Woodrow Wilson used a variant phrasing: "I promise you that this will be the final war—the war to end all wars." Address of The President of the United States Delivered at a Joint Session of The Two Houses of Congress, April 2, 1917.

CHAPTER 13

1. Quoted in Williamson Murray, "Versailles: The Peace Without a Chance," in idem and Jim Lacey, editors, *The Making of Peace: Rulers, States, and the Aftermath of War* (Cambridge: Cambridge University Press, 2009): p. 209.

2. Alan Sharp, *The Consequences of the Peace: The Versailles Settlement; Aftermath and Legacy* (Chicago: University of Chicago Press, 2015): pp. 9–70.

3. The postwar German military was known as the *Reichswehr* to 1935, then as the Wehrmacht. The latter term encompassed all the armed services: the *Luftwaffe* (air force), *Kriegsmarine* (navy), and *Heer* (army).

4. Gerhard Weinberg, *A World at Arms: A Global History of World War II* (Cambridge: Cambridge University Press, 1995): pp. 96–100, 187–263.

5. Italian dictator Benito Mussolini made the declaration public from a balcony above the Piazza Venezia in Rome. Hitler made the German declaration in a speech to the Reichstag, both on December 11.

6. On hunger in China, see Rana Mitter, *Forgotten Ally: China's World War II, 1937–1945* (London: Penguin, 2013): pp. 263–279.

7. See Kelly Crager, *Hell Under the Rising Sun* (College Station: Texas A&M University Press, 2008), and Daniel Blatman, *Death Marches: The Final Phase of Genocide* (Cambridge: Belknap, 2011).

8. Julian Jackson, *The Fall of France: The Nazi Invasion of 1940* (Oxford: Oxford University Press, 2003): pp. 60–78; Ernst May, *Strange Victory: Hitler's Conquest of France* (New York: Hill & Wang, 2000): pp. 113–194. Also see Martin Alexander, *The Republic is in Danger* (Cambridge: Cambridge University Press, 1993); E. C. Kiesling, *Arming Against Hitler: France and the Limits of Military Planning* (Lawrence: University Press of Kansas, 1996); Elizabeth Kier, *Imagining Doctrine: French and British Military Doctrine between the Wars* (Princeton: Princeton University Press, 1997).

9. A contrary view is that of Talbot Imlay, *Facing the Second World War: Strategy, Politics, and Economics in Britain and France, 1938–1940* (Oxford: Oxford University Press, 2003): pp. 8–9, 23–134.

10. Peter Jackson, "British Power and French Security, 1919–1939," in Neilson and Kennedy, *British War of Warfare*: pp. 101–134; May, *Strange Victory*: pp. 306–322.

11. Gérard Saint-Martin, *L'Armée blindée française*, Vol. 1 (Paris: Economica, 1998): pp. 44–74; Reynolds Salerno, *Vital Crossroads: Mediterranean Origins of the Second World War, 1935–1940* (Oxford: Oxford University Press, 2002): pp. 40–72; May, *Strange Victory*: pp. 8–168. An older study is F. W. Deakin, *The Brutal Friendship: Mussolini, Hitler and the Fall of Italian Fascism* (London: Weidenfeld and Nicolson, 1962).

12. William Philpott and Martin Alexander, "The French and British Field Force: Moral Support or Material Contribution?" *Journal of Military History* 71/3 (2007): pp. 743–772; Brian Bond, *British Military Policy Between the Two World Wars* (Oxford: Oxford University Press, 1980): pp. 269–276.

13. On the interwar plans of all major armies, see Allan Millet and Williamson Murray, *Military Effectiveness: The Interwar Period* (Cambridge: Cambridge University Press, 2010).

14. Philpott and Alexander, "The British Field Force," pp. 751–752, 765–770.

15. Paul Kennedy, "British 'Net Assessment' and the Coming of the Second World War," and Stephen Ross, "French Net Assessment," in Williamson Murray and Allan R. Millet, editors, *Calculations: Net Assessment and the Coming of World War II* (New York: Macmillan, 1992): pp. 19–59, 136–174. R. J. Young, "La guerre de longue durée," in A. Preston, editor, *General Staffs and Diplomacy Before the Second World War* (London: Croom Helm, 1978): pp. 41–64.

16. On the general culture in Germany after World War I, see Wolfgang Schivelbusch, *The Culture of Defeat: On National Trauma, Mourning, and Recovery* (New York: Picador, 2004): pp. 189–288. On the failure to mobilize the economy for a long war as late as 1941, see David Stahel, *Kiev 1941: Hitler's Battle for Supremacy in the East* (Cambridge: Cambridge University Press, 2012): pp. 48–65; Forster, "Germany's War in Europe," pp. 99–102. On short war thinking, see Karl-Heinz Frieser, *The Blitzkrieg Legend: The 1940 Campaign in the West* (Annapolis: Naval Institute Press, 2005): pp. 10–59; and Citino, *German Way of War*: pp. 236–237.

17. Quoted in ibid., p. 243. See Matthias Strohn, *The German Army and the Defence of the Reich: Military Doctrine and the Conduct of Defensive Battle, 1918–1939* (Cambridge: Cambridge University Press, 2011): pp. 17–130; 185–202; 219–244; N. H. Gaworek, "Hans von Seeckt," in Zabecki, *Chief of Staff*, Vol. 1: pp. 136–148; and James Corum, *The Roots of Blitzkrieg: Hans Von Seeckt and German Military Reform* (Lawrence: University Press of Kansas, 1992): pp. 1–121.

18. See Denis Showalter, *Hitler's Panzers: The Lightning Attacks that Revolutionized Warfare* (New York: Penguin, 2009): pp. 3–36; 44–61; Corum, *Roots of Blitzkrieg*: pp. 122–143; David

Stone, "Misreading Svechin: Attrition, Annihilation, and Historicism," *Journal of Military History* 76/3 (2012): pp. 677–678; Richard Simpkin, *Deep Battle* (London: Brassey's, 1987); Jacob Kipp, "Military Doctrine and the Origins of Operational Art, 1917–1936," in Willard Frank and Philip Gillette, editors, *Soviet Military Doctrine from Lenin to Gorbachev* (Westport: Greenwood, 1992): pp. 85–132; David Glantz, "Developing Offensive Success," ibid., pp. 133–174; Richard Harrison, *The Russian Way of War: Operational Art, 1900–1940* (Lawrence: University Press of Kansas, 2001): pp. 186–194.

19. Citino, *German Way of War*: pp. 253–256.

20. Gary Sheffield, "Blitzkrieg and Attrition: Land Operations in Europe, 1914–1945," in idem and Colin McInnes, editors, *Warfare in the Twentieth Century* (London: Unwin Hyman, 1988): pp. 51–79. "Blitzkrieg" usually refers to combined-arms attack seeking breakthrough to assault command and communications. Karl-Heinz Frieser makes a critical distinction between blitzkrieg as lightning *operations* but not as lightning *war* in *Blitzkrieg Legend*: pp. 4–11.

21. Jürgen Forster, "Germany's War in Europe," in Stig Forster et al., editors, *A World at Total War* (Cambridge: Cambridge University Press, 2005): pp. 89–91.

22. Translated and published entire as "Hitler's Speech to the Commanders in Chief (August 22, 1939)" at www.germanhistorydocs.ghi-dc.org/sub_document.cfm?document_id=1546. On how this policy was carried out in Poland from the first day, see Richard Evans, *The Third Reich At War* (London: Penguin, 2008): pp. 3–105.

23. Gerhard Weinberg, editor, *Hitler's Second Book* (New York: Enigma, 2006): pp. 81–98, 156–238.

24. Weinberg, *World at Arms*: pp. 6–47; Robert C. Tucker, *Stalin in Power* (New York: Norton, 1990): pp. 392–440. Zara Steiner disagrees, portraying Stalin as confused and distrustful of all sides in 1939 in *The Triumph of the Dark* (Oxford: Oxford University Press, 2011): p. 910.

25. Steven Zaloga, *Poland 1939: The Birth of Blitzkrieg* (Oxford: Osprey, 2002): pp. 32–33, 75–78.

26. Robert Kennedy, *German Campaign in Poland, 1939* (Washington: Department of the Army, 1956): pp. 81–83; Stephen Zaloga and Victor Madej, *The Polish Campaign* (New York: Hippocrene, 1991): pp. 110–112; Cathal J. Nolan, "The German Invasion of Poland (September 1–October 5, 1939)," in Gordon Martel, editor, *The Encyclopedia of War* (London: Wiley-Blackwell, 2012).

27. Showalter, *Hitler's Panzers*: pp. 88–89.

28. Alexander Rossino, *Hitler Strikes Poland: Blitzkrieg, Ideology, and Atrocity* (Lawrence: University Press of Kansas, 2003): pp. 10–18, 20–21, 31–48, 1–57, 88–120.

29. Bernard Ireland, *Battle of the Atlantic* (Annapolis: Naval Institute Press, 2003): pp. 37–73.

30. Weinberg, *A World at Arms*: pp. 48–121.

31. Rossino, *Hitler Strikes Poland*: pp. 58–87.

32. Ibid., pp. 121–190; Evans, *Third Reich at War*: pp. 3–105; Richard Hargreaves, *Blitzkrieg Unleashed: The German Invasion of Poland, 1939* (Mechanicsburg: Stackpole, 2008): pp. 224–259; Jürgen Matthias et al., *War, Pacification, and Mass Murder, 1939: The Einsatzgruppen in Poland* (Lanham: Rowman & Littlefield, 2014).

33. Roger Reese, "Lessons of the Winter War: A Study in the Military Effectiveness of the Red Army, 1939–1940," *Journal of Military History* 72/3 (July 2008): pp. 825–852; Kipp, "Soviet Operational Art," pp. 64–85; Henrik Lunde, *Finland's War of Choice* (Newbury: Casemate, 2011): pp. 1–25, 38–40, 54–59, 113–117. Reese does not quite make the revisionist case that the Red Army performed robustly in Finland, but he does show that it was not a record of undiluted incompetence as the Germans thought and was often later said and written.

34. Marc Bloch's wartime musings were written in 1940 but not published in France until 1946 as *L'Étrange Défaite* and in English as *Strange Defeat* (New York: Oxford University Press, 1949). A veteran of both wars, Bloch was arrested and shot by the Gestapo in 1944 for his work with the Resistance.

35. Frieser, *Blitzkrieg Legend*: pp. 1–3, and passim. This is the major revisionist work by a leading German historian who challenges the old view of high Wehrmacht competence.

36. The seminal, bookend works are Bloch, *Strange Defeat,* and May, *Strange Victory.* Critically important is Frieser, *Blitzkrieg Legend*: pp. 100–346.

37. Ronald Powaski, *Lightning War: Blitzkrieg in the West, 1940* (Hoboken: Wiley, 2003): pp. 33–54; Frieser, *Blitzkrieg Legend*: pp. 60–99; May, *Strange Victory*: pp. 254–270; Citino, *German Way of War*: pp. 274–290.

38. Powaski, *Lightning War*: pp. 16–32.

39. Showalter, *Hitler's Panzers*: p. 103. More precise numbers are broken down by type in Frieser, *Blitzkrieg Legend*: pp. 37–44. On the Allies, see Doughty, *Seeds of Disaster*: pp. 185–198; Powaski, *Lightning War*: pp. 7–32.

40. Henry Dutailly, *Les problèmes de l'Armée de terre française, 1935–1939* (Paris: Imprimerie Nationale, 1980). On French domestic divisions and Anglo-French diplomatic and political relations, see Joel Blatt, editor, *The French Defeat of 1940: Reassessments* (New York: Berghahn, 1998).

41. Powaski, *Lightning War*: pp. 16–32.

42. The definitive works rewriting the history of the Meuse breakthrough are Frieser, *Blitzkrieg Legend*: pp. 100–114, and Robert Doughty, *The Breaking Point: Sedan and the Fall of France, 1940* (Mechanicsburg: Stackpole Reprint, 2014): pp. 29–102. On Guderian at the Meuse, see Showalter, *Hitler's Panzers*: pp. 106–109.

43. Frieser, *Blitzkrieg Legend*: pp. 145–197, 218–245; Powaski, *Lightning War*: pp. 107–158; Doughty, *Breaking Point*: pp. 103–210.

44. Ibid., pp. 265–272; Doughty, *Breaking Point*: pp. 211–250; Showalter, *Hitler's Panzers*: pp. 113–115.

45. Frieser, *Blitzkrieg Legend*: pp. 252–272. Also see Powaski, *Lightning War*: pp. 159–202; Julian Jackson, *Fall of France*: pp. 174–177.

46. Showalter, *Hitler's Panzers*: pp. 116–119.

47. Ibid., pp. 120–121; Frieser, *Blitzkrieg Legend*: pp. 291–302.

48. Ibid., pp. 305–314.

49. Raymond Callahan, *Churchill and His Generals* (Lawrence: University Press of Kansas, 2007): pp. 7–134.

50. Powaski, *Lightning War*: pp. 248–345; Jackson, *Fall of France*: pp. 94–100.

51. See Don Alexander, "Repercussions of the Breda Variant," *French Historical Studies* 8 (1974): pp. 459–488; Anthony Adamthwaite, *France and the Coming of the Second World War* (London: Frank Cass, 1977); Robert Young, *In Command of France* (Cambridge: Harvard University Press, 1978); Jeffrey Gunsburg, *Divided and Conquered: The French High Command and the Defeat of the West, 1940* (Westport: Greenwood, 1979).

52. The apogee of negativism was Jean-Baptiste Duroselles, *La décadence: La politique étrangère de la France, 1932–1939* (Paris: Imprimerie nationale, 1979). Alternatively, see Jackson, *Fall of France*: pp. 185–227, and Martin Alexander, "The Fall of France, 1940," *Journal of Strategic Studies* 13/1 (1990): pp. 10–44.

53. R. H. Stolfi, "Equipment for Victory in France," *History* 55 (1970): pp. 1–20; Charles de Gaulle, *Vers l'armée de métier* (Paris: Berger-Levrault, 1934); Imlay, *Facing the Second World War*: pp. 23–75.

54. Robert Doughty, *Seeds of Disaster*: pp. 95–116, 141–184. Also see Dutailly, *Les problèmes de l'armée de terre française*; Elizabeth Kier, *Imagining War: French and British Military Doctrine Between the Wars* (Princeton: Princeton University Press, 1997).

55. Robert Doughty, *The Seeds of Disaster: The Development of French Army Doctrine, 1919–1939* (Mechanicsburg: Stackpole Reprint, 2014): p. x.

56. Jeffrey Gunsburg, "*La Grande Illusion*: Belgian and Dutch Strategy Facing Germany, 1919–May 1940," *Journal of Military History* 78 (2014): pp. 101–158; Herman Amersfoort and Piet Kamphuis, editors, *May 1940: The Battle for the Netherlands* (Leiden: Brill, 2010).

57. Philip Bankwitz, "French Defeat in 1940 and Its Reversal in 1944–1945: The *Deuxième Division Blindée*," in Blatt, *Reassessments*: pp. 327–353; Jackson, *Fall of France*: pp. 101–142.

CHAPTER 14

1. See Stanley Payne, *Franco and Hitler: Spain, Germany, and World War II* (New Haven: Yale University Press, 2008): pp. 87–208; 267–270.

2. On the muddled but ultimately successful British mobilization of effective armies that fought to Axis defeat, see Allan Allport, *Browned-Off and Bloody-Minded: The British Soldier Goes to War, 1939–1945* (New Haven: Yale University Press, 2015): pp. 203–276 and passim.

3. Winston Churchill, June 4, 1940, House of Commons, available at http://www.churchill-society-london.org.uk/Dunkirk.html.

4. FDR's necessary electoral mendacity is detailed in Cathal J. Nolan, "'Bodyguard of Lies': Franklin D. Roosevelt and Defensible Deceit in World War II," in idem, editor, *Ethics and Statecraft: The Moral Dimension of International Affairs*, 3rd ed. (Westport: Praeger, 2016).

5. Atkinson, "Projecting American Power," pp. 348-349.

6. Woody Guthrie wrote a song about the sinking. Its chorus was, "Tell me, what were their names? Did you have a friend on the good *Reuben James*?"

7. Nolan, "Defensible Deceit."

8. Cynthia Roberts, "Planning for War: The Red Army and the Catastrophe of 1941," *Europe-Asia Studies* 48/8 (1995): pp. 1293–1326.

9. Roger R. Reese, "The Impact of the Great Purge on the Red Army: Wrestling With Hard Numbers," *Slavic & Eurasian Studies* 19 (1992): pp. 71–90; Walter S. Dunn, *Stalin's Keys to Victory: The Rebirth of the Red Army* (Mechanicsburg: Stackpole, 2007): pp. 7–62.

10. Ibid., p. viii.

11. Alexander Statiev, "Blocking Detachments in the Red Army," *Journal of Military History* 75 (2012): pp. 475–495.

12. Reese, "Lessons of the Winter War," pp. 827–830. On the later formation of a German-Finnish alliance during the "Continuation War," see Lunde, *Finland's War of Choice*: pp. 26–54.

13. On prewar machinations, see Gabriel Gorodetsky, *Grand Delusion: Stalin and the German Invasion of Russia* (New Haven: Yale University Press, 1999): pp. 48–114.

14. The key works are Viktor Suvorov, *The Chief Culprit: Stalin's Grand Design to Start World War II* (Annapolis: Naval Institute Press, 2008), which reprises earlier work discredited by David Glantz in *Stumbling Colossus: The Red Army on the Eve of World War* (Lawrence: University Press of Kansas, 1998). A moderate view is Evan Mawdsley, "Crossing the Rubicon: Soviet Plans for Offensive War in 1940–1941," *International History Review* 25/4 (2003): pp. 818–865. Also see persuasive documentary evidence in Alexander Hill, editor, *The Great Patriotic War of the Soviet Union, 1941–1945: A Documentary Reader* (New York: Routledge, 2009), Chapter 2: "The Icebreaker Controversy and Soviet Intentions in 1941."

15. Quoted in Cynthia Roberts, "Planning for War," p. 1293.

16. December 31, 1939, German General Staff report, *Nazi Conspiracy and Aggression*, Vol. 6 (Washington: GPO, 1946): pp. 981–982.

17. Reese, "Lessons of the Winter War," pp. 827–830. On Soviet motivation, see idem, *Why Stalin's Soldiers Fought: The Red Army's Military Effectiveness in World War II* (Lawrence: University Press of Kansas, 2011), and Catherine Merridale, *Ivan's War: Life and Death in the Red Army, 1939–1945* (New York: Macmillan, 2006): passim.

18. Führer Directive No. 21 (December 18, 1940), in Hugh Trevor-Roper, editor, *Hitler's War Directives, 1939–1945* (Edinburgh: Birlinn, 2004): pp. 95–98.

19. Geoffrey Megargee, *Barbarossa 1941: Hitler's War of Annihilation* (Stroud: Tempus, 2007): p. 53–54.

20. A fundamental revision of long-held views on the Kiev cauldron is Stahel, *Kiev 1941*: pp. 274–302. On the failure of logistics, see pp. 185–187, 322–331. On Army Group North and the fight in the forests, see David Glantz, *Battle for Leningrad, 1941–1944* (Lawrence: University Press of Kansas, 2002): pp. 25–50.

21. David Glantz, *Barbarossa Derailed*, Vol. 1 (Havertown: Casemate, 2010); David Stahel, *Operation Barbarossa and Germany's Defeat in the East* (Cambridge: Cambridge University Press, 2009): pp. 260–360.

22. On the centrality of logistical denial to German failure, see Craig Luther, *Barbarossa Unleashed* (Atglen: Schiffer, 2013). This work is less reliable on the issue of criminality in the Wehrmacht. See also Showalter, *Hitler's Panzers*: pp. 129–193.

23. Stahel, *Operation Barbarossa*: pp. 84–94, 127–138.

24. Entries for July 3 and August 11, 1941, Franz Halder, *Halder War Diary, 1939–1942* (Nuremberg: Office of Chief of Council for War Crimes, 1946).

25. David Stahel, *Operation Typhoon: Hitler's March on Moscow, October 1941* (Cambridge: Cambridge University Press 2013).

26. Evan Mawdsley, *Thunder in the East: The Nazi-Soviet War, 1941–1945* (London: Hodder, 2005): pp. 44–45. Hitler quoted at p. 110.

27. Citino, *German Way of War*: p. 299.

28. Showalter, *Hitler's Panzers*: pp. 196–199; Mawdsley, *Thunder in the East*: pp. 118–148.

29. The definitive and mostly persuasive work making this argument is Citino, *German Way of War*.

30. See Robert Citino, *Death of the Wehrmacht: The German Campaign of 1942* (Lawrence: University of Kansas Press, 2007).

31. Mawdsley, *Thunder in the East*: pp. 149–182.

32. David Glantz, "Stalingrad Revisited," *Journal of Military History* 72 (2008): pp. 907–910; idem, *The Stalingrad Trilogy*, 3 volumes (Lawrence: University Press of Kansas, 2014); Anthony Beevor, *Stalingrad, The Fateful Siege: 1942–1943* (London: Penguin Books, 1999). A firsthand account, with attendant problems, by the 62nd Army commander is V. I. Chuikov, *The Battle for Stalingrad* (New York: Holt, Rinehart, & Winston, 1964), originally published in Russian 1959.

33. Robert Citino is scathing in *The Wehrmacht Retreats: Fighting a Lost War* (Lawrence: University Press of Kansas, 2012): pp. 110–144. A somewhat revisionist account is Denis Showalter, *Armor and Blood: The Battle of Kursk* (New York: Random House, 2013).

34. See Steven Newton, editor, *Kursk: The German View* (New York: Da Capo, 2003); David Glantz and Jonathon House, *Battle of Kursk* (Lawrence: University Press of Kansas, 2004); Valeriy Zamulin, *Demolishing the Myth: The Tank Battle at Prokhorovka, Kursk, July 1943* (Solihull: Helion, 2011).

35. On post-Kursk offensives, see Mawdsley, *Thunder in the East*: pp. 273–396. A different view of German performance in World War II is Murray, *Military Adaptation*: pp. 119–152.

36. Douglas Porch, *Path to Victory: The Mediterranean Theater in World War II* (New York: Farrar, Straus, and Giroux, 2004): pp. 563–613; "Situation Conference, December 12, 1942," in Helmut Heiber and David Glantz, editors, *Hitler and His Generals: Military Conferences 1942–1945* (New York: Enigma, 2004): pp. 18–21.

37. Evans, *Third Reich at War*: pp. 217–318, 541–562, 593–646.

38. Adam Classen, *Hitler's Northern War* (Lawrence: University of Kansas Press, 2001).

39. See Thomas J. Laub, "The Development of German Policy in Occupied France, 1941, Against the Backdrop of the War in the East," in Alex Kay et al., editors, *Nazi Policy on the Eastern Front, 1941: Total War, Genocide, and Radicalization* (New York: University of Rochester Press, 2012): pp. 289–313.

40. On Stalin's singular responsibility for the disaster, see David Murphy, *What Stalin Knew: The Enigma of Barbarossa* (New Haven: Yale University Press, 2005).

41. Weinberg, *Hitler's Second Book*: pp. 7–36.

42. The phenomenon is captured explicitly in Citino, *German Way of War* and implicitly in Showalter, *Hitler's Panzers*.

43. Quoted in Farrar, *Short-War Illusion*: p. 151. On pathology in Nazi policy, see Evans, *Third Reich at War*: pp. 112–214.

44. Keith Bird, *Erich Raeder: Admiral of the Third Reich* (Annapolis: Naval Institute Press, 2006): pp. xviii–xxv, 84–85, 91–96, 100–111; G. Bennett and R. Bennett, *Hitler's Admirals* (Annapolis: Naval Institute Press, 1998): pp. 191–225.

45. Scheck, *Hitler's African Victims*; Megargee, *War of Annihilation*: pp. 1–18.

46. See the important works by Klaus Arnold, Omer Bartov, Jürgen Förster, Christian Gerlach, Christian Hartmann, Johannes Hürter and Christian Streit, among others. Also Raul Hilberg, *Destruction of the European Jews* (New York: Holmes & Meier, 1985); Timothy Snyder, *Bloodlands: Europe Between Hitler and Stalin* (New York: Basic, 2010); Peter Longerich, *Heinrich Himmler: A Life* (Oxford: Oxford University Press, 2012): pp. 515–645.

47. Gerhard Weinberg, "Some Myths of World War II," *Journal of Military History* 75/3 (2011): p. 705.

48. See especially Erich von Manstein, *Lost Victories* (Chicago: Regnery, 1958); Heinz Guderian, *Panzer Leader* (New York: Dutton, 1952); more narrowly, Russell Hart, *Guderian: Panzer Pioneer or Myth Maker?* (Washington: Potomac Books, 2006). On criminality of officers, see Omer Bartov, *The Eastern Front 1941–1945: German Troops and the Barbarization of Warfare*, 2nd ed. (New York: Palgrave, 2001): pp. 40–67, 106–141.

49. Felix Römer, "The Wehrmacht in the War of Ideologies," in Kay, *Nazi Policy*: pp. 73–100, and other essays in this volume and in Hannes Heer and Klaus Naumann, editors, *War of Extermination: The German Military in World War II, 1941–1944* (New York: Berghahn, 2000).

50. Waitman Beorn, "A Calculus of Complicity: The 'Wehrmacht', the Anti-Partisan War, and the Final Solution in White Russia, 1941–42," *Central European History* 44/2 (2011): pp. 308–337; idem, *Marching into Darkness: The Wehrmacht and the Holocaust in Belarus* (Cambridge: Harvard University Press, 2014); Phillip W. Blood, *Hitler's Bandit Hunters: The SS and the Nazi Occupation of Europe* (Lincoln: University of Nebraska Press, 2006): pp. 95–213.

51. Yaron Pasher, *Holocaust vs. Wehrmacht: How Hitler's 'Final Solution' Undermined the German War Effort* (Lawrence: University of Kansas Press, 2015).

52. This powerful point is made by Omer Bartov, *Mirrors of Destruction: War, Genocide, and Modern Identity* (New York: Oxford University Press, 2000): pp. 9–43.

53. A point made by Weinberg in *A World at Arms*: p. 482.

54. Hans Mommsen, "German Society and the Resistance Against Hitler," in Christian Leitz, editor, *The Third Reich: Essential Readings* (London: Blackwell, 1999): pp. 255–273.

55. Danny Orbach, *The Plots Against Hitler* (New York: Houghton Mifflin Harcourt, 2016): pp. 121–126, and passim.

56. Wolfram Wette, *The Wehrmacht: History, Myth, Reality* (Cambridge: Harvard University Press, 2006); Stephen Fritz, *Ostkrieg: Hitler's War of Extermination in the East* (Lexington: University of Kentucky Press, 2011); Geoffrey Megargee, *War of Annihilation: Combat and Genocide on the Eastern Front* (New York: Rowman & Littlefield, 2006); Lizzie Collingham, *The Taste of War: World War II and the Battle for Food* (London: Penguin, 2011): pp. 18–48, 180–218; Alex Kay, "The Purpose of the Russian Campaign is the Decimation of the Slavic Population by Thirty Million: The Radicalization of German Food Policy in Early 1941," in Kay, *Nazi Policy*: pp. 101–129.

57. Citino, *German Way of War*: pp. 269–305; Dennis Showalter, "Prussian and German Operational Art, 1740–1943," in John Andreas Olsen and Martin van Creveld, editors, *The Evolution of Operational Art from Napoleon to the Present* (Oxford: Oxford University Press, 2011): pp. 96–136.

58. On Poland, see Blood, *Hitler's Bandit Hunters*: pp. 219–240; on the Soviet Union, see Kenneth Slepyan, *Stalin's Guerrillas: Soviet Partisans in World War II* (Lawrence: University Press of Kansas, 2006): pp. 15–59.

59. Christian Hartman, *Operation Barbarossa: Nazi Germany's War in the East, 1941–1945* (Oxford: Oxford University Press, 2013): pp. 9–18 and passim.

60. Römer, "War of Ideologies," pp. 73–100.

61. Magisterial on civilians is Karel Berkoff, *Harvest of Despair: Life and Death in Ukraine under Nazi Rule* (Cambridge: Belknap, 2004). Also see Laurie Cohen, *Smolensk Under the Nazis: Everyday Life in Occupied Russia* (New York: University of Rochester Press, 2013).

62. The English translation of the definitive German history is Bernhard Kroener et al., *Germany and the Second World War*, Vol. 5: *Wartime Administration, Economy, and Manpower Resources, 1942–1945* (Oxford: Clarendon, 2003).

63. On the wartime politics of food, see Wendy Goldman and Donald Filtzer, editors, *Hunger and War: Food Provisioning in the Soviet Union during World War II* (Bloomington, Indiana University Press, 2015): pp. 1–43.

64. Robert Pringle, "SMERSH: Military Counterintelligence and Stalin's Control of the USSR," *International Journal of Intelligence and Counterintelligence* 21 (2008): pp. 122–134; Cathal J. Nolan, "Americans in the Gulag," *Journal of Contemporary History* 25/4 (1990): pp. 523–545.

65. Mawdsley, *Thunder in the East*: p. 402.

66. Motadel, *Islam and Nazi Germany's War*: pp. 217–315.

67. R. L. Dinardo and Austin Bay, "Horse-Drawn Transport in the German Army," *Journal of Contemporary History* 23/1 (1988): p. 135; Showalter, *Hitler's Panzers*: p. 358; Omer Bartov, *Hitler's Army: Soldiers, Nazis and War in the Third Reich* (Oxford: Oxford University Press, 1992): pp. 12–28.

68. Ian Kershaw, *The End: The Defiance and Destruction of Hitler's Germany, 1944–1945* (New York: Penguin, 2011): p. 27, 207–246.

69. On interservice rivalry, see James Corum, *The Luftflotte: Creating the Operational Air War, 1918–1940* (Lawrence: University of Kansas Press, 1997): pp. 109–112; 263–266; David Isby, editor, *The Luftwaffe's War at Sea, 1939–1945* (London: Chatham, 2005); and Sonke Neitzel, "Kriegsmarine and Luftwaffe Co-operation in the War against Britain, 1939–1945," *War in History* 10 (2003): pp. 448–463. On overall dysfunction, see Williamson Murray, *Strategy for Defeat: The Luftflotte, 1933–1945* (Maxwell: Air University Press, 1983).

70. Showalter, *Hitler's Panzers*: pp. 136–139; Evans, *Third Reich at War*: pp. 321–402; and comparative essays in Allan Millet and Williamson Murray, *Military Effectiveness,* Vol. 3: *The Second World War* (Cambridge: Cambridge University Press, 2010).

71. For example, Canada ranked behind only the United States and Great Britain as a wartime ship-building nation, after expanding its capacity dramatically from a tiny prewar base. James Pritchard, *A Bridge of Ships: Canadian Ship-Building during the Second World War* (Montreal: McGill-Queen's University Press, 2011).

72. On Allied production, see Richard Overy, *Why the Allies Won* (New York: Norton, 1995): pp. 180–207; Adrian Tooze, *Wages of Destruction: The Making and Breaking of the Nazi Economy* (London: Penguin, 2006): pp. 461ff.; Mark Harrison, editor, *The Economies of World War II* (Cambridge: Cambridge University Press, 1998). David Edgerton argues that Britain could have defeated Germany on its own, based on superior war production, naval supremacy and air superiority, in *Britain's War Machine: Weapons, Resources, and Experts in the Second World War* (Oxford: Oxford University Press, 2011). A starkly materialist view of the war as won by production is Mark Harrison, *Soviet Planning in Peace and War, 1938–1945* (Cambridge: Cambridge University Press, 1985), and idem, "The USSR and Total War," in Forster, *World at Total War*: pp. 137–156.

73. Mark Reardon, *Victory at Mortain: Stopping Hitler's Panzer Counteroffensive* (Lawrence: University Press of Kansas, 2002): pp. 287–296; John Prados, *Normandy Crucible: The Decisive Battle That Shaped World War II in Europe* (New York: NAL Caliber, 2012); Peter Caddick-Adams, *Snow & Steel: The Battle of the Bulge, 1944–1945* (New York: Oxford University Press, 2014): pp. 473–502; John Eisenhower, *The Bitter Woods: The Battle of the Bulge* (New York: Da Capo, 1995): pp. 307–345, 346–375, 405–430.

74. Karen Hagemann, "Mobilizing for War: The History, Historiography, and Memory of German Women's Service in Two World Wars," *Journal of Military History*, 75 (2011): pp. 1055–1093; Perry Biddescombe, "Into the Maelstrom: German Women in Combat, 1944–1945," *War & Society* 30 (2011): pp. 61–89.

75. On raw numbers in the Red Army, see Anna Krylova, *Soviet Women in Combat: A History of Violence on the Eastern Front* (Cambridge: Cambridge University Press, 2010): pp. 162–170, 204–210, 241–245. On women infantry, see Euridice Cardona and Roger Markwick, "'Our Brigade Will Not Be Sent to the Front': Soviet Women Under Arms in the Great Fatherland War, 1941–45," *Russian Review* 68/2 (2009): pp. 240–262. Also see Reese, *Why Stalin's Soldiers Fought*: pp. 257–305; Roger Markwick and Euridice Cardona, *Soviet Women on the Frontline in World War II* (New York: Palgrave, 2012): pp. 84–116; 230–238; and Reina Pennington, "Offensive Women: Women in Combat in the Red Army in the Second World War, *Journal of Military History* 74/3 (2010): pp. 775–820.

76. Weinberg, *A World at Arms*: pp. 42–44, 364–407. Also see Edgerton, *Britain's War Machine*: pp. 12–14; 158–194; 277–278.

77. On Italy's role and experience in the Axis, see Morgan, *Fall of Mussolini*: pp. 127–266; Brian Sullivan, "The Italian Soldier in Combat," in Paul Addison and Angus Calder, editors, *Time to Kill: The Soldier's Experience of War in the West, 1939–1945* (London: Random House, 1997); Davide Rodogno, *Fascism's European Empire: Italian Occupation During the Second World War* (Cambridge: Cambridge University Press, 2006).

78. Text at http://research.calvin.edu/german-propaganda-archive/goeb36.htm Also see Mawdsley, *Thunder in the East*: pp. 186–187; Evans, *Third Reich at War*: pp. 403–432.

79. On Italy, see Philip Morgan, *The Fall of Mussolini: Italy, the Italians, and the Second World War* (New York: Oxford University Press, 2008): pp. 34–84.

80. Glantz, "Stalingrad Revisited," pp. 907–910. A study in classifications that perhaps unwittingly makes this point in its title is P. Bell, *Twelve Turning Points of the Second World War* (New Haven: Yale University Press, 2011). The text unhelpfully defines turning point as "simply a point at which a decisive or important change takes place" (p. xiii).

81. Citino, *Wehrmacht Retreats*: pp. 143–144; 227.

82. The literature on D-Day and Normandy is vast. Craig Symonds, *Neptune: The Allied Invasion of Europe and the D-Day Landings* (New York: Oxford University Press, 2014), and Anthony Beevor, *D-Day: The Battle for Normandy* (New York: Viking, 2009) provide a good start. Harshly critical of Allied performance, contemptuous of a supposed deficit in toughness and scathing about behavior toward French civilians is Olivier Wieviorka, *Normandy: The Landings to the Liberation of Paris* (Cambridge: Harvard University Press, 2008): pp. 201–270; 323–355, originally published as *Histoire du débarquement en Normandie: Des origines à la libération de Paris, 1941–1944* (Paris: Seuil, 2007). A useful contrast to this splenetic account as well as to routine American critiques of the British Army is John Buckley, *Monty's Men: The British Army and the Liberation of Europe* (New Haven: Yale University Press, 2013): especially pp. 72–145. Similarly revising the reputation of the Canadian Army is Terry Copp's fine study *Fields of Fire: Canadians in Normandy* (Toronto: University of Toronto Press, 2003): pp. 215–252.

83. J. Kaufmann and H. Kaufmann, *Fortress Third Reich: German Fortifications and Defense Systems in World War II* (Cambridge: Da Capo, 2003). *Ostwall* at pp. 274–280, 327–331.

84. Mawdsley, *Thunder in the East*: pp. 291–360; Evans, *Third Reich at War*: pp. 649–764.

85. Weinberg, *A World at Arms*: pp. 667–721, 780–841.

86. Anthony Beevor, *The Battle of Berlin* (New York: Penguin, 2003): pp. 266–406. An important corrective to the decisive-battle explanation of Allied victory and Axis defeat is Paul Kennedy, *Engineers of Victory: The Problem Solvers Who Turned the Tide in the Second World War* (New York: Random House, 2013). Also see Overy, *Why the Allies Won*.

87. See Merridale, *Ivan's War*: pp. 281–314.

88. Tami Davis Biddle, "Dresden 1945: Reality, History, and Memory," *Journal of Military History* 72/2 (2008): p. 431–436; Paul Addison and Jeremy Crang, editors, *Firestorm: The Bombing of Dresden* (Chicago: Ivan R. Dee, 2006); Richard Overy, *The Bombers and the Bombed: Allied Air War over Europe, 1940–1945* (New York: Viking, 2014). Overy's figure of 353,000 German civilian deaths is much lower than the widely accepted total of 620,000.

89. Overseas Press Club Talk, March 1, 1945, emphasis in original. Available at http://marshallfoundation.org/library/digital-archive/speech-to-the-overseas-press-club.

90. Arnold quoted in Biddle, "Dresden," p. 441.

CHAPTER 15

1. On the Kaigun, see David C. Evans and Mark Peattie, *Kaigun: Strategy, Tactics, and Technology in the Imperial Japanese Navy, 1897–1941* (Annapolis: Naval Institute Press, 1994): pp. 1–31. On the Rikugun, see Edward Drea, *Japan's Imperial Army: Its Rise and Fall, 1853–1945* (Lawrence: University Press of Kansas, 2009), and Stewart Lone, *Army, Empire, and Politics in Meiji Japan* (New York: St. Martin's, 2000).

2. I am indebted to Danny Orbach for these insights, gleaned from conversation and his doctoral dissertation in history, "Culture of Disobedience: Rebellion and Defiance in the Japanese Army, 1860–1937," Harvard University, 2015 (author's defense copy), forthcoming as *Curse on This Country: Japanese Military Insubordination and the Origins of the Pacific War* (Cornell University Press, 2017).

3. Mark Peattie, "Japan: The Teikoku Kaigun," in Vincent P. O'Hara et al., editors, *On Seas Contested: The Seven Great Navies of the Second World War* (Annapolis: Naval Institute Press, 2010): p. 157–159.

4. Richard Wright, *The Chinese Steam Navy: 1862–1945* (London: Chatham, 2000): pp. 41–84; H. P. Willmott, *The Last Century of Sea Power*, Vol. 1: *From Port Arthur to Chanak, 1894–1922* (Bloomington: Indiana University Press, 2009): pp. 19–27.

5. Ibid., pp. 85–96; S. C. M. Paine, *The Sino-Japanese War of 1894–1895: Perceptions, Power, and Primacy* (New York: Cambridge University Press, 2003): pp. 179–194; Evans and Peattie, *Kaigun*: pp. 38–51; John Perry, "The Battle off the Tayang, 17 September 1894," *Mariner's Mirror* 50 (1964): pp. 243–259; Evans and Peattie, *Kaigun*: pp. 37–51.

6. Evans and Peattie, pp. 50–51.

7. J. N. Westwood, *Russia Against Japan, 1904–1905: A New Look at the Russo-Japanese War* (Albany: SUNY Press, 1986): pp. 37–51, 72–115.

8. Evans and Peattie, *Kaigun*: pp. 102–110.

9. The account that follows draws on ibid., pp. 94–132; Westwood, *Russia Against Japan*: pp. 137–151; David Stone, *A Military History of Russia* (Westport: Praeger, 2006): pp. 139–155; Ronald Spector, *At War at Sea* (New York: Penguin, 2001): pp. 1–21; Willmott, *Port Arthur to Chanak*: pp. 74–127; Pertii Luntinen and Bruce Menning, "The Russian Navy at War," in John Steinberg et al., editors, *The Russo-Japanese War in Global Perspective* Leiden: Brill, 2005): pp. 229–260; and a firsthand account by a steward on the ironclad *Oryol*, A. Novikoff-Priboy, *Tsushima*, translated by Eden and Cedar Paul (London: Allen & Unwin, 1936).

10. John Bushnell, "The Specter of Mutinous Reserves," in Steinberg, *Russo-Japanese War*: pp. 333–348.

11. Evans and Peattie, *Kaigun*: pp. 118. Nelson's signal in 1805 was "England expects that every man will do his duty."

12. Ibid., pp. 124–125.

13. Ibid., pp. 116–124; David R. Stone, *A Military History of Russia* (Westport: Praeger, 2006): pp. 139–155; Ronald Spector, *At War at Sea* (New York: Penguin, 2001): pp. 1–21.

14. Drea, *Japan's Imperial Army*: pp. 17–18, 28–34, 57–61.

15. Orbach, *Culture of Disobedience*.

16. Drea, *Japan's Imperial Army*: pp. 35–46; Ernst Presseisen, *Before Aggression: Europeans Prepare the Japanese Army* (Tucson: University of Arizona Press, 1965). The key adviser was Jacob Meckel.

17. I am grateful to Danny Orbach for his insight on this point.

18. Paine, *Sino-Japanese War of 1894–1895*: pp. 147–149, 236–238.

19. Drea, *Japan's Imperial Army*: p.74.

20. Ibid., pp. 165–175; Drea, *Japan's Imperial Army*: pp. 84–85.

21. Ibid.

22. Paine, *Sino-Japanese War of 1894–1895*: pp. 168–169 and passim; Drea, *Japan's Imperial Army*: p. 86.

23. Paine, *Sino-Japanese War of 1894–1895*: pp. 187–192.

24. Yoshihisa Tak Matsuka, "Human Bullets, General Nogi, and the Myth of Port Arthur," in Steinberg, *Russo-Japanese War*: pp. 179–202. A junior officer participant account is Tadayoshi Sakurai, *Human Bullets: A Soldier's Story of the Russo-Japanese War* (Boston: Houghton, Mifflin, 1907), reprinted by University of Nebraska Press, 1999.

25. Drea, *Japan's Imperial Army*: pp. 104–108.

26. Oleg Benesch, *Inventing the Way of the Samurai* (Oxford: Oxford University Press, 2014): pp. 42–110.

27. Ibid., pp. 131–133.

28. See Richard J. Samuels, *"Rich Nation, Strong Army": National Security and the Technological Transformation of Japan* (Ithaca: Cornell University Press, 1996).

29. Alfred Thayer Mahan, *The Influence of Sea Power upon History, 1660–1783* (Boston: Little, Brown, 1890–1892). See also the collected essays in John B. Hattendorf, editor, *The Influence of History on Mahan* (Newport: Naval War College Press, 1991).

30. Roger Dingman, "Japan and Mahan," in Hattendorf, *Influence of History on Mahan*: pp. 49–66; Sadao Asada, *From Mahan to Pearl Harbor: American Strategic Theory and the Rise of the Imperial Japanese Navy* (Annapolis: Naval Institute Press, 2006): pp. 3–46. On Jutland, see Spector, *At War at Sea*: pp. 64–91.

31. Carl Boyd and Akihiko Yoshida, *The Japanese Submarine Force and World War II* (Annapolis: Naval Institute Press, 2012): pp. 1–7.

32. Richard Frank, *Guadalcanal* (New York: Penguin, 1992): pp. 428–492; Jeff Reardon, "Breaking the U.S. Navy's 'Gun Club' Mentality in the South Pacific," *Journal of Military History* 75

(2011): pp. 533–564; Paul S. Dull, *A Battle History of the Imperial Japanese Navy, 1941–1945* (Annapolis: Naval Institute Press, 1978): pp. 181–275; Evans and Peattie, *Kaigun*: pp. 199–212.

33. Peattie, "Teikoku Kaigun," pp. 159–160; 164; 173–174; Evans and Peattie, *Kaigun*: pp. 52–93.

34. On Japan's pre–World War I pursuit of a "Six-Six," then an "Eight-Eight," fleet to keep pace with the U.S. Navy, see Evans and Peattie, *Kaigun*: pp. 133–198.

35. Sadeo Asada, "The Revolt Against the Washington Treaty: The Imperial Japanese Navy and Naval Limitation, 1921–1927," *Naval War College Review* 46 (Summer 1993): pp. 82–97.

36. Some scholars challenge whether the U.S. Navy was battleship-centric to the eve of war. See Joel Holwitt, "Reappraising the Interwar U.S. Navy," *Journal of Military History* 76 (2012): pp. 193–210; Thomas Hone and Trent Hone, *Battle Line: The United States Navy, 1919–1939* (Annapolis: Naval Institute Press, 2006): Chapters 5, 6, and 7.

37. Edward Miller, *War Plan Orange: The U.S. Strategy to Defeat Japan, 1897–1945* (Annapolis: Naval Institute Press, 1991): pp. 77–149, 180–185, 286–312; Henry Gole, *The Road to Rainbow: Army Planning for Global War, 1934–1940* (Lawrence: University Press of Kansas, 2003); Trent Hone, "Evolution of Fleet Tactical Doctrine in the U.S. Navy, 1922–1941," *Journal of Military History* 67 (2003): pp. 1007–1048; idem, "U.S. Navy Surface Battle Doctrine and Victory in the Pacific," *Naval War College Review*, 62/1 (2009): pp. 67–105.

38. Kennedy, *British Naval Mastery*: pp. 239–298; Andrew Field, *Royal Navy Strategy in the Far East, 1919–1939: Planning for War Against Japan* (New York: Cass, 2004): pp. 123–182.

39. Enrico Cernuschi and Vincent P. O'Hara, "Italy: The Regia Marina," in O'Hara, *On Seas Contested*: pp. 125–129; 134; James Sadkovich, *The Italian Navy in World War II* (Westport: Greenwood, 1994).

40. Stephen McLaughlin, "USSR: The Voenno-morskoi Flot SSSR," in O'Hara, *On Seas Contested*: p. 254, 260–261; 278; M. G. Saunders, editor, *The Soviet Navy* (New York: Praeger, 1958); and Jürgen Rohwer and Mikhail Monakov, *Stalin's Ocean-Going Fleet: Soviet Naval Strategic and Shipbuilding Programmes, 1935–1953* (London: Frank Cass, 2001).

41. Peattie, "Teikoku Kaigun," p. 160–161; Evans and Peattie, *Kaigun*: pp. 199–298.

42. Ibid., pp. 370–383.

43. Ibid., pp. 357–360.

44. Alvin Coox, *Nomonhan: Japan Against Russia, 1939* (Stanford: Stanford University Press, 1985). Also see Stuart Goldman, *Nomonhan: The Red Army's Victory that Shaped World War II* (Annapolis: Naval Institute Press, 2012). On narrower issues, see Hiroaki Kuromiya, "The Mystery of Nomonhan, 1939," *Journal of Slavic Military Studies* 24/4 (2011): pp. 659–677.

45. Barnhart, *Japan Prepares for Total War*: pp. 198–214; Sumio Hatana and Sadao Asada, "The Japanese Decision to Move South, 1939–1941," in Robert Boyce and Esmond Robertson, editors, *Paths to War* (New York: St. Martins, 1989): pp. 383–407.

46. Nicholas Tarling, *A Sudden Rampage: The Japanese Occupation of Southeast Asia, 1941–1945* (Honolulu: University of Hawaii Press, 2001): pp. 39–79; H. P. Willmott, *Empires in the Balance: Japanese and Allied Pacific Strategies to April 1942* (Annapolis: Naval Institute Press, 1982): pp. 67–94.

47. John T. Kuehn, *Agents of Innovation: The General Board and the Design of the Fleet that Defeated the Japanese* (Annapolis: Naval Institute Press, 2008): pp. 40–143; Robert Love, *History of the U.S. Navy, 1775–1941* (Harrisburg: Stackpole, 1992): pp. 594–595, 606–607, 622–623.

48. Yoichi Hirama, "Japanese Naval Preparations for World War II," *Naval War College Review* 44 (Spring 1991): pp. 63–81. The thesis that the Kaigun was the principal mover in war with the United States is not universally accepted. It is most persuasively presented by Evans and Peattie, *Kaigun*: pp. 447–486. Supporting documentary evidence abounds in James Morley, editor, *The Fateful Choice: Japan's Advance into Southeast Asia, 1939–1941*, translations from the *Taiheiyō sensō e no michi* series, 1962–1963 (New York: Columbia University Press, 1980). Also see Michael Barnhart, *Japan Prepares for Total War: The Search for Economic Security, 1919–1941* (Ithaca: Cornell University Press, 1987).

49. On Japanese concern about Germany's intentions toward French Indochina, given the hard fact of German armies occupying part of France, see Drea, *Japan's Imperial Army*: p. 209. On Rikugun

views of its role in Asia, see Yukio Koshiro, *Imperial Eagle: Japan's Strategic Thinking about Continental Asia before August 1945* (Ithaca: Cornell University Press, 2013).

50. Evans and Peattie, *Kaigun*: pp. 510–511, 609, n.44.

51. Holwitt, "Reappraising," p. 201; Alfred Nofi, *To Train the Fleet for War: The U.S. Navy Fleet Problems, 1923–1940* (Newport: Naval War College Press, 2010): pp. 195–264.

52. Quoted in Evans and Peattie, *Kaigun*: p. 456. On complex issues and negotiations preceding the decision for war, see Dorothy Borg and Shumpei Okamato, editors, *Pear Harbor as History: Japanese-American Relations, 1931–1941* (New York: Columbia University Press, 1973), and Hilary Conroy and Harry Wray, editors, *Pearl Harbor Reexamined: Prologue to the Pacific War* (Honolulu: University of Hawaii Press, 1990). For broad cultural context, see Akira Iriye, *The Origins of the Second World War in Asia and the Pacific* (New York: Longman, 1987). On Japanese planning and crisis decision-making, see Barnhart, *Japan Prepares for Total War*: pp. 237–262; James Morley, *Japan's Road to the Pacific War* (New York: Columbia University Press, 2013): pp. 230–248; Nobutaka Ike, editor, *Japan's Decision for War: Records of the 1941 Policy Conferences* (Stanford: Stanford University Press, 1967); Donald Goldstein and Katherine Dillon, editors, *The Pearl Harbor Papers: Inside the Japanese Plans* (New York: Brassey, 1993); and Peter Mauch, *Sailor Diplomat: Nomura Kichisaburō and the Japanese-American War* (Cambridge: Harvard University Press, 2011): pp. 136–203.

53. Edward Drea, *In the Service of the Emperor: Essays on the Imperial Japanese Army* (Lincoln: University of Nebraska Press, 1998): p. 187.

54. Mauch, *Nomura Kichisaburō*: pp. 114–203.

55. Michael Barnhart, "Japanese Intelligence Before the Second World War," in Ernest R. May, editor, *Knowing One's Enemies: Intelligence Assessment Before the Two World Wars* (Princeton: Princeton University Press, 1984): pp. 424–455. Also see Edward Drea, *MacArthur's ULTRA: Codebreaking and the War Against Japan, 1941–1945* (Lawrence: University of Kansas Press, 1992); Douglas Ford, "Planning for an Unpredictable War: British Intelligence Assessments and the War Against Japan, 1937–1945," *Journal of Strategic Studies* (2004): pp. 136–167; and idem, *Britain's Secret War Against Japan* (New York: Routledge, 2006).

56. Eri Hotta, *Japan 1941: Countdown to Infamy* (New York: Knopf, 2013): p. 14. A well-reasoned contrary view is Michael W. Myers, *The Pacific War and Contingent Victory: Why Japanese Defeat Was Not Inevitable* (Lawrence: University Press of Kansas, 2015); also see James Wood, *Japanese Military Strategy in the Pacific War: Was Defeat Inevitable?* (Lanham MD: Rowman and Littlefield, 2007).

57. The classic work is Gordon Prange et al., *At Dawn We Slept: The Untold Story of Pearl Harbor* (New York: McGraw-Hill, 1981): pp. 189–306. Also see Willmott, *Empires in the Balance*: pp. 130–174; Evans and Peattie, *Kaigun*: pp. 471–479; Dull, *Battle History*: pp. 1–48; Gordon Prange et al., *Pearl Harbor: The Verdict of History* (New York: McGraw Hill, 1986).

58. Hiroyuki Agawa, *The Reluctant Admiral: Yamamoto and the Imperial Navy* (Tokyo: Kodansha International, 1979): pp. 193–200, 214–223, 227–230, 238; and Yoji Koda, "A Commander's Dilemma: Admiral Yamamoto and the 'Gradual Attrition' Strategy," *Naval War College Review* 46 (Autumn 1993): pp. 63–7; Evans and Peattie, *Kaigun*: pp. 466, 472, 480, 482.

59. Text of the grand strategy presented to the November 15, 1941, Imperial Liaison Conference by Admiral Nagano, reproduced and translated in Ike, *Japan's Decision for War*: pp. 247–249. Also see Gordon Prange et al., *December 7, 1941: The Day the Japanese Attacked Pearl Harbor* (New York: Wings Books, 1991).

60. Evans and Peattie, *Kaigun*: pp. 479–480; Ikuhiko Hata, "Admiral Yamamoto's Surprise Attack and the Japanese Navy's War Strategy," in Saki Dockrill, editor, *From Pearl Harbor to Hiroshima: The Second World War in Asia and the Pacific, 1941–1945* (New York: St. Martin's, 1994): pp. 55–72; Herbert Rosinski, "The Strategy of Japan," in B. Simpson, editor, *Development of Naval Thought* (Newport: Naval Institute Press, 1976).

61. Boyd and Yoshida, *The Japanese Submarine Force*: pp. 53–91, 134–157. Royal Navy submarines were similarly dispersed away from what might have been a more effective offensive role, which they demonstrated in the Mediterranean theater. See Richard Hammond, "Fighting under a Different Flag: Multinational Naval Cooperation and Submarine Warfare in the Mediterranean, 1941–1944," *Journal of Military History* 80 (2016): pp. 451-460.

62. Boyd and Yoshida, *The Japanese Submarine Force*: pp. xi–xii, 113–133, 158–190.
63. An exception was protection by Japanese destroyers of troop ships. Peattie, "Teikoku Kaigun," p. 127; Oi Atushi, "Why Japan's Anti-Submarine Warfare Failed," in David C. Evans, editor, *The Japanese Navy in World War II in the Words of Former Japanese Naval Officers*, 2nd ed. (Annapolis: Naval Institute Press, 1986); Evans and Peattie, *Kaigun*: pp. 199–298, 364–370, 424–446; Peattie, "Teikoku Kaigun," pp. 162–164.
64. Trent Hone, "The U.S. Navy," in O'Hara, *On Seas Contested*: pp. 228–230, and Tomas Hone and Trent Hone, *Battle Line: The United States Navy,1919–1939* (Annapolis: Naval Institute Press, 2006): pp. 110–125; Clay Blair, *Silent Victory: The U.S. Submarine War Against Japan* (Annapolis: Naval Institute Press, 2001); Kenneth J. Hagan, "American Submarine Warfare in the Pacific, 1941–1945: *Guerre de course* Triumphant," in Günther Bischof and Robert Dupont, editors, *The Pacific War Revisited* (Baton Rouge: Louisiana University Press, 1997): pp. 81–108.
65. Hans Lengerer, "The Japanese Superbattleship Strategy," Parts 1–3, *Warship*, 22/23/24 (1982).

CHAPTER 16

1. Drea, *Japan's Imperial Army*: pp. 138–141.
2. See Mark Peattie, *Ishiwara Kanji and Japan's Confrontation with the West* (Princeton: Princeton University Press, 1976).
3. See the insightful review by Stephen Pelz in *Journal of the American Oriental Society* 97 (1977): p. 344.
4. Drea, *Japan's Imperial Army*: pp. 156–159, 182–183. James Morley, editor, *The China Quagmire: Japan's Expansion on the Asian Continent, 1933–1941* (New York: Columbia University Press, 1983): pp. 3–230.
5. Barbara Brooks, *Japan's Imperial Diplomacy: Consuls, Treaty Ports, and War in China, 1895–1938* (Honolulu: University of Hawaii Press, 2000): pp. 160–207; Barnhart, *Japan Prepares for Total War*: pp. 198–214; Drea, *In the Service of the Emperor*: pp. 169–215; John Chapman, "The Imperial Japanese Navy and the North-South Dilemma," in John Erickson and David Dilks, editors, *Barbarossa: The Axis and The Allies* (Edinburgh: Edinburgh University Press, 1994): pp. 150–206; Evans and Peattie, *Kaigun*: pp. 447–486. On the Chinese side of this conflict, see Maochun Yu, *The Dragon's War: Allied Operations and the Fate of China, 1937–1947* (Annapolis: Naval Institute Press, 2006).
6. Mitter, *Forgotten Ally*: pp. 79–97.
7. Morley, *China Quagmire*: pp. 233–286.
8. Andrew Levidis, "Conservatism and Japanese Army Factionalism, 1937-1939: The Case of Prince Konoe Fumimaro and Baron Hiranuma Kiichirō," unpublished notes of research talk (2016): pp. 1-3.
9. Peter Harmsen, *Shanghai 1937: Stalingrad on the Yangtze* (Havertown: Casemate, 2013): pp. 133–148, 162–179, fall of Nanjing at pp. 233–247; Mitter, *Forgotten Ally*: pp. 98–108, 124–144. There is a cottage industry of Nanjing-denial literature in Japan. The Chinese official figure is 300,000. No one is certain, but 200,000 killed is a rough consensus.
10. Levidis, "Conservatism and Japanese Army Factionalism," pp. 4–5.
11. Morley, *China Quagmire*: pp. 309–435.
12. Chang Jui-te, "The Nationalist Army on the Eve of War," in Mark Peattie et al., editors, *The Battle for China: Essays on the Military History of the Sino-Japanese War, 1937–1945* (Stanford: Stanford University Press, 2011): pp. 83–104; Edward Drea, "The Japanese Army on the Eve of War," ibid., pp. 105–135; Peter Worthing, *A Military History of Modern China* (Westport: Praeger, 2007): pp. 1–130.
13. On Chiang Kai-Shek's decision to flood, see Jay Taylor, *The Generalissimo: Chiang Kai-Shek and the Struggle for Modern China* (Cambridge: Belknap Press, 2009): pp. 154–155; Mitter, *Forgotten Ally*: pp. 157–172.
14. Drea, *In the Service of the Emperor*: pp. 1–13.
15. Franco Macri, *Clash of Empires in South China: The Allied Nations' Proxy War with Japan, 1935–1941* (Lawrence: University of Kansas Press, 2012); Mitter, *Forgotten Ally*: pp. 239–364.

16. John Plating, *The Hump: America's Strategy for Keeping China in World War II* (College Station: Texas A&M University Press, 2011). On the CCP in the war, see Sherman Xiaogang, *A Springboard to Victory: Shandong Province and Chinese Communist Military and Financial Strength, 1937–1945* (Leiden: Brill, 2011). More modest is Dagfinn Gatu, *Village China at War: The Impact of Resistance to Japan, 1937–1945* (Copenhagen: NAIS Press, 2007).

17. S. C. M. Paine, *Wars for Asia, 1911–1949* (New York: Cambridge University Press, 2014): pp. 109–281.

18. Hara Takeshi, "The Ichigō Offensive," in Peattie, *Battle for China*: pp. 392–402.

19. Louis Allen, *Burma: The Longest War, 1941–1945* (London: J. M. Dent, 1984), and Donovan Webster, *The Burma Road* (New York: Farrar, Strauss & Giroux, 2003): pp. 243–269.

20. "Unexpected Victory," in Mitter, *Forgotten Ally*: pp. 345–364.

21. Jerome B. Cohen, *Japan's Economy in War and Reconstruction* (Minneapolis: University of Minnesota Press, 1949): pp. 1–47; Drea, *In the Service of the Emperor*: pp. 26–41; Werner Rahn, "Japan and Germany, 1941–1943: No Common Objective, No Common Plans, No Basis of Trust." *Naval War College Review* 46 (1993): pp. 47–68; Barnhart, *Japan Prepares for Total War*: pp. 162–214; Evans and Peattie, *Kaigun*: pp. 467–480.

22. A different view is Vincent O'Hara, *The U.S. Navy Against the Axis: Surface Combat, 1941–1945* (Annapolis: Naval Institute Press, 2007): pp. 297–298 and passim.

23. Evans and Peattie, *Kaigun*: p. 515. Emphasis in original. Also, Mark Peattie, *Sunburst: The Rise of Japanese Naval Air Power, 1909–1941* (Annapolis: Naval Institute Press, 2001).

24. Evans and Peattie, *Kaigun*: pp. 324–326.

25. Willmott, *Empires in the Balance*: p. 87; Mark Parillo, *The Japanese Merchant Marine in World War II* (Annapolis: Naval Institute Press, 1993); Michel Poirier, "Results of the American Pacific Submarine Campaign of World War II," Chief of Naval Operations (2009): www.navy.mil/navy-data/cno/n87/history/pac-campaign.html.

26. Lance Davis and Stanley Engerman, *Naval Blockades in Peace and War* (Cambridge: Cambridge University Press, 2006): pp. 321–382.

27. Evans and Peattie, *Kaigun*: pp. 353–391; Tarling, *Sudden Rampage*: pp. 218–251.

28. Chiyoko Man Kwong, "The Failure of Japanese Land Sea Cooperation During the Second World War," *Journal of Military History* 79 (2015): pp. 69–91.

29. Masanori Ito, *The End of the Imperial Japanese Navy* (New York: Norton, 1962): pp. 210–211; Shizuo Fukui, *Japanese Naval Vessels at the End of World War II* (Annapolis: Naval Institute Press, 1991); Williamson and Millet, *A War to Be Won*: p. 338. On general U.S. war production relative to the Pacific theater, see Jim Lacey, *Keep From All Thoughtful Men: How U.S. Economists Won World War II* (Annapolis: Naval Institute Press, 2011): pp. 20–31, 120–128; Peattie, "Teikoku Kaigun," p. 185; Hone, "US Navy," p. 248.

30. Poirier, "American Pacific Submarine Campaign"; Michael Sturma, *Surface and Destroy: The Submarine Goes to War in the Pacific* (Lexington: University Press of Kentucky, 2012); Joel Ira Holwitt, *Execute Against Japan: The U.S. Decision to Conduct Unrestricted Submarine Warfare* (College Station: A&M University Press, 2013): pp. 162–180.

31. Evans and Peattie, *Kaigun*: pp. 398–401; Daniel Blewett, "Fuel and U.S. Naval Operations in the Pacific, 1942," in *Pacific War Revisited*: pp. 57–80; Nicholas Sarantakes, *Allies Against the Rising Sun: The United States, the British Nations, and the Defeat of Imperial Japan* (Lawrence: University of Kansas Press, 2009): p. 289; Cohen, *Japan's Economy in War and Reconstruction*, pp. 48–109; 271–354.

32. Willmott, *Empires in the Balance*: pp. 181–434; Thomas Zeiler, *Unconditional Defeat: Japan, America, and the End of World War II* (Wilmington: Scholarly Resources, 2004): pp. 2–7.

33. On the loss of the Outer Defense Perimeter, see Dull, *Battle History*: pp. 293–308. Also see Alvin D. Cox, "Flawed Perception and its Effect upon Operational Thinking: The Case of the Japanese Army, 1937–1941," in Michael Handel, editor, *Intelligence and Military Operations* (London: Taylor & Francis, 1990): pp. 239–254.

34. Tarling, *Sudden Rampage*: pp. 80–99; Dull, *Battle History*: pp. 49–118; Philip Snow, *The Fall of Hong Kong: Britain, China, and the Japanese Occupation* (New Haven: Yale University Press, 2004).

35. David Dickson et al., "Doctrine Matters: Why the Japanese Lost at Midway," *Naval War College Review* (Summer 2001): pp. 139–151; Dallas Isom, "The Battle of Midway: Why the Japanese Lost," *Naval War College Review* 53 (Summer 2000): pp. 60–100; Spector, *At War at Sea*: pp. 198–204. A highly influential but also flawed account is Mitsuo Fuchida and Masatake Okumiya, *Midway: The Battle that Doomed Japan* (Annapolis: Naval Institute Press, 1955), superseded by an outstanding study from Jonathan Parshall and Anthony Tully, *Shattered Sword: The Untold Story of the Battle of Midway* (Washington: Potomac Books, 2005). Also see Dull, *Battle History*: pp. 119–179; Craig L. Symonds, *The Battle of Midway* (New York: Oxford University Press, 2011).

36. Drea, *Japan's Imperial Army*: p. 227. Shunsuke Tsurumi, *An Intellectual History of Wartime Japan* (London: KPI, 1982): pp. 75–84; Benesch, *Inventing the Way of the Samurai*: pp. 174–213; Sharon Lacey, *Pacific Blitzkrieg: World War II in the Central Pacific* (Denton: University of North Texas, 2013): pp. 1–45.

37. Unimplemented plans to occupy Hawaii are detailed in John Stephan, *Hawaii Under the Rising Sun: Japan's Plans for Conquest after Pearl Harbor* (Honolulu: University of Hawaii Press, 1984). Also see Shigeru Fukudome, "The Hawaii Operation," in David C. Evans, editor, *The Japanese Navy in World War II: In the Words of Former Japanese Naval Officers* (Annapolis: Naval Institute Press, 1986).

38. Douglas Smith, *Carrier Battles: Command Decision in Harm's Way* (Annapolis: Naval Institute Press, 2006); David Day, *Reluctant Nation: Australia and the Allied Defeat of Japan, 1942–1945* (New York: Oxford University Press, 1992); Sarantakes, *Allies Against the Rising Sun*; Prange, *At Dawn We Slept*: pp. 554–567; Willmott, *Empires in the Balance*: pp. 137–141; Fergal Keane, *Road of Bones: The Siege of Kohima, 1944* (London: Harper Collins, 2010); Frank McLynn, *The Burma Campaign* (New Haven: Yale University Press, 2011); Louis Allen, *Burma: The Longest War, 1941–1945* (London: Dent, 1984); Atkinson, "Projecting American Power," pp. 345-354

39. Peattie, "Teikoku Kaigun," p. 200.

40. Ibid., p. 201; Drea, *Japan's Imperial Army*: p. 246.

41. Drea, *In the Service of the Emperor*: pp. 39–41; Nathan Prefer, *The Battle for Tinian* (Havertown: Casemate, 2012); Matthew Hughes, "War Without Mercy? American Armed Forces and the Deaths of Civilians during the Battle for Saipan, 1944," *Journal of Military History* 75 (2011): pp. 93–123; Harold Goldberg, *D-Day in the Pacific: Battle of Saipan* (Bloomington: Indiana University Press, 2007): pp. 90–102, 195–204.

42. William Slim, *Defeat into Victory* (New York: McKay, 1961): p. 538; Charles Brower, *Defeating Japan: The Joint Chiefs and Strategic in the Pacific War, 1943–1945* (New York: Palgrave, 2012): pp. 89–148; Douglas Ford, "US Assessments of Japanese Ground Warfare Tactics and the Army's Campaigns in the Pacific Theatres, 1943–1945: Lessons Learned and Methods Applied," *War in History* 16/3 (2009): pp. 328–329.

43. Milan Vego, *The Battle for Leyte, 1944: Allied and Japanese Plans, Preparations, and Execution* (Annapolis: Naval Institute Press, 2006); Spector, *At War at Sea*: pp. 292–300; H. P. Willmott, *The Battle of Leyte Gulf, 1944: The Last Fleet Action* (Bloomington: Indiana University Press, 2005); Thomas J. Cutler, *The Battle of Leyte Gulf: 23–26 October, 1944* (Annapolis: Naval Institute Press, 1994); Tully, *Surigao Strait*; Dull, *Battle History*: pp. 325–349; Drea, *Japan's Imperial Army*: pp. 127–144.

44. Drea, *Japan's Imperial Army*: p. 245–246. Contrast to the planning record of the JCS and Combined Chiefs. See Grace P. Hayes, *History of the Joint Chiefs of Staff in World War II: The War Against Japan* (Annapolis: Naval Institute Press, 1982), and Mark A. Stoler, *Allies and Adversaries: The Joint Chiefs of Staff, the Grand Alliance, and U.S. Strategy in World War II* (Chapel Hill: University of North Carolina Press, 2000).

45. Allan Millet, *Semper Fidelis: History of the United States Marine Corps* (New York: Free Press, 1991): pp. 344–444; David Mann, "Japanese Defense of Bataan, Luzon, Philippine Islands, 1945," *Journal of Military History* 67 (2003): pp. 1149–1176.

46. Alan Powell, *The Third Force: ANGAU's New Guinea War, 1942–1946* (New York: Oxford University Press, 2003): pp. 25–91, 191–240.

47. A paragon of the genre is John Dower, *War Without Mercy: Pacific War* (New York: Pantheon, 2012). More balanced is Llachlan Grant, *Australian Soldiers in Asia-Pacific in World War II*

(Sydney: University of New South Wales, 2014). Also see Spector, *Eagle Against the Sun*: pp. 9–53. A sharply persuasive critique of the core racism thesis is Lynn, *Battle*: pp. 219–280. Hughes charges Dower with "cherry-picking random U.S. atrocities from across the Pacific war zones" to misleadingly make a case for racism. See his "War Without Mercy?," pp. 122–123.

48. Even Dower shows this to be true, in *War Without Mercy*: pp. 203ff, 234–261.

49. Douglas Ford, *The Elusive Enemy: U.S. Naval Intelligence and the Imperial Japanese Fleet* (Annapolis: Naval Institute Press, 2011): pp. 48–88, 129–163.

50. Over 35 million prisoners of war were held at some point worldwide from 1939–1945. An overview is S. P. MacKenzie, "The Treatment of Prisoners of War in World War II," *Journal of Modern History* 66/3 (1994): pp. 487–520. On Japan, see Gavan Daws, *Prisoners of the Japanese: POWs of World War II in the Pacific* (New York: William Morrow, 1994); Edward Russel, *The Knights of Bushido* (New York: Skyhorse, 2008): pp. 53–69, 96–204. Squandering access to the perpetrators while also obscuring Unit 731's real significance is James Dawes, *Evil Men* (Cambridge: Harvard University Press 2013). See this author's review in *Michigan War Studies Review* (August 27, 2014), available at http://www.miwsr.com/2014-086.aspx.

51. Contra John Dower, this argument is well-made in Lynn, *Battle*: pp. 219–280.

52. Toshiyuki Yokoi, "Kamikazes in the Okinawa Campaign," in Evans, *Japanese Navy in World War II*: pp. 454–456. Poignant recollections of kamikaze available in English include Emiko Ohnuki-Tierney, *Kamikaze Diaries: Reflections of Japanese Student Soldiers* (Chicago: University of Chicago Press, 2006), and M. G. Sheftall, editor, *Blossoms in the Wind: Human Legacies of the Kamikaze* (New York: New American Library, 2005). Also see Hatsuho Naito, *Thunder Gods: The Kamikaze Pilots Tell Their Story* (New York: Kodansha, 1989); Rikihei Inoguchi and Tadashi Nakajima, *The Divine Wind: Japan's Kamikaze Force in World War II* (Annapolis: Naval Institute Press, 1958).

53. Hiroaki Sato, "*Gyokusai* or 'Shattering like a Jewel': Reflection on the Pacific War," *Asia-Pacific Journal* 6/2 (2008), available at http://apjjf.org/-Hiroaki-Sato/2662/article.html. Rather than mere ugly fanaticism, the term *gyokusai* denotes a beautiful death in battle for a higher value. As elsewhere in this chapter, I am grateful to Danny Orbach for this clarification and insight.

54. Drea, *Japan's Imperial Army*: pp. 247–248; Roger Spiller, *In the School of War* (Lincoln: University of Nebraska Press, 2010): pp. 87–117; Drea, *In the Service of the Emperor*: pp. 60–74. For views from both sides, see Benis Frank et al., *History of the U.S. Marine Corps Operations in World War II*, Vol. 5: *Victory and Occupation* (Washington: GPO, 1968); Hiromichi Yahara, *Battle for Okinawa* (New York: Wiley, 1995); Thomas Huber, *Japan's Battle for Okinawa, April–June, 1945* (Honolulu: University Press of the Pacific, 2005); and Eugene Sledge, *With the Old Breed at Peleliu and Okinawa* (Novato: Presidio Press, 1981).

55. T. S. Eliot, "Gerontion."

56. Matome Ugaki, *Fading Victory: The Diary of Admiral Matome Ugaki*, Gordon Prange et al., editors (Pittsburgh: Pittsburgh University Press, 1991): pp. 588–622; Sarantakes, *Allies Against the Rising Sun*: pp. 168–192; Toshiyuki Yokoi, "Kamikazes in the Okinawa Campaign," in Evans, *Japanese Navy in World War II*: pp. 453–473.

57. David Wragg, "Royal Navy," in O'Hara, *On Seas Contested*: pp. 115–116; Edwyn Gray, *Operation Pacific: The Royal Navy's War Against Japan, 1941–1945* (Annapolis: Naval Institute Press, 1990); Sarantakes, *Allies Against the Rising Sun*: Chapters 10–17; Christopher Baxter, "In Pursuit of a Pacific Strategy: British Planning for the Defeat of Japan, 1943–45," *Diplomacy & Statecraft* 15/2 (2004): pp. 253–277.

58. Christian Geinitz, "The First Air War Against Noncombatants," in Chickering and Förster, *Great War, Total War*: pp. 207–225.

59. The investigation was carried out by Oxford physicist Frederick Lindemann and his assistant, David Bensusan-Butt. The "Butt Report" (PRO AIR 14/1218) is available online, in a transcription by Will Thomas, at https://etherwave.wordpress.com/2014/01/03/document-the-butt-report-1941/. For additional context, see idem, *Rational Action: The Sciences of Policy in Britain and America, 1940–1960* (Cambridge: MIT Press, 2014): pp. 51–54, but especially Tami Davis Biddle, *Rhetoric and Reality in Air Warfare* (Princeton: Princeton University Press, 2009): pp. 176–213; Butt Report at 301n1, 359n82.

60. The literature is immense. A strong overview that may nevertheless undercount civilian dead, giving lower numbers than consensus, is Overy, *Bombers and the Bombed*.

61. My neighbor in Natick Massachusetts, Karl Fasick, now deceased, was arrested and in a sense saved by the Gestapo when his bomber was shot down over Germany in March 1945 and he parachuted to the ground, breaking his leg. Another member of the crew was beaten to death by local civilians when he landed instead in a nearby town.

62. Evans, *Third Reich at War*: p. 447.

63. Memo from the Prime Minister to Minister of Aircraft Production, July 8, 1940. Emphasis added.

64. Message to the National Convention of Young Democrats. August 21, 1941.

65. Quoted in Richard Overy, "Allied Bombing and the Destruction of German Cities," in Forster, *A World at Total War*: p. 290.

66. Evans, *Third Reich at War*: pp. 443–449.

67. Making this provocative argument to the extreme is Philips O'Brien, *How the War was Won: Air-Sea Power and Allied Victory in World War II* (Cambridge: Cambridge University Press, 2015). He goes much too far in diminishing the contribution of ground forces, both Allied and Soviet.

68. Thomas R. Searle, "It Made a Lot of Sense to Kill Skilled Workers": The Firebombing of Tokyo in March 1945," *Journal of Military History* 66/1 (2002): pp. 103–133.

69. Biddle, *Rhetoric and Reality*: pp. 214–288; Weinberg, "Myths," p. 714; D. M. Giangreco, *Hell to Pay: Operation DOWNFALL and the Invasion of Japan, 1945–1947* (Annapolis: Naval Institute Press, 2009): p. 122.

70. Edward Drea, "Intelligence Forecasting for the Invasion of Japan: Previews of Hell," in Robert Maddox, editor, *Hiroshima in History: The Myths of Revisionism* (Columbia, University of Missouri Press, 2007): pp. 59–75; D. M. Giangreco, "A Score of Bloody Okinawas and Iwo Jimas: President Truman and Casualty Estimates of the Invasion of Japan," in ibid., pp. 76–115; idem, "Causality Projections for the U.S. Invasion of Japan, 1945–1946," *Journal of Military History* 61 (1997): pp. 521–582. A different view is John Skates, *The Invasion of Japan: Alternative to the Bomb* (Columbia: University of South Carolina Press, 1994): pp. 234–246.

71. Barrett Tillman, *Whirlwind: Air War Against Japan, 1942–1945* (New York: Simon & Schuster, 2010); Herman Wolk, *Cataclysm: Hap Arnold and the Defeat of Japan* (Denton: University of Texas North Press, 2010); Searle, "Firebombing Tokyo," pp. 113–115; Kenneth Werrell, *Blankets of Fire: U.S. Bombers over Japan during World War II* (Washington: Smithsonian, 1996): pp. 153–158, 346–347; William Ralph, "Improvised Destruction: Arnold, LeMay, and the Firebombing of Japan," *War in History* 13/4 (2006): pp. 495–522.

72. The numbers are from the Tokyo police count at the time. While widely accepted, some scholars believe they are too low. See Searle, "Firebombing of Tokyo," *Journal of Military History* 66/1 (2002): p. 103.

73. Testimonials in special issue on the firebombing of Tokyo, *Asia-Pacific Journal* 9/3 (2011), available at http://apjjf.org/2011/9/3/Bret-Fisk/3469/article.html. Also see the digital archive on the USAAF bombing overall at http://www.japanairraids.org/, and Frank Gibney, editor, *Sensō: The Japanese Remember the Pacific War: Letters to the Editor of "Asahi Shimbun,"* 2nd ed. (New York: Routledge, 2015): Chapter 7, "The Bombing of Japan."

74. Ross Coen, *Fu-go: The Curious History of Japan's Balloon Bomb Attack on America* (Lincoln: University of Nebraska Press, 2014): p. 200–203 and passim.

75. Jeremy Yellen, "The Specter of Revolution: Reconsidering Japan's Decision to Surrender," *International History Review* 35:1 (2013): pp. 205–226. On the other side of the debate, see John Chappell, *Before the Bomb: How America Approached the End of the Pacific War* (Lexington: University Press of Kentucky, 1997): pp. 23–38, 116–131.

76. "One Hundred Million Die Together," in Haruko Cook and Theodore Cook, *Japan at War: An Oral History* (New York: New Press, 1993): pp. 334–342.

77. Quoted in Drea, *In the Service of the Emperor*: pp. 150–152.

78. Drea, *MacArthur's ULTRA*: p. 222 on the 900,000 available Japanese troops. Richard B. Frank, *Downfall: The End of the Japanese Empire* (New York: Random House, 1999): 164–177; 197–213. Giangreco points out that, contrary to intelligence reports that Japan had only 7,000 aircraft available to face invasion, it actually had more than 12,700. *Hell to Pay*: p. xviii. These works together

form a comprehensive overview of Japanese defenses and the resistance Allied troops would have faced had they invaded. They make clear what an utter bloodbath it would have been, on both sides.

79. See Sado Asada, "The Shock of the Atomic Bomb and Japan's Decision to Surrender," *Pacific Historical Review* 67 (1998): 477–512; Yukiko Koshiro, "Eurasian Eclipse: Japan's End Game in World War II," *American Historical Review* 109/2 (2004): pp. 417–444; Wilson Miscamble, *The Most Controversial Decision: Truman, the Atomic Bomb, and the Defeat of Japan* (New York: Cambridge University Press, 2011): pp. 20–53, 94–111. Key documents are in Michael Kort, *Columbia Guide to Hiroshima and the Bomb* (New York: Columbia University Press, 2007). Alternatively, see Barton Bernstein, "The Atomic Bombings Reconsidered," *Foreign Affairs* 74/1 (1995): pp. 135–152; Alexander Downes, *Targeting Civilians in War* (Ithaca: Cornell University Press, 2008): pp. 115–155; and Tsuyoshi Hasegawa, *Racing the Enemy: Stalin, Truman, and the Surrender of Japan* (Cambridge: Harvard University Press, 2005).

80. David Glantz, *August Storm: Soviet Operational and Tactical Combat in Manchuria, 1945* (Portland: Frank Cass, 2003); and idem, *The Soviet Strategic Offensive in Manchuria, 1945* (Portland: Frank Cass, 2003).

81. Glantz, *August Storm.*

82. Drea, *In the Service of the Emperor*: pp164–165; 167; Marc Gallicchio, "After Nagasaki: General Marshall's Plan for Tactical Nuclear Weapons in Japan, *Prologue* 23 (1991): pp. 396–404.

83. The text of Hirohito's broadcast is available in English translation at https://www.mtholyoke.edu/acad/intrel/hirohito.htm. The Instrument of Surrender is available at http://archives.gov/exhibits/featured_documents/japanese_surrender_document/

84. Yellen, "The Specter of Revolution," p. 220; Drea, *Japan's Imperial Army*: pp. 250–251; idem, *In the Service of the Emperor*: pp. 187–188, 205, 211–215.

CONCLUSION

1. Tolstoy captures the essence of civilian faith in military genius, and the skepticism of officers on the same subject, in a short exchange in *War and Peace*, Book X, Chapter 25.

2. "India Prepared for Military Action, says Army Chief," and "Pak. Army Chief Warns India of 'unbearable cost' in Case of War," *The Hindu*, September 1 and 7, 2015.

Glossary

Abwehr: German military intelligence. It was headed by Admiral Wilhelm Canaris from 1935 until it was taken over by the SS in 1944. It conducted agent-based espionage, sabotage and subversion operations, counterespionage and central administration. The *Abwehr* left most military signals, electronic, and other technical intelligence to the Wehrmacht.

Allies (World War I): the Allied (and Associated) powers, with the United States insisting on the term Associated to preserve its Founding Fathers' fiction that it did not join alliances: Britain, France, Russia, Italy, Belgium, Serbia, Romania, the United States, and many overseas territories of the British and French Empires.

Allies (World War II): The wartime coalition formally called the United Nations alliance from January 1, 1942. Principal allies were the United States, the Soviet Union and Great Britain. China was a nominal fourth with little to no influence over Allied councils. "Western Allies" excludes the Soviet Union and China to mean Britain, France, the United States and minor allies.

AOK (*Armeeoberkommando*): Army Command, or main HQ, of the Habsburg army in Vienna.

Anmarsch: An approach march to close the distance between two firing lines or armies.

appatis: Ransom extorted from towns or nobles or monasteries by mercenary bands.

arme blanche: Literally "white weapon." Any weapon with a blade such as a sword or bayonet.

army of observation: A force with orders to monitor but not attack an enemy position, fortress or army, to keep the enemy's strength, movement and intentions under observation.

arquebus: Any of several types of early, slow-firing, small-caliber firearms employing a matchlock mechanism. It shot a half-ounce ball.

art of war: Broadly, all literary studies, military manuals, and guides to weapons, tactics and strategy peculiar to a historical time and place. Narrowly, the study of tactics, operations and strategy. Most narrowly, a synonym for warcraft or the command style peculiar to one of the great captains.

ASW: anti-submarine warfare.

attrition: Wearing out of military assets, of personnel and matériel, over time. It also has moral and psychological dimensions best understood as rising exhaustion or war weariness.

*Aufmarsch***:** Moving from column into line in the initial deployment leading into battle.

Ausgleich **(1867):** The constitutional compromise that produced the hyphenation of the Habsburg Empire, the "Dual Monarchy" of Austria-Hungary.

*Auftragstaktik***:** "Mission tactics." A Prussian and German principle that encouraged subordinates to aggressively pursue overarching goals and to move directly into attack in pursuit of a defined mission, rather than strictly follow a set of pre-scribed orders no matter what was happening nearby.

Axis alliance: The states opposed to the Western Allies and Soviet Union (United Nations alliance) in World War II, formally allied from signature of the Pact of Steel signed in May 1939: Germany, Italy, Japan, Hungary, Romania, Bulgaria, Finland and various puppet states such as Slovakia and Croatia.

barrage: Sustained artillery fire from many guns at once, laid down to a fire plan (firing to a grid or pattern, not by line of sight). Variations were walking, rolling and standing barrages.

battle of encounter: A battle that results when two or more armies encounter each other while on the march, either by scouting out the other's position or by acci-dent, and must rush to make dispositions in haste

*bellum se ipse alet***:** "War should pay for itself." An ancient maxim calling for armies to live off the land of foreign peoples and powers and to pay wages from plunder or collections of local taxes imposed on defeated towns and populations.

berserker: Greek and Western term for fanatic Ottoman troops paid extra to lead near-suicidal attacks, such as rushing the breach in a broken siege wall or attack-ing a firing line all-out.

*Bewegungskrieg***:** Maneuver warfare, envisioned over a campaign rather than a single battle. Used by German officers rather than the Westernized "blitzkrieg."

blitzkrieg: A combined arms attack with tanks and other armor and armored infan-try seeking breakthrough to assault command and communications. A critical distinction should be made between blitzkrieg conceived as lightning operations, but not as lightning war.

bombard: Stone throwing engine. The term is somewhat arbitrary, but generally referred to the largest guns of the medieval and early modern period. They were sometimes breech-loaders, using removable *pots de fer* containing powder, wadding and a large stone cannonball.

bombardment: Originally, shooting stone ammunition from bombards. Later, any assault from many large guns at once, most often to batter and terrorize a fortified town. In modern usage, a pummeling by artillery. Similar to a barrage.

breech-loader: A gun or cannon loading from the rear or breech rather than the muzzle or barrel.

cabinet war (*Kabinettskrieg*): War started, conducted, and then concluded by monarchs or governments (the king's cabinet), in theory for limited purposes with limited means. See *guerre de cabinet*.

cannon: Big guns cast from brass or iron and by the mid-17th century mostly standardized at six calibers (4-, 8-, 12-, 16-, 24-, and 32-pounders). Later used generically for any artillery piece.

caracole: A pistol-and-cavalry tactic prevalent in the 16th century. Riders in short columns fired into an infantry line or pike-and-musket hedge, then whirled away to reload at a safe distance before returning. It was mostly ineffective.

Central Powers: The four states that fought and lost World War I against the Allies: Germany, Austria-Hungary, the Ottoman Empire and Bulgaria. Because Austria and Hungary split apart upon defeat, there were five peace treaties negotiated at Paris.

condottieri: Contract captains. From the Italian *condotte* for military contracts. Refers first to mercenary captains who formed mercenary companies and negotiated contracts, and secondarily to the companies and men.

Concert of Europe (1815–1853): The system of consultation set up by the Great Powers (Austria, Britain, France, Prussia and Russia) to manage their affairs after the defeat of Napoleon and France in 1815. It confirmed their condominium over smaller powers on matters of international significance, but helped keep the peace for decades. Most historians date it from the Congress of Vienna in 1815. Some prefer 1822, when Britain withdrew.

contributions (*Kontributionen*): War taxes imposed by force on enemy lands. They started as a form of lawful military tax, but changed to an impost under threat of mass violence.

corning: A process for refining gunpowder developed in France ca.1429. Corning permitted standardized powder to be prepared, eventually leading to a triple division of powder grades. The finest grains were reserved as musket-grade, while coarser sorts were used in cannon and mines, and for making fuses or quick match. Gunpowder was quicker-burning and more explosive, but also more expensive. The new powder provided a great incentive to improve casting techniques, as refined powder sometimes exploded older guns.

culverin: French *coulverine*, Spanish *culebrina*. A broad range of early cannon. A secondary meaning was early handguns (*coulverines à main*). They fired lead rather than stone or iron shot. Artillery could be as small as light guns less than three feet long, with bores as small as one inch. Early types fired 1/3-pound shot 200 yards. Others were medium-sized guns that could throw six- to nine-pound shot several thousand yards. The largest hurled 32-pound stone or iron balls several thousand yards with moderate accuracy. In time, "culverin" came to mean long, thick-barreled guns throwing solid shot accurately at extended ranges.

***coulverin à main*:** See *culverin*.

cuirassiers: Cavalry named for the residual breast armor they wore, called the cuirass.

deep battle: Red Army doctrine developed in the 1930s for combined-arms offensive operations. It called for deep penetrations into the enemy's flanks and rear areas by mechanized and airborne forces, interrupting resupply and communications and paralyzing any response to encirclement.

defeat-in-detail: Beating each part of an enemy army (or other force) one part at a time, until the whole army (or other unit) is defeated. To avoid this, commanders would usually seek to remain concentrated or at least within close marching distance.

defense-in-depth: Any defensive system with multiple layers or lines rather than a single hard crust, designed to absorb a penetrating attack, muffle it and prevent breakthrough. The mature trench systems of 1915–1918 are one example; Louis XIV's Lines are another.

demonstration: A marching back and forth or other show of force by an army, demonstrating its presence to deter (or to deceive) an enemy.

destrier: The *magnus equus* or great horse of the Middle Ages in Europe. Always a stallion trained to charge straight toward the enemy. It was led to the fight by hand rather than ridden. It was never used merely for transport. It was an animal bred for battle.

devastations: Punitive cavalry raids in which whole provinces were torched to terror-coerce the local prince or deny resources to the enemy. Essentially, scorched earth on offense.

doctrine: Best available thinking on what will work in combat and operations, preferably based on experience but sometimes just abstract theory (such as *élan vital*). Principles of doctrine frequently rigidified into dogma that distorted rather than guided tactics.

dragoon: Soldiers who rode to battle but dismounted to fight on foot, as opposed to cavalry, or soldiers who rode to battle and then fought from horseback.

eat out: Living off the enemy's lands to such an extent that it is no longer possible, because all that can be consumed has been consumed. The effect might last a harvest season or years.

***élan vital*:** An early 20th-century philosophical (Henri Bergson) and crude biological concept that quickly migrated into military affairs and patriotic movements, where it reinforced ideas of offensive spirit and underlay the broad mood behind the cult of the offensive in 1914.

enfilade: To fire into or attack a flank.

Entente Cordiale: See *Triple Alliance*.

***Ermattungsstrategie*:** A slow-war "strategy of exhaustion" by attrition, to limited objectives.

étapes: A logistical system wherein towns were required to store food and fodder at preset rest stations for purchase by arriving troops.

état-major: The General Staff of the French Army.

Fabian strategy: Relying on exhausting the enemy by slow attrition and battle avoidance, mainly attacking his supply, communications and morale.

Fallschirmjäger: German airborne infantry, or paratroops.

fascines: Strands of brush 18–20 feet in length, carried to a siege by cavalry or in carts by civilian laborers, or culled from nearby woods. They were used to fill in ditches or dry moats and to top off rows of gabions along saps or around the embrasures of gun batteries.

fireships: Small vessels that were packed with explosives and their decks covered with combustibles and pitch, then fired. They usually sailed on the lee side of the line of battle, often in the vicinity of the flagship of the admiral. This hid them from enemy view until they crossed the line to attack, sailing through the gap between two ships of the line. A special type was a Hellburner, packed with the usual combustibles but also kegs of black powder. The Dutch invented these for use against Spanish canal bridges and harbors.

flèche: A fieldwork, usually earthen, forming a salient angle in front with an open gorge behind.

flintlock: Any musket or cannon in which the lock mechanism deployed a spring device that struck a piece of flint against a small iron or steel plate (frizzen). This created sparks that ignited fine firing powder in a shallow pan, which in turn set off the main powder charge. The term was first used about any gun in which the lock mechanism was used. Later, true flintlocks had striker and pan cover made in one piece, and could be both "half-cocked" and "full-cocked." This mechanism made pistols far more dependable and popular. See *fusil*.

forlorn hope: Originally, the wings of a Swiss square made of crossbowmen without protective cover of the pikemen in the strong center. Later deployed in front of the square as a type of early skirmish line or to provoke the opposing square to move or chase.

francs-tireurs: "Free shooters," Irregular fighters. Partisans or guerrillas.

Free Companies: Mixed gangs of English, Fleming and French mercenaries (or combinations thereof) that conducted private war and extorted *appatis* during the Hundred Years' War.

Freikorps: "Free Corps." Private armies of right-wing militia, many veterans, in Germany after World War I. They fought an undeclared war on the eastern border with Poland. Many were later incorporated into Nazi paramilitaries and formations.

friction: A metaphor originating with Clausewitz's depicting the fog of perception and inevitable breakdown in war of command intentions and control, caused by unforeseeable events, physical effort and enemy action. The effect is enormously accelerated in active combat.

Führerprinzip: Leader principle. The idea in Nazism that the entire nation was to be organized along military lines and in absolute obedience to the supreme *Führer* and national leader, Adolf Hitler. Lesser *führers* were in charge at lowers levels, military and civilian. In this system, the leader's decision was absolute and over-rode all else, including written law.

fu-go: Japanese balloon bombs.

fukuryu: Japanese suicide divers.

fusil: The final form of the flintlock musket. Fusils were more easily and quickly loaded and had fewer misfires, improving infantry rates of fire.

fusilier: A fusil-bearing infantryman.

gendarmerie: French heavy cavalry, noble by class and forming the core of royal armies from the late Hundred Years' War to Marignano in 1515 and for some time after.

Gestapo: Short for *Geheime Staatspolizei*. Nazi secret and political police, who had a legal right to carry out torture and executions. They were feared, and resisted, across occupied Europe.

Grand Alliance: British term for (1) the serial coalitions that formed against Louis XIV; (2) the serial coalitions that formed against Napoleon; (3) Churchill's preferred usage for the United Nations alliance of World War II that opposed the Axis.

grand battery: Forming all cannon at a battle into a single mass to perform an early form of bombardment. It was a tactic around the middle of the 18th century, seen in linear battles, to mass guns at either wing or at the center. Trying to use artillery in a mass that could bash a gap in a an opposing line, leading to a combined-arms assault and a possible breakthrough, was a tactic pioneered by Napoleon.

Grande Armée: The renamed French Army, from 1805.

Great Powers: The major military powers of any historical period. Usually a status achieved and lost in war. Sometimes, powers are misidentified as Great Powers by all the others until war clarifies matters. A case in point was Italy before World War I and World War II.

***Guandong* Army**: "East of the Barrier." A quasi-independent army that spearheaded Japan's imperial thrust on the Asian mainland during the first half of the 20th century. Its name derived from an original garrison position in the "Guandong Leased Area," between northern China at the Great Wall and three northeastern provinces of China, or Manchuria, that were long coveted by Japan. It was in place in Manchuria from 1905. In 1945, it was crushed by Chinese, Mongolian, and Soviet forces in just two weeks.

Gulag: Short for *Glavnoe upravlenie ispravitel'no-trudovykh lagerei*, or "Main Administration of Corrective Labor Camps." The most infamous subsection of the vast Soviet labor and prison camp system. At the start of the German-Soviet war in June 1941, Gulag camps confined 2.3 million forced laborers. By the end of that year, another 1.3 million were sent to the camps, with 2 million more following over the course of 1942. Officers purged during the *Yezhovshchina* were restored in 1941–1942. Polish Army prisoners from 1939 and other ethnic groups from the western Soviet Union were released to kill Germans on the Eastern Front. Other Poles were released to fight under British command in the West.

Guomindang: "National People's Party" of China, and its attendant army. Often simplified to Nationalists. It fought against the Chinese Communists as well as the Japanese.

guerre de cabinet: "Cabinet war." One run from a distance, at the ministerial or royal level, ostensibly limited in means and ends.

guerre à outrance: "War to the excess" (extreme). All-out or peoples' war.

guerre de course: "War of raids." Commerce raiding by both naval forces and privateers. Its characteristic form was targeting enemy and neutral merchants rather than seeking decisive battle in a fleet action and, as importantly, protecting friendly convoys.

guerre d'escadre: "War of squadrons" or "war of fleets." Naval strategy and maneuvers that sought fleet engagements, as opposed to commerce raiding or *guerre de course*.

guerre guerroyante: Small-scale but intense raiding and ambushes waged by widely dispersed troops, usually within a border or frontier zone that neither side fully controlled.

guerre mortelle: "War to the death." This declaration allowed a besieging army not merely to lay waste or pillage property, but legally and morally to forfeit most or all defender lives, both soldier and civilian. It was a status much abused in order to sanction wanton plunder and slaughter by cruel or disreputable commanders.

Grenzer: Balkan irregulars. They wore local costume rather than Habsburg uniform and manned fortified villages, blockhouses and watchtowers along Austria's Karlstadt and Windische borders. During the Napoleonic Wars, they retrained as regulars in line battalions.

Haufen: "Heap" or company. A Swiss square.

Hiwis: Short for *Hilfswillige* (auxiliaries) or *Hilfsfreiwillige* ("volunteer helpers"). Red Army prisoners in "helper" battalions. Most were used as drivers or cooks, and for military labor. By 1943, every Wehrmacht division had an official complement of 2,000 *Hiwis*, making up shortages arising from mass casualties. By the middle of 1945, there were 500,000 *Hiwis* working alongside the Wehrmacht. They were dreadfully treated by the Germans while in captivity, then again upon liberation. Many were shot by Smersh or the NKVD.

Hofkriegsrat (**Court War Council**): A part military, part political council to the Habsburgs.

hokushin ("**northern advance**"): The aggressive direction favored by the *Rikugun*.

hussars: Light cavalry originating in the Balkans as a frontier force in late 15th-century Hungary. Other armies adopted lighter cavalry formations, using the term "hussar" and in many cases also the famously elaborate dress and brilliant colors of the Hungarian horsemen.

Hutier tactics: German infiltration tactics using *Sturmtruppen* ("assault troops") to infiltrate through, rather than try to storm over, opposing trenches. They by-passed strongpoints under orders to maintain momentum of attack. Prevalent in 1917–1918 assaults.

impressment: A forced (press masters and gangs) recruitment used to man navies. Press gangs generally tried to persuade men to join the service, but used force when necessary.

investment: A preliminary encirclement of a fortress by cavalry or dragoons marking the opening of a siege. Once the main body of the besieging army arrived, the opening of the trenches was marked, as lines of contravallation and of circumvallation (or parallels) were started.

Jacobites: Supporters of the claims to legitimacy of the Catholic House of Stuart, onetime ruling house of Scotland and England. In exile from the deposition of "Jacobus," or James II of England (James VII in Scotland), in favor of the Protestant ascension of William III in the "Glorious Revolution" of 1688. They were in rebellion and in league with France and other foreign monarchs to the mid-18th century, when their last rebellion was crushed.

Jacobins: Republican political clubs which ultimately grew into the most radical faction in the French Revolution. Dominated by Danton and Robespierre, from 1792 the Jacobins gained increasing control over the course of the Revolution. Through the Committee on Public Safety they conducted the Terror, called for the *levée en masse*, took credit for throwing back invading monarchist armies, and proclaimed revolutionary war against the established governments and governing principles of Europe.

jacquerie: Violent peasant uprisings named for the French sobriquet "Jacques Bonhomme," the first in 1358 and sporadically after that. Like most peasant armies, the Jacques lacked cohesion, strategic planning, and a precise and articulate agenda of reform. They were, as a result, savagely repressed by the crown and nobility, which set aside differences when faced with the common enemy of rebellion by armed peasants.

Janissary Corps: From Turkish *yeniçeri* ("new militia" or "new army"). Heart of the *kapıkulu askerleri*, the Ottoman sultan's personal or household troops. Janissary infantry at first included enslaved prisoners of war and began as infantry archers, but evolved into a premier firearms corps. Starting in 1438, the Ottomans raised an annual levy of boys from subject Christian populations through the *devşirme* recruiting system. By the 1470s, there were nearly 10,000 Janissaries, surpassing every palace guard in Europe. They were not allowed to engage in commerce. Trained from an early age solely for war, and sporting a white felt cap (*börk*) that distinguished them from the regular Ottoman troops wearing red, janissaries were the most professional and tactically disciplined troops of their time.

Kaigun: The Imperial Japanese Navy.

kaiten ("**turn to heaven**"): Suicide boats of several types, also called "human torpedoes."

Kempeitai: Japanese military police. They ran an extensive domestic political intelligence net.

Kessel: See *Kesselschlacht*.

Kesselschlacht: "Cauldron battle." German doctrine for a battle of encirclement, a concentric mobile surrounding of an entire enemy army leading to its physical elimination. In a *Keil und Kessel* ("wedge and cauldron"), a mechanized panzer wedge punched through an enemy line, with follow-on motorized infantry support on the expanding flanks and rear supplied by panzergrenadiers. The armored wedge itself was called the *Panzerkeil*.

kokutai: "National essence." The term had multiple meanings: linguistic, cultural and political. It underlay the Meiji imperial system after 1868, serving as a unifying national ideology celebrating the special virtue of the Japanese, centered on the unbroken succession of emperors. During World War II, it usually referred to the imperial Japanese principle of a "family state" with the emperor at its summit as divine and human father to the nation. Its retention in 1945 was the condition asked for and allowed in surrender talks. Afterward, it was redefined in a more modern and democratic form.

König-Feldherr: "King-general." A Prussian idealization of the warrior-king, combining policy and operations in one set of hands, aiming at a singular goal.

Kriegskasse: "War chest." Prior to the development of modern economies and systems of taxation and expenditure, national leaders and generals literally kept chests of gold and other precious metals to finance war. It is where "contributions" were kept by generals.

Landser: A private in the German army.

Landwehr: Prussia's military reserve, set up in 1813. Originally slated for home defense and separate from the Prussian Army; Moltke added it to the main force marching into France in 1914. Austria belatedly established a *Landwehr* or reserve but was never as comfortable with arming the population and subject minorities.

levée en masse: "mass rising." The first modern, universal conscription system, introduced in France in 1792. It vastly expanded the size of the Army of the Republic.

Lines: 17th–18th century field fortifications built to connect forts and fortified cities, to enhance defenses for positional warfare. They comprised communications and support trenches as well as the main fighting trenches. Long sections were often empty of troops.

logistics: Problems and methods of supplying an army (or navy) on the move, or feeding an in-place garrison. For much of this period, even into World War II in the case of the *Ostheer*, this meant foraging, contributions, expropriations and otherwise living off occupied lands. Logistics included water and fodder. A single horse consumed upwards of 20 pounds of dry fodder or 50 pounds of grass each day. The ratio of total mounts and draft or pack horses to men in most pre–20th-century armies was 1:2. An average soldier consumed three pounds of food per day but could only carry 65–80 pounds of equipment, weapons and supplies. That limited soldiers to about ten days food supply (30 pounds) at the start of a march. A pack-horse carried 250 pounds burden, of which 100 pounds were devoted to its fodder. No military action can take place without logistical support, famously referred to in Roman times as the "sinews of war." In World War II, that meant production, provision and movement of all supplies necessary to establish and maintain armies, navies and air forces in the field, at all levels from tactical to operational to strategic. Items produced or moved included everything from mail and medicine to vehicles, fuel, food, shoes, pack and feed animals, ammunition and men. Logistics was necessarily concerned with long-term management of ships, roads, bridges, railways, aircraft, airfields and all other requirements of transportation necessary to the basic task of moving men, equipment and supplies into battle. Unintentionally bowing to the gods of logistics, the U.S. Army called its heavy towing vehicles "prime movers."

Machstaat: "Power state." In Nazism and more generally, an exaltation of the state as a reified organic whole, imbued with a moral force and worth unto itself which far exceeded that of any individual citizen. This view underlay the Nazis' appeal to extreme nationalism, and encouraged support for their war policy by the Party and the Wehrmacht officer corps.

magazine: Supplies prepositioned along the expected line of march of armies, usually stopping at the frontiers, where foraging began.

matchlock: A firing mechanism for early muskets and pistols invented sometime before 1411, but with the first reliable military versions appearing between 1450 and 1470. It was the first major improvement in firearms from early hand cannon that were little more than metal tubes fixed to boards with a drilled touchhole. The matchlock permitted the gunman to fire while steadying the stock and barrel with both hands, instead of using a forked rest or a second man to apply a slow match or a heated wire to the touchhole. It gripped several feet of slow match in a lock that descended into a pan of priming powder when a serpentine was lowered, at first by hand, but later when a trigger released a spring-and-tumbler that moved the serpentine and match to the pan. The powder in the priming pan set off the main charge in the barrel, providing the signature two-step ignition of early firearms. The matchlock was one of three essential parts—lock, stock and barrel—that turned primitive hand cannons into recognizable guns that could be aimed and fired while holding them against the chest or shoulder.

matériel: Also, war matériel. The physical supplies necessary to make war: guns, carts, shells, tanks and all other necessities of modern war.

Materialschlacht: "Battle of matériel." The Germans feared it, the Allies won with it.

***Militärgrenze* (*vojna krajina* or *vojna granica*):** "Military frontier." The Habsburg borderland zone with the Ottoman Empire, a frontier zone of land-based military obligations for Serbs and Bosnian Vlachs. On the other side of the frontier, the Ottomans also employed local Christian troops, so that each empire fought the other for decades via Vlach and Serb proxies. The *Militärgrenze* grew in time into a band of territory that ranged from 20 to 60 miles in width and over 1,000 miles in length. During the 17th century, it was measled with about 90 fortresses, most of a rudimentary form rather than full-bastioned defenses.

mission tactics: See *Auftragstaktik*.

Murbräcker: "Wall-breaker." 16th- and 17th-century siege guns. They were in use in Germany much longer than elsewhere. Barrels were often inscribed with boasts of special prowess in knocking down fortifications, praise for their royal owners or religious pieties.

musket: A matchlock or flintlock infantry firearm. The first flintlock mechanism for firing guns was introduced in Germany in the mid-15th century, but it did not catch on for another hundred years. Around 1547, primitive flintlocks appeared in Florence and Sweden. More advanced models were made in France, but not outside it until the 1640s. By the 1660s, knowledge of the flintlock diffused throughout Europe. The new lock displaced the old matchlock as the preferred firing mechanism for the infantry musket from the 1680s in most advanced armies, though later on wilder frontiers.

muzzle-loader: Any gunpowder weapon that was loaded via the muzzle (mouth) of the gun rather than through the end or breech.

nanshin ("**southern advance**"): The aggressive direction favored by the *Kaigun*.

nation-in-arms: Mass armies, made up primarily of conscripts. This was a phenomenon first clearly seen during the French Revolution with the *levée en masse*. The term expands in military history to mean the arousal to peoples' wars, leading ultimately to total war.

new model army: A term for several early modern armies patterned on that of the United Provinces, with standardized weapons, drilled by Maurits of Nassau in volley fire. The Swedish Army reshaped by Gustavus Adolphus on the Dutch model was also widely seen as a new kind of model army. In England it is used for the army founded on February 17, 1645, by Parliamentary ordinance, trained in the Dutch and Swedish fashions and infused with Puritan zeal. It was principally the creation of Thomas Fairfax, its first commander. Oliver Cromwell was responsible for the Ironsides cavalry. The army then put him in power as dictator, after the execution of the king.

Niederwerfungsstrategie: Literally "overthrow strategy" or "throwing down" the enemy. An all-out effort to win fast and completely, as opposed to a slower and more limited strategy of exhaustion or attrition.

nikudan: "Human bullets"; literally, "bullets made of flesh." Japanese propaganda term to hide the mass casualties taken from Russian machine guns in 1904–1905 as an expression of *seishin* spirituality. It was revived in all subsequent Japanese wars.

NKVD: *Narodnyi Komissariat Vnutrennikh Del* (People's Commissariat of Internal Affairs). The Soviet secret police, 1934–1954, including during the *Yezhovshchina*. Previously, it was known as the Cheka and then as the OGPU. In 1954, it was renamed the KGB. It was responsible for millions of deaths among the kulaks during forced collectivization, for running blocking detachments and executions of deserters, punishment battalions, and the forced labor camps of the Gulag.

Oberkommando des Heeres (OKH): German Army High Command. As planning for *Barbarossa* got underway, the OKW was relegated to oversight of Germany's southern and western fronts, while OKH took charge of the Soviet or eastern front. That division became more pronounced after the failure of Operation *Blau* by late 1942.

Oberkommando der Wehrmacht (OKW): German Armed Forces High Command. Overarching headquarters of the German Armed Forces, comprising all three services: *Heer* (Army), *Kriegsmarine* (Navy), and *Luftwaffe* (Air Force). It was established in 1938 when Hitler purged the Wehrmacht of top generals who opposed his aggressive war plans. OKW was supposed to work on grand strategy, but never developed one. From the onset, Hitler merged political and military authority in his own person while consulting on operational matters, making planning what he had already decided the main function of OKW. He thus reduced the military leadership to little more than a technical elite without a policy role. From 1938 to 1945, the key officer was Wilhelm Keitel. The *Wehrmachtsfuehrungsstab* (Armed Forces Operations Staff) was headed by Alfred Jodl. It advised on operations until Hitler took over direction even of detailed movements late in the war. The Luftwaffe remained largely independent of the OKW due to the political clout of Hermann Göring with Hitler and in Nazi circles, though that role waned after Stalingrad, from 1943 to 1945.

oblique order: Frederick's trademark tactic that "refused" (held back) a weakened wing of the battle line, using detached troops from its second echelon to conduct a wheeling march around the far enemy flank. See *enfilade; rake.*

Ohka: "Cherry blossom." Piloted jet-bombs, a Japanese anti-ship suicide weapon used in 1944–1945. The MXY-7 was a 20-foot-long rocket made from a light aluminum fuselage. It had wooden wings and carried a 2,600-lb explosive charge. Its nose was armor-piercing. It had three rockets at the rear that propelled it to over 500 mph. Carried under the belly of a land-based medium bomber, once released the *Ohka* glided unpowered until the pilot engaged short-range rockets that accelerated it faster than any aircraft. Alternatively, they were launched from elevated rails on cliffs along the coastline. The "Divine Thunder God Corps" of *Ohka* suicide pilots was approved in 1944. Pilots got one training mission in unpowered gliding. Six small U.S. warships were struck by *Ohka*, and three were sunk.

order of battle: The chart of organization, command and actual units available to a commander or a state at war. A listing of military assets.

Ostheer: The German army on the Eastern Front in World War II.

operations: The intermediate level of warfare between small-unit tactics and war-winning (or losing) strategies. It refers to command and movement of large units, in the period considered here divisions, corps, armies and army groups. It is a 20th-century term that is nevertheless used retroactively in military history about earlier campaigns.

passage of Lines: 17th–18th centuries. Moving an army through a fortified frontier (Lines), so rare an achievement it was viewed as a pinnacle act of war, a measure of highest generalship.

pell-mell: A mêlée at sea, looking to win by individual ships or squadrons. Replaced by the line of battle and permanent fighting instructions. Nevertheless, they sometimes occurred in smaller actions. During a pell-mell, all effort was made to rake the enemy with ships' cannon while crews and marines engaged with short-range weapon and small arms, from swivel guns to grenades, muskets and pistols.

petite guerre (**"little war"**): A 17th-century term for what the mid-18th century called "partisan war," which became known from the early 19th century as "guerrilla war": irregular fighting, scouting and foraging, collecting contributions and hostage-taking, fast raids (courses), burning crops and villages, harassing garrisons, mountain ambushes, brutal punishments and reprisals. Its practitioners used multiple weapons and were often highly skilled at maneuver and deception. They almost always rode as dragoons, sometimes double-riding with light cavalry hussars.

poilus: "Hairy ones." Ordinary French soldiers in World War I, the privates and NCOs, not officers.

raison d'état: Reason of state. A modern equivalent is *Realpolitik* or "the national interest."

rake: Firing along the length of a flanked position of enemy troops or line of ships, or down the length of a single ship from ahead or astern. This avoided exposing oneself to a volley or broadside, while bringing maximum fire to bear on the enemy. In field battles, this full enfilade position was often sought after but seldom achieved. Militating against infantry enfilade on more than a minor scale in fighting in Europe was basic equality of military technology and comparable tactics among European armies. That is why Frederick's oblique order was initially so successful and became so famous.

ranker: A private. A simple G.I. or grunt or Tommy or Ivan or *poilu* or *Landser*.

rasputitsa: The twice-yearly (spring and fall) Russian "season of no roads." Seasonal rains turned the mostly dirt roads and red-soil fields of the western Soviet Union into knee-deep mud that sucked boots off feet, snapped the legs of draft horses, clogged the wheels and tracks of military vehicles. In operational terms, the *rasputitsa* had far greater effects on combat, logistics and strategic timing than did the more frequently commented-upon Russian winters.

refuse the flank or wing: See *oblique order.*

res publica Christiana: "Christian Commonwealth." A medieval European concept expressing an admixture of pride in the Roman heritage of Latin Christian civilization and faith in the presumed unity of a godly community (*"Corpus Christianum"*) of all Latin Christians.

revanchist: A policy seeking to reverse a prior defeat and regain territory that was lost last time.

Rikugun: The Imperial Japanese Army.

Rikusentai: "Special Naval Landing Forces." *Kaigun* marines. They were organized in brigade-strength units of 2,000. They first saw action at Shanghai in 1932, where their inability to hold ground drew more heavily armed and numerous Japanese Army troops into the fighting. They were again assaulted in Shanghai by elite *Guomindang* troops in 1937. They were reformed into 12 battalion-strength units of about 800–1,200 each in 1940, two trained for airborne operations. They were instrumental in the Hundred Days Campaign of 1941–1942, including in airborne assaults on Celebes, Sumatra and Timor.

roi-connétable: A medieval French military office; more than just commander-in-chief, closer to lieutenant ruler or second to the king.

routiers: Rootless, roving, impoverished, unemployed mercenary *routes* ("bands") that lived off the land by intimidating the peasantry of medieval France.

seishin: "National spirit." As with so many Japanese ideas in this period, what began as a more or less benevolent cultural and patriotic concept devolved into malevolent assertions of superiority during the 1930s and 1940s. It also fed into a military mysticism that denied Japan's material disadvantages versus the Great Powers it proposed to fight.

shock: Delivering a stunning, smashing attack directly and bluntly into an enemy line or square with the weight and force of a whole military unit.

Spanish muskets: An early design six feet long, weighing at least 15 pounds (more often 18–20 pounds), that took two men to carry and load and could only be aimed and fired using a fork rest or hooked to a wall. It shot a heavy ball (1½ ounces) with sufficient force to pierce plate armor out to 240 yards, making it the anti-tank weapon of its day. While this punching power greatly exceeded that of any other missile weapon, Spanish muskets were extremely poor weapons in several regards. They were too heavy and inaccurate, with an effective sniping or aimed range barely passing 50 yards. They were difficult and very slow to load and reload, with a poor rate of fire, and took 28 discrete steps to reload.

spike the guns: The poor rate of fire and the limited range of early gunpowder cannon were inherent weaknesses that led opposing armies to adopt a simple and effective counter: wait until the enemy's guns fired, then rush the position and overwhelm the gun crews. From the early 15th century, the additional precaution was taken of "spiking the guns." Once the guns were taken, iron spikes were hammered into the touchhole, which was the quickest and surest way to put cannon out of action. This rendered them inoperable even if the position was retaken by the original owners. This threat to the artillery led to ever larger protective contingents of infantry, which meant more men on the other side were dedicated to charging the guns, which led to still more defenders, and so on. Over time, the proportion of an army's strength devoted to protecting or attacking artillery grew to a considerable size, much of it on the defensive side devoted to digging blocking trenches in front of the guns or constructing earthworks and palisades.

spoiling attack: Attacking with the intent to impair a building enemy attack, spoiling his preparations and thereby avoiding being attacked on his schedule, if at all.

standing armies: *Militum perpetuum.* A permanent professional army, paid for and barracked by the monarch or state; one not demobilized in times of peace, nor seasonally recruited as was in the case in medieval armies. The Ottomans, Mughals and Ming all had far larger standing armies than any in Europe into the late 17th century.

Staatsräson: "reason of state." Equivalent to *raison d'état.*

Stavka: Short for *Stavka Verkhovnogo komandovaniya* or "Main Command of the Armed Forces." The GHQ of the Russian Army. From July 10, 1941, it was headed by Stalin under his title *Verkhovnyi glavnokomanduyushchii* (*VKG*), or "Main Commander-in-Chief." The *Stavka* did not meet formally. Appointees served as military advisors to Stalin, but membership was not reflective of who had real influence. From mid-1942, senior officers planned and oversaw all major Red Army operations, notably after failure at the First Battle of Kharkov (May 12–29, 1942) revealed basic problems of command and control. In the final campaign of the war, against Japan in Manchuria during August 1945, *Stavka* relinquished direct operational control to a Far Eastern Command that coordinated fighting by three army groups.

Schwerpunkt: "Weight of effort" or "stress point." A strategic concept in Clausewitz, changed in German thinking to an operational idea before World War I. It found resonance in the Schlieffen plan massing on the right wing. Again before World War II, *Schwerpunkt* evolved in German operational planning as the idea that an overwhelming superiority of force should be applied at decisive points of maximum enemy weakness. Once the enemy front cracked, German armor would penetrate behind his broken line prior to achieving envelopment of his main force in a *Vernichtungsschlacht* ("battle of annihilation"). If a succession of such decisive battles could be strung together into a *Vernichtungskrieg* ("war of annihilation"), Germany could avoid losing a contest of attrition. Only in that distant sense did the term vaguely retain its original Clausewitzian strategic meaning.

SS (*Schutzstaffel*): "Guard detachment." Subdivided into the *Allgemeine* ("General" or Political) SS and Waffen ("Armed") SS. Headed by Heinrich Himmler. The SS grew to over 50,000 by the end of 1932 and over 200,000 a year later, and much larger after that. *Einsatzgruppen* death squads roamed Poland as the SS carried out the dirtiest tasks of the Nazi regime. It oversaw the murder of millions in purpose-built death camps from 1942. Women's units served on the frontlines as nurses, in signals work and SS offices, and as camp guards.

steal a march: Maneuver stealthily or use a ruse in such a way as to leave behind an army of observation, thus stealing a day's march and putting distance and confusion between the two armies.

Stellungskrieg: Positional war, implying in later German usage also positional stalemate.

Sturmtruppen: "Assault troops."

Sublime Porte: Translation of Ottoman Turkish *Bâb-ı âli* ("High Gate" or "Gate of the Eminent"). A diplomatic and protocol term for the government of the Ottoman Empire, taken from the High Gate that led into the central government complex in Constantinople, which included the courts of justice, the foreign ministry and from the 17th century also the palace of the Grand Vizier.

sutlers: Large-scale merchants who carted goods for sale and followed along in the baggage train of armies. Sutlers played a critical role in medieval and early modern warfare, since soldiers were responsible for obtaining their own food, clothing, arms and equipment. They became a regular feature of the logistical systems of early modern armies as well, which could not maneuver as they did without contracted supplies moving with them.

tercio: "Third." Spanish infantry formation. Derived from the tripartite division common to Spanish squares. It was the main infantry unit in the 15th–16th-century Spanish system.

Triple Alliance: (1) 1668: A league of England, the Netherlands and Sweden against Louis XIV and France. (2) 1882–1915: A secret alliance among Austria-Hungary, Germany and Italy, pledging mutual assistance in the event of an attack by France. Unbeknownst to Austria or Germany, Italy signed a secret nonaggression pact with France in 1902. As it was Germany which attacked France in 1914, Italy was therefore within its legal rights in refusing to accept that the Triple Alliance came into effect. Rome instead joined the Allies, declaring war on Germany and Austria-Hungary in 1915.

Triple Entente: A loose term for three-way British, French and Russian cooperation between 1907 and 1914, often too loosely called the Entente Cordiale (Russia and France). It applies more properly to the formal military alliance signed on September 3, 1914. The 1914 military pact was disavowed by the Bolsheviks when they signed a separate peace with Germany in March 1918.

United Nations alliance: The armed league, more commonly known as the Allies, which won World War II against the Axis states. Its principal members were the United States, the Soviet Union and Great Britain, with a nominal but distant fourth major member in China and a badly wounded member in Free France. It had many smaller members.

van: At sea: the lead of any three squadrons in a fleet. On land: the foremost major division of an army; the lead force of a moving army divided in three parts.

Vernichtungskrieg: "War of annihilation."

Vernichtungsschlacht: "Battle of annihilation."

Vernichtungsstrategie: A short-war "strategy of annihilation."

victor's disease: The idea that winning in war teaches fewer lessons than losing, and tends to breed complacency about how to win next time. Shorthand for military conservatism.

Waffen SS: "Armed SS." The prefix "Waffen" in a unit's formal designation meant armed but additionally referenced an initial plurality of foreign volunteers. All ethnic-German units were at first designated "SS-Division." However, the term "Waffen" came to be applied over time to all armed SS-divisions. It is used that way by most historians. The Waffen SS evolved as ideological and battlefield shock troops, eventually given better transport, weapons, men, and supplies than the Wehrmacht. Reflecting an emphasis on ideological zeal, some Waffen SS troops exhibited a marked *Einsatzfreude*, or love of combat. It reached 100,000 men by June 1940, 230,000 in January 1942, 594,000 men in June 1944, and a peak of 910,000 men in 38 divisions in October 1944. Many units were shattered by then, badly undermanned and underequipped and reeling in defeat. Not all late-war SS were volunteers, though all had to meet superior height and other physical requirements.

warcraft: See *art of war*.

Weltmacht: "World power." German conception and ambition to become a Great Power of the first rank, with an empire and global reach and influence.

Wehrmacht: "Armed Forces." It incorporated the *Heer* (army), *Luftwaffe* (air force), and *Kriegsmarine* (navy). Military casualties of all types—killed, wounded, missing, taken prisoner—averaged nearly 400,000 per month over the last five months of World War II.

Weltpolitik: "World policy." First applied to Imperial Germany's policy from the 1890s, to its seeking to become a *Weltmacht* or first-rank world power. It abandoned Bismarck's caution and continentalism to prod and provoke, particularly at the British. It encouraged belief before 1914 that Germany's future required a military confrontation with one or more Great Powers that were "encircling" it with a ring of iron, denying German destiny.

Westheer: The German army on the Western Front in World War II.

Westphalia, Peace of (1648): The set of agreements that codified the political arrangement ending the Thirty Years' War.

Yezhovshchina: "The time of Yezhov." The greatest of the Stalin purges, lasting from 1936 to 1938, and named for Nikolai I. Yezhov, head of the NKVD. After serving as Stalin's willing and eager executioners, Yezhov and other top NKVD officers were themselves purged. Estimates vary as to the number of victims of the *Yezhovshchina*, from a low NKVD-supplied figure of just under 700,000 to a serious scholarly estimate by Robert Conquest of nearly two million. Stalin's purges as a whole may have taken 10 million lives. A later KGB report said 20 million were arrested under Stalin, of whom seven million were shot. Stalin killed perhaps 20–25 million, counting purges, forced famine, internal deportations and executions in the slave camps of the Gulag archipelago.

Index